# WILLIAM DONALDSON'S

# ROGUES, VILLAINS AND ECCENTRICS

William Donaldson was born in Sunningdale, Berkshire and was educated at Winchester and then Cambridge where he read English. He went into the theatre and produced, among other shows, *Beyond the Fringe* and *The Bedsitting Room*. His novels include *Both the Ladies and the Gentlemen*, *Nicknames Only* and *Is This Allowed?*. His other books are *The Henry Root Letters*, *The Further Letters of Henry Root*, *Henry Root's World of Knowledge* and *Root Into Europe* (which was filmed by ITV in 1991). From 1989 to 1995 he was a columnist on the *Independent*.

# WILLIE DONALDSON'S

# ROGUES, VILLAINS AND ECCENTRICS

An A-Z of Roguish Britons
Through the Ages

BREWER'S

BREWER'S
An imprint of Chambers Harrap Publishers Ltd
7 Hopetoun Crescent, Edinburgh, EH7 4AY

Chambers Harrap is an Hachette Livre UK company

This edition published by Chambers Harrap Publishers Ltd 2008
First published as *Brewer's Rogues, Villains and Eccentrics* by Cassell in 2002;
paperback edition published by Phoenix, an imprint of Orion books, in 2004

A CIP catalogue record for this book is available from the British Library.

ISBN 978 0550 10496 0

www.chambers.co.uk

Cover design by Stuart Polson
Printed and bound by Clays Ltd, St Ives plc

# contents

# introduction

My invitation to compile *Brewer's Rogues, Villains and Eccentrics* was itself eccentrically delivered. Since they had not heard of me, much less knew my whereabouts, my own publishers of 25 years sent it to a Mr Wilfred Donaldson of Kilmarnock in Scotland, an expert on the history of bagpipes. He turned it down, which was my good fortune. Within no more than a few months, the invitation reached me and we were off to the races (*see* SMIRKE, CHARLIE), albeit with a problem, at least with decisions to be made in matters of inclusion and good taste.

The publisher's proposal was for 'a browsable and addictive collection of pen-portraits of 1500 extraordinary characters, drawn from the "undergrowth" rather than the mainstream of British and Irish history. It should take its inspiration from that strand within *Brewer's Dictionary of Phrase and Fable* that is serendipitous and mildly eccentric in nature, and from the century-old Brewer's practice of recording information that is not generally available in other reference books'. An attractive idea, but by putting a murderous East End villain (*see* KRAY, RONALD) cheek by jowl in the same book with a no more than fairly mad 19th-century travelling woman (*see* KINGSLEY, MARY) might we not seem to be suggesting that the categories 'Rogues', 'Villains' and 'Eccentrics' are not discrete? Indeed, which would be offensive to the latter, that there is a 'family resemblance', as it were, between Mr Kray and Miss Kingsley?

It is a problem which has confronted others, most notably Hugh Massingberd in his matchlessly funny collections from the *Daily Telegraph*'s obituary pages. In his introduction to *The Daily Telegraph Fourth Book of Obituaries: Rogues* (1998) – in which the lives of Ronnie Kray and Anthony 'Fat Tony' Salerno, 'Godfather' of the New York-based Genovese crime family, are celebrated next to that of Lord Havers, a former Tory lord chancellor, and father of the matinee actor Nigel Havers (*see* WIGMORE STREET MASSAGE PARLOUR SCANDAL, THE) – Mr Massingberd writes, 'Readers would sometimes take exception to our including a notorious villain (such as, say, a Mafia hitman or an East End gangster) beside a gallant war hero or blameless bishop in the Obituaries page. The outraged inference seemed to be that we were thereby conferring some form of moral approval by granting such unworthy figures the "honour" of an obituary at all. In reality, of course, we were merely applying straightforward "news values".'

The argument is very weak, as Mr Massingberd himself seems to acknowledge when he later refers to the 'deadpan detachment' and 'the bemused indifference' with which these lives are chronicled. Respectability is conferred by the sheer perfection of the comic style adopted by his various contributors. Better, I think, to admit that by writing about 'Mad' Frankie Fraser or Freddie 'the Mean Machine' Foreman in a (excuse me) 'marketable' way, one is inevitably glamorizing them – a service one would not wish to perform for the Yorkshire Ripper, say, or Fred West.

'Rogues' and 'eccentrics' present no such difficulties, though it is customary to point out that the selection process has been purely subjective, as if it could have been otherwise. One man's loveable rogue is another man's drunken fat show-off (*See* REED, OLIVER), his agreeable parliamentary eccentric a witless Scot in silly clothes (*See* FAIRBAIRN, NICHOLAS). Certainly I have found many candidates for inclusion under these two categories to be tiresome in their behaviour rather than amusingly unorthodox. In her introduction to *The Emperor of The United States of America and Other Magnificent British Eccentrics,* 1981 (one of the two entirely successful books in this genre, I think, the other being Peter Somerville-Large's wildly funny *Irish Eccentrics,* 1975), Catherine Caulfield writes, 'An interval of time or distance may be necessary before we can recognize eccentricity as something other than inconvenient or offensive behaviour.' I'm sure this is so. One day in the distant future, the gauche antics of various Soho louts and layabouts may seem as amusing as those of Buck English, an 18th-century Irish character who once shot a waiter and had him put on the bill for £50. The behaviour of true eccentrics (if I may use a question-begging phrase) must have an innocence about it, and an iron logic of its own. When the brothers, Tony and Douglas GRAY, trading as the Alberts, had a hit show in the West End with *An Evening of British Rubbish*, they refused to form themselves into a limited company on the grounds that before being sent to prison defendants always describe themselves as company directors. Their decision made perfect sense.

Even the most devoted admirers of *Brewer's Dictionary of Phrase and Fable* admit that it is sometimes difficult to find in it exactly what one's looking for.

Accordingly, I have introduced an innovative system of cross-referencing, though whether I have improved matters or made them worse I'm far from clear. Suppose your special interest is bombs: rather than go through the whole book in search of them, simply look under the appropriate letter of the alphabet and you will find various dummy entries, each with helpful cross-references attached. Thus:

**bomb, blowing up one's father with a.** *See* BROWN, ERIC.

**bomb, suspecting one's guest's suitcase contains a.** *See* SINCLAIR, DONALD.

**bomb down a pensioner's chimney-pot, threatening to drop a.** *See* FORSTER, JAMES.

**bomb inadvertently detonated by pet Rottweiler.** *See* ARISTIDES, SUSAN MARY.

**bomb with one's umbrella, poking a.** *See* CECIL, LORD HUGH.

**bombing hotel lavatories.** *See* MOON, KEITH.

**bombs, ticking time.** *See* DEMPSEY, ANDREW; KEELER, CHRISTINE; MANN, PAUL; THORPE, JEREMY.

Equally, and in the appropriate place, you will find:

**drunk and indecent in South Eaton Place.** *See* VIVIAN, ANTHONY CRESPIGNY CLAUDE, 5TH BARON.

**drunk in his shirtsleeves at four in the afternoon.** *See* POULSON, JOHN (for Reginald Maudling).

**drunks, convivial.** *See* KEAN, EDMUND; NEWTON, ROBERT.

**drunks, nightmare.** *See* BERNARD, JEFFREY; FARSON, DANIEL; REED, OLIVER.

Just where you would expect them you will find:

**dwarf, knocked over by a.** *See* WILLIAMSON, NICOL.

**dwarfs, bank-robbing.** *See* MCCRAY, RAYMOND.

**dwarfs, Cavalier.** *See* HUDSON, JEFFREY.

**dwarfs, sacrifice of.** *See* HELL-FIRE CLUB, THE IRISH.

Or:

**Love, Abode of.** *See* PRINCE, HENRY.

love, giving and receiving the last charming proofs of an
unbounded. *See* HERVEY, AUGUSTUS.
love, powerfully agitated in the delights of. *See* GRAHAM, JAMES.
love and presents, fraught with. *See* HARRIS, JOHN.
Lovebody, Jane, nightclub hostess and mistress. *See* BLOOM, JOHN.
love in broad daylight, alleged unlikelihood of any woman
making. *See* COLLUSION, DIVORCE BY.
love in ditches, making. *See* CRIPPLE, MARGARET AND WILLIAM; DAVID-
SON, THE REVEREND HAROLD FRANCIS (the rector of Stiffkey).

Or:

pig, riding through Edinburgh on a. *See* GORDON, LORD GEORGE.
pig destroys Angelic Organ. *See* POCKRICH, RICHARD.
pigs, priest steals parishioners'. *See* OATES, TITUS.
pigs and potatoes, paying the fees at Eton in. *See* SITWELL, SIR
GEORGE RERESBY.
pigs in fox-hunting, unsuccessful attempt to use. *See* HIRST, JEMMY.
pigs rooting up graves. *See* FREE, THE REVEREND EDWARD DRAX.
pigs to jump hurdles, teaching the headmaster's. *See* HIRST, JEMMY.

It is the convention at this point to express one's thanks to various people 'but for whose patience and encouragement my lonely task … etc. etc.'. I have never before felt the need to follow this practice – if anything, the opposite. On this occasion, however, I do owe an enormous debt of gratitude to Richard Milbank, who has been an inspiration and source of strength throughout, and to Ian Crofton and Patricia Moore, who have edited the manuscript. They both know everything and have therefore been able to repair much of the damage done by my inexperience in this area and lack of academic virtues. I would not wish either of them to carry the blame for any lapses of taste or occasional spasms of attitude, but it is fair to say that, thanks to them, all the toothcombs and magnifying glasses in the world will avail you nothing in an officious search for errors and omissions.

*William Donaldson*
LONDON

# A–Z of Rogues, Villains and Eccentrics

# a

**abandoned wretches who confine themselves to a horrid course of life.** *See* TRACEY, MARTHA.

**Abberline, Chief Inspector Frederick** (*c.*1830–?), investigating officer in the notorious Cleveland Street Brothel Scandal of 1886 (*see* NEWTON, ARTHUR). Abberline applied for a warrant, but before it could be executed the brothel's proprietor, Charles HAMMOND, posing as a clergyman, had fled to the Continent with his wife, a French prostitute known as 'Madame Caroline'. It was later suggested that Abberline had been deliberately slow to act – the delay enabling Hammond's aristocratic clientele to be elsewhere at the time of the raid. Public interest was fanned by the rumour that the brothel had been patronized by the prince of Wales's eldest son, the duke of CLARENCE, known as 'Eddy'. Under the assumed name of 'Victoria', Eddy was already a member of The Hundred Guineas, a transvestite club in Portland Place, run by a Mr Inslip. Here, there was dancing until 2 a.m., at which point the lights were lowered, allowing various forms of sexual contact until 6 a.m. when the club closed.

**Abbott, George** (1562–1633), priest, academic and archbishop of Canterbury (1611–33). Had he not shot a gamekeeper dead when aiming at a deer, Abbott would be remembered, if at all, as one of the least distinguished of English archbishops. Described by Hugh Trevor-Roper as 'simply indifferent, negligent, secular', he was notable only for a keen sense of his own importance and the zeal with which he persecuted heretics. When vice chancellor of Oxford University, he sent 140 undergraduates to prison for failing to remove their hats in his presence. As a member, and sometime ruling spirit, of the High Commission Court – whose methods have been described as 'equal to those of the Spanish Inquisition' – he was remarkable for the savagery of his punishments. In

*Age of Reason Begins*, Durant notes that one preacher, Alexander Leighton, 'was tied to a stake and received thirty-six stripes with a heavy cord upon his naked back; he was placed in the pillory for two hours in November's frost and snow; he was branded in the face, had his nose split and his ears cut off, and was condemned to life imprisonment'. Owing his appointment to James I, Abbott was careful to protect his patron. A Somerset clergyman, Edmund Peacham, who criticized the king in a sermon, was more fortunate than Alexander Leighton. He was merely suspended in chains on the archbishop's instructions.

On 24 July 1621 Abbott joined a hunting party at Bramshill Park, Hampshire, the estate of Lord Zouch. The archbishop was known to be an indifferent marksman, but a gamekeeper, Peter Hawkins, failed to take due care and was hit by an arrow. A coroner recorded a verdict of 'death by misfortune, and his own fault', and the king was quick to defend his senior prelate. 'An angel', he said, 'might have miscarried in that sort.'

Abbott's unpopularity ensured that the incident would not be overlooked. Three newly elected, but unconsecrated, bishops – William Laud, Dr Valentine Cary and John Williams – were all ambitious to replace him. 'To leave a man of blood as primate is a thing that sounds very harshe in the counsels and canons of the church', wrote Williams to the king's favourite (and sometime lover), Charles Villiers, 1st duke of Buckingham, and all three bishops refused to be consecrated by Abbott. The king was forced to set up a commission to investigate the incident. Although the three bishops who had most to gain from Abbott's downfall were among its members, it failed to reach a verdict and referred the matter back to James. Abbott duly received a pardon from his royal patron and continued uneasily in office until his death.

Since then, none of his fellow citizens has been shot by an archbishop, though one has by a deputy prime minister. In 1984 Sir Joseph NICKERSON, who had taught himself to 'think like a partridge', had invited Viscount Whitelaw to his Lincolnshire shoot. The deputy prime minister slipped in the butts and winged his host and a gamekeeper, Waddle. A statement from 10 Downing Street announced that 'Lord Whitelaw is naturally deeply upset but is relieved that no lasting damage has been done either to Sir Joseph or to Mr Waddle'.

The present Lord Zouch – the 18th Baron – lives in Australia.

**abducting a performing parrot.** *See* RUBELL, IDA.

**abduction clubs.** Informal associations of indigent rakes who in 18th-century Ireland kidnapped any young lady entitled to a fortune. A typical abduction occurred in 1797 when Sir Henry Hayes kidnapped Mary Pike, described as unremarkable in appearance but a substantial heiress. Taken to Sir Henry's house, struggling and kicking up the length of its long avenue, she was set down in his parlour and married to Sir Henry by a man dressed as a parson. Miss Pike courageously tore off the ring which had been forced on her finger and threw it across the room. Sir Henry admitted defeat, and Miss Pike was returned unharmed to her parents.

The 2nd Viscount Mountmorres, who in 1797 was so affected by the troubles in Ireland that he shot himself, may have become deranged by a failed attempt at abduction 20 years previously. Learning one morning that a young woman, who had already turned him down, was staying at a nearby inn, he surprised her at breakfast and bundled her into his coach. Her cries of alarm alerted her servants who gave Mountmorres a beating from which he never fully recovered.

*See also* BALTIMORE, FREDERICK CALVERT, 6TH BARON; PINKINDINDIES, THE.

**Abercorn, John James Hamilton, 1st marquess of** (1756–1818), rank-conscious Irish peer notorious for the extravagance of his lifestyle. Even in the trying circumstances of a marriage breakdown, Abercorn was anxious that aristocratic conventions be observed. When he discovered that his second wife was on the point of eloping, he requested that she meet her lover in the family carriage so that 'it can never be said that Lady Abercorn left her husband's roof in a hack chaise'.

Abercorn maintained a style of living that was lavish even by the spendthrift standards of a prodigal age. On his way to visit the marquess in Carlisle, the novelist Walter Scott (a friend of the Abercorn family) met a procession of five carriages, 20 outriders and a man on horseback wearing the blue ribbon of the Knights of the Garter. It turned out to be Abercorn himself – on his way to dine alone at a public house in the small village of Longtown.

A preference for solitude influenced Abercorn's approach to the entertaining of house guests. Visitors to his home at Bentley Priory were generously accorded the 'run of the house' and were free to do what they wished – save in one respect: under no circumstances were they permitted to speak to Abercorn himself.

**Abercrombie, Helen** (*c.*1771–1830), woman murdered by her son-in-law in the Case of the Thick Ankles (*see* WAINEWRIGHT, THOMAS GRIFFITHS).

**Aberystwyth, having your bicycle stolen in.** *See* BOAKS, BILL.

**ablutions, rarely purified by.** *See* FOX, CHARLES JAMES.

**Abominable Snowmen living in the Cairngorms.** *See* RANKIN, SIR HUGH.

**Abrahamson, Fred.** *See* VERONICA MUTINEERS, THE.

**abroad, the unacceptability of.** *See* REDESDALE, CLEMENT NAPIER THOMAS FREEMAN MITFORD, 2ND BARON; SIBTHORP, COLONEL CHARLES DE LAET WALDO.

**absent-minded, the.** *See* BAKER, PETER; DEVONSHIRE, ANDREW ROBERT BUXTON CAVENDISH, 11TH DUKE OF; DUDLEY, JOHN WILLIAM WARD, 1ST EARL OF; HAMILTON, ROBERT; MATURIN, CHARLES ROBERT; SALISBURY, ROBERT ARTHUR TALBOT GASCOYNE CECIL, 3RD MARQUESS OF; TYRRELL, LADY MARGARET-ANN.

**Absolon, Charles** (1817–1907), cricketer. At the age of 76, Absolon took 209 wickets in a season for his London club, Osterley Park, but his statistics declined steadily over the next few years. In 1897, at the age of 80, he took only 101 wickets. Absolon had greatly admired William Adlam who in 1888 had opened the innings for Taunton at the age of 104, scoring three.

**academics and other scholars who ought to have known better.** *See* ALLEGRO, JOHN; ARAM, EUGENE; BARRETT, JOHN; WATSON, THE REVEREND JOHN SELBY.
  *See also* TEACHERS WHO HAVE STRAYED.

**Acid Bath Murders, the.** *See* HAIGH, JOHN GEORGE.

**Acke, Peter** (1928–2000), market speculator and benefactor. Known in the village of Midgham, Berkshire, as Cynthia Watson, a spinster, Acke was held in affection by other residents. Some were surprised to discover when she died that she had been a multi-millionaire, none by the revelation that she had been a man.

Glynis Snow, landlady of Midgham's only public house, The Swan, was enthusiastic about her former customer. 'She had a good sense of humour. She didn't like the French. She used to say, "Down with the French!" Then she had another glass of wine. Her wig was always a bit skew-whiff.'

Miss Watson, a former pupil at Stowe School, had been a carpenter in the Merchant Navy and a cowboy on an Argentine ranch. Mystery surrounds how she made her fortune. Glynis Snow thinks that it might have been on the Stock Exchange. 'She was in here one evening, having her glass of wine, then she said she had to get up early in the morning to ring her broker in Tokyo.'

Miss Watson, who had previously lived on Osier Island in Wyre Piddle, Worcestershire, left her £3.3 million estate to the Royal National

Lifeboat Institute for the purchase of a new lifeboat, to be named *The Witch of Osier*.

**acting the old fool in Barclays Bank, Camden Town.** *See* CHANEY, SID.

**actors.** *See* HOOLIGANS, THEATRICAL; KEAN, EDMUND; NEWTON, ROBERT; REED, OLIVER; WILLIAMSON, NICOL.

**actresses, Australian.** *See* HOLME, LORD RICHARD.

**Adams, Donny 'The Bull'** (1913–83), unlicensed fistfighter.
*See also* BRADSHAW, BRIAN 'THE MAD GYPSY'; MCLEAN, LENNY.

**Adams, Dr John Bodkin** (1899–1983), physician and alleged poisoner. A general practitioner in Eastbourne, Dr Adams is thought by many to have got away with murder, not once, but several times. He was tried in 1957 after one of his patients, Edith Morrell, had died in suspicious circumstances. Like other elderly patients before her, she had made him a beneficiary of her will before succumbing to a course of morphine. That the jury found Adams not guilty was due in no small part to the poor opinion they had formed of the prosecuting counsel, later to be an undistinguished Tory Lord Chancellor, Sir Reginald Manningham-Buller (dubbed 'Sir Bullying Manner' by the journalist Bernard Levin, and thought by some to be the model for the character of Widmerpool in Anthony Powell's novel sequence *A Dance to the Music of Time*), and to the painstaking defence advanced by Geoffrey Lawrence QC. It may have further added to the prosecution's difficulties that Sir Reginald's junior was Melford STEVENSON, later a controversial judge.

After his acquittal, Adams ended his association with the National Health Service and was struck off the Medical Register. He continued to treat a few private patients without mishap, and was reinstated by the General Medical Council in 1961. Some have argued that he merely practised a form of euthanasia, but most students of the case believe that he dispatched at least nine elderly ladies for personal gain.

**Adams, Thomas** (1957– ), gangster and senior member of the notorious Adams family, which continues to inspire unparalleled fear in the London underworld. Financial expert, Philip Beresford, who compiles the *Sunday Times*'s annual 'Rich List', estimates that Tommy Adams has acquired a fortune of £50 million from drugs and extortion. He is known to have ordered the killing of at least 30 informers and competitors, but because the violence is generally subcontracted to gangs of Afro-Caribbean hoodlums he is viewed with suspicion by old-style gangsters (*see* DIAMOND GEEZERS) from east and south London.

The family's popularity was further diminished in July 1991 when 'Mad' Frankie FRASER, the RICHARDSON gang's former enforcer, was shot at point-blank range as he came out of Turnmill's 'Nite' Club in Clerkenwell. Although Fraser took the incident in good part, claiming later that it had made for a good night out, underworld figures saw the shooting as a destabilizing outbreak of lawlessness on the London crime scene. 'It was well out of order,' said one. 'Frank's a romantic. It's common knowledge that he was shot by a hired killer employed by the Adams brothers. What's the point of shooting a man like that? He's getting on in years. It was done as a demonstration of strength.'

In 1998, Freddie FOREMAN's son had his ear bitten off in Marbella by Tommy Adams's brother. A former henchman of Ron and Reggie KRAY and a leading underworld figure in his own right, Foreman demanded a sit-down with the family. 'If my boy's been harmed,' he said, 'your brother will be coming home in a body bag.' The quarrel was patched up, and Foreman later declined to lead an alliance of south and east London gangs against the Adamses. However, members of the Metropolitan Police who are not on the family's payroll are thought to be keeping an eye on its arrangements.

**Adams, Tommy** (1960– ), rugby player. A 25-stone lock forward with the Cornish club Camborne, Adams was recruited when the club's coach, Bill Strides, was driving past a farm and saw a large young man ploughing a field without a horse or tractor. When Strides stopped to ask the way, he was impressed by the way Adams used the plough to point him in the right direction.

Adams's idea of warming up before a match is to drink nine pints of beer, and when he feels the need to practise he tackles parked cars. On one occasion he galloped through a knot of players and tackled a mounted policeman, knocking the horse unconscious. He was less successful when he lost his bearings in an away match and tackled the opposition's outside lavatory. When Adams came round he said to his team-mates, 'that last fellow hit me rather hard'.

In spite of his size, Adams is a keen exponent of the seven-a-side game. The team he plays for, Billie's Bulldozers, requires its members to be over 17 stone and to drink three pints of beer between each round of a tournament. Adams is rumoured to have drunk 38 pints of Guinness in one afternoon.

**Adams, Victoria.** *See* BECKHAM, BROOKLYN; BECKHAM, DAVID; MCAVENNIE, FRANK.

**Adam the Leper** (*c.*1320–60), the most feared of the many itinerant cut-throats who terrorized England in the 14th century. Adam and his gang would descend on a town when a fair was taking place, plunder and set fire to the houses and then withdraw – safe from capture since householders were too busy saving their properties to organize pursuit. According to Luke Owen Pike (*History of Crime in England*, 1873), 'Men and women were captured, ransom was extracted on pain of death, and even those who paid it might think themselves fortunate if they escaped some horrible mutilation.' In 1347 Adam and his men took over Bristol, robbing the ships in the harbour – including some commissioned by King Edward III – and forcing a trader to hand over jewellery belonging to Queen Philippa. The king was obliged to send Thomas, Lord Berkeley, to restore order, but when Adam was taken, and tried, his gang waited outside the court in Winchester and attacked everyone who came out. The authorities preferred not to pursue the matter, and Adam continued with his depredations.

**aesthetes, treacherous.** *See* BLUNT, SIR ANTHONY.

**affray, causing an.** *See* ANDREWS, THE REVEREND BASIL; DIMES, ALBERT; MR SMITH'S; PORTEOUS, CAPTAIN JOHN; SPOT, JACK.

**Africans, sex and.** *See* MARKS, HOWARD; MONTROSE, JAMES ANGUS GRAHAM, 7TH DUKE OF.

**Agar, Edward** (1816–81), stock-market speculator, investment manager, master safe-cracker and leading conspirator in what became known as the 'Great Train Robbery' of 1855. At Agar's trial in 1857, the judge, Sir Samuel Martin, acknowledged that he was a man of genius, albeit of genius misapplied. 'One tenth of the care and perseverance given to this, and perhaps to other robberies', Sir Samuel mused, 'must, if directed to honest pursuits, have raised you to a respectable station in life and enabled you to realize a large fortune.'

In fact, Agar had, by the age of 37, and by careful speculation, acquired a fortune in stocks and shares and was living a life of apparent probity in the middle-class environs of Shepherd's Bush with his 19-year-old mistress, Fanny Kay. None of his neighbours, nor Sir Samuel himself, perhaps, would have suspected that this well-mannered, silk-hatted investment manager had been a career criminal since the age of 18.

The crime for which he became something of a romantic hero was not originally conceived by Agar but by one of his four accomplices, William Pierce, an embittered betting clerk who had been sacked by South Eastern Railways in 1850. Pierce had discovered that gold ingots and other valuables were being sent by train and boat from bullion merchants in the City of London to the Banque de France in Paris. He passed this information on to Fanny Kay, who worked as a barmaid at a public house frequented by Pierce, and it was she who persuaded Agar that the robbery would be possible. Thereafter, it was meticulously planned by Agar and executed with considerable aplomb by him, Pierce and three other conspirators: 'Barrister' SAWARD, who had a substantial law practice as a Queen's Bench defence counsel and was the reality behind an elusive forger known to Scotland Yard as 'Jem the Penman'; James Burgess, a guard on South Eastern Railways who was unhappy with his wages; and William George Tester, an adventurer and dandy (*see* BOLLOCKS, A SILLY), temporarily employed in the public traffic department at London Bridge.

Chubb had recently installed a new safe in the train with two keys, copies of which the thieves would need in their possession. An impression of one was made by Tester when a safe was sent back to Chubb's for repair, and Pierce obtained the other by walking into the Folkstone railway office and removing it from under the nose of its guardian. Carrying large carpet bags, and tipped off by Burgess that the train was carrying a full cargo of bullion, Agar and Pierce boarded it at London Bridge on the night of 15 May 1855. By the time the train reached Folkestone, they had transferred several hundredweight of gold ingots from the bullion chests to their carpet bags, substituting lead shot so that the chests would weigh the correct amount when checked at Boulogne.

Agar and Pierce returned to London, where the gold was melted down and disposed of as recast bullion, principally through the agency of 'Barrister' Saward. The money was then distributed equally among the four thieves, who might have got away with the crime but for a lack of that good faith without which no business enterprise can hope to succeed.

Agar was arrested, quite fortuitously, when a pimp called HUMPHREYS, with whom he had fallen out, falsely accused him of fraud. Agar was sentenced to life imprisonment for this imaginary crime and to transportation to Australia. At the time of his arrest, he had entrusted his share of the bullion robbery to Pierce, on the understanding that Pierce would settle it on Fanny Kay. While held in a convict hulk in Portland, Agar heard that Pierce had kept the money for himself. Disappointed by this act of treachery, Agar turned informer, and Pierce, Burgess and Tester were arrested.

At their trial in 1857, all three were convicted on Agar's evidence. Because of extensive newspaper coverage, everyone knew that Agar had been the criminal genius behind the robbery. But he had not been charged with it, let alone convicted. By legal anomaly, the South Eastern Railway had no right to the money entrusted to Pierce by Agar. To the dismay of prosecution lawyers, the judge, seized by the romance of Agar's sacrifice, ruled that his share should be handed over to Fanny Kay. Thus it was that a young woman who customarily had to be taken home in a wheelbarrow received the proceeds of the most celebrated robbery in criminal history.

**agents provocateurs.** *See* HAMPSON, KEITH; HITCHIN, CHARLES; POPAY, WILLIAM STEWARD; THIN BLUE JEANS, THE.

**Aherne, Caroline** (1966– ), actress and comedienne whom happiness has eluded. In July 1998, and on the theory that laughter is the best therapy, the troubled funnywoman was advised by her psychiatrist to watch *The Mrs Merton Show* on television. 'But doctor, I *am* Mrs Merton,' replied Miss Aherne. The story may be apocryphal. In an unrelated incident, Miss Aherne was seen to French kiss another actress at the British Academy of Film and Television Arts awards ceremony in 1999. The next day she faxed her apologies to the press from the Priory Hospital, a drug and alcohol rehabilitation clinic in Roehampton, London. She later moved to Australia.

**Air, Donna.** *See* ASPINALL, JOHN.

**Aitken, James.** *See* PAINTER, JOHN THE.

**Aitken, Jonathan** (1940– ), cabinet minister, entrepreneur and perjurer. Once considered by himself and others to be a candidate for high office (and 'my old standby for many a dirty trick' by Alan CLARK), Aitken's downfall stemmed from a misguided decision to sue the *Guardian* for libel. Peter Preston, the paper's editor, had wanted to know why a bill for almost £1000 run up by the minister of state for defence procurement at the Ritz Hotel, Paris, had been paid by Said Ayas, a Saudi businessman involved in an arms contract. Aitken's explanation was that his wife, Lolicia, had subsequently settled the matter with a cash payment to Ayas's account. Had he left things at that, all might have been well. Instead, he embarked on a complicated story in which he sought to explain why a woman he said was his wife had paid for a hotel room in which it emerged later she had never stayed. The fabrication was repeated at the libel trial, and George Carman QC, for the *Guardian*, was able to show that Lolicia Aitken had been in Geneva with her daughter Victoria at the time Aitken claimed she was at the Ritz Hotel in Paris. Aitken was subsequently jailed for perjury. On his release he became a born-again Christian under the influence of the Reverend Nicky Gumbel, a charismatic preacher practising at the Holy Trinity Church, Brompton. At Gumbel's so-called Alpha courses participants make animal noises and then fall over backwards. Other converts include Samantha Fox, the former topless model.

**Alamo building, putting on your girlfriend's party frock and relieving yourself on the.** *See* OSBOURNE, JOHN MICHAEL ('OZZY').

**Alberts, the.** *See* GRAY, DOUGLAS and TONY.

**Albery, Sir Donald.** *See* PAPERING THE HOUSE.

**alcoholics.** *See* BERNARD, JEFFREY; BEST, GEORGE; FARSON, DANIEL; KEAN, EDMUND; LANGAN, PETER; MOON, KEITH; NEWTON, ROBERT; OSBOURNE, JOHN MICHAEL ('OZZY'); REED, OLIVER; THOMAS, DYLAN.

**Aldborough, Benjamin O'Neill Stratford, 6th earl of** (1808–75), landowner and balloonist. The 6th earl was marked by an inherited eccentricity. His great-grandfather, John Stratford, the 1st earl (1689–1777), had, on receiving the title, restyled himself 'The earl of Aldborough in the Palatine of Upper Ormonde', a place as fictitious as the family tree he then commissioned tracing his family back to William the Conqueror's lord great chamberlain. The 2nd earl, Edward Augustus Stratford, built five houses and a model town called Stratford-on-Slaney in County Wicklow. His death in 1801 interrupted a house party to which he had invited 100 young people with the intention of marrying them off to one another. He left 54 wills. Edward's brother John, the 3rd earl, had a very sociable wife but hated company himself. As soon as one of his wife's guests arrived, he would say: 'When do you leave? The coach passes every morning and I can get you on it tomorrow.' He would get up very early in the morning to pick fruit from the garden and hide it from his visitors.

The 6th earl was preoccupied by a 20-year project to build the largest hot-air balloon in the world. To satisfy his ambition he shut himself away at Stratford Lodge, outside Baltinglass, with one reliable servant. His meals were cooked in Dublin and sent up daily in the mail coach. His plan was to fly his balloon from Ireland to England and then across the Channel to France, where he had bought a plot of earth on the banks of the Seine as a landing ground. When the Crimean War broke out, however, he altered the proposed schedule, imagining instead that he would fly on across Europe, shooting at the Russian army from his balloon. The whole plan had to be abandoned when the hangar in which the balloon was kept caught fire on the day of its maiden flight. The fire spread to the main house but, unconcerned by the fate of his home, Aldborough cried, 'Save the balloon hangar!', and this was achieved under his direction. But the long chain of buckets which he'd organized was unable to save its contents; a spark caught the silk and the balloon was consumed in seconds. With it went the purpose of Aldborough's life. Since the big house had been burned to the ground, he moved for a time into the blackened balloon hangar with a few pieces of salvaged furniture. Later, he moved to Alicante in Spain, where he became a recluse in a hotel. He had his meals sent up to him, but refused to let anyone collect the used crockery. When one room filled up with dirty plates and glasses, he moved into another room. The earldom became extinct on his death.

*See also* BALLOONISTS.

**Aldeburgh, wearing pyjamas out of doors in.** *See* BROWN, CRAIG.

**Alexander, James** (*c*.1700–?), hooligan. From *The Justicing Notebook of William Hunt* (1744–9, ed. Elizabeth Crittall, Wiltshire Record Society, 37, 1982) it can be discovered that the 'yob culture' is not a modern phenomenon. The point is made by a case that came before Hunt, a magistrate, on 15 May 1747. John Swan, a labourer, complained against James Alexander for 'pissing in my hat'. The matter was settled, Hunt notes, 'by the defendant making the complainant satisfaction for the hat'. Dr J.A. Sharpe, professor of history at York University, has pointed out that the case is instructive since it indicates leniency at the time towards minor offenders when there were extenuating circumstances.

*Alexander vs Alexander and Amos. See* COLLUSION, DIVORCE BY.

**aliases.**
William ARCHER: William Grimwood.
Graham BARTON: Peter Poodle.
Ronnie BIGGS: Terry Cook.
Harry BENSON: Hugh Montgomery; the Marquess Montmorency; the comte de Montagu; the mayor of Chateaudun.
Paul BINT: the earl of Arundel; Lord Forte.
Kenneth DE COURCY: the duc de Grantmesnil.
Duke of EDINBURGH and Commander Michael Parker: Murgatroyd and Winterbottom.
Anthony Claud Frederick LAMBTON: Mr Lucas.
John HATFIELD: the Honourable Alexander Augustus Hope.
Rachel LEVERSON: Granny.
Andrew NEWTON: Peter Keene.
Frederick PARK: Fanny.
John STONEHOUSE: Joseph Markham; Donald Mildoon.
John VASSALL: Auntie.
Sara WILSON: Princess Susanna Caroline Matilda.
Lieutenant Colonel A.D. WINTLE: the earl of Norbury.
    *See also* NAMES, STREET.

**Alington, John** (1795–1863), farmer. Alington believed that he had a responsibility to educate the workers on his Letchworth estate. He read to them from Shakespeare and transformed a pond on his farm into a scale model of the world. While they rowed him round the different countries in his constructed microcosm he gave introductory lectures on geography, followed by discussions and quizzes. Before taking them to London for the Great Exhibition of 1851, and fearing that they might get lost, Alington required them to build a large model of the streets of London, fashioned out of logs and covering the area between Hyde Park and King's Cross. For a week he drilled his workers on the route from the railway station to the Exhibition and back again. Those learning the way from the station to the Crystal Palace wore a ribbon on their right legs; those responsible for mastering the return journey wore the ribbon on their left legs. The experiment was unsuccessful, and the trip was cancelled.

Alington was a generous man, and he held open house six days a week. Tramps, Gypsies and outcasts of all sorts were particularly welcome. Those on horseback could ride straight into his drawing room, where Alington would entertain them with ribald songs, accompanying himself on the grand piano. He enjoyed being carried round his garden in an open coffin, but was defiant at the end. In his last illness, he refused to take the prescribed medicine until his gardener had tried it for three days. Then he called for a tumbler of brandy, drank it and fell backwards, dead.

**alive, taking one's own pulse to check one is still.** *See* SPENCER, HERBERT.

**Allegro, John** (1923–88), philologist of the Semitic languages and author. As a senior, and greatly admired, lecturer in Old Testament and intertestamental studies at Manchester University (1962–70), Allegro argued – against most authorities in the field – that Jesus was a walking mushroom and the God of the Old Testament 'a mighty penis in the heavens who in a thunderous climax of the storm ejaculated semen upon the furrows of Mother Earth'. The argument was based on his belief that Christianity was a cryptic version of ancient sex cults inspired by the hallucinogenic mushroom *Amanita muscaria*.

After service in the Royal Navy (1941–6) and research at Magdalen College, Oxford, in Hebrew dialects, Allegro was appointed in 1952 to a lectureship in comparative Semitic philology and in Hebrew at Manchester University, where he taught until his retirement. His books, which include *The Dead Sea Scrolls* (1958) and *The People of the Dead Sea Scrolls* (1958), are generally regarded as the most authoritative on the subject. As the 1960s wore on, however, his theories became increasingly idiosyncratic and his obsession with mushrooms grew. In 1967 he acquired a following among adherents of the counter-culture by tracing the roots of Christianity to 'a phallic, drug-taking mystery cult', and in *The Sacred Mushroom and the Cross* (1970) he preached a new humanism that was to replace the ancient faiths discredited by his findings.

Allegro's theories were not accepted by everyone in the academic establishment. The historian Dr Henry Chadwick wrote in the *Daily Telegraph* that there was 'no particle of evidence for all this exciting conjecture. Allegro's work reads like a Semitic philologist's erotic nightmare after consuming a highly indigestible meal of hallucinogenic fungi'.

Allegro denied that he ever consumed the mushroom himself. 'I wouldn't be so bloody stupid,' he said.

**Allen, Margaret** (1906–49), bus conductress. On 28 August 1948, in Rawstenall, Lancashire, Allen, who liked to be called Bill, battered to death 68-year-old Nancy Chadwick, who told fortunes and counted her money in the park. 'I was in one of my funny moods,' Miss Allen explained. The police had wanted to speak to Allen because Miss Chadwick's body had been found outside her house at 137 Bacup Road. At first she denied any involvement, but later admitted hitting Miss Chadwick with a hammer, putting her body in the coal cellar and then, in the early hours of the morning, dumping it in the street in the hope that it would look as though the injuries had been caused by a traffic accident rather than from nine hammer blows. A defence of insanity was put forward at Allen's trial, but without success. Her friend, Annie Cook, organized a petition for clemency but succeeded in collecting only 17 signatures. Allen was hanged at Strangeways Prison, Manchester, on 12 January 1949.

For references to similar murders, *see* INSTRUMENTS, BLUNT.

**Allen, Maud.** *See* BILLING, PEMBERTON.

**Allen, Peter Anthony** (1931–64), dairyman and small-time thief. Allen and his accomplice, Gwynne Owen Evans, were the last men to be hanged in Britain. On 7 April 1964, during a robbery of a Preston laundry that went wrong, Allen and Evans murdered laundry-worker John Alan West by hitting him with a poker and then stabbing him. Allen left behind his mackintosh and a Royal Life Saving Society medallion bearing his name.

Allen had been behind with his rent, and together with Evans had been on a small crime spree, later being fined by Preston Borough magistrates. Needing money to pay their £10 fines, they called on West, who was known to leave cash lying around. At their trial each blamed the other for hitting West with the poker. The jury convicted both after a retirement of three hours, and their appeals and applications for a reprieve were refused. In the letters signing their death warrants, the permanent undersecretary of state at the Home Office said, 'It seems kinder to let the prisoners go on hoping until the last possible moment.' Allen was executed at Walton Prison, Liverpool, and Evans at Strangeways, Manchester, on 13 August 1964.

*See also* CAPITAL PUNISHMENT.

**all the ceremony natural to a Frenchman.** *See* CARLETON, MARY.

**amateur fist-fighters.** *See* ARGYLE, MICHAEL; BARKER, COLONEL LESLIE IVOR GAUNTLETT; BERNARD, JEFFREY; BROMLEY-DAVENPORT, LIEUTENANT COLONEL SIR WALTER; CHAMPION, SIR CLAUDE; WILLIAMSON, NICOL.

**ambassador kicked downstairs, Belgian.** *See* DROITWICH BAMBRIDGE, LIEUTENANT COLONEL SIR WALTER.

**ambassador's wife up a tree.** *See* TYRRELL, LADY MARGARET-ANN.

**ambassador turned upside down, Austrian.** *See* WILKES, JOHN.

**Ambrose, Bert.** *See* NASH, JIMMY.

**Amherst, Jeffrey John Archer, 5th Earl** (1896–1985), soldier, war hero, BOAC pilot and inspiration for *Private Lives* (1931), a light comedy by Noël Coward (1899–1973), thought by some to be his masterpiece. In 1929 Coward departed on an extended tour of the Far East with 27 pieces of luggage, a gramophone and Jeffrey Amherst, an old Etonian and former officer in the Coldstream Guards. Suffering from a sudden loss of confidence, Coward had become unsure of his talent, and of his friends. He was sure of his love for Amherst, however, a dashing aristocrat who had won the Military Cross in World War I and was to become a commercial airline pilot after World War II.

Unhappily, Coward's feelings were not reciprocated. Amherst preferred a boxer called Gerry MacCarthy whom he had met in Jersey City. The resulting tension surfaced in the play that Coward sat down to write in the Cathay Hotel, Shanghai – *Private Lives*. Among the many penetrating observations about the human condition in this remarkable work, perhaps the most profound is Amanda's declaration in Act 1, 'I think very few people are completely normal, deep down.'

Amherst was a popular member of Pratts and the Garrick.

For Eton College as 'an absolute hotbed of buggery', *see* COOK, ROBIN. For references to other Old Etonians, *see* ETONIANS.

**Amiri, Julie** (1952– ), housewife. In 1993, 35-year-old mother of three Mrs Amiri claimed to have orgasms when detained by police or security guards. Arrested for shoplifting in Oxford Street, she said in court that she only stole to get arrested so that she could have an orgasm. Mrs Amiri managed to convince doctors that her condition was genuine. Although she was arrested 53 times between 1985 and 1993, she was not convicted once.

*Amorous Prawn, The.* *See* AMPTHILL, JOHN RUSSELL, 3RD BARON.

**Ampthill, John Russell, 3rd Baron** (1897–1973), naval officer and petitioner in notorious divorce proceedings, which, over several decades, involved two trials, two appeals and a hearing before the Committee of Privileges in the House of Lords.

In 1916, Christabel Hart, a headstrong young woman with a taste for hunting and ballroom dancing – in which she excelled, particularly in the tango – answered an advertisement in *The Times* placed by three lonely sailors, one of whom was John Russell. They met her when next on leave, and all three were smitten. Russell proposed marriage, but Christabel rejected him and departed for Gretna Green with his friend, Gilbert Bradley. There they failed to satisfy the residency qualification and returned to England unmarried. In 1918, Christabel consented, after all, to marry Russell, but ruled that these altered circumstances should not be a restriction on her social life. Russell agreed that they should not have children for several years, not realizing, perhaps, that to Christabel this meant no sexual relations either. The honeymoon was spent with Russell's parents, and although there was a certain amount of kissing during his Christmas leave, sex consisted of his climaxing between her legs – a practice that Christabel described as 'Hunnish'.

When Russell left the navy he took a job with Vickers. The couple no longer shared a bedroom, and in two years they dined together twice. On one occasion, Christabel spent the night at Gilbert Bradley's flat and in the morning Bradley telephoned Russell, asking him to bring round day clothes for his wife. Later she wrote to a friend, 'I have been indiscreet all my life and he has enough evidence to divorce me once a week.' In June 1923 Christabel visited a clairvoyant, who told her she was pregnant – a state of affairs confirmed by a gynaecologist, in spite of the fact that she was still a virgin. She passed the news on to Russell, adding 'I suppose I must be another Virgin Mary.' On 15 October 1921 she gave birth to a son, Geoffrey.

Russell petitioned for divorce, citing Bradley, an unnamed man alleged to be Geoffrey's father, and a Lieutenant George Cross about whom little else is known. At the first trial, which began in July 1922 before Lord Merrivale, Russell's parents, Lord and Lady Ampthill, were the chief witnesses. They described their son as thunderstruck when learning of his wife's pregnancy since she had always denied him his conjugal rights. They could see no similarity between the baby and their son at the same age. The baby was brought into court and inspected by the jury during the luncheon adjournment. Christabel admitted indiscreet behaviour, but denied adultery. Her husband was Geoffrey's father, she insisted, conception having taken place without penetration – possibly when Russell was sleepwalking in his pyjamas. After a ten-day hearing, the jury was unable to agree a verdict. On 28 February 1923 a retrial began before Mr Justice Hill. This time, the jury found that Christabel had had intercourse with an unknown man and the baby was declared illegitimate. In 1926 Christabel, as her son's guardian, brought an action to establish his legitimacy. She won the case and Geoffrey was declared the rightful heir.

John Russell succeeded to the Ampthill title in 1935. After he was at last divorced from Christabel in 1937, he remarried twice and, by his second marriage, had a son, John, who, on his father's death in 1973, claimed the title. Geoffrey Russell, by this time a producer of West End plays, wrote to the House of Lords requesting that he might take the seat, but was told that his half-brother had already lodged an application. In February 1976 the Committee of Privileges in the House of Lords heard the claim for succession brought by John Russell and contested by Geoffrey Russell 'to protect my mother's reputation'. The evidence from the 1926 illegitimacy dispute was heard again and John Russell offered to withdraw if Geoffrey would make available blood tests carried out on himself and his mother, who by now had died. Geoffrey declined, but in April the Committee ruled in his favour. As the 4th Baron Ampthill he was henceforth able to devote himself to the production of theatrical entertainments, the most successful of which to date had been *The Amorous Prawn* (1960), which had included in its cast Miss Evelyn 'Boo' Laye.

After World War II Christabel Russell went to live in Ireland, becoming joint master of the Ballymacad Hunt in County Meath, and continuing to hunt side-saddle until well into her seventies. At the age of 78 she rode across Australia and then drove home in a van. Back in London, she discovered that it had been unlicensed and uninsured. She died in Galway at the age of 80.

**Amsterdam, known to have visited.** *See* GARVIE, SHEILA.

**anagrams.** *See* PAISLEY, IAN; PALMER TOMKINSON, TARA; URQUHART, SIR THOMAS.

**Anderton, James** (1932– ), policeman. Known as 'Holy Jim', Anderton became chief constable of Greater Manchester at the age of 44, thereby finding an ideal platform from which to exercise his authoritarian disposition and command of evocative imagery. Describing himself as 'the Lord's prophet', he accused homosexuals of 'swirling around in a cesspit of their own making' and pornographers of 'floating in a sea filth'. Criminals, deserved to be 'flogged until they begged for mercy'.

During Anderton's boyhood his father, a coal miner, made him read the Bible every morning, and beat him with a strap for the slightest misdemeanour. After winning a scholarship to Wigan grammar school, he joined the Manchester police in 1953, rising to the rank of chief superintendent by the age of 35. He is proud of the fact that he arrested his first wrongdoer at the age of 6 – a neighbour's 4-year-old daughter who had stolen an orange from his mother's kitchen. She became a Sunday-school teacher 21 years later. Satisfied that the infant criminal had learned the error of her ways, Anderton married her in 1959.

Anderton was revered by his men. He was the first chief constable to equip his force with rubber bullets and he customarily described defence lawyers as 'belonging to a society for the prevention of the conviction of the guilty'. Some of his supporters were disappointed by his opposition to the death penalty, and have remained unconvinced by his belief that only God can take away life.

A former lay preacher, Anderton converted to Catholicism after being inspired by the Pope's visit to Manchester in 1982. Disappointed by his failure to become commissioner of the Metropolitan Police, he retired from the force in 1987. He lives in Sale, Cheshire, where he likes to ramble and write poetry.

**Andrews, the Reverend Basil** (1867–1958), clergyman and gambler. When Jack SPOT engaged fellow Soho gangster Albert DIMES in a knife fight in Frith Street in 1955, the police supposed that they had at last netted two of London's leading underworld figures. They had overlooked the intervention of the Reverend Andrews. At Spot's trial, Andrews, an 88-year-old clergyman who had suffered many recent disappointments at the race track and in Soho gambling rooms, informed the court that the altercation, such as it was, had been instigated by Dimes.

It later emerged that one of Spot's business associates, Morris 'Moishe Blue Boy' Goldstein, had given Andrews £63 to provide false witness. Andrews admitted the deception and was then used by the prosecution to give evidence against Goldstein, who, with Spot's wife Rita and Bernard 'The Yank' Schach, was tried for conspiracy to pervert the course of justice. Asked by the judge whether he ever spoke the truth, Andrews replied, 'No' – an interesting example of the 'Liar Paradox', but one which the judge on this occasion preferred not to discuss. Goldstein, Rita Spot and Schach were convicted and sentenced to terms in prison.

In *The Theory of Types* (1903) and *The Ramified Theory of Types* (1905), Bertrand Russell attempted to solve the semantic paradoxes, such as the 'Liar Paradox', and, more importantly, his own paradox, known as 'Russell's Paradox', which in the opinion of Gottlieb Frege had threatened the foundations of mathematics. Logicians have judged the attempt to have been only partially successful.

**Andrews, Jane** (1962– ), dresser who killed her lover, Tom Cressman, in the celebrated Cricket Bat Murder of June 2000.
  *See* YORK, SARAH MARGARET, DUCHESS OF; INSTRUMENTS, BLUNT.

**Andy from the Sixties.** *See* DEMPSEY, ANDREW; EYRES, TONY.

***anglais, le vice.*** *See* ASHBEE, HENRY SPENCER; JEFFRIES, MARY; PAYNE, CYNTHIA; POTTER, SARAH; PROCTOR, HARVEY; ST CLAIR, LINDI; SALA, GEORGE AUGUSTUS; STOCK, LIEUTENANT ST GEORGE H.

**anglers.** *See* BIRCH, THOMAS; MATURIN, CHARLES ROBERT.

**Ankles, the Case of the Thick.** *See* WAINEWRIGHT, THOMAS.

**antics, zany.** *See* STANSHALL, VIVIAN.

**aphrodisiac, arsenic used as an.** *See* MAYBRICK, FLORENCE ELIZA-
BETH.

**aphrodisiacs, peddlers of.** *See* FORMAN, SIMON (and also his accomplice Anne TURNER); GRAHAM, JAMES; SOLOMON, SAMUEL.

**apples, bad.** *See* ASHTON, HORACE; CHALLENOR, DETECTIVE SERGEANT
HAROLD; GARNER, ROY (for Dectective Superintendent Tony Lundy);
HUMPREYS, JAMES (for Commander Kenneth Drury and Commander
Wally Virgo); KELAHER, DETECTIVE CHIEF INSPECTOR VICTOR; LILLEY,
DETECTIVE CONSTABLE NIGEL; MOODY, DETECTIVE CHIEF SUPERINTEN-
DENT WILLIAM; RHINO-WHIP CASE, THE; ROBSON, DETECTIVE INSPECTOR
BRIAN.

**Aram, Eugene** (1704–59), scholar, linguist, teacher, lexicographer and
murderer. Born in the village of Netherdale, Yorkshire, to an ancient and
respected family, (one of whose members had served as high sheriff for
that county in the reign of Edward III), Aram was working as a school
teacher in Knaresborough when he committed a particularly brutal
murder. His trial in 1759 occasioned a timely reminder from the bench that
academics should have no need of income. 'So horrid a crime,' declared
the judge, 'could not naturally have been expected from a man of so studious a turn, as the inducement that led to it was merely a gain in wealth, of
which a scholar should not be covetous.'

Contemporary chroniclers were as shocked as the judge that a man
who had Latin and Greek, who had mastered Chaldee and Arabic and had
studied Celtic in all its dialects – thereafter making comparisons between
Celtic, English, Latin, Greek and Hebrew, and, having found many similarities between them, had then embarked on a comparative lexicon –
should have committed such a crime. 'The criminal was a man of extraordinary endowments,' wrote the compilers of the *Newgate Calendar*. 'On the
very slender stock of learning found in a day school, he built a fabric which
would have been worthy to stand on the shoulders of our literary Atlas, Dr
Johnson.'

In spite of his many learned enquiries, Aram, on 8 February 1745, and
in the company of one Richard Houseman, murdered a Knaresborough
shoemaker, Daniel Clarke, who had advertised the fact that his wife was
soon to inherit a considerable fortune. Persuaded by Aram and Houseman

that he should seek to impress his wife's trustees with a display of his own riches, Clarke obtained a quantity of silver plate and other valuables on credit. On the pretext that they would advise him on the disposal of this windfall, Aram and Houseman took Clarke into Knaresborough Forest, where Aram killed him with a single blow to the head. The treasure was then divided equally, and Aram carried his share to London, where he sold it. He thereafter took a job as an usher in a school in Piccadilly, later obtaining the same employment at schools in different parts of the country. For the next 14 years he worked quietly in his chosen field of comparative linguistics. He corresponded with no one, and was presumed dead – except by his wife, whom he had abandoned at the time of his crime.

In 1759 the bones of a human body were dug up in a field near Knaresborough. Aram's embittered wife had for some time been claiming that Clarke had been murdered by Houseman and her husband, and Houseman was brought before a coroner. Invited to inspect the recently discovered skeleton, Houseman fell into the coroner's trap. 'These are no more Dan Clarke's bones than they are mine!' he exclaimed. Asked how he could be so sure, he replied that Clarke's remains were buried in St Robert's Cave, in quite another part of Knaresborough.

A search was made for Aram, and he was eventually discovered quietly pursuing his studies at a school in Norfolk. Tried for murder at the county assizes, he spoke eloquently in his own defence, arguing that it would be most unsafe to convict. After 14 years it was not possible, he reasoned, to identify the bones as Clarke's. In this he was certainly correct, but the judge was unimpressed and the jury took only 20 minutes to return a guilty verdict. Aram was hanged on 6 August 1759. The proceeds from his crime – of which, as the judge had pointed out, a scholar should have had no need – amounted to £16. His career inspired a ballad by Thomas Hood, and a novel, *Eugene Aram* (1832), by Bulwer-Lytton, which asserted his innocence.

**Archer, Jeffrey.** *See* ARCHER, WILLIAM.

**Archer, Mary.** *See* ARCHER, WILLIAM; DUTY, LOYALTY ABOVE AND BEYOND THE CALL OF.

**Archer, William** (1879–1957), soldier, bigamist and confidence trickster. In 1914 Archer was charged with defrauding the public while posing as a mortgage broker. He jumped bail and departed for France, where he called himself William Grimwood and worked as a hospital orderly. In 1916 he travelled to America on a false passport and posed as an army surgeon recovering from a war wound. To back up this story he had compiled an album of false photographs that showed him in uniform. With the help of a bogus degree from Oxford University he then set up a charity that claimed to be raising money for injured soldiers. In 1917 Archer was arrested for taking money by false pretences and was sentenced by a United States court to three years in prison. He was released after 10 months and departed for Canada. Here, he re-offended and was sentenced to a year's hard labour. Before he could serve the sentence he was deported to Britain, where he was arrested and sent back to the Old Bailey to face a charge of jumping bail. He spent seven weeks in prison on remand before the prosecution dropped the case after one witness died and another moved to France.

Archer's criminal activities, while suggesting a systematically dishonest nature, were undistinguished; certainly they were less remarkable than those of his son, Jeffrey, born in 1941 to William and his wife, Lola, a journalist on a local newspaper. After a career of flamboyant dishonesty, including the theft of a pair of trousers in Canada, Jeffrey (later, Lord) Archer was charged, in 2001, with perjury and conspiracy to pervert the course of justice. The allegations referred to an earlier civil action in which Archer had won substantial damages from the *Star* newspaper for suggesting that he had slept with a prostitute, Monica Coghlan. In the criminal trial he was found guilty and sentenced to four years in prison. A moral philosopher from Bradford University pointed out at the time that, since punishment can never be justified for its own sake but only by reason of its deterrent value (and even that – against Kant – is to treat a person as means), Mr Justice Potts's purpose in sending Archer to prison must have been not to punish him but to discourage deputy chairmen of the Conservative Party in future from committing perjury in libel trials. Throughout his ordeal, Archer was supported by his wife Mary. He is the author of several airport novels, poorly received by the critics.

**Argyle, Michael** (1915–99), circuit judge, sportsman and parliamentary candidate. Argyle's pronouncements from the bench at the Old Bailey, where he sat as an additional judge, were a constant source of controversy. An accomplished heavyweight boxer in his youth, he preferred sporting events not to be interrupted by court proceedings, acts of God or technological breakdowns. He always kept a television set in his robing room and was enraged when a union dispute temporarily interfered with the coverage of a cricket tour of the West Indies in 1985. 'Here we are struggling in a cold temperature,' he told a surprised court, 'while in the Caribbean in glorious sunshine 22 of the best cricketers in the world are engaged in a test match. There is television yet none of us can watch the game. It is enough to make an orthodox Jew join the Nazi Party.'

Celebrated for such outbursts, and for a sentencing policy that was at best erratic, Argyle first gained notoriety when he presided at the *Oz* 'School Kids Issue' trial in 1971. John Mortimer, appearing for the magazine, had no difficulty in representing Argyle as an out-of-touch reactionary. When the trial was dramatized for television, Leslie Phillips, a broad comedian who had achieved popularity in the *Carry On* series of films, was cast as Argyle.

The caricature was not without justification. Offence was taken in some quarters when Argyle, paying tribute to a woman detective, said, 'You are far too attractive to be a police woman. You should be an actress.' Speculating on the number of immigrants in Britain, he said, 'I don't have the figures, but just go to Bradford.' A British-born black defendant was told to 'get out and go back to Jamaica'. A bar room bouncer convicted of rape received more practical advice, 'You come from Derby. That is my part of the world. Off you go, and don't come back.' On one occasion, a juror, who had talked briefly to a witness, was fined £2000 and placed in the cells for the afternoon.

In a short farewell speech from the bench in 1988, Argyle admitted that he might have made a few mistakes. 'For which I apologize,' he said.

**Argyll, Margaret duchess of** (1912–93), society beauty, hostess and gossip columnist. A formidable litigant herself, it is as the defendant in an acrimonious divorce case that the duchess will be remembered. The action, brought by her second husband, the 11th duke of Argyll, involved the production in court of a diary, stolen by the duke, in which the duchess had listed the physical attributes of her many lovers as if – in the words of her *Daily Telegraph* obituary – 'she was running them at Newmarket'. Still more sensationally, Polaroid photographs were distributed in the jury box in which the duchess, naked but for three strings of pearls, was seen to be fellating someone who was soon to pass into folklore as 'the Headless Man'.

The only daughter of George Wigham, a self-made businessman from Glasgow, Margaret was voted 'Deb of the Year' in 1930. She turned down an offer of marriage from Lord Beaverbrook's son, Max Aitken, and broke off her engagement to Prince Aly Khan in favour of the earl of Warwick, whom she subsequently deserted for Charles Sweeney, an American golfer. She was not noted for her intelligence, nor did she have a sense of humour, but her striking looks and vivacious personality ensured that the couple soon became the toast of London and New York. She was even immortalized in a song by Cole Porter, 'You're the Top':

> You're the nimble tread
> Of the feet of Fred
> Astaire.
> You're Mussolini,
> You're Mrs Sweeney,
> You're Camembert ...

Sweeney discouraged his wife from leading an ostentatious social life during World War II, so she consoled herself with American servicemen.

She and Sweeney had two children – Frances, later the duchess of Rutland, and Brian but the marriage failed, as did her second, to the duke of Argyll. In 1963, he instigated divorce proceedings in Edinburgh before Lord Wheatley. In his 40,000-word summing-up, Wheatley found that the duchess had committed adultery with at least four men: the West German ambassador to the United Nations, the public relations officer at the Savoy Hotel, an American businessman whose habits the judge likened to those of a tom cat, and the unidentifiable man in the Polaroid photographs. The images in these of oral sex proved to Lord Wheatley that the duchess was 'a highly sexed woman'; even worse, that 'she indulged in what I can only describe as disgusting sexual acts'.

The duke was granted his divorce, but the duchess's many feuds continued to entertain the public. She sued at one time or another her daughter, her landlord, her bankers and her recently widowed stepmother, whom she accused (correctly, as it turned out) of having an affair with her ex-husband.

In her later years, the duchess was much exercised by the servant problem. In the early 1980s she fell out with Mrs Springett, who had looked after her for many years. Mrs Springett had been found unconscious next to an empty whisky bottle on the floor of the duchess's bedroom. Good relations were restored, but the duchess was later obliged to send solicitor's letters instructing Springett to stop calling her 'a silly old whore' in front of her guests. In 1989, her Moroccan maid was prosecuted for running up a phone bill of several thousand pounds. Had the duchess not been permanently drunk, the maid pleaded, she would have remembered that she had given her permission to telephone her family in Morocco. The maid was acquitted.

Throughout the 1970s and 1980s, the duchess continued to entertain lavishly in her Grosvenor House apartment, but her final years were sad. Evicted from her Park Lane suite in 1990 she became a resident in a Pimlico nursing home.

Speculation over the identity of the 'Headless Man' continued after her death. Popular candidates were Sir Winston Churchill's son-in-law, Duncan Sandys, and the duke of Edinburgh. It was generally judged to be a disappointment when in 1999 the 'Headless Man' was finally revealed to be the film actor, Douglas Fairbanks Jr.

**Aries, Robert** (1919–93), racehorse owner, art collector and corporate blackmailer. A dapper, invariably cheerful operator, Dr Aries liked to refer to himself as a latter-day Robin Hood. Multinational companies who had suffered from his depredations took a less romantic view, perhaps. In 1980 the *Sunday Times* estimated that corporations as formidable as ICI, Marks and Spencer and de Beers had been fleeced of at least £50 million.

Dr Aries's method was to register the trademarks of large companies before they thought of doing so themselves. He then invited them to buy these back at his price. One of his most successful coups involved Exxon, the giant oil company. In 1972 it came to his attention that Standard Oil, as it was then called, was thinking of changing its name. After lengthy research, Aries discovered that Exxon was to be the new title. He immediately registered it in France, which gave him the right to trade as Exxon in 22 other countries. It was rumoured that Exxon had to pay Dr Aries over £1 million to recover their rights.

Another of Dr Aries's ploys was to bribe laboratory workers to reveal the development research their companies were involved in. He would then take out patents on drug compounds that he now knew were needed to develop new products. As a consequence, drug companies would be obliged to buy back the patents on compounds that they assumed they already owned. Nor did Aries shrink from blatant blackmail. He liked to research the trading practices of large companies and then to threaten them with exposure if he found evidence of price-fixing schemes or tax avoidance. Many paid for his silence.

Dr Aries liked to keep negotiations on a friendly basis. A joke that particularly pleased him was to be photographed – trilby hat doffed in jaunty salutation – outside the offices of his intended prey. He would then send the photograph to the organization's chief executive. Nor did he bear malice towards those who rejected his demands. He would be quite satisfied if the chairman treated him to an expensive lunch. He thought there was little point in risking unpleasantness when there were enough fools already willing to finance his art collection and string of racehorses. 'I'm not some sort of crook,' he explained to the *Sunday Times*.

**Arif, Dogan** (1951– ), head of the gangland family that took over the control of drugs and extortion in south London after the downfall of the RICHARDSONS, and which continues to exert its influence in spite of the fact that many of its leading members are serving long prison sentences. According to a senior police officer, 'It doesn't matter whose name is over the door of a pub, restaurant or club in this area, it is the Arifs who own it.'

In 1983 Dogan Arif had been acquitted of taking part in a bogus arms deal to swindle Ayatollah Khomeini out of £34 million. In 1992 he was imprisoned for 14 years in connection with an £8.5 million drug-smuggling plot. At the time of his sentence, and in the tradition of other high-profile crooks such as Robert MAXWELL, he owned a football club, Fisher Athletic. During his time as chairman, the club, which on one occasion won the Gola League, was involved in paying substantial transfer fees for well-known players and employed Malcolm Allison (known as 'Big Mal' during his days in the 1970s as Manchester City's coach) as its manager.

In November 1990, two of Dogan's brothers, Dennis and Mehmet, had ⁓⁓⁓⁓⁓⁓⁓⁓ in Reigate High Street wearing Ronald Reagan masks and armed with 12-bore Browning self-loading shotguns. They had intended to rob a Securicor van to finance the drug deal. The police, who had been targeting the Arifs for some months, surrounded the van and, in the ensuing fire-fight, shot dead an old-time bank robber called Kenny Baker, who had accompanied the Arifs. At the subsequent trial, Mehmet Arif pleaded guilty to conspiracy to rob, but Dennis Arif ran the imaginative defence of duress, saying that he owed Baker £60,000 and that Baker had threatened to shoot him unless he settled the debt by taking part in the robbery. He was not believed. Earlier in the year, he and Baker had attended an Arif family wedding at the Savoy Hotel along with other powerful crime families, including the ADAMS family and the FRASERS. Dennis Arif received a sentence of 22 years and Mehmet 18 years.

Dogan Arif, who continues to control the family's fortunes from prison, was upset when, in September 2000, he was relegated to seventh place in the *Sunday Times*'s 'Criminal Rich List' with a fortune of a mere £7.5 million. He blamed his poor showing on his current circumstances.

*See also* DALY, JOSEPHINE; DURESS.

**Aris, Doris** (1921– ), pensioner, community worker and bootlegger. When Customs and Excise officers carried out a dawn raid on the Community Centre run by Mrs Aris in the Sneinton area of Nottingham, they found 13 kilograms of narcotics. They also found the widowed grandmother's diary, which identified her as the mastermind behind an international drug-smuggling gang, and listed the name of her main supplier, a shadowy underworld figure known to her only as 'Big Albert'.

David Faulkener, the Customs officer who carried out the raid, was surprised that Mrs Aris had abused her position in the community to build up a client list of vulnerable old folk willing to experiment with banned narcotics. Trevor Brown, Nottingham Council's assistant director of housing, confirmed that the bespectacled pensioner had been a popular chairwoman of the Citywide Flatdwellers and Residents Association. 'She was greatly appreciated for her community work,' he said. 'A lot of old people will be disappointed if the court decides that a custodial sentence would be appropriate.'

Mrs Aris was sentenced to 96 hours of community service.

*See also* BUS PASS BANDITS.

**Aristides, Susan Mary** (1957–2001), housewife and gangster. Aristides (*née* Hicks), who was born in London and lived there until her marriage at the age of 21, was the first woman, and the first foreigner, to rise to a prominent position in the Greek underworld – a milieu famous for its entrenched chauvinism. By 1998 she had become the greatly feared enforcer-in-chief for the Dridbrakos crime family, the most powerful in Athens. In May 2001 she was blown up when her Rottweiler, Boris, sat on a bomb she had in her car. Athens police chief Giorgos Angelakos told reporters that the home-made contraption was under the handbrake and a remote control device was found in Mrs Aristides's bag. Her ears were tightly packed with cotton wool. Boris, who did not survive the blast, was next to her in the car. Detectives concluded that Mrs Aristides was on her way to avenge the murders of two members of the Dridbrakos family. Mrs Aristides's Greek-Australian husband disappeared five years ago.

**Armstrong, Major Herbert Rowse** (1861–1922), soldier, provincial solicitor and murderer. A diminutive, mild-mannered man who practised law in Hay-on-Wye, Major Armstrong fitted the stereotype of the poisoner – usually defined by criminologists as a gentle, ineffectual person who feels compelled to right through poison an injustice dealt to him by life, but who in his other dealings is punctiliously correct. For example, when handing a buttered scone laced with arsenic to an intended victim, Major Armstrong still remembered to say, 'Excuse fingers.' He departed from the Dr Crippen mould in just one respect: having, as he supposed, solved his domestic problem, he became over-confident and tried by the same method to solve a professional one.

Major Armstrong's wife, Katie, was a tyrant. She would inform her husband in company that it was his bath night, or that he had had enough to drink. Once, at a tennis party, she told him in the middle of a game that it was time to leave. 'Six o'clock, Herbert,' she said. 'You can't expect punctuality from the servants if their master is late for meals.' When, early in 1921, she died after an attack of abdominal cramps, diagnosed by the family GP, Dr Hinks, as neuritis, the major's many friends judged it a happy release.

Two months later, and after repeated invitations, Oswald Martin, a rival solicitor in Hay with whom Armstrong was in dispute, went to tea at Armstrong's house. Martin ate a buttered scone and a slice of currant loaf, and soon after he got home he was seized with severe stomach pains. Dr Hinks was summoned and, recognizing the symptoms of a bilious attack, prescribed accordingly. When the sickness continued, the doctor had an analysis made, which discovered in the sample submitted a third of a gram of arsenic. It struck him then that the symptoms of arsenic poisoning are the same as those of neuritis, for which he had treated Mrs Armstrong.

Dr Hinks went to the police, Mrs Armstrong's body was exhumed and a considerable amount of arsenic was found in her stomach. Major Armstrong was arrested and later tried before Mr Justice Avory, who was unimpressed by the major's 'not guilty' plea. 'To find three and a half grams of arsenic in a solicitor's pocket is surely rare?' he observed at one point. The jury convicted, and Armstrong was sentenced to death. The hangman at his execution, John ELLIS, was surprised to discover that his client weighed only 8 stone 3 lb, obliging him to prepare the longest drop he'd ever used. He adjusted the noose and Armstrong said, 'I'm coming, Katie!' Afterwards, Ellis, who was a follower of rugby league, met a Rochdale Hornets player in the town, and spent a pleasant hour with him before returning home by train, arriving in time for tea.

**Arnett, Richard** (1674–1728), hangman. Arnett was an incompetent executioner, even by the standards of his day. Appointed London's hangman in 1719 after the previous incumbent, William Marvel, had himself been hanged for stealing ten silk handkerchiefs valued at 12 shillings, Arnett was late for his first job. By the time he turned up the crowd had become impatient and they threw him into a horse pond. The three condemned men were returned to Newgate while Arnett was taken away for treatment by a physician.

The following year, knowing that he had two people to despatch, but confused by drink, Arnett tried to hang the Ordinary of Newgate, the Reverend John Villette, and a Catholic priest who had come to administer the last rites. After this confusion had been sorted out, the platform collapsed and the three officials fell ten feet to the ground, landing in a heap on top of the two prisoners. Arnett had forgotten to secure the bolt that held the platform together.

No mishaps are reported to have occurred when in November 1724 Arnett executed the notorious Cockney thief and highwayman, Jack SHEPPARD, but when he hanged Jonathan WILD at Tyburn seven months later, he took so long in his preparations that Wild's pickpockets had plenty of time to relieve the spectators of their watches and wallets. Irritated by the delay, the mob threatened to return Arnett to the horse pond again unless he got on with the job.

Arnett died at Deptford in August 1728, and was succeeded by John Hooper, the 'Laughing Hangman', who made himself welcome to his prisoners by his gift of mimicry and fund of jokes. One of his victims, Major Oneby, left Hooper five shillings in his will.

**arsenic.** *See* ARMSTRONG, MAJOR HERBERT ROWSE; COTTON, MARY ANN; CRIPPEN, DR HAWLEY HARVEY; JACKSON, THE REVEREND WILLIAM; MAYBRICK, FLORENCE ELIZABETH; SMITH, MADELEINE.

**Arsenic and Old Face.** *See* WINTERTON, CECIL TOURNOUR, 6TH EARL.

**arsonists.** *See* ADAM THE LEPER; BRIAN, JOHN HERMAN; CREAM, DR THOMAS NEILL; GLASGOW, JAMES CARR-BOYLE, 5TH EARL OF; HARRIS, LEOPOLD; LANCEY, JOHN; PAINTER, JOHN THE; RICHARDSON, CHARLIE.

**arsonists, inadvertent.** *See* HELL-FIRE CLUB, THE IRISH; MYTTON, JOHN; PAGET, DOROTHY; SALISBURY, FRANCES MARY, 1ST MARCHIONESS OF.

**art forgers.** *See* DREWE, JOHN; KEATING, TOM.

**'Artful Dodgers'.** *See* PICKPOCKETS, 'ARTFUL DODGERS' AND CUT-PURSES; SHEPPARD, JACK.

**artful women, the softer deceptions of.** *See* BAKER, MARY; CALVEY, LINDA; CARLETON, MARY; DIVER, JENNY; DOWSE, MARGARET; FLECKNEY, EVELYN; GOLDSTEIN, LILIAN; JONES, JANIE; LEVERSON, RACHEL; PRIDDEN, SARAH; WALTERS, CATHERINE; WILSON, HARRIET; WILSON, SARAH.

**Ashbee, Henry Spencer** (1834–1900), senior partner in a Hamburg-based trading company, wealthy book collector and pornographer, with a special interest in flagellation. Married with four children, Ashbee was a corresponding member of the Royal Academy of Madrid, and in his lifetime he amassed the finest collection of books about Cervantes outside Spain. He also formed an unrivalled assortment of 'Kruptadia', which was book dealers' code for pornography. In 1877 he published *Index Librorum Prohibitorum*, the first major English bibliography of erotic and pornographic writing, which borrowed its title from the Vatican's list of proscribed books. By his will, he proposed to leave his unrivalled collection of erotica to the trustees of the British Museum, who were initially offended by the offer. However, they were keen to have his library of Spanish literature and, on being offered both or neither, they accepted Ashbee's erotica. This proved extensive enough to form the original 'Private Case' of the museum's forbidden books.

Speculation has always pointed to Ashbee as the author of *My Secret Life* (1888–92), a lengthy account by 'Walter', an anonymous diarist, of his sexual relations with 1200 prostitutes and domestic servants over a period of 40 years. The work runs to eleven volumes and the social underworld in which the events occur is described in vivid detail. Experts have generally opposed this attribution on the grounds that Ashbee's dates do not match Walter's, and, further, that the leaden prudishness of his own diaries is in stark contrast to the explicitness of Walter's. A characteristic passage from the latter might be:

> I put my hand down and felt around. What rapture to feel my machine buried! In another minute nature urged a crisis, and at once I spent in a virgin cunt; my prick virgin also. Thus ended my first fuck!

Ashbee attempted no such effects in non-pseudonymous works and the conclusion has hitherto been that he merely arranged publication of *My Secret Life*, which he was able to do because of his clandestine contacts with the Dutch and Belgian pornographic book trade. However, in *The Erotomaniac: The Secret Life of Henry Spencer Ashbee* (2001), Ian Gibson claims that Ashbee's diaries do in fact provide strong evidence for his authorship of *My Secret Life*. Against previous experts (notably, Steven Marcus in his *The Other Victorians*, 1966), Gibson finds similarities between the diaries and *My Secret Life*, not least a penchant for Germanic sentence structures, misspellings and a shared obsession with classification.

In *Index Librorum Prohibitorum* (1877), Ashbee usefully listed the London brothels where men could be whipped by women, or women by men. The best appointed of these were run, it seems, by Mrs Emma Lee, *née* Richardson, of 50 Margaret Place, Regent Street; Mrs Phillips of 11 Upper Belgrave Place; Mrs Shepherd of 25 Gilbert Street and Mrs Sarah POTTER at various addresses in Chelsea and Soho.

Ashbee's entry in *The Dictionary of National Biography* omits his scandalous disinheriting of his four children, who sided with their mother when she and Ashbee separated. The cause of their separation remains unclear. It may have been because Elizabeth Ashbee became increasingly offended by her husband's right-wing views, or because she discovered he was the author of pornography. There is the possibility that he maintained a second *ménage* in Paris.

**Ashpole, Ian** (1955– ), adrenalin sports 'junkie'. In October 2001 Ashpole, who lists tightrope walking among his hobbies, floated 11,000 feet above the Cambridgeshire countryside attached to 600 balloons. Inspired by the 1956 Oscar-winning film, *The Red Balloon*, he launched himself from a hot-air contraption at 5000 feet and thereafter climbed a further 6000 feet in six minutes – beating his previous best of 10,000 feet over Ross-on-Wye in 1998 – before parachuting to safety as the helium-filled balloons began to burst 'like machine guns firing'.

Asked whether this was a record, a spokesman for *The Guinness Book of Records* said, 'A record what?'

*See also* BALLOONISTS.

**Ashton, Sir Frederick.** *See* BERNERS, GERALD HUGH TYRWHITT-WILSON, 14TH BARON.

**Ashton, Horace** (*c.*1870–*c.*1935), corrupt policeman. Ashton merits a footnote in legal history since one of his cases led to the setting up of a Royal Commission to inquire into methods and discipline in the force. This case was also the first to be taken up by the Public Vigilance Society, established in May 1905 to investigate police malpractice. In *My Life and Adventures* (1929), the East End villain Arthur HARDING, who later led an armed siege of Old Street Police Court, describes Ashton as:

... having a nice wife, but always after the women. He wasn't intelligent enough to catch a thief, but he was good at perjury and he could do a man an injury by strength.

In August 1906 Ashford came across a young man named Gamble in the company of a prostitute, Ethel Griffiths. Wanting the girl for himself, Ashton told Gamble to 'clear off'. Mrs Griffith rejected Ashton, whereupon he attacked Gamble so violently that he was hospitalized for six months. One member of the Royal Commission, which was assisted in its deliberations by the Public Vigilance Society, compared his injuries to those which would have been sustained by falling on spiked railings.

The Royal Commission found that Ashton was guilty of the misconduct alleged, but that he had not intended to do Gamble any serious injury. The publication of the Commission's report resulted in Ashton's prosecution, but at the Old Bailey in September 1908 the jury was instructed to ignore the evidence of Ethel Griffiths on the grounds that she was a prostitute. Nevertheless, the jury convicted, and Ashton was sentenced to nine months' hard labour.

Within days of the Royal Commission's report it was inundated with complaints of police corruption, perjury and bribery, often in language that its members found 'foul and intemperate'. After investigating 64 cases over eleven months, the Commission exonerated the police of all malpractice and declared that far from harassing street offenders, they were 'kind and conciliatory'. While there had been some evidence of reprehensible conduct in a few cases, on the whole 'the Metropolitan Police is entitled to the confidence of all classes of the community'.

*See also* APPLES, BAD.

**aspersing a clergyman of the established religion.** *See* BYRNE, JAMES.

**Aspinall, John** (1924–2000), gambler, animal-rights enthusiast and zoo owner. Aspinall's ideas on politics and society belonged, in the opinion of his critics, to less enlightened times. He believed that women's main use was to 'serve the dominant male' and that what Britain needed was a 'bout of beneficial genocide'. To a wider public, he was known for his close friendship with Lord LUCAN and for the habit of the animals in his private zoos of killing their keepers.

Aspinall was born in colonial India as a result of a liaison between his mother and Major General McKiltrie Bruce, conducted with the approval of another major general to whom she happened to be married. The young John was sent back to England to be educated. He was expelled from Rugby for idleness, and periods at Oxford and in the Royal Marines were cut short. He liked to boast that he had missed an important exercise with the Marines by simulating a fainting fit so that he could attend the Ascot Gold Cup.

Before the 1960 Gaming Act made gambling legal, Aspinall held floating games of chance for wealthy friends around Belgravia. When one of these was raided, his mother – by now Lady Osborne – protested, 'It's a poor thing if you can't hold a party in a private house without the police arriving.' In 1962 he founded the Clermont Club in Mayfair where he encouraged young men to fritter away their inheritances. Sir James Goldsmith, Lord Lucan and Dominick ELWES, the society painter who had been in the news in 1957 when eloping with an heiress, Tessa Kennedy, were founder members.

In 1975 Aspinall sold the Clermont Club in order to finance his other great enthusiasm: the preservation of endangered wildlife species. He opened two private zoos, Howletts and Port Lympne, where his policy of encouraging the animals to develop close relationships with their keepers aroused some controversy. Over the years, three keepers were killed by tigers and one was crushed by an elephant. In another incident, a boy's arm was torn off by a chimpanzee. Aspinall was unperturbed. 'I would happily sacrifice the lives of my loved ones,' he insisted, 'if that meant saving an endangered species.' His life was summed up by one critic who described him as a 'knee-jerk right-winger with simple-minded and frightening views'.

Since Aspinall's death, the zoos' practices and traditions have been adhered to by his son, Damian. In June 2001 Howletts was fined £43,000 after an experienced keeper was squashed to death by an Indian elephant. Damian Aspinall's partner is the 21-year-old Geordie model and television presenter, Donna Air.

**assassins, political.** *See* BELLINGHAM, JOHN; DESPARD, EDWARD MARCUS; LAMBOURNE, LADY MARGARET; MCNAUGHTON, DANIEL; OXFORD, EDWARD; THISTLEWOOD, ARTHUR.

**assault, indecent.** *See* BAKER, COLONEL VALENTINE; BICKFORD, CHARLES ARTHUR.

**assistance, baronets living on national.** *See* RANKIN, SIR HUGH.

**Aston, John** (*c*.1650–*c*.1700), hooligan. Aston's behavioural difficulties are as instructive as those of his near contemporary, James ALEXANDER, suggesting, as they do, that the 'yob culture' is not a modern phenomenon. He is described in R. Gough's *The History of Myddle* (ed. Peter Razzle, 1979, cf. Hey, *English Rural Community*) as 'a sort of silly fellow, very idle and much given to stealing of poultry and small things', whose petty larcenies were tolerated for some time. Finally, however, he was tried at Shrewsbury assizes, where he was whipped after the jury saved him from a more serious fate by undervaluing by elevenpence the poultry he had stolen. The experience apparently left him chastened, but we are informed that 'hee left not his old trade whoally'. Like Alexander's, Aston's story is instructive, too, in that it indicates a parish's readiness to extend leniency if a malefactor is considered to be 'a sort of silly fellow'. His return to Myddle after the trial, and his refusal to abandon totally his old ways, emphasize the apparent ability of villagers to tolerate a level of delinquency in their midst.

**Astor, William Waldorf, 3rd Viscount.** *See* KEELER, CHRISTINE; WARD, STEPHEN.

**Atherton, Bishop John** (1598–1640), priest, collector of erotica and alleged sodomite. Since he already had a reputation as a philanderer and persistent theatregoer, with a taste for pornographic books, drunkenness and swearing, it came as no surprise to his flock in the see of Waterford and Lismore when, in 1640, Bishop Atherton was arrested after prayers in the cathedral and accused of buggering his tithe collector, John Childe, a man of an inferior social class. The charges were put before Parliament and on 28 November he was found guilty and sentenced to death. It was during the last week of his life in the condemned cell that Atherton redeemed himself in the eyes of many by a display of public contrition – albeit contrition for a crime he had not committed. His miraculous reformation was due to the tactics employed by his final confessor, Nicholas Bernard, the dean of Ardagh. Confined in the dark, Atherton was denied all company except that of Bernard, a morose and unforgiving puritan. He was encouraged by Bernard to scourge himself, and his coffin was placed in his cell.

In fact, Atherton had not committed the act of indecency for which he stood accused, but three visits a day from his disagreeable confessor soon drew him into an orgy of remorse and self-castigation for his love of pornographic books, his drunkenness and his unceasing visits to the theatre. Decapitation (a privilege enjoyed by an aristocrat) would be too good for the sort of man he was, Atherton decided, and he asked to be thrown into the sea with a stone round his neck. Later, he amended this instruction. He should be buried in a corner of the churchyard where the rubbish was left. From the scaffold on 5 December 1640 Atherton delivered a final self- lacerating speech. 'I am the first of my profession that ever came to this shameful end,' he cried. 'I pray God that I may be the last. You are come hither to see a comedy turned to a tragedy, to witness a miserable catastrophe of a life ...'

Atherton's co-accused, John Childe, was hanged the following March. Disqualified by his social standing from receiving final instruction from Dr Bernard, he died unredeemed. The chief prosecution witness, a servant who had been dismissed by Atherton, was himself executed shortly after ~~wards for an unrelated offence.~~ On the scaffold, he confessed that he had fabricated his evidence against the bishop – and against Childe, too, it may be assumed. Atherton clearly had his faults, but it is not obvious what Childe's offence had been.

**attitudes, Lady Hamilton's.** *See* HAMILTON, LADY EMMA.

**Attlee, Martin, 2nd Earl** (1927–91), merchant seaman, Social Democrat Party spokesman for transport and maritime affairs, public relations officer and jewellery salesman. A more convivial man than his taciturn father Clement, the Labour prime minister (1945–51), Martin Attlee kept his many friends entertained by his idiosyncratic career choices and unusual views. In the House of Lords he campaigned vigorously against drug dealers, arguing on one occasion that they should be forcibly injected with heroin to give them a taste of their own medicine. Wishing to emphasize that he spoke as an authority, he confessed to his lordships that he had experience of drug abuse himself. Once, while on holiday in Portugal, he had inadvertently smoked a cannabis joint, thereafter finding himself 'on a high'. He was able to tell the House that he had fought hard against the sensation, which he had found disagreeable.

After Millfield School and Southampton College (now, in the way of things, Southampton University), Attlee served in the merchant navy for five years, and then stumbled into the public-relations business. From 1970 to 1976 he was assistant PR officer at Waterloo station, but this employment was discontinued when he published a humorous book, *Bluff Your Way In PR*, which was amusingly dedicated to 'those clients I'd most like to handle – Gina Lollobrigida and Miss World'.

After he lost his job at Waterloo station, Attlee had the idea of selling identity talismans to the armed forces in Saudi Arabia. He was disappointed to discover that Muslim law discouraged the wearing of personal jewellery. Despite such setbacks, he continued to enjoy a challenge. He spent most of 1985 working on a way to improve helicopter safety and could often be seen running up and down his garden with a model helicopter on a stick.

Shortly before his death, Attlee took up a campaign against the unnecessary brutality dealt out by the Metropolitan Police. In a letter to the *Daily Telegraph*, he drew attention to 'horrific stories of police arrogance, especially when it comes to picking up boys with a public school accent'. It later emerged that he himself had had a disagreeable encounter with uniformed authority. Having fallen asleep on an underground train and woken up at the end of the line, he had made his way to a police station to enquire about late-night taxi services. Here, he had been bundled into a cell before being charged with being drunk and disorderly.

**Audley, Mervyn Castleford, 2nd Baron** (1573–1631), peer and libertine. In April 1631 Audley was accused at Westminster Hall of:

> Abetting a Rape upon his Countess, Committing Sodomy with his servants, and Commanding and Countenancing the Debauching of his daughter.

The erotic evolutions devised by Lord Audley were an attempt to enliven his second marriage. His first wife, Elizabeth Barnham, had died young. His second, Lady Ann, a famous beauty, had been married before, to Lord Chandos of Sudeley. On their wedding night, Lady Ann was surprised when Lord Audley's manservant, Anthill, appeared suddenly at the bedside. She told the court that:

> Anthill came to our bed, and the Lord Audley talked lasciviously to me and told me that my body was his and that if I lay with any man with his consent 'twas not my fault but his.

To add variety to these arrangements, other servants were encouraged to take part. Skipwith, a groom, 'came naked into our chamber,' said Lady Ann, 'and to our bed.' Lord Audley invited his wife to decide which, between him and Skipwith, was the better endowed:

> He took delight in calling up his servants to show their nudities and forced me to look upon them and commend those that had the longest.

If Lady Ann demurred, force was employed. When Broadway, a butler, came to her bed, Lord Audley held her firmly by the hands and feet:

> He delighted to see the act done, and made Broadway lie with me in such a way that he might see it, and though I cried out, he never regarded the complaint I made but encouraged the ravisher.

At Lord Audley's trial, Broadway told the court that, after he had taken Lady Ann, he was in turn sodomized by his lordship, as was Fitzpatrick, a cook. The court was then told that Lady Ann was not the only ill-treated woman in the family. She had a daughter, Elizabeth, by her first husband, Lord Chandos of Sudely. At Audley's trial, Elizabeth testified that she had been forced to submit to Skipwith, the groom:

> He used oyl to enter my body first for I was then but twelve years old and he usually lay with me by the Baron's privity and command.

Elizabeth was in time married off to Skipwith.

It was Lord Audley's son, James, who eventually informed on his father. Charged with a capital offence before a jury of his peers, Audley admitted that a servant might occasionally have shared his bed, but that that contingency was due to the shortage of rooms in his various houses.

The court was inclined not to accept this defence and Lord Audley was sentenced to death. Nothing is known of Lady Ann's fate, but Elizabeth, having rid herself of Skipwith, married James, Audley's heir and nemesis, and thus shared in her stepfather's estate. Despite her early experiences, she enjoyed a long life and is buried at St Martin-in-the-Fields, London. Lord Audley was executed on Tower Hill on 14 May 1631 for, in the words of *The Oxford History of Britain*, 'every known sexual felony'.

**Australian homosexuals.** *See* IMRIE, DEREK.

*autrefois acquit.* An English law by which, in general, once a defendant has been acquitted on the facts, he or she cannot be retried. *See* MONEY, SIR LEO CHIOZZO.

**axemen, mad.** *See* BROMLEY-DAVENPORT, LIEUTENANT COLONEL SIR WALTER; FRASER, FRANCIS ('MAD FRANKIE'); MITCHELL, FRANK.

**Ayley, John** (*c*.1570–1636), delinquent. We learn from J.A. Sharpe's *Crime in Seventeenth-Century England: A County Study* (Cambridge University Press/Editions de la Maison des Sciences de l'Homme, 1983, ch. 10. 'Crime and the Local Community') that between 1613 and his death in 1636, John Ayley, keeper of the Unicorn inn, Kelvedon, Essex, was before the leet (manorial court) for:

> ... habitually failing to attend church, and leaving early when he did; living immorally with his maidservant; committing adultery with a married woman; obstructing the highway with a dunghill; assaulting the constables; playing cards, dice, tables and other unlawful games; committing fornication during the archbishop of York's visitation; leaving ditches in disrepair; using scandalous words against his neighbours; being drunk in sermon time; and contempt of court.

Recognized, like John ASTON, as 'a sort of silly fellow', he was treated leniently, in the manner of the day.

*See also* ALEXANDER, JAMES.

# b

**babes, tormented soap.** *See* PALMER, PATSY; WESTBROOK, DANIELLA.

**Bacchus, Reginald** (1858–1921), theologian, novelist and pornographer. An Oxford graduate, contributor of learned articles to the religious press and an admired translator of French literary fiction, 'Reggie' Bacchus epitomized the late Victorian pornographer. Like his near contemporaries, James Glass Bertram (who, as 'the Reverend William Cooper', wrote the perennially popular *History of the Rod*), and George Augustus SALA (the respected war correspondent of the *Daily Telegraph* and the author of *Prince Cherrytop and the Good Fairy Fuck*), Bacchus was a cultured, middle-class man happy to augment an income derived from more serious endeavours by providing an educated readership with highly charged erotic material. Nor were his books the pious frauds that street-traders all too often palmed off on the lower classes. Unlike purchasers of *The Dreadful Disclosures of Maria Monk* (who had been promised lesbianism by its cover and a hint of bizarre chastisement, only to discover that it had been issued by the Presbyterian Tract Society in 1833 and that its earnest sermonizing was unenlivened by anything stronger than an innuendo against Catholicism), Bacchus's customers were never disappointed.

Married to the young actress Isa Bowman, who was the first to play Alice on stage and was one of the children who enjoyed seaside holidays at the Reverend Charles Dodgson's Eastbourne lodgings, Bacchus was part of a circle that included Oscar Wilde and Ernest Dowson, and whose centre was the Sheffield solicitor and publisher of expensive pornography, Leonard Smithers. Another friend was Thomas Wirgham, who occupies a unique place in legal history as the only defendant ever convicted of 'publishing' an obscene toothpick. The charge, according to Cox's *Criminal Cases*, was that its cover depicted 'the naked persons of a man and a woman in an indecent and filthy attitude and practice'.

Bacchus's literary reputation as the respected translator into English of such novels as *Dolly Morton* by the French right-wing poet and contributor to Action Française, Hugues Rebell (the pseudonym of Georges Joseph Grassal) survived simultaneous publication of *The Nemesis Hunt* series of erotic novels, whose titles included *The Confessions of Nemesis Hunt*, *Pleasure Bound Afloat* and *Pleasure Bound Ashore*.

**back, to hell and.** *See* COPPE, THE REVEREND ABIEZER; PALMER, PATSY; STANSHALL, VIVIAN; WESTBROOK, DANIELLA.

**Bacon, Francis** (1561–1626), philosopher and corrupt politician. Bacon combined in his person intellectual distinction of the highest order with defects of character that drove him to commit crimes unbecoming in a philosopher, namely bribery, favouritism and extortion.

Inspired by the Renaissance, and in revolt against Aristotelian logic, Bacon proposed an inductive method of discovering truth founded on empirical observation and verification of hypotheses through experiment. For Voltaire, Bacon was the father of experimental philosophy. In his *Lettres philosophiques* (1734), Voltaire wrote:

> As Lord Chancellor, amidst the intrigues of a Court, and the affairs of his exalted employment, Lord Bacon yet found so much leisure for study as to make himself a great philosopher, a good historian and an elegant writer. No one before him was acquainted with experimental philosophy. It was a hidden treasure which Lord Bacon had some notion of, and which all philosophers, encouraged by his promises, endeavoured to dig up.

And yet, as lord chancellor, Bacon accepted money from defendants to influence court judgements. In 1621 he confessed to his peers that he was 'guilty of corruption and do renounce all defence'. It is possible that most of the bribes were pocketed by his staff, but he was not helped by his easy-going attitude to his servants' misdemeanours, one of whom, Godrick, he kept as 'a catamite and bedfellow'. According to the historian, A.L. Rowse, Bacon confessed to corruption in order to avoid an imminent sodomy charge.

After Trinity College, Cambridge, Bacon studied law at Gray's Inn, and was called to the Bar in 1582. The law failed to satisfy his ambitions and in 1584 he entered Parliament as MP for Melcombe in Dorset. He assiduously courted the favour of Robert Devereux, the 2nd earl of Essex, from whom he received a gift of land, only to betray his benefactor when the earl was accused, and then convicted, of treason. Bacon's rise was swift under James I, who recognized his remarkable abilities, and he was appointed lord chancellor in 1618. In 1620 he took the title of Viscount St Albans.

The publication in 1621 of his great work on logic, *Novum Organum*, established Bacon's reputation abroad, but he had made many enemies at home, the most formidable of whom was the lord chief justice, the puritanical Sir Edward Coke. Coke wanted an excuse to attack the court, to whose excesses Bacon had contributed in no small measure. Coke's real target was the king's lover, the earl of Buckingham. The court needed a scapegoat, and Bacon was more expendable than Buckingham. Disappointed litigants were persuaded to accuse Bacon of accepting bribes when he was presiding in the Court of Chancery. A man named Aubrey claimed that he had lost his case even though he paid the lord chancellor 100 guineas. Another man, Egerton, made a similar accusation, but in his case the lord chancellor's price had been 400 guineas.

Within a month there were 23 charges for Bacon to answer, and Parliament pronounced the items of impeachment. Bacon made a qualified admission of guilt, but the House of Lords wanted more. It resolved that the lord chancellor:

> ... should be charged with the briberies and corruption alleged against him, and that he should make a particular answer thereunto with all convenient expedition.

Bacon confessed, and on 3 May 1621 he received his sentence: a fine of £40,000, imprisonment in the Tower at the king's pleasure, and banishment from court, Parliament and any other public office.

In his years of disgrace, Bacon completed some of his most important work, including his influential *Advancement of Learning*, but he never received a full pardon. His end, ironically perhaps, was caused by an experiment in scientific method. While out on a walk in the depth of winter, he came across a dead fowl lying by the road. Wishing to observe the effect of refrigeration on the preservation of flesh, he stuffed it with snow and took it home. He contracted pneumonia, and died

Bacon's character remains a mystery. Perhaps it is explained in a footnote provided by an equally distinguished philosopher, G.E. Moore (1873–1958). When lecturing at Cambridge on the naturalistic fallacy, and wishing to demonstrate the logically idiosyncratic behaviour of the word 'good', it was Moore's habit to take Bacon as a model. Just as a man who shot his grandmother at a distance of 100 yards could be described as a good shot, but not as a good man, so Bacon, 'the wisest, brightest, meanest of his kind', could be described as a good philosopher, but not a good man.

The genealogist Sir Iain Moncrieffe, of that ilk, established the agreeable fact that P.G. Wodehouse – the creator of the immortal Jeeves – was able, through the marriage of his 18th-century forebear Sir Armine Wodehouse, to claim Sir Francis Bacon as his ancestral uncle.

One of Sir Edward Coke's descendants, Lady Carey Coke, was debutante of the year in 1953. Her coming-out dance at Claridges was judged to have been even more splendid than that held in the same year by Margaret duchess of ARGYLL and Charles Sweeney for their daughter Frances Sweeney (later the duchess of Rutland) and her friend Florence ('Flockie') Harcourt-Smith. During the late 1950s, Miss Harcourt-Smith summered at 'La Reserve', Beaulieu, in the south of France, where she excelled on the high diving-board in a one-piece bathing suit.

**bad boys, soccer.** *See* BEST, GEORGE; GASCOIGNE, PAUL; MCAVENNIE, FRANK.

**bad company, murdering one's son to prevent him falling in with.** *See* MAYES, JOY.

**Bad Earl, the.** *See* LONSDALE, JAMES LOWTHER, 1ST EARL OF.

**Badger Club, the.** *See* HELL-FIRE CLUB, THE IRISH.

**badger game, the.** A confidence trick in which a wealthy man of reputation is lured into a brief liaison, usually in a hotel bedroom, with an apparently respectable young woman whom he has just met. At a compromising moment, the woman's supposed husband bursts into the room and threatens the victim with public exposure unless he hands over a large sum of money. Past experts at the game have included William Cooper HOBBS and May Churchill SHARPE ('Chicago May').

**badgers.** *See* IMRIE, DEREK.

**Bagenal, Beauchamp** (1741–1802), Irish hell-raiser and duellist. Reputed to be the most handsome man in Ireland, Bagenal inherited the family estates in 1752 at the age of 11. A high-spirited young man, his behaviour on the Grand Tour caused surprise even among his contemporaries. According to Sir Jonah Barrington (*Personal Sketches of His Own Time*, 1869), he:

> ... fought a prince, jilted a princess, intoxicated the Doge of Venice, carried off a duchess from Madrid, scaled the walls of a convent in Lisbon and fought a duel in Paris.

The jilted princess, Charlotte of Mecklenburg-Strelitz, afterwards married George III of England.

At his home, Dunleckney in County Carlow, 'King' Bagenal entertained on a lavish scale – his nickname deriving from the autocratic manner in which he ran what was virtually a court. Guests were expected to behave according to his whims. Meals were primarily drinking contests. At table, he kept a brace of pistols handy, one for tapping the barrel of claret, the other for dealing with any of his guests who failed to drink enough to send him reeling from the table. Dinner was followed by compulsory all-night revels. Rather than take part, one guest, a clergyman, hid in the grounds till morning. Later, he described the scene:

> Such of the company as were still able to walk had acquired a flat-backed car on which they heaped the bodies of those who were insensible and delivered them to their respective homes.

Bagenal was less violent than his reputation suggests. There is no proof that he shot all, or even many, of his guests. He fought as few as a dozen duels, a derisory number compared to those logged by such celebrated duellists as 'Hairtrigger' Dick Martin and 'Fireball' Macnamara. One of the twelve was against his cousin, Bagenal Hervey. Hervey shot first, and missed. Bagenal was delighted. 'You damn young villain! Do you know you had like to kill your own godfather? Go back to Dunleckney, you dog, and have a good breakfast ready for us. I only wanted to see if you were stout.'

Bagenal was lame and compelled, when fighting, to lean against a tombstone. As an old man, and wishing to provoke a quarrel, he sent an insulting note to a neighbour whose pigs had strayed on to his land. In due course he received a challenge. Bagenal faced his opponent sitting in a chair. He was getting old. 'Time was', he said, 'that I could have risen before breakfast to fight at sunrise – but we cannot do these things at sixty.' In the event, he was unscathed and his adversary was badly wounded. 'Rest upon your pistols, my boys,' he advised his guests shortly before his death. 'Occasions will rise in which use of them is absolutely indispensable.'

**Baker, Mary** (1795–1865), vagrant, thief and impostor By assuming an exotic alternative persona, complete with an invented language, Mary, a barely literate country girl, deceived not just the cream of society but also the most eminent linguists of the day, thus assuring herself a place among the great impostors.

On 3 April 1817 Mary was found wandering in the grounds of Knole Park in Gloucestershire, the home of Samuel Worrall, a magistrate of the county. She was wearing a turban and some sort of oriental garb. Mrs Worrall took pity on the confused young girl and invited her into her home. During the days that followed, Mary's behaviour provided some clues to her background. Shown a map of the world by the vicar, she recognized images of China. She then identified herself as Princess Caraboo. As her fame spread, she received many visitors, several of them foreigners who hoped to discover her place of origin through language. None was successful, until a young Portuguese sailor, who had recently landed in Bristol, claimed to understand the girl's dialect. He was able to inform Mrs Worrall that her guest was a princess from an island called Java in the East Indies, whence she had been abducted by pirates, brought to England and then abandoned. Fired by the romance of this revelation, Mrs Worrall told Princess Caraboo that she could remain at Knole for as long as she wished.

No sooner had the local farmers and tenants grown fond of the exotic stranger in their midst, however, than she disappeared. After a week, word reached Mrs Worrall that her protégée was in Bath, where she later discovered her 'at the very pinnacle of her glory, enthroned in the drawing-room of a lady of *haut ton*, surrounded by rich admirers of both sexes'. Among the latter was a Dr Wilkinson, who the next day informed readers of Bath's *Chronicle* that the princess's:

> … mode of diet seems to be Hindoostanic, as she lives mainly on vegetables; water is her beverage and she expresses great disgust at the appearance of intoxicating liquors; she is very cautious of her conduct with respect to gentlemen.

Dr Wilkinson's report solved the mystery, albeit fortuitously. The story reminded a Mrs Neale, who ran a boarding house, of a certain Mary Baker who had lodged with her several months before. Mary had stuck in her mind because of her habit of telling preposterous stories. When Princess Caraboo was brought before her, Mrs Neale identified her immediately as her ex-lodger. Mary confessed to everything. The daughter of a Devon cobbler, she had run away to London at the age of 18, where she had worked as a maid for three years until she was dismissed for stealing from her employer. She had then married a man named Baker, who had travelled in the Orient. Deserted by Baker, she had worked for a short time as a barmaid and then briefly in a brothel before devising her plan to become – with the aid of her Portuguese sailor – Princess Caraboo from Java.

After her exposure as an impostor, Mary's former admirers among the mercantile classes failed to act quickly enough to recover the expensive silks, dresses and gems they had bestowed on her in the hope of securing future patronage. Princess Caraboo and her sailor escaped to America, taking with them an estimated £10,000 in goods and jewellery. From Philadelphia she wrote wistfully to a friend:

> Although I have the best of everything and live as I ought as a Princess, yet I hope to see old England again and those kind friends I left in it, as I can never forget the attention they showed me.

In fact, Mary did return to England, as a contemporary newspaper report makes poignantly clear:

> In 1824, Caraboo, having returned from America, took apartments in New Bond Street, where she made a public exhibition of herself –

admittance one shilling each person; but it does not appear that any great number went to see her.

*Princess Caraboo*, a film based on her life, was released in 1994, to no great acclaim. 'Delve deeper into this period meringue and the whole concoction deflates into fluffy nothingness' (*Halliwell*, 1995).

**Baker, Peter** (1921–66), MP, publisher, wine merchant and forger. Captain Baker, the Conservative member for South Norfolk, blamed alcohol and mental exhaustion not only for the fraudulent transactions that landed him in Wormwood Scrubs in 1954 but also for his inability to remember them. 'There are whole weeks in 1953 and 1954 that I cannot remember at all,' he said after his arrest. 'Often I had to check up in *Hansard* at the time to make sure that I had attended the Commons.' His attendance was not as frequent as it might have been. On one occasion he was approached in the Smoking Room by the deputy speaker, Sir Charles McAndrew, who prided himself on knowing every MP. He was puzzled that he couldn't recall Baker. 'Please don't apologize,' said Baker, 'I have no idea who you are either.'

By the time he entered Parliament in 1950, Baker was already running several businesses, including four publishing houses, a brewery and an investment trust. As with Robert MAXWELL ('a remarkable man', in Baker's opinion, and one to whom he sold his New York-based British Book Centre), it was publishing that brought about his difficulties. In 1953, in an attempt to shore up his ailing Falcon Press, he obtained a loan from the Bank of America by means of a forged guarantee from the industrialist, Sir Bernard Docker. He then borrowed £49,000 from Barclays Bank, secured again by Sir Bernard's forged signature. From this account, Baker transferred £11,000 to the Bank of America, £23,000 to his Peregrine Press and £15,000 to his personal account at the National West minster.

In May 1953, the MP for South Norfolk was invited to attend on Sir Bernard Docker, who confronted him with the fraudulent guarantee. Baker broke down. 'I have been ill for a long time,' he cried. He checked into Holloway Sanatorium, where he shortly received a visit from the police. 'During the last twelve months,' he said, 'I have had at least 30 blackouts. My mind has veered from pinpoint brilliance to a total inability to remember events and conversations. The rest that I have refused to take has now been forced upon me.'

At his Old Bailey trial, Baker pleaded guilty to six charges of forgery and was jailed for seven years. His prison escort was sympathetic. 'Sounds like a long time,' he said. 'Sounds a bloody sight longer to me,' said Baker. In 1963, he petitioned unsuccessfully for a Queen's pardon. On his release, he retired to Eastbourne, and died three years later.

**Baker, Colonel Valentine** (1825–87), soldier and alleged rapist. An attempt by Colonel Baker, a close friend of the prince of Wales (later EDWARD VII), to rape a young lady on the Portsmouth-to-London train was one of the most widely publicized scandals of the 1870s.

On the afternoon of 17 June 1875, 21-year-old Rebecca Dickenson boarded the train at Midhurst in Sussex. She was alone in the compartment with 49-year-old Colonel Baker, an expert on cavalry tactics. For the first 50 minutes of the journey, Baker, a married man with two daughters, and until recently the commanding officer of the 10th Hussars, made polite conversation, but as the train pulled out of Woking he tried to put his hand inside Miss Dickenson's underwear. With a cry of alarm, she jumped to her feet, somehow opened the door and scrambled backwards out of the compartment. As the train passed through Walton station, a bricklayer named William Burrowes saw her standing on the running board, clinging to the handle of the door. He alerted the stationmaster, who signalled to Esher, where the train was stopped. A clergyman named Baldwin Brown got in with Rebecca and travelled with her to London. Baker was obliged to use another compartment. At Waterloo, Rebecca, Baker and the Reverend Baldwin Brown were taken to the inspector's office, where Rebecca reluctantly agreed to report the matter to the police.

Three days after the assault, Baker was arrested in Guildford. His trial opened at Croydon Assizes on 2 August 1875. Huge crowds gathered outside the courtroom long before the trial was due to start. Two society ladies, who had climbed through a window, were thrown back into the street. Many of Baker's friends were in court, including Lord Lucan and the marquess of Tavistock. Most people believed that Baker, as an intimate friend of royalty, would be acquitted, and it came as no surprise when the judge in his summing-up emphasized that Baker's chief concern had been to save Miss Dickenson from falling off the train's running board. He could find no evidence, he said, that there had been 'intent to ravish'. Baker had merely tried to 'win the girl's consent to intercourse by exciting her passions'. The jury took the hint, but seemed reluctant to exonerate Baker entirely. He was found not guilty of intent to ravish, but guilty of indecent assault. He was sentenced to one year in jail and fined £500.

The public felt that Baker had got off too easily, but he was disgraced in any case. He tried to resign his commission but was told that he was to be cashiered. It was widely believed that this step was taken at the suggestion of Queen Victoria, who disapproved of the raffish company kept by her son (dubbed in society 'Edward the Caresser' and, less elegantly, 'Dirty Bertie'). Having served his prison term, Baker left England with his wife and two young daughters. He became a lieutenant general in the Ottoman army and fought bravely during the Russo-Turkish War. He then went to Egypt and accepted an appointment as commander of police. While attempting to relieve Tokar during the Sudan war he was shot in the leg.

When he came back to London to recuperate, he was greeted at Victoria Station by a cheering crowd. His friends tried to have him reinstated in the British army, but their efforts failed against Queen Victoria's determined opposition. In November 1887 Baker died in Egypt after an attack of typhoid. Victoria finally relented and cabled that Baker was to be buried in Cairo with full military honours.

For another military debaucher, *see* CHARTERIS, COLONEL FRANCIS.

**balloonists.** *See* ALDBOROUGH, BENJAMIN O'NEILL STRATFORD, 6TH EARL OF; ASHPOLE, IAN; PRICE, DILYS; VENTRY, ARTHUR FREDERICK DAUBENEY EVELEIGH DE MOLEYNS, 7TH BARON.

**ballroom dancers.** *See* AMPTHILL, JOHN RUSSELL, 3RD BARON; BOURNEMOUTH; DIGGLE, ANGUS; HAMILTON, LADY EMMA; MATURIN, CHARLES ROBERT; RATTENBURY, ALMA; ROCHE, TIGER.

**Balon, Norman** (1926– ), publican and author. Having achieved celebrity in middlebrow literary circles as a 'character' – a consequence of frequent appearances in Jeffrey BERNARD's popular *Spectator* 'Low Life' column – Balon, the licensee of the Coach and Horses public house in Greek Street, London, has built on his reputation as the most insolent landlord in London. Customers who fall short of his exacting proprietorial standards are ejected with a volley of abuse. Although he had published his own memoirs in 1989, he disappointed his many admirers in 1990 by suing a fellow author for libel. In a book of collected essays, Val Hennessy, the respected contributor to the *Daily Mail's* book pages, mistakenly described Balon's condition as 'crapulous' when returning to London by train from the Brighton races. Balon, a teetotaller, sued, and Miss Hennessy's publishers, Harrap, were obliged to withdraw her book. In the early days of the spoof magazine *Private Eye,* its editor, Richard Ingrams, recognized the Coach and Horses as a congenial venue for the magazine's fortnightly lunches, and they have continued to be held there since Ingrams's transfer to *The Oldie.*

**Baltimore, Frederic Calvert, 6th Baron** (1706–78), aristocrat and traveller. Baltimore – whose father had been born in Dublin but whose connections with Ireland had since become sufficiently remote for him to consider himself a gentleman – became celebrated in London when he widened the scope of ABDUCTION CLUBS by recruiting a harem. While travelling in Turkey in the 1730s, and having noted certain benefits accruing to men under the local customs, he assembled a small troupe of professional women, thereafter taking them with him on his trips abroad. In this he had been assisted by two procuresses, Mrs Harvey and Madame Griffenburg. Sometimes there were difficulties. When Baltimore arrived in

Vienna accompanied by two Negro eunuchs and eight of his troupe, the chief of police asked him which was his wife. He replied that as an Englishman it was not his custom to discuss his personal arrangements, and then offered to settle the matter with a fist fight. When the chief of police refused, Baltimore continued with his travels.

Back in London in 1767, Baltimore became attracted to Miss Sarah Woodcock, a young woman of excellent reputation who worked in a milliner's shop. With the help of Mrs Harvey he had her kidnapped and brought to his house. Baltimore's bloated and rheumy-eyed appearance no doubt contributed to the ease with which she resisted him for a week before being brought to his bed, 'her handkerchief wet with tears as if she had dipped them in water'. When he was sued by her outraged family, Baltimore conducted his own defence and convinced the jury that Miss Woodcock had enjoyed sitting on the knee of a portly 60-year-old and had at all times been 'happy, cheerful and playful in his house'.

**BANG, I just walked in, put the gun to Tommy's head and.** *See* ELLUL, PHILIP.

**Bang Bang Charlie.** *See* CURZON, CHARLES.

**Barber, Susan** (1956– ), housewife and murderer. In May 1981 Michael Barber came home from a fishing trip to discover his wife, Susan, in bed with his partner in the local darts team, Richard Collins. He hit his wife and then threw Collins out of the window. Harmony was restored, but the next day, Susan put half a teaspoonful of weedkiller in Barber's steak-and-kidney pie, causing him to be admitted to hospital with suspected pneumonia. Later his illness was diagnosed as Goodpasture's syndrome, a rare nervous condition. He was transferred to Hammersmith hospital in west London, where he died; cause of death was said to be pneumonia and kidney failure. Susan Barber collected £15,000 from her husband's pension fund and set up home with Richard Collins. When the romance cooled, she advertised for new admirers on citizen's band radio, under the call-sign 'Nympho'.

However, David Evans, the pathologist who conducted the postmortem, had lingering suspicions about the cause of Barber's death. Organs preserved from his body were sent to ICI, manufacturers of the weedkiller, Gramoxone, and traces of the poison were discovered. The police began an enquiry, seven months after the murder had been committed. Susan Barber was arrested with Collins in April 1982. Collins was charged with conspiracy to murder and sentenced to two years imprisonment. Susan Barber was jailed for life.

For other female poisoners, or alleged poisoners, *see* BARTLETT, ADELAIDE; MAYBRICK, FLORENCE ELIZABETH; SMITH, MADELEINE.

**Barker, Colonel Leslie Ivor Gauntlett** (1889–1960), farmer, teashop manager, manservant and impostor. Colonel Barker was a useful welter-weight boxer, a talented cricketer and a leading member of the National Fascist Party. It was only after his arrest at the Regent Palace Hotel on bankruptcy charges in 1925, and subsequent medical examination in the reception area at Brixton prison, that the colonel was found to be a woman. The next day he appeared at the Old Bailey, charged with making a false entry in a marriage certificate.

Born in Jersey, the daughter of a sportsman who had wanted a son, Lillias Valerie Barker was educated at a convent in Brussels. In 1918, she married an Australian, Harold Arkell-Smith, but she left him after a year to run a teashop in Warminster. She then met another Australian, Pearce Crouch, by whom she had two children, a boy and a girl. By 1923 she had taken to dressing as a man and had changed her name to Captain Barker. In November of that year, and believing that her son, Tony, would benefit from a woman's influence in the home, she 'married' the daughter of a Brighton chemist, giving her marital status as 'bachelor'. She told her wife that she couldn't consummate the marriage because of war wounds. Later, she promoted herself to colonel and awarded herself the DSO.

At Barker's Old Bailey trial, Sir Ernest Wild, an unpublished poet, sentenced her to nine months in prison for making a false entry in a marriage register. He then took her counsel, Henry Curtis-Bennett, back to his rooms, where he explained the reasons behind the sentence:

> I sentenced her for the profanation of holy matrimony and for her unfeminine conduct. She outraged the decency of nature and broke the law of man.

Sir Ernest then read Mr Curtis-Bennett some of his poetry – a habit of his after a disagreeable case.

Undeterred, Lillias awarded herself a bar to her DSO and, as Colonel Barker, toured Britain, playing male roles with repertory companies. She ran an antique shop, joined a cricket club and became a member of the National Fascist Party. In 1927, after a raid on the party's headquarters, she was charged as Colonel Barker with keeping a gun without a licence. She was led into court with bandages over her eyes, claiming to be blind from a war wound. In 1934, and having changed her name to John Hill to escape the attention of the tabloid press, she was charged with stealing a handbag. In 1937, while living with an actress in Mayfair as man and wife, she worked as a butler, but was arrested for stealing £5 from her employer, who described her in court as 'the perfect manservant'. During World War II she moved with her 'wife', Eva, to a Suffolk village, where she served in the Home Guard. She was known by then as Geoffrey Norton. Her son, who was killed in the war, never knew that his father was in fact his mother. When Colonel Barker died in 1960, her secret was revealed by the newspapers. Everyone in the village was surprised – except the vicar, who said he had always guessed.

**Barn Murder, the Red.** *See* CORDER, WILLIAM.

**barred from one's own restaurant.** *See* LANGAN, PETER.

**barrel of tar, standing on one's head in a.** *See* BOLD BUCKS.

**Barrett, John** (1753–1821), scholar, miser and recluse. A distinguished classicist, Dr Barrett rose to the position of vice provost of Trinity College, Dublin. The son of a clergyman, he entered Trinity as a student in 1767 at the age of 14 and spent the rest of his life behind its walls, venturing further afield just three times a year: once to accompany the other fellows on their annual outing to the new observatory at Dunsink, and twice to cross the street to pick up his half-yearly dividend from the Bank of Ireland. His many academic achievements included the discovery and editing of a rare copy of St Matthew's Gospel written in Greek, which he came across in the college library.

In his novel, *Charles O'Malley* (1842), Charles Lever provides a portrait of Barrett in old age:

> Dr Barrett was, at the time I speak of, close upon seventy years old, scarcely five feet in height, and even that diminutive stature lessened by a stoop. His dress was a suit of the rustiest black, threadbare and patched in several places, while a pair of large leather slippers, far too big for his feet, imparted a sliding motion to his walk that added an indescribable meanness to his appearance.

Barrett's rooms were dark and gloomy – a consequence of the windows never being cleaned – and quite unfurnished apart from books. Dusty volumes were piled high on a table and two stuffed chairs. His quarters were never heated, even in the coldest weather, since it was more economical to warm himself in the college kitchen than light a fire. On one occasion a party of students had to resuscitate him with a tumbler of rum after they had found him nearly frozen to death, sitting in the dark with one flickering candle by his chair. Because he could eat in college, the only provisions he was normally obliged to buy were for his breakfast, which consisted of a pennyworth of bread and a halfpennyworth of milk. Once he sent his servant, an old lady called Catty, for the milk with a penny and instructions to bring back the change. She slipped, broke her leg and was carried off to hospital, where she was visited by Barrett. 'Do you hear me, Catty, where's the jug?' he asked. 'Oh, Doctor dear,' she managed to say, 'sure the jug was broken and I couldn't help it.' 'Very good, Catty,' Barrett reassured her, 'that's true, it couldn't be helped; but do you see me now, where's my halfpence change?'

In an age of wigs, Barrett wore his own hair, but he powdered it properly when he had to take examinations. His invigilating duties done, he combed out the powder on to a sheet of paper, and preserved it for the next occasion. He saved up his guineas – acquired, some claimed, by the sale of accumulated candle ends – and kept them in a sock until he had enough to buy a debenture. The only person he ever lent money to was Magee, afterwards archbishop of Dublin. Once, while he was lending Magee five pounds the stocking broke, scattering guineas all over the floor. 'Stop, stop, Magee!' cried Barrett, 'do you see me now, stand on the table and I'll pick them up.' It was then discovered that one guinea was missing. 'They are all right but one. One is gone, and maybe it rolled into a mousetrap and maybe it didn't.' The quarrel lasted a lifetime and when Magee was promoted to bishop, Barrett remarked: 'Do you see me now – I don't care if he was made Bishop of Hell so long as I am not in his lordship's diocese.'

The doctor was equally unforgiving of Miss Anne Plumptre, who offered her impressions of him in her *Narrative of a Residence in Ireland* (1817). She paid tribute to Barrett's erudition but also noted his 'simplicity of manners and utter ignorance of the world'. She then pointed out that although his income as a fellow was £2000 a year, he spent no more than £20 of it except on books. He clearly read hers with care, for in the Minutes of the Library dated 9 September 1817 he wrote:

> I put up in the Library and entered in both catalogues the 46
> volumes sent in by Mullens last Saturday, with the exception of Miss
> Anne Plumptre's Narrative which I hope the Board will order to be
> locked up as too silly and too ill-mannered for a public library.
> Travel in savage countries by all means, Miss Plumptre, and publish
> their conversations if you can, but spare the feelings of those who
> are accustomed to the rules and decencies of civilized life.

Dr Barrett died a wealthy man, having spent a lifetime accumulating money and avoiding his relatives. Catty received an annuity from the £80,000 he left, and the remainder was given to the college fellows in trust for charitable purposes.

**Barrie, Paddy** (1888–1935), racehorse ringer. Born in Edinburgh, Barrie was one of the most successful fixers in turf history. His method was simple. He would buy two horses, only one of which was quick, and then he'd paint the quick one to look like the other. His first success was at the expense of Lady Mary Cameron, who employed him as a groom on her estate near Edinburgh. He paid her £50 for a broken-down mare, painted it a different colour and sold it back to her for £750. A week after it had rejoined Lady Cameron's stables, it became listless and its colour started to run. Barrie left immediately for America, where his most successful coup

took place in 1931 at Havre de Grace, Maryland. He had bought a quick
four year old called Aknahton for $2000 and a known loser called Sham
for $200. He painted Aknahton to look like Sham and entered it for a valu-
able race at Havre de Grace. Mrs Payne Whitney's Byzantine was an
odds-on favourite to win, and the unregarded 'Sham' started at 50 to 1.
Though trapped in the stalls, 'Sham' caught the field with little difficulty
and to the disappointment of Byzantine's supporters came home an easy
winner. Barrie and his gambling partners were thought to have profited by
as much as $500,000.

Barrie altered Aknahton's appearance at three other meetings and
although the authorities were on to him by now he was able to escape
arrest by the same method as he had used on horses. He was let down
finally by the misjudgement that had caused him to leave Lady Cameron's
employ in such a hurry. The false moustache he had painted on his upper
lip began to run on a wet day at Saratoga racetrack in New York state.
Barrie was arrested, and although, by legal anomaly, he was guilty of
nothing more than unlawful entry to the United States, he was sent back to
Edinburgh. He died two years later of a broken heart, brought on, according to his obituaries, by Scotland Yard's determined surveillance.

For other ringers, *see* COYLE, FRANCIS; DILL, SIR VICTOR ROBERT
COLQHOUN.

**Barry, Dr James Miranda** (1792–1865), medical practitioner. Few people
have been able to impose their version of reality on the world as successfully as Dr Barry, who, when he died from influenza, brought on by
London's drainage system, was discovered to have been a woman who had
once had a child. The distinguished army physician was immediately
embraced by feminists as a heroine in the struggle for equal professional
rights. 'For high courage,' one tribute ran, 'nothing could exceed the spirit
of this woman who was so far ahead of her time that, to achieve her
purpose, she renounced her sex.'

Having graduated at Edinburgh University at the age of 17, Barry
joined the army, serving thereafter as a military surgeon in Canada, Africa
and the West Indies. Wherever he practised, he quickly gained a reputation
for his considerable talents. When he arrived at the Cape of Good Hope
in 1816 he was soon appointed physician to the governor. One of his
patients among the Cape's fashionable set wrote to the governor of St
Helena:

> I have here quite a prodigy as a physician, a Doctor Barry, whose
> skill has attested wonders since he arrived. Indeed it would be well
> worthwhile for an invalid to come here solely for the purpose of
> obtaining his advice.

St Helena's most celebrated inhabitant at the time was the exiled Napoleon

Bonaparte, and when the son of his private secretary, the count de la Cases, fell ill, the highly recommended Dr Barry was immediately sent for. The count recorded in his diary that Barry had been described to him as 'an absolute phenomenon' and that he had performed 'extraordinary cures' at the Cape, one of which 'had saved the life of the governor's daughter'. When, after a 2000-mile voyage, Barry arrived, escorted by a sea captain from St Helena, the count was so confounded by his youthful looks that he mistook him for the captain's nephew. In his diary he wrote, 'The grave doctor I had expected was a boy of 18.' Dr Barry prescribed fresh air, exercise and regular baths, duly effecting a complete recovery in his patient and causing his fame in the colony to spread still further.

While on duty in the Cape, Barry enhanced his reputation as a ladies' man, first gained at Edinburgh University. As Mark Twain recorded in one of his travel books, *A Tramp Abroad* (1880), 'There were plenty of pretty girls, but none of them caught him, none of them could get hold of his heart; evidently Dr Barry was not the marrying kind.' He was very much the fighting kind, however, happy to accommodate anyone who challenged him to a duel. After his death, a letter appeared in *The Lancet* from Sir Josias Cleote:

> I am the only officer in the British army who has fought a duel with a woman. When I was aide-de-camp to Lord Charles Somerset at the Cape, a buxom young lady called to see him on business of a private nature, and they were closeted for some time. Dr Barry made some disparaging remark about this. 'I say, Cleote,' he said, 'that's a nice Dutch filly the governor has got hold of.' 'Retract your vile expression, you infernal cad!' said I, advancing and taking hold him by the neck. Barry challenged me and we fought with pistols, fortunately without effect.

On another occasion, Barry shot his opponent dead.

In spite of his quarrelsome disposition, which was exacerbated, no doubt, by the pretence he was obliged to maintain, Barry was always able, after a heated confrontation with the military authorities, to continue his distinguished career, rising in time to the rank of medical superintendent general. When he died in 1865, the army physician who examined him, and who had been a close colleague for many years, was astonished to discover that he had been a woman. Barry's fellow former students at Edinburgh University were equally surprised. The only unusual characteristic they could recall was a reluctance to box.

In death, hindsight took over, particularly among male colleagues, who now remembered Barry as 'shrewish' and 'governed by her emotions'. In one account, Barry had so irritated a superior that he had 'seized the little fellow by the collar and dangled him out of the window'. In another version, it is Barry's superior who 'was taken by the doctor and thrown through the window', If these reports satisfied a male audience who preferred to believe that Barry was, like other women, emotionally unstable, the accounts of her many duels may have had an erotic appeal at a time when cross-dressing heroines were a popular feature of the contemporary stage.

For want of any other identification, the tombstone of this courageous woman, who so successfully imposed her will on an unsympathetic world, is still inscribed, 'Dr James Barry'.

**Barry, Tony.** *See* DURESS.

**Barrymore, Michael** (1953– ), troubled funnyman. He's been to hell and back, but he's looking more relaxed now that he's discovered who he really is.

**Bartlett, Adelaide** (1856–?), alleged poisoner. Doubt hangs over Bartlett's case, as it does over those of her near contemporaries and fellow alleged murderers, Madeleine SMITH and Florence MAYBRICK. All were acquitted after sensational trials, not least, perhaps, because the jury on each occasion took the view that their supposed victims deserved no better than they got. Additionally, the reserved manner and attractive appearance in the dock of those variously accused was thought not to have gone against them.

In April 1886 Adelaide was tried at the Old Bailey on a charge of murdering her husband with liquid chloroform. At the age of 19, Adelaide had married Edwin Bartlett, a prosperous grocer who was ten years her senior. Edwin's unorthodox attitude to married life appeared to have left Adelaide unsatisfied. When, in 1885, she became friendly with the Reverend George Dyson, a young Wesleyan minister, Edwin encouraged the liaison and in the same year made a will leaving everything to Adelaide and naming Dyson as an executor. Within a few weeks Edwin became ill. The doctor diagnosed sub-acute gastritis. Hitherto a fit man, Edwin was reduced to an invalid and died on 1 January 1886. A large quantity of chloroform was found in his stomach and Adelaide was charged with murder.

The problem for the prosecution was to show how the chloroform had been administered. No one would have taken it voluntarily because of the burning sensation it induced. Prosecution experts admitted that it would have been difficult for Adelaide to have given it to her husband while he was unconscious, and traces of it would have been found in any case in Edwin's windpipe. Edward Clarke, counsel for the defence, was able to show that no such traces had been found.

Adelaide Bartlett was triumphantly acquitted. What became of her subsequently remains a mystery. Some believe she went to America, taking her secret with her. Others think she committed the perfect murder. Sir

James Paget, consultant surgeon at St Bartholomew's, was clearly of that opinion. 'Now that she has been quite properly acquitted,' he said, 'she should tell us, in the interests of science, how she did it.'

**Barton, Graham** (1930– ), business executive and forger. In May 1977 Barton, using the code name Peter Poodle, approached the *Daily Mail* with what he described as a 'hot potato'. He had in his possession, he said, a letter to Alex Park, British Leyland's managing director, from the company's chairman, Lord Ryder. According to Poodle, the letter showed that Leyland had been paying bribes and conspiring to defraud foreign governments on a massive scale. The bribes involved commissions often 20% higher than usual and free dentistry. David English, the *Mail*'s editor, agreed to meet Poodle at a public house in Richmond. Poodle admitted that his real name was Graham Barton and that he was employed by Leyland. 'I don't want to see my country associated with banana-republic business methods,' he said. After two or three hours, English was persuaded that the letter from Ryder to Park was genuine.

The *Mail* paid Barton £15,000 and led the next day with a world exclusive. The paper had evidence, it said, of 'an international bribery web at Leyland'. Printing Lord Ryder's letter, which showed that a slush fund of over £1 million had been set aside for this purpose in 1976, the *Mail* suggested that the proposed fund for the year 1977–8 might be as high as £25 million.

Lord Ryder immediately dismissed the letter as a clumsy forgery. Further investigations exposed Barton as its author and in July 1977 he was charged with intent to defraud. In court, Lord Ryder admitted under cross-examination that a government report had indeed uncovered a slush fund at Leyland of £127,000. This was a trivial amount, he argued. Barton was found guilty and sentenced to four years in prison. In an out-of-court settlement, Lord Ryder received an undisclosed sum in damages from the *Daily Mail*. David English's career prospered.

**Bass, Harry 'The Doctor'** (1901–73), thief. With his partner, Johnny 'No-Legs' Mancini, who was of Italian descent, Bass formed a criminal double-act better suited to vaudeville than to serious thieving. Their farewell performance in a jewellery shop in Blackpool might have been more successfully staged at one of that popular resort's many light-entertainment venues.

The pair's most celebrated routine involved the legless Mancini entering a jewellery shop in his electric chair. He had mislaid the key to his toolbox, he would say, and wondered whether the jeweller might have one of the same fit. Sometimes the jeweller would hand over his bunch of keys, at which point, 'Dr' Bass, wearing an Anthony Eden hat, and with a stethoscope round his neck, would hurry into the shop, urgently seeking directions to Acacia Avenue. While the jeweller was distracted, Mancini would make an impression of his keys. Later, he and 'Dr' Bass would return to the shop and empty it.

That, at least, was the plan. Since Bass and Mancini never thought to vary it, the routine became as familiar as that of any other cross-talk act. When they tried it out at Bravington's in Blackpool in 1951, the police, alerted by the fact that the duo had already performed it at six other shops in the vicinity, were waiting for them. Both were jailed, and the partnership was later disbanded.

**Bate, the Reverend Henry** (1745–1824), priest, journalist, playwright and magistrate. It was a matter of surprise to his contemporaries that Bate had chosen the priesthood as an occupation rather than a career such as the military, in which his confrontational approach, often involving fist fights, might have found more appropriate expression. As rector of North Fambridge in Essex – a living he had inherited from his father – Bate fought five duels, edited two muckraking newspapers, wrote plays that caused riots, was named as co-respondent in a celebrated adultery trial and spent a year in prison for a criminal libel against the duke of Richmond.

Bate claimed to be a doctor of divinity from Oxford University, but there is no record of this honour having been bestowed. In 1773 he was appointed editor of the *Morning Post*. After an incident in Vauxhall Gardens, the *Morning Chronicle* referred to him as 'the bullying, boxing Vauxhall parson'. On an evening walk with the actress, Mrs Hartley, Bate had taken exception to the way his companion was being looked at by a Captain Croft. He called Croft an 'impudent puppy' and challenged him to a duel. Captain Croft decided to involve his friend, George Robert FITZGERALD, a mentally unstable aristocrat who had lost part of his skull in a previous altercation. Fitzgerald brought in his footman, a former professional boxer, and the dispute was settled at the Turk's Head Coffee House on the following afternoon. Bate prevailed, and his three opponents were helped home in a coach.

The incident, which became known as 'the Vauxhall Affray', was fully chronicled by Bate in the *Morning Post*, whose circulation rose sharply as a result. This was a lesson Bate never forgot. From then on, and hoping to provoke trouble, he lost no opportunity to goad public figures with inaccurate slurs. One such libel backfired. In 1780, Bate accused the duke of Richmond of treacherously opposing increases in the country's military strength. What he wanted was a duel that would boost circulation, and had Richmond, who was famously volatile, acted in character, he would have been accommodated. Instead, Richmond sued for libel. Bate received a custodial sentence, postponed for a year until the prison, which had been destroyed in the anti-Catholic riots provoked by Lord George GORDON, had been rebuilt. Afraid that he too might receive a libel writ, the *Morning*

*Post*'s owner, Mr Richardson, warned Bate to be more circumspect in future. Bate called him a coward, Richardson challenged him to a duel, and the editor shot his proprietor in the arm.

Bate then turned his attention to writing plays for London's West End. It seemed unlikely that those who had suffered from the *Morning Post*'s insults would let slip this chance to avenge themselves, nor did they. When the curtain rose on Bate's first effort – a musical comedy called *The Black-amoor Washed White* – the actors were greeted with catcalls and the box in which Bate sat with his friends was pelted with fruit. (For other examples of theatrical hooliganism, *see* HOOLIGANS, THEATRICAL.) Bouncers hired by Bate against just such an eventuality moved into the auditorium, provoking fist fights in the aisles. In spite of an enthusiastic review in Bate's own paper, written by himself ('this fine new opera promises to become a favourite'), the play failed to find an audience and closed within a week.

By 1788 Bate had slowed down somewhat – was in danger, even, of becoming respectable. He now edited the *Morning Herald*, a sober broadsheet, and had become a magistrate. However, he was to be involved, not too unwillingly, in one further scandal. This arose because his current mistress, a Mrs Dodwell, had other lovers, including a French general with whom she had conducted an affair on a yacht. To secure a divorce, Mr Dodwell, an amateur anatomist, would have to prove her infidelity, and Bate could be more conveniently cited than the general. In December 1788, Bate was charged with 'the seduction of, and conversation with, Mrs Dodwell' (*see* CRIMINAL CONVERSATION). Bate defended his position vigorously, arguing that Mrs Dodwell could not be blamed for consoling herself away from home since Mr Dodwell was in the habit of dissecting bodies in the bedroom. Bate was acquitted and the case received widespread publicity, except in the *Morning Herald*. Bate no longer craved the limelight. Having been made a baronet for his work as a magistrate in Ireland, Bate moved back to Essex as rector of Willingham in 1819, and lived there in respectability until his death.

**Bath, Alexander Thynn, 7th marquess of** (1932– ), peer, novelist, autobiographer, sonneteer and muralist. Dubbed 'The Loins of Longleat' (the play on words deriving from Bath's advocacy of free love, involving 'wifelets', and the wild animals in the grounds of his stately home), the 7th marquess inherited the title in 1992 on the death of his father, a noted eccentric who had admired Hitler and who, with the assistance of the circus proprietor, Jimmy Chipperfield, had built Longleat's famous safari park.

After Eton, Oxford University and national service in the Life Guards, Bath travelled extensively in South America in a Jaguar and in the company of a Hungarian actress named Anna Gyarmathy (later to achieve some success in French films under the name Anna Gael). In the 1960s he arrested his tendency towards reclusion by acquiring a maisonette in

North Kensington. In 1966 he gained some notoriety by contracting what he called an 'anti-marriage' with a girl from Ceylon. The match was unsuccessful and she moved to Rome in 1968. In 1972, he married Miss Gyarmathy in order to legitimize the son and heir, Ceawlin, to whom she was about to give birth. During this period he was able to complete *The Ages of History Mural*, *The Heaven and Hell Mural* and the *Kama Sutra Mural* in his Longleat quarters. Later he received an offer from Des O'Connor involving the production of an LP of the 7th marquess singing 16 of his own songs, entitled 'I Play the Host'.

In 1987, Bath started work on his autobiography, *Strictly Private*, an expurgated version of which is being published on the Internet. He has completed Series I (*A Plateful of Privilege*) which subdivides into three books, *The Early Years*, *Top Hat and Tails* and *Two Bites of the Apple*, dealing respectively with his time at prep school, the years at Eton and his national service. In 1999, he introduced a helium balloon at Longleat to enable daytrippers to obtain panoramic views over the estate.

**bathing in public during the course of a battle.** *See* BULLER, SIR REDVERS.

**bathroom plumbing, allegedly committing sodomy amidst the.** *See* THORPE, JEREMY.

**bats, biting the heads off.** *See* OSBOURNE, JOHN MICHAEL ('OZZY').

**'bawd of the seamen, the great'.** *See* PAGE, DAMARIS.

**bawds who have won clog-dancing competitions.** *See* JONES, JANIE. *See also* BROTHELS, KEEPERS OF 'CONVENTIONAL'.

**Bawdy House Bob.** *See* ROBERTS, 'BAWDY HOUSE' BOB.

**Bean, Sawney** (*c.*1400–?), robber, mass murderer and cannibal. The narrative of Bean's life, as described in the *Newgate Calendar*, 'presents such a picture of human depravity that were it not attested to by the most unquestionable historical evidence, it would be rejected as incredible'. The details are indeed obscene.

Born near Edinburgh in the reign of James I, Bean moved to Galloway as a young man, accompanied by a woman as mad as himself. Here they took up habitation in a seaside cave, reported to have been a mile in length and penetrated to its dank and murky depths by the incoming tide. With their extended family – which consisted eventually of 8 sons, 6 daughters, 18 grandsons and 16 granddaughters, all by incest – they lived by robbing and killing any man, woman or child who travelled the vicinity, thereafter quartering, salting and pickling them as food. Such was the extent of their activities that they were sometimes over-provided with rations, in which circumstance they would throw the arms and legs of dried human bodies into the sea at night. These were washed ashore, to the mounting horror of local residents, who had until then been ignorant of the fate of their many disappearing relatives and friends.

When as many as a thousand had been robbed, slaughtered and cannibalized, the king himself was forced to act. Accompanied by 400 heavily armed men and a pack of hounds, James led a search of the area, eventually penetrating the Bean family's cavernous black slaughterhouse. Here, they were confronted, according to the *Newgate Calendar*, by:

> ... legs, arms, hands, feet of men, women and children, suspended in rows like dried beef. Some limbs and other members were soaked in pickle; while a great mass of money, both of gold and silver, watches, rings, pistols, and an innumerable quantity of other articles were either thrown together in heaps, or suspended from the sides of the cave.

Bean and his insane extended family, now 50 in number, were seized and taken in chains to Edinburgh. Within 48 hours, and with the utmost brutality, they were executed without trial: a departure from natural justice against which the most rigorous liberal might not wish to argue.

**bear, a microphone concealed in the nose of a teddy.** *See* LAMBTON, ANTONY CLAUD FREDERICK.

**bears, performing.** *See* MISS STEVENS, THE PIG-FACED LADY.

**bears, pet.** *See* BUCKLAND, FRANCIS TREVELYAN; FITZGERALD, GEORGE ROBERT; HIRST, JEMMY; MYTTON, JOHN.

**Beaton boxed on the jaw, Cecil.** *See* HEBER-PERCY, ROBERT.

**Beaton thrown into a river, Cecil.** *See* HERBERT, DAVID.

**Beauty of Buttermere, the.** *See* HATFIELD, JOHN.

**Beckford, William** (1759–1844), writer and art collector. Beckford spent the latter part of his life as a recluse in a 300-foot octagonal tower in the company of his Spanish dwarf, his heraldic advisor and his four dogs: Viscount Fartleberry, Mrs Fry, Nephew and Tring. Sometimes, he would enliven his solitary existence by ordering a lavish meal for twelve. With twelve servants in attendance, he would sit down alone and eat one dish, thereafter rising from the table.

Born in Fonthill, Wiltshire, the son of Alderman Beckford, who had made his fortune in the West Indies, William was educated at home at the insistence of his doting mother. This decision can only have reinforced his tendencies to misanthropy and oddness, while benefiting his precocious intelligence. At the age of 6 he took music lessons from Mozart, himself aged 9. He learnt Persian and was writing Gothic narratives in his adolescence. At the age of 10, when his father died, he inherited an estate worth £1 million and an annual income of over £100,000. When he was 21, he wrote his masterpiece, *Vathek*, an oriental romance in the style of Voltaire. It was published in France in 1787 and in an English translation (by Samuel Henley) in 1786. When the rumour broke of an improper relationship with a family friend, the 11-year-old William 'Kitty' Courtenay – heir to Powderham Castle and future earl of Devon – Beckford escaped to the Continent. He went on to make a happy marriage with Lady Margaret Gordon, but she died in childbirth at Lake Geneva in1786.

In *Gothic: 400 years of Excess, Horror, Evil and Ruin* (1999), Richard Davenport-Hines writes:

> The death of his wife, together with the previous sexual scandal, splintered his life. After she died, Beckford became resolutely misanthropic and preferred objects to people.

He spent the next 13 years travelling in Europe, accompanied by his doctor, his *maitre d'hotel*, baker, cook, valet, three footmen and 24 musicians. He also took with him his bed, cutlery, plate, books and prints. He required any inn at which he stopped to have his rooms repapered for him, and on one occasion, in Portugal, he imported a flock of sheep from England to improve the view from his window.

In 1799, Beckford returned to England. Still ostracized by society, he devoted the rest of his life to the building of Fonthill Abbey; this Gothic-Revival extravaganza was designed by James Wyatt, and its chief feature was to be the 300-foot octagonal tower. Beckford was so eager to see the edifice completed that he bribed Wyatt's builders to work in relays through the night, seven days a week, by supplying them with large quantities of alcohol. Fonthill was thus built by men in an advanced state of intoxication, and the tower collapsed three times. At one point the distracted Wyatt had to divert to Fonthill 500 men who were working on a job for George III at Windsor. In 1800, Beckford insisted on having Christmas dinner in the abbey in spite of the fact that the mortar in the kitchen was still wet. As the servants carried the food into the dining room, the kitchen collapsed behind them. No one was injured, and rebuilding began immediately. The following spring, Beckford was able to bring off one of his few social successes by entertaining Lord Nelson to dinner in the course of his triumphant tour of the west of England. This had been possible because Beckford was related to Emma HAMILTON's compliant husband.

In 1822 financial reverses forced Beckford to sell the, still unfinished, abbey. He was undisturbed by losing what had been his major interest in life for 22 years, remarking that it had been just a plaything. He sold the estate to John Farquhar, a businessman, for £300,000. Three years later, the tower collapsed for the fourth time. Although there were people living inside it at the time, no one noticed that it had been slowly crumbling. The building materials had been so flimsy that the fall had been silent. Farquhar took the incident in good part, pointing out that Fonthill was now a more manageable size.

Beckford moved to Bath, where he bought two adjoining houses in Lansdown Crescent and built a bridge to connect them. He also built a tower on Lansdown Hill, now a museum devoted to his life. The tower was 130 feet high, crowned with a cast-iron model of the temple of Lysicrates, and incorporating a chapel and a graveyard. His dog, Tiny, was buried there in a marble tomb. In 1844 Beckford was laid to rest beside him in a pink sarcophagus.

One of the many ironies of his life was the fact that in 1940 his Fonthill estate was bought by the Morrison family from Glasgow. Beckford had harboured an abiding hatred of all blood sports, but for the second half of the 20th century Fonthill was occupied by John Morrison, 1st Baron Margadale, one of the best shots of his day and for many years Master of the South & West Wilts hounds – and a man with no interest in the arts.

**Beckham, Brooklyn** (1999– ), celebrity toddler. It was revealed in October 2001 that Brooklyn Beckham, the infant son of the soccer player David Beckham and his wife, Victoria (formerly Posh Spice of the Spice Girls singing group), suffers from obsessive-compulsive disorder. According to his mother, Brooklyn becomes fretful unless all his toys are lined up in the right order. A spokesman for the charity Obsessive Action said that Brooklyn might have inherited the disorder from his father, who is similarly afflicted. David Beckham becomes fractious unless everything in the fridge is in its place and each piece of furniture on its correct spot. 'David is so from another planet!' said his wife, Victoria:

> We've got three fridges – food is in one, salad in another and drinks in the other. In the drinks one everything is symmetrical. If there's one extra can of Diet Coke, David will put it away in the cupboard so it doesn't look out of place. It has to be an even number. I mean, what is he like?

Medical experts say that a chemical imbalance in the brain compels some people to rearrange their environment. Research shows that the condition can be passed through the genes, but there is also evidence that it can be learned behaviour.

Brooklyn derives his name from the fact that he was conceived while his parents were driving over Brooklyn Bridge in New York.

*See also* TODDLERS CHERISHED AS FASHION ACCESSORIES AS MUCH AS FOR THEMSELVES.

**Beckham, David** (1976– ), soccer player. He can cross a ball and land it on a sixpence. He lets his boots do the talking.

*See also* BECKHAM, BROOKLYN; DRESS SENSE, A COMEDIC; MCAVENNIE, FRANK.

**bed, naked Arab under the.** *See* PROCTOR, HARVEY.

**bed, three (or more) in a.** *See* AUDLEY, MERVYN CASTLEFORD, 2ND BARON (with Lady Audley, Skipwith, a groom, Fitzgerald, a cook, and others); BLACK-BURNE, ARCHBISHOP LANCELOT (with Lydia and Dolly); BLOOM, JOHN (with Miss Lovebody and others); BRISTOL, FREDERICK WILLIAM JOHN AUGUSTUS HERVEY, 7TH MARQUESS OF (for Georgiana, duchess of Devonshire, the 6th duke of Devonshire and Lady Elizabeth Foster); CHARTERIS, COLONEL FRANCIS (with Ann Bond and Mrs Mitchell); DILKE, SIR CHARLES (with Virginia Crawford and Fanny Stock); DRIBERG, TOM (with Daniel FARSON and Mrs Shufflewick); GARVIE, SHEILA (with Mr Garvie and Mrs Birse); LAMBTON, ANTONY CLAUD FREDERICK (with Norma Levy and Gina); WELDON, GEORGINA (with Harry Weldon and Charles Gounod; and with Angèle and Anarchasis Menier).

**Bedford, John Robert Russell, 12th duke of** (1888–1953), peer, politician and naturalist. The 12th duke was accused of fascism during World War II, and, after it, of being a communist. In 1939 he became chairman of the British People's Party, which was made up for the most part by ex-members of Sir Oswald Mosley's British Union of Fascists. In 1952 the duke spoke in the House of Lords in defence of Dr Hewlett Johnson, the 'Red Dean' of Canterbury, who was an apologist for the Soviet Union in the 1940s and 1950s. As a socialist, he suggested that 'if every man in the country went to work for ten seconds a day he would produce the country's total requirements'. Alternatively, one could do away with money and return to a system of barter. Neither suggestion was taken up.

The 12th duke inherited his interest in the natural history of birds from his father, with whom he was on poor terms. The 11th duke, who had served as aide-de-camp to the viceroy of India, Lord Dufferin, became a recluse after World War I, retiring to Woburn Abbey, where he devoted himself to the study of rare animals and birds. During World War II the old duke quarrelled with his son, who was a pacifist, and they did not speak, or communicate in any way, for 20 years. The present duke, the 13th, did not know of his grandfather's existence, or that he was the eventual heir to the dukedom, until he was 16, when a servant accidentally let the information slip.

A respected naturalist, and ardent ornithologist, the 12th duke developed a strain of homing budgerigars and wrote a piece in *Country Life* on the subject, illustrated by a photograph of himself surrounded by 3000 birds. He was also devoted to the study of parrots. Birds eventually caused his death: he shot himself when aiming at a hawk that was threatening one of his budgerigars.

*See also* HINCHCLIFF, GRANT.

**Behan, Brendan Francis** (1923–64), writer. Behan was born in Dublin into a family which, on both sides, was traditionally anti-British. He left school at 14 and worked as a house painter. From the age of 9 he had served in a youth organization connected with the IRA, and in the late 1930s he was an IRA messenger boy. In 1939, he was arrested on a sabotage mission in England and sentenced to three years in Borstal for attempting to blow up a battleship in Liverpool harbour. In 1942, he was sentenced to 14 years for the attempted murder of two policemen. In 1947 he was in prison again, serving a short sentence in Manchester for helping an IRA prisoner to escape.

During his years in prison, Behan started to write, mainly short stories in a highly original version of Dublin vernacular. His best known novel *Borstal Boy* (1958) shows the narrator moving from a rebellious bravado to a greater understanding of himself and the world, 'Prison had cured me of any idea that religion had anything to do with mercy or pity or love.' In spite of his experiences, his writing rarely shows signs of anger or political fervour:

> It seemed a bit disloyal to me, that I'd sooner be with Charlie and Ginger and Browny in Borstal than with my own comrades and countrymen any place else; that I should prefer to be with boys from English cities than with my own countrymen and comrades from Ireland's hills and glens.

Behan's first play, *The Quare Fellow*, was presented, to critical acclaim, at an avant-garde theatre club in 1956. Covering the twenty-four hours before a hanging, it is a riotous attack not only on the depravity of capital punishment but on public attitudes to sex, politics and religion. His most successful play, *The Hostage* (1958), is set in a Dublin brothel owned by a former IRA commander. In it, Behan used song, dance and direct speech to the audience, thus displaying his debt to Bertolt Brecht. The style was also in accord with that of the English director, Joan Littlewood, whose Theatre Workshop was largely responsible for establishing Behan's reputation in Britain. The notoriety and critical acclaim that came to Behan in the late 1950s no doubt contributed to his early death. His life gradually collapsed into bouts of heavy drinking and uncalled-for fist fights. His life-long battle with alcohol was finally lost in a Dublin hospital on 20 March 1964, at the age of 41.

In an essay, collected in *Tread Softly for you Tread on my Jokes* (1966), the journalist Malcolm Muggeridge describes an occasion when he was engaged to interview Behan on the television programme, *Panorama*:

> As Behan grew drunker and more boisterous, doubts began to be felt in the higher echelons of the BBC as to whether he should be allowed to appear at all. I argued that he should. Leonard Miall, the BBC official in whose jurisdiction *Panorama* fell, in the end agreed, only adding, 'If he uses the word cunt, don't laugh.' On the set it was apparent that Miall need have had no apprehension. Behan was incapable of talking coherently at all. He took off his shoes and said he 'wanted to go for a leak'. Since he would have been unable to negotiate his way off the set, I decided to risk disaster by refusing this request. When the cameras came on us, I put my first question, and, allowing Behan to mumble a little, answered it myself. All television interviews are really like this. I liked him, except, of course, that, like all drunks, he was a fearful bore.

**Belaney, Archibald ('Grey Owl')** (1887–1937), author, lecturer, conservationist and impostor. The career of Grey Owl, a self-proclaimed Native American who had in fact been brought up in Hastings by his Aunt Ada, usefully illustrates a point made by Hillel Schwarz in *The Culture of the Copy* (1996). According to Hillel, 'Impostures succeed because, not in spite of, their fictitiousness. They take wing with congenial cultural fantasies.' By this account, the crowds who attended Grey Owl's lectures and eagerly bought his books wanted to believe that a life like his, led in perfect harmony with nature, was superior to the materialistic bustle of their own.

According to the historian Sarah Burton (*Imposters: Six Kinds of Liars*, 2000), Grey Owl never claimed that he was 100% North American Indian. His blue eyes were explained by his mixed parentage. He had been born, he said, in Mexico to a Scottish father and an Apache mother, later settling with the Ojibwa Indians in Canada. Like many Native Americans, he had fought in World War I, in the course of which Indians had been renowned for their marksmanship. Returning from the war, and horrified by the devastation wrought by the mining and timber industries, he became a prototype eco-warrior. He owed much of his enlightenment, he said, to his wife, Anahareo, an Iroquois Indian, who was 18 years his junior. It was she who adopted two beaver kittens whose mother had been caught in one of Grey Owl's traps, thereby causing him to rethink his approach to the natural environment. He gave up trapping and hunting, and described his conversion in his first book, *Pilgrims of the Wild*. He was a talented writer and an accomplished speaker. On his first tour of Britain in 1934, a quarter of a million people attended his lectures, among them the two young daughters of the duke of York, later King George VI. In 1937, exhausted by a gruelling tour of North America, he caught pneumonia and died.

Only after his death was Grey Owl's true identity revealed. An obituary in the Toronto *Star* claimed that he was an Englishman named Archibald Belaney. In the ensuing debate, those who had served with him in Flanders spoke of the way he had crawled undetected across no-man's-land; of his sharp-shooting and knife-throwing skills; and of his gift for absolute immobility for long periods of time – the unique accomplishments, they argued, of a true Indian. His publisher, Lovat Dickson, also supported his story, but facts began to emerge that cast doubt on Grey Owl's origins.

Archibald Belaney was born to an English father and a European-American mother. His father was a drunk and a womanizer. When the couple separated, Mr Belaney left the country (he later died in a bar-room brawl) and Mrs Belaney moved to London, leaving the 4-year-old Archie with his Aunt Ada in Hastings. Left to his solitary pursuits, the boy spent hours reading and fantasizing about 'Red Indians'. When he was 18, he persuaded his aunt to send him to Toronto – ostensibly to study farming, in fact to 'become' an Indian.

For most impostors, the motive is personal gain. This was not the case with Grey Owl. His publisher, Lovat Dickson, wrote that 'he never showed the slightest interest in how we were doing from a sales point of view.' Belaney was driven to his elaborate deception by an unhappy childhood. Abandoned by both parents, he was brought up by a domineering aunt, whom he feared and hated. 'She was a snob and a perfectionist,' he told Anahareo, his wife. 'She lacked a human heart.' He became a champion of the underdog, whether the Indian people or a threatened animal, because that was how he perceived himself. The success of his deception can be explained as a product of the time. In the words of Lovat Dickson:

> The voice from the forests momentarily released us from some spell.
> In contrast to Hitler's screaming, ranting voice, and the remorseless
> clang of modern technology, Grey Owl's words evoked an unforget-
> table charm, lighting in our minds the vision of a cool, quiet place,
> where men and animals live in love and trust together.

A film, *Grey Owl*, directed by Richard Attenborough and featuring Pierce Brosnan as the eponymous 'Indian' was judged a failure on its release in 1999.

**Belcher, Harry** (1904–64), politician, railway clerk and recipient of 'gifts'. A former employee of the Great Western Railway, and MP for Sowerby in

Yorkshire, Belcher was the only member of Clement Attlee's rigorously honourable governments (1945–51) to be involved in a scandal – and that misfortune might have been avoided had his barrister not referred to 'bribes' received by his client when he had meant to say 'gifts'. As parliamentary secretary of the Department of Trade, Belcher prided himself on always keeping his door open to leading figures in the commercial world. Among those to take advantage of such easy access was Sir Horace Bloch, head of the Glasgow distillers, Bloch Brothers Ltd. In a two-month period, Sir Horace furnished Belcher with 56 bottles of sherry, in return, it was claimed, for three import licences for 'essential' business supplies. A more sinister visitor to Belcher's office was Sydney Stanley, also known as Solomon Wulkan Hymans, a key fixer in the black market that thrived after World War II. Belcher gratefully received gifts and favours from Stanley, including a three-piece suite, a £68 gold cigarette case, two pounds of Walls pork sausages and a holiday in Bournemouth. A man of no great sophistication, Belcher enjoyed Stanley's company and was happy to be his guest at boxing contests in Bethnal Green and on visits to Harringay's dog track.

In 1948 the Board of Trade under its president, Harold Wilson, brought a prosecution against Sherman Pools for a breach of the paper rationing regulations. Stanley told the Sherman brothers that Belcher was in his pay and that he could persuade him to have the prosecution stopped. Harry Sherman reported this to the police, though it is not clear why. As a result, a tribunal was set up under Mr Justice Lynsky to investigate these rumours. At one of the hearings, Belcher's barrister admitted that his client had accepted 'small bribes' when he had meant to say 'small gifts', and in Lynsky's 50,000-word report Belcher was found guilty of having dishonestly used his influence as a member of the government. He resigned as an MP on the day the report was debated in the House of Commons. He went back to work on the railways, rising in time to the position of assistant goods master at King's Cross. He died in 1964, leaving £600.

*See also* BOURNEMOUTH.

**Belcher, Muriel** (1910–79), club owner. Belcher maintained only one rule at the Colony Room Club, which she opened in Soho in the early 1950s: that no one should be boring. On the other hand, the membership included Dan FARSON, Tom DRIBERG and Jeffrey BERNARD.

At the age of 16, Muriel left Birmingham for London, where in time she fulfilled the role of 'queens' moll' at Le Jardin des Gourmets, a restaurant in Dean Street frequented by Noël Coward and Graham Payne. When she opened the Colony Room Club, she named it after her lifelong companion, Carmel, who came from the colonies. The painter, Francis Bacon, was an early member and he and Muriel became close friends. Bacon had no money at the time, so Muriel gave him £10 a week to act as a 'hostess'.

In August each year, Bacon and Muriel liked to holiday in the casino towns of the south of France. Bacon always kept out of the sun because it made his hair dye run. In the evenings Muriel watched him play roulette. On one occasion they were stranded without funds, so they decided to rob an acquaintance who was staying nearby. Muriel climbed up a lamppost outside his apartment, while Bacon stood lookout. Then they went to the casino, where Bacon staked their return fare to London at the gambling tables. He began to win heavily, but as he did so his face slowly turned black. He had run out of hair dye and had used boot polish instead. Once Bacon had won the cost of their fare back to London, Muriel climbed up the lamppost and replaced the stolen money.

When she died, Muriel left the Colony to Ian Board, whom she had met when he was a commis-waiter at Le Jardin des Gourmets. Board had run away from home in Devon when his father slapped him for wearing too much lipstick. Known as Ida to the Colony's long-standing members, Board's manner was deceptive. He once picked up Dan Farson and threw him down the stairs.

**Bell, Terence** (1932–97), building-society clerk. Bell, of Southsea, Hampshire, made seven attempts to kill his wife without her noticing that anything was wrong. In 1980 he took out an insurance policy that would yield £250,000 in the event of her accidental death. He then put a lethal dose of mercury in her strawberry flan, but it rolled off the plate. Next he laced her mackerel with the entire contents of the bottle. This time she ate it, but with no side effects at all. He then took her on holiday to Yugoslavia. Recommending the panoramic views, he suggested she sit at the edge of a cliff. She refused, prompted by what she later described as 'a sixth sense'. When Mrs Bell was in bed with chickenpox, he started a fire outside her bedroom door, but a neighbour put it out. He then started another fire that burnt down the house, but Mrs Bell escaped unhurt. Finally, he asked her to stand in the middle of the road so that he could test the brakes on his car by driving straight at her. Since nothing could destroy her, Bell gave up and made a full confession to the police. According to Detective Constable Harry Legge of the Hampshire CID, Mrs Bell was dumbstruck when told of her husband's plot to kill her.

**Bell, Tricia.** *See* GREEN, HUGHIE.

**Bellingham, John** (1771–1812), shipping merchant, insurance broker and political assassin. In 1812 Bellingham, a forebear of the present MP for Southwest Norfolk, Henry Bellingham, shot the prime minister, Spencer Perceval, dead in the House of Commons. He had allowed a minor grievance against the government to become a festering obsession.

When employed in the Russian Arctic port of Archangel as a shipping merchant, Bellingham was involved in a pecuniary dispute with some Russian traders, in settlement of which he felt he had not received due assistance from the British ambassador in that part of the world, Lord Granville Leverson Gower. Back in England, and working as an insurance broker in Liverpool, Bellingham was unable to let the matter drop. Thinking that he was entitled to some redress from the government for what he judged to have been culpable negligence by its appropriate agent, Leverson Gower, he petitioned first the Privy Council, then the Treasury, and finally the prime minister himself, Spencer Perceval. When Perceval refused to intervene, Bellingham adopted an unprecedented way of making himself heard. Armed with a pair of pistols, he took up a position in the lobby of the House of Commons and when the prime minister entered he shot him at point blank range. Perceval reeled a short distance and cried, 'I'll have one of Belamey's veal pies!' and fell down dead. (Bellamy's Pies of Parliament Square, Est. 1698, were particularly popular among prime ministers, including Pitt the Younger.) Shouts of, 'Shut the door! Let no one out!' were heard, and then someone said, 'Where's the murderer?' Bellingham, who was still holding the pistols, replied, 'I am the unfortunate man!' and was taken into custody.

During his trial at the Old Bailey in May 1812, Bellingham denied any personal animosity towards Perceval, for whose death he expressed the greatest sorrow. His motives for committing such an act, he said, had been, 'want of redress and denial of justice'. He was taken to the scaffold in a cart, followed by a crowd of the lower class, who shouted, 'God bless you!' and other expressions of their approval.

**belly dancers.** *See* MOYNIHAN, ANTONY PATRICK ANDREW CAIRNE BERKELEY, 3RD BARON.

**Belvedere, Robert Rochfort, 1st earl of** (1708–74), Irish aristocrat whose behaviour was contrary to the spirit of the 18th-century ABDUCTION CLUBS in that his chosen bride had great beauty and many accomplishments but no fortune. In 1736 Belvedere, then merely Viscount Belfield, married a 16-year-old girl, Mary, whose father, Viscount Molesworth, was as brutal as her future husband. At first Lord Belfield's rages so frightened Mary that she escaped at night to her father's house, only to be sent back to her husband the next morning. She settled down eventually at Gaulstown, the dispiriting residence where Belfield's father had once entertained Dean Swift, and they seemed to be reasonably happy. Several children were born and Belfield devoted his time to the construction of a magnificent villa 6 miles away overlooking Lough Ennell.

However, while visiting London, where he hoped to ingratiate himself at the court of George II, Belfield was sent anonymously an exchange of love letters between his wife and his brother, Arthur Rochfort, a married man with a large family. When confronted, Lady Belfield admitted everything, including the confession that Lord Belfield's last son was in fact his nephew. Belfield sought the advice of Lord Molesworth, who suggested that his daughter be transported forthwith to the West Indies as a vagabond, but Belfield's choice of punishment proved more effective in the long run. He imprisoned his wife in Gaulstown for the next 30 years. She was allowed servants, to whom she could give orders, but they were not allowed to speak to her. She could walk in the grounds, preceded by a footman who rang a bell to keep everyone away, but she was forbidden to leave the estate. After she had been confined for twelve years, she managed to escape to her father's house in Dublin. He refused to admit her, and the next day she was back in the peculiar prison devised by her husband.

Lady Belvedere's lover, Arthur Rochfort, had escaped to Yorkshire, having heard that Belfield had threatened to shoot him. He had then spent some time in France, before returning to Ireland 15 years later. He assumed that his brother, now Lord Belvedere, would ignore him, but in this he was wrong. Belvedere immediately had him arrested and charged with £20,000 damages for CRIMINAL CONVERSATION. When he couldn't pay, Belvedere had him confined in the Marshalsea debtors' prison, where he died.

Lady Belvedere passed her captive years at Gaulstown attended by mute servants, never once receiving a visit from her family. Her face became wild and haggard and she almost lost the power of speech. Meanwhile, her husband lived in luxury at his new villa 6 miles away, entertaining on a lavish scale, but finding time to quarrel with another brother, George, who had established himself within sight of Belvedere's residence. This aspect so offended Belvedere that he decided to block out the view by building a sham ruin between their two properties. At great expense, he imported a number of Italian artists to design and build a ruined abbey, complete with Gothic windows, to stand between his house and his brother's.

When Belvedere died in 1774, his son – somewhat belatedly some might think – came to Gaulstown to release his mother, whom he found dressed in the fashions of 30 years before. 'Is the tyrant dead?' she whispered. To entertain her, the 2nd earl of Belvedere took her to Rome, where she became a Catholic.

## Belvoir, the Witches of. *See* FLOWER, JOAN.

Belvoir is pronounced 'Beevor' – a convention peculiar to this part of England. Other Lincolnshire villages pronounced idiosyncratically are those of Bolsom and Mulf.

## Benson, Harry (1848–1911), linguist, newspaper proprietor, musician, confidence trickster and key figure behind the 'Trial of the Detectives',

which shocked Victorian society in 1877. Known also as Hugh Montgomery, the Marquess Montmorenci and the comte de Montagu, Benson, who had been educated in France, lived in elegant circumstances in a large house in the Isle of Wight, attended by several maids and a French valet. He was the proprietor of three local newspapers and moved only in the best circles, in which he was recognized as a talented musician and linguist.

In fact, Benson's income derived entirely from swindles, including one in 1872 in which he had posed successfully as the mayor of Chateaudun, supposedly raising money for refugees from the Franco-Prussian War. On that occasion he had extracted £1000 from those of a charitable disposition before being arrested. Afraid of imprisonment, he had set fire to the bedding in his cell and was carried into court on the back of a warder to receive a twelve-month sentence.

On his release, Benson teamed up with William Kurr, a Scottish fraudsman, who had been bribing Inspector John Meiklejohn, one of Scotland Yard's senior detectives. Meiklejohn kept Kurr informed about the progress of police inquiries in connection with racing scams. Chief Inspector George Clarke was also recruited, after a suggestion of blackmail by Benson, as was one of Scotland Yard's most able detectives, the multilingual Nathaniel Druscovitch. Druscovitch had backed a bill for his brother in the sum of £60, and when he couldn't pay he was lent the money by Kurr and Benson. The fourth officer involved, William Palmer, was recruited through Meiklejohn. The sums of money they received from Benson and Kurr were considerable. For informing Benson that a fraud charge could be settled, Meiklejohn received £200. Druscovitch received £1000 for not travelling to Scotland to pursue a fraud inquiry, and on another occasion accepted £100 and a piece of jewellery for his wife. He was also given a cigar box containing £200 in gold. For assisting in the exchange of bank notes, Meiklejohn received £2000 from Benson.

In September 1876 Benson set in motion an audacious racing swindle against a number of wealthy French citizens, including the comtesse de Goncourt. Having been contacted by Benson – posing as Mr Hugh Montgomery, whose gambling activities had been so successful that British bookmakers would no longer accept bets in his name – the comtesse was persuaded to back various nonexistent horses on his behalf through a commission agent in London. In a matter of weeks, she had been swindled out of £10,000. Her lawyer engaged the services of Mr Abrahams, a tenacious London solicitor, who pestered Scotland Yard with complaints. Chief Inspector Clarke and Inspector Meiklejohn were put in charge of the investigation. This made little progress, since both were on Benson's payroll, but Clarke advised Benson to leave the country for a while. Benson went to Amsterdam under the alias 'Morton', but was eventually arrested on an extradition order from London. When Clarke heard of this, he sent a telegram to the Dutch police, 'Morton is not man we want. An officer will not now be sent to pick him up. Free him immediately. Letter follows.' Clarke signed the telegram 'Frederick Carter, Scotland Yard'.

The Dutch police were about to release 'Morton', but then decided to wait for the promised letter from the nonexistent Inspector Carter. When it failed to arrive, Benson was returned to England in handcuffs. Having received a sentence of 15 years penal servitude, he decided to cooperate with the authorities, in return, he hoped, for an early release. On his evidence, Meiklejohn, Palmer, Druscovitch and Edward Froggart – a dishonest solicitor who had brokered the various *douceurs* – were each sentenced to two years, but Clarke was acquitted.

Druscovitch died shortly after his release from prison. Palmer became a successful publican, as did Clarke, who retired on a pension after his acquittal. Meiklejohn became a private enquiry agent, having lost a libel action over his participation in Benson's racing swindle. Froggart, the solicitor, was later imprisoned for tricking Lord Eustace into marrying a lady with a doubtful reputation. He embezzled £10,000 from the marriage settlement, of which he was a trustee. He died in Lambeth workhouse.

On his release, Benson moved to the United States, where he operated a series of swindles. He committed suicide in the Tombs prison, New York, on discovering that he was about to be extradited to Mexico for selling fake tickets for a tour by Madame Patti, a soprano.

Writing of the affair in *The Rise of Scotland Yard* (1956), D.G. Browne dismisses it as 'a net of corruption happily unique in the history of the Metropolitan Police'. Others might argue that by accepting bribes, suppressing evidence and giving advance notice of raids, the activities of the detectives involved provided the Metropolitan CID with an operational blueprint for the next 120 years.

*See also* APPLES, BAD.

**Berkeley, Humphry John** (1926–94), ill-mannered politician, broadcaster and occasional writer, now remembered only as the organizer of a spoof book, *The Life and Death of Rochester Sneath* (1974), the first in a chain of laborious epistolary pranks, culminating in the facetious *Henry Root Letters* (1980).

**Berkley, Theresa** (*c.*1780–1836), madam. Berkley ran a notorious brothel in Hallam Street, London, which specialized in flagellation and whose appointments were recognized as second to none. On arrival, clients were offered a choice of whips and restraining devices. Popular among the latter was Theresa's own invention, the Berkley Horse, of which there were two types: a padded ladder to which the customer was pinned like a butterfly and then whipped, and a wheel which revolved at various speeds, flogging the customer as it turned. Favoured clients were personally chastised by Theresa, others were attended to by 'assistant governesses', one of whom,

'One-Eyed Peg', had a particularly strong hand. When Theresa died in 1006, she left her fortune to her brother, a missionary in Australia. On discovering how the money had been acquired he renounced all claim to it. Having become the executor of Theresa's estate, the Crown suppressed her autobiography in which she had named many royal and aristocratic clients.

**Bernard, Jeffrey** (1934–97), fairground boxer, scene-shifter, theatrical extra, journalist and drunk. Less talented in many people's judgement than his two brothers – the poet, Oliver, and the art historian, Bruce – Bernard, in the way of things, achieved greater celebrity than either with his long-running, bar-room performance as a loveable rogue and little boy lost. Educated, through the unstinting devotion of his mother, an opera singer, at Pangbourne Naval College, he drifted through Soho, and many occupations, before finding a natural home in the pages of the *Spectator*, where he used his 'Low-Life' column to provide a middle-class readership with an amusing, if largely fraudulent, account of a bohemian existence. In 1991 the column was adapted as a West End entertainment by Keith Waterhouse under the title *Jeffrey Bernard is Unwell* – a reference to the announcement that regularly explained the absence of Bernard's column during his many indispositions.

Truculent and disorganized, Bernard was dismissed by many as a conventional Soho drunk whose radicalism amounted to having his first large vodka at 10 a.m. and then picking an argument with the man standing next to him in the Coach and Horses, Soho. To his critics, his was merely the acceptable face of dissent. His targets were the Arts Council, feminists, Americans, subsidized poets and intellectuals; his heroes were Lester Piggott, Mr 'Sugar Ray' Robinson and Lord Nelson. Some were amused by the performance; others failed to see the charm. Among Bernard's four wives was the talented actress, Jacqueline Ellis.

*See also* BALON, NORMAN.

**Berners, Gerald Hugh Tyrwhitt-Wilson, 14th Baron** (1883–1950), composer, artist and writer. Visitors to Faringdon in Oxfordshire, the home of Lord Berners, were confronted by whippets wearing diamond collars, doves painted pink and blue, and an antique Rolls Royce with a clavichord built into its rear seat. This eccentric display sometimes obscured the fact that Berners was a skilful parodist and an accomplished composer of opera and ballet music. In 1926, his first ballet, *The Triumph of Neptune*, to a scenario by Sacheverell Sitwell, was produced by Diaghilev's Ballets Russes. He was one of only two British composers – the other being Constant Lambert – to be commissioned by the great impresario. His last three ballets, *A Wedding Bouquet*, *Cupid and Psyche* and *Les Sirènes*, were written in collaboration with Frederick Ashton as choreographer and Constant Lambert as musical director. In 1944, he contributed a song, 'Come on Algernon', to the Ealing film *Champagne Charlie.*

Berners acquired his sense of humour, and taste for practical jokes, during ten years in the diplomatic service. He took a particular dislike to a senior member of chancery in one embassy who signalled the end of any pronouncement by solemnly putting on his spectacles. One day Berners attached the spectacles by a piece of thread to the ink bottle on his desk. When his superior next raised his spectacles to signal the end of a speech he covered himself in ink. Terrified of bores, Berners had various ways of avoiding them, particularly on trains. According to his friend, the artist and writer Michael Ayrton, Berners, wearing a black skull cap and humorous black spectacles, would lean out of the window of his compartment and beckon passengers to join him. Those foolhardy enough to accept the invitation soon departed when he took his temperature anally every five minutes with a large clinical thermometer.

From Faringdon House, Berners was able to look across to the 140-foot-high Faringdon Folly which he built in 1935. There was some public objection to the scheme when planning permission was originally sought. Asked to justify his request, Berners replied, "The great point of the tower is that it will be entirely useless.' The authorities were convinced and the project was approved. The completed folly had a sign stating that, 'Members of the public committing suicide from this tower do so at their own risk.'

On his death in 1950, Berners left Faringdon House to his friend of many years, Robert HEBER-PERCY, known as 'the Mad Boy'. According to Diana Mosley, wife of the Fascist leader, Sir Oswald Mosley, Heber-Percy 'so enchanted Gerald Berners that he no longer needed a drug to give him contentment'. Coincidentally, it has recently come to light that a canine sedative, 'Calm Doggie' (intended to keep pets quiet during air raids) was used recreationally by Berners's collaborator, Sir Frederick Ashton, to replace his usual indulgence, which had become scarce during World War II.

**Bessell, Peter** (1922–88), politician, lay preacher and entrepreneur. Bessell, who drove round his Cornish constituency in a Cadillac and who was known to be haphazard in both his business and his personal arrangements, would not have been most people's choice as a reliable ally in times of trouble. It was the Liberal MP for Bodmin, however, to whom Jeremy THORPE turned when Norman SCOTT, a male model, first threatened the Liberal leader with allegations of a homosexual relationship.

At first Bessell did what was asked of him, attempting to pay Scott off with sums of money, which over a period totalled £700. However, when Fleet Street uncovered evidence of these payments, Bessell, who was deeply in debt, saw that there was money to be made from betraying his friend. In April 1976 he sold his story to the *Daily Mail*, which ran it under the headline, 'I Told Lies to Protect Thorpe'.

Thorpe retired to the back benches, and the police interviewed Bessell in California, which had become the centre of his business operations. In return for immunity from prosecution, Bessell provided the police with an 11,000-word statement, which implicated Thorpe in a conspiracy to murder Scott. The *Sunday Telegraph* agreed to pay Bessell £50,000. Half of this was paid in advance; the balance would be paid if, and when, Thorpe – whose trial on a conspiracy charge now seemed inevitable – was convicted. Some have argued that this arrangement amounted to a conspiracy to pervert the course of justice. Certainly it ensured that the prosecution at Thorpe's trial would fail. Bessell, with his peculiar tan and summer suit, was an unconvincing figure in the witness box, and George Carman QC, for the defence, easily destroyed what little credibility he had. He pointed to many unresolved contradictions in Bessell's evidence, and made much of the fact that he would be substantially enriched, thanks to the terms of his deal with the *Sunday Telegraph*, were Thorpe to be convicted.

Mr Justice Cantley, presiding, was equally unimpressed by Bessell, whom he referred to in his summing-up as 'an obvious humbug'. Thorpe, though disgraced, was acquitted, and the one-time Liberal member for Bodmin departed for California with a mere £8000 with which to shore up his several ailing ventures.

**Best, George** (1946– ), Irish soccer player, sometimes dubbed 'The Fifth Beatle' – a reference to the fact that he achieved a status among 'teenyboppers' in the 1960s more usually enjoyed by pop bands and crooners. Described by soccer enthusiasts as the most naturally gifted player of all time, Best's self-proclaimed inability to adjust to 'life in a goldfish bowl' brought about a sharp downturn in his affairs, which embraced alcoholism, a spell in prison over Christmas, and guest appearances with Scunthorpe United and Dunstable Town. He has survived as a skeletal bearded presence on the after-dinner celebrity circuit, exchanging banter with his friend, the former player, Rodney Marsh. 'When Marshy was picked for England,' Best jokes, 'he told the manager, Sir Alf Ramsey, that he wasn't 100% fit. "Don't worry," said Sir Alf. "I'll pull you off at half time." "Great," said Marshy. "At Queens Park Rangers we just get half an orange."'

*See also* MCAVENNIE, FRANK.

**Beswick, Hannah** (1680–1758), spinster. Miss Beswick, of Cheetwood Hall, Manchester, was morbidly afraid of being buried alive. To avoid this circumstance, she left her doctor, Charles White, £25,000 in her will on condition that he continue to visit her regularly after her death. When she died in 1758, Dr White had her embalmed and placed her at the top of his house in a grandfather clock. Each year, on the anniversary of her death, he paid her a morning visit, accompanied by a witness.

When Dr White himself died in 1813, Miss Beswick was moved to the Lying-In Hospital (now St Mary's) and from there to the Manchester Museum of Natural History. When the museum transferred to new premises in the mid-19th century, Miss Beswick was examined and the trustees came to the unanimous decision that she was definitely dead. On 22 July 1868 she was finally buried in the Manchester General Cemetery.

**Betty Ford Clinic, asking the way to the bar in the.** *See* OSBOURNE, JOHN MICHAEL ('OZZY').

**Beverley, Anne** (1949– ), punk. Beverley was the mother of Sid Vicious, a guitarist with the 1970s pop band, the Sex Pistols, which had been assembled by the style entrepreneur, Malcom McLaren, and his partner, the fashion designer Vivienne Westwood. When Vicious killed his girlfriend, Nancy Spungen, during a drunken fight in their New York hotel room in 1979, Anne spoke vigorously in her son's defence. 'I called her Nauseating Nancy,' she told reporters. 'She was a bad influence on Sid.'

Vicious was released on £25,000 bail on condition that he enlist at a detoxification clinic. Instead, Mrs Beverley took her son to a party at the flat of his new girlfriend. There, he injected himself with heroin and had a fit. Since he then appeared to recover – briefly – no one called an ambulance. The next morning he was dead.

When *The Great Rock and Roll Swindle*, a feature film featuring the Sex Pistols, opened in London in 1981, Mrs Beverley arrived at the première on a 750 cc motorcycle dressed as a punk. Interviewed by the *News of the World*, she explained that it was she who had bought the heroin that had killed her son. She had got it from a New York street dealer, and it had been unusually pure. 'I suppose it's fate,' she said. 'Sid died because I tried to help him.'

**Bibby, John** (1780–1814), vagrant. Sentenced to death at the Old Bailey for sheep stealing on the duke of Richmond's estate, Bibby ran up the ladder to the scaffold, shouting, 'I am the Duke of Wellington! I am the Duke of Wellington!' When the trapdoor opened, Bibby bounced up as if on a trampoline, shouting, 'What did I tell you?' He was subdued after a struggle, and eventually dispatched.

**Bickford, Charles Arthur** (1940– ), unemployed scaffolder. In 1978, Bickford broke into a house in Birmingham and threatened the owner, Mrs Meriweather, with indecent assault unless she gave him £20 in cash. She didn't have it, so he told her to write him a cheque. When she asked him whom she should make it out to, he said, 'Charles A. Bickford'. He then robbed a store, but his trousers fell down as he was making his getaway.

**Bidwell, Austin** (1839–1911) and **Bidwell, George** (1841–1915), confidence tricksters, notorious for defrauding the Bank of England of £100,000 in 1873 – the equivalent of £30 million in today's terms. The feat was accomplished with the assistance of George MACDONNELL, a master forger. Their plan involved the lodging of bogus bills of exchange with the Bank of England, and it fell to Austin Bidwell to open an account there in the name of F.A. Warren – an entrepreneur supposedly financing the building of American-style Pullman cars in England.

To open an account with the Bank of England, however, Bidwell needed a recommendation. Since 1855, the Bank had had a Western Branch in Burlington Gardens, which had been established to gather private customers in that fashionable area of London. Savile Row, with its exclusive tailors and expensive shops, ran north from Burlington Gardens. Bidwell was sure that some of these businesses would have accounts at the Bank of England's Western Branch. In April 1872, and posing as a window-shopper in Burlington Arcade, he saw the military clothier, Edward Hamilton Green, emerge from the Western Branch and return to his shop at 35 Savile Row. A few days later, 'Mr Warren' called at the shop and ordered a range of expensive suits. 'Mr Warren' was soon on excellent terms with Mr Green. After a few weeks, and several fittings, he confided in Mr Green that he was carrying a large sum of cash and was uneasy about leaving it at his lodgings. He would be grateful, he said, if he could put it in the shop's safe. Mr Green advised him that such a substantial sum should be deposited at once in a bank. As luck would have it, he said, his own bank was close at hand, and he offered to introduce 'Mr Warren' to the manager. A few hours later, Austin Bidwell had an account with the Bank of England's Western Branch.

For six months, Bidwell deposited and withdrew money and bought and sold bonds. The account was impressively active, and in November 1872, he asked the manager, Colonel Francis, to accept a few genuine bills of exchange for relatively small amounts. Colonel Francis explained that the Western Branch was not authorized to deal with such matters, but he agreed to ask head office in Threadneedle Street if they could accommodate his customer. Head office were happy to do so, and within a short time, acceptance of Bidwell's genuine bills through the Western Branch was routine. The account of a man who had the exclusive rights to manufacture Pullman cars for British and European railways was an important acquisition, even for the Bank of England.

Austin Bidwell now travelled to Paris, where he bought from Rothschilds Bank a bill for £4000. On 17 January this was changed by the Bank of England. Six days later the Bank of England exchanged three more such bills, apparently identical, but in fact the work of the master forger in the Bidwells' employ, George Macdonnell. The name of Rothschild seemed to guarantee their authenticity, not least because Lionel Rothschild was a director of the Bank of England. By the end of February 1873 the Bank had changed forged bills in the amount of £100,405 7s 3d. 'It appeared,' said George Bidwell later:

> ... as if the bank managers had heaped a mountain of gold in the street with a notice saying, 'Please do not touch this', and then left it unguarded with the guileless confidingness of an Arcadian.

In the event, the robbery was discovered because of a simple mistake: Macdonnell had forgotten to date the bills. Colonel Francis spotted this at last, and the conspirators were eventually arrested – but only after they had found temporary safety in the United States thanks to assistance from Inspectors John Meiklejohn and Nathaniel Druscovitch, the corrupt policemen who were later on the payroll of Harry BENSON. Before their trial, allegations were made that guns had been smuggled to them by a third Bidwell brother, and Mr Justice Archibald was thought to be the first judge in English legal history to sit through proceedings with a gun under his robes. The defendants were found guilty and sentenced to penal servitude for life. George Bidwell was released in 1887, on the grounds of ill health, and his brother, Austin, in 1890.

**bigamists.** *See* ARCHER, WILLIAM; CARLETON, MARY; CHUDLEIGH, ELIZABETH; HATFIELD, JOHN; ROUSE, ALFRED ARTHUR; SMITH, GEORGE JOSEPH.

**bigamy.** During the 19th and early 20th centuries, bigamy was the only method by which impecunious members of the working class were able to relieve an unhappy marriage. In 1843 Lord Maul, before sentencing an itinerant beggar who had pleaded guilty to this offence, was helpful enough to instruct him in what would have been the correct course of action:

> I will tell you what you ought to have done under the circumstances, and if you say you did not know, I must tell you that the law conclusively presumes that you did. You should have instructed your attorney to bring an action against the seducer of your wife for damages; that would have cost you about £100. Having proceeded thus far, you should have employed a proctor and instituted a suit in the Ecclesiastical Courts for a divorce *a mensa et thoro*: that would have cost you £200 or £300 more. When you had obtained a divorce *a mensa et thoro* you had only to obtain a private Act for divorce *a vinculo matrimonii*. The Bill might possibly have been opposed in all its stages in both Houses of Parliament and altogether these proceedings would cost you £1000. You will probably tell me that you never had a tenth of that sum, but that makes no difference.
>
> Sitting here as an English judge it is my duty to tell you that this is

not a country where there is one law for the rich and another for the poor.

From *The Life of Richard, Lord Westbury* (1888).

Financial dishonesty is generally regarded by the courts to be a more serious offence than bigamy. In October 1993, Victor Harris, a solicitor, who had used both his wives to obtain mortgages, received six months for bigamy and three years for false accounting.

In the present day, bigamy is usually undertaken to provide British citizenship, which is otherwise unavailable to one of the parties. Professional brides are paid as much as £1000 a time. In 1998 Samantha Parry was charged with marrying eight times in the course of five years, with four marriages in 1996. Susan Coates, a former lap dancer, married seven illegal immigrants from West Africa in 14 months.

**Bigg, John** (1629–96), scholar and recluse. Known as the Dinton Hermit, Bigg spent the last 30 years of his life in a cave in Buckinghamshire. At one time he had been a man of parts, a respected scholar and clerk to Simon Mayne, one of the judges who passed sentence on Charles I. It was Charles II's restoration to the throne in 1660 that caused Bigg to fall into the depression from which he never recovered – his case being the exact opposite of Sir Thomas URQUHART, in whom the Restoration gave rise to a fatal fit of laughter.

Throughout his 30 years in the cave, Bigg never begged, but relied on the kindness of local people, who provided him with food and drink. He asked for nothing but a constant supply of leather straps. He nailed these to his clothes, whose original fabric had long since disintegrated. One of his shoes, made up of 1000 pieces of leather, is in the Ashmolean Museum, Oxford.

*See also* RECLUSES.

**Biggar, Joseph** (1841–1911), politician and philanderer. Biggar combined his parliamentary duties with many amorous adventures. These gained him great favour with the public, and not only in his Belfast constituency. When W.S. Caine introduced a bill in 1883 that would relieve men in breach-of-promise actions unless actual pecuniary loss could be proved, it was popularly known as the 'Biggar Relief Bill'.

Biggar was sued many times by disappointed women, on one occasion by a barmaid, Fanny Hyland, to whom he had proposed marriage in the course of a trip to Paris, sealing the offer with the gift of a parrot. When he broke off the engagement, he compounded his bad behaviour by suing for the return of the parrot. Miss Hyland counter-claimed, alleging breach of promise. The judge awarded her £300, and she left the court in tears. 'I would rather have kept the parrot,' she said.

On another occasion Biggar spoke in court of certain impediments in the way of a proposed marriage to a cabaret dancer, Fay Sinclair. The judge asked him what these impediments might be. 'Four illegitimate children,' Biggar replied. 'Is the mother still alive?' asked the judge. 'Yes, m'lud,' said Biggar. 'All four are.' The judge was unamused and Miss Sinclair was awarded £500.

See also PARROTS.

**Biggs, Ronald** (1928– ), carpenter and thief. Biggs played only a minor roll in the Great Train Robbery of 1963. He was recruited by Bruce REYNOLDS because he happened to be decorating the house of a retired train driver. The train driver was recruited, too, but turned out to know nothing about driving trains. In the event, Biggs's contribution to the robbery almost caused a disaster. However, by his daring escape from Wandsworth prison and the affable contributions he subsequently made to law-and-order debates, he achieved a fair measure of sympathy, not to say iconic status. He was greatly helped in this by Detective Chief Superintendent Jack Slipper's good-natured, but dogged, attempts to return him to his south London prison cell.

Having scaled the prison wall by means of a rope ladder provided by Paul Seabourne, a former colleague, Biggs made his way to Australia, where he worked as a jobbing carpenter under the name of Terry Cook. Informed on by a neighbour, who mistook him for Lord LUCAN, Biggs moved to Brazil, where he quickly made his girlfriend, Raimunda, pregnant, thus ensuring that he was safe from extradition. Thereafter, he made a living as a radio personality, advising on crime prevention. In 1977 he felt bound to offer an explanation for an apparent lapse of taste in a record cut with the Sex Pistols, a popular rock group. This had contained a less than condemnatory reference to Martin Boorman, the Nazi war criminal. 'If we are going to make a better Christian society,' Biggs argued, 'we must start with some basic tenets, the most fundamental of which is forgiveness for everyone. We cannot discriminate between Martin Boorman and the Good Samaritan.'

In later life, following a decline in his health, Biggs came to the idiosyncratic decision that his declining years could be spent more pleasantly in Peckham, south London, than on the sun-kissed beaches of Brazil. Accordingly, he returned voluntarily to the United Kingdom in April 2000, with financial assistance from the *Sun* newspaper. Those of a vindictive disposition demanded that the frail old thief should spend the rest of his life in prison. Others pointed out that, by escaping justice, he had saved the tax payer £900,000 – considerably more than he had received from the train robbery. They further argued that his condition at least merited the sympathy recently extended by the home secretary, Jack Straw, to Augusto Pinochet, the Chilean torturer and mass murderer. At the very least, they said, Biggs should be housed – as General Pinochet had been – in comfort on a private estate in Wentworth Surrey, while his case was reviewed. This was taken to be a facetious suggestion, and those of a retributive constitution won the argument. The bewildered old villain, who had suffered three strokes and two heart attacks, was thereafter handcuffed to the bedpost and fed through a drip.

**Big Sal.** *See* FLOOD, MATTHEW.

**billiard cue, duelling on the Malabar Coast with a.** *See* MAGUIRE, BRIAN.

**Billing, Pemberton** (1870–1946), politician, journalist and casino owner. The Independent member for East Hertfordshire, Billing edited *Vigilante*, a magazine which existed to cause sensation in the guise of reforming zeal. He was anti-German, anti-Semitic and homophobic. When the popular actress, Maud Allen, who was thought to be a lesbian, announced that she would be appearing in two performances of Oscar Wilde's *Salome* at the Prince of Wales theatre, the *Vigilante* ran an article under the title 'The Cult of the Clitoris'. Maud Allen sued for obscene libel before Lord Darling, who was as prejudiced as the defendant. Billing appeared for himself, and was allowed as much latitude as he needed. He opened his cross-examination of Miss Allen with the question, 'Was your brother executed in San Francisco for murdering two young girls and outraging them after death in a belfry?' Mr Ellis Hume-Williams, on behalf of Allen, objected, but Lord Darling allowed the question on the basis of Billing's argument that since the brother was a necrophiliac and *Salome* an obscene play there was a relevant connection. Darling then expressed the hope that when women were able to have their influence on legislation they would make it their business to ensure that more purity was introduced into public representations than was the case at present. The jury took the hint, and deliberated for only half an hour before acquitting Billing.

Billing's behaviour became more idiosyncratic with time. In 1934 he was suspended from Parliament and carried out drunk. He moved to Mexico, where he ran a casino unsuccessfully with the former heavyweight boxer, Jack Dempsey. In 1941 he wrote a book, *The Aviation of Tomorrow*, on the subject of rocket refuelling. He died in 1946, ten years before Maud Allen, who had retired from the stage to become a teacher.

**Bindon, John** (1943–93), actor and celebrity thug. Until he was discovered by the film director, Ken Loach, and given a small part in *Poor Cow* (1966), Bindon was a minor London villain, who according to his own account had once hit 'Big' Jim Connolly, a KRAY brothers henchman, with a soda-water siphon from behind. He later cropped up in other films and on television, and in the company of his girlfriend, the model Vicki Hodge, he became a token 'hard man' at Chelsea parties. Miss Hodge introduced him to Princess Margaret, whom he entertained by balancing six glasses of beer on his penis.

According to his obituary in the *Independent*, Bindon 'could make a horse laugh', but many people were wary of his uncertain temper. John Hobbs, the owner of Fulham's Furniture Cave, was on one occasion knocked unconscious for some minor breach of bar-room etiquette. He came round to find Bindon cradling him in his arms, and kissing him. 'It was worse than the slapping,' said Hobbs.

In 1978, in the course of a fight at the Ranelagh Yacht Club in Chelsea, Bindon killed Johnny Darke, an alleged informer, with a machete hidden in his trouser leg. Underworld rumour had it as a contract killing, for which Bindon had received £10,000, but at his trial he pleaded self-defence and was acquitted.

**Bint, Paul** (1959– ), hairdresser and con man. Bint's career met a temporary setback in August 2000 after he had persuaded Virgin Rail to put him up for three nights at a luxury hotel in Newcastle. Claiming to be a barrister and, to lend authenticity to the impersonation, wearing a wig borrowed from Birmingham Crown Court, he had told staff on the Birmingham-to-Edinburgh train that his laptop computer, which contained crucial defence details, had been stolen. The train stopped for so long while a search was made that the other passengers had to be taken by taxi to their destinations. Bint was booked into the Newcastle hotel at Virgin Rail's expense.

Newcastle Crown Court was told that Bint had appeared in court 17 times since 1980, charged with 116 offences. His record included posing as a locum doctor, as a member of the Royal Ballet and as a landed aristocrat. In 1984 he had been jailed for five years at the Old Bailey for tricking a salesman out of an £83,000 Ferrari while posing as the earl of Arundel. In 1988 he had received four years for test-driving a Porsche as a relative of the lord chancellor, and disappearing with it. On another occasion, and as the grandson of Lord Forte, he had done the same with a Rolls Royce.

Bint's favourite role had involved posing as a doctor and touring the wards of various hospitals. He was caught in 1983, but only after he had attended a man with a collapsed lung, put twelve stitches in another man's head wound and assisted at a by-pass operation. He was in trouble again in 1993 when he was found walking the corridors of St James's Hospital, Leeds, carrying a stolen bleeper and attending patients. In the course of this impersonation, and against the prognosis of a senior consultant, he told the parents of a 17-year-old girl that she would recover in six months. She died a week later.

Judge William Crawford, at Newcastle Crown Court, was impressed by Bint's career. 'You are a most imaginative trickster,' he said. 'I have been greatly impressed by your counsel's speech in mitigation. You will receive

a lesser sentence than you might have expected.'
Blint was sent to prison for six years.

**Birch, George 'Parrots are my Business'.** *See* RUBELL, IDA.

**Birch, Thomas** (1705–66), librarian. Birch, a keeper of books at the British Museum, was a keen fisherman who devised an unusual way of disguising his intentions. Dressed as a tree, he stood by the side of a stream in an outfit designed to make his arms seem like branches and the rod and line a spray of blossom. Any movement, he argued, would be taken by a fish to be the consequences of a mild breeze.

Sir Humphrey Davy, the distinguished chemist, improved on the idea half a century later. His preferred costume consisted of a green coat, green breeches and an old green hat. 'In this attire,' wrote Cordy Jeafferson, 'Davy flattered himself he resembled vegetable life as closely as it was possible for mortal man to do' (*Humphrey Davy*, Sir H. Hartley, 1966). On shooting expeditions, Davy made himself as conspicuous as possible in order not to be shot at by mistake. Usually, he wore a large scarlet hat. One of his friends amusingly pointed out that the hat put him in danger of being shot by an anti-cleric who mistook him for a cardinal.

**Bird, Harold ('Dickie')** (1933– ), county cricketer and umpire. A moderately talented batsman for Yorkshire, Bird had a quirky personality that brought him international celebrity as an umpire. Sometimes he became so involved with the game that he would forget his role as a non-participant, taking a sharp catch at square leg or bellowing 'No!' when a batsman was about to attempt what he thought was a suicidal run. In his first season as an umpire, Bird was standing in a match between Hampshire and Lancashire when the Lancashire wicketkeeper, Keith Goodwin, set off on a quick single. 'Go back, Goody!' shouted Bird. Goodwin was so startled that he stopped half way down the pitch and fell over, stranding himself in no-man's-land. Bird was obliged to give him 'run out'.

In all respects a worrier, Bird has a morbid fear of being late – an idiosyncrasy that resulted in his arriving hours early for any appointment. His first county match as umpire was Surrey against Yorkshire at the Oval in 1970. He arrived at the ground at 5.30 a.m., and since the gates were locked he decided to climb over them. He was perched at the top, with one leg on either side, when he was seen by a policeman, who immediately arrested him. When he was invited to lunch by the Queen, Bird arrived in time for breakfast and was asked to go away. John Major, who had better manners, had him sent in straight away when he turned up for lunch at Chequers at 9 a.m.

**Birdwood, Jane, the Dowager Lady** (1901–87), founder of the British

Movement's Women's Division (BMWD). Lady Birdwood's task within the British Movement was to recruit young women who might be attracted to National Socialist policies on race and immigration. She particularly admired Benito Mussolini, the Italian dictator, and, to a lesser extent, Adolf Hitler. As well as issuing a steady stream of political pamphlets, Lady Birdwood launched many unusual initiatives as a moral watchdog. The oddest of these was a private prosecution under the 1376 Blasphemy Act against Oscar Panniza's irreligious satire, *Council of Love*, produced in 1970 at the Criterion Theatre, London, in an English translation by the writer and comedian, John Bird. Lady Birdwood's objections centred on the fact that God, Christ and the Virgin Mary were impersonated on stage; further, that Pope Alexander VI and his cardinals were shown participating in orgies with naked women and oiled wrestlers during the celebration of divine Mass at the Vatican. By the time of the trial, the producers were already hiding in foreign bank accounts, so Lady Birdwood named the play's director, Eleanor Fazan, as defendant, in spite of the fact that she wasn't the director, merely the choreographer. If found guilty, Miss Fazan would, under the 1376 Blasphemy Act, have been burned as a witch, but John Mortimer, for the defence, was able to show that since she had not been in the theatre on the night of Lady Birdwood's visit she could not be held responsible for what might have happened on stage. The Bow Street magistrate, who was the grandson of George Robey, the 'Prime Minister of Mirth', agreed with Mr Mortimer. He dismissed the case and awarded Miss Fazan her costs. John Bird later consolidated his reputation with his appearances in the popular *Rory Bremner Show* on television and with his colleague John Fortune in *The Two Johns* and *The Long Johns*.

**bishop, performing an act of fellatio on a newly consecrated.** *See* CLEVELAND, BARBARA VILLIERS, DUCHESS OF.

**bishops, bicycling.** *See* CECIL, LORD WILLIAM.

**Blackbeard.** *See* TEACH, EDWARD.

**Blackburn, Raymond** (1915–91), politician, journalist, alcoholic and minor fraudster. Blackburn's career spiralled downwards after a promising start. The one-time Labour MP, whose maiden speech had been praised by Sir Winston Churchill, ended up as a public nuisance, scuffling in county courts and joining Lord Longford on anti-pornography campaigns. Had he been less independent (his speeches as a rule gave greater comfort to the opposition's front bench than to his own), and less drunk, he might have been more successful. In 1947, two years after entering Parliament as MP for King's Norton in Birmingham, he was charged with being incapable in Piccadilly, the first of many such incidents.

By 1952 Blackburn was on a steep downward path, albeit one he negotiated with a bankrupt's customary panache. Late after lunch at his own insolvency proceedings, he was told by the registrar that he had been seen at an expensive restaurant smoking a large cigar. In 1956 he was charged with fraudulently inviting the public to lease plots on a caravan site. In spite of a seven-hour speech in his own defence, he was sentenced to two years in prison. His fighting spirit remained intact. On appeal, he rebuked Lord Chief Justice Goddard for 'a very wrong remark', adding that his lordship was clearly prejudiced, and had already decided to send him back to prison. Goddard angrily denied this. 'You'd better be very careful,' he said, and then he sent him back to prison.

After two failed marriages, one to a woman from Brazil, Blackburn in 1959 embarked on a third, to Tessa Hulme. This was a success, and brought stability to his life. He gave up alcohol and founded an import–export agency, which thrived. In the late 1960s he cropped up again in public life as a moral vigilante, keen to bring those in authority – often the commissioner of the Metropolitan Police – to a clearer perception of their duties. His campaign against gaming clubs was not a success, but in 1975 he persuaded an Old Bailey jury that the film, *More About the Language of Love*, was grossly indecent. The following year, he prosecuted the film's predecessor, *The Language of Love*, but on this occasion failed. He had some harsh words for Judge Neil McKinnon, whose daughter, Gail, was a popular topless model.

Among the several books Blackburn published, *I Am An Alcoholic* (1981) explained how drink had ruined his political career.

**Blackburne, Archbishop Lancelot** (1658–1743), priest, philanderer and pirate. Blackburne's behaviour was seldom of a standard to be expected of an archbishop. In many respects it was seldom of a standard to be expected of a pirate. He was rumoured to have employed the highwayman, Dick Turpin, as his butler, and, which is more plausible, to have married George I to his German mistress. Successively a freebooter in the Caribbean, bishop of Exeter and archbishop of York, Blackburne was educated at Christ Church, Oxford, and ordained in 1681. The life of a parish priest held little appeal, so he accepted a posting to Antigua. Here, he was disappointed to discover that the living, though generous, was paid in sugar. He moved his ministry to St Paul's, Falmouth, a settlement on the island of Nevis. He then served on board a pirate ship, assiduously claiming his share of any booty captured from Spanish galleons. He was popular with the crew. When an elderly pirate arrived in England after years at sea, his first question was, 'How's old Blackburne?' He was surprised to be told that his former shipmate was now the archbishop of York.

By 1683 Blackburne was back in England and keeping an eye out for clergymen in poor health whose desirable livings he might inherit. 'The incumbent, Mr Bonhomme, almost 70 years of age, is at the point of death,' he wrote in his diary of the rector of Calstock before succeeding him. In 1694 he became sub-dean at Exeter Cathedral, but in 1702 scandal caught up with him. His bishop was informed that Blackburne was cuckolding one of Exeter's most eminent citizens, Mr Martyr. A local carpenter, Mr Stibbs, was said to have constructed a passage leading from Blackburne's house to Mr Martyr's next door, allowing Blackburne to call on Mrs Martyr secretly. Blackburne resigned, an inconclusive investigation was carried out, and, after two years, he was reinstated.

When George I acceded to the throne in 1714, Blackburne ingratiated himself at court by standing firm against the following year's Jacobite rebellion, and was rewarded when he was chosen to accompany the king on a visit to the royal estates in Germany. Returning to Exeter in 1716, he noted in his diary that the bishop was in poor health. By the time the bishop died three days later, Blackburne had drafted an obsequious letter to the archbishop of Canterbury suggesting himself as Exeter's successor. With the king as his mentor, he was appointed to the see.

Blackburne was seldom in Exeter, preferring to lead the life of a libertine in London. After several years of well-rewarded idleness, he was made archbishop of York – an elevation which brought about no change in his habits or behaviour. On one occasion, it was necessary to draft in the bishop of Gloucester to carry out the archbishop's duties, and during the last decade of his ministry he failed to ordain any new clergy, devoting himself, rather, to his amorous adventures. In 1743, a satirical poem suggested that the archbishop enjoyed the attentions of two women at the same time:

> One had her charm below, and one above
> So I together blended either bliss
> Lydia lay on, Dolly had my kiss.

When Blackburne died, the balladeers were kept busy. One of the more popular squibs marked his funeral with the lines:

> All the buxom damsels in the North
> Who knew his parts lament his going forth.

**blackmailers.** *See* ARIES, ROBERT; DENNIS, CEREDIG DAWYL; HOWELL, CHARLES AUGUSTUS; LEVERSON, RACHEL; NEWTON, ARTHUR; RAUCH, MICHAEL; SCOTT, LADY SELINA.

**blackmailer's charter.** *See* BOULTON, ERNEST; LABOUCHERE, HENRY.

**Black Widow, the.** *See* CALVEY, LINDA.

**Blake, Joseph** (1688–1724), pickpocket, cut-throat and robber. A sometime associate of Jack SHEPPARD, and protégé of the notorious, double dealing thief-taker general, Jonathan WILD, Blake – known as Blueskin because of his dark and brooding features – lacked the ambition and organizing skills of his treacherous mentor, but surpassed him, as Wild discovered to his cost, when savagery was required. 'His enormities,' according to a contemporary report, 'are the subject of public conversation, and the dread of travellers.'

Born in London, Blake was a resourceful pickpocket while still at school, and by the age of 15 he had already been in prison several times. He soon graduated to street robbery, joining a gang of young thieves under Wild's direction. When arrested with three others, he escaped conviction and demonstrated that he had learned one lesson at least from Wild, by informing on his colleagues. While on remand, he received a retainer from Wild of 3s 6d a week, but on his release he teamed up with Jack Sheppard, who had always refused to join Wild's gang. With Sheppard he robbed a Mr Kneebone of goods worth £36.

Sensing an opportunity to have his revenge on Sheppard, Wild, in his capacity of authorized thief-taker, went with a posse to Blake's house. When Blake denied them entry, the door was broken down by Quilt Arnold, one of Wild's associates. Blake drew a knife and swore that he would kill the first man who entered, to which Arnold replied:

> Then I am the first man, and Mr Wild is not far behind, and if you do not deliver your knife immediately, I will chop your arm off.

Blake, uncharacteristically, allowed himself to be taken, thinking, perhaps, that a better opportunity to avenge himself on Wild might soon present itself.

In this he was correct. Wild was listed to give evidence at Blake's trial, but in the event it had to go ahead without him. Hoping that they might reach a mutually beneficial accommodation, Wild visited Blake in prison and had his throat cut with a blunt knife. 'The wound, though dangerous, did not prove mortal,' noted the *Newgate Calendar*, 'and Jonathan was preserved for a different fate.'

Even without Wild's evidence, Blake was found guilty. While under sentence of death, he failed to show 'concern proportionate to his calamitous situation'. When asked whether his attack on Wild had been premeditated, he said that it had not. 'Had it been,' he said, 'I would have provided a knife sharp enough to cut his head off.'

**Blazing Car Murder, the.** *See* ROUSE, ALFRED ARTHUR.

**Blood, Colonel Thomas** (1630–?), soldier, courtier and thief. On the morning of 15 March 1671, Colonel Blood, dressed as a parson, and accompanied by three friends, visited the Tower of London, where he produced a mallet from under his cassock and knocked out the guard who was looking after the crown jewels. Blood and his companions then tried to ease their escape by filing the valuable, but conspicuous, sceptre in half. This proved impossible, so they made off with only the orb and ceremonial crown. They got no further than the main gate, however, where they were arrested.

Thereafter, rumour took over. The punishment for stealing the crown jewels would normally have been torture and death. Most unusually, Blood and his companions received a free pardon from King Charles II, and Blood himself was rewarded with a position at court. The supposition was that Charles, who was always short of money, had organized the robbery himself. Since this seemed to be the only explanation, it came as no surprise when Blood was further rewarded with the deeds to rich tracts of land in Ireland.

When Charles died in 1685, officials were shocked to discover that jewels were missing from the coronation crown and had been replaced by cheap imitations. Thereafter, they became accustomed to his many former mistresses appearing in public wearing the originals.

**Bloom, John** (1934– ), washing-machine salesman, nightclub owner and restaurateur. It was Bloom's misfortune that he operated at a time when *arrivistes* were viewed with suspicion in the City. Instead of bearing an ancestral crest, his cufflinks were fashioned in the manner of twin-tub washing-machines, and at his wedding in 1961 he and his wife cut a cake in the shape of a dishwasher. The publication of his memoirs in a Sunday newspaper under the headline 'Secrets of the Bedroom', illustrated by a picture of the couple reclining on a water bed, was the final straw. When his business affairs began to unravel, patrician bankers politely turned the other way.

A compulsive salesman from an early age (at school he had negotiated with other children over sweets and comics), Bloom hit the jackpot in 1958 when he had the idea of buying washing machines in Holland for £29 and selling them directly to British housewives for £50. The venture was so successful that he was soon unable to satisfy demand. Though dangerously under-capitalized, he decided to expand. He merged with Rolls Razor, financing his side of the arrangement by a series of share deals in which the same shares were sold backwards and forwards with bewildering speed. Bloom ended up with a £2 million fortune, and might have survived had a key associate not left at this point to set up a rival business, taking Bloom's Dutch suppliers with him. Though inexperienced as a manufacturer, Bloom set up his own production lines. The machines broke down, causing wash-day disasters up and down the land. Undeterred, Bloom expanded into discount stores and holidays in Bulgaria. Meanwhile, his washing machines sold at a loss.

In 1964 the house of cards collapsed. Rolls went into liquidation with a deficit of £4 million. The Board of Trade announced an inquiry and in 1908 Bloom was arrested and charged with intent to deceive shareholders. He was found guilty and fined £30,000.

Thereafter, Bloom embarked on many ventures, none of which met with success. He opened The Crazy Horse Saloon, a nightclub with hostesses, one of whom, Jane Lovebody, became his mistress. He was no match for the protection gangs then operating in the West End of London, and The Crazy Horse Saloon was shortly taken over at the point of a gun by the gangster, Jo Wilkins, a man feared even by Ron and Reggie KRAY. Bloom shut himself away in his apartment at 55 Park Lane, where he and Miss Lovebody entertained couples who looked, increasingly, as if they had been recruited through an advertisement.

In the mid-1970s Bloom departed for America. When FBI agents raided his home and took away a collection of bootlegged video cassettes he moved back to Europe. John Bloom was last heard of running a restaurant bar in Majorca, far away from what he described as 'the drugs and muggings in America'.

**Blueskin.** *See* BLAKE, JOSEPH.

**Bluffstein, Sophie.** *See* MILES, LOUISA.

**Blunt, Sir Anthony** (1907–83), art historian and spy. Some students of espionage have argued that Blunt was in the second division of traitors, compared with Kim Philby or Guy BURGESS. Others disagree. For Chapman Pincher (*Their Trade is Treachery*, 1981):

> Blunt was one of the most damaging spies ever to operate in Britain. His crimes against his country are such an indictment of wartime security that every effort has been made to cover them up.

When exposed to the public in 1979 by the prime minister, Mrs Thatcher, he was nevertheless entertained in the boardroom of *The Times* to a lunch of trout and white wine – treatment starkly in contrast to that meted out, for instance, to the less aesthetically refined Ronald BIGGS.

Blunt was the son of a London vicar who became British embassy chaplain in Paris during World War I. He won a scholarship from Marlborough College to Trinity College, Cambridge, where he stayed for eleven years, becoming a don. He was recruited to Marxism at Cambridge by his friend and fellow homosexual, Guy Burgess, whom he succeeded as chief 'talent spotter' of future Soviet sympathizers. In 1940, Blunt joined MI5 via the Army Intelligence Corps, thereafter, and throughout World War II, passing on to the Russians whatever classified information came his way. He and Burgess shared a flat in Bentinck Street, in London's West End, which became a favourite meeting place for intelligence officers, inverts and fellow travellers – many of whom became vulnerable to blackmail by participation in the homosexual orgies held there by Blunt. From Bentinck Street, Blunt and Burgess took their notes and stolen documents to the former's quarters at the Courtauld Institute, where Blunt was a lecturer in the history of art. Here, the material was photographed for delivery to the Soviet embassy in Kensington Palace Gardens.

After he left MI5 in 1945, Blunt remained in close touch with Burgess. On 7 May 1951 he met Burgess off the *Queen Mary* at Southampton and was told that he, Blunt, was under KGB orders to warn Donald Maclean of his imminent arrest. Blunt himself came under suspicion almost immediately after Burgess and Maclean defected. However, he bluffed his way through no less than eleven interrogations until, on promises of immunity from prosecution, he confessed in 1964. Remarkably, he retained his Palace appointment as surveyor of the Queen's pictures, and was allowed to keep his knighthood. Still more remarkably, further honours were bestowed upon him throughout the years of his many interrogations and, indeed, after he had confessed. In 1956 he was made a knight commander of the Royal Victorian Order – an honour that led to his prestigious appointment as Slade professor of fine art at both Oxford and Cambridge Universities. In 1972 he was appointed adviser of the Queen's pictures and drawings, a position he held until his retirement in 1978. He remained director of the Courtauld Institute, whose photographic facilities he had used as a spy in World War II, until 1974.

There was disquiet in some quarters over the kid-glove treatment accorded Blunt by the security authorities and others. After his 'trout and white wine lunch' in *The Times*'s boardroom, the *Daily Express* observed that 'Professor Blunt would not have been offered so much as a stale kipper in the *Express* offices.' In his book *Their Trade is Treachery* (1981), Chapman Pincher revealed that:

> Sir Michael Adeane, the queen's private secretary, asked what action the authorities would like Her Majesty to take regarding Blunt's royal appointment if Blunt agreed to confess. He was told that it would be advisable for the queen to take no action whatsoever, because otherwise traitors to whom Blunt might point would take evasive action. The queen was properly told of Blunt's treachery by Adeane as soon as he had received the brief of his confession. She merely asked what the official advice was, and, on being told, immediately agreed to accept it in the national interest.

Alan Bennett's play, *A Question of Attribution* (1990), starring Prunella Scales as Her Majesty, speculates elegantly on the relationship Blunt may have enjoyed with his royal employer.

**Blythe, Jenny.** *See* MCAVENNIE, FRANK.

**Boaks, Bill** (1921–86), naval officer and parliamentary candidate. Standing as a rule on behalf of the Land, Sea, Air, Road and Public Safety, Democratic Monarchist, White Resident and Women's Party, Boaks was the most unsuccessful parliamentary candidate of all time. At the 1974 general election he stood in three constituencies simultaneously – polling 240 votes in Wimbledon, 45 in Streatham and 35 in Westminster. He was candid in his disappointment, but optimistic about the future. 'I failed,' he said, 'but, had I been elected, I think I would have become the next prime minister.'

Boaks spent 30 years in the Navy, joining at 16 and rising to the rank of lieutenant commander. He was awarded the DSC after his destroyer sank under him in 1941. 'Always steer towards the gunfire' became his political maxim. As a civilian, road safety became his abiding interest. He bought a 1935 Vauxhall that he painted black and white, thereby turning it into a mobile zebra crossing. He covered it with placards advising pedestrians 'not to rush to cross the road' and fitted it with loudspeakers through which he shouted, 'I am now stopping for pedestrians in my path!'

In 1951 Boaks planned to stand for Parliament against the prime minister, Clement Attlee, in Walthamstow West, but nominated himself for the wrong constituency, Walthamstow East. He nevertheless polled 174 votes, having campaigned vigorously, and on behalf of the Association of Democratic Monarchists Independently Representing All Ladies Party, for equal rights for women. He painted his Vauxhall with the slogan 'She loves me, she loves me not' and lost his deposit.

In 1952 Boaks provided the Vauxhall with a mast and a mainsail and re-launched his campaign for greater safety on the roads. He was arrested and fined £5. His offence had been to 'use a vehicle wholly or mainly for advertising purposes within three miles of the statue of Charles I at Charing Cross' – thereby constituting a hazard to other motorists. He was concerned too with safety in the air. This may have been triggered by his experience of taking part in the *Daily Mail* London-to-Paris air race on roller skates. Convinced that Richmond was in danger of an air crash because of its location on the flight path to Heathrow, he argued for the re-siting of the airport at Bodmin Moor. Passengers could be transported in helicopters to pick-up pads sited every few hundred yards in parks and open spaces. Most usefully, the helicopters could take the place of undertakers, winching up a body from a bereaved family and dropping it into the sea.

In 1974, Boaks set out his political testament:

> I want to reform Parliament on democratic lines. Scrap the division lobbies and have secret ballots. MPs could vote as they thought best. White resident is exactly what I am. Sometimes, when I am being nominated, I find a black, give him a pound and tell him to find another 149 people to do the same so he can stand against me as a

Black Immigrant. No one has ever taken me up. More people have
been killed on the roads this century than in war. One Remembrance
Day, I laid a wreath at the Cenotaph in memory of road accident
victims. People thought it was in very poor taste.

At the Glasgow Hillhead by-election in 1982, Boaks had his most
notable result. He secured only five votes, which was remarkable since he
had needed the support of ten voters to get on the ballot paper in the first
place. Fortunately for his self-belief, securing votes was never his primary
concern. 'The thing which matters,' he said after his latest setback, 'is to
give people the chance to vote; it is a matter of complete indifference to me
how they vote as long as they have a choice.'

This public-spirited attitude caused Boaks some privation on his
modest naval pension. On one occasion, his bicycle was stolen in Aberystwyth, and he couldn't afford a new one. Being immobilized had no bearing
on the effectiveness of his canvassing methods, however. 'Once I am nominated,' he explained, 'I don't go back to the constituency. For one thing, I
can't afford to. For another, it would be wrong for someone who holds two
commissions (as an RAF pilot and as a naval officer) to go knocking on
doors in support of Her Majesty.' Supporting Her Majesty had not always
been an overriding concern. When Prince Philip, driving a Rover, and with
the Queen as passenger, collided with a Ford Prefect driven by a Mr
Cooper of the White Caravan Site, Holyport, Berkshire, Boaks issued a
summons against the Queen for aiding and abetting. That prosecution
fared no better than his many political campaigns.

**Bobbed-Haired Bandit, the.** *See* GOLDSTEIN, LILIAN.

**Bodkin, Sir Archibald** (1864–1941), lawyer and moral watchdog. As
director of public prosecutions, Sir Archibald was conscientious in maintaining the illiberal traditions associated with that office. In 1923, when
representing the United Kingdom at a League of Nations conference on
the international trade in obscene material, he surprised delegates from
more enlightened parts of the world by speaking out powerfully against
any attempt to define pornography. To right-thinking men, he argued, it
was self-evident what was, and what was not, pornographic. A definition
would only confuse the issue, making it more difficult for him to imprison
those who privately exchanged such material.

Included in what was, to Sir Archibald, self-evidently obscene, were the
works of Sigmund Freud, which he described as 'disgusting filth', and
whose publisher, the distinguished firm of Allen & Unwin, he threatened
with prosecution. It was only after Sir Stanley Unwin had personally
assured him that Freud's works would be stocked in brown wrappers
on top shelves beside the naturist magazines that Sir Archibald allowed

publication to proceed. Other serious people fell within his net. In 1921 Sir Archibald's suspicions were aroused when a Dr F.R. Leavis sought permission to import a copy of James Joyce's *Ulysses* from America. Sir Archibald instructed the police to check the credentials of this sinister sounding academic and in due course Leavis was visited in Cambridge by two uniformed constables. The latter were unconvinced by Leavis's arguments, and permission was denied.

*See also* MORAL WATCHDOGS.

**bodyline bowling.** A term in cricket to denote fast, short-pitched deliveries aimed at the batsmen rather than the stumps. Australian cricketers were particularly intimidated by this tactic, and, after alarmed representations from that quarter, the practice was discontinued.

*See also* JACKSON, JOHN; JARDINE, DOUGLAS.

**body snatchers.** *See* BURKE, WILLIAM; HARE, WILLIAM.

**body snatchers, Irish.** Body snatching flourished in Ireland towards the end of the 18th century. Bully Acre near the Royal Hospital in Dublin and the Poor Man's Burial Ground provided work for at least 50 resurrection men. Sometimes they dug up more bodies than they could sell, in which circumstance the public highway was strewn with abandoned corpses. William Rae, a Scots naval surgeon on half pay, was better organized than most and conducted an export trade in cadavers. The goods were sent over the Irish Sea marked 'pickled pork' and 'pianos'. Crazy Crow, who also made a living as a porter to musical bands, had mixed success, with a period of imprisonment for stealing corpses from St Andrew's graveyard. He was caricatured in a contemporary engraving, which showed him weighed down with musical instruments. It was accompanied by the verse:

> With looks ferocious and with beer replete
> See Crazy Crow beneath his minstrel weight;
> His voice is frightful as great Etna's roar
> Which spreads its horrors to the distant shore,
> Equally hideous with his well known face
> Murders each ear – till whiskey makes it cease.

**Bogard, Isaac.** *See* COONS; HARDING, ARTHUR.

**Bold Bucks.** A society of English gentlemen who in the late 18th century were dedicated to 'doing all possible hurt to their fellow creatures'. On recruitment, they had formally to deny the existence of God and swear to eat a dish known as Holy Ghost Pie every Sunday. To work themselves up to the necessary pitch of enthusiasm for their ferocious games they first drank so much that they were 'quite beyond the possibility of attending to any notions of reason or humanity' (Christopher Hibbert, *The Roots of Evil*). The ravages of the Bold Bucks were more specifically sexual than those of a rival gang, THE MOHOCKS, who liked to jeer at foreigners and pelt them with mud as they walked through the streets of London. A Portuguese visitor who got into a fight with the Mohocks had his ear nailed to the wall, and when he broke away he was stabbed to death. The Bold Bucks derived their entertainment from forcing a prostitute or an old lady to stand on her head in a barrel of tar. Alternatively, they made their victim jump up and down to avoid the swinging blades of their swords.

**bollocks, a silly.** A term used in the underworld to describe someone, usually, but not always, a man, who, while leading a life of bourgeois rectitude, draws vicarious excitement from moving at the edges of criminal circles. A 'silly bollocks' will not always be aware of the low regard in which he is held by his 'glamorous' new acquaintances.

*See also* FIELD, BRIAN; OSBOURNE, COLIN 'DUKE'; TESTER, WILLIAM GEORGE.

**bomb, blowing up one's father with a.** *See* BROWN, ERIC.

**bomb, suspecting one's guest's suitcase contains a.** *See* SINCLAIR, DONALD.

**bomb down a pensioner's chimney pot, threatening to drop a.** *See* FORSTER, JAMES.

**bomb inadvertently detonated by pet Rottweiler.** *See* ARISTIDES, SUSAN MARY.

**bomb with one's umbrella, poking a.** *See* CECIL, LORD HUGH.

**bombing hotel lavatories.** *See* MOON, KEITH.

**bombs, ticking time.** *See* DEMPSEY, ANDREW; KEELER, CHRISTINE; MANN, PAUL; THORPE, JEREMY.

**BOMP! Leave them in the piss.** *See* SPOT, JACK.

**Bongo Bongo Land.** A humorous name for Africa, coined by the Tory intellectual, Alan CLARK.

**Bonny, Anne** (*c*.1692–?), pirate. Notwithstanding the heartless ferocity with which she carried out her buccaneering duties, none of Bonny's shipmates ever suspected her of being a woman. In courage and cold determination she was equalled – as contemporary accounts make clear – only by another female pirate in male attire, Mary Read. 'In times of action, no persons among them were more resolute, or ready to board, or undertake anything that was hazardous, than she and Mary Read' (*The Lives and Adventures of the German Princess*, 1760). Nor might her imposture have been discovered had not Mary Read, taking her to be a man, attempted to seduce her.

Born in County Cork, the daughter of a lawyer and his maid, Anne demonstrated her fiery temper at an early age by killing a servant girl with a case knife. Later, when a young suitor pressed his attentions on her, she 'beat him so badly that he lay ill for a considerable time'. Disinherited for marrying a man of her choice rather than her father's, she sailed with her husband to the Bahamas, where she fell in with the notorious pirate, Captain John Rackham, known as 'Calico Jack'. Rackham courted her so successfully that she agreed, though already pregnant, to elope with him to sea, disguised as a man. At an appropriate moment Rackham landed her in Cuba, where she was looked after by friends, in due course giving birth. As soon as she was able, she abandoned the child and rejoined Rackham at sea and proved in future expeditions that:

> ... when there was business to be done, nobody was more forward or courageous than she; and particularly when they were taken, at which time she and Mary Read were all the persons that durst keep the deck, calling to those below to come up and fight like men, and when they did not stir, fired her arms down the hold amongst them, killing one and wounding others.

Apart from such displays of fighting spirit, Bonny was 'remarkable for her modesty, according to her notions of virtue'. Thus, no one on board, other than her lover, 'Calico Jack', would have suspected her true sex had not Mary Read, taking her to be a handsome young man, conceived a passion for her. Her attentions may have surprised Bonny, who, equally, had taken Mary to be a boy. Being in possession now of Mary's secret, and:

> ... knowing what she would be at, Bonny, being very sensible of her own capacity that way, was forced to come to a right understanding with her, and so, to the great disappointment of Mary Read, she let her know that she was a woman also.

This misunderstanding caused no serious breach in their friendship, but a further complication then arose. 'Calico Jack' was so disturbed by their intimacy that he became furiously jealous, informing Bonny that he would cut her supposed lover's throat. At this point, Bonny felt obliged to divulge Mary's secret, at least to 'Calico Jack'.

Harmony was restored on board, but in October 1720 the governor of Jamaica sent an armed sloop to capture Rackham and his crew. Rackham's ship, the *Revenge*, was caught by surprise and, to Bonny's dismay, the pirates fought like cowards and were taken far too easily. Rackham was hanged and Mary Read died of fever while in prison, but Bonny's fate remains a mystery. She escaped from prison and disappeared, but not before demonstrating her unrelenting cruelty. On the day Rackham was executed, she was brought to his cell as a special favour. Even at this extremity, she could offer him no comfort other than to say that she was sorry to see him there, but that 'if he had fought like a man he might not have died like a dog'.

**Bonzo Dog Doo-Dah Band, the.** *See* GRAY, DOUGLAS AND TONY; STANSHALL, VIVIAN.

**boogie-woogie clubs.** *See* HEMP SAID TO INDUCE SEXUAL DESIRE IN WHITE GIRLS; MARKS, HOWARD.

**booing one's own play.** *See* HOOLIGANS, THEATRICAL (for Charles Lamb).

**Bookie Peer, the.** *See* ST GERMANS, NICHOLAS RICHARD MICHAEL ELIOT, 9TH EARL OF.

**Boomerangs.** *See* CROWLEY, ALEISTER; JORDAN, JOHN.

**Booth, Anthony.** *See* FOWLER, MAJOR NIGEL.

**Boothby, Robert** (1900–86), politician and television personality. Boothby was an inflated character of the sort referred to from time to time under the wistful heading, 'Great Prime Ministers we never had', and whose death is generally accompanied by a claim, baffling to some, that 'the gaiety of the nation is hereby much diminished'. (*See* Alan CLARK and Nicholas FAIRBAIRN.) His biographers have been generous. He was impulsive, they admit, reckless even, but a man of brilliant gifts, fearless and charming. The suggestion is that, but for a trivial mishap early in his career (he had not declared an interest when, as a junior minister, he helped a foreign businessman to unfreeze his UK assets), he would have attained high office. His friend, Ronnie KRAY, and his cousin, Ludovic Kennedy, were not so lenient in their judgements. In Kennedy's opinion, Boothby was 'a shit of the highest order'; in Kray's, 'a silly old queen'.

A compulsive seducer of other men's wives, by whom he fathered at least three children, Boothby was a regular guest, with his friend Tom DRIBERG, at Ronnie Kray's sadomasochistic homosexual orgies. While these pursuits might be considered by some to be less harmful than a dogged ambition for power, Boothby's willingness to instigate libel proceedings against newspapers whose allegations he knew to be true (a habit that would have involved him in lying to his lawyer, had that not been the equally reckless Arnold Goodman, and which would have required him, had the need arisen, to repeat the lie on oath), raises questions about whose transgressions are overlooked by commentators, and by the establishment, and whose are not. Less clubbable wrongdoers have not been so easily forgiven. Harold Macmillan, whose wife's affections Boothby stole, might not have been alone in concluding that loveable rogues are as much of a nuisance as professional thieves.

**boots, eating one's own.** *See* MORGAN, SIR HENRY.

**boots arranged calendrically.** *See* BRIDGEWATER, FRANCIS HENRY EGERTON, 8TH EARL OF.

**Bootscraper, the Case of the Iron.** *See* INSTRUMENTS, BLUNT; MAYES, JOY.

**Bose, Douglas** (1915–36), writer and dabbler in black magic. Bose was living above a restaurant in Charlotte Street, London, when he took up with Sylvia Gough, a diamond heiress and ex-dancer who had appeared in New York in *The Ziegfeld Follies*. She had also modelled, sitting for Augustus JOHN, who became her lover and was cited in her second divorce. Bose, who was half her age, treated her badly, was even rumoured to have mesmerized her with various forms of hypnotic hocus-pocus. One day in 1936 she appeared in the Fitzroy Tavern with a black eye. A 30-year-old jobbing book reviewer named Douglas Burton offered his apartment as a sanctuary. When, later that evening, he saw Bose at a party, he battered him to death with a sculptor's hammer. Burton was duly declared insane, the suggestion being that he was in love, not with Gough, but with an artist's model known as Betty 'Tiger Woman' May and had gone mad when she rejected him. Miss May was a disciple of Aleister CROWLEY and earned her sobriquet following a knife fight in Paris with a rival. In later life, she was known for taking off her skirt in Wally's, a basement club in Fitzroy Street, and twirling it in front of her while she sang 'The Raggle-Taggle Gypsies'.

**bottom, Mick Jagger's.** *See* HERBERT, DAVID.

**Bottomley, Horatio** (1860–1932), journalist, politician, company promoter and fraud. The most remarkable swindler of his, or any other, time, Bottomley exploited human greed on a scale that is unlikely to be equalled. That he was able to transfer £60 million of the public's money into his own accounts while facing as many as 50 bankruptcy petitions and numerous trials for fraud – at all of which the evidence pointed overwhelmingly to his guilt – attests not so much to his billowing oratorical gifts as his victims' masochistic desire to subside before a force of nature.

Born in the East End of London, the orphaned Bottomley acquired his first lesson in the art of fraud from the dishonest managing clerk of a solicitor's firm that he joined as an errand boy at the age of 14. From the clerk's practice of levying a fictitious tax on many City businesses, Bottomley arrived at the conclusion that, if hard-headed financiers could be so easily defrauded, there must be no end to human gullibility. He first put this theory into practice with the *Hackney Gazette*, which published reports of local debating societies. Its success encouraged his own political ambitions and in 1887 he stood as the Liberal candidate in a Hornsey by-election. Being temporarily short of funds, he took the unusual step of persuading his opponent, H.C. Stephens (of Stephens ink), to lend him the money to pay for his campaign. Stephens won, and the loan was never repaid.

Bottomley's political ambitions received a further setback when he was forced into his first bankruptcy. Undeterred, and following a pattern that he used thereafter to enrich himself while impoverishing his investors, he set up the Anglo-Austrian Union, ostensibly to acquire companies in Austria with paid-up capital of £93,000. The company never acquired any assets other than the shareholders' funds, but Bottomley declared a dividend of 8% on the preference shares and 15% on the ordinary shares. The accountants' report on the first year's trading make instructive reading:

> Receipts – £93,000 in shares and debentures. Expenditure – cash to Mr Bottomley, £88,500, balance at bank, £26 ...

The report concluded:

> The company has acquired no business in Vienna or elsewhere, has no property whatsoever, and its whole capital appears to be lost.
> There are insufficient funds to pay the expense of printing this report.

The public were not discouraged from investing in Bottomley's next venture, which was to set up the Hansard Union with an initial capital of £1 million. The Debenture Corporation underwrote £250,000 and, when interest payments failed to appear, it put in a receiver. This led to the first of Bottomley's many appearances in a criminal court. Since £600,000 was unaccounted for out of the starting capital of £1 million, he was charged with fraud. Heard before Mr Justice Hawkins, the case seemed straightforward enough. However, Hawkins took a liking to Bottomley that was as strong as his aversion to Sir John Rigby, who led for the prosecution, and throughout the trial he assisted Bottomley, who was defending himself, in any way he could. During Sir John's closing speech, and tried beyond endurance by the latter's interminable loquacity, the judge passed a note to the jury that read, 'Patience Competition. 1st Prize, Henry Hawkins. Honourable mention, Job.' Bottomley was acquitted.

Though still bankrupt, Bottomley now bought a substantial property in Pall Mall, in which he entertained his many mistresses. This was paid for by the flotation of an Australian gold-mining company, for which he issued 10 million five-shilling shares with forged certificates. Charged with fraud, he was once again acquitted – though not before he had corrected the judge's observation that he kept a string of race horses. 'I don't keep them,' said Bottomley. 'They keep me.' It is unclear what he meant by this since there is no record of any of them having won.

In 1906 Bottomley launched *John Bull*, a jingoistic newspaper that reflected its proprietor's tub-thumping disposition and which he used to promote his various financial and political endeavours. In the same year, he entered Parliament for the first time as Liberal MP for South Hackney, recontesting the seat successfully in 1910. In 1912, he went bankrupt again, this time with liabilities of £233,000, and was obliged to give up his seat in Parliament. Happily, he was able to recover his position by entering the lottery business, routing the public's money through Switzerland to remain within the law. With the outbreak of World War I, he further enriched himself by selling Victory Bonds at £1 each against Whitehall's price of £5. The enticement to buy from Bottomley was the opportunity to win a prize of £20,000 in a sweepstake, but instead of buying Victory Bonds with his customers' money, he used £42,000 to set up two other newspapers, which he ran at a loss. The balance, which was considerable, found its way into his personal bank accounts.

When pamphlets were circulated denouncing the Victory Bonds obtainable through *John Bull* as fraudulent, Bottomley, whose instinct was always to go on the offensive, sued for libel. This was a mistake. The director of public prosecutions began to take an interest, shortly bringing an action for fraudulent conversion. At his trial, Bottomley did manage to persuade the court to adjourn each day at 11.30 a.m. so that he could refresh himself with a bottle of champagne, but he was found guilty and sentenced to seven years in prison.

After his release Bottomley was supported, during his final attempt at a comeback, by his devoted mistress, the actress Peggy Primrose. Still something of an attraction, he toured variety shows throughout the land, but in 1932 he suffered a heart attack on stage at the Windmill Theatre in London – later famous for its fan dancers, *tableaux plastiques* and apprentice comedians – and died a few months later. He is remembered for his reply to a prison visitor who, finding him at work on mailbags, asked, 'Sewing, Bottomley?' 'No, reaping,' he replied.

**Boulton, Ernest** (1841–?), transvestite. Caught up in one of the three scandals of the late 19th century that brought about Henry LABOUCHERE's notorious Criminal Law Amendment Act 1885, Boulton and his companion Frederick Park live on as bit-part players in legal textbooks. In 1861 the death penalty for the crime of buggery had been replaced by life imprisonment, and, to the unease of those of a regulating disposition, sexual misconduct between men short of penetration wasn't an offence at all. If there was any doubt in the minds of respectable people that a new offence had to be created it was dispelled by the case of Boulton and Park.

On this occasion, and unlike those that followed (*see* NEWTON, ARTHUR and QUEENSBERRY, JOHN SHOLTO, 8TH MARQUESS OF), there was no suggestion that Boulton and Park were working-class prostitutes. Boulton, who had a fine soprano voice and was known as Stella, was the son of a stockbroker. From an early age he had been encouraged by his mother to wait at table dressed as a French maid. Park, whose father was a master at the Court of Common Pleas, was articled to a solicitor. Both lived at the home of Lord Arthur Clinton, MP for Newark and third son of the 5th duke of Newcastle. Boulton, who was treated by Lord Clinton as his wife, had visiting cards printed in the name of 'Lady Arthur Clinton'. To avoid feelings of jealousy, Clinton was also on intimate terms with Park, who signed himself 'Fanny'.

In April 1870 Boulton and Park were arrested as they left the Strand Theatre (later, in the 1960s, to be the home of the long-running entertainment, *No Sex Please, We're British*). Boulton was wearing a scarlet dress with white *moiré* antique petticoats, stays and a wig. Park was in dark green satin trimmed with black lace. Without waiting for a court order, the police doctor, James Peel, carried out an examination to discover whether the crime of buggery had been committed, thereafter ruling that it had. Boulton and Park were charged with frequenting the Strand Theatre with intent to commit a felony. The evidence was that Boulton and Park, in the company of Lord Clinton, had met a Mr Cox in a City public house, where, after a champagne lunch, Cox had kissed Boulton, believing him to be a woman. Told later of his mistake, Cox had followed Boulton to Evans's Coffee House in Covent Garden, where he had cried, 'You infernal scoundrel! You ought to be kicked out of the place!' (Evans's Coffee House was the model for the cave of Harmony in Thackeray's *The Newcomes*, 1853).

The prosecution failed for a number reasons. Lord Clinton, who had been named in the indictment, and another witness, John Stafford Fiske, a United States Consular representative (who disapproved of crossdressing), had already died after an attack of scarlet fever, and Mr Cox was unable to attend. The defendants were homosexual, but there was no evidence that they had broken the law as it then stood.

The judge, Lord Chief Justice Cockburn, was sympathetic towards the defendants from the outset, rebuking both the police and Dr Paul. 'Had you examined two strong young men rather than effeminate ones,' he said, 'you might have met with summary punishment for your unwarrantable conduct.' There were cries of 'Bravo!', the jury acquitted and Boulton fainted.

Not everyone was pleased by the outcome, or by its unfortunate sequel.

By Labouchere's Amendment, known thereafter as a Blackmailer's Charter, an act of gross indecency between males became a misdemeanour, punishable by a prison sentence not exceeding two years.

**Bourke, Patrick** (*c.*1706–45), thief. The law in the 18th century was unequivocal in the matter of sheep stealing:

> If any person or persons shall feloniously drive away with, or shall wilfully kill, one or more sheep, with intent to steal any part of the carcasses, the person or persons so offending shall be sentenced to death, without benefit of clergy.

In fact, not everyone suffered this extreme punishment. Sometimes judges, in their humanity, concluded that the offence had been committed 'from a dread of hunger'. In such a circumstance, they were content to impose a sentence of life imprisonment.

Bourke and his associate Ellis were not so fortunate in this regard. In 1744 they were indicted at the Old Bailey for killing 15 ewe sheep, the property of Mr John Messenger of Kensington, with intent to steal the fat near the kidneys. Mr Messenger deposed that the prisoners had confessed their crime to Sir Thomas Devil, and that Bourke had acknowledged that they had sold the fat to a tallow-chandler for 42 shillings and twopence halfpenny.

Both were convicted, but the circumstances surrounding their capture suggest an early example of police malpractice. At their trial, Joseph Agnew, a constable, swore that Ellis had come to him with two black eyes, claiming that Bourke had beaten him up. Agnew testified that he had then gone to Bourke's house, where he had found him asleep. On being woken up, Bourke had admitted the assault on Ellis, which had been the consequence of their having fallen out over the division of the spoils. They had recently sold the fat of the stolen sheep, Bourke had admitted, and Ellis had refused to hand over Bourke's share – hence the black eyes. Constable Agnew further testified that he had found a knife among Bourke's possessions.

This was all denied by Bourke and Ellis. It was Constable Agnew who had given him the black eye, claimed Ellis, thereafter forcing him to concoct the story against Bourke. They had then gone to Bourke's house, where Agnew had forced a confession out of Bourke by getting him drunk. The knife, he said, had been planted by Agnew. The jury chose to believe the police evidence, and Bourke and Ellis were executed in February 1745.

**Bournemouth.** South-coast resort celebrated for the quality of its *thés dansants*. *See* BELCHER, HARRY; RATTENBURY, ALMA.

**bowler hats, armed robbers in.** *See* GOODY, GORDON.

**Bow Street Runners.** Established in 1748 by the novelist Henry Fielding
– then senior stipendiary magistrate at Bow Street – the Runners were also
referred to as thief-takers, a label they disliked since it seemed to bracket
their activities with those of their predecessor in law enforcement, the
notorious criminal thief-taker, Jonathan WILD. At first theirs was a spare-
time occupation, but under Henry Fielding's brother, Blind John Fielding,
who succeeded him as Bow Street magistrate, the Runners were awarded a
weekly salary of 11s 6d, later increased to 25s. This was not a living wage,
so they continued to undertake private work, acting as security men at the
Bank of England and hiring themselves out as bouncers to London
theatres. Acting in the latter capacity, a runner, Donaldson, provided an
early example of police brutality. A man sitting in the pit at the Drury Lane
Theatre, 'applauding and booing', was seized by Donaldson and thrown
into the street with such force that his neck was broken (*see also* HOOLI-
GANS, THEATRICAL).

Evidence of corruption on a large scale suggests that it was disingenu-
ous of the Runners to resent comparisons with Jonathan Wild. On his
modest weekly salary of 25s, Townshend, the best remembered of the
Runners, managed to leave an estate of £20,000. Much of this must have
been acquired by acting as an intermediary between thieves and insurance
companies. There were complaints, too, that the proceeds of robberies
were habitually handed over to Townshend and his colleagues in return for
a promise not to prosecute.

In 1828 Sir Richard Birnie, the chief magistrate at Bow Street, told a
House of Commons Committee that such practices were unheard of –
thus establishing the official response to charges of police malpractice and
one that stayed in place until 'The Fall of Scotland Yard' in the 1970s. One
typical case that Sir Richard preferred to overlook was a Paisley bank
robbery, which was investigated by a colleague of Townshend's, John
Sayer. Sayer had recently arrested two notorious thieves, James Mackoull
and Huffey White. Mackoull had offered to hand back all the money in
return for an undertaking not to prosecute. This had been accepted by
Sayer, but the bank had recovered only a fraction of the stolen money. The
assumption – never proved – was that Sayer had kept most of it for himself.
He and Mackoull worked the same trick on two further occasions. On the
first they were successful. On the second Mackoull was unable to escape
prosecution; he was found guilty and sentenced to death. His wife
obtained a reprieve, but he went mad and died in prison. Sayer eventually
left an estate as valuable as Townshend's.

The days of the Runners were numbered once they had demonstrated
their inability to control the streets of London. In 1768 John WILKES, a
former MP for Aylesbury, returned to London following his exile in Paris
for publishing a libel on King George III. The Runners were unable to dis-
perse the crowds that gathered to celebrate Wilkes's re-election to

Parliament, and which later freed him from the King's Bench prison. More curious than the Wilkes disturbances was the destruction of the Newgate prison in the anti-Catholic Gordon Riots of June 1780. The Runners in general were absent, and for a week London was in the hands of a looting and rioting mob, led by the unstable and fanatical Lord George GORDON. In 1785 the government introduced the London and Westminster Police Bill, which divided the capital into nine administrative divisions, each presided over by a stipendiary magistrate and manned by 25 properly equipped, full-time constables.

**Boyce, Samuel** (1708–49), poet and ingrate. Boyce forfeited every opportunity that came his way of securing patronage. The son of a dissenting minister, he went to school in Dublin and then to Glasgow University, where he married unwisely before he was 20 and proclaimed himself a poet. For a while he kept himself afloat by living off his father. When his father died, Boyce returned to Scotland and embarked on a lifetime of financial destitution. Once, after writing an elegy mourning the death of Viscountess Stormont, he was offered a sinecure in the Customs Office by her grateful husband. It happened to be raining on the day of his appointment and Boyce preferred to lose the job rather than get wet. When mounting debts forced him to leave Scotland, he went to London, where he had a letter of introduction to Alexander Pope. When he called at Pope's lodgings the better-known poet happened to be out, and Boyce never called again.

Boyce's wife, who according to Theophilus Cibber (son of the more famous Colley) was 'little better than a strumpet', was kept busy by her husband, begging on his behalf from a circle of acquaintances, who had a duty to support him, or so Boyce thought. On more than one occasion, Samuel Johnson collected sixpences on his behalf. The money was intended to redeem Boyce's clothes from the pawn shop, but they were always back in pawn within a day. 'Can it be believed,' wrote Cibber, 'that when he received half a guinea in consequence of a supplicating letter, he would go to a tavern, order a supper to be prepared, drink of the richest wines and spend all the money that had just been given him in charity, while his wife was starving at home.'

When the begging letters failed, Boyce would resort to subterfuge, seeking subscriptions for poems that he hadn't written. Alternatively, and with the intention of securing a widow's pension, he sent his wife out to circulate the news that he was dead. When the clothes he had pawned could not be redeemed, he lay in bed under a single blanket. If there was a poem to be written, he would sit up in bed with the paper on his knee and with the blanket wrapped around him, having cut a hole large enough to accommodate his writing arm. He invented a paper collar and shirt – a makeshift garment, consisting of strips of paper at his neck and wrists. Wearing a coat over this arrangement, but without trousers (which he didn't possess), he sometimes visited friends, to the distress, it was reported, of any ladies who were present.

In 1745 his wife died. Boyce had no money for mourning clothes, so he bought a piece of black ribbon for his dog to wear. Four years later, he died himself at the age of 41. No one was inclined to pay for his funeral. A Mr Stewart of Edinburgh, who canvassed possible contributors, reported that:

> ... he has quite tired out his friends, and the general answer that I received was that such a contribution was of no service to him for it was a matter of no importance how or where he was buried.

Writing of Boyce's indolence and ingratitude, R. Ryan in *Worthies of Ireland* (1821) concludes that:

> ... men of genius have no right to expect more favourable consequence from impudence and vice than what are common to the mass of mankind.

**Boyle, Jimmy** (1944– ), gangster and sculptor. Formerly a leading figure in the Glasgow underworld, with an unsurpassed record for violence, Boyle subsequently won a reputation as a talented artist and authoritative spokesman for penal reform. The son of a Gorbals 'hard man', Boyle worked in his youth for Frank 'Tarzan' Wilson's loan-sharking operation. The interest charged was 25% per week and if this wasn't forthcoming Boyle called on the debtor with a bayonet wrapped in a copy of the *Glasgow Herald*. He was in demand, too, as a bar-room bouncer. In 1964 he was charged with murder, but this was later dropped and he didn't stand trial. Ten days later he attacked two men and took the eye out of one with a broken bottle. 'I felt good after that,' Boyle said in a television film of his life, *The Hard Man*. 'I felt I had proved myself.' Following another fight in a house in Govan, during which a man was scalped, he faced a new murder charge, but this too was dropped.

In 1966, after the death of Glasgow gang leader, 'Babs' Rooney, Boyle headed for London, where he was protected by Ronnie and Reggie KRAY. Rooney had died in his Kinning Park home after a visit from Boyle and another man. There had been an argument that had ended with Boyle slashing Rooney's face. Rooney was later found dead, and Boyle was tracked down to the British Lion, an East End pub where the Krays were hiding him. He was returned to Scotland, and sentenced to life imprisonment.

In prison, Boyle underwent a remarkable transformation. Transferred to the Special Unit in Barlinnie he came under the administration of one of the few enlightened penal projects in the country. Boyle responded by becoming a successful writer and artist.

Some experts believe that hard men like Boyle are peculiar to Glasgow and belong in any case to a bygone era. Joe Beltrami, a respected Scottish lawyer, has argued that 'hard men might have been regarded in the past as "bonny fechters", and admired. Nowadays, they would be dismissed as hoodlums with a high pain threshold.'

**Bradshaw, Brian 'the Mad Gypsy'** (1937– ), unlicensed fist-fighter who in March 1979 lost his bare-knuckle world championship to Lenny 'The Governor' MCLEAN. Bradshaw was unconscious for 45 minutes after head-butting McLean before the bell went for the first round.

**brandy, bringing one's mother round with a quart of.** *See* SHEP-PARD, JACK.

**Braun, Heide** (*c*.1939– ), housewife. CRIMINAL CONVERSATION, by which a man could claim damages from his wife's lover, remained a tort in British law until abolished by Matrimonial Causes Act 1857, but it was a civil offence in Ireland until the 1970s. In June 1972, Werner Braun brought an action in Dublin claiming damages from a Mr Roche, who admitted an affair with Braun's wife, Heide, but denied that he had caused Braun any suffering. Heide's own counsel argued that since she had indeed committed adultery her stock was of diminished value. Mr Justice Butler instructed an all-male jury that their task was not to punish the defendant, Mr Roche, but to put a price on Mrs Braun. 'In this country,' he said, 'a wife is regarded as a chattel, just as a thoroughbred mare or cow.' In the event, and against the opinion of her own counsel, the jury valued Mrs Braun highly, tagging her at £12,000.

**Brian, John Herman** (1683–1707), manservant, incendiary and alleged thief. The case of the crown versus Brian in the matter of Mr Persuade's fowling piece excited some controversy at the time due to the unsatisfactory nature of the evidence offered at the trial. As a young man, Brian had moved to Geneva, where he lived for some years in the service of a gentleman, thereafter touring Italy with a person of fortune. On his return to England he served several reputable families without giving his employers grounds for complaint, and finally entered the employ of a Mr Persuade, who discharged him, for no reason that can be discovered, after a few months. Two days after his dismissal, Brian broke into Mr Persuade's house – or so it was alleged – and, having plundered it, burned it to the ground. This was a capital offence, and he was brought to trial in October 1707.

It was said in evidence that on the night in question Mrs Persuade secured the house and, having locked up her gold watch, etwee case and her savings of 17 guineas, retired to bed with Mr Persuade at about 10 p.m. At 3 o'clock in the morning she smelt a fire, which spread so rapidly that she and Mr Persuade were fortunate not to be burned alive in their bed.

It also came out in evidence that an elderly woman of the lower class, who happened to be passing, had been involved in a disagreeable confrontation with a man who she saw clambering over Mr Persuade's garden wall. The intruder had acted with great presence of mind. 'Damn you!' he'd cried. 'Calling on people at this time of night! Are you drunk?' He had then made off in a hurry.

Brian told the investigating constable that on the night of the fire he was at home in lodgings that he had recently taken in Soho, London. He even produced a witness to support this story, but the latter was of a shifty disposition and was not believed. It further went against Brian that a trunk, which he had used to convey his belongings to his new address, was found on examination to contain Mr Persuade's fowling piece. Brian claimed that he had bought this from a stranger, but the jury at his trial chose not to believe him, and he was found guilty.

While waiting to be executed, Brian, instead of preparing himself for his future circumstances, clung obstinately to his version of events. Even on the scaffold he denied the charge. Asked why he refused to repent, he replied:

Life is sweet and any man would save it if he could.

This was not well received, and the hangman hastened to dispatch him.

Six weeks later the old woman who claimed to have seen Brian climbing over Mr Persuade's garden wall attempted to sell Mrs Persuade's etwee case to Messrs Stevenson and Acton, jewellers of Covent Garden. No prosecution was brought, the authorities feeling, no doubt, that to reveal such a miscarriage of justice might bring the judiciary into disrepute.

*See also* JUSTICE, MISCARRIAGES OF.

**bribes.** *See* TWO POUNDS OF WALLS PORK SAUSAGES AND A WEEK IN BOURNEMOUTH.

**bricks planted on demonstrators.** *See* CHALLENOR, DETECTIVE SERGEANT HAROLD.

**Brides in the Bath Murders, the.** *See* SMITH, GEORGE JOSEPH.

**Bridgewater, Francis Henry Egerton, 8th earl of** (1756–1829), recluse. For 30 years Bridgewater lived in Paris, a city for which he had an abiding hatred. Nor did he have much time for his fellow humans, believing, rather, that dogs were better behaved. His dogs ate with him every day. A large table would be laid for twelve, and the dogs would be led in, each with a white napkin round its neck. Servants would circulate with silver dishes, one servant to each dog. Bridgewater's other interest was boots. His dogs wore handmade boots, and he himself put on a new pair every day. At night he ranged them round his bedroom and, since he could remember on which day he had worn which boots, he used them as a calendar.

Although he employed the great chef Viard, Bridgewater would allow him to cook nothing but English boiled beef and potatoes, a menu that disappointed his few acquaintances when they came to dinner. He missed English hunting and sometimes liked to dress in pink and chase an imported fox in his Paris garden. He also kept 300 partridges, which he would sometimes shoot (*see also* NICKERSON, SIR JOSEPH). Bridgewater once set off to the country for the summer, the move involving 16 carriages laden with luggage and 30 servants on horseback. The procession returned after a few hours, the change of plans occasioned by the earl's inability en route to find English boiled beef on the menu in country restaurants.

When Bridgewater died, each of his servants was left a mourning suit, a cocked hat and three pairs of worsted stockings. The will made no mention of his dogs.

**Brighton.** Now 'the heaving Sodom of the south coast' (Robert Hanks, *The Independent*, 4 April 2001), formerly the preferred venue for the establishment of adultery by agreement.
*See also* COLLUSION, DIVORCE BY; HALL, NEWMAN.

**Brighton Trunk Murders.** *See* MANCINI, TONY.

**Brinks-Mat Robbery, the.** *See* NOYE, KENNETH; ROBINSON, BRIAN.

**Bristol, Frederick William John Augustus Hervey, 7th marquess of** (1954–99), collector, car enthusiast, drug addict and old Harrovian. The 7th marquess inherited a family characteristic of stylish decadence. 'When God created the human race,' said Voltaire, 'he made men, women – and Herveys.'

Among the 7th marquess's ancestors was John, Lord Hervey of Ickworth (1696–1743), who wore rouge and conducted himself in such an effeminate manner that Alexander Pope called him Lord Fanny. Despite having a wife and many mistresses, Hervey took a male lover, Stephen Fox, whose attentions were so ardent that Hervey thought of exposing his scars in public to 'excite compassion'. Hervey eventually evicted his wife and children from their London home and handed it over to Fox. When Fox married a girl of 13, Hervey acted as the witness. Later, he consoled himself with an Italian youth, known as the Swan because of his ability to glide smoothly round the courts of Europe.

Nobody was surprised when another of the 7th marquess's forebears, Frederick Hervey, the 4th earl of Bristol, better known as the earl-bishop of Derry (1730–1803), was imprisoned in a castle in Milan. In an earlier incident in Siena, the bishop had been forced to run for his life after he had seized a tureen of pasta and dropped it out of the window on to a Corpus Christi procession. The British ambassador in Naples, reporting the trouble in Milan, said that 'his lordship's freedom in conversation, particularly after dinner, is such as to make him liable to accidents of this nature.' After his release from prison, a young Irish girl spotted the bishop out on the town. 'He was sitting in his carriage,' she wrote, 'between two Italian women, dressed in a white bed-gown and night-cap like a witch and giving himself the airs of an Adonis.' Hervey died in Italy, which was not a comfortable place for a Protestant bishop to meet his end. The crew of the ship nominated to return the 4th earl to England refused to allow the corpse on board. He had to be smuggled back to England in a packing case labelled as an antique statue.

The 4th earl's daughter, Lady Elizabeth Foster (1759–1824), combined charm and a formidable sex drive, the latter embracing bisexual tastes. As a young widow, Lady Elizabeth's relationship with the 6th duke of Devonshire and his gambling-mad wife, Georgiana, evolved into a notorious *ménage-à-trois*. Elizabeth's perseverance was rewarded, and after bearing two illegitimate children by the duke, she became his second wife in 1809.

The 6th marquess (1915–85) was known as 'Victor Hervey, Mayfair Playboy No 1' in society columns written by himself. On one occasion he drove his car into a taxi rank to discover whether they buckled like a concertina. He was able to report that they did. He later tried to relieve his financial situation by becoming a gun runner in the Spanish Civil War, but failed through incompetence. Soon after this disappointment he received a three-year prison sentence on two counts of robbery. Asked why he needed the money, he explained that he was waiting for an unpaid commission of £83,000 on an arms sale to China. Living as a tax exile in Monaco in the 1970s, the 6th marquess explained that fear of crime in dangerous areas such as Belgravia had driven him abroad. He was the father of the 'posh tart' (*see* PALMER TOMKINSON, TARA), Lady Victoria Hervey (1979– ), who ran a Mayfair boutique until it went bankrupt. Lady Victoria has made her mark on the public imagination by appearing in nightclubs in her foundation garments.

Family decadence reached its apotheosis with the drug-addicted John Bristol, the 7th marquess. Before the death of his father, with whom he was on poor terms, Bristol lived as a tax exile in France on the proceeds of a £4-million family trust. On one occasion, when driving through Paris, he was shot at by a Frenchman. Happily, he was in his six-door, armour-plated Mercedes that had been built for Pope John Paul II. Had he been driving either of his Rolls Royces, with the numberplates 'TWINK 1' and 'TWINK 2', the offence to the Frenchman might have been greater and the damage to Bristol worse.

Though slightly built, Bristol never lacked courage, and he took the incident in good part. When his father died in 1985, he moved into one wing of the ancestral home in Ickworth, Suffolk, thereafter keeping existential angst at bay with copious amounts of heroin. A favourite source of amusement was to organize midnight rabbit shoots for his inebriated young guests, firing from competitive limousines; another was to shoot holes in a rubber dinghy in which a guest was fishing on the lake. A more unpleasant idiosyncrasy was to feed his wolfhound on a diet of cats culled from the Ickworth estate. In all, 47 cats were thought to have been eaten by the 12-stone dog.

Bristol was married briefly to Francesca, the daughter of a property tycoon, Douglas Fisher, but he preferred the company of young men who were delivered in the middle of the night like pizzas. A helicopter, parked on the lawn, was used for this purpose, as well as for the ferrying in of drugs. Targeted by the police, he was arrested more than once for dealing in heroin and cocaine, and he spent a year in prison. There is no reason to suppose that this experience provided any sort of cure, and he continued to throw parties until his death at the age of 44. The diagnosis was 'multi-organ failure attributable to chronic drug abuse'. By then, the 7th marquess's friends had helped him to dissipate a fortune of £16 million.

*See* also HERVEY, AUGUSTUS.

**Britton, Thomas** (1654–1714), coal merchant, musician and bibliophile. Born in Northamptonshire, Britton came to London at an early age and by 1677 had established himself near Clerkenwell Green as a coal merchant, living with his wife above a modest stable from which he ran his business. At this ramshackle address, accessible only by an outside builder's ladder, he held musical evenings every Thursday for 40 years.

The high standards of the concerts attracted the best professional musicians of the day, notably Handel. Although Britton's harpsichord was said to be of good quality, Handel preferred to play a five-stop organ, accompanied by Britton on the viola da gamba. Leaders of society, including the duchess of Queensbury, joined distinguished musicians in climbing the rickety approach to the concert room. At first these evenings were free, but later there was a subscription of ten shillings a year with coffee served at a penny a cup.

Britton also achieved recognition as a bibliophile, acting as an agent to many wealthy collectors. Every Saturday a group of enthusiasts, including the earls of Oxford, Pembroke and Winchelsea, searched London for rare books and met afterwards at Christopher Bateman's shop in Paternoster Row. Here they were joined by Britton, still wearing his blue apron after a morning humping coal in the street. Britton formed the collection of pamphlets now known as 'the Somers Tracts', which he later sold to Lord Somers; he was involved, too, in the formation of the Harleian Library, which is now part of the British Library.

Britton's own collection of books displayed an interest in the occult sciences, particularly Rosicrucian philosophy. He was certainly superstitious, a characteristic that led to his death. Intending no more than to play a small practical joke, a Mr Roe, who often attended the Thursday evening concerts, brought with him on one occasion a ventriloquist named Honeyman, who had won fame as 'the talking blacksmith' but was unknown to Britton. Throwing his voice, Honeyman announced that Britton would die on the spot unless he fell to his knees and recited the Lord's Prayer. The shock to Britton was so great that he took to his bed and died within a few days. He left no money, but his collection of books fetched high prices when sold at auction. The painting of Britton by Woolaston now in the National Portrait Gallery shows him dressed, appropriately, as a coalman – a trade he pursued with pride throughout his life.

For other coal merchants of note, *see* HANGER, GEORGE.

**Brodie, Deacon William** (1741–88), carpenter and burglar. Born in Edinburgh, the son of a respected cabinet maker, Brodie followed his father in business and also became a deacon of the town council. Though highly regarded in society, his taste for gambling, and a private life that involved several mistresses and many illegitimate children, soon brought about financial difficulties. By 1785 he had squandered his considerable inheritance, and so turned to burgling the homes of his well-to-do friends. In this occupation he was greatly helped by knowledge of their circumstances acquired on social occasions. Becoming more ambitious, he enlisted the services of three professional criminals, with whom he carried out a number of thefts, including that of the silver mace from Edinburgh University. In 1788 he and his associates were disturbed when attempting to rob the Excise Office of Scotland, and Brodie fled to Holland. He was brought back to Edinburgh, tried and convicted. Before he was executed, his carpentry skills were put to use for the last time. He was allowed to design and construct the gallows on which he was hanged outside St Giles High Kirk in February 1788. Robert Louis Stevenson supposedly used Brodie as a model when writing *The Strange Case of Dr Jekyll and Mr Hyde* (1886). A public house called Deacon Brodie's Tavern has for many years stood at the corner of the Royal Mile and the Mound in Edinburgh.

**Bromley-Davenport, Lieutenant Colonel Sir Walter** (1903–89), soldier and politician. One of the last of the 'knights of the shires' at Westminster, Sir Walter was a parliamentay 'character' of the sort the British are supposed to admire. As such, he was happy throughout his years on the back benches to flesh out this logical fiction by playing the buffoon. A former lightweight boxing champion of the army, he liked to startle new Labour MPs when they rose to make a speech by bellowing, 'Take your hands out of your pockets!' On one occasion, Brigadier Otho Prior-Palmer, MP for Worthing, attempted to speak at the same time as Bromley-Davenport. 'Sit down!' thundered the colonel, which the brigadier immediately did. He used his voice, which was reputed to be the loudest in the house, away from the Commons too. Boarding an over-crowded train at

Crewe, he walked up and down the corridor, shouting 'All change! All change!' This had the desired effect. Everyone got off and he was able to find a seat. When he was attacked in his home by a madman with an axe, he shouted 'Don't let the NHS get me!' so loudly that his assailant fled.

During the 1987 general election, Neil Hamilton, whom he regarded as his spiritual heir and who had succeeded him as MP for Knutsford in Cheshire, invited him to address a meeting. When Hamilton's attention was drawn to a pile of dog-eared notes, he asked Bromley-Davenport when the speech had been composed. Sir Walter replied that he had written it in 1945, having returned from the war. He had delivered the same speech, he said, at every general election for 42 years. For this, and other, reasons, he never achieved high office, though he was elevated to the post of junior whip in 1949. This ended disappointingly two years later when he approached the Belgian ambassador from behind and kicked him down the stairs. He had mistaken him for a colleague leaving the Commons before the 10 o'clock vote. Sir Walter was keen on amateur dramatics, and had a theatre in his home.

**Bronson, Charles** (1952–  ), armed robber and unlicensed fist-fighter. Bronson, whose real name is Michael Gordon Peterson, was first jailed for 7 years in 1974 after he robbed a Liverpool jeweller of £35. Since then he has enjoyed just 69 days of freedom: 25 years have been added to his original sentence, of which he has spent 22 years in solitary confinement. To the surprise of the authorities, this experience has not altered his behaviour for the better. He has led eight roof-top protests, assaulted more than 20 prison officers, taken two governors and seven Iraqi terrorists hostage, lassoed a visiting teacher with a skipping rope and caused £500,000 worth of damage to prison property. He has been moved 150 times and housed in all three of the country's top-security hospitals – Ashton, Rampton and Broadmoor. He possesses unusual strength, which he likes to demonstrate by bending the bars on his cell door and by performing 2000 press-ups with a prison officer on his back.

First certified insane in 1978, Bronson was sectioned for life and sent to Broadmoor. He caused so much damage there that the authorities calculated that it would be cheaper to reverse the verdict and return him to prison. Released in 1993, he fought as an unlicensed boxer under the name of Charles Bronson. This was his manager's suggestion. He himself had never heard of the Hollywood actor. Within eight weeks he was back in prison after another bungled robbery, sentenced this time to eight years. Ten years were subsequently added for various misdemeanours, including the incident with the Iraqi highjackers and with the teacher, Phil Danielson, whom he held hostage for two days with a skipping rope round his neck. Mr Danielson contracted a nervous disorder after the experience, and has not been able to work since.

A visit from his son, Michael, who had been born in 1971, and the intervention of an enlightened prison governor, who awakened in Bronson an interest in art, seemed to hold out hope of rehabilitation. He turned out to be a talented cartoonist, but when carrying out chef's duties in July 2000 he was so disappointed by the non-delivery of a consignment of mushrooms that he smashed up the prison kitchen. After a five-hour stand-off, 24 prison staff wearing riot clothes moved in and after a fierce tussle were able to restrain him.

Bronson's friends in Liverpool have expressed surprise at his continuing difficulties. 'He was never violent,' said one. 'He just liked a punch-up.' Further hope for the future accompanied the news in June 2001 that in a simple ceremony at Woodhill prison, near Milton Keynes, Bronson had married Miss Saira Rehman, who works as a translator in Luton. Miss Rehman had started to write to Bronson after seeing his photograph in a paper. At the conclusion of the ceremony the groom sang a version of Louis Armstrong's 'What a Wonderful World' before being returned to his cell. The late Frank Packenham, the campaigning 7th earl of Longford, had acted as best man. Asked whether he had been frightened of Bronson, the 95-year-old peer said, 'Certainly not. We did press-ups together. I managed one.'

**brothels, keepers of 'conventional'.** *See* DALY, JOSEPHINE; FERNSEED, MARGARET; JEFFRIES, MARY; JONES, JANIE; PAGE, DAMARIS; PAYNE, CYNTHIA; TURNER, ANNE.

**brothels, keepers of 'sodomitical'.** *See* CLAP, MARGARET; COOKE, JAMES; HAMMOND, CHARLES.

*See also* CLARENCE, PRINCE ALBERT VICTOR, DUKE OF; NEWTON, ARTHUR.

**brothels, measures to prevent the police putting young people into.** *See* RUSSELL, JOHN CONRAD, 4TH EARL.

**brothels with a chaplain on the premises.** *See* PRIDDEN, SARAH (for Mother Wisebourne).

**Brothers, Richard** (*c.*1769–?), naval officer, author and prophet. In March 1795 Brothers, a former lieutenant in the Royal Navy and self-proclaimed 'nephew of the Almighty', was arrested in Paddington Street, London, on a warrant from the duke of Portland and charged with high treason. A few months earlier, a bookseller, George Ribeau, had published the first volume of Brothers's *A Revealed Knowledge of the Prophecies and Times* from his premises in the Strand. Brothers had forecast that on 19 May 1795 he would be revealed as the Prince of True Hebrews and Ruler of the World.

He further suggested that George III should prepare to hand over the crown.

To the alarm of the authorities, Brothers's pamphlet had attracted a large number of supporters. In it he declared that the rebuilding of Jerusalem would begin in 1798, and this struck a chord with millenarians, whose numbers were growing rapidly in the 1790s. One of them, Nathaniel Brassey Halhed, MP for Lymington, had been studying the prophecies in the Book of Daniel. On 31 March 1795 he rose in the House of Commons and delivered a three-hour speech in Brothers's defence. A month later another bookseller, Benjamin Crosby, published Halhed's speech at 1s 6d. In the same year, a Halhed pamphlet testifying to the authenticity of Brothers's prophecies was published by Henry Delahoy Symonds at the price of 1s. Symonds had already been in trouble for publishing controversial material. In May 1793 he had been sentenced to a year in Newgate prison for publishing Thomas Paine's *The Rights of Man*. There was little to link the prophecies of Brothers with Paine's rationalism, but with France in revolutionary turmoil the British government lived in fear of civil unrest. They were quick to link any non-conformist religion with republicanism.

To make matters worse, two of Brothers's followers raised suspicions because of their involvement with the secretive Avignon Society in France. John Wright, a carpenter from Leeds, had come to London in 1788 to attend the first services of the New Jerusalem Church, founded the previous year by followers of the aristocratic Swedish scientist turned mystic, Emanuel Swedenborg. Once in the capital, Wright fell in with William Bryan, a London druggist who held similar religious convictions. In January 1789 they had travelled together to Avignon and stayed for some months in a Freemason's lodge. Both Wright and Bryan now published pamphlets supporting Brothers and detailing their adventures in Avignon. These included a chance meeting with the Archangel Raphael.

It was all too much for the authorities. On 27 March 1795 the Privy Council found Brothers guilty of treason. Having ignored evidence of his mental instability, they sentenced him to eleven years in prison. Later they reversed the decision and transferred him to an asylum for the criminally insane, where he was shortly joined by Wright and Bryan. Halhed escaped a similar fate by resigning his parliamentary seat.

**Brown, Craig** (1959– ), writer and journalist. Brown works at his desk from breakfast until luncheon dressed in his pyjamas. He says that he would otherwise walk around Aldeburgh in his day clothes instead of composing his many excellent columns. Brown is married to the writer Frances Welch, the gifted daughter of Colin Welch. They have two children, Talullah and Silas.

*See also* PAGET, DOROTHY; PYJAMAS, BUYING THE CHAUFFEUR SILK;

**Brown, Eric** (1924– ), bank clerk and murderer. At the age of 19, and unusually in a domestic, as opposed to a military, dispute, Brown killed his father, Archibald, by blowing him up with an army land mine. Brown senior, aged 47, had been injured in a motorcycle accident and had gradually developed paralysis of the spine. By 1942 he was confined to a wheelchair at his home in Rayleigh, near Southend, where he lived with his wife and two sons. On 23 July 1943 his nurse, who was called Mitchell, took Archibald Brown on one of his favourite walks. They stopped a mile from home to enjoy the tranquillity of the countryside, and while parking the wheelchair, nurse Mitchell was thrown high into the air by a loud explosion. She was shocked, but unharmed. Archibald Brown was blown to pieces. Eric Brown had somehow acquired an antitank device known as a Hawkins No 75 grenade mine, which he had fitted to his father's wheelchair. At his trial for murder at Chelmsford assizes in November 1943, Eric Brown said that he hadn't liked his father's attitude. He was found guilty but insane.

**Brown, James** (1863–?), cabinet maker and zoophilist. In 1888, Brown a young man of previously good conduct, appeared before Lord Coleridge, the lord chief justice, at Chelmsford assizes and was sentenced to one year's hard labour for committing an offence with a duck. As Lord Coleridge was leaving court his clerk drew his attention to an unreported decision in the case of *Dod* in which it had been held that a duck was not an animal within 25 & 26 Vict. C100.61. Coleridge was a conscientious jurist, so he immediately referred his own decision to the Court of Crown Cases Reserved, over which he happened to preside. Here he argued with himself for several days, representing both sides of the case even-handedly and ruling finally that the defendant referred to by his clerk had in fact been acquitted on other grounds. Brown was sent back to prison to serve his sentence and Coleridge's decision went into the law books. Here, it is one of the first to be read by students – though not, it seems, by defence counsel for a visitor from Nigeria who in 1952 was accused of indecency with a pigeon in Trafalgar Square. Counsel produced the old argument that a duck was not an animal, but the defence failed when prosecuting counsel cited *Brown*. The Nigerian was fined £50 and another £10 for taking the pigeon home and eating it.

**Bruce-Wallace, Andy** (1951– ), recluse, known to his neighbours as 'the Yeti'. At the age of 24, Bruce-Wallace became an environmentalist and a follower of some aspects of Taoism. He moved into the bombed-out shell of a house in Northern Ireland whose previous occupant had been an officer in the Royal Ulster Constabulary recently blown up by the IRA. He grows all his own food in a large organic garden and travels on a tricycle of his own design, with his camping facilities packed on the back.

Bruce-Wallace's reclusive disposition first showed itself when he was a boy growing up in the Lake District. He converted the garage into a room of his own, where he shut himself off from the rest of the household, even refusing to be photographed in family groups. He then moved out of the house altogether, establishing himself in a tent in the garden. Finally he arrived at the point where he stayed out of doors all the time, braving the elements on the mountains of northern England and the Scottish Highlands. Bruce-Wallace has been known to walk very long distances, and he writes tongue-in-cheek letters to the newspapers under the name of Gerald Winstanley.

**Brummagem Boys versus the Sabini family, the.** *See* SABINI, CHARLES.

**brush manufacturers, murderous.** *See* WAINWRIGHT, HENRY.

**buccaneers.** The word derives from the French *boucanier*, from *boucan*. The native inhabitants of the West Indies used a method of preparing and preserving meat by roasting it on a barbecue and curing it with smoke. *Boucan* was the French name for this, derived from Tupi, *mukem*. In time, the great variety of hill-dwelling pig hunters, international refugees, escaped slaves, transported criminals and indentured servants who roamed along the Caribbean island coasts became known as buccaneers. They were encouraged by the English government – which initially had no colonies in the West Indies – to wage guerrilla war against the enfeebled Spanish empire.

*See also* BLACKBURNE, ARCHBISHOP LANCELOT; BONNY, ANNE; KIDD, WILLIAM; LANCEY, JOHN; MORGAN, SIR HENRY; TEACH, EDWARD; TRELAWNY, EDWARD.

**Buchan, Elspeth** (1738–91), Scottish salvationist residing in Tayside who identified herself with a character from the first verse of Revelations, chapter 12:

> There appeared a great wonder in Heaven; a woman clothed with the sun, and the moon under her feet, and upon her head a crown of twelve stars.

Miss Buchan was assisted in her mission to save the world by the Reverend Hugh Whyte, a minister of the Relief Church and her chief apostle. Whyte preached that God would at any moment make himself known to Miss Buchan and her followers, thereafter translating them straight to Heaven without having to die first. On the other hand, divine vengeance and the flames of hell would be visited on such Scotsmen as refused to recognize Miss Buchan as God's emissary. Soon enough, the Reverend Whyte announced that the day of the cult's happy translation to heaven was imminent. With their hair cut short, leaving only a tuft on top by which they could be caught up from above, they assembled on rising ground. Here, according to the historian A.S. Morton, they erected a fragile wooden stage, on to which they climbed, with Miss Buchan mounted on a higher platform in the middle. The air was filled with their singing and invocations, and then, as the sun rose over Templand Hill, a gust of wind caused the platform to collapse and instead of ascending to heaven Miss Buchan and her followers fell to the ground in a heap.

Miss Buchan preached her own immortality, so when it became clear that in this she was about to be confounded, she announced to her followers that while she might appear to die she would in fact be going to heaven to prepare the way for them. She would return in six months to escort them to paradise, or, if their faith was not sufficient, she would give them a second chance and return in ten years. If that failed, she would be back in 50 years to announce the end of the world. A few days later she died. The six-month anniversary passed uneventfully, as did the one ten years later. By the 50th anniversary there were only two Buchanites left, Mr and Mrs Andrew Innes. When the day came and went without an appearance by Miss Buchan, Mr and Mrs Innes renounced their faith.

**Buck, Bienvenida** (1952– ), self-proclaimed expert on how to secure a rich husband. Initially the wife of Tory MP, Sir Antony Buck, Lady Buck first came to prominence in 1989 when a Sunday newspaper published the story of her affair with Sir Peter Harding, Chief of the Defence Staff. This contained the revelation that the couple had a preference for kissing with a mouthful of champagne ('the champagne kiss of love'). Sir Peter resigned, but Lady Harding stood by him. Lady Buck's second husband was a mustachioed art dealer, Count Nicholas Sokolow, but the marriage was not a success. Her third husband was Eduardo Jimeno, a Spanish lawyer. She was last heard of living in a Chelsea flat, where for a fee of £5000 she was offering a two-day course in seduction techniques.

**Buckingham, George Villiers, 2nd duke of** (1627–87), politician, courtier and playwright. Buckingham's celebrated misdeeds illustrate the extent of aristocratic delinquency in the Restoration. Born in London, the son of James I's lover, he was brought up with Charles I's children. At the outbreak of the Civil War he joined the royalists. He followed Charles II to Scotland, but after the latter's defeat at the battle of Worcester he went into exile. Returning secretly to England in 1657, he married the daughter of Lord Fairfax, the parliamentary general to whom his forfeited estates had been assigned. At the Restoration he recovered his offices, became a privy councillor and for the next 25 years exceeded all other courtiers in the extent of his debauchery.

Buckingham was among the first to embrace duelling as a recognized social institution among the aristocracy. In 1666 his disparagement of the Irish nation during a debate in the House of Lords angered Lord Ossory, who demanded satisfaction. On this occasion Buckingham avoided trouble by having Ossory locked in the Tower. Four years later, however, he killed the earl of Shrewsbury in a duel, provoked by Buckingham's adultery with Shrewsbury's wife, who watched the fight disguised as a page.

In 1674 Buckingham was dismissed from government for alleged Catholic sympathies. He was the author of several comedies, written for the stage – of which *The Rehearsal* (1671) is thought to be the most amusing – but he is better known as the 'Zimri' of Dryden's *Absalom and Achitophel*.

*See also* DORSET, CHARLES SACKVILLE, 1ST EARL OF.

**Buckingham Palace sold to an American.** *See* FERGUSON, ARTHUR.

**Buckingham Palace twice penetrated.** *See* FAGAN, MICHAEL.

**Buckland, Francis Trevelyan** (1826–88), naturalist, 'experimental zoöphage' and writer. The Victorian layman's idea of a working naturalist reached its highest representation in the person of Frank Buckland. His *Curiosities of Natural History*, appearing in four volumes, and his many articles in *Land and Water*, *The Field* and other periodicals brought him constantly before the public. Nor was the public ever disappointed. Whether bottle-feeding a porpoise in a railway waiting room or striding down Albany Street with a giant on one arm and a dwarf on the other, he satisfied every popular expectation. He usually had a variety of wildlife in his pockets. Meeting a Mr Bell in Carlisle, who happened to mention that he kept storks, Buckland was disappointed that he had no frogs about his person to give to the storks, 'But happily I had a Lucifer-matchbox full of little toads, about the size of beans.' (*Notes and Jottings from Animal Life*, 1882.)

Buckland was the son of William Buckland, a distinguished Oxford geologist who was the first to make the discipline a respected subject of study in Britain. It was from his father that he inherited his boundless energy and habit of outspokenness – characteristics that prompted Charles Darwin to say of William Buckland:

> Though very good-natured, he seemed to me a vulgar and almost coarse man. He was incited more by a craving for notoriety, which sometimes made him act like a buffoon, than by a love of science.

On his honeymoon, William and his wife were taken to the shrine in

Palermo of St Rosalia. The moment he saw her bones, preserved as relics, Buckland exclaimed, 'Those are the bones of a goat!' Furious priests escorted the Bucklands out, and later removed the bones from public view. Some years later, on a visit to a foreign cathedral, William and his son Frank were shown a patch of floor marked with the blood of a martyr – stains that miraculously appeared fresh every day. William dipped his finger in the blood, tasted it and said, 'I can tell you what this is – bat's urine.'

Frank Buckland was educated at Winchester College and Oxford, where he kept a chameleon, some marmots, an eagle, a jackal and a bear called Tiglath-Pileser, named after a king of ancient Assyria. Tiglath-Pileser, dressed in a cap and gown, attended the Oxford meeting of the British Association in 1847 where Lord Houghton attempted to mesmerize him. This made the bear angry, but he gradually yielded to the influence, and at last fell senseless to the ground (George C. Bompas, *Life of Frank Buckland*, 1887). Buckland's original ambition was to be a surgeon, but he fainted at his first operation and soon decided that operating on live human beings was less enjoyable than dissecting dead chickens.

By the 1860s Buckland was installed with his wife, Hannah, and numerous pets at 37 Albany Street. Here he was visited by Mrs Priestly from *World* magazine, who wrote an account of his domestic arrangements as part of her series on 'Celebrities at Home'. After describing the monkeys, the jaguar, the jackass, the tame mice, the cats and a parrot that kept shouting for cabs out of the window, Mrs Priestly turned her attention to the kitchen, and wrote:

> Quaint and original must be many of the dishes which issue from Mr Buckland's kitchen. The long-suffering cook, were she free to speak, might tell some strange tales of young crocodiles boiled down for stock, of food misapplied, and of diets given to the wrong animals. Mr Buckland's housekeeping books cover a wide range.

Mrs Priestly is alluding to that branch of zoological research that Frank Buckland made his own and to which he contributed his most original research – the gastronomy of the subject. Even as a boy he had experimented with squirrel pie and mice cooked in batter, hedgehogs, frogs and garden snails. 'A roast fieldmouse – not a house mouse – is a splendid *bonne bouche* for a hungry boy, it eats like a lark.' At Oxford, he had feasted on a panther, sent to him from the Surrey Zoological Gardens. 'It had been buried for two days, but I got them to dig it up. It was not very good.'

Once he was established as a naturalist, Buckland's opportunities for zoophagy greatly increased. Summoned to Gravesend to examine a whale that had been washed ashore, he tasted a portion but 'found it too strong, even when boiled with charcoal'. Mr Bartlett of the London Zoo supplied him with many delicacies: elephant trunk, which he made into soup ('rubbery'), rhinoceros, which he baked into a huge pie for one of his lecture audiences ('like very tough beef'), porpoise, which tasted like 'broiled lamp-wick', and giraffe, which had been cooked on the hoof as a result of a fire in the giraffe house. The giraffe was one of his great successes. The meat was white, and tasted like veal. In this it resembled boa constrictor, which also reminded him of veal.

Buckland's successful attempt to institutionalize zoophagy began with the celebrated 'Eland Dinner', held in 1859 at the London Tavern. On this occasion the country's most eminent naturalists assembled to discover whether eland should be introduced to the national diet. In 1860 he initiated the Acclimatization Society to further the search for new food. Having enlisted the marquess of Breadalbane as president, he arranged an inaugural dinner for 100 guests at Willis's Rooms. The meal began with bird's-nest soup, tripang (Japanese sea slug) and soup made from the sinews of the axis deer. This was followed by 'kangaroo steamer', which, as Buckland admitted, 'was a little gone off, but not bad for all that'. The main course of guan, curassow, Honduras turkey and kangaroo ham was a great success, though it emerged afterwards that the waiters had mixed up the menu cards and the kangaroo ham was really wild boar.

The society flourished and produced annual reports for a decade. Lord Breadalbane raised yaks and American bison on his Taymouth estate; Lord Bute stocked his Scottish islands with beavers and thereby killed all the trees for miles around; and Buckland urged anyone who would listen to turn his park over to kangaroos.

With naturalists and circus performers constantly coming and going, Buckland's house was never dull. A relative of Mrs Buckland, who as a small child often visited the Buckland home, told her grandson, the zoologist John Napier, that on one occasion while descending a dark staircase she tripped over a large, soft object and fell down several flights. It turned out to be a dead hippopotamus. Frank Buckland picked her up and said, 'Do be more careful. Hippopotamuses don't grow on trees, you know.'

*See also* WYKEHAMISTS.

**budgerigars.** *See* BEDFORD, JOHN ROBERT RUSSELL, 12TH DUKE OF; CHANEY, SID; MITCHELL, FRANK.

**budgerigars taught to say 'Bertie's a fucking grass'.** *See* SMALLS, BERTIE.

**buggery, self-improvement through mystic.** *See* CROWLEY, ALEISTER.

**Bugle, the Grand.** *See* HELL-FIRE CLUB, THE IRISH.

**Buller, Sir Redvers** (1840–1913), soldier, of whom it has been said that his command of the expeditionary force against the Boers in South Africa brought a new level of ineptitude to the British war effort. His idea of fair play accorded with General Herbert Kitchener's assessment of the Boers as 'not being like the Sudanese, who stood up to a fair fight, but are always running away on their little ponies'. Like Kitchener, Buller (known as Sir Reverse Buller) believed that the enemy should stand in the open and be shot down by British rifles. Before embarking for South Africa he had therefore prepared his men at Aldershot with a comically inept course of military manoeuvres. No trenches could be dug for fear of damaging the country-side, the soldiers were not allowed to take cover lest they get their uniforms dirty and the manoeuvres could only take place between 9 a.m. and 5 p.m. so that they would not interfere with the officers' social arrangements.

Within days of Buller's arrival in South Africa in 1899 his master plan lay in ruins. His first mistake was to send his most incompetent commander, General William Gatacre (known to his men as 'Backacher'), to capture the strategic railway junction at Stormberg with a surprise attack. This entailed 2700 men undertaking a difficult night march during which they lost their way. They had forgotten to take with them the only man who had a map. As dawn broke, the British troops discovered to their surprise that they were stranded at the base of a steep cliff on top of which the Boers were taking their morning coffee. It was then the Boers' turn to be surprised. Instead of retiring with as much dignity as they could muster, the British troops were ordered by Gatacre to advance up the almost sheer rock face into a hail of bullets. Seeing his men fall back, Gatacre ordered a retreat, congratulating himself that he had suffered only 90 casualties. He then remembered that he had forgotten 600 men who had received no orders to retreat and were still clinging to the precipice. Surrounded by Boers, they had no option but to surrender. 'Better luck next time,' Buller telegraphed to Gatacre.

Meanwhile, and not to be outdone, Buller had been bombarding a hill near Magersfontein in the belief that the Boers were entrenched at the top. In fact, they were dug in at the bottom, and greatly enjoyed the display of fire power mounted by Buller for their amusement. Assuming that the Boers must have been thoroughly rattled by this bombardment, Buller ordered his second most incompetent general, Lord Methuen, to take the hill with a force of 3500 men from the Highland Brigade. Since he didn't know the location of the Boers, he was sending Lord Methuen into a trap. As the sun came up, the Boers saw the Highlanders marching confidently towards them across open country. When the Boers opened fire, some men took to their heels, but most fell to the ground or tried to take cover behind anthills. With his men trapped in the open and under murderous fire, Lord Methuen was paralysed by indecision. In the end, the men of the Highland Light Infantry gave way to panic and fled, many of them being shot in the back. British losses amounted to 900 men.

After this setback, Buller was reinforced by a new division under Sir Charles Warren, whose previous occupation had been that of London's police commissioner. In that capacity, he had recently failed to catch JACK THE RIPPER. It was Warren's habit to bathe in public. At the height of the battle for Hussar Hill in February 1900, Buller discovered his second-in-command splashing about in a tub of water instead of directing his troops. During the crossing of the Tugela at Trickhardt's Drift, Warren spent 26 hours supervising the transfer of his personal baggage across the river. When he had arrived at the river, it was defended by only 600 Boers; by the time Warren's baggage had been taken across, a further 6000 had moved into position, and Warren's advance was blocked. Buller's reaction was to put Warren in command of the British forces at the important battle of Spion Kop. They agreed that the hill of Spion Kop must be taken since it commanded the Boer positions. Buller ordered Warren to occupy the top, though it was never decided what he should do once he was there. In thick fog, the assault troops, mainly from the Lancashire Brigade, set off up the steep-sided hill, while the rest of Buller's army – approximately 2000 men – stood and watched. When Warren's men reached what they took to be the summit, they started to dig in. At this point, they realized that they had left the sandbags behind, but luckily had remembered to take 20 picks and shovels with them. As visibility improved, they discovered that they weren't at the summit at all, but on an exposed plateau half way up the hill. From higher up, the Boers opened fire on Warren's men from three sides. The British troops were massacred. When Winston Churchill, who was present as a war correspondent, told Buller that his men were trapped, the general ordered his arrest. Later, Buller wrote to his wife, 'We were fighting all last week, but Warren is a duffer and lost me a good chance.'

**Bum Bathsheba.** *See* SYMONDS, JOHN.

**Bumtickler's Revels, Lady.** *See* HOTTEN, JOHN CAMDEN.

**'Bunnies will go to France'.** *See* THORPE, JEREMY.

**Burgess, Guy Francis de Moncy** (1911–63), spy. After Eton and Cambridge – where he had been recruited by the Russians – Burgess worked for a short time at the BBC before drifting into one of the mushrooming intelligence services. Gifted amateurs, if considered amusing, were welcome in this milieu, even if, like Burgess, they had previously been associated with a fashionably pro-German faction in pre-war London. This former connection rather confused Burgess's friends but appeared not to hinder his future career either as a British diplomat or as a Soviet agent.

In 1944 Burgess was offered a temporary job at the Foreign Office. This employment shortly became permanent in spite of his poor behaviour in the personal sphere. From being a spokesman, he was taken on as personal assistant to the minister of state at the Foreign Office, Hector McNeil, who thought him brilliant. However, he was dismissed from another department by a minister who described him as 'dirty, drunk and idle'. At the same time, a firm of London solicitors tried to evict him from his flat in New Bond Street. According to a partner in the firm:

> Soon after Burgess moved in, there were complaints from other tenants of rowdy parties, shouts, screams and fights throughout the night. The parties were all-male affairs. Whenever I saw him, he seemed to have some part of his body in bandages. Early one morning, another of the tenants rang us in a panic. The noise from the flat above was indescribable. Then an ambulance drew up and Burgess, with his head and arms bandaged, was taken out on a stretcher. Quite obviously, there had been a first-class fight. I rang the hospital and was told that he had a fractured skull and a broken jaw and was on the danger list.

Later, a ballet dancer called Jack Hewitt, who lived with Burgess at the time, explained that, 'Guy was thrown down the stairs by a fellow diplomat. It wasn't Maclean.'

Despite such setbacks, and while Burgess was passing on confidential papers to his Soviet employers, he was appointed in 1950 to the British embassy in Washington to look after Far Eastern affairs. Here he stayed at the home of his old Cambridge friend and fellow Soviet agent, Kim Philby. In May 1951 the KGB discovered that Donald Maclean, now back in London after his stint in Washington, was about to be uncovered by British counter-intelligence, and they decided that he must be warned. The method chosen was complicated. In order that he might alert Maclean personally, Burgess was to be sent back to London in disgrace – a feat that he easily accomplished. He simply drove round Washington in his customary state of advanced inebriation, insulted police officers who stopped him and threatened to invoke diplomatic immunity from arrest. He returned to Britain on the *Queen Mary* and was met at Southampton by Anthony BLUNT, who helped him with the escape arrangements. Burgess visited Maclean at his home in Surrey and then drove him in a hired car to Southampton, en route for the Soviet Union via France. Either by accident or through panic, but certainly not by prior intent, he decided at the last minute to sail with Maclean – after which there was no going back.

From then until his death in 1963, Burgess's value to the Russians, as a working defector and as a propaganda symbol, progressively declined. From all accounts (the best, perhaps, being Alan Bennett's television play, *An Englishman Abroad*, 1987), Burgess's final years in Moscow were far from happy.

**'Burglar to the Gentry'.** *See* CHATHAM, GEORGE

**buried in a stolen Zandra Rhodes creation.** *See* PITTS, SHIRLEY.

**Burke, William** (1792–1829), labourer and body snatcher. Born in County Cork, Burke arrived in Scotland as an immigrant labourer in 1818, meeting fellow Irishman, William HARE, at Logue's lodging house, a squalid building in Edinburgh's West Port. Sharing the same building was an army pensioner, known as Old Donald, who died in 1827, owing Hare £4. Hitting on a way of recovering this debt, Burke and Hare opened the coffin and substituted a sack of bark for the old soldier's body, which they sold for £7 10s to Dr Robert KNOX of Edinburgh's Anatomy School. Over the next ten months Dr Knox became a good customer of the newly formed body-snatching partnership. At first, corpses were dug up from among the recently buried at local graveyards. But as the trade became more lucrative, Burke and Hare broadened the scope of their operations, and began to create their own supply. Their method rarely altered. Either Burke's common-law wife, Helen McDougal, or Hare's, Maggie Laird, would lure a victim back to the lodging house, where he would be knocked unconscious with drink. Burke would then kneel on his chest, while stopping his nose and mouth with his hands. In recognition of its originator, this method of causing death became known as 'burking'.

Dr Knox first became suspicious when he was offered the body of an attractive young woman named Mary Paterson whom he recognized as a prostitute he had recently patronized. His suspicions turned into certainty when Burke and Hare sold him the body of a well-known local idiot called Daft Jamie, but he preferred to keep quiet.

The partnership was involuntarily discontinued in 1828 when, through carelessness, they left the body of Margaret Docherty where other lodgers could find it. Hare and Maggie Laird escaped prosecution by turning King's evidence, leaving Burke and McDougal to stand trial at the High Court of Justiciary. The case against McDougal was found 'Not Proven', but Burke was publicly hanged on 27 January 1829. McDougal was pursued through the streets of Edinburgh by a furious mob and escaped lynching only through the intervention of the police. William Hare died in London, a blind beggar.

By some accounts, Dr Knox spent his final days in the position of showman to a tribe of Ojibwa Indians in a travelling circus.

**burking (as a cause of death).** *See* BURKE, WILLIAM.

**bus conductresses, murderous.** *See* ALLEN, MARGARET ('Bill').

**bus-pass bandits.** *See* ARIS, DORIS; CHANEY, SID; CURZON, CHARLES; DALY, JOSEPHINE; MCSKIMMEY, BUNTY.

**Butler, Lady Eleanor** (1738–1821), recluse. In 1774 Lady Eleanor, the daughter of an Irish peer, and her kinswoman Sarah Ponsonby met in Kilkenny and fell in love. Lady Eleanor was 39, Miss Ponsonby ten years younger. Their subsequent decision to withdraw from the world and set up home together in the Welsh village of Plas Newydd brought them enduring fame as 'the Ladies of Llangollen'. Here they lived in complete seclusion with one maidservant, Flirt the dog and Mrs Tatters the cat. Neither spent a single night away from their little farmhouse, or from each other, until their deaths 50 years later.

Dressed in men's clothes, Lady Eleanor and Sarah Ponsonby occupied themselves by tending their lovingly planted garden and model farm, the beauty of which struck every visitor. Fashionable people liked to make the difficult journey over the mountains to see their hermitage and admire the advantages they found there. According to Prince Puckler-Muskau, these included:

> ... a well-furnished library, an even-tempered life without material cares, a most intimate friendship and community among themselves.

Among their other visitors were Wordsworth, Southey, De Quincey and the Darwins. The duke of Wellington was a close friend, and Queen Charlotte asked for the plans for their cottage and garden.

Sarah Ponsonby herself described their idyllic existence in a letter to a friend:

> In the Mornings after breakfast I try to improve myself in drawing. My Beloved is also improving herself though this is scarce possible in Italian. After dinner She reads aloud to me 'till nine o'clock when we regularly retire to our dressing room, where we generally employ ourselves 'till twelve.

Apart from games of backgammon during which Eleanor would cry 'Faith!' after a lucky throw, no one knows what these employments consisted of, nor would it have occurred to anyone at the time to ask. Romantic friendship between women was approved of, but strictly circumscribed. Had the ladies' friendship been discovered to be sexual, social opprobrium would have immediately followed.

**butler, running off with the.** *See* KAGGS, JOHN.

**Butler, Detective Chief Superintendent Thomas** (1915–77), policeman. Known as 'One Day' Tommy, because of the speed with which he got his man, Butler was famously corrupt, though not in order to enrich himself. His unwavering belief in law and order led him, when investigating a crime, to speed up the judicial process by supplying the evidence himself, rather than discovering it at the scene of the crime or on the person of the suspect. Professional criminals took this *modus operandi* in good part, acknowledging that those 'fitted up' by this method of crime detection were usually guilty of something, if not always of the crime under investigation. There is general agreement, however, that when Butler, as head of the Flying Squad, investigated the Great Train Robbery of 1963, his enthusiasm got the better of him and at least one of those convicted, William Boal, was innocent. Butler placed him at the scene of the crime by putting yellow paint on his shoes from a can found at the robbers' hide-out, Leatherslade Farm. Gordon GOODY, one of the leaders of the gang, and convicted by the same planted evidence, is still indignant on Boal's behalf. 'OK, I was there,' he has admitted:

> ... but Boal wasn't even a criminal, never mind on the robbery. His crime in Butler's eyes was to be a friend of Ronnie Biggs. It wasn't right.

Boal was sentenced to 15 years and died in prison. Other officers on the case, including Detective Sergeant Jack Slipper, agree that Boal played no part in the robbery.

It is generally acknowledged, on the other hand, that Butler knew nothing about the £50,000 in used notes (and part of the proceeds from the robbery) that was placed in a south London telephone box by Freddie FOREMAN at the request of Butler's second-in-command, Superintendent Frank Williams.

*See also* KEYHOE, MICKEY.

**butlers, disgraced bishops masquerading as.** *See* JOCELYN, THE REVEREND PERCY.

**butlers, indecently assaulted.** *See* AUDLEY, MERVYN CASTLEFORD, 2ND BARON; JACKSON, THE REVEREND WILLIAM.

**butlers, levitating.** *See* GREATRAKES, VALENTINE.

**butlers, murderous.** *See* HALL, ARCHIBALD.

**Butterbottom, Miss Sarah.** *See* SALA, GEORGE AUGUSTUS.

**Byrne, James** (1797–?), coachman. Having been the victim of a homosexual rape, Byrne made the mistake of naming his assailant – a man of a superior social class to his own – in a letter to the mayor of Dublin.

In 1822 Percy JOCELYN, bishop of Clogher, was discovered in the back room of a public house in the Haymarket with a soldier named John Moverley. His defence – that he had taken the trooper to be a woman – was not accepted, and he was disgraced. It was only then that it emerged that while bishop of Ferns and Leighlin he had committed the same offence. His accuser on that occasion, James Byrne, had protested not just to the mayor of Dublin but also to the bishop's brother. Byrne was prosecuted for criminal libel. Jocelyn was the only witness for the prosecution, so it was a bishop's word against a coachman's. The bishop was believed. The trial was notable for an unusual argument put forward by Jocelyn's lawyer, the Right Honourable C. Kendal Bushe, Ireland's solicitor general. His claim was that Ireland, being so far from the 'corrupted manners' of the Continent, remained untouched by homosexual practices. 'There is no instance of its memory by any professional man,' declared Kendal Bushe.

When a guilty verdict was announced it was the judge's turn to register astonishment at Byrne's allegations. 'You have thought to asperse a Clergyman of the Established Religion,' thundered Mr Justice Fox:

> ... one elevated by those virtues which are not made known by casual ebullition of a day or years, but by the whole period of a life devoted to the enormous exercise of duty which becomes a man and a Christian.

Regretting that he could not impose a harsher punishment, Fox sentenced Byrne to two years imprisonment and ordered that he be whipped three times through the streets of Dublin. The next day he was tied to a cart and flogged to the Royal Exchange and back – a distance of a mile. Under the threat of a second flogging, Byrne withdrew the allegation.

**Byron, George Gordon, 6th Baron** (1788–1824), poet and philanderer. Famously described as 'mad, bad and dangerous to know' by one of his many mistresses, Lady Caroline Lamb, Byron has the misfortune to be better known for his 'life' than his work. Before dealing with the various scandals that make up the legend, it might therefore be appropriate to allow the Cambridge critic, F.R. Leavis, to 'place' Byron in the great tradition of English poets:

> Byron's incapacity for Augustan satire could only be suggested in long quotations. For success in an Augustan mode there would have to be an easy sureness of diction and tone, a neat precision and poise of movement and gesture, an elegant constancy of point and an even decorum: none of these things can Byron command. Byron speaks as a man of the world and a gentleman, but not only is he not polite, the very essence of his manner is a contemptuous defiance of decorum and propriety. Irreverence about religion is something we cannot imagine in Pope, and when he is ironical about the House of

Hanover, it is with perfect decorum. The impudent, high-spirited recklessness of the Byronic irreverence is alien to Pope's formal urbanity and perfect manners. Between Byron and Pope come Voltaire and Rousseau and the French Revolution, and Byron the satirist has less affinity with Pope than with Burns. The positive to which he appeals is a generous common humanity, something that is indifferent to forms, conventions and classes, though in Byron's recklessness there is something of the aristocrat. His generosity is a cynical man-of-the-world good humour, and the irreverence moves towards the burlesque comedy that, in its high spirits, is sometimes schoolboy.

From *Revaluation* (1936).

Such a critique, greatly extended, would illuminate what is significant in Byron. The rest is mere biography. He was born on 28 January 1788 to a Scottish heiress, Catherine Gordon, and 'Mad Jack' Byron, a notorious rake and gambler. 'Mad Jack' died in France three years later, possibly committing suicide. The boy's childhood was unhappy. He had a deformed right foot, which made him the butt of schoolboy jokes. It has been suggested that his mother's violent changes of mood instilled in him a lifelong mistrust of women. At the age of 9 he had his first sexual experience with a young servant girl, Mary Gray. It was her habit to take a succession of lovers with the boy Byron looking on.

At the age of 10, on the death of his grandfather, he became the 6th baron. For the next four years he attended Harrow School, where he was introduced to homosexuality. His mother meanwhile had started an affair with 23-year-old rake, Lord Grey de Ruthyn, who made advances to Byron when he came home for the holidays. Byron rejected these since his own homosexual inclinations always took as their object men younger than himself.

When he went up to Cambridge University in 1805, he visited prostitutes with such frequency that even his French procuress advised him to slow down. He also fell in love with a choirboy named Edleston. His various excesses during this period caused him to put on weight. This was intolerable to a man of Byron's vanity and he took to playing cricket in half a dozen waistcoats to induce perspiration. At this time he published his first poems, but these were judged to be so poor that he thought for a while of killing himself. Before leaving Cambridge, he acquired his first mistress, a girl named Caroline, whom he dressed in boy's clothes and passed off as a male.

In 1809, Byron set off on a tour of Europe, visiting Greece, Albania, Turkey and Spain with his friend Hobhouse, who was writing a book called *Sodomy Simplified*, which is thought not to have found a publisher. When Hobhouse left him in Greece, Byron took up with a boy named

Nicolo, who was 15. He also spent a great deal of money on prostitutes. (In his life, he was thought to have visited more than 200.)

Byron returned to England in 1812, and in the same year John Murray published *Childe Harold's Pilgrimage*. This dark and romantic poem, describing the exploits of a young man who has tasted every forbidden pleasure in his twenties and thereafter finds life insupportably boring, brought him overnight celebrity. He was adored by young women, while young men imitated his brooding demeanour, his dangerous silences, even his limp. One of the most affected of the women was Lady Caroline Lamb, the beautiful but wilful wife of William Lamb (later Lord Melbourne). (*See* NORTON, GEORGE CHAPPLE.) They became lovers, but Byron's attitude towards her was detached, even ironical, and he in fact preferred her mother-in-law, Lady Melbourne. Byron's indifference caused Lady Caroline to behave in a way which might be described as clumsy. On one occasion she disguised herself as a pageboy and hid in Byron's carriage. When, with the help of Lady Melbourne, he broke off the affair, she burned his image in effigy. Byron repaired to Cambridge, where he began an incestuous affair with his half-sister Augusta. After he had been seduced by the promiscuous Lady Oxford, he and Augusta moved to the family home, Newstead Abbey, where she became pregnant.

By now, Byron's louche behaviour dominated society gossip. Lady Caroline Lamb was still a source of embarrassment, and his affair with Augusta was common knowledge. He decided to silence the gossips by making a suitable marriage. Lady Melbourne's niece, a prim and demure heiress named Annabella Milbanke, accepted him at the second time of asking – rather, it was thought, to his dismay. The marriage was never a success. Byron continued to flirt openly with his half-sister, and he was frequently drunk. Annabella was soon pregnant, which may have added to his feeling of being trapped. Sexual abstention may also have increased his irritability, although gossip had it that he continued to sodomize his wife late into her pregnancy. Exhausted by a difficult birth and by quarrels with her husband, Annabella decided to recuperate at her mother's house. She had probably not intended a permanent separation, but once Sir Ralph and Lady Milbanke knew that she had participated in an act of 'criminal perversion' with a man who was reputed to be his half-sister's lover, nothing would have induced them to allow their daughter to return home.

The collapse of Byron's marriage caused him to become the most vilified man in London. The celebrated poet was suddenly unwelcome in fashionable drawing rooms. Rather than be snubbed, Byron left England for the last time in April 1816. The sale, for £94,500, of Newstead Abbey allowed him to rent a grand palazzo in Venice. There, in the words of his biographer Frederick Raphael, 'he embarked on an orgy to challenge even the Venetian capacity to remain unshocked.' The Palazzo Mocigeno became virtually a brothel. Though still in his early thirties, Byron was growing fat and his hair was fast receding. After one last great affair, with Teresa Guiccioli, a married woman whom he had met at an art exhibition, he decided it was time to leave Italy – a feeling to which Shelley's death by drowning no doubt contributed. He set off for Greece, where, instead of becoming a freedom fighter, as he had intended, he caught a fever and died at the age of 36.

*Lady Caroline Lamb*, written and directed by Robert Bolt, was filmed in 1980. Sarah Miles gave one of her finest screen performances in the title role. The part of Lord Byron was taken by the American actor Richard Chamberlain, formerly Dr Kildare in the television series.

**Bywaters, Frederick.** *See* THOMPSON, EDITH.

# C

**cabaret dancers.** *See* ARTFUL WOMEN, THE SOFTER DECEPTIONS OF; HAMPSON, KEITH (for Luscious Leon, the undercover policeman); LAMBTON, ANTONY CLAUD FREDERICK (for Norma Levy); PENNY GAFFS.

**cabinet ministers dressed as cocktail waitresses.** *See* KEELER, CHRISTINE.

**cactus, landing on a.** *See* PRICE, DILYS.

**Caddy, Eileen** (1918– ) and **Caddy, Peter** (1911–84), hotel managers and New Age evangelists. In 1962 Eileen Caddy's 'inner voice' instructed her to move her family into a caravan. Accordingly, she and her husband Peter, a retired RAF officer, together with their friend Dorothy Maclean, moved with their three young sons to a trailer park on the Scottish Moray coast, a mile from the village of Findhorn. The old caravan site was bought up by the Findhorn Foundation in 1983, and became home to 100 permanent members. By 2001 the Caddy's caravan – preserved like a shrine – had become the 'Vatican of the New Age' and the old trailer park was able to attract 14,000 New Age visitors a year, and scores of 'associated' alternative groups, bringing with them Reiki therapists, psychotherapists, fortune-tellers and faith healers. There were meditation rooms, Japanese peace poles, a meeting hall and an internationally praised human-waste disposal system, chemically flushed.

Eileen Caddy's inner voice had issued its instructions after she and her husband had been sacked as hotel managers in nearby Forres, their dismissal being a consequence of an experience they had had with spaceships. In Peter Caddy's autobiography, *Perfect Time: Memoirs of a Man for the New Millennium* (1993), he describes how in 1961 he and Eileen cut down all the trees behind the Cluny Hill Hotel in Forres without the owner's permission.

On this occasion, it wasn't Eileen's inner voice that had given the orders, but extraterrestrials. In the middle of the Cold War the Caddys had opened up a dialogue with their 'space brothers' to negotiate an evacuation of selected earthlings in the event of a nuclear disaster. The brothers wanted to land their spaceships at Cluny Hill, so the trees had to go. The hotel owner was angry about the loss of his trees and the Caddys were moved to a hotel in the Trossachs, where they lobbied ceaselessly to be moved back to Forres and their 'mission'. They were dismissed for a second time, and Eileen's inner voice told them to make for the caravan park at Findhorn.

It was then that the Caddy's friend Dorothy Maclean began communicating with plants. In the late 1960s Peter Caddy was on Scottish television showing off his vegetables, and giving the credit for their condition not to fertilizer but to Dorothy's conversations with the plant spirits. Soon pilgrims started to arrive, including the film actress Shirley Maclaine. Mike Scott of the rock group The Waterboys also sought spiritual renewal.

Relations have never been good between the Foundation and the village of Findhorn, whose 650 residents are scathing about their neighbours. In the local pub the tendency is to see Foundation members as 'airy fairy'. The publican's wife attended a concert there that she did not enjoy. 'At the end, they asked you to hug the people on either side of you,' she says. 'It's not our way.' Others point disapprovingly at the Foundation's shop, laden with books about UFOs, mystical stone circles, and how the spirit of Diana, princess of Wales can help you find love. Most serious was the scandal in 1999 when one of the Foundation's members, Verity Linn, died of dehydration during a fast on a Scottish mountain while following the teachings of the Australian guru, Jasmuheen. Verity had been following Jasmuheen's teaching that human beings can 'live on light alone'.

Despite the negative energy emanating from the village, the Caddys and Dorothy Maclean are still revered by the community. Dorothy is a regular visitor and Eileen, now aged 83, lives quietly on the site. Peter, who married twice before he met Eileen, and twice thereafter, died in a car crash in 1993.

**Cahill, Martin** (1950–94), notorious Irish gangster, known as 'the General'. In a 22-year career marked by obsessive secrecy, extreme brutality and meticulous planning, Cahill and his gang netted over £40 million in a series of bank robberies, art gallery thefts and household burglaries. When he was executed by the IRA in August 1994, no one was more relieved than the Dublin police, whom Cahill had consistently mocked. During one court appearance on a dangerous driving charge, he had amused his followers by stripping down to his Mickey Mouse boxer shorts and performing a comic dance; on another occasion, he had emerged from the District Court in Dublin wearing a white nightshirt and with a model of a bird's nest strapped to his forehead. Antics such as these fostered the idea that he was a 'loveable rogue' or latter-day Robin Hood, with a hatred of all forms of authority. The reality was different. The only beneficiary of his crimes was Cahill himself, and those who crossed him were treated with great brutality. A suspected traitor within his organization had his hands nailed to a snooker table in a mock crucifixion.

Cahill grew up in the Holyfield slums, some of the worst in Dublin. At the age of 11 he was convicted of housebreaking, and when he was 15 he was sent to St Conleths, a young offenders' institution. The regime was harsh, with a discipline strap in constant use. In 1969 he married Frances Lawless, whom he met while working in Goodbody's making sacks. That was his last known job. In 1973 Cahill carried out a £90,000 robbery at Rathfranham Shopping Centre, and in July 1983 he was the prime suspect in the £2-million robbery of the Thomas O'Connor and Sons jewellery factory in Harold's Cross. With only 25 of the 100-strong staff at work, Cahill's gang hid in a boiler house at the back of the premises. As each employee arrived he or she was locked in a lavatory, and when all had been accounted for the manager, Dan Fitzgibbon, was made to open the strong-room. This was emptied in 30 minutes, and by the time the Gardai were notified the jewellery was in parcels all over Dublin. The company was insured for only £900,000 of its £2-million loss, and it went into receivership four years later.

In February 1988 the General was named on Irish television as the mastermind behind the Beit art robbery of 21 May 1986. The collection had had an unhappy history. It had been established at Russborough House in 1952 by Sir Alfred Beit, a former British MP who had retired to County Wicklow. On 26 April 1974 a gang of four armed men and the heiress Dr Rose Dugdale had stolen 19 paintings from the 100-strong collection. Sir Alfred and his wife had been assaulted and tied up, while a Vermeer, a Goya, two Gainsboroughs and three Rubens had been removed. Rose Dugdale had been sentenced to nine years for her part in the robbery, and after the recovery of the paintings, Sir Alfred had donated the collection to the state under the care of the Alfred Beit Foundation. This time, under Cahill's supervision, the stolen paintings included Vermeer's *Woman Writing a Letter*, which was valued at £5 million, and a Goya portrait.

On the evening of 30 November 1988 Ann Gallagher, the postmistress at Kilmanagh, and her landlady were kidnapped from their home. The next morning one of Cahill's henchmen, who had a radio-controlled bomb strapped to his chest, drove her to Kilmanagh post office and made her withdraw £30,000 in cash and stamps. It was an escapade too far for the Gardai. A 70-strong surveillance unit was set up to harry the General and his gang, who retaliated by digging up the greens at Stacksdown Golf Club, which was used almost exclusively by the Gardai. They also rammed 20 of the Gardai's cars with stolen vehicles, and announced that Detective Superintendent Ned 'the Buffalo' Ryan was to be eliminated. There were other notable confrontations. On one occasion, after the Gardaí had surrounded the General's house, a detective reported:

> He wouldn't let us in; came to the door with a great big butcher's knife. One of our lads shot a dog which he thought was attacking him. Meanwhile a girl with a baby in a pram left and after that Martin came to the door and in we went, peaceful as anything. The lad said he was sorry about the dog but Martin didn't seem to mind and said it was no fucking good anyway. Of course the girl should have been stopped.

On Thursday 19 August 1994 Cahill was shot dead in his Renault 5 by two men, one on a motorcycle, the other posing as a council worker who appeared to be checking registration numbers. A man using a recognized IRA code word later told a Dublin radio station that the General 'had been executed because of his involvement with, and assistance to, pro-British death squads'.

*The General*, a film written and directed by John Boorman, was criticized on its release in 1998 for glamorizing Cahill's exploits. 'He was a remarkable man,' claimed Boorman, 'very clever, very cunning. In an earlier incarnation he would have been a leading mafioso. He felt he owed nothing to society. And he did it all with a great deal of wit.' The *Republican News* took a different view:

> Cahill was no hero. He was an oppressor of people of his own class whom he used and abused and brutalized in order to fulfil his own selfish ambitions. His motive was pure, unadulterated greed.

Boorman was sharply rebuked by James Donovan, a forensic scientist, for calling Cahill a 'Celtic chieftain' because of his hatred of authority. 'The mythical Celtic stuff is nonsense. Boorman is in some Celtic twilight of his own,' said Donovan, who testified against Cahill several times and suffered severe injuries in a car bomb blast when he was scheduled to present evidence linking Cahill to an armed robbery in a 1982 trial. He continued:

> Nobody is denying that Cahill committed crime, yet there is an attempt to excuse it, as if it were fun. People say Cahill was humorous, but my experience of his humour was his laughter when the bomb went off in my car.

At the time Donovan faced the prospect of losing his left leg because of poorly healed wounds, and he had developed cataracts from shards of metal that blew into his eyes.

## Cairngorms, Abominable Snowmen living in the. *See* RANKIN, SIR HUGH.

**Calico Jack.** *See* BONNY, ANNE.

**Calvey, Linda** (1948– ), armed robber. Calvey earned the sobriquet 'the Black Widow' after her husband, Mickey Calvey, was killed by a police marksman while robbing Caters supermarket in Eltham, southeast London. She later claimed that she was the original on which one of the characters in the popular ITV series, *Widows* (1991), had been based.

In 1979 Calvey became romantically involved with another armed robber, Ronnie Cook. When he was jailed for 15 years in 1982 after a raid in which £1 million was stolen from a security van in Dulwich, she swore she would wait for him, and, as a mark of her good intentions, had 'True Love Ron Cook' tattooed on her leg. In the event she soon took up with Cook's friend Brian Thorogood. Thorogood left his wife and bought a house in Harold Wood, Essex, into which he and Calvey moved. The proceeds of the Dulwich robbery kept them in some style (on a trip to Las Vegas, they spent £30,000 of Cook's money in one week), but in 1986 Thorogood was jailed for 18 years for robbing a post office. Calvey served 3 years of a 5-year sentence for conspiracy.

In 1990 Cook was due for release. Expecting violent retribution from that quarter when he discovered that Calvey had been spending his money, she put out a £10,000 contract on his life. This was accepted by Daniel Reece, a convicted rapist, who needed the money and was, in any case, under Calvey's spell. In theory Cook, who was on day release, had a cleaning job outside the prison, but he preferred to spend his time more pleasantly in Calvey's company. On 19 January 1990 she picked him up outside Maidstone prison and drove him to London, while Reece, whom she had already collected from another prison from which, like Cook, he was on day release, waited outside her flat. Cook brought in the milk and when he took it into the kitchen, Reece shot him in the elbow. Reece later told the police that he could not bring himself to commit murder. Calvey, who had no such qualms, grabbed the gun, ordered Cook to kneel and then shot him in the back of the head. Reece took a train back to Bristol to continue a 13-year sentence for rape, buggery and false imprisonment.

At first the police accepted Calvey's story that an unknown gunman had burst in and shot Cook while she cowered in a corner. They then discovered that Reece was her lover and that he had been with her over the weekend. They interviewed Reece, who confessed immediately. In court Calvey insisted that Reece's version of events was a fabrication. 'Ron meant everything to me,' she claimed. The jury was unimpressed, and she and Reece both received life sentences for murder.

**Camb, James** (1915–81), ship's steward and alleged murderer. When in 1948 Camb, a steward on board the liner *Durban Castle*, pushed a passenger through a porthole, he was under the impression that in the absence of a body he was unlikely to be convicted of any crime related to it. The victim was Gay Gibson, a cabaret dancer described in reports as 'neurotic', though no evidence of this was offered other than that she had a high sex drive and that her real name was Eileen.

Up to a point, there was no dispute over the sequence of events leading to Miss Gibson's disappearance. Camb admitted at his trial that he had entered her cabin, No 126, and that he had made love to her – by force, according to the prosecution; with her consent, according to Camb. She had then had a fit and choked to death, said Camb. He had strangled her and bundled her through the porthole, alleged the prosecution.

Camb, who made a poor showing in the witness box, was sentenced to death, but was then reprieved because the abolition of the death penalty was being debated in Parliament. There was a feeling, too, that his conviction had not been safe, and he was released in 1959. His supporters took Miss Gibson's known promiscuity as evidence of his innocence, on the grounds that highly sexed women can expect to be pushed through portholes. Whatever the rights and wrongs of the verdict, the case is of interest since it has been used to point up the dangers of capital punishment by those who object to the practice merely because an innocent person might be hanged. The argument is that, while hanging the guilty is unobjectionable, Camb might have been executed for something he hadn't done. Twelve years for something he hadn't done was a satisfactory outcome.

**canary that fell from its perch, the.** *See* O'MAHONEY, MAURICE.

***Canetti et Moi*** (by Rachel Garley). *See* STRACHEY, WILLIAM.

**Cannibals, King of the.** *See* DE ROUGEMONT, LOUIS.

**cannibals and cannibalism.** *See* BEAN, SAWNEY; CARSTAIRS, MARION BARBARA; GUERIN, EDDIE; KINGSBOROUGH, EDWARD KING, 4TH VISCOUNT; KINGSLEY, MARY; LABOUCHERE, HENRY; PSALMANAZAR, GEORGE.

**capital punishment.** *Homo sapiens* is the only animal to experience a desire for revenge. This is frequently exercised at the expense of self-interest. Sometimes it can only be satisfied by killing another person, and with a high sense of self-righteousness – as it is in acts of capital punishment. The source of this emotion remains a mystery, since it has no survival value in evolutionary terms. Some have argued that it is a gift of God – one of the many from that source that lift man above the animal kingdom. A short history of capital punishment in Britain:

**1671**. The Coventry Act made it a capital offence to lie in wait with intent to disfigure someone's nose.

**1699**. The Shoplifting Act made it a capital crime to steal from a shop goods valued at more than 5s. In 1722, James Appleton was hanged at Tyburn Tree for the theft of three wigs. In 1750, Benjamin Beckonfield was hanged for stealing a hat.

**1723**. The Waltham Blacks Act was passed to combat the increasing amount of poaching and damage to forests and parks owned by the nobility. The act increased the number of capital crimes from approximately 30 to 150.

**1782**. A 14-year-old girl was hanged for being found in the company of Gypsies.

**1810**. There were by now 222 capital crimes. These included rape, sodomy, burglary, horse stealing, forgery, adopting a disguise and stealing.

**1816**. Four boys aged between 9 and 13 were hanged in London for begging.

**1835**. Sacrilege, letter stealing and returning from transportation before finishing a sentence ceased to be capital crimes.

**1861**. The Criminal Law Consolidation Act reduced the number of capital crimes to four: treason, piracy, mutiny and murder.

**1868**. The Capital Punishment Within Prisons Act put an end to public execution. On 26 May Michael Barrett was the last man to be publicly hanged.

**1875**. The hangman William Marwood introduced the 'long drop'.

**1908**. People under 16 could no longer be executed.

**1931**. Pregnant women could no longer be hanged.

**1948**. Suspension of capital punishment for experimental period of five years approved by the House of Commons, but this was reversed by the House of Lords.

**13 July 1955**. Ruth ELLIS was the last woman to be hanged in Britain.

**March 1957**. The Homicide Act limited capital murder to five categories: murder in the course or furtherance of a theft; by shooting or causing an explosion; while resisting arrest; murder of a policeman or a prison officer; two murders committed on different occasions.

**13 August 1964**. Last British hangings: Peter Anthony ALLEN and his accomplice Gwynne Owen Evans for murder in the course of a theft.

**9 November 1965**. The Abolition of the Death Penalty Bill Act suspended capital punishment for murder for a trial period of five years.

**December 1969**. Parliament confirmed the abolition of capital punishment for murder.

**Captain Calamity.** *See* HILL, STUART.

**Captain Whip'em.** *See* PRIDDEN, SARAH.

**Caraboo, Princess.** *See* BAKER, MARY.

**Cardigan, James Thomas Brudenell, 7th earl of** (1797–1868), soldier, politician and duellist. Had an action for CRIMINAL CONVERSATION, brought against him in 1843, succeeded, Cardigan, who had an uncertain temper, might not have been in a position to lead the ill-fated charge of the Light Brigade at Balaclava in October 1854.

The action arose from Cardigan's affair with Lady Frances Paget, the wife of Lord William Paget, second son of the marquess of Anglesey. Paget was reputed to be unfaithful as well as brutal. He was obsessively jealous and in the habit of having Lady Paget watched. One day, when Cardigan called on Lady Frances at her town house in Berkeley Square, Paget's butler, Winter, was concealed under the sofa in the drawing room, on the instructions of his employer, while Cardigan and Lady Frances were in the bedroom. Later that day a quarrel broke out between Lord Paget and his wife, and she was subsequently seen with a black eye.

Challenged to a duel, Cardigan informed Lord Paget that he would be unable to accommodate him. His reason was that he had already fought a duel and, for that offence, had been fortunate to escape transportation. His opponent on that occasion, Captain Harvey Tuckett, had been seriously wounded. In October 1840 a grand jury at the Old Bailey had found a true bill of intent to murder, maim and cause grievous bodily harm to Captain Tuckett on Wimbledon Common. Quite fortuitously the indictment omitted any mention of wounding, which took away the risk of deportation. Further, Tuckett refused to give evidence. Sir William Follett, appearing for Cardigan, told the court that 'the prosecution is bound to prove the Christian and surnames of the person against whom the offence is alleged; if it fails in either, it fails in proof.' Because Tuckett was absent, there was no legal proof that Cardigan had wounded him on Wimbledon Common. Cardigan was found not guilty, but another duel was something he dared not risk.

It was against this background that Lord Paget brought an action for criminal conversation at the Guildhall in December 1843. The public had expectations of a long and enjoyable trial, but their hopes were quickly dashed. On this occasion, it was Paget's man, Winter, who failed to appear, and the action failed with him. The public had to be content with the continuation of the dispute in the correspondence columns of *The Times*, in the course of which Lord Paget accused Cardigan of 'the infamous crime of having bought and sent away the principle witness against him'. Cardigan angrily denied this, but it was generally supposed that that was what he had done.

Cardigan's descendant, David Brudenell-Bruce, the 11th earl, appears to have inherited his forebear's disputatious nature, and a preference, once the law has been invoked, for not appearing in court. In June 2001 he became embroiled in an argument with a neighbour, William Smith, over the use of a track through Savernake Forest in Wiltshire, part of Lord Cardigan's 4000-acre estate. Mr Justice Pumfrey clearly found the matter trivial. 'I don't want the High Court to be used as a staging post for some future dispute between these two parties,' he said. 'I am unhappy that this is just one broadside in a continuing naval engagement which will stretch on till the crack of doom.' He was even unhappier when the earl failed to appear in court. 'This is the second time there has been a no-show,' said Mr Justice Pumfrey. 'I expect to sit tomorrow in the settled expectation that the witness will be here. If the witness is not here, he will have to have a blindingly good explanation, backed up to the hilt.' Two weeks after the matter was settled, Lord Cardigan was injured in an altercation with another neighbour, who tried to drive into the forest. Lord Cardigan blocked the road and the neighbour drove straight into him, knocking him down. Since 1996 the 11th earl has twice been fined for firearms offences.

**card sharps.** *See* CHARTERIS, COLONEL FRANCIS.

**Carleton, Mary** (*c.*1625–63), actress, playwright, impostor and confidence trickster. It is unusual for criminals to exploit their celebrity status until after they have retired, but Mary Carleton risked detection by dramatizing her offences publicly while still committing them.

Married to a Canterbury shoemaker, and the mother of two children, Mary grew dissatisfied with her humdrum domestic existence and took off one day to Dover. Here she discovered in herself a gift for extracting cash from men who, in the words of Captain Johnson's *Lives of the Highwaymen*, 'have more money in their pockets than wit in their heads'. Her first victim was a rich surgeon whom she shortly married. Faced with a bigamy charge she left for Germany, where she took an older lover – later leaving him at the altar and departing with the money and jewels he had lavished upon her. Having assumed the identity of a German princess, she returned to England in 1663. Visiting an inn in Billingsgate she told such a sad story that all the men present gave her their money. They then departed, promising that they would shortly return with some more.

The innkeeper, Mr King, was so taken with Mary that he introduced her to his brother-in-law, John Carleton. Offended, at first, that a commoner would presume to court a princess, she relented at last and agreed to marry him. The union was short-lived. She was informed on to the authorities and was once again charged with bigamy. On this occasion she escaped prosecution by running away and joining a theatrical group. With them she appeared successfully in *The German Princess*, a play written by herself. This, remarkably, was a boastful account of her own exploits to date – an act of audacity that greatly increased her notoriety. Far from deterring admirers – and potential victims – it seemed to sharpen their interest. Two young suitors 'for want of that commodity in themselves were particularly beguiled by her wit and humour'. Mary encouraged them both, even to the bedroom door, at which point she relieved them of £300 each and then departed. She was astonished at their impudence, she said, that they had supposed they might make love to a princess.

Now in funds, and using her title of 'princess', Mary called on a French weaver in Spitalfields, from whom she bought silks to the value of £40, thereafter persuading him to carry the goods to her house, where he would receive his money. Here, with 'all the ceremony natural to a Frenchman', he sat down to write out his account, while she took the silk into another room to 'show it to her niece'. Thanks to a bottle of wine, with which the Frenchman had been provided, an hour passed pleasantly enough. Then, growing uneasy, he went in search of his customer, only to be told by another woman in the house that 'the princess' had been a lodger there and had now departed with her belongings.

Mary then took lodgings with a master tailor, whom she employed to make dresses with the silk stolen from the Frenchman. Having been told that she would be holding a party in the near future, the tailor employed several journeymen to ensure that the dresses would be ready in time. The day arrived, the guests, many of whom were the tailor's friends and assistants, appeared, and much wine was consumed. The tailor's glass was replenished so frequently that his wife was shortly obliged to help him to his bed. Mary then departed, taking with her silver tankards, cutlery, money, jewellery and the fine clothes that her guests, in the pursuit of pleasure, had strewn around the house.

While carrying out these, and similar, robberies, Mary continued to write and appear in dramatic entertainments, based on her exploits. Celebrity – however earned – seemed to be an end in itself, as it is today. Inevitably, she was recognized by a thief-taker and brought before the Old Bailey to face the original bigamy charge. Found guilty, she was hanged at Tyburn, confessing on the scaffold that she had been 'a very vain woman and hoped that her fate would deter others from the same evil ways'.

**Carlton, Sydney** (1949– ), painter and decorator. Those who argue that bestiality should be treated with understanding had a setback in 1998 when Carlton, a married man from Bradford, was sentenced to a year in prison for having intercourse with a Staffordshire bull terrier, named Badger. His defence was that Badger had made the first move. 'I can't help it if the dog took a liking to me,' he told the court. This was not accepted.

**Carrington, Charles** (1851–1921), bookseller, publisher and pornographer. Carrington, who had worked as a lavatory attendant and van driver before entering the book trade, became the most celebrated publisher of English-language pornography in France between 1890 and 1914. The fugitive trade flourished in Paris until a more liberated view prevailed in England through the Obscene Publication Act of 1959.

Preferring to operate beyond the reach of Scotland Yard and the Vice Society, Carrington found premises in the rue du Faubourg-Montmartre, a narrow commercial street off the boulevards of central Paris. His list was a curious mix of learned tomes, such as Forberg's *Manual of Classical Erotology* (1899), and exotic pornographic fiction. *Dolly Morton* (1899) mingled sex and sadism in the hot-house climate of America's Deep South. *Woman and Her Master* (1904) was a steamy account of well-bred Englishwomen held captive in the Mahdi's harem after the fall of Khartoum. *Raped on the Railway: A True Story of a Virtuous Lady Ravished and Chastised on the Scotch Express* (1894) caused some offence to readers north of the border. They complained that it made the pride of the North Western Railway sound like a whisky dray.

Chief Inspector Drew of Scotland Yard also took offence. 'During the past 14 years,' he told the Parliamentary Committee on Indecent Advertisements:

> Carrington has been a source of considerable embarrassment to the police in this country by the persistent manner in which he has been carrying on his business through the post in the shape of catalogues of a very obscene and disgusting nature.

To Inspector Drew's continuing disappointment, the books were being smuggled into England and 'gentlemen who should know better' were having them delivered to their clubs. Carrington's plain-cover novels, often masquerading as 'Social Studies of the Century' or as private publications issued by 'the Society of Bibliophiles', easily passed the scrutiny of Customs and Excise officers.

Among the books that got through safely was *Flossie: A Venus of Fifteen* (1900), said to be the work of Algernon Charles Swinburne's old age. Though Swinburne corresponded with Carrington, and privately wrote schoolboy flagellation epics, scholars find little in the novel that reflects his work. Another enduring Carrington favourite was *Two Flappers in Paris*

(1903), a story about a finishing school in which the pupils try out a variety of French vices under the tutelage of 'Uncle Jack'. Among Carrington's curiosities, the first part of 'Walter's' anonymous diary, *My Secret Life,* was published in 1901 as *The Dawn of Sensuality* (*see* ASHBEE, HENRY SPENCER). Carrington also became Oscar Wilde's publisher after the playwright's conviction in 1895.

Carrington's career ended with the outbreak of World War I, but his books continued to be enjoyed by the British Expeditionary Force on the Western Front. Sir Maurice Bowra, later warden of Wadham College, Oxford, recalls in his memoirs that when the German bombardment was at its height his commanding officer would read to his men from Carrington's edition of Edward SELLON'S (*The New Lady's Tickler: The Adventures of Lady Lovesport and Audacious Harry*). Sir Maurice Bowra's reputation among metropolitan *literateurs* was bracingly demolished by the distinguished Cambridge critic, F.R. Leavis, in his paper *The Progress of Poesy,* collected in *The Common Pursuit,* (1953): 'The Warden of Wadham', wrote Dr Leavis, 'has just applied his classical scholar's ripeness and percipience to an extended appreciation of the poetry of Edith Sitwell.'

**Carstairs, Marion Barbara** (1900–94), powerboat racer and traveller. The daughter of a Scottish army officer and an American heiress, 'Joe' Carstairs led an eventful life. In 1916 she claimed to be 20 and drove ambulances for the Women's Legion in France. In 1921 her mother died, leaving her $4 million on condition that she took a husband. Accordingly she married Count Jacques de Pret, and left him as soon as the service was over. She had other male admirers, though an Italian acrobat's advances stemmed from hopes of an on-stage partnership. Such broad shoulders were greatly valued in professional tumbling circles.

In 1924 Marion Carstairs became the fastest woman in the world on water in a speedboat designed by herself. With three friends – Molly, Betty and Bardie Colclough – she later ran a Daimler car hire company from Cornwall Gardens, London. Among her clients was the shah of Persia, whom she drove round Europe. In the 1930s she travelled more widely, dressed, as usual, in Savile Row suits and walking shoes from Lobb's in St James's. She took a large party to the Cocos Islands on a treasure hunt, shot big game in India, fished for tunny off the coast of Africa, and, in spite of the language problem and incompatible value systems, established good relations with a tribe of pygmy cannibals in New Guinea. She settled eventually in the Caribbean, where she bought Whale Island for £8000. Here she built 26 miles of sign-posted roads, a mansion for herself, a lighthouse, some kennels and a church. These improvements cost a further £180,000.

Disappointed that the 500 islanders showed little respect for conventional standards, she made it a rule that only couples who married in church, and lived respectably in the small houses she provided, could stay.

She banned alcohol and voodoo practices, and told residents to eat more vegetables. She dotted the island with admonitory notices, one of which read, 'If brown rice is good enough for me, it's good enough for you. M.B. Carstairs'. Outsiders were unwelcome. Four guards with sawn-off shotguns were stationed round the island with instructions to shoot unauthorized visitors.

During World War II Carstairs built a deep-water harbour for the use of the Royal Navy. In 1951 she moved to Florida, from where she made occasional trips to New York, equipped with a revolver.

**Cartland, Barbara** (1901–2000), novelist and nutritionist. In 1933 Barbara Cartland wrote:

> The real woman should be completely feminine. She should have no desire to take up a career or flaunt herself in public. Women should stick to managing their men.

Few people's lives have so remarkably contradicted their expressed principles. After a slow start, Miss Cartland pursued money and fame with ineffable purpose. Before 1963, when she became a widow, her output had been a modest 100 titles in 40 years. During the next 37 years she produced six times as many. By dictating at the rate of 3000 words an hour, and fuelled by 29 varieties of vitamin pills, she could finish a book in two weeks. In all, she sold 1 billion books worldwide.

Credit for this accomplishment is due to Lord Beaverbrook. 'One of his tips was never to be boring,' Miss Cartland said. 'And so I reduced all the paragraphs in my novels to three lines. If they were longer, the reader skipped them.'

Miss Cartland could be a formidable opponent. Asked by an interviewer on BBC Radio 4 whether social barriers had been greatly reduced during her lifetime, she replied, 'Of course. Why else would I be talking to you?' Richard Ingrams, who published her in *The Oldie*, and General Gadafi were both admirers of her work.

**castaways.** *See* KINGSLAND, GERALD.

**Cast-Iron Pol** (*c*.1830–?), legendary coster girl who had been hit on the head by an iron cooking pot and had suffered no apparent damage.

**cat burglars.** *See* CHATHAM, GEORGE; EDGAR, HENRY; HOLLIDAY, BERT; PEACE, CHARLES; SCOTT, PETER.

**catching a Tartar by his mustachios.** *See* TRELAWNY, EDWARD.

**Cato Street Conspiracy, the.** A plot in 1820 to assassinate the entire

British cabinet and to seize power. Lord Castlereagh, the widely hated foreign secretary, was to have been decapitated.

*See also* THISTLEWOOD, ARTHUR.

**cats, talking.** *See* WENHAM, JANE.

**cavalrywomen.** *See* STANLEY, SARAH.

**cave-dwellers.** *See* BEAN, SAWNEY; BIGG, JOHN; SLATER, JOHN.

**Cavewomen, the.** *See* HUNTER-COWAN, MAJOR BETTY.

**Cecil, Lord Hugh** (1869–1956), peer, politician and provost of Eton College. The fifth son of the 3rd marquess of Salisbury, Lord Hugh held unconventional views that he adhered to vigorously throughout his life. One of the less idiosyncratic was that gentlemen didn't grow beards. Algernon Cecil, a cousin, was asked why he was wearing one. 'Our Lord wore a beard,' Algernon reminded him. 'Our Lord wasn't a gentleman,' replied Lord Hugh. As MP for Greenwich between 1895 and 1906, his only interest was implacable opposition to an attempt to repeal the Deceased Wife's Sister Bill. A canon of 1604 had made it illegal for a man to marry the sister of his dead wife. For many years Lord Hugh frustrated all attempts to effect a reform, denouncing any such marriage in the strongest terms. 'It is an act of sexual vice as immoral as concubinage,' he informed the House. When he discovered that his brother Robert's next-door neighbour in the Weald of Sussex had married his deceased wife's sister, he persuaded Robert to ostracize him. The neighbour took his revenge by planting a line of trees along the boundaries of his country estate, thus cutting off the Cecils' view of the South Downs.

Believing that Sussex was infested with poisonous snakes, Lord Hugh advised residents 'not to sit in the garden unless on a very high chair. I have been told that snakes find the sound of the human voice disagreeable, so you must talk loudly all the time – reciting poetry, perhaps.'

In 1936 Lord Hugh became provost of Eton College. This appointment afforded him many opportunities to practise his lifelong contempt for schoolmasters. During World War II, the headmaster, Elliott, was concerned to protect the boys from aerial bombardment. Cecil took a different view. He had already written to *The Times* denouncing the building of air-raid shelters as smacking of hysteria ('Would it matter a jot if a theatre full of people were bombed?'), and he now opposed a move by Elliott to take similar precautions at the school. 'May I remind you,' he wrote to Elliott, 'that under the statutes of the school the headmaster is responsible only for the studies and disciplines of the school – from which a right to protect the boys from bombs cannot be inferred.' Elliott disagreed. 'How can I possibly teach or discipline the boys if they are dead?' he replied.

The matter was settled by Eton's governing body, who voted for shelters. From then on, provost and headmaster were scarcely on speaking terms. Asked later what he would do if a bomb did drop on the school, Cecil said he would ring for his butler, Tucker. In December 1940 the headmaster's house was hit by a bomb, but it didn't explode. Cecil did indeed ring for Tucker, who handed him a battered old hat which would be no great casualty were it to get dirty. 'No no, Tucker,' said Cecil. 'Me best 'at to see the ruins.' Arrived at the headmaster's house, he poked the bomb with his umbrella, shouting, 'It's a dud! It's a dud!' The bomb then exploded – an incident referred to in a letter to Cecil from Winston Churchill:

> It will be good to have you in the House of Lords, to sustain aristocratic morale, and to chide the bishops when they err, and now that I read in the newspapers that the Eton flogging-block is destroyed by enemy action, you may have more leisure and strength.

Correctly pronounced, Cecil rhymes with 'whistle'.

**Cecil, Lord William** (1867–1936), priest. The second son of the 3rd marquess of Salisbury, and brother of Lord Hugh CECIL, Lord William sat in the House of Lords for 20 years as the bishop of Exeter. Called 'Fish' by the family, he married Lady Florence Bootle-Wilbraham, known as 'Fluffy'.

Fluffy was the more socially adept. In company, Lord William usually remained silent, leaving it to Fluffy to keep the conversation going. Sometimes he would fall into a deep sleep. On one occasion, when making a courtesy call on important new arrivals in the see, Fluffy decided that the visit had gone on for long enough. 'Well,' she said to their hostess, 'we must be going now. We only dropped in to say "How do you do?"' The bishop, waking with a start, heard only the last few words. He jumped up and held out his hand. 'How do you do?' he said. Following his wife to the front door, and thinking they'd just arrived, he wiped his feet on the mat, returned to the drawing room, sat down and once again fell asleep.

On trips abroad with his seven children, Lord William's behaviour changed and he liked to take the lead. At home he would have nothing to do with money. Abroad, he wore a money belt to confound pickpockets, but he usually put this on upside down, thereby losing the family's travelling expenses and return tickets. On his many trips to the south of France, often by bicycle, he wore yellow glasses, a broad-brimmed hat and a brown silk suit. Believing that the colour red was a protective against the sun, he dressed the girls in red dresses and the boys in red shirts. When they got home, Fluffy always checked the bishop's suitcase to ensure that he'd remembered to pack his pyjamas, and not the hotel's towels and sheets.

When Lord William became bishop of Exeter he declined to live in the palace, preferring to travel in by bicycle from a small house outside the city. The bicycle was painted orange so that he could recognize it when parked among others. Even so, he often made mistakes. On one occasion he realized when he was halfway home that he was on someone else's bicycle – a woman's machine, painted black. He pedalled back to Exeter, apologized to its anxious owner and, raising his hat, climbed on to the same bicycle and pedalled away.

An enduring interest was the invention of scientific improvements to the home. Lord William was particularly proud of a new central heating system that involved naked electric light bulbs wrapped in a hockey mask. This was plugged into the mains and placed under armchairs. When his nephew, the literary historian Lord David Cecil, pointed out that this wasn't very safe, the bishop replied, 'My dear boy, when one is putting in a heating system, safety must go to the wall.'

**celebrity villains.** *See* BINDON, JOHN; BOYLE, JIMMY; BRONSON, CHARLES; CARLETON, MARY; FRASER, FRANCIS ('MAD FRANKIE'); FOREMAN, FREDDIE; KNIGHT, RONNIE; REYNOLDS, BRUCE.

**'Celestial Bed' as a specific against impotence.** *See* GRAHAM, JAMES.

**Challenor, Detective Sergeant Harold** (1925– ), policeman. In June 1964 Detective Sergeant Challenor, known as 'Tanky', was tried at the Old Bailey for conspiracy to pervert the course of justice. Three colleagues were jailed for a total of eleven years on the same charge, but Challenor was found unfit to plead. The distinguished psychiatrist, William Sergent, for the defence, said he was 'as mad as a March hare'. Others took a less lenient view. For some time, pretending to be mad in court was known as 'doing a Challenor'.

Insane or not, Challenor was a resourceful man. He had served in the Special Air Services during World War II, and, before being moved to West End Central, had played an active role in the Flying Squad. His policing methods were always unorthodox. Once he persuaded a small-time thief to take him to a criminals' pub in Soho so that other crooks could be pointed out to him. Since the man was reluctant to be seen drinking with a known policeman, Challenor wore a woman's wig and borrowed an evening frock, nylon stockings, high-heel shoes and a handbag from his wife, Doris. Dressed like this, and heavily made up, he sat nursing a gin and tonic while his informer identified the villains present. All went well until he almost blew his cover by visiting the gentlemen's lavatory by mistake. 'I have recently had a miscarriage,' Challenor explained to its occupants, 'and still feel a little light-headed.' Later, he was propositioned by one of the men from the lavatory, but was rescued by his companion who maintained the deception by calling him 'a silly old cow'.

Challenor's behaviour became increasingly erratic. On 23 July 1963 there was a demonstration outside Claridges hotel against Queen Frederika of Greece, who was seen as symbolic of her country's right-wing regime. Enraged by what he saw as anti-royalist activities, Challenor gave some of the demonstrators a slapping and planted bricks on others with the words, 'That will be two years, me old darling, for carrying an offensive weapon.' Donald Rooum, one of the men arrested, was a member of the National Council For Civil Liberties and was able to prove that since there was no brick dust in his pocket he could not have been carrying a brick. Rooum was cleared, and Challenor was suspended. Later he announced, somewhat obscurely, 'The whores danced outside the Old Bailey when Oscar Wilde was jailed, glad to see a menace to their profession locked away.'

**champagne and cockroaches.** *See* LANGAN, PETER.

**champagne in exchange for taking off one's clothes.** *See* LANGAN, PETER.

**'champagne kiss of love'.** *See* BUCK, BIENVENIDA.

**Champion, Sir Claude** (1847–1935), soldier, sportsman and adventurer. Sir Claude believed that the best indication of a man's character was a willingness to participate in a fair fist fight. His obituary in *The Times* noted that 'as a man of honour, he regretted the passing of the duel as the proper means of obtaining satisfaction'. Men who applied to work at his home, Champion Lodge, had first to box with their future employer. Only those who put up a good fight were taken on. If he came across a tramp, Sir Claude would invite him to box for a meal. His friends once dressed a professional boxer in rags and stationed him in Sir Claude's path. The usual challenge was given and accepted, and Sir Claude took a severe beating. He greatly enjoyed the joke, and continued to issue his challenges.

'Where there is a daring deed to be done in any part of the world,' declared Sir Claude, 'an Englishman should be there to accomplish it.' Though he enjoyed a long and adventurous career, many of his initiatives were thwarted by the caution of others. Henri Blondin, the French equilibrist, who crossed Niagara Falls on a tightrope, refused to let Sir Claude take his turn on the high wire. On a trip to Havana he was hauled out of a bullring before he could sustain serious injuries – not from a bull but from other spectators. Aficionados of the *corrida* had become impatient with Sir Claude's failure to grasp its rules. Having confused the present spectacle with Wild West rodeos, Sir Claude tied a rope round the bull's testicles (an ordeal suffered by rodeo bulls in order to make them buck and rear) and rode it round the ring while he tugged on the rope. In 1888 he made his way to Egypt where there was a Dervish uprising, but in spite of his claim that he was war correspondent for the *Sporting Times* he was refused permission to go to the front. He tried to get over this disappointment by volunteering, at the age of 52, for the second Boer War.

Following family tradition, Sir Claude pursued a military career. He joined the navy at 13, but five years later transferred to the King's Royal Rifle Corps. He was stationed in Ireland, where he took up steeplechasing and earned the nickname 'the Mad Rider'. Although he had broken 14 bones before middle age, he continued to accept challenges better undertaken by the young and fit. At 42 he became the first Englishman to swim the Nile rapids. When he was 61 he walked the 45 miles from Champion Lodge in Essex to London to win a bet of 2s 6d. He participated, erratically, in steeplechases until he was 67. In 1920, at the age of 73, he challenged his cousin to a duel and was greatly disappointed when the offer was rejected.

Sir Claude taught his two sons to swim by throwing them overboard while sailing on Blackwater. They survived this and other lessons, and grew up to become distinguished soldiers and accomplished sportsmen.

**Chaney, Sid** (1919– ), bus-pass bandit. At the age of 75 Sid conceived a grudge against financial institutions of all kinds, and thereafter devoted his energies to defrauding banks, building societies and credit-card companies. In 1994 he acted the old fool in Barclays Bank, Camden Town. He had £25,000, he said, but he kept forgetting where he'd put it. The bank eagerly accepted him as a customer and he opened an account in the name of his ferret, Sir Andrew Large. He then visited the National Westminster Bank, City Branch, London N1, where he opened an account in the name of his cat, Mr Sniffles. Having been furnished with all the necessary credit cards, Sir Andrew Large and Mr Sniffles ran up debts of £117,000 in six months.

Chaney's *modus operandi* meant he could never stay long in one place. 'Once I get naughty at one address I have to move on,' he explained in a television documentary, *Bus Pass Bandits*, in April 2001. Relocation seldom presented a difficulty. One method was to throw a brick through his own window, thereafter telling the council that the neighbourhood was becoming too dangerous for a man of his age. As a rule, the council hastened to relocate him. On another occasion, when established on the 13th floor of a block in Essex, and having 'got naughty' with a new account opened in the name of his budgerigar, Captain Mainwaring, he told the council that he liked to stand on his balcony, gaze down on the lights of Basildon and imagine he could fly. 'They thought, "silly old fool, we'd better move him on."'

As a rule, institutions defrauded by Sid decided not to prosecute, but in July 2000 American Express sued him for £11,500. The court ruled that he should discharge this debt by paying £1 a week for 230 years. Sid remained cheerful despite this burden. In April 2001 he visited Las Vegas, courtesy of Barclaycard, where, as secretary of the Jeanette Macdonald Fan Club, United Kingdom Branch, he was delighted to meet the secretary of the American branch.

**Chant, Laura Ormiston** (1847–1923), ordinary mother, member of the general public and moral watchdog. In 1894, Mrs Chant (*née* Dibben) tried to bring about the closure of the Empire Theatre, Leicester Square. Its productions of drama and grand opera had not generated the profits expected by its shareholders and to drum up customers the management had resorted to acrobats and dancing girls. What particularly concerned Mrs Chant, however, was what went on at the back of the dress circle, which, she believed, amounted to little short of open prostitution. Middlesex County Council, alerted by Mrs Chant, informed the Empire that unless appropriate steps were taken she would raise an objection at the next meeting of the licensing committee.

There are grounds for supposing that Mrs Chant had a point. Young men, including Winston Churchill, were advised not to visit the Empire. Churchill received a letter from his former nanny, Anne Everest, in which she wrote:

> I hope you will be kept from all evil and bad companions & not go to the Empire & not stay out at night, it's too awful to think of, it can only lead to wickedness and everything bad.

Churchill didn't heed her words, nor did the Empire heed Mrs Chant, who duly lodged her objection at the next council meeting. She gave evidence that 'dressed in my prettiest frock, I myself was accosted by men behind the Empire's circle'. The stage show had also given great offence. Two Americans had been outraged, said Mrs Chant, by the vulgar coster songs of Albert Chevalier, and a Frenchman had not cared for a cross-talk skit in which a low comedian, playing a shopwalker, had said to the ingénue, 'I want to see your underwear.' '*C'est trop fort!*' the Frenchman had protested to his companion, and both had left. Mr Edwards, the Empire's manager, told the Licensing Committee that the scripts had been carefully vetted and that this line must have been overlooked.

Mrs Chant was supported in her campaign by the Central Prayer Meeting Branch of the YMCA, but she had equally formidable opponents. The London Cab Drivers Union supported the Empire, as did the Reverend Stewart Headlam, who later stood bail for Oscar Wilde. Mrs Helen Matthews, the novelist, suggested that 'Nature, by establishing a considerable excess of women over men, seems to say that men should have special privileges' – for which she was called a harlot by the campaigning journalist, W.T. Stead.

Edwards, the Empire's manager, made the sensible point that prostitutes would be driven on to the streets if the theatre were closed, and Victoria Clafin, the editor of *The Humanitarian*, kept interest going with a column asking whether 'the same standard of morality should be required from men as from women'.

By a majority of 43, the Middlesex County Council refused to renew the Empire's license. With a chorus of 'Rule Britannia' and a *tableau vivant* of weeping dancing girls, the Empire closed its doors. The *Methodist Times* called it 'a great defeat of lust and lying', and described the Empire's supporters as 'the very epilepsy of licentiousness'.

The *Sporting Times* called Mrs Chant 'a nasty-minded busybody' and a 'member of the shrieking sisterhood'. At a mass meeting in Hyde Park she was burned in effigy, but was well received when she appeared in person at a rival meeting at the Queen's Hall, also attended by George Bernard Shaw. Shaw departed after the prayers, leaving the floor to Mrs Chant. 'I am 47,' she said, 'and I don't mind telling you I'm proud of it.'

It turned out to have been a fuss about nothing. The Empire was back in business within a week, and on the opening night the crowd tore down the screen that separated the bar from the promenade. One of those who joined in the celebrations was the young Winston Churchill, who, in his autobiography, said that this was the occasion of his maiden speech. He wrote to his brother, 'Did you see the papers about the riot at the Empire last Saturday? It was I who led the rioters and made a speech to the crowd. My cry was "Ladies of the Empire! I stand for liberty!"'

*See also* MORAL CRUSADERS.

**Chapman, Eddie** (1910–87), safe-cracker and double agent. Born in a small mining village outside Newcastle, and originally apprenticed to the shipbuilding trade, Chapman became the leading cracksman of his time, nightclubbing in London on the proceeds and day-tripping to Brighton with an ingénue on either arm. 'The one thing we had was money. If we ran out, we'd blow another safe. Sweet as that.' (*See* BRIGHTON.) In World War II he distinguished himself by working simultaneously for the British and German secret services.

The 1930s were innocent times in Britain. When an American gangster arrived in London, Chapman was shocked by his professed methods and ambitions. 'Don't you do heists?' the American asked. 'What's a heist?' said Chapman. 'You knock on the door and stick a fucking gun in their face,' the American explained. He was told that this wasn't the English way of doing things. It was the American, however, who persuaded Chapman, and his partner Jimmy Hunt, to explore the possibilities offered by gelignite.

Chapman and Hunt set off for Wales, where they stole 400 detonators and two packets of gelignite from unattended mines. They practised in the countryside and, having blown up a few trees, decided they were expert enough to use it on safes. Their first target was Edgeware Road underground station, which they relieved of the day's takings, and they progressed steadily from there. 'Every week we were knocking something out. Every time we did a job it was on the BBC. "There's been another attack by the Gelignite Gang," said the BBC.' A specially formed police unit decided that the American gang must be responsible because of the bits of chewing gum that Chapman used to fix the explosives.

Odeon cinemas were popular targets. Chapman would hide in the gents lavatory, perched above a cubicle, until the cinema closed. He would then break into the manager's office and go to work on the safe. On one occasion, when robbing the Odeon at Swiss Cottage, he miscalculated the timing device and blew himself backwards through the office wall. After he recovered, he stuffed the takings into a bag and made his escape. On the underground he noticed that cleaners on their way to work were staring at his injuries, and at a bag on his knee which bore the words 'Property of Odeon Cinemas'.

There were other mishaps, usually caused by using too much gelignite. This was rectified by the introduction of the condom as a useful tool of the trade. The condom would be filled with gelignite and water, knotted, and then poked through the lock. The condom kept the explosive together, and prevented dangerous overspill.

For a while in the 1930s Chapman lived at a hotel near Burlington Arcade. 'They were good times,' he later said. 'The Four Flash Devils were playing at the Nest, Lady Mountbatten would arrive with a black man and a bottle of whisky was 12s 6d.' The good times were temporarily interrupted when Chapman moved up to Scotland, having read about a record dividend being offered at a Co-Op store in Edinburgh. With the cover story that they were on their way to participate in a tournament at the Royal and Ancient, he and two accomplices drove north with the gelignite in their golf bags. When they came to do the job, they overestimated the size of the Co-Op's safe, too much gelignite was used and tins of fruit were sent flying into the street. Chapman escaped, and, back in London, hid out at the Regent Palace Hotel. When he read an advertisement for 'Sunny Jersey' on the back of a hotel menu, he thought, 'That sounds nice,' and he departed for the Channel Islands with his two accomplices.

In Jersey they said they were film producers, but their cover was blown when one of the gang sent a bottle of perfume to a girl he had met at a tea dance in Bournemouth. She told her brother, who was in the CID, and the hunt for Chapman moved to Jersey. Realizing that the hotel was under surveillance, Chapman escaped along the beach. He then broke into a cinema and stole £1000, planning to ship out to France the next day. He was arrested that night, but confessed to the local police that he had just robbed a cinema. They insisted that he stand trial in Jersey.

When the Germans invaded the Channel Islands in 1940 they found Chapman in jail, and immediately recruited him as an agent. As soon as he was free, he informed the British authorities of his role, and he became a double agent. 'The deal was that any money I made with the Germans I kept,' said Chapman. 'I was working under British Intelligence and they behaved like gentlemen.' Throughout the war he kept up his old profession, taking shots of cocaine before a big job to ease the pain brought on by old injuries. 'It was murder. If it had come on top, I'd never have got away.'

In recognition of his services the outstanding charges against Chapman were dropped after the war, thus sparing him a possible sentence of 20 years for more than 40 emptied safes. His story was later filmed as *Triple Cross*, starring Christopher Plummer, Trevor Howard and Yul Brynner. He retired from crime in the 1950s and, with his wife, Betty, opened a health club in Essex. Among its clients were the boxers, Frank Bruno and John Conteh. The venture was a success, enabling Chapman to buy a castle in Ireland, and to send his daughter to a good school. Yul Brynner will be remembered for popularizing the No 1 haircut, later adopted by the TV detective Kojak and by the soccer player David BECKHAM.

**Charteris, Colonel Francis** (1675–1732), soldier, cardsharp, libertine and rapist. Charteris was a notorious figure in London in the early 18th century. He was an inveterate gambler and cheat, who acquired his great wealth by taking his winnings in land rather than cash. He debauched women from all sections of society, including Sally Salisbury, the most celebrated courtesan of her day.

Few of Charteris's victims were brave enough to challenge him, but one who did was Anne Bond, a naïve serving girl whom he hired in 1729 with the sole purpose of seducing. One night, Anne was told by the housekeeper, Mrs Mitchell, that some new, and unusual, sleeping arrangements would be in place that night. Normally Anne slept in Mrs Mitchell's room, but because their master was indisposed, she and Mrs Mitchell would be obliged on this occasion to sleep in the colonel's chamber, with Anne 'lyeing with her in the truckle-bed'. Once she had been assured that the curtains would be so closely drawn about the bed that the colonel would not see her undress, Anne agreed to this arrangement. During the night, however, Mrs Mitchell was ordered to move into her master's bed, which she did, thereafter telling Anne to join them. When Anne refused, Charteris became so enraged that he stuffed his nightcap into her mouth to prevent her crying out, and then ravished her at gunpoint. Finally he whipped her, accused her of stealing and threw her out of the house.

Anne, most courageously, accused him of rape. Charteris was convicted, but after the manner of the time, was immediately pardoned by George II. Anne's fate is unknown. After Charteris died of venereal disease in 1732 he was pilloried as an example of depravity in Epistles I and II of Alexander Pope's *Moral Essays*. A portrait of him can be seen hovering esuriently in the background of the first plate of Hogarth's *Harlot's Progress*.

**Chatham, George** (1903–82), cat burglar. 'Taters' Chatham was London's most celebrated housebreaker in the years following World War II. Known as 'Burglar to the Gentry', his list of clients, according to his distinguished contemporary, Eddie CHAPMAN, 'read like a page from *Debretts*'. But Chatham lacked Chapman's knack of staying out of trouble, and was rumoured to have his own room at Chelmsford prison. His first conviction was in 1931, and he spent a total of 35 years in jail.

Targeting only the titled and famous, Chatham would break into a house and if the valuables on offer were of an inferior quality he would leave quietly and try the house next door. The hairdresser, Mr 'Teasie Weasie' Raymond, and Madame Prunier, the restaurateur, were two clients whose possessions satisfied Chatham's exacting standards. Some rings and a fur coat belonging to Lady 'Bubbles' Rothermere, wife of the newspaper proprietor and a former 'starlet' with the Rank Organization, failed the test, and were returned.

Chatham's tools were a screwdriver, a pair of gloves and a small torch, and he preferred to let himself into a house while its owner was at home. This ensured that the alarm would be switched off, and that the jewellery would be on the premises. He researched his targets carefully, spending long hours in the local library studying *Who's Who* and *Burke's Peerage*, and society magazines such as *Tatler* and *Country Life*. He referred to these as his *Exchange and Mart*.

Chatham once attempted to break into the home of Raine Spencer (the daughter of Barbara CARTLAND and stepmother of Diana, princess of Wales), but he stepped off the roof and fell four floors into the street. He was in hospital for six weeks, but as soon as he was discharged he returned, in plaster and a neck brace, to finish the job. This time he was disturbed by a maid just as he was about to pocket the Spencer jewels. The maid screamed, the police arrived and Chatham made one of his visits to Chelmsford prison.

Chatham's most successful robbery was the theft in 1948 of the Wellington swords from the Victoria and Albert Museum. He broke in via a window 40 feet above the ground by tying two ladders together. It was a simple job. 'I smashed the glass, took the swords and was away.' He removed the stones, sold some and gave the rest to his girlfriend, Ivy.

Steady accumulation, in the manner of more prudent thieves, was not for Chatham. He gambled his loot away as quickly as he acquired it, stealing and spending more than a million pounds in the course of his career. In his late 60s he was still stealing fur coats and jumping traffic lights to escape police cars. At 76 he was arrested for shoplifting. 'What have I got?' he said. 'A lot of sad memories. And 30 years inside.'

**Chatterton, Thomas** (1752–70), liar, exhibitionist, literary fraud, and by some accounts a genius. For Samuel Johnson, Chatterton was 'the most extraordinary young man that has encountered my knowledge'. He was praised by Coleridge, Shelley and BYRON for his contribution to their understanding of medieval poetry. Keats dedicated *Endymion* to him, Wordsworth called him 'the marvellous boy', and the French Romantics were influenced by his work. Yet everything he produced was a forgery, and by his early teens the habit of deception had become second nature.

Born in Bristol, and raised by his widowed mother, Chatterton had begun to 'medievalize' himself by the age of 11, brooding over old parchments in Bristol churches. In 1763 he produced his first literary forgery, *Elinore and Juga*, allegedly the work of a 15th-century poet. He wrote some poetry in the English of his own day, but publishers and critics thought it undistinguished. His greatest work was *The Legend of Thomas Rowley*, supposedly a priest of the Church of St John in Bristol during the reign of Henry IV. He sent this to Horace Walpole, who had himself published *Otranto* as a medieval original before admitting his authorship in the second edition. Walpole was impressed and he asked Chatterton to send him some more poems. These were passed on by Walpole to Thomas Gray, who immediately recognized them as forgeries. Walpole wrote severely to Chatterton, advising him to seek a position in commerce rather than continue as a forger.

Chatterton ignored this advice and made his way to London, where his new life began well enough. He lodged with a cousin, Mrs Ballance, in Shoreditch, and became friendly with various writers and politicians, including the radical John WILKES. Through his new contacts he began to contribute to Whig journals. He even managed to sell a few Rowley poems, but payments were slow in coming, and he was obliged to move into an attic room in Brooke Street, Holborn. Loneliness and hunger plunged him into self-pity and on 24 August 1770 he tore up all his poems, took a dose of arsenic – bought to poison the rats with which his attic was infested – and died in agony.

In 1777 the Rowley poems were published by Thomas Tyrwhitt with the question of their authorship left open. Some experts believed they were forgeries, others that they were genuine. Horace Walpole was denounced as Chatterton's murderer, and the myth that, by rejecting a genius, he had brought about his suicide would pursue him for the rest of his life. In 1780 Herbert Croft's novel, *Love and Madness*, based on the murder of Martha RAY, the mistress of the earl of Sandwich, by a lovesick priest, James HACKMAN, created a sensation. It contained a long account of Chatterton's life and brought him the fame he had always craved.

*See also* IRELAND, WILLIAM HENRY.

**Cheese, a duellist named.** *See* DUELLING.

**cheetah racing introduced to England.** *See* DOWER, GANDAR.

**Chelsea, aggrieved drug users of.** *See* FLECKNEY, EVELYN.

**Chelsea, Cecil Beaton boxed on the jaw in.** *See* HEBER-PERCY, ROBERT.

**Chelsea, flagellation house in.** *See* POTTER, SARAH.

**Chelsea, philandering MPs who have represented.** *See* CLARK, ALAN; DILKE, SIR CHARLES.

**Chelsea Football Club shirt, making love in a.** *See* DE SANCHA, ANTONIA.

**Chelsea public house with one's throat cut, found outside a.** *See* HOWELL, CHARLES AUGUSTUS.

**Chenevix-Trench, David Brian Robert** (1927–2000), Wykehamist. The outstanding scholar of his day at Winchester College, Chenevix-Trench won the Goddard (twice) and was last behind the hot in VIs canvas. After a double first in classics at New College, Oxford, he joined Sir Robert McAlpine and Sons, but he preferred a different career and in 1951 he went to Geneva to study catering. He and his second wife, Betty, took relief management jobs and catered for a number of organizations, including West Byfleet Golf Club and Exeter Country Club. Later, he learned to record Crown Court proceedings on a tape recorder, and enjoyed this work. He had a stroke in 1994, and died on 30 April 2000. He was survived by his wife.

For references to other Wykehamists, *see* WYKEHAMISTS.

***Cherrytop and the Good Fairy Fuck, Prince.*** *See* SALA, GEORGE AUGUSTUS.

**Chicago May.** *See* GUERIN, EDDIE; SHARPE, MAY CHURCHILL.

**Child, Benjamin** (*c*.1686–1722), teacher, philanderer and highwayman. Child deserves a less disobliging memorial, perhaps, than that provided by a contemporary biography, *The Whole Life and History of Benjamin Child, lately Executed for Robbing the Bristol Mail* (1722). Having noted that Child 'was brought into the world when Mercury, the god of thieves, and Venus, the goddess of love, had the joint ascendancy', and having been discourteous about his subject's mistresses, the anonymous writer concludes that it was clear from an early age that Child 'would die of the pox or on the gallows'.

As a young man, Child studied arithmetic and became a clerk, but was soon dismissed for insubordination. He turned to teaching, but was dismissed for a second time when he seduced the two daughters of the elderly clergyman who owned the school. He then moved to London, now hardened, in the words of his disapproving biographer, 'into a more confirmed state of wickedness'. Worse, he took up residence in Covent Garden, 'that receptacle of sharpers, pickpockets and strumpets'.

Here he soon made the acquaintance of two highwaymen, Spickett and Lindley, and being in urgent need of funds to pay off gambling debts, was persuaded to join them in robbing an Islington baker of £200. The partnership flourished and Child soon acquired a livery stable in Finsbury, three fine geldings and as many mistresses in other parts of town. His favourite was Mrs Anne Watkins, by whom he had three children, and who escapes censure by Child's anonymous biographer; his second was a Mrs Elizabeth Stukely, by whom he had another child 'after her ground had been tilled by half the sparks in town without bearing fruit before'; and the third was a Mrs Mary Chance, 'as errant a jilt as ever stood on two legs, and could no more be true to one than twenty'.

In fact, Child was of a most charitable disposition. He used his profits to help others, on one occasion securing the freedom of every inhabitant of Salisbury prison by paying off their debts. Such expansiveness of spirit, together with the cost of maintaining several mistresses, caused him to take unnecessary risks. In June 1721 he was captured while trying to rob the heavily guarded Bristol Mail and was sentenced two months later to be hanged. He died as gracefully as he had lived, repenting with dignity on the scaffold, and forgiving those who had brought him there:

> I heartily ask pardon of all that have been injured by my means,
> either by open assaults on the road, or collusory practices in private,
> to cheat and defraud them. And I forgive all men whatsoever,
> without distinction or reserve, even my prosecutors, among whom
> my particular thanks are due to Captain Blathers, who took me on
> the Mail.

Child left £10,000 in his will, to be divided equally between Mrs Anne Watkins, Mrs Elizabeth Stukely and Mrs Mary Chance.

**China, believing oneself to be the empress of.** *See* HELL-FIRE CLUB, THE IRISH.

**chinchilla on one's head, dancing with a.** *See* JONES, JANIE (for Miss Zelda Plum).

**Christ.** *See* JESUS.

**Christ, the Bride of.** *See* SOUTHCOTT, JOANNA.

**Christmas card showing a naked woman with a whip, a.** *See* FORSTER, JAMES.

**Chudleigh, Elizabeth** (1720–91), society beauty. By engaging in a biga-mous marriage with the duke of Kingston, Chudleigh involved her husband, Lieutenant Augustus HERVEY RN, in a scandal as notorious in its day as that occasioned 50 years later by Admiral Nelson's affair with Lady Emma HAMILTON. Miss Chudleigh had been appointed a maid of honour to the princess of Wales at Leicester House when, in the summer of 1744, she met Lieutenant Hervey at Winchester races. She had already been courted by the 19-year-old duke of Hamilton, who had promised to marry her when he returned from the Grand Tour of Europe. In his absence she allowed herself to be seduced by Lieutenant Hervey. Both were impetuous by nature and within weeks they were married.

As a married woman Miss Chudleigh would lose her position as maid of honour, and the £400 a year that went with it, so the ceremony was carried out in secret, and remained a secret from English society until its details emerged during the bigamy scandal 20 years later. Apart from the vicar and the bride and groom there were only three other people present – Miss Chudleigh's aunt, her maid, and a Mr Mountenay, who was acting as a witness. Precautions were taken to ensure that the domestic staff of all concerned had no idea what was planned, and the brief ceremony took place in semi-darkness, the only light coming from a taper attached to Mr Mountenay's hat. A few days later Hervey rejoined his ship at Portsmouth and sailed for the West Indies.

Apart from a brief reunion when Hervey returned from Jamaica in 1746, the couple drifted apart, and both took lovers elsewhere. Miss Chudleigh, as she continued to be known, acquired an increasingly scandalous reputation. This was in no way diminished by her appearance at the Venetian ambas-sador's ball at Somerset House in 1749, an occasion on which she wore a costume so revealing that she might as well have been naked. George II and the other men present were reported to be delighted, but the women were less amused. The princess of Wales tried to cover her maid of honour with a wrap, and afterwards Mrs Elizabeth Montagu noted:

> Miss Chudleigh's undress was remarkable. She was Iphigenia for the sacrifice, but so naked the high priest might easily inspect the entrails of the victim. The Maids of Honour were so offended they were lost for words.

By the late 1760s Miss Chudleigh had become the mistress of the duke of Kingston, a wealthy and generous man whom she wished to marry. In her opinion the ceremony she had gone through with Hervey was 'such a scrambling shabby business and so much incomplete' that it didn't count. In spite of a certain amount of society gossip about the true state of affairs, she managed to satisfy the Ecclesiastical Court that she was a spinster and in March 1769 she became the duchess of Kingston. Hervey, who had been thinking of divorcing her in any case, remained silent. However, when the duke of Kingston died four years later, the eldest of his heirs, who had been disinherited, decided to contest his will and challenge the legality of his father's marriage. The former Miss Chudleigh became the first woman to be tried on a charge of bigamy in the House of Lords —the only legitimate venue since Hervey had recently succeeded to the family title and was now the earl of Bristol. If Miss Chudleigh's marriage to Hervey was legal she was the countess of Bristol; if it was not, she was the duchess of Kingston. Either way she was a peeress, and must be tried by her peers. The Lords ruled that Chudleigh's marriage to Hervey was legal and that she was therefore guilty of bigamy. However, no action was taken against her. She departed for the Continent, spent some time in the convivial company of Catherine the Great and died in Paris in 1788.

*See also* JACKSON, THE REVEREND WILLIAM.

**Church, the Reverend John** (1783–?), priest, exhibitionist and self-dramatizing sodomite. In his autobiography, *The Child of Providence* (1823), Church identifies strongly with many martyred Biblical characters, not all of them inverts, including Samson, John the Baptist and Christ himself. His many persecutors, by contrast, are Philistines, Pharisees and various of the more coarse-grained inhabitants of the animal kingdom. His description of his time in prison after he had been convicted of sodomizing an apprentice potter is characteristically inflated:

> I arrived at Anchor Vale, glad enough that I was delivered at last from the noise of the archers, the horns of rams blown by goats, the braying of asses ...

That future ministries would be controversial became clear in 1808 when the 25-year-old Church was appointed rector at Banbury, in Oxfordshire. Within weeks, a pamphleteer was circulating rumours that involved a hairdresser, a porter and a grocer from Warwick. It was also suggested that when staying with a friend in the neighbouring village of Kingham, Church had seduced his host's son and later, when he had tired of the boy, his host's butler. Church admitted the truth of the accusation, but said that any impropriety must have been inadvertent:

> If there was anything of which you speak it must have been when I was asleep and supposing I was in bed with my wife.

His explanation was not accepted and Church was obliged to leave the village.

Church moved to London, where he became a preacher at the Obelisk Chapel in Vere Street, a homosexual brothel, attached to the Swan Hotel. Here he officiated at transvestite weddings, and carried out funerals of men who had been executed for sodomy. In 1810 the Swan's proprietor, James COOKE, was charged with what *The Times* called 'detestable practices', and the scandal was written up in *The Phoenix of Sodom: or The Vere Street Coterie* (1813) by a journalist, Robert Holloway. Among other revelations, Holloway reported that the Swan's regular customers disported themselves as women: 'Pretty Harriet' was a guardsman, 'Lady Godiva' a coachman, and 'Miss Sweet Lips' a butcher.

Holloway's pamphlet didn't mention Church by name, but a prominent picture of him on the front cover alerted the father of a young man, William Clarke, whom Church had sodomized the previous year in a barn near Colchester. The first Church knew of impending difficulties was when the boy's father arrived at the Obelisk Chapel armed with two cocked pistols. In the event, the excitement of the occasion caused Clarke senior to pass out before he could get off a shot, and Reverend Church escaped.

Such incidents only served to increase Church's notoriety, raising him to the status of 'gay icon', as it might now be called. Such was his popularity that he was compelled in 1813 to open a larger and more profitable Obelisk Chapel. Opposition pamphlets denouncing him as 'JOHN CHURCH, INCARNATE DEVIL' merely served to swell his congregations.

For the next few years Church was left in peace while his enemies regrouped. Then, in 1817, he was charged at the Old Bailey with attempting to sodomize Adam Foreman, an apprentice potter. In the witness box Foreman said he had been startled out of his sleep one night by 'someone laying hold of me very tight'. When he had asked who was there, he had received the reply, 'Don't you know me, Adam? It is your mistress.' Church was found guilty of 'intending to commit that most detestable and sodomitical crime (among Christians not to be named) called buggery', and was sentenced to two years in prison.

Church consoled himself with the characteristically enlarged thought that Samson's locks had grown again. His resilience had its just reward. He emerged from prison with an increased and devoted following which, for the next five years, flocked in ever greater numbers to hear his sermons. In his autobiography, published in 1821, he marvels at the many strange things – all beyond his control – that had happened to him.

**Churchill, Sir Winston.** *See* CECIL, LORD HUGH; CHANT, LAURA ORMISTON.

**clairvoyants.** *See* CADDY, EILEEN; CRADDOCK, FANNY, ICKE, DAVID, SLADE, HENRY; STOKES, DORIS.

**Clancarty, William Francis Brinsley Le Poer Trench, 8th earl of** (1911–95), peer, advertising agent and ufologist. Clancarty, who had been educated at the Nautical College, Pangbourne, and later sold advertising space for a gardening magazine whose offices were opposite Waterloo Station, claimed that he could trace his descent from 63,000 BC, when beings from another planet had landed on earth in spaceships. Most humans, he maintained, were descended from these aliens. No other theory could account for the variety of shapes, sizes and skin colours to be seen on the streets of South Kensington as one went about one's business. Not all of these aliens came from space, however. Some emerged through tunnels from a civilization that still existed beneath the earth's crust. There were six or seven of these tunnels altogether, one at the North Pole, another at the South Pole, and others in places such as Tibet. 'I haven't been down one of these tunnels myself,' the earl admitted, 'but from what I gather, these beings are quite advanced.'

For many years the earl was frustrated in his attempts to spot a flying saucer. According to his obituary in the *Daily Telegraph* he installed a UFO detector in the bedroom of his South Kensington flat, but the results were disappointing. 'It did buzz one Saturday afternoon,' he said, 'but when I ran out into the street I found that the sky was completely overcast.'

When he succeeded to the earldom on the death of his half-brother in 1975, Clancarty founded the UFO Study Group at the House of Lords, and introduced the *Flying Saucer Review* to the library. He also instigated a debate in which Lord Strabolgi, speaking on behalf of the government, said that he was not convinced that alien spacecraft had ever visited this planet. Lord Clancarty's books, written under the name Brinsley Le Poer Trench, included *The Sky People, The Flying Saucer Story* and *Secrets of the Ages*. He married first, Diana, daughter of Sir William Younger, second, Mrs Wilma Belknap, third, Mrs Mildred Spong, and, fourth, Mrs May Beasley, widow of Commander Frank R. Beasley RN. He was succeeded by his nephew, Nicholas Power Richard Le Poer Trench.

**Clap, Margaret** (*c*.1682–1727), brothel proprietor. In July 1726 'Mother' Clap was convicted of running a 'sodomitical house' in Holborn, generally supposed to be the one visited by the notorious double-dealing thief-takers Jonathan WILD and Charles HITCHIN, and the occasion of the latter's downfall. According to the trial records, Constable Samuel Stephens, accompanied by Constable Joseph Sellers, visited the house in December 1725 and found as many as 50 men indulging in gross behaviour. Sometimes, according to Constable Stephens:

... they would sit in one another's laps, kissing in a lewd manner and using their hands indecently. Then they would get up, dance and make curtsies, and mimic the voices of women. 'Oh fie, Sir!', 'You're a wicked devil!', 'I swear I'll cry out!' Then they'd hug and play and toy.

To satisfy themselves that their eyes had not deceived them on their first visit, Constables Stephens and Sellers returned to the house on the following Sunday, and again on the Sunday after that. They were then able to report that they'd found as much to be disgusted by in the course of these later visits as on the first occasion. Stephens told the court that 'the company talked all manner of gross and vile obscenity in "Mother" Clap's hearing, and she appeared wonderfully pleased with it.' He further divulged that 'one Eccleston, used to stand pimp for her, to prevent strangers disturbing her clients in their diversions' – and failing in his duties, he might have added, at least with regard to himself and Constable Sellers.

'Mother' Clap defended herself with vigour. 'I hope it will be considered that I am a woman,' she said, 'and therefore it cannot be thought that I would ever be concerned in such practices.' The court took a different view and she was sentenced to stand in the pillory in Smithfield, to pay a fine of 20 marks and to serve two years in prison. The sentence was unnecessary. When placed in the pillory, Margaret Clap was assaulted so viciously by the crowd that she died of her injuries within a week.

*See also* AGENTS PROVOCATEURS; HAMPSON, KEITH.

**Clarence, Prince Albert Victor, duke of** (1864–92), heir to the British throne. The eldest son of the prince of Wales (later EDWARD VII), and a grandson of Queen Victoria, Eddy, as the duke of Clarence was known, barely escaped involvement in one of the great scandals of the late 19th century. In 1889 Charles Swinscow and others admitted that they supplemented their incomes from the receiver general's department by working as prostitutes at a homosexual brothel in Cleveland Street, catering for the nobility. Lord Arthur Somerset, a major in the Blues and an extra equerry to the prince of Wales, was named as a client. Somerset engaged the services of Arthur NEWTON, a resourceful but suspect solicitor, who warned the assistant director of public prosecutions, Hamilton Cuffe, that if Somerset were prosecuted he would name a still more illustrious client of the brothel – the duke of Clarence. Under the assumed name of 'Victoria', Clarence was already a frequent visitor to the Hundred Guineas, a transvestite club in Portland Place, run by a Mr Inslip, so there may have been truth in the allegation. It was sufficiently serious in any case for Cuffe to inform his superior, Sir Augustus Stephenson, who in turn informed the prime minister, Lord Salisbury. Somerset avoided scandal and the duke of Clarence, who had enough troubles already (engaged to Princess May of Teck, he had syphilis and gonorrhoea, both in a communicable usage) avoided it too.

Clarence was later suspected, somewhat more fancifully, of being JACK THE RIPPER. For that to have been the case, however, it must be assumed that from time to time he was released from the insane asylum in which he was kept. Princess May of Teck fared better. She changed her name to Mary and married the future George V.

*See also* HAMMOND, CHARLES; NEWTON, ARTHUR.

**Clarendon, John Cornbury Hyde, 3rd earl of** (1669–1738), diplomat. When appointed governor of New York and New Jersey by his cousin, Queen Anne, Clarendon decided that as the representative of a woman he should dress accordingly. At the opening of the New York Assembly in 1702 he wore a blue silk frock and satin shoes, and he carried a fan. Lady Clarendon was unhappy in America because the earl spent all the money he had on dresses for himself. He took to wearing elaborately decorated hooped silk gowns, and since there was no money left over after he had shopped for himself, Lady Clarendon was obliged to steal her clothes from unattended stores. When he returned to England in 1708, Clarendon continued to dress as a woman and he remained a favourite of the queen.

**Clark, Alan** (1927–99), politician, historian and sexual profligate. According to an after-dinner jest circulating in Whitehall in the 1990s, and attributed to the Conservative politician Michael Hesletine, Clark's failure to achieve the worldly success that Clark, if no one else, might have thought his gifts merited, arose from the fact that he had inherited his father's furniture but not his intellect. The attribution may be false and the story, in any case, apocryphal. His father was Lord Kenneth Clark, the distinguished art historian, amusingly dubbed Lord Clark of Civilization by the spoof magazine *Private Eye*. Labelled politically incorrect, which he took to be a compliment, Alan Clark, according to the Right Honourable Tony Benn, was 'an independent man who always says what he thinks and means what he says' – though it is not obvious how the first proposition could in any case be true and the second false. Benn's unorthodox logic notwithstanding, it can be taken for granted, then, that Clark's frequently expressed admiration for Adolf Hitler was genuine, and his indignation at being called a fascist by the *Guardian* newspaper sincere. 'I am not a fascist,' he said in a letter to the paper. 'Fascists are shopkeepers, I am a Nazi.' Admirers took this to be an attempt at humour, but that was probably not the case. Clark liked to refer to Africa as 'Bongo Bongo land', and he kept an attack dog called Eva, named after Hitler's mistress. Clark was admired in some quarters as a popular historian with a special interest in military affairs, but he achieved little as a politician – other than to use his influence, when working in the Ministry of Defence, to advise Matrix

Churchill on how to get round sales embargoes to President Saddam Hussein of Iraq. Later he admitted that at the trial of three of Matrix Churchill's directors he had committed perjury – or, as he put it (with characteristic affectation), 'I was economic with the *actualité.*' He is best known for his *Diaries*, published in two volumes by Weidenfeld & Nicolson in 1994 and 2000. The lengthy accounts in these of his various sexual adventures (including affairs with Judge James Harkness's wife and both his stepdaughters – a trio he amusingly dubbed 'the Coven') guaranteed Clark an extensive readership in Middle England. His wife Jane stood by him throughout his various escapades.

*See also* DUTY, LOYALTY ABOVE AND BEYOND THE CALL OF.

**Cleft Chin Murder, the.** *See* JONES, ELIZABETH MAUD.

**clergymen who have set a poor example.** *See* ABBOTT, GEORGE; ANDREWS, THE REVEREND BASIL; ATHERTON, BISHOP JOHN; BATE, THE REVEREND HENRY; BLACKBURNE, ARCHBISHOP LANCELOT; CHURCH, THE REVEREND JOHN; COPPE, ABIEZER; DAVIDSON, THE REVEREND HAROLD FRANCIS (the rector of Stiffkey); DAVISON, JANE; DODD, THE REVEREND DR WILLIAM; FREE, THE REVEREND EDWARD DRAX; FREESTONE, VERITY (for Dr Brandon Jackson); GAMBLE, THE REVEREND PETER; HACKMAN, THE REVEREND JAMES; HUNTER, THE REVEREND THOMAS; JACKSON, THE REVEREND WILLIAM; JOCELYN, THE REVEREND PERCY; TYLER, THE REVEREND TOM; WATSON, THE REVEREND JOHN SELBY.

**Cleveland, Barbara Villiers, duchess of** (1641–1709), courtesan. Described as 'the fairest and lewdest of the royal concubines', Barbara became the mistress of Charles II at the age of 19, and bore him six children. Her appetite for scandalous behaviour survived the king's death. On one occasion she was said by Lord Coleraine to have performed an act of fellatio on a recently consecrated bishop and to have bitten off his penis. She had an affair with a notorious highwayman, Cardonnel 'Scum' Goodman, who was later jailed for attempting to poison her sons, the dukes of Grafton and Northumberland. At the age of 64, she married a celebrated rake, Robert 'Bean' Fielding, who already had a wife. She escaped punishment, but Fielding was convicted of bigamy and had his hand burned. In her later years, she became grotesquely swollen by dropsy. The duchess's descendants include the late Lady Diana, princess of Wales (1962–97) and Sarah Ferguson, the duchess of YORK (1959– ).

**Cleveland Street Brothel Scandal, the.** *See* ABBERLINE, CHIEF INSPECTOR FREDERICK; HAMMOND, CHARLES; NEWTON, ARTHUR.

**Clonmell, John Scott, 1st earl of** (1711–80), gourmand, libertine and chief justice of Ireland, known as 'Copperfaced Jack' from his Hibernian appearance and the unorthodox methods by which he was rumoured to have made his fortune. Clonmell was suspected of having held land in trust for Catholics, who until 1778 were not allowed to own property, and then to have reneged on the contracts. Like most of his contemporaries he was an experienced duellist, having fought at one time or another the lord chancellor, the chief justice common pleas, the master of the rolls, the leader of the House of Commons, Lord Tyrawly, three privy councillors and his predecessor as chief justice King's Bench (*see also* DUELLING).

Clonmell kept a diary, published after his death, which recorded many resolutions, few of which he kept. The most endearing, perhaps, was one he made six years after his appointment as chief justice of Ireland, when he determined '*seriously* to set about learning my profession'. In 1774 he resolved to refrain from 'snuff, sleep, swearing, gross eating, sloth, malt liquors, indulgence – and never to take anything after tea but water or wine and water at night'. Notwithstanding these intentions, he grew so fat that he became immobile and at night had to be carried to bed by his servants. When he died, the undertaker's men were unable to negotiate his body down the stairs and were obliged to lower it from the bedroom window by a system of ropes and pulleys to the waiting hearse.

**coal merchants, remarkable.** *See* BRITTON, THOMAS; HANGER, GEORGE.

**Cock Lane Ghost, the.** *See* ROBINSON, ANNE.

**cockroach washed down with champagne, a.** *See* LANGAN, PETER.

**coconuts in Western Samoa, hanging up one's.** *See* KINGSLAND, GERALD.

**codpiece, using a tortoise as a.** *See* MOON, KEITH.

**coffin, collapsing into one's son's.** *See* DUDLEY, CAPTAIN RICHARD.

**coffin, keeping one's beloved in a.** *See* LONSDALE, JAMES LOWTHER, 1ST EARL OF; MAGUIRE, BRIAN; VAN BUTCHELL, MARTIN.

**coffins, white slaves exported from Kew in.** *See* JEFFRIES, MARY.

**coffins suspected of concealing arms.** *See* OATES, TITUS.

**Cole, Horace de Vere** (1883–1936), art student, dilettante and practical joker. An inveterate prankster, Cole was the brother-in-law of the future

Conservative prime minister, Neville Chamberlain, but bore a strong physical resemblance to the leader of the Labour Party, Ramsay MacDonald. A favourite joke was to appear as MacDonald at election rallies and, when called on to make a speech in support of the local candidate, to denounce everything the Labour Party stood for. He would condemn the unions and heap praise on the Tories, announcing that he wished to have nothing more to do with the absurd activities of Labour. He would then depart, leaving his audience in a state of confusion.

Cole pulled off his most celebrated stunt when still an undergraduate at Cambridge University. He and five other students, masquerading as African princes visiting England, were entertained to a lavish dinner by university and government officials. Cole, impersonating the sultan of Zanzibar, expressed his gratitude by presenting his hosts with 'the dorsal fin of the Sacred Shark of Zanzibar – a token of everlasting remembrance'.

On another occasion, as Mr Herbert Cholmondeley of the Foreign Office, Cole escorted his student friends – masquerading this time as Abyssinian princes – on a tour of England. At Portsmouth, senior naval officers in full dress showed Cole and his party round HMS *Dreadnought* and other specially assembled ships of the Home Fleet. His fellow practical jokers on this occasion were the naturalist Andrew Buxton, the artist Duncan Grant, Guy Ridley, a judge's son, and Adrian Stephen and his sister Virginia, later the novelist Virginia Woolf. Miss Stephen, who, like the others, was in black face for the occasion, was fearful that she might be uncovered as a woman and therefore confined herself in conversation to grunting like a monkey. The others recited passages from Virgil's *Aeneid*, assuming – correctly, as it turned out – that naval officers would be unable to identify this as Latin.

Cole's English victims usually took his jokes in good part, but he was once shot in the leg by a Corsican.

**Collins, Dennis** (1781–1832), able seaman. In 1832 Collins, who had lost a leg at the battle of Trafalgar, limped 21 miles from London to Ascot, where he attended the races and threw a stone at William IV as a protest against the removal of his pension rights. The stone dented the king's top hat and Collins was sentenced to be hanged. This was later commuted to deportation, but Collins died before he could be shipped out to the Caribbean.

**Collins, Jonathan** (*c.*1680–?), barrister. Collins, a resourceful advocate, is thought to be the only barrister in British legal history ordered to bear the costs of a failed action. In 1725 two highwaymen fell out over the proceeds of a recent robbery. One of them, Joseph Williams, took the unusual step of suing the other, John Everitt, for £200. Since Everitt was reluctant to appear in court, the action was undefended and Williams obtained his judgement. Believing that Williams had cheated him out of more than £200 from the robbery, Everitt was aggrieved enough to consult a solicitor, William Wreathock, who, in turn, instructed Jonathan Collins of counsel to start an action in the Court of Exchequer for an account to be taken between the two highwaymen.

The statement of facts drawn up by Collins is an ingenious document. He lays out that his client, John Everitt, is 'most skilled in dealing and in buying and selling several sorts of commodities', and that the defendant, Joseph Williams, 'knowing Everitt's great care and diligence in managing the said dealing, invited him into partnership'. They agreed on this, and further agreed that they should 'severally provide all sorts of necessaries at the joint and equal expense of both such as horses, bridles, saddles, assistants and servants'. The statement then alleges that:

> ... pursuant to the said agreement, Everitt and the said Joseph Williams went on and proceeded jointly in the said dealing with great success on Hounslow Heath, where they dealt with a gentleman for a gold watch.

Later Mr Williams told Mr Everitt that:

> Finchley was a good and convenient place to deal in, and so they dealt there with several gentlemen for divers watches, rings, swords, canes, hats, cloaks, horses, bridles and other things to the value of £200 and upwards.

In pursuit of business, they then rode to Bagshot, Salisbury and Hampstead, and their profits amounted to over £2000. Mr Williams took charge of the goods, and Mr Everitt, finding that Mr Williams 'began to shuffle with him', asked for an account, but was refused. Mr Collins ends the statement with a flourish:

> My client, John Everitt, is relievable only in a Court of Equity before Your Honours where just discoveries are made, frauds detected and just accounts settled.

Collins was confident that the threat of exposure would bring about an out-of-court settlement, but Williams kept his nerve and Mr Sergeant Girdler, on his behalf, persuaded the court to dismiss the action as 'a scandal and an impertinence'. A week later Collins, who sensibly had kept away from the hearing, was ordered to pay the costs himself – thus achieving for himself a unique place in legal textbooks.

Two years later Joseph Williams was hanged for carrying out further 'dealings' with travellers. In 1730 John Everitt was hanged for a highway robbery on Hampstead Heath. Jonathan Collins continued in practice, in this respect faring better than his instructing solicitor, Mr Wreathock. In 1735 Wreathock was himself condemned to death for a highway robbery, but was reprieved and transported for life. Later, he received a royal pardon and resumed work as a solicitor. He was eventually struck off.

**collusion, divorce by.** The Divorce Reform Act of 1923 made it possible for women to obtain a divorce on the grounds of their husbands' adultery. Opponents of the act, as well as believing that adultery by a husband was hardly as serious as adultery by a wife, feared that it would cause a rise in collusive divorces since under the new law only a single act of adultery need be proved. In this they were correct. The 1920s were the heyday of the Brighton divorce. London nightclub hostesses, more usually employed by Kate MEYRICK and her colleagues, travelled to the south-coast resort for the weekend to provide evidence – confirmed by breakfast waiters and chambermaids – that a husband had committed adultery. Brighton was not the only seaside town specializing in this service, but it was the most popular. Evelyn Waugh's *A Handful of Dust* (1934) contains an amusing account of a weekend spent in this disagreeable way.

Divorce by collusion was one thing, perjured evidence another – as was illustrated by the case of *Alexander vs Alexander and Amos* (1925). Mr Alexander had married beneath him, and deciding that he must rid himself of Mrs Alexander, he cited Amos, the butler. The evidence was that a farm labourer, Sullivan, had, by climbing on to a stable roof, seen Amos and Mrs Alexander in the latter's bedroom. On another occasion he had come across them in an outhouse. When Sullivan first reported this to Mr Alexander, he had been kicked and abused for his pains. Gradually, however, Mr Alexander had come to believe him. The judge, Sir Cresswell Cresswell, took a different view. Unable to credit that any woman would make love in broad daylight (thereby allowing Sullivan a full view of what she and the butler might be doing), Sir Cresswell Cresswell concluded, for this reason alone, that the action was a put-up job, and Alexander was denied his divorce. Whether Sullivan was well rewarded for his stressful appearance in court is not known.

*See also* BRIGHTON; CONJUGAL RIGHTS.

**coloured men.** 'The principal motive of the coloured man in smoking hemp is to stimulate sexual desire in innocent white girls' – *The Times* (1957). *See* MARKS, HOWARD.

**condemned by onanism to imbecility and an early grave.** *See* ROBERTS, 'BAWDY HOUSE' BOB; SALA, GEORGE AUGUSTUS.

**confidence tricksters.** *See* ARCHER, WILLIAM; BENSON, HARRY; BIDWELL, AUSTIN; BINT, PAUL; BOTTOMLEY, HORATIO; CARLETON, MARY; CORRIGAN, MICHAEL; COWDEN, CHARLIE; DAY, ALEXANDER; DIVER, JENNY; DREWE, JOHN; FERGUSON, ARTHUR; GORDON-GORDON, LORD;

GREGORY, MAUNDY; HALL, ARCHIBALD; HATFIELD, JOHN; HOBBS, WILLIAM COOPER; KAGGS, JOHN; MILES, LOUISA.

**confidence tricksters, assistant.** *See* COOK, ROBIN.

**conjugal rights.** Before the Law Reform (Matrimonial Causes) Act 1949, the law presumed that a husband owned his wife's body. A long-standing ground for divorce had been that an erring wife had failed to comply with an order for restitution of conjugal rights. In 1891 the Court of Appeal established that a man could 'confine his wife if she was about to be guilty of misconduct touching upon her husband's honour' (*see* JACKSON, EDMUND HAUGHTON). Wives had the same rights under the law, but seldom acted on them. An exception was the singer, Dorothy SQUIRES, whose husband, the film actor Roger Moore, deserted her in 1972 for an Italian starlet. Squires brought an action for restoration of conjugal rights, and, although successful, didn't immediately present the divorce petition to which the order would have entitled her.

*See also* HALL, NEWMAN; OWEN PEEL, CLARISSA.

**Connolly, Cyril.** *See* DEVONSHIRE, ANDREW ROBERT BUXTON CAVENDISH, 11TH DUKE OF; HERBERT, DAVID.

**Continent, corrupted manners of the.** *See* BYRNE, JAMES.

**convent, love in a.** *See* HERVEY, AUGUSTUS.
For *Venus in the Cloister or the Nun in her Smock, see* CURLL, EDMOND.

**Conyers, David** (1932–95), literary agent and theatrical producer. An outstanding undergraduate at Cambridge University, where in 1953 he displayed an agreeably light touch in the spoof revue mounted annually by the Footlights Club, Conyers suffered many disappointments in his subsequent career, in the course of which he was variously a writers' and choreographers' agent with MCA, an assistant drug dealer, the producer in Holland of the American musical comedy *Hair* (1969), and an operator on the Hampstead telephone exchange.

In October 1970 Conyers tried to strangle the film director Guy Ritchie's mother, Amber, to whom he was engaged at the time. But for that he might have ended up as the step-father-in-law of Madonna, the American pop singer, instead of suffering a heart attack, brought on by exhaustion, while working the night shift at the telephone exchange.

When MCA was closed down in 1960 by the American anti-trust laws, Conyers became a partner in London Management Ltd, a talent agency backed by the powerful light-entertainment impresarios, Lew and Leslie Grade. An early indication of mental instability arose when he threw his secretary's typewriter out of a second- floor window into Regent Street, quickly followed by the secretary herself. His partners, who included Robin Fox, father of the actors Edward and James Fox, put him into hospital; thereafter, while he was sedated, they secured his shares in the agency for themselves. When he came out of hospital he joined the theatrical management firm, Jack Waller Ltd, with whom he was involved in 1961 in the production at the Comedy Theatre, London, of J.P. Donleavy's wry comedy *Fairy Tales of New York* (*see* PAPERING THE HOUSE). This relatively successful period in his life was cut short when he threw Jack Waller's 73-year-old general manager, Bert Leywood, out of the window into Leicester Square. The directors of Jack Waller returned him to the mental hospital; later, while he was sedated, they stole back his shares in the company. Nothing was heard of him for some years, until in 1969 – and in spite of the fact that he was now kept going by electro-convulsive shock therapy powered by a pocket dynamo hidden under his waistcoat – he managed to obtain the rights to produce *Hair* in Holland.

The production was beset with many difficulties. Having failed to raise the necessary capital from various sources (his plans received a setback when one potential backer, the Soho gangster Raymond Nash, sat down in the arrival lounge at Tokyo airport and the chair collapsed under the weight of smuggled gold secured about his person), Conyers decided to go ahead in any case. He invited the Dutch royal family to the first night, but forgot to book a theatre. When this was pointed out to him, he hired a circus tent, whose bench seats were poised unevenly, causing a see-saw effect. When the band played the national anthem, everyone stood up except the Dutch royal family, who were sent sprawling in the sawdust. Then the audience sat down and the Dutch royal family were fired into the air like tumblers on a variety bill. This might have gone on all night had not Dutch creditors soon arrived to repossess the set, such as it was.

Conyers went to live in north London with his friend, Tim Williamson, who was married to the daughter of the commissioner of the Metropolitan Police, Sir Robert Mark. At the time, Williamson was supplementing his income as a theatrical agent by selling drugs in the bohemian milieu frequented by Princess Margaret and her louche companions. Conyers was invited to assist in a minor capacity, but the partnership quickly faltered. At the time Williamson was himself on the verge of a nervous breakdown. He suspected that his father-in-law, Sir Robert Mark, was following him around in a police helicopter. Less plausibly, he believed that he had the power to stop buses, and was able to prove the point more than once by stepping suddenly into the street in front of one. Williamson ended up in hospital, and Conyers went to work on the Hampstead telephone exchange, which he enjoyed. He died two years later. Nothing might have come of his relationship with Guy Ritchie's mother, Amber, who is on poor terms in any case with her daughter-in-law, Madonna. She is now

living in Torremolinos, Spain, where she is studying to become a physio
therapist.

**Cook, Robin** (1931–94), writer, pornographer, minicab driver and assistant
confidence trickster. Cook, an old Etonian whose father was prominent in
the City of London, was never ambitious for mainstream literary success.
'I've watched people like Kingsley Amis struggling to get on the up-
escalator,' he said, 'while I had the down-escalator all to myself. I've no
time for those who see writing as a means of social advancement.' While
not everyone would accept that as an accurate description of Amis's literary
*raison d'être*, Cook's own ambitions were amply fulfilled in this regard since
his career followed a steep downward path from a social point of view.

After national service in the Brigade of Guards, Cook went to Spain,
where he became involved in smuggling tape recorders. On his return to
England in 1960, a chance encounter in a Soho pub with a confidence
trickster, Charles de Silva, provided him with the opportunity to front de
Silva's fraudulent property company. 'I was plausible, and I didn't have any
form,' Cook later explained. In the summer of that year, he was questioned
by the police after he reported the theft from his flat of a Rubens, a Renoir
and various works by Dutch masters. 'It was an insurance scam,' Cook
admitted in 1990. 'My father was the chairman, rather conveniently, of the
company which had insured them.' He also helped to run illegal gambling
clubs and at one stage worked in a pornographic book shop in Soho. 'We
had to pay money to the police,' he recalled. 'Prominent public figures
used to shock us with their requirements. We put up a sign saying "The following MPs must not be served."'

It was this shadowy milieu, where well-born idlers meet the criminal
classes (*see* BOLLOCKS, A SILLY), which Cook described in comic novels
such as *The Crust On Its Uppers* (1965) and *The Legacy of the Stiff Upper Lip*
(1966). In 1973 his muse deserted him, or so he claimed, and he moved to
Averron in France, where he lived in a tower. In the 1980s inspiration
returned, and he began to write thrillers. *How the Dead Live* (1986) and *He
Died With His Eyes Open* (1988) were less well received in England than in
France, where he was made a Chevalier des Arts et des Lettres.

In his autobiography, *The Hidden Files* (1992), Cook gives Eton College
the credit for what success he had. 'It was an absolute hotbed of buggery,'
he wrote. 'An Eton background is essential if you are at all into vice.'
*See also* ETONIANS.

**Cook, Thomas** (*c*.1661–1703), butcher, prize-fighter and murderer. Like
many criminals, Cook, through loquacity and drunkenness, was the cause
of his own downfall. The son of a butcher, a man of reputation in Gloucestershire, Cook was belligerent by nature, this trait causing him to be
dismissed from the many jobs he took – barber, gentleman's gentleman,

barman – after violent altercations. Advised that he might do better as a fist-fighter, he moved to London, where he took up residence in Mayfair and followed this profession with some success. At the time, Mayfair was one of the loucher parts of the capital, frequented for the most part by thieves and women of bad character, who came to enjoy the puppet shows and other low distractions. In time, Queen Anne issued a proclamation against vice and immorality. When Cooper, the high constable, assisted by all the inferior constables at his disposal, came to suppress the puppet shows, Cook boxed six inferior constables to the ground, and then the high constable himself, causing him to die two days later of his injuries.

Cook fled to Ireland, where he might have survived happily enough had he not taken to boasting of his exploits. Drunk in a pub one night, and using profane language, he was reprimanded by the landlord and threatened with arrest. 'Informing Irish dogs, are you?' cried Cook, continuing:

> I'll tell you this. In London at a fair, called Mayfair, there was a noise which I went to see, the constables played their part with their staves, and I played mine, and when the man dropped I went away.

The Irish landlord, to his credit, seemed to follow this, and the police were called. Cook was taken into custody, shipped back to England, tried at the Old Bailey and sentenced to be hanged. Having received the sacrament on 21 July 1703 he was taken from Newgate to Tyburn on a hurdle, but was reprieved before he got there. Back in Newgate, he was visited by his family and friends, who rejoiced at his narrow escape. On 11 August he was taken back to Tyburn and, on this occasion, hanged without interruption.

**Cooke, Adolphus** (1792–1876), soldier and landowner. Cooke, a believer in reincarnation, was unfailingly courteous to a turkey cock whom he took to be his father. Menservants were instructed to doff their hats when they passed the bird, and serving girls were required to perform a small curtsy.

Cooke was the illegitimate son of Robert Cooke, inheriting Cookesborough, a large estate in Mullingar, when Robert died in 1835 without a legitimate heir. Adolphus, who had been educated in England, and had thereafter served in the army, ran his 4000-acre inheritance in an unconventional way. Positions of trust were given to two employees whom he called 'gentlemen of nature's stamp'. His steward, Tom Cruise, whom he had selected from the workhouse, had a passion for sport, on one occasion interrupting Sunday Mass by calling out, 'Father, you are forgetting to tell them about the races at Longfield today.' Next in seniority was Billy Dunn, who liked to drill imaginary troops and greatly admired the newly created police force. On public days he would himself dress up as a policeman, wielding a stick which he called his bayonet.

Cooke's ideas on animal husbandry were unorthodox by the standards of the time. One day, he was informed that a bullock had stumbled into the river and was on the point of drowning. After consultation with Cruise and Dunn, he ordered all the other cattle to be driven to the river's bank. They would have the opportunity, Cooke said, 'of seeing their companion drowning, and it will be a warning and a caution to each and every one of them during their mortal tenure to shun the water.' On another occasion, a bull which threatened Cooke in the paddock was challenged to a fight. The bull was gaining the upper hand until a maidservant came to her master's aid, managing to open a heavy iron gate through which he was able to escape. She was sacked on the spot for altering the conditions of a fair fight.

Cooke's belief in reincarnation led to a last-minute reprieve for Gusty, a large and affectionate red setter. Gusty had a habit of straying, and when brought home would be kept in solitary confinement for three days and placed on short rations. After many such imprisonments, Gusty was warned that if he went missing one more time he would be hanged like a common criminal. To press the point home, Gusty was shown the rope and the tree from which he would be suspended. The dog ignored the warning, and within days was discovered in Mullingar in 'common company'. A trial took place the following morning in the Great Hall. Dunn and Cruise were appointed as special advisers to the court, and a jury was sworn in. Evidence was given by two labradors that Gusty had resisted arrest. After an absence of three hours, the jury returned a verdict of 'guilty of misbehaviour'. Having passed sentence, Cooke informed Gusty that a tombstone would be erected over his grave with the following inscription, 'Gusty – executed for high crimes and misdemeanours. It is earnestly hoped that his sad fate will be a warning to other dogs against so offending. Tuesday 8th May, 1860'. The problem was to find a hangman. None of the staff was keen to carry out the execution since instant dismissal was the expected outcome. Eventually a man known as 'The Bug Mee' agreed to do the job. 'To please your honour I'll hang him', he said, 'and I'd hang the missus and children too, if it came to that.' The next morning, Bug Mee disappeared with Gusty and a rope, but soon returned with Gusty still alive. His explanation was that while he was putting the rope round Gusty's neck, the dog had spoken to him in some kind of foreign language. 'So I said to myself, I'll bring him back to the master, because there is something in him.' Gusty was readmitted to the house, and like the turkey cock he lived to a considerable age.

As he grew older, Cooke became obsessively concerned with his own burial arrangements. He built a huge marble vault on the estate, 40 feet underground so that he would not be disturbed by the screechings of jackdaws, which he detested. Marble steps led down into a large book-lined room, with a great fireplace, in front of which he put a marble table and chair. He directed that he should be embalmed and placed in a sitting position by the fire, which should be kept perpetually alight. When he died in 1876, the rector of Killucan, with whom he had been on poor terms, had him buried in a stone beehive. The marble vault has been demolished, but the beehive, which looks like a large egg, survives in Reynella churchyard, near the Cookesborough estate.

**Cooke, James** (1760–1829), pimp. In September 1810 Cooke, the proprietor of the Swan Hotel in Vere Street, was convicted at the Old Bailey of running a homosexual brothel. A journalist, Robert Holloway, later revealed in his pamphlet, *The Phoenix Of Sodom: The Vere Street Coterie*, that there was a room at the Swan, known as 'the Chapel', in which John CHURCH officiated at transvestite weddings, sometimes solemnized, according to Holloway, 'between a six foot six Grenadier Guardsman wearing a frock and a *petit maître* not more than half the altitude of his beloved wife'. Cooke was sentenced to two years imprisonment and to stand in the pillory in the Haymarket – an ordeal he endured better than his predecessor 'Mother' Margaret CLAP, who had died of her injuries. Cooke survived, completed his prison sentence and returned to his previous occupation.

**Coons.** *See* HARDING, ARTHUR.

**Coppe, the Reverend Abiezer** (1605–72), priest. After studying at Oxford University, Coppe was ordained first as a Presbyterian, then as an Anabaptist, minister. For a while he carried out his duties in an inconspicuous manner, but in 1649 he started to appear in the pulpit naked, and to sleep with members of his congregation. He then joined the Ranters, a radical religious group that rejected morality and the law, and particularly espoused total sexual liberty. Inspiration had come to him, apparently, after he was taken on a four-day trip to hell and back, in the course of which he had been chosen by God to be his instrument against 'the Great Ones of the World'. The latter had been identified by God as 'the ministers, fat parsons, Vicars, Lecturers &c who serve Christ only to maintaine their pride, paunches and purses'. Henceforth, they would be well advised to abase themselves before thieves, beggars, harlots and publicans. God had further demanded the subversion of all 'honourable' things, which were in fact corrupt and hypocritical. 'Elderships, Fellowships, Churches, Ordinances, Prayers, Holiness, Righteousness, Religions of all sorts' were all in God's eyes part of the vile conspiracy of 'Honour'.

In his first book, *The Fiery Flying Roll* (1650), Coppe wrote:

> I have chosen, and cannot be without, BASE things, to confound some in mercy, some in judgement, though also I have concubines without number, which I cannot be without. I can if it be my will, kisse and hug Ladies, and love my neighbour's wife as my selfe, without sin.

The argument is coherent, attractive even, but the ministers and fat parsons of the time took a different view. Upon publication of *The Fiery Flying Roll*, Coppe was arrested and thrown into prison. A month later, Parliament ordered that all copies of the book should be burned by the hangman, and in August 1650, an act was passed against the Ranters.

At first Coppe was defiant. Brought before Parliament's committee of examinations, he pretended to be mad and threw apples at his inquisitors, but after languishing in prison for a few more months he published a complete retraction. In *Coppe's Return to the Wayes of Truth*, he declares, 'mine UNDERSTANDING is returned to me,' and he catalogues all the errors attributed to him. However, he vigorously denies responsibility for the numerous children whose mothers were claiming him as their father. 'Some of them indeed look somewhat like my children,' he concedes, 'but I will not be so full of foolish pity as to spare them. I will turn them out of doors, and starve them to death.' Parliament was impressed, and Coppe was at last released from prison. He changed his name to Dr Higham and moved to Surrey.

**'Copperfaced Jack'.** *See* CLONMELL, JOHN SCOTT, 1ST EARL OF.

**Corder, William** (1805–28), farmer, school teacher and perpetrator of the celebrated 'Red Barn Murder' of 1827. Corder, a prosperous farmer's son, had become engaged, against his will, to Maria Marten, a mole-catcher's daughter. Maria had established 'a reputation' in Polstead, Suffolk, having lost her virginity to one local youth and bearing a child by another. She also became pregnant by Corder's brother Thomas, but the infant died soon after birth. William Corder himself was considered shifty and devious. On one occasion, he secretly sold all his father's pigs. He was sent to London in disgrace, but returned when his brother Thomas was drowned trying to cross a frozen pond. In 1826 William became Maria's lover, and when she became pregnant he promised to marry her – albeit in secret, since she might be arrested, he said, for having illegitimate children. On 18 May 1827 Corder told her to meet him at the Red Barn, a building on his father's land, whence they would travel to Ipswich to be married. Maria was never seen again. Corder returned home and told Maria's family that, for the time being, he had placed her in lodgings in Ipswich. He then moved to London, where he advertised in the newspapers for a wife – shortly meeting a young woman, Mary Moore, whom he married. Mary Moore had enough money to set up a girls' school in Ealing. Corder bought a pair of spectacles and appointed himself headmaster.

Meanwhile, Maria's mother was having dreams in which she saw Corder shooting her daughter at the Red Barn and burying her body there. Her persistence caused the barn to be searched, and on 19 April 1828 Maria's murdered body was dug up. Corder was arrested and his defence –

that Maria had committed suicide after a quarrel – was not believed. He was hanged before a huge crowd outside Bury St Edmunds prison on 11 August 1828.

Maria's story and Corder's execution became classic entertainments of the Victorian period, in print, on the stage as *Murder in the Old Red Barn* and in fairground peepshows. The latter became so popular that the travelling impresario, 'Lord' George Sanger, was obliged to fit his stalls with 26 glass apertures so that 26 customers could watch simultaneously, while outside the patter-man drummed up new customers:

> Walk up! Walk up! See the death of Maria Marten at the hands
> of the villain Corder in the famous Red Barn! See how the ghost
> of Maria appeared to her mother on three successive nights at the
> bedside, leading to the discovery of the body and the arrest of
> Corder at Everley Grove House, Brentford, seven miles from
> London!

*See also* CURTIS, JAMES; FAIRS, TRAVELLING.

**corporate loyalty, master criminals brought down by a lack of.** *See* AGAR, EDWARD; SAWARD, JAMES TOWNSHEND.

**corpse, arriving at Mrs Cornely's masque dressed as a.** *See* LUTTRELL, COLONEL JAMES.

**corpse, objection to sharing one's husband with a.** *See* VAN BUTCHELL, MARTIN.

**corpse, put off pork chops for life after viewing a dissected.** *See* HACKMAN, THE REVEREND JAMES

**corpse, substituting oneself for a.** *See* EDGAR, HENRY.

**'corpse' beats up undertaker.** *See* INGRAMS, HAROLD.

**corpse's beer, finishing the.** *See* MADDOCK, WILL.

**corpses clattering in the wind, ironed.** *See* JEFFREYS, GEORGE.

**corpses of soldiers sold as edible meat.** *See* LABOUCHERE, HENRY.

**corpses passed off as live sailors.** *See* KELLY, SHANGHAI.

**Corrigan, Michael** (1881–1946), confidence trickster. Born in Fermoy, Ireland, 'Major' Corrigan was the most successful confidence trickster in

London during the 1930s and 1940s. A handsome man of military bearing, and an accomplished actor, he promoted himself to the rank of general in the Mexican army and sold oil concessions to the British government. As a chief inspector in the Canadian Mounted Police he seconded himself to Scotland Yard and persuaded a West End jeweller to lend him his stock for the day in order, he said, to entrap a gang of Canadian thieves. He sold the Tower of London, London Bridge (twice), and, on numerous occasions, 145 Piccadilly to American tourists. His most imaginative exploit, however, was the Liverpool Street Station Information Booth Swindle, based on a stunt already pulled off in New York, where it had been known as the Grand Central Station Swindle.

In March 1935 two successful Covent Garden fruiterers, Tony and Nick Mancini, were visited by Major Corrigan, who introduced himself as Mr T. Remington Grenfell, chairman of the Liverpool Street Station Holding Company Ltd. According to Mr Grenfell, the company had decided that all travel enquiries at Liverpool Street Station would be handled in future by the ticket office, thus clearing the information booth for commercial purposes. The board had decided that a fruit stand would best meet travellers' needs. After an intensive search, the Mancini brothers had been chosen to put this idea into practice. The rent would be a mere £350 a week, with the first year's rent in advance. The Mancinis signed a contract on the spot, and paid the first year's rent in cash. In return, Mr Grenfell gave them papers authorizing them to take over the information booth the following day.

At 9 o'clock the next morning the Mancini brothers arrived at the booth with a gang of carpenters who would turn it into a fruit stall. Wood was stacked up outside the booth and measurements were taken by the carpenters. When the travel clerks refused to vacate the premises, the Mancinis tried to eject them by force. A fight broke out and railway guards were summoned to remove the carpenters, who were in the way of travellers seeking information about the train service to East Anglia. The Mancinis, brandishing their authorization papers, were escorted to the station's offices, where they were told that the Liverpool Street Station Holding Company Ltd didn't exist. Believing that they were being discriminated against as second-generation immigrants, the Mancinis started another fight and were only subdued when the police arrived.

In 1946 Major Corrigan was arrested in the bar of the Ritz hotel, London. His guest at the time was the director of public prosecutions, and one-time commissioner at Scotland Yard, Sir Richard Jackson, to whom he was trying to sell a pension plan. Facing a long prison sentence for fraud, he hanged himself in Brixton prison with his Guards tie.

**Costa del Crime.** *See* FOREMAN, FREDDIE; KNIGHT, RONNIE; MOYNIHAN, ANTONY PATRICK ANDREW CAIRNE BERKELEY, 3RD BARON.

**Cotton, Mary Ann** (1833–73), district nurse. Cotton, three times married and a resident of West Auckland in County Durham, has strong claims to being England's foremost mass murderer, Dr Harold Shipman apart. 21 people close to her died within 20 years, and she was suspected of a further 15 murders. Her motive was either to collect insurance money or to open the way to a new marriage. Among her proven victims were her bigamous second husband Frederick, his two stepsons, her lodger and sometime lover Joseph Natrass, and a local excise officer named Quick-Manning, by whom she became pregnant.

It was when Cotton's second stepson died that a suspicious neighbour went to the police. The doctor, who had seen the child the previous day, refused to sign a death certificate. A post-mortem was carried out and analysis of the stomach contents proved positive for arsenic. Cotton was charged with murder and taken to Durham prison where her child by Quick-Manning was born. At her trial, defence counsel claimed that the dead boy had been poisoned accidentally by arsenic contained in green floral wallpaper used in the home. But Cotton's recent purchase of arsenic – ostensibly for killing bedbugs – told against her. She was found guilty and sentenced to death. Her baby by Quick-Manning was taken away from her five days before she was executed. The hangman bungled the operation and it was three and a half minutes before her body stopped convulsing at the rope's end.

**countesses who have lived to 140.** *See* DESMOND, CATHERINE FITZGERALD, COUNTESS OF.

**Coven, the.** *See* CLARK, ALAN.

**Cowden, Charlie** (1917– ), confidence trickster. In November 2000, 83-year-old Cowden admitted in court that he had obtained the sum of £37 from Mrs Khadijeh Khedri by deception. Posing as Colonel J.P. Kenneally VC, Cowden told Mrs Khadijeh, who ran a fruit stall in Peckham, that he had several million in stocks and shares but that this was a bad time to sell. He needed the cash urgently, he said, to tide him over. Mrs Khadijeh was not able to fund Kenneally from the day's takings, so she borrowed the money from the bank.

Snaresborough Crown Court was told that Cowden had 571 previous convictions and had spent 20 years in prison – twice for bigamy and, in 1940, for 'idling in on War Department land'. Judge Timothy King put him on probation for two years.

**cows used as secret weapon, herd of.** *See* MORGAN, SIR HENRY.

**coxcombs.** *See* DODD, THE REVEREND DR WILLIAM; MACLEANE, JAMES; MASSEREENE, CLOTWORTHY SKEFFINGTON, 2ND EARL.

**Coyle, Francis** (*c*.1801–?), farmer and ringer. Coyle, a successful Berkshire farmer, was the most resourceful 'switcher' of his day – a time when horse racing was systematically corrupt. According to the *Sporting Times*, he was 'the most unutterable of all the unutterable scoundrels who ever disgraced the Turf'.

Coyle's most daring betting coup was an attempt to rig the Derby in 1844. There is no doubt that two suspect horses, one a 4-year-old, the other a 5-year-old, were entered that year for a race that is famously for 3-year-olds. The latter were an indifferent bunch on this occasion and the best of them, Rattan, had in any case been poisoned just before the off.

At the start of the race, one of the suspect horses, Running Rein, kicked and disabled the other, Leander. With Rattan already dead, and with Leander crippled, Running Rein, which was owned by Coyle, came home an easy winner at 10–1. Colonel Peel, who owned the second-placed horse, Orlando, obtained an injunction to prevent the prize money being distributed. Coyle, who now feared prosecution, pre-empted this by bringing a civil action to recover the prize money, which, after an interval, had been given to Colonel Peel. He didn't dispute the fact that he had backed Running Rein for large sums of money, and it was admitted by the court that he might have done so if the horse had been entered legitimately. His case was not helped, however, when, on being asked to produce Running Rein for examination by the stewards, he said that the horse had disappeared.

At this point a Mr Worley, a farmer who had attended the Derby, announced that he had recognized Running Rein as Maccabeus, an excellent 4-year-old that had won a valuable race at Newmarket the previous summer. He was able to identify Maccabeus with such confidence, he said, because the horse had wintered at his farm in Northamptonshire – at least until it had disappeared after a visit from Coyle. Coyle, it turned out, had ridden to Mr Worley's stables on a hack, passed the time of day, waited until Mr Worley was otherwise occupied and had then ridden away on Maccabeus, later to win the Derby as Running Rein.

Orlando was reinstated as the winner of the 1844 Derby, but his owner, Colonel Peel, was rebuked by Baron Alderson in the Court of the Exchequer Chamber:

> If gentlemen would make it a rule to associate only with other gentlemen such incidents would not occur. But if gentlemen will condescend to race with blackguards they must expect to be cheated.

Francis Coyle went to prison for five years and was warned off for life.

**Cracksman, the Gentleman.** *See* HOLLIDAY, BERT.

**cracksmen, master.** *See* AGAR, EDWARD; CHAPMAN, EDDIE; HINDS, ALFRED; RAMENSKY, JOHNNY.

**Cradock, Fanny** (1909–94), novelist, journalist and cook. Mrs Cradock
has some claims to being the first of the celebrity cooks who subsequently
came to dominate the television schedules. Though best remembered for
her overbearing manner and inappropriate wardrobe – she cooked as a rule
in a Hartnell ball gown – her contribution to improved standards of catering shouldn't be entirely overlooked.

Fanny Cradock was born as Phyllis Peachey in the Channel Islands.
Her father was a butterfly collector and a writer of novels and pantomimes.
Her mother Bijou was an actress and singer. At the age of 1 the infant
Phyllis was given to her grandmother as a birthday present. In later life she
would claim that it was her grandmother who had taught her everything
she knew about food and wine. Grandma insisted that she was seated, and
properly dressed, by the time the food was served – a condition Fanny
could only satisfy by cooking in her Hartnell frock. 'That's how I learned
to cook in evening dress,' she said. Away from the table she spent her childhood communing with the dead. 'I was on intimate terms with the court of
Louis XIV,' she recalled.

At the age of 17 Fanny eloped to Brighton with her first husband, who
died soon after, leaving her as a pregnant widow. She made ends meet by
washing up at a Roman Catholic canteen. In 1939 she met Johnnie
Cradock, an old Harrovian. They were together for the next 50 years, but
didn't marry until 1977. While Johnnie was away in the army during World
War II, Fanny occupied herself by writing erotic fiction under the name
Frances Dale. *The Lormes of Castle Rising* and *Storm Over Castle Rising* were
among the most successful. After the war she turned her hand to cookery
writing with *The Practical Cook* (1949) and *The Ambitious Cook* (1950).

Fanny had many contretemps with the general public. On one occasion, some youths refused to surrender a parking space that she had her eye
on. 'I went in kicking low,' she said. The youths quickly moved their car.
When charged in 1964 with careless driving, her manner was described by
the arresting officer as 'abusive in the extreme'. Asked to move her Rolls
Royce, which was holding up the traffic while she chatted to a friend, she
had called the constable 'a uniformed delinquent' and had told him to wait
until she had finished her conversation. When he insisted that she move
her car, she reversed into the one behind. 'He told me to back up,' she told
the court. 'I was just doing as I was told.'

By the 1970s Mrs Cradock's memory was fading. When she finally
married Johnnie in a register office she seemed to be confused about her
name and her age. She claimed to be 55, even though she had a son of 50,
and she gave her family name as de Peche rather than Pechey. When questioned further she changed it to Valentine.

In 1983 Mrs Cradock was again prosecuted for dangerous driving after
she had caused a collision by swerving out of her lane. When the other
driver tried to discuss the matter with her she shouted, 'Dog's poo!' and

then drove off. The other driver followed her for 15 miles, blowing his horn and signalling. When he finally overtook her, and stood in the road waving her down, she drove straight into him and ran him over. She told the judge that his threatening behaviour had made her afraid to stop.

In 1984 Mrs Cradock was appointed *Grande Dame de la Tripière d'Or*, a much coveted gastronomic award.

**Crapp, Jack** (1915–89), cricketer. Crapp is remembered as an accomplished batsman and alert fielder in the slips who played for Gloucestershire from 1936 to 1957 and appeared on seven occasions for England. On retiring from the game he stood as an umpire for a further 22 years. Throughout his 43-year career Crapp wore the same pair of boots. They were handmade by the Bristol shoemakers Stubbs and Burt, had cost five guineas and travelled with him all over the world. He once lent them to the local Boy Scouts who put them on sale at a jumble sale with a sign reading, 'See the boots Jack Crapp wore – 5p'.

**Crazy Crow.** *See* BODY SNATCHERS, IRISH.

**Cream, Dr Thomas Neill** (1850–92), physician, known as 'the Cross-Eyed Lambeth Poisoner'. Cream was born in Glasgow and graduated in medicine at McGill University, Canada, in 1876. He practised as a physician in Chicago, where he developed an alternative career in crime, involving murder, arson, abortion and blackmail. In 1881 he murdered with strychnine a man called Stott, the husband of his current mistress, and then took the unusual step of writing to the district attorney, advising that Stott's body be exhumed. He was arrested and sentenced to life imprisonment. It was an example of the exhibitionism that eventually caused him to be hanged.

Released from Chicago's Joliet prison, Dr Cream arrived in London in October 1891 and took lodgings at 103 Lambeth Palace Road. During the next few months he glided cross-eyed and silk-hatted through south London, preying on prostitutes to whom he gave pills laced with strychnine. By this method he poisoned Ellen Donworth, Matilda Clover, Emma Shrivell and Alice Marsh. As he had done in Chicago, he indulged in various forms of self-advertisement that led to his arrest. He made an offer to name the 'Lambeth Poisoner' for a reward of £30,000, and brought himself to the attention of Scotland Yard with complaints that he was being followed. He was arrested on 3 June 1892 and charged with acting under false pretences. A murder charge followed when a prostitute named Louisa Harvey reported that she had picked up the cross-eyed doctor some months before and had spent the night with him. He had offered her some pills to combat her poor complexion, and his insistence that she swallow these whole had made her suspicious. She had pretended to swallow them, later dropping them on the floor.

Cream was tried in October. Louisa Harvey's testimony and a chemist's evidence that he had recently bought *nux vomica* and gelatin capsules from his shop, together with the discovery of seven bottles of strychnine at the doctor's lodgings, were enough to convince the jury of his guilt. He was hanged on 15 November 1892.

In a letter to *The Times*, Cream's optician suggested that the condemned man's moral degeneracy might have been attributable to the fact that his squint had not been corrected when he was a child.

**Cresswell, Sir Cresswell.** *See* COLLUSION, DIVORCE BY.

**cricket as a cause for divorce.** *See* ROWLEY, MICHAEL.

**Cricket Bat Murder, the.** *See* INSTRUMENTS, BLUNT; YORK, SARAH MARGARET, DUCHESS OF.

**cricketers, idiosyncratic.** *See* TENNYSON, LIONEL, 3RD BARON.

**cricketers, intimidation by.** *See* GRACE, DR W(ILLIAM) G(ILBERT); JACKSON, JOHN; JARDINE, DOUGLAS; MORRIS, WILLIAM; SLEDGING.

**cricketing dogs.** *See* TRUMPER, FRANCIS.

**cricket umpires.** *See* BIRD, HAROLD ('DICKIE'); CRAPP, JACK.

**criminal conversation.** A term formerly used for the activities of the lover of an adulterous wife; at one time criminal conversation could be subject to a civil action for damages by the wronged husband (*see* BATE, THE REVEREND HENRY; BELVEDERE, ROBERT ROCHFORT, 1ST EARL OF; CARDIGAN, JAMES THOMAS BRUDENELL, 7TH EARL OF; NORTON, GEORGE CHAPPLE).

Shortly before the law was abolished by the Matrimonial Causes Act 1857, an upholsterer, Mr Lyle, fearing that his wife's affections had been transferred to his business partner, Mr Herbert, employed a cabinet maker, Mr Taylor, to construct what the judge called a crimconmeter that would show how many people were in a bed at one time. Having taken delivery of the apparatus, Mr Lyle rented a room in the house next door, bored a hole through the wall and set up the device, which was in the form of a lever that fell to a certain level when one person got into bed and dropped further when a second, third or fourth person joined in. Once the lever had fallen to the second level, Lyle and Taylor went into Lyle's home and shone a torch at Mrs Lyle and Mr Herbert. Taylor then appropriated Mr Herbert's bottle of gin, taking the view that in the circumstances it was rightfully Lyle's, and that he, Taylor, deserved a bonus. Lyle and Taylor then went to

a pub, where they drank themselves insensible. Mr Herbert was allowed to
remain in Lyle's house for the rest of the day, and to ensure that he did so,
Lyle and Taylor confiscated his boots. Lyle was awarded a farthing's
damages against Mr Herbert.

*See also* BRAUN, HEIDI.

**crimping.** The profession, common in the 19th century, of supplying merchant ships with sailors by means of kidnap. As a rule, the victims would
be incapacitated by drink or drugs, later waking up at sea.

*See* KELLY, SHANGHAI.

**Crippen, Dr Hawley Harvey** (1862–1910), patent medicine salesman,
physician and murderer. Crippen's poisoning of his second wife, Cora
Turner, an amateur music-hall artiste calling herself Belle Elmore, was one
of the most sensational crimes of the early 20th century.

Born in Michigan, the nervous and mild-mannered little doctor
enjoyed poor relations with women throughout his life. His first wife was a
guilt-ridden woman who hurried off to confession after the couple had
made love. His second marriage, to Cora Turner, with whom he moved to
London in 1900, was equally unenjoyable. Since Crippen's American qualifications didn't allow him to practise as a doctor he took various jobs
connected with selling patent medicines. Cora, a strong-willed woman,
had him under her thumb, taunting him with her many adventures and
forcing him to do the housework at 39 Hilltop Crescent, where she took in
paying guests. In time, Crippen became infatuated with his secretary, Ethel
le Neve, with whom, as he later said, he was happy for the only time in his
life.

In 1910 Crippen poisoned his wife after a party at their home, later dissecting the body and burying the remains in the coal cellar. Cora's friends
were told that she had died on holiday in the USA, but after the police had
unsuccessfully investigated Cora's disappearance, Ethel took fright and the
pair fled to Canada on board the SS *Montrose*, Crippen calling himself Mr
Robinson and Ethel disguising herself as his son. The ship's captain, who
had read that a second police search at Hilltop Crescent had unearthed
Cora's remains, and whose suspicions had in any case been aroused by le
Neve's ill-fitting disguise and by the couple's affectionate behaviour, contacted Scotland Yard by radio telegraphy (famously the first use of radio
for police purposes) and Crippen and le Neve were arrested.

Crippen was tried for murder at the Old Bailey on 18 October 1910,
found guilty and hanged at Pentonville on 23 November. Ethel le Neve was
tried separately as an accessory after the fact. Defended by F.E. Smith, she
was acquitted. She remarried, and died in 1967.

**Cripple, Margaret** (*c.*1590–?) and **Cripple, William** (*c.*1590–?), exhibitionists. The public satisfaction of lust was not encouraged in the early years of the 17th century, and in 1619 the Cripples appeared before the Archdeacon's Court in Somerset for offending the moral values of their co-parishioners. A farmer reported that he had come across a young couple 'having intercourse in a plot of grass under a hedge'. According to G.R. Quaife's *Wanton Wenches and Wayward Wives: Peasants and Illicit Sex in Early Seventeenth Century England* (1979):

> The informant stepped up to them and took William by the tail of his shirt and demanded of them why they were so wicked as to do such a thing in a public place. To which William replied that Margaret was his wife by promise and that he intended to marry her the next morning at eight of the clock.

The Cripples appear not to have learnt their lesson from whatever punishment they received on that occasion. The following year a case surfaced in Star Chamber in which a couple, identifiable as the Cripples, formerly resident in Somerset, and now living in Burton-on-Trent, cited 18 other residents of the town for unjustly punishing them for sexual incontinency. The Cripples, according to their account of what happened, were dragged from their bed, and barely had time to dress before they were driven through the streets by a group of townsmen, 'many of them being disguised'. This group made a 'rough music' as they dragged Mr and Mrs Cripple along, 'with greate noyce and with ringing cow bells, basons, candlesticks, fryingpannes and with the sound of a drumme', crying out, 'a whore and a knave, a whore!' as they went, and throwing 'dourte and mier of the streets at them'. The Cripples, whose punishment had by now attracted some 400 spectators, were put in the town stocks, where the town folk not only threw more dirt at them but also 'pissed on their heads'. After which they were dragged by their feet, with their heads down, through 'the durty channells' of the streets. Edward Lambe, the constable who led the proceedings, explained to Star Chamber that the treatment was intended to 'make soe notorious an abuse exemplarye whereby other evill disposed might be discouraged from committing the like' (from *The English Village Constable 1580–1642: A Social and Administrative Study*, Joan R. Kent, 1986). Constable Lamb later deposed that the Cripples' swift departure from Burton-on-Trent was occasioned by their fear that they would also be 'carted' – the standard punishment for sexual immorality in borough towns.

For references to other sexual exhibitionists, *see* EXHIBITIONISTS.

**crocodile from one's canoe, dislodging a.** *See* KINGSLEY, MARY.

**crocodile in one's front room, keeping a.** *See* DALY, JOSEPHINE (for Thomas Carrington).

**crocodile in the Scottish Borders, surprising appearance of a.** *See* DOUGLAS-HOME, WILLIAM.

**crocodiles, eaten by.** *See* DE ROUGEMONT, LOUIS.

**Crombie, having a meat cleaver concealed under one's.** *See* RATCLIFFE, OWEN.

**cross-dressers.** *See* ACKE, PETER; BARKER, COLONEL LESLIE IVOR GAUNTLETT; BARRY, DR JAMES MIRANDA; BONNY, ANNE; BOULTON, ERNEST; BUTLER, LADY ELEANOR; CARSTAIRS, MARION BARBARA; CHALLENOR, DETECTIVE SERGEANT HAROLD (for professional purposes only); CLARENDON, JOHN CORNBURY, 3RD EARL OF; DAVISON, JANE; DE BEAUMONT, CHEVALIER D'EON; HALL, ARCHIBALD; LAMBOURNE, LADY MARGARET (for purposes of assassination); LLOYD, SOPHIE (for professional purposes only); PAYNE, CYNTHIA (*re* some of her clients); SNELL, HANNAH; STANLEY, SARAH.

**Cross-Eyed Lambeth Poisoner, the.** *See* CREAM, DR THOMAS NEILL.

**Crowhurst, Donald** (1932–69), electronic engineer and yachtsman. On 31 October 1968 Crowhurst, a married man with four children, set sail aboard a trimaran ketch, *Teignmouth Electron,* in a bid to win the prestigious *Sunday Times* Golden Globe single-handed round-the-world yacht race.

It was sometime during the first week of December that he decided to cheat. On 10 December he claimed to have sailed 243 miles in a day, which, had it been true, would have set a new world record for any lone sailor. The field by now had narrowed to four, including himself, Robin Knox-Johnston, Bernard Moitessier and Commander Nigel Tetley. Because of his startling burst of speed, newspapers at home were already naming Crowhurst as the likely winner. By 12 December he was keeping a fictitious log book and had evolved a plan to hide in the wastes of the South Atlantic while reporting record-breaking progress round the world.

On 16 March 1969 Crowhurst contravened a further rule by putting ashore in Argentina for running repairs. With these completed, and having set a northeasterly course to convince the local coastguards that he was heading for Britain, he headed south to continue the deception. By now there were only three competitors for the Golden Gold trophy: Crowhurst, Nigel Tetley and Robin Knox-Johnston. Knox-Johnston was sighted homeward bound on 6 April and was clearly set to win the Golden Globe as the first man home. However, his monohull boat was slower than either of the trimarans, so Tetley (round the Horn by 20 March and already well into the Atlantic) and Donald Crowhurst, who was supposedly in record-breaking pursuit, were both well placed to beat him for the fastest passage prize.

On 4 May Crowhurst began sailing in earnest so that he could claim a faster time home than Tetley. It was only then that a disturbing truth dawned: with the fastest passage time a near certainty, and the £5000 prize his for the taking, he suddenly realized that the obligatory log-book inspection would expose him as a fraud. He decided to slow down and arrive a close second (thus avoiding the log-book inspection), forgoing the prize-money but winning nationwide acclaim as a gallant loser. On 16 May, he radioed, 'No chance overtake Tetley now. Probably very close result.' On 21 May, however, Commander Tetley's ship sank under him with only 1200 miles to go.

Since there was no way now in which Crowhurst could fail to win the £5000, he broke under the strain and, in the month that followed, went mad. The last words he wrote, and which appear to have been addressed to God, were:

> It is time for your move to begin I have not need to prolong the game
> It has been a good game that must be ended at the I will play this
> game when I choose I will resign the game 11 20 40 There is no
> reason for harmful ...

He is presumed to have jumped overboard at that point and to have drowned in the Sargasso Sea. His body was never found.

When the truth was finally established, Robin Knox-Johnston, now undisputed winner of both the Golden Globe trophy and of the fastest passage prize, handed the £5000 to the Appeal Fund established for Donald Crowhurst's widow and four children. 'None of us should judge him too harshly,' he said.

**Crowley, Aleister** (1875–1947), writer and magician. Born into a family of wealthy brewers and religious dissenters, Crowley became interested in the occult as an undergraduate at Cambridge, his time there coinciding with the magic revival of the late 19th century. For a time he was a member of the Order of the Golden Dawn, which the poet W.B. Yeats also joined. When he was expelled for 'extreme practices', Crowley founded his own order, the Silver Star, which handed out comic-opera degrees in mysticism and related hocus-pocus. He liked to be known as 'the Great Beast' (the name given to him by his mother, who had brought him up after his father died when he was 11) and as 'the wickedest man alive'.

In receipt of a substantial inheritance, Crowley spent the first part of his life trying to combat boredom. He travelled, climbed mountains, dabbled in mysticism, designed boomerangs and invented a gadget for indoor golf. When the money ran out he had little choice but to sell himself as an apparently serious occult hierophant, peddling an inconsistent brand of sex magic. Among other practices, he recommended self-improvement through mystic buggery. In 1920 he founded an experimental Thelemic community near Cefalu, in Sicily. He claimed he could conjure up demons, and the community's watchword, 'Do what thou wilt shall be the whole of the Law', excited the condemnation of the popular press.

Crowley's sexual relations became increasingly intertwined with his magical work as he grew older. He aspired to guilt-free sex, and, with some psychological insight, recognized that this was best achieved through humiliation, involving the total destruction of the personality. However, his sadistic impulses were too strong to allow him to reach this point himself. His emotional prison turned out to be not, as he had supposed, a respectable English childhood, but the fact that he came to prefer the humiliation of others for its own sake to any sexual pleasure derived therefrom. This tension had unfortunate consequences both for himself and for those with whom he came in contact. On his travels he beat his porters and guides. At home he beat his lovers of both sexes. If he could have been bothered with his children he would no doubt have beaten them too. And, privately, he may have recognized that his inability to overcome his heroin addiction was a poor reflection on his teaching that 'Will is the whole Law'.

Crowley's ideas on sex and drugs brought about a revival of interest in the 1960s, particularly in America, where he has always been taken more seriously than in his native country, and where Wicca, the neo-pagan cult that he had some influence on founding, is now recognized as an official religion by the United States army. In England, Crowley was always treated as something of a joke. His many appearances in the libel courts, where it was consistently decided that he had no reputation worth defending, were a constant source of public entertainment. When his third wife, Marie De Miramar, was committed to an insane asylum, her identification as Mrs Aleister Crowley was taken as a further symptom of her condition.

**Culley, Robert** (c.1800–33), police constable. The stabbing to death of PC Culley by a mob in 1833 turned out to be a blow for freedom of speech. In October of that year the police commissioner banned a meeting in Coldbath Fields, London, of a revolutionary group that called itself the National Political Union. The ban was ignored and a crowd gathered round a speaker on a soapbox. A police spy reported that sedition was being preached, and a senior officer ordered his men to advance slowly, with their truncheons at the ready. The crowd booed and pelted them with stones. The police reacted badly, hitting out wildly and knocking down women and children. A man drew a knife as a policeman tried to snatch an anarchist banner and stabbed him in the chest. Constable Culley staggered a few yards and fell dead.

A coroner's jury, consisting of respectable tradesmen, returned a verdict of justifiable homicide against the unknown person who had stabbed PC Culley. The spectators cheered, and the jury were treated as

ABOVE Having announced his decision to sue the *Guardian* for libel – a misjudgement on his part that led to a prison sentence for perjury – former cabinet minister and entrepreneur **Jonathan Aitken** leaves a news conference with his wife Lolicia and daughter Victoria.

LEFT **Jane Andrews**, once a dresser to the duchess of York, seen here with her boyfriend Tom Cressman, whom she shortly afterwards bludgeoned to death in the celebrated Cricket Bat Murder of June 2000.

BELOW LEFT Former Tory Party chairman and fiction writer **Jeffrey Archer** attends a book launch at Claridges with his loyal wife, Mary.

LEFT **Margaret duchess of Argyll** with the French miniature poodle that she customarily 'walked' in the lobby of the Grosvenor House Hotel, Park Lane – obliging the management to suggest that she find alternative accommodation.

RIGHT The late **John Aspinall**, casino owner and animal-rights activist, romps with a tiger at his zoo, Howletts in Kent. The zoo has a poor safety record. Three keepers have been killed by tigers and one has been squashed to death by an elephant.

LEFT **Francis Bacon**, one of England's most distinguished philosophers and jurists, yet a voluptuary who, as James I's lord chancellor, accepted money from defendants to influence court judgements.

RIGHT **William Beckford**, writer and art collector, spent the latter part of his life building a 300-foot tower at his home, Fonthill Abbey, in Wiltshire. He lived there as a recluse with his Spanish dwarf, his heraldic advisor and his dog, Viscount Fartleberry.

BELOW The late **Jeffrey Bernard** (right), Soho 'character' and author of the *Spectator*'s 'Low-Life' column, enjoys a drink with the Coach and Horses' proprietor Norman Balon (centre), reputed to be the rudest publican in London.

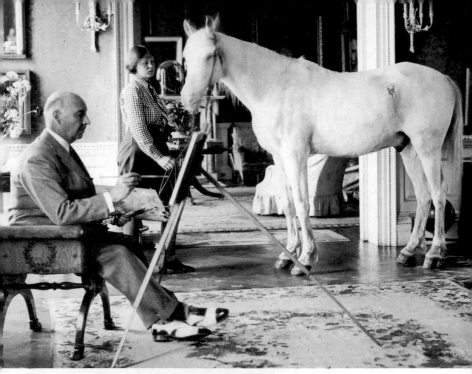

ABOVE Mrs P. Betjeman and her horse pose for their portrait in the drawing-room of Faringdon House, the home of **Gerald Hugh Tyrwhitt-Wilson, 14th Baron Berners**. Lord Berners also composed ballet music and contributed a song, 'Come on Algernon', to the Ealing comedy, *Champagne Charlie*.

LEFT **Peter Bessell**, formerly the MP for Bodmin in Cornwall. In 1979, Bessell gave evidence against his friend Jeremy Thorpe when the former leader of the Liberal party was accused, and later acquitted, of conspiracy to murder Norman Scott, a male model.

RIGHT **Ronnie Biggs**, the Great Train Robber and prison escapee, enjoys the good life in Brazil, advising on crime control, and, as a beach-bar celebrity, accepting *pina coladas* on the house.

BELOW The Queen enjoys a reflective moment at the Courtauld Institute of Art with its director **Sir Anthony Blunt** (right), formerly a spy for the Soviet Union. Sir Anthony remained in this position, and continued as surveyor of the Queen's pictures, after he confessed in 1964.

RIGHT **Lord Boothby**, Tory politician, television personality and participant with his friend, the gangster Ronnie Kray, in homosexual orgies, seen here in celebratory mood after his marriage to Wanda Sanna, a Sardinian, in 1967.

BELOW Journalist, politician and the most remarkable swindler of all time, **Horatio Bottomley**, leaves the Old Bailey after one of his numerous appearances charged with fraud. He had persuaded the judge to adjourn early so that he could enjoy a bottle of champagne.

RIGHT **The 7th marquess of Bristol**, who died of a heroin overdose in 1999, and had previously been in constant need of funds, attends an auction of ancestral treasures at his home, Ickworth in Suffolk.

RIGHT **Lord Byron**, philanderer and poet, famously dubbed 'mad, bad and dangerous to know' by one of his many mistresses, Lady Caroline Lamb. His 'work' – bridging the Augustan and Romantic modes – has been obscured inevitably by the 'life'.

LEFT **Sir Redvers Buller** (known as Sir Reverse Buller), who commanded the expeditionary force in the 2nd Boer War, and of whom it was said that he brought a new level of ineptitude to the British general-ship.

RIGHT **Burke and Hare**, legendary 19th-century body-snatchers, who supplied the anatomist Dr Robert Knox with corpses not only by robbing graves but also by suffocating fellow guests at their Edinburgh lodging house.

TOP **Barbara 'Joe' Carstairs**, at the wheel of her speedboat Estelle IV, which she had designed herself, and in which she became the world's fastest woman on water in 1924.

ABOVE **Thomas Chatterton**, literary fraud and precocious genius – praised by Wordsworth, Keats and Byron – at work on a forgery in his rat-infested London attic shortly before his suicide in 1770 at the age of 17.

**Barbara Cartland**, the romantic novelist, seen here in 1929 modelling the gown she wore at the Santa Claus charity ball in aid of London's Queen Charlotte's Hospital.

RIGHT **Prince Albert Victor, duke of Clarence**, the eldest son of the prince of Wales (later Edward VII) enjoys a fishing expedition. A member of the Hundred Guineas Club, where transvestites could dance with one another, the duke was involved in the Cleveland Street Brothel Scandal and was later suspected of being Jack the Ripper.

BELOW **Alan Clark**, the Tory intellectual and philanderer, poses with his inherited possessions for a 1988 *Observer* feature, 'A Room Of My Own'. His long-suffering wife Jane makes herself scarce at the edges of the scene.

ABOVE **Dr Hawley Harvey Crippen** is escorted off the SS *Montrose* following his arrest for the murder of his wife, Belle Elmore, a music-hall artiste. He had hoped to escape to Canada with his mistress Ethel le Neve.

RIGHT The writer and occult hierophant **Aleister Crowley**, who liked to be known as 'the Great Beast' and 'the wickedest man alive'. In the 1920s, he peddled a brand of beneficial sex magic and recommended self-improvement through mystic buggery. The 1960s brought about a brief revival of interest in his ideas.

ABOVE **The Reverend Harold Davidson**, whose
mission as the rector of Stiffkey was the salvation of
fallen women, seen here in compromising circumstances with a young 'model'. Brought before a
consistory court, Davidson claimed that he had
walked into a trap, but he was not believed. He was
eaten later by a performing lion.

ABOVE RIGHT **Sir Francis Dashwood**, politician,
profligate and founder of the notorious Hell-Fire
Club, a society for sots and the sexually depraved
that met at Dashwood's estate, Medmenham Abbey,
West Wycombe.

RIGHT **The Reverend Dr William Dodd**, cleric, dandy and fraud, bids his wife a tearful
farewell on the eve of his execution in 1777 on a charge of forgery.

TOP Having been exposed as an impostor, **Louis de Rougemont** – self-proclaimed explorer, King of the Cannibals, alligator hunter and Great White God – but in reality, Louis Grin, a former butler – demonstrates his turtle-riding skills in a tank at the London Hippodrome in 1906.

ABOVE **The duke of Edinburgh** enjoys a relaxing night out during the early 1950s with (from left to right), the film stars Frank Sinatra and Ava Gardner, Mrs Latter and Dorothy Kirsten.

RIGHT Former ski-jumper **Eddie 'the Eagle' Edwards** promotes his first single, 'Fly, Eddie, Fly', which climbed to number 2 in the charts in Finland, but failed to make a similar impact in the United Kingdom.

BELOW **Sir Nicholas Fairbairn**, the Tory politician and 'character', seen here in one of the comic outfits designed by himself and in which he customarily attended the House of Commons.

RIGHT Gillray's celebrated cartoon of **George IV**, 'A Voluptuary under the horrors of Digestion', depicts the king's enormously distended belly, his face on the verge of apoplexy. An overflowing chamber pot acts as a paperweight for a pile of unpaid bills.

heroes. The long-term result was to establish an Englishman's right to stand on a soapbox and say whatever he likes.

**Curll, Edmond** (1675–1747), publisher and pornographer. Curll has claims to be regarded as the father of pornographic publishing in England. More significantly, his many brushes with the law – from which he invariably emerged unscathed – established eventually that corruption of morals was a misdemeanour, and obscenity went into the statute books as a crime. In 1708, when James Read and Angelo Carter were indicted for publishing *The Fifteen Plagues of Maidenhead*, the Queen's Bench dismissed the indictment for obscene libel on the grounds that the book was not a reflection on the government, the church or any individual. Mr Justice Powell ruled:

> If there is no remedy in the Spiritual Court, it does not follow that there must be a remedy here. There is no law to punish it. I wish there were. But we cannot make law.

Twenty years later, Curll's publication of *Venus in the Cloister or the Nun in her Smock* caused the judiciary to change its mind. It was not Curll's first appearance in a court of law. In 1719 he had been acquitted of publishing an obscene libel against the proprietor of a brothel. Peter Motteux, a translator of Rabelais, had died in curious circumstances in a brothel near the sign of the Dial and Bible in Fleet Street, where Curll had offices. The prosecution alleged murder against the brothel-keeper and her daughter, who were both unexpectedly acquitted, thus leaving Curll exposed to a libel charge. The defence at the murder trial claimed that Motteux had suffered a fit, which may have been the case since he was almost certainly indulging in masochistic practices at the time.

Curll, who combined his publishing trade with the sale of patent medicines, and had been successful with John Marten's *The Charitable Surgeon – being a new way of Curing (without Mercury) the several degrees of the Venereal Distemper in both Sexes* (1715), next published a translation of a work by Johann Heinrich Meibom, who held the chair of medicine at the University of Helmstedt. The English title was *A Treatise of the Use of Flogging in Venereal Affairs,* and Curll embellished it with a good deal of pornographic detail. He was duly prosecuted, but his defence that he had published with 'the least moral intent' was accepted by the jury.

Then in 1727 Curll published *Venus in the Cloister or The Nun in her Smock*, but later denied that he was the publisher, admitting only that he had sold one copy of the book, which – written by the Abbé Du Prat under the pseudonym Abbé Barin – described behaviour in French convents. The secretary of state, Viscount Townshend, immediately ordered Curll's arrest, and for good measure had *A Treatise of the Use of Flogging in Venereal Affairs* seized. Curll pleaded that *Venus* had appeared 40 years earlier, published by a Henry Rhodes, and that no action had been taken against him. He further pleaded that the *Treatise on Flogging* was a medical work beyond reproach. He was released on bail while the Court of the King's Bench considered the matter, and in November 1727 he was convicted, with Mr Justice Fortescue dissenting. 'There should be a breach of the peace,' argued Fortescue, 'or something tending to it, of which there is nothing in this case.' The court found the corruption of morals to be a misdemeanour at common law, and obscenity became accepted as a crime. Curll was fined £100, and sentenced to a term in the pillory, which he survived.

**cursed by the Nine Bards of Ireland.** *See* KINGSALE, JOHN DE COURCY, 35TH BARON.

**Curtis, James** (*c.*1800–70), biographer and court reporter. Curtis was obsessed with the proceedings at the Old Bailey's New Court, and for 25 years he attended there daily. He had no interest in what happened in the Old Court and he never set foot in it. On rare occasions he could be tempted out of London by a particularly noteworthy case in another part of the country. Though he had little money, the reports he wrote were entirely for his own pleasure. He did, however, devise an improved system of recording hours of spoken evidence, which he published under the title, *Shorthand Made Shorter*.

Nothing could persuade Curtis to miss a day in court except a public execution. Having followed the progress of a trial, Curtis liked to witness the finale. This habit seems not to have been prompted by a sadistic or ghoulish impulse – indeed, he befriended many of the convicted and frequently kept them company during their final days. Since he couldn't afford public transport, he walked 25 miles before breakfast to witness the execution of Captain Moir at Chelmsford. In 1828 he befriended William CORDER, the notorious perpetrator of the Red Barn Murder. Corder, a prosperous Suffolk farmer, promised to marry, and then killed, Maria Marten, the attractive daughter of a mole-catcher who lived in the village of Polstead, near Bury St Edmonds. Throughout Corder's trial, Curtis stood with him in the dock, and later wrote his biography. Their close relationship caused an artist from a provincial paper to mistake Curtis for Corder. Corder's name appeared the next day under a picture of Curtis, bringing about the latter's arrest as he walked in Ipswich.

This was not the only occasion on which Curtis was the victim of mistaken identity. On his only visit to Dover he was arrested as a French spy, and when he attended Captain Moir's execution, he was evicted from his lodgings by the landlady, who mistook him for the hangman.

**Curzon, Charles** (1918– ), bus-pass bandit and armed robber. Formerly a professional con man with 579 convictions, Curzon took up armed robbery at the age of 72, although blind in one eye and going deaf. Wearing a stocking mask and carrying a sawn-off shotgun, he robbed Glasgow banks and building societies of £271,000 between 1990 and April 2000. Known as 'Bang Bang Charlie', and dressed, when off-duty, in the immaculate manner of George Raft in the great days of Warner Brothers and *film noir*, he reacts badly to being called an 'old rogue' saying, 'That's a stupid name. I'm a successful fucking bank robber.' Asked by a television reporter in April 2001 whether he felt sorry for any of his victims, he admitted that 'some may have been mentally harmed, but there you are. Plenty of quacks around to sort them out.'

*See also* BUS-PASS BANDITS.

# d

**'Daft Highland Laird', the.** *See* ROBERTSON, JAMES.

**Daft Jamie.** *See* BURKE, WILLIAM.

**dairymen, murderous.** *See* ALLEN, PETER ANTHONY.

**Dally, Simon** (1952–87), publisher. A protégé of Lord Weidenfeld, Dally was a director of Weidenfeld & Nicolson at the age of 27. Educated at Winchester College and the son of two distinguished psychiatrists (one of whom had treated members of the British royal family), he decided in October 1980 that knowledge was power. Accordingly, he installed surveillance devices in his own Notting Hill apartment and let it to a call girl, having it in mind to blackmail her clients. He then bugged Lord Weidenfeld's office with a view to organizing a palace revolution. He planned thereafter to run the business from a fortified hilltop castle in northern Tuscany, not yet acquired. The conspiracy was uncovered when he invited Weidenfeld's managing director, Ray Compton, to join it as his second-in-command, and Dally was given just 30 minutes to clear his desk.

Dally's proven ability to unearth bestselling books (he had recently published Mr Robert Morley's amusing *Book of Bricks* (1977), as well as the memoirs (1979) of Jimmy Greaves (the famous soccer player and one half of the popular television double act, Saint and Greavsie), secured him a position with Hutchinson, which in those days was still a distinguished house. However, his ambitions no longer lay in books – least of all in publishing them. When Lord Keynes, the grandson of the economist, and his neighbour in north London, went on holiday, Dally let himself into his house and stole his library. He then made the mistake of offering it to Christie's, who had recently catalogued it and valued it at £1.5 million. The police were called and Dally was arrested. While on bail he bought a gun, which he kept beside the bed. One night when the telephone rang, Dally picked it up instead of the receiver and shot himself in the head.

Jim Cochrane, a director of Hutchinson, later remarked that it was unusual for a publisher to show any interest in selling books.

**Daly, Josephine** (1936– ), pensioner and brothel-keeper. In September 2000 Philip Beresford, the compiler of the *Sunday Times*'s annual 'Rich List', named Daly as the sixth richest criminal in the country with an estimated fortune of £7.5 million. She fell some way behind Curtis Warren, the Liverpool crime lord (£50 million from drugs and property), Thomas ADAMS (£50 million from drugs and extortion) and Thomas Carrington, who keeps a crocodile in his front room (£20 million from cars and cocaine). However, she was ahead of high-profile gangsters such as Dogan ARIF, whose family took over south London after the fall of Charles and Eddie RICHARDSON (£5 million from used cars and heroin). Arif, who is an Arsenal supporter, blamed his poor showing on the fact that he was serving 14 years for armed robbery.

Daly was quick to dispute the extent, and the source, of her wealth. When she was charged, in July 2000, with controlling London's largest vice operation, her defence counsel pointed out that a short-sighted pensioner confined to a wheelchair could not be expected to keep a close eye on all her business interests. Asked to account for the £100,000 in cash found in her house, Daly said she had saved the money from her pension. She had always been frugal, she said. The sophisticated security system that ringed her property could be explained by the fact that she liked to keep an eye on her Rottweilers when they played in the street. Now that it had been brought to her attention that some of the employees at her several massage parlours had in her absence been offering unauthorized services she would ensure that such irregularities didn't occur again – difficult though this would be. No one could be everywhere at once, least of all a grandmother in a wheelchair. Equally, if the prime minister, Mr Tony Blair, cared to employ her as a roving 'vice tsar', checking on massage parlours throughout the country, she would happily undertake the task. This offer was judged to be facetious, and was not taken up. Daly escaped a prison sentence, however – in this respect being more fortunate than her predecessors Cynthia PAYNE (six months for running a brothel in Streatham), and Janie JONES (seven years for introducing Miss Franie Kum, later the wife of Mr Johnnie Walker, the popular Radio 2 presenter, to a peer of the realm).

At a later confiscation hearing, Daly was ordered to forfeit £3 million. She was wheeled away from court, complaining that she might have to sell some of her houses.

**Dancer, Daniel** (1716–94), farmer and miser. Dancer was the son of one minor and the grandson of another, but he exceeded both in his parsimonious habits. As the eldest son he inherited an 80-acre farm in Harrow Weald, Middlesex. Although he knew his father had hidden £15,000 somewhere on the property, he preferred not to search for it lest its discovery alert his brothers to its existence and oblige him to share it with them. With his sister as unpaid housekeeper, he lived in a run-down shack on the estate rather than in the main house. Every Saturday she cooked one piece of mutton and 14 dumplings. This was made to last for a week.

Miss Dancer's duties kept her for the most part indoors, but her brother liked to roam outside collecting cow dung, which he built into a hiding place for his money. In 1766 Miss Dancer died. Dancer had refused to call a doctor, arguing that 'if the old girl's time has come, all the quacks in Christendom cannot save her. She may as well die now, as at a future time.' He then replaced her with a servant named Griffiths, a man whose temperament was similar to his own. Before joining Dancer, Griffiths had managed to save £500 from wages that never came to more than £10 a year.

A neighbour, Lady Tempest, concerned about Dancer's health, persuaded him one day to buy a hat for a shilling. The next time she saw him, he told her that he had sold the hat to Griffiths at a sixpence profit. On another occasion Lady Tempest presented him with a difficult choice by giving him a dish of trout stewed in claret. Dancer was fond of trout, but the cost of lighting a fire to heat it was hardly to be contemplated. On the other hand, cold foods gave him toothache. He solved the problem by sitting on the trout until it was warm enough to eat.

Rumours of piles of gold hidden under the floorboards of his shack caused Dancer to be in constant danger from thieves, but he hid his money well and they seldom got away with much. On one occasion a gang of robbers had to hang him by the neck several times before he agreed to lead the way to a small portion of his hidden treasure.

According to Cyrus Redding (*Memoirs of Remarkable Misers*, 1863), Dancer was harsher with himself than with others. His servant Griffiths ate whatever he wanted, and slept in a comfortable bed. Dancer could also be generous to his friends. Once, after a day's riding (with Dancer as usual perched on a sack rather than a saddle) he and a friend reached an inn, and Dancer said, 'Pray, Sir, do you go into the house, order what you please and live like gentleman, I will settle for it readily.' He bought a penny's worth of bread for himself, slept under the horse's manger, and the next morning paid his friend's bill of £15.

**dancing on the dead.** *See* RABBETT, MARMADUKE.

**Daniels, Duane** (1974– ), youthful gang leader who in the early 1990s brought terror to the William Bonny estate in Clapham, south London. Some members of his team, the 28 Posse, had been recruited by intimidation. One boy who declined to join was set on fire. By the time Duane's career was interrupted at the Old Bailey in December 1993 he had committed 959 identifiable offences. Most had been carried out to finance his drug habit, which was said at his trial to be a daily intake of half an ounce of cannabis, 20 rocks of crack, ten pints of extra strength lager, two doses of LSD, quarter of a bottle of spirits and handfuls of tranquillizers. In one month alone the gang stole £100,000 worth of electronic hardware, but recently they had taken to kidnapping and torture. Having forced his victims to reveal their personal identification numbers, Daniels was able to empty their bank accounts through high-street cash machines. A woman who was attacked in a veterinary surgery refused to give up her PIN number so the gang threw her guinea pig out of the window. Daniels was sentenced to nine years in prison. Within four months of his release in November 2001, he was involved in an affray outside a club in New Cross, south London and knifed a bouncer, George Napier. Charged with murder, Daniels was returned to prison for life.

**Daniels, Paul** (1961– ), financial adviser and garden designer. Daniels, the son of the former television conjuror, was charged in May 2001 with the cultivation of cannabis with a street value of £89,000. Police found 89 marijuana plants when they raided his home in Hartlepool, County Durham. After appearing in court, he was asked by journalists what his father thought about it all. They had hoped for the reply, 'Not a lot!', which had been the conjuror's catch phrase. They were disappointed when Daniels Jnr answered, 'We haven't spoken for five years so how the fuck would I know?'

**Dansey, Colonel Sir Claude** (1879–1944), soldier and intelligence officer. Dansey graduated to intelligence work during World War I by way of the Territorial Army. By the time of his retirement he had become vice chief of the Secret Intelligence Service. The title had been carefully chosen for him in order not to offend Colonel Valentine Vivian, who already held the title of deputy chief. Dansey and Vivian had always been on poor terms, though their differences had not been caused by the fact that Vivian's main achievement had been to recruit Kim Philby (*see* BLUNT, SIR ANTHONY; BURGESS, GUY FRANCIS DE MONCY). On Philby's merits they had always agreed. 'We've been joined by a bright young man,' Dansey had said at the time. 'Used to know his father in the old days.' Dansey and Vivian must share the credit for building up the service penetrated with such conspicuous ease by the Soviet Union's KGB.

Between the wars Dansey involved himself in a series of unsuccessful business ventures. For a while he ran an English country club in the United States, offering croquet on a lawn and staffed by theatrical butlers in silk tights and buckled shoes, but this was not a success. Realizing that he was nnl rnl nvn fai uny career other than intelligence work, he returned to the SIS in London and worked conscientiously to establish networks of agents on the Continent. These were rolled up with ease by the Germans in the first week of World War II, and Himmler was able to name publicly the chief officers of the British secret service from 'C' downwards. Professor Hugh Trevor-Roper, who worked in intelligence during the war, commented that 'When I looked at the world in which I found myself, I thought that if this was our intelligence system we were doomed to defeat.'

Dansey was always sharply critical of Vivian, whose staff he described as 'a lot of old women in red flannel knickers'. One reason for his dislike was that Vivian was in charge of security, an aspect of intelligence work for which Dansey had nothing but contempt. He preferred the aggressive expansion of overseas networks – a policy responsible for the blunder that finished his career. In the last months of the war a German liaison officer presented himself at the British embassy in Berne offering information. Dansey ordered his people to ignore the offer. The German officer got in touch with Allen Dulles, then running the American OSS (Office of Strategic Services) operation in Switzerland, and handed over valuable information. When copies of the documents reached Dansey, he rejected them as having been planted on the Americans. He was invited to resign, and died on D-Day in 1944.

**Darke, Johnny.** *See* BINDON, JOHN.

**Dashwood, Sir Francis** (1708–81), politician and profligate. Sir Francis, who on the death of his uncle in 1770 became the 15th Baron Le Despencer, was postmaster general (1770–81) and chancellor of the exchequer (1761–3). His behaviour was seldom of a standard to be expected from someone who had occupied these offices, equally from someone who had not. He was expelled from Italy for 'scandalous behaviour', seduced the Empress Anne of Russia while disguised as King Charles of Sweden, and, most famously, founded the Hell-Fire Club, a society for sots and the sexually depraved, whose members included John WILKES and the 4th earl of Sandwich. He also set up the Society of Dilettanti, described by Horace Walpole as 'a club of which the nominal qualification is having been to Italy, and the real one of being drunk'.

It was in Italy that Dashwood conceived the idea of the Hell-Fire Club, or, more formally, the Order of Medmenham Monks. It came to him when he attended a service in the Sistine Chapel at the Vatican, during which the worshippers scourged themselves with whips. Disappointed that the chastisement was only simulated, Dashwood attended a Good Friday service with a horsewhip under his waistcoat and when the lights dimmed for the flagellation scene he thrashed the congregation properly. The worshippers fought back, and Dashwood was obliged to retreat.

Dashwood delighted in structural puns and visual jokes. He erected a statue of Priapus in the grounds of Medmenham Abbey, near West Wycombe, carrying the amusing motto, '*Peno Tento Non Penitento*' ('I feel my penis ...'), At meetings of the Hell-Fire Club, he and his twelve 'Franciscans' – so called in order that their excesses could be passed off as anti-Catholic mockery – indulged in public fornications. A girl would be laid naked on an altar, to be enjoyed in turn by the Mad Monks. Sometimes the religious aspect of these ceremonies was taken too seriously, at least in the opinion of John Wilkes. On one occasion the Franciscans decided to say a prayer to the Devil. Wilkes procured a baboon, dressed it in red garments, strapped horns to its head and shut it in a cupboard in the 'Chapel'. When Dashwood began his Satanic incantations, Wilkes released the baboon, which leapt on to the back of Lord Sandwich, who supposedly cried out, 'Spare me gracious devil! Spare a wretch who was never your servant! I am but half a sinner.' It was Dashwood's turn not to be amused, but the various cavortings were soon continued.

Dashwood, like Wilkes, was a supporter of American independence, and among those who visited West Wycombe between 1764 and 1765 was Benjamin Franklin, who liked to walk out of doors in the nude. Dashwood and Franklin collaborated on *The Abridged Book of Common Prayer*, their explanation being that they had found the original laborious.

**date rape.** *See* DIGGLE, ANGUS.

**David, Peter** (1935– ), lay preacher stopped by the police in south Wales for driving from chapel to chapel in an uninsured Ford Sierra with the registration DEUT 818. David explained that it referred to the Book of Deuteronomy, chapter 8, verse 18, which acknowledges God as the only source of power. On 11 May 2001 magistrates in Skewen, near Swansea, reserved judgement on whether driving a car with God in the passenger seat counts as insurance cover under the Road Traffic Act (1959). David had earlier informed the court that God, who customarily travelled as his passenger, had told him that he was covered by His Divine protection, and that this was sufficient for most purposes. The case was referred to a crown court, but David remained confident. 'The court will have to accept that God is on my side,' he said. A solicitor for the Crown Prosecution Service remained calm. 'We get all sorts in court,' he said, 'but I don't expect to see God in the witness box.' Before the hearing, David sold his Ford Sierra and bought a Vauxhall Cavalier with the number plate JOHN 316 – referring to John 3:16, which promises that those who believe will not perish but have everlasting life. The judge banned David for two years.

*See also* WELSH, THE.

**Davidson, the Reverend Harold Francis** (1875–1937), priest. In the course of his ministry as the rector of Stiffkey, Davidson, on his own assessment, saved the souls of more than 1000 fallen women. He also photographed actresses in their pyjamas, was ejected from a nudist camp in Harrogate, exhibited himself in a barrel, and was eaten in the end by a lion named Freddy.

Educated at Whitgift School, Davidson recited comic monologues after the manner of George Grossmith in end-of-term entertainments, thereafter deciding that he preferred the stage to the church – the career chosen for him by his father, the vicar of Sholing in Hampshire. At the age of 19 he was a hit in a touring production of *Charley's Aunt*, playing the title role. However, the church was in his blood and when on tour he made a habit of calling on vicars to find out if any of their ageing parishioners would like to hear the Bible read aloud. Once he persuaded a 16-year-old girl not to jump into the Thames on a foggy night. He gave her money to return home and seems to have acquired a lifetime habit of helping young ladies.

Davidson studied for holy orders at Exeter College, Oxford, and in 1905, after a short curacy at Holy Trinity, Windsor, he was awarded the living of Stiffkey, a small village in Norfolk. It was his habit thereafter to catch the first train to London on Monday morning and the last train back to Norwich on Friday night. During the week he rescued the fallen – at first of both sexes, latterly only pretty girls. He believed that young women of unremarkable appearance were less vulnerable, through lack of opportunity, to the temptations of the flesh. 'I like to catch them between 14 and 20,' he said. 'I believe with all my soul that if Christ were born again in London in the present day He would constantly be found walking in Piccadilly.'

In fact Davidson preferred Oxford Street as a field of missionary activity. Waitresses in tea shops seemed to him to be particularly at risk. Instead of leaving tips, he distributed theatre tickets, and, having told a waitress that she had nice eyes and a pretty smile, he would show her a picture of an actress who, he said, had come to him for confession, later to be saved. Eventually, he was banned from tea shops. 'But what if my bishop invites me here?' he once protested. 'The bishop will be served, but you will not,' the manageress replied.

In September 1920 Davidson met Rose Ellis, a 20-year-old prostitute, and embarked on a rescue mission that lasted for ten years. He paid her rent and introduced her to landladies as 'my secretary, Mrs Malone'. It was later alleged that Rose was his mistress, the evidence being that he had on one occasion taken her to Paris. Davidson countered by saying that he had taken her there to find her a job as an *au pair*. Later, Rose made a statement that severely compromised her benefactor – a betrayal that she afterwards regretted.

However, it was Barbara Harris, a 16-year-old prostitute encountered at

Marble Arch in 1930, who was to get Davidson into greater trouble. His first words to her – or so she later alleged – did not suggest a missionary intent. 'Has anyone ever told you that you look like the film actress, Mary Brian?' he asked. Thereafter, he appears to have treated Barbara with paternal kindness, finding her jobs and lodgings, and cultivating her mind with improving literature. Though she had a habit of disappearing for months at a time, she always returned to 'Uncle Harold' after she had been abandoned by her latest lover – among them, an Indian prince, and a professional strong man who performed in the street.

Meanwhile, nemesis was approaching in the form of Major Philip Hammond, a Boer War veteran and a magistrate in Davidson's parish. The major disapproved of the fact that the rector usually arrived for Sunday service after the congregation had gone home. Nor did he like it that young ladies were staying at the rectory, with the result that villagers were likely to stumble over couples making love in ditches. When Davidson failed to return from London for an Armistice Day service, Hammond complained to the bishop of Norwich, Dr Pollock. The bishop engaged a firm of private detectives who persuaded Rose Ellis, over several glasses of port in a Charing Cross hotel, and on receipt of 40 shillings, to speak at length about her relationship with 'Uncle Harold'.

Davidson wrote angrily to Dr Pollock, protesting his innocence and claiming that Rose had been 'bribed with money and drugged with alcohol'. He continued:

> For years I have been known as the 'Prostitute's Padre', to me the proudest title that a true priest of Christ can hold.

Meanwhile, Rose Ellis, overcome with remorse, sold her story to the *Daily Herald*, accusing the detectives of having bribed her to make up stories against Davidson, and insisting that he was innocent.

The Rector of Stiffkey was now famous. Sightseers from all over the country arrived in charabancs to hear him proclaim his innocence from the pulpit. 'No character in the world's history suffered from misunderstanding and vituperation more than Christ,' he declared to his cheering audience. But in February 1932 Barbara Harris set out a list of accusations in a long letter to the bishop – alleging among other things rape and breach of promise.

In March Davidson appeared before a consistory court, presided over by F. Keppel North, chancellor of the diocese of Norwich. He was charged with adultery with Rose Ellis, making an improper suggestion to waitresses in a Lyons Corner House, and 'habitually associating with women of a loose character for immoral purposes'. He denied all the charges, but the case went against him when a photograph was produced that showed him with a naked girl. Chancellor North, peering at the photograph through a magnifying glass, was visibly taken aback. 'I am trying to be as

much like a machine as I can,' he said, 'but I am only human.' 'I hope you
will be not only human, but judicial too,' observed Mr Richard Levy for
the defence. (Earlier, Mr Levy had proved to be no match for Barbara
Harris. Asked in cross-examination whether she usually remained on good
terms with those who had tried to rape her, she had replied, 'I do if they
come in useful.')

Davidson insisted that the photograph was a set-up. He had been
advised that he was walking into a trap, he said, but he had ignored the
warning. 'I was told three weeks earlier that I was about to be compromised. I would be telephoned by a lady of title and asked to go to her
house. When I got there I would find that she had removed all her clothes
and then two detectives would step out into the room and so discover me in
that position ...' It went against Davidson that the naked figure in the photograph was not a woman of title but 15-year-old Estelle Douglas, who had
been told by Davidson that he could help her in her career as a bathing-suit
model.

Chancellor North declared Davidson's evidence 'a tissue of lies' and
sentenced him to be deprived from holy orders. At the suggestion of the
Blackpool showman, Luke Gannon, Davidson exhibited himself in a
barrel on the promenade, charging 2d, and using the time to prepare
various appeals against the court's verdict. The crowds that came to see
him grew so large that he was prosecuted in a magistrates' court for
causing an obstruction. Having obtained a licence, he then performed a
variety act in a Birmingham music hall and took five curtain calls. Returning to Blackpool he stayed in his barrel for ten days before being
prosecuted, tried and acquitted of starving himself with intent to commit
suicide. In July 1937 he moved to Skegness, where, in a cage measuring
14 ft by 8 ft, and in the company of a lion named Freddy, he began a series
of performances in which he denounced the archbishop of Canterbury, the
bishop of Norwich and the entire leadership of the Church of England.
One evening Freddy, who was normally a docile animal fed and looked
after by an 8-year-old girl, turned on the rector and fatally mauled him.

Davidson's former parishioners refused to believe any ill of him. The
guide to Stiffkey's St John the Baptist Church contains the following
tribute:

> Here in the parish he was respected and above all loved by the vil-
> lagers who relished his sermons, recognized his humanity and
> forgave him his transgressions. May he rest in peace.

A less dignified memorial may be provided by a film that Mr Kenneth
Russell plans to make about his life.

*See also* GREGORY, MAUNDY.

**Davis, Richard** (1948– ), magazine publisher. Davis, who had previously enjoyed a modest lifestyle in Mill Hill, north London, and was, by his own account, a sexual virgin, went off the rails in 1989. He fell into the habit of buying himself two new suits on the way back to the office after lunch and several expensive gifts for his secretary. He set up a British version of *Playboy* magazine and spent £20,000 on photographic equipment. He frequently woke up drunk at 5 a.m. in hotel toilets, having spent thousands of pounds on high-class call girls. On one occasion he bought a diamond ring for a nightclub hostess whom he had known for five minutes. He pursued women down the street and bought pornographic video equipment. He joined a country club and became involved in a bar-room brawl with Paul Merson, of Aston Villa and England, after making unwelcome advances towards Merson's wife. He was left with huge debts, his company went into liquidation and his Bentley was repossessed. By way of compensation, he sued Novartis Pharmaceuticals (UK) Ltd, Camden and Islington Health Authority, the Middlesex Hospital and Professor Howard Saul Jacobs, who had been treating him with an experimental drug, Bromocriptine. The case cost him a further £2.5 million. Afterwards he said:

> Would I recommend someone else to do what I have done? I would say, 'Don't bother.'

**Davison, Jane** (*c.*1768–?), Methodist preacher. In 1793, according to William Benbow's *Crimes of the Clergy*, an itinerant preacher travelled through the north of England and parts of Scotland, claiming women's souls for the Lord. Settling in Alnwick, Northumberland, in 1794, Jane Davison was taken into the house of another Methodist minister, Mr Hastings, who had two unmarried daughters. Davison stayed with the family for six months, before mysteriously absconding. It was then discovered that both daughters were pregnant. Jane, who was in fact a Mr Thomas Heppel, had not only managed to seduce each girl without her sister knowing, but had also arranged to elope with both of them. Having told them to wait for him in different parts of Alnwick – with all their clothes packed for a long journey – he disappeared with their entire wardrobes. With his own wardrobe now replenished, he made his way to York where he was arrested for wearing a dress. He was transported to Australia, where he settled happily.

**Davy, Sir Humphrey.** *See* BIRCH, THOMAS.

**Dawkins, Queenie** (1921–98), property mistress. In the course of the annual pantomime at the Yvonne Arnaud Theatre, Guildford, in 1976, the Wicked Fairy was concocting an evil spell over a bubbling cauldron. With a cry of 'abracadabra!' she brought the spell to its peak, but instead of turning the Good Fairy into a frog, a faulty electronic flash under the mouldron blew the Wicked Fairy's knickers off. The theatre's property mistress, Mrs Dawkins, admitted she was undergoing a series of misfortunes. The previous year an exploding oven had blown Mother Hubbard 20 feet across the stage. She told reporters that she was leaving the theatre to become an undertaker.

The Yvonne Arnaud Theatre is named after the fine comedienne who always claimed that she couldn't speak English. On at least one occasion, however, Miss Arnaud showed that she was familiar with the folklore of her adopted country. While staying with Lord and Lady Olivier in Buckinghamshire, Miss Arnaud looked out of the French windows into the garden and saw Evelyn 'Boo' Laye sitting on the grass. 'Doesn't that mean it's going to rain?' she said.

**Dawson, Charles** (1864–1916), solicitor, antiquarian and hoaxer. In 1912 Dawson, an amateur archaeologist, announced the discovery of some bones in a gravel pit near Piltdown Common in East Sussex. Experts from the British Museum hailed the find as the 'missing link' between man and ape, and the confirmation of Darwinian theory. It would take the scientific community 40 years to agree that Dawson's discovery was a hoax.

The remains consisted of parts of a skull and a jaw. The skull was human, but the fragments of the jawbone seemed to be ape-like in their contours. Some scientists doubted whether the skull and the jaw had ever belonged together, and anthropologists pointed out that if 'Piltdown Man' was genuine it meant that the earliest Englishman had lived on earth half a million years ago. This did not seem to match the evolutionary tree based on earlier discoveries. As the years passed, Piltdown's authenticity was repeatedly challenged, but there was no way to prove fraud until the late 1940s when Kenneth Oakley, a geologist at the British Museum, devised a way of determining if ancient bones were of the same age. By 1953 he had come up with a sophisticated radioactive fluorine test that proved that 'Piltdown Man's' skull was 50,000 years old but the jaw much younger.

The explanation was that in 1911 someone, presumably Dawson, had planted a human cranium in the gravel excavation together with the doctored jaw of an orang-utan. As Sir Richard Milner states in *The Encyclopaedia of Evolution*:

> The orang-utan's teeth had been filed to make them look more human, and the jaw had been deliberately broken at the hinge to obscure the correct identification. All the fragments had been stained brown with potassium bichromate, which made them appear equally old.

And in his book *The Piltdown Forgery* Dr J.S. Weiner offers evidence that Dawson was known to stain bones and otherwise to forge ancient remains. Most experts agree that Dawson was the creator of the fraud – some, like Professor Stephen Jay Gould of Harvard suggesting that he started the deception as a prank but was swept up in the interest it aroused. A more fanciful theory was advanced by Professor John Winslow, who suggested that the culprit was in fact Sir Arthur Conan Doyle. The evidence for this theory is hardly persuasive – merely that Sir Arthur lived a short distance from the Piltdown gravel pit and was a fanatical spiritualist; by this account, the hoax would have been Sir Arthur's revenge on the scientists who ridiculed his beliefs. More interesting, perhaps, is a fictional 'missing link' provided in 1987 by Professor Charles Blinderman in *The Piltdown Inquest*. The hoax, according to Blinderman, was obviously the work of Doyle's Professor Moriarty, who wished to discredit the creator of his nemesis, Sherlock Holmes.

Dawson, in any case, died greatly honoured, and safe in his lifetime from scientific exposure. He was known for years as 'The Wizard of Sussex', and a monument commemorates his most famous 'find'.

**Day, Alexander** (*c.*1681–?), sharper, hoaxer, duffer and swindler. Confidence tricksters in all their varieties were rife in the 18th century, and Day was the most notorious of his time. However, his career and working methods might dissuade all but the most patient and devoted from entering the profession. The complicated preparations and the risk capital involved seem to have yielded so little by way of profit that the pleasure in duping others, rather than any subsequent reward, must have been the motive. To swindle Mrs Scrimshaw out of a gold chain worn by her squirrel, Day needed the assistance of two stooges, a rented house at an enviable address, a coach, a horse, several false names and an expensive wardrobe. The same help and appurtenances were required to relieve Mr Gravestock of a quantity of Spanish lace worth £48.

In 1723 Day – calling himself Marmaduke Davenport – set out to defraud Mr Hinchcliffe, a silk mercer. He first instructed Hinchcliffe to call at his house (a large property rented for the occasion in Queen Square), where he would receive a substantial order. When Hinchcliffe arrived there the next morning, he was told by a servant – one of Day's stooges – that his master would be with him shortly. While they waited the servant took the opportunity to inform Hinchcliffe that Mr 'Davenport' was the son of a Yorkshire baronet, and possessed a large fortune in that county.

When Day/Davenport at last appeared, he told Hinchcliffe that he wanted to purchase a large quantity of valuable silks, and asked that samples might be sent to him so that a selection could be made. When Hinchcliffe pointed out that this could be more conveniently accomplished by viewing patterns in his shop, Day took him there in his coach (hired for the occasion), on the way talking of his father, Sir Marmaduke Davenport, and dropping the information that he was affianced to the daughter of a Counsellor Ward. In the circumstances, he would need to refurnish his London house to his finaccr's tasto und would want goods from Mr Hinchcliffe to a large amount.

Having arrived at Hinchcliffe's shop, Day selected materials for furniture and hangings to the value of £1000, and he asked Mr Hinchcliffe to deliver these to his house in Queen Square. In the meantime he would like to depart with two pieces of brocade, worth £30, to show to his fiancée, Counsellor Ward's daughter. Mr Hinchcliffe agreed to this arrangement, but he seems to have become suspicious at this point, since he later called on Counsellor Ward, who told him that his daughter was already married. Hinchcliffe went immediately to Mr 'Davenport's' town house, but found it deserted. Day had made off with goods worth £30 – hardly enough, it might seem, to justify the capital outlay.

Worse was to come. In May 1723 Day was arrested on suspicion of fraud. After a long trial he was sentenced to two years imprisonment in Newgate, to stand twice in the pillory and to give security for his good behaviour for a further two years on his release. The last condition was not one which Day found it possible to satisfy. On leaving prison he went immediately, and again as Mr Davenport, to the house of a goldsmith, Mr Markham, from whom he ordered an equipage worth £50. For whatever reason, Mr Markham accompanied Mr 'Davenport' back to his (rented) London house, where he noticed that Davenport's squirrel was wearing a gold chain similar to one he had recently sold to a customer of his, Mrs Scrimshaw. Finding this suspicious, Mr Markham called on Mrs Scrimshaw and asked her whether she knew a Mr Marmaduke Davenport. She said that she didn't, but when Mr Markham offered a description she recognized it as belonging to a Mr Alexander Day, who had recently cheated her out of a considerable amount of property, including the gold chain usually worn by her squirrel. Day was returned to Newgate prison.

**death by drowning, faking one's own.** *See* STONEHOUSE, JOHN.

**debagged by factory women.** *See* TASTE TICKELL, KIM DE LA.

**debauched and put on the streets.** *See* FERNSEED, MARGARET.

**debauched when young by the earl of Sandwich.** *See* RAY, MARTHA.

**debauchees.** *See* BLACKBURNE, ARCHBISHOP LANCELOT; BUCKINGHAM, GEORGE VILLIERS, 2ND DUKE OF; CHARTERIS, COLONEL FRANCIS; CLONMEL, JOHN SCOTT, 1ST EARL OF; DASHWOOD, SIR FRANCIS; DORSET, CHARLES SACKVILLE, 1ST EARL OF; FOX, CHARLES JAMES; HELL-FIRE CLUB, THE IRISH; MYTTON, JOHN; WILKES, JOHN.

**debauchery, a specific against.** *See* SOLOMON, SAMUEL.

**de Beaumont, Chevalier D'Eon** (1728–1810), soldier, duellist and courtier. Born in France, the chevalier fled to England disguised as a woman after a scandal involving a gross libel on the Swedish ambassador to the court of Louis XV. He became a popular figure at the court of George III and for 15 years lived in London as a woman with another woman, who claimed never to have known that the chevalier was a man. It was rumoured that £20,000 was wagered on the London Stock Exchange as to de Beaumont's true sexual identity. Another rumour claimed that he had been discovered in Queen Charlotte's bedroom and had been obliged thereafter to dress as a woman to scotch rumours that he was the father of the prince of Wales. Eonism, as a synonym for transvestism, derives from the chevalier's name.

**de Breffney, Brian** (1931–89), author, genealogist and architectural historian. Baron O'Rourke de Breffney (on some occasions the 7th Baron of the Holy Roman Empire, on others Count O'Rourke), who lived for some years on the Tipperary/Kilkenny border at Carrick-on-Suir in a Palladian pile staffed by Indian servants, was in fact the son of an Isleworth taxi driver called Leese.

As a young man, Leese/de Breffney lived in Rome, sometimes working as a professional genealogist. His interest in the subject had been stimulated when he discovered that his great-grandmother's name was Breffni. From this he inferred that she must have been related to the Irish O'Rourkes, princes of Breffney. Thereafter, he identified strongly with the French and Russian branches of that ancient Irish family. His American clients were delighted when he was able to produce pedigrees showing that they too were of Irish ancestry, sometimes descended from the 17th-century exiled and dispossessed Irish landowners known as the Wild Geese.

De Breffney had a serious side. His *Bibliography of Irish Family History* (1979) is considered to be an authoritative reference book of its kind. *The Irish Ancestor* (1982) and *The Houses of Ireland* (1984), written in collaboration with the Irish genealogist, Rosemary ffolliott, are equally well regarded.

It was de Breffney's habit, when researching the latter project, to let himself into a country house and to wander around making notes. Few resented this, but in Munster once he was shown the door when the owner's wife came across him examining the plasterwork. Retreating down the drive, he bumped into the owner, returning on a horse. 'One of your servants has just been very rude to me,' he said. 'That was no servant, that was my...', the owner began, before realizing that he was about to participate in a cross-talk skit.

De Breffney married twice, first Princess Jyotsna, daughter of the Mahrajadhiraja Bahadur of Burdwan, and second Ulli, widow of Sir

Stafford Sands, minister of tourism and finance in the Bahamas, and daughter of Lauri Castren of Helsinki. In 1987 their daughter, Sita-Marie, married the 7th viscount de Veski, nephew of the earl of Snowdon.

**de Clifford, Lord Edward Southwell Russell** (1907–86), racing driver. In 1935 Lord de Clifford, 26th holder of the barony created in 1299, became the last person to be tried by 'God and his peers' in the House of Lords. His alleged offence was the manslaughter on the Kingston bypass of Douglas George Hopkins, a fellow motorist. It was the only time in the last century that the House was convened for such a trial, and de Clifford was unanimously acquitted. The right to trial by peers was abolished by the Criminal Justice Act of 1948.

De Clifford had already been in the news when, in 1926, it was announced that at the age of 19 he had secretly married Dorothy Evelyn Meyrick (known as Dolly), the daughter of Mrs Kate MEYRICK, the celebrated nightclub owner. Dolly was a dancer, and de Clifford, fearing that his mother Eve (herself a former member of a dance troupe known as the Gibson Girls) might oppose the marriage, falsely gave his age as 22, and for that offence came up before the lord mayor at Mansion House. After explaining that he was not yet a man of means, de Clifford was given two weeks to pay the fine of £100. 'Elsewhere,' observed the lord mayor, 'the penalty would have been seven years in prison.'

Lord de Clifford tried his hand at many occupations. He ran a quarantine kennels in Somerset, worked for a time as a door-to-door dog food salesman and was briefly a racing driver. He and Dolly separated in the 1950s, and the marriage was dissolved in 1973. His mother Eve, the former Gibson girl, who had perhaps been the cause of his earlier difficulties, changed her name to Eva and in 1929 married Vernon Tate, of Tate and Lyle, the sugar manufacturers. Vernon and Eva Tate moved to Sunningdale, where their daughter, Virginia, was educated at Hurst Lodge, a stage school run by Doris Stainer, the sister of Leslie Howard, the film actor. Sarah Ferguson, later the duchess of York, was a pupil there in the 1970s, and the school is mentioned in *101 Things You Didn't Know About The Royal Lovebirds* by royal insider Talbot Church (1986).

*See also* YORK, SARAH MARGARET, DUCHESS OF.

**de Courcy, Kenneth** (1909–99), author and fraudsman. The changes of fortune experienced by de Courcy were as extravagant as the fantasies that sustained his several ventures. In the 1930s he was on terms with Mussolini, toured Europe as secretary to the right-wing Imperial Policy Group, reported directly to the prime minister, Neville Chamberlain, and was a dining companion of the duke of Windsor. In the 1960s, after a failed plan to build a garden city in Rhodesia obliged him to defraud the investors, he was sharing a cell in Wormwood Scrubs with the Soviet spy, George Blake.

De Courcy's father, a clergyman from County Galway, founded an evangelical mission that gave magic-lantern lectures about the Holy Land, and was killed when the projector exploded during the Boxing Day show. His mother claimed to be descended from the last duc de Granmesnil, a French title that became defunct in the Middle Ages. In later life de Courcy liked to style himself the duc de Granmesnil. In the 1920s he made money by buying up shops in the north of England, obtaining licences to operate them as sub-post offices and selling them on at a considerable profit. In the 1930s his newly acquired wealth, together with his knowledge of foreign affairs, allowed him to publish *Intelligence Digest*, a private-subscription newspaper that served as a platform for his belief that Hitler should be appeased. This position enhanced his standing with Chamberlain, and relations were further improved when he took on as his assistant William DOUGLAS-HOME, the brother of the prime minister's parliamentary private secretary, Lord Dunglass, the future prime minister, Alec Douglas-Home.

After World War II de Courcy continued to publish *Intelligence Digest*, together with another periodical, the *Weekly Review*. Their straightforwardly anti-Soviet stance brought them more than 100,000 readers, most of them in America. Greatly enriched, de Courcy bought an apartment in New York's Empire State Building, waterproofed his Rolls Royce for underwater driving and hired a chauffeur who came with a certificate from Lord Mountbatten testifying to his bravery as a commando. Now a public figure, de Courcy hosted dinner parties in Belgravia at which Churchill's son-in-law, Duncan Sandys, and the future lord chancellor, Quinton Hogg, were guests. After dinner they were invited to pray with him 'for the future of Britain' in his private chapel.

This period of affluence might have continued but for his scheme to build a garden city in Rhodesia. When this failed, and finding himself unable to return some of the £1 million put up by investors, de Courcy resorted to forgery and in 1963 was sentenced to seven years in prison. A year later, while on day release to discuss an appeal with his solicitor in Lincoln's Inn, he walked through the front door of the solicitor's office and straight out through the back. He was arrested two days later at a hotel in Fareham. The manager had become suspicious when de Courcy had kept his dark glasses on throughout dinner, despite obvious difficulties in filleting his poached salmon.

Released from prison in 1969, de Courcy moved to a small house in Gloucestershire, where he made himself unpopular with neighbours by enforcing rights due to him, he thought, by manorial titles purchased. He cropped up from time to time on television, recalling his friendships with Mussolini and the duke of Windsor, and arguing that his conviction for fraud had been a plot by left-wingers who wished to silence him.

**Dee, Simon** (1932– ), former disc jockey and television presenter. Simon

The Syndrome derives its name from Matthew Sweet's discovery (reported in the *Independent on Sunday* 19 August 2001), that those who suffer from it are better remembered for having been forgotten than they would be if they were still remembered, which indeed they are, but only for having been forgotten, which they are not. There may be a formal paradox, or antimony, here, but one which Mr Sweet did not discuss. Media specialists believe that, unusually, early detection of the disease only serves to speed up onset of the full-blown disease. The jury is thought to be out in the cases of Helen Shapiro and Showaddywaddy.

**Defoe, Daniel** (1660–1731), pamphleteer, spymaster and author. Defoe's character combined with exceptional clarity two opposing tendencies in human nature: criminality and creativity. Instinctively of a criminal disposition, in that he believed that his ambitions could be best realized by expediency and manipulation, he yet possessed the honesty of a serious artist. Paradoxically, it was only in fiction that he could tell the truth.

Born in Stoke Newington, London, the son of a butcher, Defoe set up in the hosiery trade and quickly made a fortune. Extravagance and bad management soon led to bankruptcy, however, and he was forced to flee from his creditors. He went to Bristol, where he became known as 'the Sunday gentleman', since that was the only day he could leave his lodgings without fear of arrest. In 1694 he issued a tract supporting King William's unpopular war with France. The king was glad of a supporter, and Defoe was given a profitable government post. At the same time his entrepreneurial instincts drove him to take advantage of the new fashion for Dutch tiles. He opened a tile factory in Tilbury, and was able to pay off his creditors.

In 1702 Defoe ran into trouble with his famous satire *The Shortest Way With Dissenters.* Under William III dissenters had been allowed to hold public office, provided they paid occasional lip service to Anglicanism. After the king's death, reactionaries demanded that dissenters be banned from office. In *The Shortest Way With Dissenters* Defoe appeared to side with the Establishment, suggesting that all dissenters should be banished or hanged. Many reactionaries missed Defoe's ironic intent and greeted the pamphlet with enthusiasm. One bishop said he valued it above all books except the Bible and prayed that Queen Anne would carry out its suggestions. It was then discovered that it was one of Defoe's satires. Parliament issued a warrant for his arrest on a charge of libelling the governing class by making it out to be insane. Defoe's 'joke' cost him a ruinous fine, two days in the pillory and a year in Newgate prison. He obtained his freedom by approaching a man as devious as himself, the Tory minister, Robert Harley, described by a contemporary in words that applied as well to Defoe:

He loved tricks, even where not necessary, but from an inward satisfaction he took in applauding his own cunning. If any man was ever born under the necessity of being a knave it was he.

Defoe suggested to Harley that the government needed a network of informers to uncover potential enemies. Queen Anne was prevailed upon to release Defoe from prison, and, under Harley's patronage, he travelled the country, building up a network of agents and laying down the basic rules of spying. Each agent had to appear to be an ordinary citizen, and all had to be unknown to the others. The scheme was successful and it would not be an exaggeration to say that Defoe's network was the foundation of the British Secret Service.

In 1710 the Whig government fell and Defoe, who had made his reputation as a liberal, hastily announced that he cared more for his country than for party prejudice and had become a Tory. But in 1714 the Whigs returned to power under George I and Defoe went back to prison. Once again he offered his services as a spy. The Whigs decided that a discredited Tory, an 'enemy' of the government, might well find out what their opponents were planning. Defoe gained the confidence of various anti-government newspapers and was able to use his devious skills to suppress anything the Whigs disliked. In time, however, one of his dupes, a man called Mist, who ran a Jacobite newspaper, printed a letter criticizing the government. When he was summoned to explain himself, he tried to put the blame on Defoe. The Whigs began to suspect that Defoe was doubly treacherous.

The breach was healed, but Defoe seems to have realized that his career in treachery was over. Casting around for an alternative livelihood, he remembered the case of a Scottish pirate named Alexander Selkirk who in 1704 had been marooned at his own request on an uninhabited island off the coast of Chile called Juan Fernandez. He had spent five years there before he was rescued, and when he returned to England he had become a celebrity. Defoe may have visited him in prison in Bristol in 1713, thereafter acquiring his papers for a small sum of money. Using this material as a basis, he wrote *Robinson Crusoe* in a matter of weeks. The book appeared in 1719 and was an immediate success. A writer of great versatility, Defoe published more than 250 works in all, including the novels *Moll Flanders* (1722), *Journal of the Plague Year* (1722) and *Roxana* (1724).

In August 1730, at the age of 70 and with old debts catching up with him, Defoe suddenly disappeared. He could have satisfied his creditors with the money from his novels, but typically he preferred to abscond. He died in April the following year in an obscure lodging house near the place of his birth. Literary historians maintain that while his defective personal morality died with him the honesty of his imagination created an artistic revolution of lasting importance.

*See also* SHEPPARD, JACK.

**Dempsey, Andrew** (1944– ), actor and publisher. A former 'Mr Hammersmith' who can still squat-lift a grand piano at the age of 56, Dempsey is known on the 'street' as Andy From the Sixties (for other street names, *see* NAMES, STREET). The sobriquet derives from an association with Brian Epstein, manager of the Beatles pop group, early exponents of 'the Mersey sound'. It was Dempsey's role to supply Epstein not only with drugs but also with rent boys, who were encouraged to steal things from Epstein's Belgravia house – not by Dempsey, but by Epstein himself. The troubled impresario could only achieve satisfaction by concealing himself behind the furniture and watching while a common boy from the West End pocketed his *objets d'art*.

*See also* EYRES, TONY; MELLOR, DAVID.

**Dennis, Ceredig Dawyl** (1921–92), librarian and blackmailer. In 1978 Dennis, who worked in a Swansea library, involved his girlfriend in a plan to blackmail a solicitor, Mr Shoemaker, against whom he held a grudge. He hid in a cupboard and waited for her to lead Mr Shoemaker into the room. At a compromising moment he jumped out of the cupboard, took a Polaroid photograph and demanded money. When developed, the photograph showed only a large refrigerator in the corner of the room.

*See also* WELSH, THE.

**Dennis, Edward** (1717–86), hangman. Dennis has the distinction among hangmen of appearing in a book by Charles Dickens. In *Barnaby Rudge* (1841), Dickens involves Dennis in the anti-Catholic Gordon Riots of 1778 (*see* GORDON, LORD GEORGE), having him hanged as one of the ringleaders in the attack on Newgate prison. Prior to his execution Dennis begs for his life in terror:

> The government can't know it's me, or they wouldn't bring me to this dreadful slaughterhouse. Stop my execution – for charity's sake stop my execution, gentlemen …

In fact, Dennis's participation in the Gordon Riots was inadvertent rather than planned, and certainly less serious than Dickens imagined it to have been. He was arrested for aiding a mob that was looting a Catholic shopkeeper's premises in High Holborn, and brought to trial at the Old Bailey in July 1780. Dennis claimed in his defence that someone in the mob had recognized him with the cry, 'Here's bloody Jack Ketch!' and had threatened to burn him alive unless he helped them. The judge tried hard in his summing-up to convince the jury that Dennis was innocent, but he was found guilty and sentenced to death. He dropped to his knees and begged for mercy, but was taken with the other convicted rioters to Tothill Fields prison to await his execution.

In due course, and perhaps in recognition of his former satisfactory work as hangman, Dennis was granted a free pardon – in this respect being more fortunate than his own first client had been. In 1771 he had hanged 18-year-old Mary Jones at Tyburn for the theft of four pieces of muslin valued at ten shillings. The girl's husband had recently been press-ganged and she had been turned out into the street with her two children to beg. One of her children was at her breast when she was taken in a cart to Tyburn.

Dennis's most illustrious former clients had included Dr William DODD, who committed a clumsy forgery against his friend and patron, Lord Chesterfield, and the Reverend James HACKMAN, condemned to death for the murder of Martha Ray, mistress of the earl of Sandwich. Dennis died in his bed at the age of 76.

*See also* CAPITAL PUNISHMENT.

**Dent, Fred.** *See* STOLL, SIR OSWALD.

**Dering, George Edward** (1831–1911), inventor and recluse. Dering's work, which was mainly to do with electrical devices, was not without its merits and earned him a fellowship of the Royal Society. But as the squire of Lockeleys, his estate in Welwyn, he was known to locals, somewhat derisively, as 'the tightrope-walking inventor'. His interest in stunts on the high wire had brought him to the attention of the French equilibrist, Charles Blondin. In the late 1850s, shortly before Blondin made his crossing of Niagara Falls, he and Dering practised together on a rope stretched across the River Mimram, near Lockeley. The blindfolded Blondin carried the squire across in a sack.

In other respects, Dering preferred to live quietly. He rarely entertained and spent most of his time reading. A local bookseller had a standing order for every book published, in any language, on the subject of electricity. Dering went to considerable lengths to obtain the peace he needed for his work. He lived largely at night, and dined at 2 o'clock in the morning. The window shutters were closed all day to keep out the noise, and he bought the farm next door rather than put up with his neighbour's bleating lambs and barking dog. He even built a new public highway at his own expense to divert traffic that might otherwise pass his house.

In 1879, Dering disappeared. For the next 30 years his whereabouts were a mystery, but his staff had been left with a standing order for one mutton chop to be ready against his sudden reappearance. As a rule, this took place once a year, shortly before Christmas. He would then settle accounts, pay the wages, read his mail and leave promptly on Christmas morning.

In 1907 he returned to Lockeleys as mysteriously as he had left it, but henceforth, and without explanation, he lived in just one room, which no one else was allowed to enter. His love of solitude had by now become so extreme that he dismissed all his servants and let the estate run wild. When

During died It was discovered that for 30 years he had been living in Brighton under the name of Dale with a wife and a child. His daughter was surprised to find herself heir to Lockeleys and a large fortune, neither of which she had known about in her father's lifetime.

**Dermody, Thomas** (1775–1802), poet and soldier, celebrated for his ingratitude to patrons. Born in Ennis, County Clare, Dermody wrote verse as a child and was hailed by some as another Thomas CHATTERTON. That there would be difficulties ahead was suggested by the fact that he was an alcoholic by the age of 10 – a condition inherited from his father, a schoolmaster and lifelong drunk. By the age of 9, Thomas was helping his father to teach Latin and Greek, at the same time finding that writing poetry was as easy as speech. One of his earliest poems, in which he expresses his sorrow at the death of his brother from smallpox, survives:

> What dire misfortune hovers o'er my head?
> Why hangs the salt dew on my aching eye?
> Why doth my bosom pant, so sad, so sore,
> That was so blithe before?

Soon after completing this the 11-year-old Dermody ran away from home, taking with him two shillings, a copy of *Tom Jones* and a spare shirt. After wandering the streets of Dublin for a while, he met the first of his many, and shortly to be much abused, patrons, a Dr Houlton, who found him in a book shop poring over a Greek text. The doctor took him home and encouraged him to perform for his friends. Dermody would recite 'The Sensitive Linnet', which he had composed on the way to Dublin, and discuss classical subjects.

Bored in this circle, the boy took to the streets again, shortly being befriended by an out-of-work theatrical set painter named Coyle. When Coyle found a job in a Dublin theatre Dermody was persuaded to assist him in various undemanding tasks. While performing these, he found time to compose a lampoon on the rival merits of two actors, one of whom, Robert Owenson, was so impressed that he offered the boy a home, first buying him some new clothes. Dermody decided to burn the old ones in a sacrificial rite, but at the last moment he snatched his breeches from the fire and wrote a poem to them:

> … yet though I cast you off like lumber
> Your fame shall chime in jingling number.

Just as his future seemed bright, Dermody, who by now was drinking heavily, began to flit backwards and forwards between patrons, displaying towards each an even-handed lack of gratitude. His benefactors included the dowager countess of Moira, Lord Kilwarden, the attorney general, the Reverend Gilbert Austin, Henry Grattan and Henry Flood. The Reverend

Mr Boyd tried to put him through Trinity College, while a certain Mr Tighe mistook him for a beggar, thrashed him, and then, realizing his mistake, gave him a snuffbox, a suit of clothes and a cocked hat. These were soon pawned, and the poet was once again forced to peddle his verses around the countryside in rags.

Obliged to get money from somewhere, Dermody wrote to the dowager countess of Moira, whose kindness he had previously repaid with a savage essay entitled 'The Old Bachelors'. Lady Moira sent him half a crown, eliciting the response:

> My Lady, thankful for every former instance of your noble and generous favour, I cannot but wonder at receiving half a crown from that hand which had bestowed many guineas.

Dermody then decided to seek his fortune in England, but while waiting for his ship to sail he fell into the hands of a press gang, and shortly found himself in the hold of a tender on the Liffey. He sent an appeal to a former patron, Mr White, who managed to secure his release, but over the next few weeks he was pressed on two more occasions. Deciding that this must be his fate, he enlisted in the normal way and embarked for England on 17 September 1794 as a private in the Wagon Corps.

To the surprise of everyone who knew him, Dermody was an excellent soldier, serving courageously against the French and being wounded twice. When a truce was called in 1802 he retired on half pay and, by embracing his former dissolute habits, was soon reduced to poverty. In London he was taken up by two new patrons – a Mr Johnson, who presented him with a fashionable suit and a frilled shirt, and Sir James Bland Burgess, who helped him to obtain ten guineas from a literary fund. Again Dermody treated his benefactors with disdain. There was some unpleasantness over a cheque that he said he had lost but which in fact he had cashed, and there was the recurring problem of his vanishing wardrobe. He had been given another suit by Sir James but soon afterwards appeared at his house 'without either shoes, stockings, hat, neckcloth or waistcoat and in a state of intoxication not to be endured'. Sir James refused him any further help.

Dermody became ill with consumption and his last years were disagreeable. Sometime in 1802 he escaped his creditors and left London for an abandoned cottage near Sydenham in Kent. There he was discovered by his one friend, also his biographer, John Raymond, 'in a retreat more suitable for a horde of robbers than for a dying man. There was a stool, some wood scattered on the floor, and a crazy bedstead on which the poet lay beneath a leaking roof.' By the time Raymond had found him more comfortable accommodation in Sydenham, Dermody was dead. He was buried in Lewisham Church under a tombstone on which Raymond inscribed 'The Fate of Genius'.

**de Rougemont, Louis** (1847–1920), footman, explorer, inventor and impostor. During World War I a stooped and mumbling figure, dressed in a ragged greatcoat, could be seen selling matches in Shaftesbury Avenue, London. It was an undistinguished postscript to the career of the man who had once been the King of the Cannibals, alligator hunter, pearl diver, Great White God and author of the publishing sensation of the 1890s, *The Adventures of Louis De Rougemont – As Told By Himself.*

In his autobiography, serialized in *World Wide* magazine, de Rougemont described how as a young man he had set off on a pearling expedition to New Guinea. His ship had been wrecked in a storm, and he would have drowned with the rest of the crew had he not been able to paddle ashore clinging to the tail of the ship's dog, Bruno. Washed up on a deserted island off the coast of Australia, he and Bruno survived for two and a half years, sleeping in a hut made of shells and existing on a diet of sea birds and turtles' eggs. He warded off depression by taking up gymnastics, becoming proficient in tumbling and acrobatics, and amusing himself by taking rides on the backs of turtles.

In time, a party of Aborigines was washed ashore, a couple and their two boys apparently more dead than alive. De Rougemont nursed them back to health and they, in turn, overcame their fear of this strange white creature, whom they took to be 'a kind of Supreme Spirit from another world'. When they were fit enough, the family helped de Rougemont to build a boat, in which they all set sail for mainland Australia. By this time de Rougemont was able to communicate with Yamba, the mother of the family, and she warned him that her tribe, with whom they made contact once they were ashore, were cannibals. Happily, the tribesmen were so impressed by the various conjuring tricks that de Rougemont was able to perform that they invited him and Bruno to remain with them for as long as they wished. De Rougemont was even offered a wife, and an exchange that satisfied all parties was negotiated with Yamba's husband.

Readers of *Wide World* were kept enthralled by de Rougemont's adventures in the ensuing years. By confounding the local witch doctor with his tricks and predictions, by leading Yamba's tribe in a war with a tribe of hostile cannibals and by saving them from a party of white explorers who fired their rifles at them, de Rougemont convinced his new friends that he was indeed a god. At one point they came across a chief who had two white wives in attendance, both of them naked. Although by now a cannibal king, de Rougemont was still at heart a Victorian gentleman, and uncomfortable, therefore, in the presence of unclothed white girls. He was moved, too, by the way they clung to him and cried, 'Oh save us! Take us away from this brute!' Having dressed them in cockatoo feathers, he discovered that they were Blanche and Gladys Rogers, daughters of a sea captain. They had been separated from their father and kidnapped by cannibals, who had cooked and eaten the sailors who had accompanied them.

Taken as wives by the savage chieftain, Blanche and Gladys had tried on many occasions to escape but had always been restrained by the women who guarded them. De Rougemont challenged their captor to a wrestling match, with the two girls as the prize. The cannibal chief was 'magnificently muscular', but de Rougemont was able to secure him in a headlock before finishing him off with a blow to the chest.

Gladys and Blanche were treated as daughters by de Rougemont and Yamba, who derived great pleasure from their company, conversing in English, singing hymns and reciting passages from Shakespeare. Gladys and Blanche taught Yamba the Irish jig, and de Rougemont taught them how to yodel. This happy interlude came to a disagreeable end when, setting off on the long trek back to civilization, Gladys and Blanche became separated from de Rougemont and Yamba and were eaten by crocodiles. Yamba also succumbed en route, but after further adventures de Rougemont came across a trail of litter and realized that he had at last reached civilization after many years lost in the Australian bush. A group of prospectors – the first people to hear his story – took him for a madman, but once he had worked his passage to England and presented himself in the offices of *World Wide* magazine, he found a receptive audience.

The serialization of his story excited immediate controversy. An Australian, Ferguson, wrote to the *Daily Chronicle*, casting doubt on de Rougemont's claim that he had ferried himself around on the backs of turtles. He had never come across a turtle, Ferguson said, that wouldn't drop like a stone to the seabed if touched on any part of its body. Admiral J. Moresby, writing from Sherringham in Norfolk, disagreed:

> I have considerable experience of turtles, and know of a midshipman who got on a turtle's back and enjoyed a ten minute ride.

Other correspondents wanted to know why de Rougemont had not come across the telegraph line that connected Adelaide and Port Darwin.

Most vehemently contested, however, was de Rougemont's claim that he had been fired on by white settlers. Colonel Henry Greenaway of Devizes in Wiltshire pointed out, with justified indignation, that white men never attack a black camp 'except as a punitive measure'. A Mr David Carnegie agreed with the colonel:

> It is not the custom of any white man to fire on unoffending blacks, as if they were rabbits.

The *Daily Chronicle* felt obliged to launch a full investigation, and de Rougemont was soon uncovered as a fantasist and fraud. It turned out that his real name was Louis Grin, that he had been born in Switzerland and had come to London as a young man, working as a travelling servant for, among others, the celebrated actress Fanny Kemble. He had indeed embarked on a pearling expedition, and had been shipwrecked. However, he had been lost for three years at the most. As the *Daily Chronicle* put it, 'Mr de Rougemont has merely added a zero to the truth.' The paper also located a wife abandoned by Louis Grin, now living in poverty in Sydney, Australia, with several children, among whom were two girls called Blanche and Gladys. What *World Wide* called 'the monstrous fraud' that Louis Grin had committed on its readers had been concocted in the Reading Room at the British Library. In *The Adventures of Louis de Rougemont*, Grin had reinvented his failed life as a success story. He remained out of the public eye for many years, but in 1906 he appeared at the London Hippodrome, demonstrating his turtle-riding skills in a large tank – without any great success. He emerged again briefly during World War I, first as an inventor of a meat substitute, and then as a ghostly presence in London's West End, selling matches from a tray. The King of the Cannibals died in poverty in 1920.

**de Sancha, Antonia** (1960–  ), actress and 'other woman' in the David Mellor scandal that contributed to the downfall of the Tory cabinet minister. Miss de Sancha's revelations in the *Sun* newspaper that the heritage secretary in John Major's government liked to make love wearing a Chelsea Football Club shirt and had a penchant for spanking left their mark on the public imagination. Her later memoir in the *Sunday Mirror*, in which she described a bisexual affair with the former model Michelle Davis, aroused little interest by comparison.

*See also* MELLOR, DAVID. For references to other women, *see* OTHER WOMEN.

**Desmond, Catherine Fitzgerald, countess of** (*c*.1480–*c*.1615), second wife of the 12th earl of Desmond of Dromana in County Waterford, whom she married in 1529. The countess apparently lived to the age of 140, danced with RICHARD III, met Sir Walter Raleigh more than a century later and died in the early 17th century having outlasted nine English sovereigns. Her encounter with Raleigh took place in 1589 and her name is mentioned in a deed dated a year later. A portrait of her at Knole in Kent is inscribed, 'Catherine, Countess of Desmond at ye court of our sovereign James in present A.D. 1614 in the 140th year of her age.'

Shortly before her death, the countess walked from Bristol to London to make a personal appeal to King James I over some property that had been confiscated. Robert Sydney added to her legend by contributing the information that she had a new set of teeth not long before her death and might have lived much longer had she not fallen out of a tree that she had climbed in search of nuts. Some say it was a cherry tree, others an apple tree.

**Despard, Edward Marcus** (1753–1803), soldier and traitor. Despard's plan to overthrow the government in 1802 was described by the *Newgate*

*Calendar* as 'the most vain and impotent attempt ever engendered in the distracted brain of an enthusiast'. The writer's contempt seems to have been particularly aroused by the fact that among the conspirators only Despard was a gentleman:

> Without arms, or any probable means, a few dozen men, the very dregs of society, led on by a disappointed and disaffected chief, were to overturn a mighty empire; nor does it appear that any man of their insignificant band of conspirators – Colonel Despard alone excepted – was above the level of the plebeian race, and not a few of them were Irish.

Despard was descended from an ancient family from Queen's County (now Laois) in Ireland. Having joined the army, he served with distinction and was appointed superintendent of his majesty's affairs on the coast of Honduras. There various differences arose between the inhabitants and the king's ministers, and Despard was accused of unspecified misdemeanours. On returning to England he demanded that his conduct should be properly investigated, but was told that there was no charge against him worthy of an enquiry. Indeed, he would have been reinstated in the office of superintendent at Honduras had it not been abolished.

Dissatisfied by the outcome, Despard began to vent his indignation in such an unguarded manner that he was judged a suspicious character and imprisoned in Coldbath Fields under the Habeas Corpus Act. Imprisonment did little to assuage his anger; indeed it provided him with an opportunity to enlist a small army of toughs and malcontents whom he would lead in a conspiracy to assassinate George III and seize power.

On 16 November 1802, some time after Despard's release, a party of police officers armed with a search warrant went to the Oakley Arms in Oakley Street, Lambeth, where they arrested the Colonel together with 40 labouring men and soldiers, many of them Irish. Having been examined by the magistrates at Union Hall, Despard was committed to Newgate prison, 12 of 'his low associates' were sent to Totwell Fields Bridewell, and 20 to the New Prison, Clerkenwell. Ten other people, who had been drinking in the Oakley Arms, though not with the colonel, were beaten up anyway, and then released.

Despard's trial opened on 7 February 1803. The evidence against him was provided by treacherous co-conspirators, chiefly one Thomas Windsor. Windsor testified that the assassination attempt was to be made on the day that George III went to Parliament. According to Windsor, Despard said, 'I have weighed the matter well, and my heart is callous.' Windsor and three soldiers were instructed by Despard to 'post themselves as sentries over the great gun in the Park' and fire on his majesty's coach as it passed by on its way to the House. After the king had been killed, the mail coaches were to be stopped, as a signal to the country that the revolt had taken place. Windsor was to meet Despard at 11.30 the next morning on Tower Hill and to bring with him 'four or five intelligent men' to consider the best manner for taking the Tower and securing the arms.

Lord Nelson appeared as a character witness for Despard, testifying that they had served on the Spanish Main together, where Despard had been a loyal and good officer. On cross-examination, his lordship admitted that he had not seen the defendant since 1780, and the jury returned a verdict of guilty. Lord Ellenborough, presiding, 'in a style of awful solemnity highly befitting the melancholy but just occasion', pronounced sentence:

> You will be taken from the place from whence you came, and from thence you are to be drawn on a hurdle to the place of execution, where you are to be hanged by the neck, but not until you are dead; for while you are still living your body is to be taken down, your bowels torn out and burned before your face, your head then cut off, and your body divided into four quarters, and your head and quarters to be then at the King's disposal; and may Almighty God have mercy on your soul!

The *Newgate Calendar* reports that Mrs Despard was greatly affected when she first heard the sentence passed, but afterwards recovered her fortitude. She and Colonel Despard 'bore up with great firmness at parting, and when she got into a coach, as it drove off she waved her handkerchief out of the window'. At 7 o'clock on 21 February 1803 Despard was taken from his cell and his arms were bound with rope. He thanked his solicitor 'very cordially for all his kind attentions', and then, observing the sledge and apparatus, cried, 'Ha! Ha! What nonsensical mummery is this?' He was carted to Horsemonger Lane, Shoreditch, where he was executed at seven minutes to nine.

**Devil encountered in St Audoen's Church, Dublin, the.** *See* HELL-FIRE CLUB, THE IRISH.

**Devil impersonated by a baboon, the.** *See* DASHWOOD, SIR FRANCIS.

**Devil's work, the.** *See* ROBINSON, ANNE; and *passim*.

**Devonshire, Andrew Robert Buxton Cavendish, 11th duke of** (1920– ), politician and racehorse owner. Devonshire is said to exemplify the finest characteristics of the English aristocracy. Diffident and dishevelled – he goes out in a new suit only after his head gardener has worn it in – he is unfailingly generous to those less fortunate than himself. Some have taken advantage of his otherworldly disposition and shortsightedness. In 1985, the duke courageously prosecuted the boyfriend of a young woman who stole his chequebook and used it to buy photographic equipment.

During this disagreeable ordeal, Devonshire was publicly supported by his wife Debbo, the youngest of the Mitford sisters.

The 11th duke's forgetfulness is legendary. According to Anthony Powell's *Journals 1982–86* (1995), Cyril Connolly was dining one night with Lady Cunard. Devonshire was another guest. After dinner, he said to Connolly, 'Come to a club I belong to.' The two of them went to Pratts, where Devonshire said, 'You're just the sort of chap we'd like as a member. Would you care to join?' 'Yes,' said Connolly. Devonshire approached old So-and-So. 'Do you know Cyril Connolly?' 'No.' 'Would you all the same second him for membership?' 'By all means,' said old So-and-So. Connolly heard nothing more. Two years later, he dined again with Lady Cunard. Old So-and-So was another guest. After dinner, he said to Connolly, 'Come to a club I belong to.' The two of them went to Pratts, where old So-and-So said, 'You're just the sort of chap we'd like as a member. Would you care to join?' 'Yes,' said Connolly. Old So-and-So approached Devonshire, who happened to be there. 'Do you know Cyril Connolly?' said old So-and-So. 'No,' said Devonshire. 'Would you all the same second him for membership?' 'By all means,' said Devonshire. Connolly didn't hear from him again.

In her collection of occasional essays, *Counting my Chickens* (2001), the duchess of Devonshire reveals that her grandmother 'used to preserve the family furniture by banging it with a mallet to give concussion to the woodworm'. An earlier work, *The British Goat Society Year Book* (1972), includes an account of her travelling from Mull to London by train at the outbreak of World War II with her goat. 'At Stirling, in the middle of the night, I milked the goat in the first-class waiting room, which I should not have done as I only had a third-class ticket.'

*See also* REDESDALE, CLEMENT NAPIER THOMAS FREEMAN MITFORD, 2ND BARON.

**Dia, Ali** (1968– ), footballer and impostor. Dia was an enthusiastic, but unskilful, part-time footballer whom Barry Jackson, the manager of Blyth Spartan – a club in the lower leagues – was happy to release after a few games. Some months later Jackson was surprised to see Dia playing in a Premiership game televised on *Match of the Day*. Ali Dia's moment of glory came after Graeme Souness, the manager of Southampton Football Club, apparently received a telephone call from George Weah, the Liberian international and former Footballer of the Year. Souness would be well advised, said Weah, to take a look at Dia, whom he described as a Senegalese international of outstanding talent, now living in England. The phone call was followed by one apparently from the French international, David Ginola, who seconded this advice. Weah and Ginola were not people to disregard, so Souness engaged Dia without a trial and played him against Manchester United. He missed an open goal and was otherwise careful not to get too involved, so Souness substituted him after 20 minutes. At the end of the season Souness let him go. Dia then joined Gravesend, another club in the lower leagues, turning out twice in the reserves before being released again. It was then discovered that he was a mature student taking a course in business studies at Newcastle University, but he continued to deny that he had impersonated Weah and Ginola on the telephone to Graeme Souness.

'At least he played in the Premiership,' said his former manager at Blyth Spartan, 'which is more than I ever did.'

**diamond geezers.** All diamond geezers are hard bastards, though not tautologically so, since not all hard bastards, less than a majority, perhaps, are diamond geezers.

Diamond geezers are old-style gangsters who honour their mothers and inflict serious injury – nailing wrong-doers to the floor, removing their teeth with pliers – only on their own kind. In other respects they display the characteristics of 'a perfect gentleman', a description they customarily bestow on a colleague from whom they have just received a beating. In the heyday of diamond geezers (see FOREMAN, FREDDIE; FRASER, FRANCIS ('MAD FRANKIE'); GOODY, GORDON; HILL, BILLY; KRAY, REGGIE) the streets of London were safe for women and children. By contrast, contemporary celebrity villains, such as 'Dodgy' Dave Courtney, the Kojak look-alike who organized Ronnie KRAY's funeral in 1995, are hard bastards but not diamond geezers. Courtney lives with a black lingerie model as bald as himself and has ambitions to follow the soccer player Vinnie JONES, into films.

**Dickenson, Mother** (c.1600–?), witch. She was burnt at the stake for indulging in obscene rituals in Rochdale, turning herself into a horse and riding off with young men.

**Diggle, Angus** (1940– ), solicitor and ballroom dancer. After attending a Highland Ball at the Grosvenor House Hotel, London, in 1993, Diggle was invited back to the flat of the girl with whom he had attended the function. She had expected him to spend the night on the sofa, but she woke up to find him wearing a luminous green condom and trying to have sex with her. When the police were called, he said, 'I have spent £200 on this woman.' Diggle was jailed for three years and suspended from practice for one year. Later, he was bound over to keep the peace after he had quoted passages from Shakespeare to a woman on a train. In 1996 he was struck off the rolls of solicitors after being found drunk in Bolton.

**Dilke, Sir Charles** (1843–1911), politician and philanderer. Such was the complexity of the divorce case in which Dilke was notoriously involved that it might have played better in the theatre as a French farce. In fact, *The Right Honourable Gentleman*, a dramatized version of the events starring Anthony Quayle and Coral Browne, was produced by Emile LITTLER at Her Majesty's Theatre in 1960.

In July 1885 Sir Charles – the MP for Chelsea, a cabinet minister in Gladstone's government and thought by many to be a future prime minister – was warned by a friend, Mrs Christina Rogerson, that he was to be cited in a divorce action brought by a Mr Donald Crawford, alleging a confession of adultery with Dilke by his wife, Virginia. There is no doubt that Dilke had had affairs with many women, including Mrs Rogerson, and also with Virginia Crawford's friend, Mrs Eustace Smith. But he always strenuously denied any impropriety with Mrs Crawford, whose confession also alleged troilism involving herself, Dilke and Fanny Stock, a maid in Dilke's household.

Virginia Crawford, together with her sister Harriet, had always been promiscuous. Donald Crawford, a Tyneside shipowner, was twice her age and the sisters – like many women of this type – frequently enjoyed the company of medical students and young men of a lower social class. On one occasion they visited a Knightsbridge brothel, where Virginia met a Captain Henry Foster. One theory has been that it was to protect Captain Foster that Dilke was named as co-respondent. It was suggested too, that Mrs Rogerson might also have been involved in the plot. She was displeased with Dilke, who was now engaged to a respectable widow, Emilia Pattison, whom he later married.

In law there was no evidence against Dilke. Virginia Crawford's confession was evidence against her, but not against him. However, Dilke's lawyer, Sir Charles Russell, made a fatal blunder. 'In the life of any man,' he informed the court, 'there may be found to have been indiscretions.' Although Mr Justice Butt dismissed Dilke from the case, he granted Donald Crawford his divorce, and the damage had been done. The campaigning journalist W.T. Stead demanded in the *Pall Mall Gazette* that Dilke should clear his name. Dilke applied to the Queen's Proctor to annul Crawford's decree nisi before it was made absolute, and a second hearing was ordered. Fanny Stock was found, and she was happy to deny the allegation of troilism. There was still a problem, however. Dilke was not a defendant on this occasion, but a witness. His lawyer had no right to cross-examine Mrs Crawford, who now amended her evidence. She admitted to an affair with Captain Foster, but she stuck to her story that she had committed adultery with Dilke. The jury took only 15 minutes to decide that the decree nisi had not been improperly obtained.

Repeated efforts were made over the years to clear Dilke's name, but none was successful. By the time of the second hearing he had been defeated in his Chelsea constituency and, although he was re-elected for Forest of Dean, he never again held public office. Virginia Crawford fared better. She converted to Catholicism and entered public life herself, as a Labour councillor and a campaigner against fascism.

**Dill, Sir Victor Robert Colqhoun** (1897–1986), soldier, actor and race-horse ringer. Educated at Eton and Sandhurst, and a relation of Sir John Dill, one-time chief of the Imperial General Staff, Sir Victor won the Military Cross in World War I, distinguished himself in World War II, and went to prison for nine months in 1953 for his part in a horse-switching scandal.

Finding himself at a loose end after World War I, Dill first tried his hand at acting, securing a part in *Funny Face* at the Princes Theatre. Thereafter, he worked variously as a garage attendant, sandwich-bar assistant and waiter at a club in Putney. When in funds, he dabbled as a racehorse owner. Sir Gordon Richards, the 28-times champion jockey, once rode for him in a selling plate at Chepstow, finishing last.

In July 1953, when his fortunes were at a low ebb, Dill was persuaded to join a racecourse gang that planned to run a horse called Francasal at Bath races in the name of a considerably slower animal called Santa Amaro. Shortly before the 'off', the gang placed bets totalling £6000 on 'Santa Amaro' with bookmakers throughout the country. 'Santa Amaro' duly won with something to spare, but the circumstances aroused suspicion and payment of bets was withheld. At the gang's subsequent trial, Mr Justice Byrne said how distressed he was to see a man with Dill's background in such a situation. 'I imagine you were brought in to add an air of respectability,' he said. 'Not in the least,' replied Dill affably. 'I was doing odd jobs for a bookmaker at the time – sweeping up and so forth.'

Dill served his nine months in prison and then moved to Maison Lafitte, near Paris, where he set up as a bloodstock agent. Never without his monocle, and usually to be seen riding an English bicycle, he became a popular figure in French racing circles.

**Dimes, Albert** (1906–72), gangster best known for his part in the Frith Street affray of 1954, which marked the end of Jack SPOT's career as a Soho overlord (*see* ANDREWS, THE REVEREND BASIL). As Billy HILL's former right-hand man, Dimes inherited many of the gang's interests when Hill retired to Sunningdale in 1958. In the early 1960s he acted as an unseen 'godfather' of London crime, keeping an uneasy peace between the various young pretenders – including the NASH brothers and the KRAY twins – striving to take over the territories formerly controlled by Spot and Hill. Through an early connection with the Sabini family, known as the 'Italian Mob', Dimes was the trusted representative in Britain of the American Mafia. Between 1965 and 1969 he had frequent meetings, both in London and America, with Angelo Bruno of the Philadelphian crime family. In November 1972

Dimes died of cancer. The imprisoned Krays sent a wreath with the inscription 'To a fine gentleman' (*see* DIAMOND GEEZERS). The message was destroyed by friends on the grounds that it brought shame to the family.

**dinner guests, robbing one's own.** *See* MYTTON, JOHN.

**Dinosaurs, last of the City.** *See* LOWSON, SIR DENYS.

**dirty bastard who gets himself noticed, a.** *See* JONES, VINNIE.

**discount carpets.** *See* THORPE, JEREMY.

**disease, the Scotch.** *See* GREEN, MARY.

**ditch, tipplng one's biographer into a.** *See* MYTTON, JOHN.

**Diver, Jenny** (c.1650–1710), pickpocket and confidence trickster. Jenny was the most skilful pickpocket of her day, bringing to the profession sophisticated new techniques that put her at the head of any gang she cared to join and earned her a graceful tribute from the compilers of the *Newgate Calendar*:

> Her depredations, executed with the courage of a man and the softer deceptions of an artful woman, surpass anything which we have yet come to in our researches into crimes and punishments.

Diver's most imaginative innovation was to equip herself with a pair of false hands and arms, allowing her to conceal her real ones under her dress. With her extensions in place, and having stuffed a cushion under her stays to simulate pregnancy, she would proceed to a church service in a sedan chair, with one of her gang going ahead to secure her a seat among the wealthier members of the congregation, and with another in attendance as her footman. Having taken her seat between two elderly ladies of quality, she would wait until they were crouched in prayer and then relieve them of their watches and jewellery, which she would pass to an accomplice in an adjoining pew. Should one of her elderly victims discover her loss, the other would exonerate 'the pregnant lady' whose hands, she could vouch, had never left her lap.

Another stratagem was to suffer a fainting fit in a public place. On a day when James II was on his way to the House of Lords, Jenny sank gracefully to the ground in Hyde Park and was immediately surrounded by a sympathetic crowd. By indicating that she was too weak to be moved she gave her accomplices ample time to relieve the anxious onlookers of their watches, girdle-bracelets, purses and snuffboxes.

On another occasion, and again accompanied by her footman, Jenny knocked on the door of a house in Wapping, whose owner, Mrs Mapplebeck, was told by the footman that his mistress had been taken ill and had mislaid her smelling salts. Jenny and the footman were invited in, and while Mrs Mapplebeck was upstairs searching for her bottle of salts, Jenny had time to conceal many of Mrs Mapplebeck's priceless *objets* under her dress. Later, while Mrs Mapplebeck was holding the bottle of salts under her nose, Jenny picked her pocket of a purse containing 60 guineas. Meanwhile, the footman, who had been told to wait in the kitchen, stole six silver spoons, a pepper box and a salt cellar. Once she was strong enough to leave, Jenny thanked her benefactress for her help and then drove off in Mrs Mapplebeck's coach.

The following evening, and still in Mrs Mapplebeck's coach, Jenny went to a theatre where she attracted the attentions of a rich young man from Yorkshire. At first, she resisted him with all due modesty, saying she was married, but she relented at last and invited him to come to her house the following day, when her husband would be away on business. On arrival at her lodging house, the young man from Yorkshire was taken straight to the bedroom. No sooner had he undressed than Jenny's maid knocked on the door in some agitation with the news that the master of the house had unexpectedly returned. Panic-stricken, Jenny begged the Yorkshireman to hide under the bed, which he immediately did. When he dared to emerge, half an hour later, he discovered that Jenny had departed with his clothes, a gold-headed cane, a sword with a gold hilt, his watch and a diamond ring.

A victim in time of her own success, Jenny was compelled by her growing notoriety to move her business to Bristol, where she was soon arrested for theft, and subsequently sentenced to deportation. Finding that America offered few opportunities for the practice of her skills, she persuaded an infatuated young man to pay her passage back to England. She was arrested on the day she arrived when attempting to rob an old woman of 13s 6d. Sentenced to be hanged at Tyburn, she was taken there in a coach instead of a wagon, which was an unheard-of mark of respect. She was commemorated by John Gay as one of Macheath's attendant loose women in *The Beggar's Opera*.

**Dobson, Rodney** (1928– ), burglar. In 1971 Dobson was arrested for the 43rd time when he drove the wrong get-away car into two parked vans. Sentencing him to a suspended sentence of 18 months, Judge Lionel Percy offered some advice from the bench:

> I think you should give up burglary. You have a withered hand, an artificial leg and only one eye. You have been caught in Otley, Leeds,

Harrogate, Norwich, Beverley, Hull and York. How can you hope to succeed? You are a useless burglar.

**Docker, Sir Bernard.** *See* BAKER, PETER.

**dockers, queer.** *See* FARSON, DANIEL.

**doctors, homicidal.** *See* ADAMS, DR JOHN BODKIN; CREAM, THOMAS NEILL; CRIPPEN, DR HAWLEY HARVEY; PALMER, WILLIAM.

**Dodd, the Reverend Dr William** (1729–77), priest, writer, dandy and fraud. The execution of Dr Dodd on a charge of forgery in 1777 caused a sensation. He was an elegant scholar and, in the opinion of many, the finest preacher in the land. He was the promoter, and sometimes the instigator, of many public charities. The Magdalen, for reclaiming fallen women, the Society for the Relief of Poor Debtors, and the Humane Society for the Recovery of Persons Drowned at Sea all owed their existence to Dr Dodd. He was a former royal chaplain to George III and he held the lucrative office of prebend of Brecon. His income, however, could never cover his extravagant lifestyle, and a desperate shortage of cash led him eventually to commit a clumsy forgery against his friend and pupil, Lord Chesterfield.

It wasn't Dodd's first attempt to advance his own interests at the expense of others. In 1774 the lucrative living at St George's, Hanover Square, became available after the elevation of its incumbent. The living was in the gift of the lord chancellor, to whose wife, Lady Apsley, Dodd sent a letter offering her £3000 if she succeeded in persuading her husband to grant him the living. Lord Apsley traced the letter back to Dodd, who was immediately disgraced. He fled to Switzerland, where he stayed with his loyal friend and former pupil, Philip Stanhope, now Lord Chesterfield. He was away for several months. On his way back to England he stopped briefly in Paris, where he was seen at the races, reeling from the effects of alcohol and losing heavily on the horses.

Back in England, Dodd resumed his extravagant lifestyle, which he maintained by borrowing heavily. In desperation, he embarked on the fraud that was to cost him his life. On 1 February 1777 he forged a bond for £4200 in the name of Lord Chesterfield. Under the 'Bloody Code' of the 18th century, this was one of 350 capital offences on the statute books. The method he adopted was remarkably clumsy. Pretending that Lord Chesterfield was in urgent need of a loan, but reluctant to be his own agent, Dodd employed Lewis Robertson, a broker, to negotiate the bond. Robertson was able to borrow the money from Messrs Fletcher & Peach and to pass it on to Dodd. When the bond reached Lord Chesterfield he immediately disowned it, and Dodd was arrested. The forgery was a temporary ιεσουιce, hē said, and the money would have been repaid within six months. He added:

> My Lord Chesterfield cannot but have some tenderness for me as his tutor. I love him, and he knows it. I am sure my Lord Chesterfield does not want my life. Mercy should triumph over justice.

Mercy was withheld, and on 19 February Dodd went on trial at the Old Bailey. His behaviour in court was unimpressive. Escorted to the dock on the arm of a friend, he burst into tears as he sat down. Lord Chesterfield testified that the handwriting on the bond was that of his old tutor, and the jury took only ten minutes to return a verdict of guilty. When Dodd was sentenced to be hanged, he collapsed in the dock, groaning, 'Lord Jesus receive my soul!'

The public mood, formerly hostile, now became extravagantly sympathetic. Those who had previously dismissed Dodd as a painted fop, a sentimental preacher and a third-rate writer (in his youth he had written a vulgar farce for the theatre and a prurient novel), now argued that it would set a bad example if such a respected clergyman were to be publicly hanged. The most notable intervention came from Samuel Johnson, who wrote Dodd's speech from the prisoners' chapel at Newgate, entitling it 'Convict's Address to His Unhappy Brethren'. This and other speeches and letters written on Dodd's behalf are considered to be among Dr Johnson's most powerful compositions.

Dodd's execution took place at Tyburn on 27 June 1777 and the outcry it occasioned has been recognized by some historians as a key moment in focusing public attention on the brutality of CAPITAL PUNISHMENT. It seems more likely, however, that it was caused less by any broad change in public opinion than by the fact that Dodd was of the same class as those who protested against his execution. A 15-year-old orphan, John Harris, who was hanged on the same day for stealing two and a half guineas, received no such support, least of all from Dr Johnson.

**dog, running a man through for stepping on one's.** *See* FITZGERALD, GEORGE ROBERT.

**dog appointed to a company directorship.** *See* SLATER, JOHN.

**dog called Bruno, rescued by the tail of a.** *See* DE ROUGEMONT, LOUIS.

**dog lovers.** *See* BECKFORD, WILLIAM; BERNERS, GERALD HUGH TYRWHITT-WILSON, 14TH BARON; BRIDGEWATER, FRANCIS HENRY EGERTON, 8TH EARL OF; FITZGERALD, GEORGE ROBERT; JONES, VINNIE; MYTTON, JOHN; THORPE, JEREMY (for Norman Scott).

**dog on a diet of cats, feeding one's 12-stone.** *See* BRISTOL, FREDER-ICK WILLIAM JOHN AUGUSTUS HERVEY, 7TH MARQUESS OF.

**dogs, hunting one's children with.** *See* REDESDALE, CLEMENT NAPIER THOMAS FREEMAN MITFORD, 2ND BARON.

**dog saves 'dirty bastard' from suicide by licking his nose, small.** *See* JONES, VINNIE.

**dogs in mourning.** *See* BOYCE, SAMUEL; MASSEREENE, CLOTWORTHY SKEFFINGTON, 2ND EARL OF.

**'Dog's poo!', celebrity chefs who have shouted.** *See* CRADDOCK, FANNY.

**dogs who have defeated county cricketers at their own game.** *See* TRUMPER, FRANCIS.

**Donaghue, Albert** (1934– ), unlicensed fist-fighter and gangster. In 1963 Donaghue was having a quiet drink in an East End pub when Ronnie KRAY shot him in the leg. Donaghue took the incident in good part (*see* DIAMOND GEEZERS) and as a reward for not complaining he was given £15 and a place on the 'Firm'. Among his duties thereafter was the collection of 'rents' from protected premises, and he also acted as Ronnie Kray's body-guard. In 1966 Donaghue played a leading part in the escape from Dartmoor of Frank MITCHELL, known as the 'Mad Axeman'. When the Krays and their associates were arrested in 1967 by Superintendent Leonard 'Nipper' Read, Donaghue was charged with Mitchell's murder. Read suspected that Donaghue, who had merely acted as one of Mitchell's minders, would be unwilling to take responsibility for his death. In this he was correct. Donaghue named Freddie FOREMAN and Alfie Gerrard as Mitchell's killers, pleading guilty to being an accessory after the fact and receiving a prison sentence of two years. He and Foreman have since made frequent appearances together on television as celebrity villains and, given their history, seem to be on good terms.

**Dorset, Charles Sackville, 1st earl of** (1630–1701), peer, debauchee and murderer. A member of the 2nd duke of BUCKINGHAM's circle, Dorset was prominent among those who gave the Restoration a reputation for upper-class hooliganism, largely unpunished. In 1662 Dorset, his brother and three aristocratic cronies were accused of robbing and murdering a tanner named Hoppy during an evening of drunken revelry. Their defence was that they had mistaken him for a highwayman. This was accepted and the case was dropped. On another occasion, and in the company of the

2nd earl of Rochester – also a member of Buckingham's circle – Dorset was involved in a fight between a group of gentlemen roisterers and the watch at Epsom, in the course of which one of his aristocratic friends was killed. A year later he was in the company of another of Buckingham's circle, Sir Charles Sedley, when the latter carried out a vicious assault on an actor named Edward Kynaston, to whom he happened to bear a physical resemblance. Kynastan's offence had been to appear in public dressed like Sir Charles. Sedley later distinguished himself by being fined £500 for running an orgy at the Cock tavern in Bow Street.

The misdeeds of Dorset and his fellow delinquents had an unfortunate influence on the lesser gentry who, in the way of things, tended to ape the manners of their social betters. Reports of crime in late 17th-century London contain numerous references to would-be aristocrats who were ready to commit acts of violence in defence of what they conceived to be their honour. A pamphlet in 1684, describing the death of a watchman who was murdered after accidentally bumping into a gentleman in the street, deplored the common attitude that felt 'nothing but the blood of a man were a satisfaction for a neglectful stumble upon one of these night-walking gentlemen'. (*A True Account of a Bloudy and Barbarous Murder, committed on the Body of John Sparks, Waterman, by John Hitchins, in Fleet Street, near Serjeants-Inn*, 1684.)

The malign influence of Dorset and those like him was not confined to London. Northern assize records give an unfavourable picture of Yorkshire gentry. In 1681 the earl of Eglington killed a Mr Maddox in an ale house in Doncaster after the latter had made some disobliging remarks about the Scottish peerage. And in 1664 Lionel Copley was indicted for assault. He had saddled up a man of the lower class, put a bridle in his mouth and ridden him round Sheffield. As the historian J.A. Smart observed in *Crime in Early Modern England – 1550–1750* (1984), 'Renaissance concepts of aristocratic behaviour evidently arrived late in south Yorkshire.'

**doss house, dressing for dinner in a.** *See* SITWELL, SIR GEORGE RERESBY.

**double agents, safe-cracking.** *See* CHAPMAN, EDDIE.

**Douglas, 'Mother' Jane** (1700–61), madam. Known as 'The Empress', Douglas ran a lavishly appointed brothel at the King's Head tavern in the Euston Road. Uniformed footmen supplied clients on arrival with beribboned condoms and aphrodisiac pills. In spite of her notoriety, and frequent spells in prison, she was able to attract, and retain, an upper-class clientele. This included Prince William, duke of Cumberland, Lord Fitzwilliam and Admiral Charles Homers – one of whom fathered her daughter, Elizabeth. Shortly before her death Douglas was described by the playwright Charles Johnson as 'a nice cheerful old woman although much bloated by drink and debauch'. John Cleland used her as the model for Mother Cole in *Fanny Hill* (1748).

**Douglas-Home, William** (1912–92), playwright, parliamentary candidate and cashiered army officer. Douglas-Home wrote undemanding light comedies that seldom challenged the convictions of his audience. Away from his desk he was a courageous man who stood by his principles. His own convictions, indeed, led to a spell in Wakefield prison for disobeying an order in World War II. 'Willie's always fightin',' said Lady Astor at the time. 'Fightin' to get into the army. Fightin' to get out of it by fightin' to get into Parliament, then fightin' to get into prison.'

Douglas-Home was born in Edinburgh, the younger son of Lord Dunglass, who succeeded to the earldom of Home in 1918. His mother, the former Lady Lilian Lambton, daughter of the 4th earl of Durham, was a noted eccentric. She had all her teeth out at one go without an anaesthetic and then went to a formal lunch ahead of her false ones. When they arrived, they flew out of her mouth as she shook hands with an admiral.

After Eton and Oxford, Douglas-Home trained at the Royal Academy of Dramatic Art to be an actor, sharing a flat in London with two old school friends – Jo Grimond, the future leader of the Liberal Party, and Brian Johnston, later a popular cricket commentator. In 1937 he secured a small role in the West End production of Dodie Smith's *Bonnet Over the Windmill*, but his career was interrupted by the outbreak of World War II. When he received his call-up papers he replied to the War Office by telegram:

> Prepared to be conscripted on the understanding that if my most
> strongly held principles should be challenged by Winston
> Churchill's government to a point beyond endurance I cannot be
> relied on.

That point was reached on 8 September 1944, when, as a tank commander with the Royal Armoured Corps, Douglas-Home received an order to attack Le Havre, which contained a large number of civilians whom the Germans had not allowed to evacuate. Needing time in which to examine the moral grounds for such an action, Captain Douglas-Home drove 25 times round a turnip field before informing his colonel that he would be unable to obey the order. He was court-martialled and sentenced to a year in prison. His brother, Alec, later to be prime minister, visited him in Wormwood Scrubs but was so put off by the beard he had grown that he stood with his back to him and discussed cricket with the warder. After his mother had visited him in Wakefield prison, she wrote to the governor, thanking him for having her son to stay.

After the war Douglas-Home turned to writing plays and was successful almost immediately with *The Chiltern Hundreds*, starring A.E. Matthews. Matthews preferred to make a play up as he went along and kept boredom at bay by handing round plums among the cast, thus making it difficult for them to speak. During the run Douglas-Home sent a telegram to the company saying:

> Propose to visit theatre Monday. A brace of pheasants to anyone still speaking my lines.

A.E. Matthews replied:

> Majority decision to return to your script.

Other successful plays followed, including *The Jockey Club Stakes*, which reflected Douglas-Home's love of racing. He himself enjoyed only mixed fortunes as an owner, once entering a 3-year-old, Goblin, for the Derby against the advice of its trainer. When Goblin got off to a poor start, Douglas-Home thought it had got its tail caught in the starting stall, but in fact it had fallen asleep. In spite of this, Goblin finished tenth.

Douglas-Home was fond of practical jokes. He once smuggled a stuffed crocodile out of the Hirsel, the family's Scottish seat, and then took his mother and a party of friends on a walk in the grounds. As they crossed a bridge, an accomplice pushed the crocodile out into the stream. Lady Home's reaction was disappointing. She passed by unperturbed, remarking, 'I hadn't realized they came this far north.'

**Dower, Gandar** (1881–1950), sporting gentleman. In 1937 Dower introduced cheetah racing to England as an exciting alternative to greyhounds. He imported eight cats and staged highly publicized events at Romford and Haringey. He had not discovered that cheetahs are remarkably uncompetitive, and too intelligent to mistake a length of rag on a stick for a Thomson gazelle or other prey. The cheetahs wandered round in a state of indifference and the experiment was abandoned.

**Dowse, Margaret** (1911–83), thief. In the years immediately after World War II, professional crime was a male preserve. With a few notable exceptions (Billy HILL's sister Maggie, 'Queen of the Forty Elephants', was one, Lilian GOLDSTEIN, 'the Bobbed-Haired Bandit', another), wives and girlfriends were expected to carry out their domestic duties and remain loyal. Against this background Margaret Dowse's extrovert criminal activities so bewildered the Metropolitan Police that its exasperated commissioner, Sir Robert Jackson, was moved on one occasion to question her understanding of appropriate feminine behaviour. 'She can hardly be described as an ornament to her sex,' he said. At selection boards, one of the first questions put to CID officers was, 'What would you do about Margaret Dowse?'

With her boyfriend, Stanley Turner, who was the firm's junior partner, Margaret was constantly on the move, choosing a town and then using her considerable charm to secure a position in a sub-post office. Having manipulated her employers to the point where she was trusted to collect and deposit the cash, she would pocket the takings and move with Stanley to another part of the country. By the time she was caught she was wanted in 43 different towns. When she was jailed for five years at Lewes Crown Court in 1960 she asked for 38 other offences to be taken into account. She retired in 1970 and settled with Stanley in Westcliffe-on-Sea, where they ran a boarding house.

**dress sense, a comedic.** *See* BECKHAM, DAVID; BROMLEY-DAVENPORT, LIEUTENANT COLONEL SIR WALTER; CARTLAND, BARBARA; CLARENDON, JOHN CORNBURY, 3RD EARL OF; CRADOCK, FANNY; FARSON, DANIEL (for Mrs Shufflewick); LOLE, WILLIAM; MCAVENNIE, FRANK; MATURIN, CHARLES ROBERT; SALISBURY, FRANCES MARY, 1ST MARCHIONESS OF; SIBTHORP, COLONEL CHARLES DE LAET WALDO; SPENCER, HERBERT; TASTE TICKELL, KIM DE LA; WARING, FRANCIS.

**Drewe, John** (1949– ), confidence trickster. In 1987 Drewe instigated what critics accept as the greatest art-forgery 'caper' of the 20th century – a deception which caused as many as 200 fakes to be passed off as works by Marc Chagall, Alberto Giacometti, Graham Sutherland, Georges Braque, Paul Klee and Ben Nicholson. It began when John Myatt, a 41-year-old artist who had been abandoned by his wife and was struggling to support himself and his two young children, placed an advertisement in *Private Eye* offering 'genuine fakes' for £150. Myatt received a telephone call from Drewe, who commissioned a Chagall, which Myatt shortly completed, using a modern canvas and, as was his custom, household emulsion (Dulux being his favourite). The partnership prospered, and the following year Drewe told him that a cubist painting Myatt had done in the style of Albert Gleizes had been valued by a London auctioneer at £25,000. After that the works poured out, the only requirement being that the paintings had to be by deceased modern masters. One of Myatt's Giacometti fakes sold at auction for more than £100,000, but Myatt later claimed that he only received a fraction of the money that Drewe made on this and other sales. He knew nothing, for example, about the Giacometti sale until he was told about it years later by the police.

The secret of the 'scam's' success rested with Drewe, who is thought to have netted at least £1 million. Born in Uckfield, Sussex, to Kathleen and Basil Drewe, a telephone engineer, he attended Bexley Heath Grammar School without distinction, leaving at the age of 17 when he secured a lowly paid job with the Atomic Energy Authority. Later he surfaced as a teacher, claiming expertise in physics and supporting this story with a fake degree. When Myatt first met him, he said he was a research scientist who inspected nuclear submarines for the government.

Drewe's masterstroke was the realization that the provenance of a work of art counts as much with experts as the brushwork. He saw that if he gave Myatt's paintings histories, he stood a better chance of passing them off as genuine. Accordingly, he made a donation of £20,000 to the Tate Gallery, thus gaining access to the reading room – a privileged area restricted to 'readers' who use the archive's records to date paintings and to check their authenticity. At the same time he gained access to the Victoria and Albert Museum's archives under the guise of 'Dr' Drewe, backed up by a reference written by himself as a 'Dr Crockett'. Once he had access, Drewe was able to insert photographs of paintings by Myatt into the files, thus creating false histories and laying a trail that led experts to believe they were genuine.

On one occasion Drewe stole the catalogue of an exhibition held at the Hanover Gallery in London, replacing it with a fake version showing some of Myatt's paintings. On another occasion he forged a receipt dated 1958 for a Giacometti, apparently sold at auction for £1900 but in fact painted by Myatt in 1991. Among the experts taken in was Peter Nahum, one of the team on BBC television's *Antiques Roadshow*. Nahum was reported to have lost £40,000 through the purchase of a fake Graham Sutherland. One London gallery, Whitford Fine Arts, complained about a fake Nicolas de Staël, but were compensated with four fake Sutherlands. The largest loss was sustained by an American gallery that paid £105,000 for a Giacometti. The gallery's owner became suspicious at one point and hired a specialist firm to check the painting's authenticity. This firm happened to be owned by Drewe, who charged the gallery £1140 to report that the work was genuine.

The conspiracy came to an end in 1995, when Myatt's estranged wife Bathsheva Goudsmid found some incriminating documents and went to the police. Drewe maintained his innocence, insisting that the fakes had been put on the market by foreign arms dealers in search of currency. The jury at Southwark chose not to believe him and he was sentenced to six years in prison. Myatt pleaded guilty and was jailed for twelve months, serving just four. In April 2000 it was announced that Further Films, a production company owned by the Hollywood actor Michael Douglas, was to make a film based on the story of Myatt and Drewe.

**Driberg, Tom** (1905–76), politician and predatory homosexual, befriended by Lord Beaverbrook, the proprietor of the *Daily Express*, and by the East End gangster Ronnie KRAY, whose homosexual orgies Driberg attended, sometimes in the company of Lord BOOTHBY. Even admirers as loyal as Michael Foot may have been disappointed by the lack of judgement displayed in Driberg's pornographic and uncompleted memoirs, published posthumously. ('I was about to attend to his long, uncircumcised and tapering but rock hard erection when we were caught almost wet-handed by a policeman ...' may be a characteristic passage but this could only be confirmed by reading the entire book.) Driberg was rumoured to have dabbled in espionage either for the KGB or MI6, or possibly both.

**drinking 'brain damage' while composing a speech for Michael Heseltine.** *See* HAMPSON, KEITH.

**Dripping, in the pay of Lady Deborah.** *See* JACKSON, THE REVEREND WILLIAM.

**drug dealers.** *See* ADAMS, THOMAS; ARIF, DOGAN; DEMPSEY, ANDREW; EYRES, TONY; FLECKNEY, EVELYN; KELAHER, DETECTIVE CHIEF INSPECTOR VICTOR.

**drugs, hard.** Under the Misuse of Drugs Act 1971, the law was changed in the United Kingdom to ensure that the production and supply of dangerous drugs should henceforth be in the hands of criminal organizations (*see* ADAMS, THOMAS; ARIF, DOGAN). Some people have argued that this is not an ideal arrangement.

*See also* MARKS, HOWARD.

**Druitt, Montague** (1840–88), barrister and sexual deviant. Educated at Winchester College and Balliol College, Oxford, where, unusually for a Wykehamist, he failed to shine academically, Druitt was strongly suspected of being JACK THE RIPPER, the serial killer who caused terror in Victorian London. Whether Druitt's poor showing academically was enough to arouse these suspicions remains unclear, but Sir Melville Macnaghten, assistant commissioner at Scotland Yard and the leading expert on the case, had no doubts that Druitt was the Ripper:

> From private information I have discovered that his own family thought he was the Ripper, and it was certainly known that he was sexually insane.

According to anecdotal evidence it is less unusual for a Wykehamist to be a sexual deviant than to put up a poor show academically. An interesting footnote on the subject is provided in her memoirs by the improperly convicted madame, Janie JONES. Miss Jones tells us that one of her girls, Franie Kum (who later married Johnnie Walker, the popular Radio 2 presenter), was once invited by a client to accompany him to Paris for the weekend. Miss Kum was a little uncertain whether to accept, so the client said, 'Don't worry. I'm a Wykehamist.' Miss Jones continues:

We didn't know what a Wykehamist was, so we looked it up in the dictionary. When we couldn't find it, we assumed that it must mean pervert. So Franie went, and he was.

As well as practising as a barrister of the Inner Temple, with chambers in King's Walk, Druitt studied medicine, which accords with the theory that the Ripper had some knowledge of anatomy. When he drowned himself in the Thames in 1888, the killings stopped. Druitt's name has been removed from the Winchester College records.

**drunk and indecent in South Eaton Place.** *See* VIVIAN, ANTHONY CRESPIGNY CLAUDE, 5TH BARON.

**drunk in his shirtsleeves at four in the afternoon.** *See* POULSON, JOHN (for Reginald Maudling).

**drunks, convivial.** *See* KEAN, EDMUND; NEWTON, ROBERT.

**drunks, nightmare.** *See* BERNARD, JEFFREY; FARSON, DANIEL; REED, OLIVER.

**Drury, Commander Kenneth.** *See* HUMPHREYS, JAMES.

**Dudley, John William Ward, 1st earl of** (1781–1833), peer and politician. Dudley was heir to one of the largest fortunes in England. As a child he lived away from his family in a house in London with only a tutor as company. After Oxford, he stood for Parliament, and was described by Lord BYRON as 'studious, brilliant, elegant', but his lonely upbringing ensured that he became more reclusive and emotionally constrained as he grew older. His absent-mindedness increased, and he used to forget where he was. On one occasion, when dining at the house of a woman who prided herself on the excellence of her cuisine, he apologized to the other guests on the poor quality of the meal. 'My cook isn't feeling well,' he explained. When visiting another woman, he failed to respond to his hostess's hints that it was time for him to leave. 'A pretty enough woman,' he whispered to the assembled company, 'but she stays a devilish long time. I wish she'd go.'

Dudley's loneliness eventually caused him to invent a wife for himself, of whom he always spoke with great affection. In 1832 he behaved so oddly at one of his own dinner parties that one of the guests, who was a doctor, had him confined. He suffered a stroke and died in 1833.

**Dudley, Captain Richard** (1681–1708), soldier and highwayman. According to the *Newgate Calendar*, Dudley was a disappointment to his loyal father, a Leicestershire landowner who moved to London just so that his eldest son could receive a liberal education at St Paul's. An early report had the boy as 'possessing a natural vicious disposition which baffled all restraint'. At the age of 9 he robbed his sister of 30 shillings and ran away from home. He was found, and sent back to school, but later stole money from his father and absconded for a second time. On this occasion he was tracked down to a brothel where he was disporting himself with 'two lewd women'.

Like many concerned fathers before and since, the elder Dudley now enlisted the boy in the navy, in which employment he conducted himself with great gallantry and was commissioned as an officer. Back on shore, however, he left the ship, joined up with a gang of thieves and assisted them in robbing the country house of Admiral Carter. He was soon arrested, charged with robbery and sentenced to death. Still undefeated, the father, by relentless petitioning, secured the boy a royal pardon, thereafter buying him another commission, this time in the army.

Dudley, now a captain, carried out his duties in an exemplary fashion for a while, and married a respectable woman from whose family he received £140 a year. This emolument, together with his army pay, should have allowed him to live in comfort, but he soon became bored, abandoned his family and joined up with another gang of robbers. More reprehensibly, he enlisted the services of his vulnerable younger brother Will, with whom he stopped Sir John Friend on the highway and robbed him of his watch, his sword, a whip and ten shillings. Again he was quickly arrested, and again he was saved by his father, who persuaded the court to change the sentence of death to transportation. Captain Dudley and his brother Will were put on a ship bound for Barbados, but managed to escape when it reached the Isle of Wight.

At this point Dudley abandoned Will and set off on his own. Soon enough he met a farmer, whom he robbed of his horse and his clothes. He then came across a gentleman who was better dressed, and more expensively mounted, than the farmer had been. This gentleman was led into a thicket, where his clothes were removed by Dudley and exchanged for the farmer's. 'Never say that I robbed you,' Dudley advised him, 'since according to the proverb, exchange is no robbery.' He then wished the gentleman good day and rode on to London on his horse. Here he joined up with his old associates and with his brother Will. With Dudley at its head, the gang was so successful that:

> ... no stage, nor coach, nor passenger, of which they had intelligence, could escape their depredations, and scarcely a day passed without some notorious robbery being committed.

Their luck ran out when they robbed a nobleman on Hounslow Heath of £1500, after an exchange of small-arms fire with his servants, of whom three were wounded and two had their horses shot from under them. A proclamation was issued against Dudley and his gang, offering a substantial reward to anyone who brought them in. One of the gang turned informer and Dudley was arrested, along with Will and four accomplices. All six were tried, convicted and sentenced to death. Dudley appeared cheerful on the way to the scaffold, but Will lay sick in the cart.

The bodies of Dudley and his brother were put into separate coffins to be conveyed to their inconsolable father. At the sight of them he was so overwhelmed that he fell into their coffins and expired, thus being buried in the same grave as his sons.

**Duell, William** (*c*.1710–40), murderer. Duell was sentenced to death for murdering Sarah Griffin in Acton in 1740. The case is of interest, not because of the crime, but because Duell survived the punishment. Having been hanged at Tyburn, he came back to life as students prepared to dissect his body at Surgeons Hall. In two hours he was able to sit up in his chair, and in the evening he was committed to Newgate. His sentence was later changed to transportation.

*See also* SHEPPARD, JACK.

**duelling.** The first fencing school in England was opened in Blackfriars in 1576 by an Italian named Rocco Bonetti, and the art of fencing rapidly acquired upper-class patrons. Bonetti advertised his aristocratic clientele by hanging his students' coats of arms on his walls. Vincentio Saviola, another Italian fencing master, was the protégé of the earl of Essex. Although duelling in England never became as extensive a problem as it did in France, and later in Ireland, it enjoyed a vogue among the English gentry. One of them, named Cheese, became proficient enough to get the better of Jeronimo Saviola – Vincentio's brother, and himself a fencing master – and to run him through with his rapier. In the 17th and 18th centuries those wishing to mimic the manners of the upper class could do no better than model themselves on members of the political elite, such as George Villiers, the 2nd duke of BUCKINGHAM, who was involved in a number of duels.

In Ireland the fashion for fighting caused even greater mayhem, and when violence was legitimized through the conventions of duelling, Irishmen fought more wildly than other European gentlemen. It was a sport for the rich and respectable, rather as golf became in later times. Inns kept a special pair of duelling pistols on the premises in case travellers arrived unequipped in this respect. Duels were fought on the flimsiest excuse. Richard Daly, the manager of the Crow Theatre, fought 16 times in a year. Brian MAGUIRE used to throw dirt on the heads of passers-by in order to get a challenge. If they looked up, he spat on them and immediately offered the chance of satisfaction. The Right Honourable George Ogle fought Barney Coyle, a distiller, because he was a Papist. Crow Ryan of Carrick-on-Suir challenged everyone he met.

*See also* ABDUCTION CLUBS; HANGER, GEORGE; HELL-FIRE CLUB, THE IRISH; PINKINDINDIES.

**duellists.** *See* BAGENAL, BEAUCHAMP; BARRY, DR JAMES MIRANDA; CARDIGAN, JAMES THOMAS BRUDENEL, 7TH EARL OF; CLONMEL, JOHN SCOTT, 1ST EARL OF; FITZGERALD, GEORGE ROBERT; ROCHE, TIGER.

**Duff, James** (*c.*1720–88), Scottish eccentric. Duff, a character of the Edinburgh streets, first gained notoriety when he entered himself as a runner in the Leith horse races, whipping himself with a switch, and finishing last. Later, he acquired a taste for ceremonial dress and solemn occasions, and for 40 years he attended every funeral in Edinburgh, leading the procession in his mourning costume of black cravat, cape and a hat that he dyed a deeper shade of black for important funerals, such as that in 1776 of the philosopher David Hume. His appearances became expected and a payment of 6d for his services was customary, taken up by way of a street collection. Mischievous small boys sometimes sent him after non-existent funerals, on which occasions he would fly into a rage and lash out at the first person he saw, without as a rule inflicting any serious damage.

Duff's one anxiety was that he might be conscripted by the army, which at the time was deceiving men into joining up by surreptitiously offering them coins in the street. 'Taking the king's shilling', even inadvertently, meant that one contracted oneself into the army. Duff became so worried that he might be tricked into enlisting that he decided to refuse all offers of money in case the donor turned out to be a recruiting officer. Since he relied for his income on street donations this policy caused him great hardship and distressed his friends. Eventually, his mother – with whom he lived – persuaded him to take his nephew with him on his daily walks. Since the boy was too young to join the army he could safely accept money on Duff's behalf. This arrangement worked successfully.

**Dugdale, Dr Rose.** *See* CAHILL, MARTIN.

**Dugdale, William** (1800–68), publisher, bookseller and pornographer. Dugdale was the most persistent purveyor of pornographic material in Victorian London. Trading from premises in Drury Lane and Holywell Street, he was imprisoned nine times in a 30-year career. Unlike less flamboyant operators, such as Charles CARRINGTON and John HOTTEN, he openly bribed the police and was an accomplished street fighter, able to hold his own in a scuffle with members of the Vice Society. As a young man he had been implicated in the Cato Street Conspiracy of 1820 (*see* THISTLEWOOD, ARTHUR), and on one occasion, when sentenced before Lord Campbell, he pulled out a knife and attacked a member of the Vice Society who was standing nearby. With such a record he was inevitably a target criminal and his premises became a battleground.

A typical raid took place on 8 September 1851, when Inspector Lewis and a party of constables (who had the powers of Customs and Excise officers to search and seize), set off for Holywell Street, accompanied by street bruisers hired by the Vice Society. Dugdale, who was as well organized as any late 20th-century Soho bookshop baron, was waiting for them. As soon as the law enforcement posse reached Holywell Street, his lookout gave the alarm. The doors, which had been reinforced against just such an emergency, were slammed and bolted. Other inhabitants of the street closed in and began to threaten the police, whom they regarded as cynical takers of bribes. They also attacked members of the Vice Society, whom they saw as 'miscreants in white chokers, who croak for the safety of Christian England'.

For 15 minutes the police tried to break in without success. Then Dugdale opened the door and said, 'All right, Lewis, you can come in now.' The police were able to take away a few books and prints, and Dugdale was later imprisoned for two years, but he had had time – like his 20th-century counterparts, James HUMPHREYS and Bernie Silver, in similar contingencies – to conceal his most incriminating stock.

Dugdale occupies an important niche in legal history by reason of his successful argument, advanced at a later trial, that intent to sell rather than mere possession must be established for a prosecution to succeed. He died in the House of Corrections in Clerkenwell in 1868.

**dum casta.** A draconian provision in a Victorian separation agreement, by which a divorced wife would be paid maintenance provided she thereafter led a chaste life: *dum casta et sola vixit.* The clause, which was still being inserted in contracts until the 1960s, frequently had disastrous consequences, not least in the case of the celebrated advocate, Edward Marshall Hall and his estranged wife, Ethel Moon.

**Dunn, Lennie 'Books'.** *See* MITCHELL, FRANK.

**Dunsany, Edward John Moreton Drax Plunkett, 18th Baron** (1878–1957), novelist, poet, playwright and big-game hunter. Born in London and educated at Eton College and Sandhurst, Dunsany served in the Second Boer War and then settled in Ireland. He was associated with the Irish revival led by W.B. Yeats, and achieved success with his poetic and imaginative literary works, such as *The King of Elfland's Daughter* (1924) and his 'Jorkens' stories, beginning with *The Travel Tales of Mr Joseph Jorkens* (1931). At the invitation of Yeats, he wrote many plays for the Abbey Theatre in Dublin, of which the most popular was *The Laughter of the Gods* (1919).

In 1934 Dunsany was appointed Byron professor of poetry in Athens, but he arrived to take up his duties 18 months late. Such was his distinction as a scholar that the post was held open for him, and his explanation, when he finally turned up, was readily accepted. He had journeyed to Athens via India, where he had been delayed by his consuming passion – the hunting of big game.

Big-game hunting was an activity Dunsany followed as the circumstances allowed. In the 1930s the proprietors of Lobb & Co., the gentlemen's shoe shop in St James's, advertised their premises by means of a trap drawn by two zebras. Never having bagged a zebra, Dunsany took up a position between Fortnum and Mason and Hatchards, the bookshop, and shot them both dead as they trotted down Piccadilly.

**duress.** In English law the defence of duress is difficult to establish. In essence the accused must show that he, or his family, was in a life-threatening situation and had no opportunity to report the matter to the police. It was a defence run with success by the East End club owner, Tony Barry, who provided the gun with which Reggie KRAY attempted to kill Jack 'The Hat' McVitie.

*See also* ARIF, DOGAN.

**Durrell, Lawrence.** *See* HUNTER-COWAN, MAJOR BETTY.

**duty, loyalty above and beyond the call of.** *See* ARCHER, WILLIAM (for Jeffrey and Mary Archer); CLARK, ALAN (for Jane Clark); DEVONSHIRE, ANDREW ROBERT BUXTON CAVENDISH, 11TH DUKE OF (for Debbo); GUPPY, DARIUS (for Patricia Guppy); HOLME, LORD RICHARD (for Lady Kay Holme); KEELER, CHRISTINE (for Valerie Profumo); MELLOR, DAVID (for Judith Mellor).

**Duval, Jack 'the Rat'.** *See* RICHARDSON, CHARLIE.

**du Vall, Claude** (1643–70), highwayman. Born in Dumfort in Normandy, du Vall moved to Paris, where he trained as a footman. According to Captain Johnson's *A General History of the Lives of the Highwaymen*:

> He continued in this humble station until the Restoration of Charles II, when multitudes from the Continent resorted to England. In the character of a footman to a person of quality, du Vall also repaired to that country. The universal joy which seized the nation upon that happy event contaminated the morals of all – riot, dissipation and every species of profligacy abounded. The young and sprightly French footman entered keenly into these amusements. His funds, however, being soon exhausted, he deemed it no great crime for a Frenchman to exact contributions from the English. In a short time, he became so dextrous in his new employment that he had the

honour of being first named in an advertisement issued for the apprehension of some notorious robbers.

It was not unusual for footmen to become highwaymen. Hired to protect an equipage from robbery, they had been trained in the requisite skills of riding and shooting. Further, they had been encouraged to assume a haughty manner, since an insolent attitude was thought to reflect well on their employers. Du Vall's particular flair, courage and taste for the high life mirrored the values of the Restoration aristocracy that he had once served. Among his victims was Hooper, master of hounds to Charles II, whom he ambushed in a thicket. He took his purse, which contained 50 guineas, tied him to a tree and then rode away. It was some time before the huntsmen discovered their master. Once released, and unwilling to venture a second time into a thicket ('whatever might be the fortune of the hunt'), Hooper made his way to Windsor, where he was accosted by Sir Stephen Fox. Sir Stephen asked him if he had had any sport. 'Sport!' bellowed Hooper, and continued:

> Yes, sir, I have had sport enough from a villain who bound me neck and heel, contrary to my desire and then took fifty guineas from me, to pay him for his labour, which I had much rather he had omitted.

Du Vall was finally captured when drunk in Chandos Street, London. He was committed to Newgate, convicted, condemned and hanged at Tyburn at the age of 27. 'So much had had his gallantries rendered him the favourite of the fair sex,' writes Captain Johnson, 'that many a bright eye was dimmed at his funeral, and his lifeless corpse was bedewed with the tears of beauty.' Du Vall's career was later celebrated by Charles II's favourite, Samuel Butler, the author of *Hudibras*, a satire on Puritanism.

**dwarf, knocked over by a.** *See* WILLIAMSON, NICOL.

**dwarfs, bank-robbing.** *See* MCCRAY, RAYMOND.

**dwarfs, Cavalier.** *See* HUDSON, JEFFREY.

**dwarfs, sacrifice of.** *See* HELL-FIRE CLUB, THE IRISH.

**Dyer, Ernest** (1891–1922), farmer and murderer. Dyer was unusual among murderers in that he himself was dead before his victim was discovered. At the end of World War I, two ex-officers in their 20s, Ernest Dyer and Eric Gordon Tombe, went into business together as breeders of horses. After two failures, Tombe put up the money for the purchase of a stud farm called the Welcomes at Kenley in Surrey. In April 1921 the Welcomes was destroyed by fire, but Dyer's claim was rejected by the insurance company. Later that month Tombe disappeared after a quarrel with Dyer over money. The Reverend Harold Tombe, the missing man's father, learned for the first time of his son's association with Dyer, and he traced them to the Welcomes. He then went to his son's bank, where he was told by the manager that he had received letters from Eric Tombe, in one of which he gave power of attorney to Ernest Dyer. The distraught clergyman dismissed the signature as a forgery and then discovered that his son's current account, once healthy, had been reduced to nothing in a matter of months.

Over a year later, in November 1922, a man calling himself Fitzsimmons, who had been working a confidence trick in the north of England, was visited by a policeman at his Scarborough hotel. A struggle took place in the course of which Fitzsimmons shot himself with his own gun. Fitzsimmons turned out to be Ernest Dyer, and cheques belonging to Eric Tombe were discovered in his hotel room.

The mystery of Tombe's disappearance was only solved after his mother had nightmares in which she saw her son's body lying at the bottom of a well. Ten months after Dyer's death in Scarborough, detectives were persuaded by Tombe's parents to search the Welcomes. There they found the body of Eric Tombe at the bottom of a well with a bullet in his head.

**Ear, More Voices in My.** *See* STOKES, DORIS.

**ears, bagfuls of drying.** *See* KINGSLEY, MARY.

**ears, nailing to floor.** *See* BOLD BUCKS.

**ears with treacle, filling one's daughter's.** *See* GLENCONNER, PAMELA LADY.

**ecstasy (i.e. 3,4-methylenedioxymethamphetamine), considerable quantities of.** *See* MCAVENNIE, FRANK.

**Edgar, Henry** (1811–?), cat burglar. Edgar was not the most successful thief of the day, but he became notorious as one of the most difficult to apprehend. Since his escapades invariably ended in failure, he grew practised in the stratagems of escape, earning the sobriquet in police circles of 'Edgar the Escaper'.

Edgar was finally caught in September 1850, when he set out one night with his partner Edward Blackwell to rob a furrier in Regent Street. Having concealed themselves in the lavatory of a public house, he and Blackwell waited until the landlord locked up for the night. They then went up the fire escape, from which they could reach the roof parapet of the furrier's premises. There they began to cut out the panes of glass from a garret window, and were surprised to come face to face with a serving girl who was preparing to go to bed. Blackwood was so startled that he stepped backwards and fell three floors into the yard, killing himself outright. The commotion alerted the furrier, who now appeared at the window with two loaded pistols and told Edgar that he would shoot him if he tried to escape. Edgar leapt ten feet on to the roof of the next house in Regent Street, dropped through a trap door and managed to find his way to a second-floor bedroom fronting on to Argyle Street. Once again, the room was occupied, this time by a married couple whose startled cries persuaded Edgar to jump out of the window into the street.

By now the alarm had been raised, and the police, who had already gathered up Blackwell's dead body, were waiting for him. Edgar landed on top of Blackwell, the fall causing him to break a leg and dislocate his shoulder. Temporarily out of action, he was arrested and taken by cab, with Blackwell's dead body, to Vine Street police station. Here he managed to change places with Blackwell, and was shortly removed to the mortuary in a body bag. From there, and in spite of his injuries, he managed to make his escape, limping all the way to Corbett's Place, Spitalfields, where he was lodged by friends in a safe house.

Within a week Edgar was back at work, once again in Regent Street, but armed now with two pistols in recognition of the fact that he was less agile than he had been. Ambushed by the police, he pulled both triggers, but neither pistol went off. He was arrested, and later sentenced to transportation.

**Edgecombe, Johnny.** *See* KEELER, CHRISTINE.

**Edgeler, Keith** and **Edgeler, Roy.** *See* GAUL, JOHN.

**Edgworth Bess.** *See* SHEPPARD, JACK.

**Edinburgh, Prince Philip, duke of** (1921–   ), consort. The son of Prince Andrew of Greece and Princess Alice of Battenburg, grandson of George I of Greece and great-grandson of Queen Victoria, Philip was born in Corfu and educated at Gordonstoun in Scotland and the Royal Naval College, Dartmouth. It is fashionable to blame him for many of the misfortunes that have befallen his family – a consequence, it is said, of an absence of paternal affection during their formative years – but it can be persuasively argued that the example set by those responsible for his own upbringing may have been more at fault. They were at best absent, at worst notably odd.

Philip's mother, Princess Alice, believed she was enjoying carnal relations with Christ; his father, Prince Andrew, lived on a boat with a French actress named Andrée de la Bigne; his grandfather, George I, was assassinated in 1913; his uncle, King Alexander, died after being bitten by a monkey; and his father was condemned to exile after being tried by a kangaroo court. His surrogate father, the marquess of Milford Haven, is best remembered for having assembled the most comprehensive library of sadomasochistic pornography in Europe. It is understandable, perhaps, that Philip wanted to set his own children a more orthodox example.

From 1925, when Philip was just 4 years old, to 1936, when he was 15, his mother Princess Alice alternated between being harmlessly eccentric (playing Ouija, receiving messages from packs of cards) and clinically insane (announcing a dinner engagement with Jesus, cutting up objects and putting them in parcels, believing herself to be magnetic and thinking she had a band of disciples in Bedfordshire). She was interned in a succession of Freudian clinics, in one of which her analyst, Dr Binswanger, reported that she talked incessantly about prostitutes and pulled faces at her doctors. Dr Binswanger diagnosed a neurotic pre-psychotic libidinous condition and sedated her with morphine.

From 1948 until her death in 1969 Princess Alice dressed as a nun, although she had never been accepted into an established order. For the last few years of her life she lived in Buckingham Palace, where the staff found her 'strange but likeable'. Some commentators have not been surprised that Prince Philip tried to instil in his children the lessons of self-discipline and common sense. That said, he was in the habit, during the 1950s, of slipping away from Buckingham Palace to tour London's nightclubs with his friend Commander Michael Parker. On these occasions, they used the aliases 'Murgatroyd' and 'Winterbottom'.

*See also* ARGYLL, MARGARET DUCHESS OF.

**Edmund (II) 'Ironside'** (*c.*990–1016), English king remembered mainly for the unpleasant circumstances of his death. The son of Ethelred (II) the Unready and half brother of Edward the Confessor, Edmund was appointed to the throne when Cnut Sveinsson (Canute) invaded England in the summer of 1015. He raised an army and, though routed by Cnut at Ashingdon in Essex, held out bravely until an English traitor – one of Edmund's thanes, Edric Streona – hoping to ingratiate himself with Cnut, arranged to have Edmund murdered. After dinner one evening, Edmund retired to the outside lavatory, which was little more than a hole in the ground. As he sat down, Edric's son, who had previously concealed himself inside this primitive depository, drove his dagger upwards into Edmund's bowels. Another version has Edmund killed by an even more complex method. According to a Norman chronicler named Geoffrey Gaimar, a device had been fixed in the lavatory by Edric's son in such a way that when Edmund sat down he triggered a crossbow whose arrow flew upwards and penetrated him deeply from beneath.

Edric failed to profit from his ingenuity. He presented himself to Cnut with the confident salutation, 'Hail! thou who art sole king of England!' Cnut replied, 'I will exalt you higher than all the nobles of England!' He then ordered that Edric be decapitated and his head placed on a pole on the highest battlement.

**Edmunds, Christina** (1828–1907), poisoner. In 1870 Miss Edmunds, a spinster living on her own in Brighton, conceived a passion for her physician, Dr Beard. Although Dr Beard seems not to have encouraged his patient, he did allow her to send him a stream of romantic letters, which he kept hidden from Mrs Beard.

In September of that year Miss Edmunds managed to obtain a quantity of strychnine on the pretext that she was being plagued by stray cats. One evening, when Dr Beard was out, she took some poisoned chocolates round to his house and offered one to Mrs Beard. Mrs Beard spat it out, later saying that, 'It had a very unpleasant taste. The next day I had an attack of diarrhoea and felt very unwell.' For some reason, Mrs Beard didn't report this incident to her husband, but, still more inexplicably, Miss Edmunds did. Dr Beard told Miss Edmunds that she would no longer be welcome in his house and, having warned Mrs Beard to be on her guard, he left Brighton for three months.

Thinking that Dr Beard might recover his good opinion of her if she could show that Mrs Beard had been poisoned by accident, Miss Edmunds bought a large quantity of chocolates from Mr Maynard, the local confectioner, laced them with strychnine and distributed them among Brighton's children. Mr Maynard would be revealed as a purveyor of poisoned sweets, Miss Edmunds reasoned, and she would be forgiven by Dr Beard.

The plan seemed to be working when, on 12 June 1871, 4-year-old Sydney Barker died of convulsions within minutes of eating one of Mr Maynard's chocolates. However, the coroner's verdict was accidental death, so Miss Edmunds began a campaign against Mr Maynard, sending poison-pen letters, writing to Sydney Barker's father suggesting that he instigate proceedings, and sending poisoned fruit and cakes to selected beneficiaries, some of whom ate them and survived.

Soon enough a comparison of letters sent to the police, to Sydney Barker's father and to the recipients of the poisoned fruit showed Miss Edmunds to be the sender. She was arrested on 17 August 1871. At her trial in 1872 at the Old Bailey, her mother told the jury of a long history of insanity in the family. Miss Edmund's father had suffered from acute mania, her maternal grandmother had died of the same affliction at the age of 43, her brother was lodged in a mental institution and Miss Edmunds herself suffered from hysterical paralysis.

The jury was unimpressed by this catalogue of misfortune, as it was by Miss Edmunds's declaration – when asked if she had anything to say – that she was pregnant by Dr Beard. The death sentence was passed, but was commuted by the home secretary. Miss Edmunds died in Broadmoor in 1907.

**education blamed for decline in criminal standards.** *See* GUERIN, EDDIE.

**Edward VII** (1841–1910), king of Great Britain and Ireland. Bertie, as he was known in the family, was a keen disappointment to his mother, Queen Victoria, and to his father, Prince Albert. 'The systematic idleness, laziness and disregard for everything is enough to break one's heart and fills me with indignation,' wrote the queen in her diary. Her worst fears – that her son had inherited the 'tainted blood' of her licentious Hanoverian uncles – seemed to be confirmed by an unfortunate incident when Edward, aged 19, was sent on army manoeuvres at the Curragh in Ireland. One night, some of his brother officers arranged for an actress to be smuggled into his tent. Prince Albert died a few weeks later. Victoria believed that his grief at 'Bertie's misconduct' at the Curragh had shortened his life, and she declared that she would never be able to look at 'that boy' without a shudder.

Marriage at the age of 22 to Princess Alexandra of Denmark afforded the prince of Wales some relief from his mother's domination, but she still denied him any official governmental role. He in return rebelled by indulging himself in women, food, gambling and sport. Alexandra seemed not to mind her husband's escapades, referring to him as 'my naughty little man'. At his coronation a special pew, known as 'the Loose Box', was reserved for his many mistresses. These included the actresses Lillie Langtry and Hortense Schneider, and French and English society beauties such as Princesse de Sagan, the duchess de Mouchy and Lady Brooke (the future countess of Warwick).

However, the most enduring and by far the most astute of the future king's lovers was Alice Frederika Edmonstone, the wife of the Hon. George Keppel, an officer in the Gordon Highlanders. The prince of Wales met Mrs Keppel in 1898. She was 29, he a man of nearly 60, who stood 5 feet 7 inches, weighed 19 stone and had a 48-inch waist. In an average day he smoked 20 cigars, ate five enormous meals and drank quantities of whiskey, wine and brandy. She was captivated, and he in return showered the Keppels with gifts and money, allowing them to acquire, among other things, a magnificent estate in Italy named Ombrellino. In London, the king entertained Mrs Keppel in a private room at Kettners in Soho, now the flagship restaurant in the popular Pizza Express chain. (In deference, perhaps, to its former eminence, a pianist in the strict tempo style plays dance tunes in the early evening.) Mrs Keppel's daughter Violet, who liked to claim that Edward VII was her father, became the (far from discreet) lover of the writer Vita Sackville-West, the wife of Harold Nicolson.

Mrs Keppel's great-granddaughter, Camilla Parker-Bowles, became the mistress of the latest prince of Wales, Prince Charles (1948– ). It is thought that Mrs Keppel, who died in 1947 – the year of Mrs Parker-Bowles's birth – would have been dismayed by the ineptitude with which Prince Charles and Mrs Parker-Bowles handled their arrangements. In 1936, when her former lover's grandson, Edward VIII, abdicated the throne for a twice divorced American woman, she was heard to say, 'Things were done much better in my day.'

*See also* CLARENCE, PRINCE ALBERT VICTOR, DUKE OF; GORDON CUMMING, COLONEL SIR WILLIAM.

## Edward VII, reputedly illegitimate son of. *See* JAMES, EDWARD.

**Edwards, Eddie 'the Eagle'** (1963– ), ski jumper, pop singer and author. In 1988 Edwards, a plasterer from Essex, distinguished himself at the Calgary Winter Olympics by coming last by a considerable distance in the 70-metre ski jump. For his own safety, Edwards, who trained by running up and down stairs and was known as Mr Magoo because of his thick spectacles, was urged by Olympic officials not to jump on the 90-metre hill. Rob McCormack, chief of competition at the Games, said, 'Edwards doesn't jump – he drops like a stone. In such near-perfect conditions, with no wind, an 11-year-old child could jump further.' Nevertheless, the British delegation decided he could cope in the 90-metre event. Since there was every chance that he'd kill himself, the cheers when Edwards landed were greater than those for the winner, Pirmin Zurbriggen of Switzerland.

Edwards himself was in no doubt that his achievement had been greater than Zurbriggen's. He explained it thus on American television:

> I made a splash in Calgary because I had created an international profile. There were a lot of good jumpers there, but they were very boring. The Swiss were the worst. You've got to be good with the media. That goes for any sport.

After working in Lake Placid, New York State, where he was reported to have had them in stitches during his many media appearances, and where his date of birth is still a public holiday in hospital casualty departments, Edwards returned to England to enjoy his 15 minutes of fame. He wrote his autobiography, *On The Piste* (1990), cut a record, 'Fly, Eddie, Fly', which climbed to number 2 in the charts in Finland, but failed to make a similar impact in the United Kingdom, and opened the Crystal Peaks Shopping Centre in Sheffield. This flurry of celebrity was followed by years of obscurity, momentarily brightened by the news in 1996 that he had joined a male escort agency in Wolverhampton. 'I'm open and friendly, and I have a good sense of humour,' he said, 'so I expect to be very popular.' Alas, this turned out not to be the case.

In September 2000 Edwards enjoyed a moment of retrospective celebrity when a Nigerian swimmer, nicknamed Eric the Eel, made an even bigger fool of himself in his event at the Sydney Olympics than

Edwards had in his at Calgary. Interviewed by the television personality, Jeremy Clarkson, Edwards revealed that while he still had ambitions to be a pop singer he had for the first time in his life moved out of his mother's house to study law at university.

**Eel-in-the-Mud, the.** *See* MASSEREENE, CLOTWORTHY SKEFFINGTON, 2ND EARL OF.

**Egan, Joe** (1967– ), publican and boxer. When Lennox Lewis defended his world heavyweight title at the London Arena against Frans Botha in July 2000, four of the spectators – Egan, Al Malcolm, Lew Gerrard and Steve Garber – gathered at the ringside to share their memories. Lewis had fought each of them early in his career and had beaten all four, starting with Egan in 1985. Egan was visiting his sister in New York at the time, and was invited to stand in for the New York All Stars, who were short of a man, against Lewis's Canadian team. 'My mistake was to hit him,' recalled Egan:

> It seemed to annoy him. He hit me back and the fight was over. Otherwise it might have gone either way.

The other three were no more successful than Egan had been. Al Malcolm was chosen as Lewis's opponent for his professional debut at the Albert Hall in 1989. Malcolm recalled:

> I was a puncher, so I was in with a chance. He's a puncher too. We were toe to toe. I prepared to hit him with a big right. He hit me first. I went clean over the top rope.

Lew Gerrard was Lewis's third opponent:

> I put Lewis in hospital. He broke his hand on my head. The referee stopped the fight after 20 seconds. I said, 'Ref, what took you so long?'

Steve Garber met Lewis at Hull in October 1989:

> I was well up for it. I was looking for an edge, so I hit him before the bell. Lewis still talks about how angry it made him. It was all over in 12 seconds including the count. I've been silly twice in my life. The first time I ended up in prison. The second time was when I hit Lewis before the bell.

'To me and the rest of the boys it was great to have shared a ring with him,' said Egan. The other three seemed less convinced.

**Egg, the Sitwell.** *See* SITWELL, SIR GEORGE RERESBY.

**Eglintoune, Susanna Kennedy, countess of** (1696–1787), one of the great beauties of the 18th century. The countess claimed at the end of her long life that she had never received true gratitude except from animals, particularly rats. She kept hundreds of rats, summoning them to the dining room at meal times by tapping on an oak panel. At this cue, dozens of rats would appear from the woodwork and join her at table. After dinner, at a quiet word of command, the rats would retire in an orderly fashion.

**elderly homosexuals and predatory thin women.** *See* NASH JIMMY.

**elephants.** *See* FAIRS, TRAVELLING; KEECH, WILLIAM; SACKVILLE, VICTORIA-JOSEPHA, BARONESS.

**Elephants, Queen of the Forty.** *See* HILL, BILLY.

**Elephant's Graveyard, being beaten up by queer dockers in the.** *See* FARSON, DANIEL.

**elephant-trunk soup.** *See* BUCKLAND, FRANCIS TREVELYAN.

**elixir of eternal youth.** *See* EMMETT, HORACE.

**Elizabeth II** (1926– ), queen of Great Britain and Northern Ireland and head of the Commonwealth. According to the historian, Professor Ben Pimlott, the entrenched snobbery of Elizabeth's court extends to the royal stables. The queen rejected one likely stallion as a suitable mate for a royal mare because it was owned by a bookmaker. She is thought to be as tight-fisted as Queen Victoria. On one occasion she rebuked her private secretary for making a full declaration to HM Customs of foreign goods she had brought into the country.
*See also* MISERS.

**Elliott, Grace Dalrymple** (*c.*1758–1823), wife. The daughter of a successful Edinburgh lawyer, Grace married Sir John Elliott MD in 1771. Thereafter she was consecutively, and sometimes simultaneously, the mistress of, or the other woman in the lives of – among many others – Lord Valentia, Lord Cholmondeley, Charles Windham, George Selwyn (the bishop of Lichfield, in whose name Selwyn College, Cambridge, was founded) and the duc d'Orléans, who changed his name after the French Revolution to Phillippe Egalité, and who shared her favours with the prince of Wales, later George IV. Sir John Elliott divorced her in 1794.

**Ellis, John** (1874–1932), publican, hairdresser and hangman. There was little in Ellis's background that seemed to point to a career as public executioner. Indeed, when he applied for the post in 1901 the chief constable of Rochdale recommended him as 'a man of good character' – not previously thought of as a necessary qualification for the job, if anything the opposite (*see* ARNETT, RICHARD; DENNIS, EDWARD). The son of a local hairdresser, Ellis had married Annie Beaton at the age of 20 and was working as a stripper and grinder at the Eagle Mill, Rochdale, when he was appointed assistant hangman in 1902.

In appearance Ellis was undistinguished and, as one newspaper put it, 'never looked what he was'. What a hangman should look like isn't clear, but Ellis, in any case, was slightly built, with pale blue eyes and a pale complexion. He was going bald, but sported a bushy moustache. He carried out his duties efficiently enough – hurrying round the country with his Gladstone bag dispatching men and women – without seeming too obviously to enjoy it. Indeed, sometimes it quite upset him, particularly when it was a woman to be hanged. Not that he ever faltered in his duties, even when they prevented him from taking his whippets for a walk or from attending a game of rugby league involving the Rochdale Hornets.

In January 1922 he received a letter from the sheriff's office in Chelmsford informing him that Frederick Bywaters and Edith THOMPSON, who had been convicted together of murdering Thompson's husband, would have to be hanged on the same day at different prisons. The letter continued:

> In which case it will be necessary to employ two executioners. We would be glad to know whether you would be prepared to act at the execution of Mrs Thompson on Tuesday the 9th January at Holloway, or on Friday 5th January at the same place.

After pondering the matter for a day, Ellis's sheer professionalism – supported, perhaps, by the expectation of a fee of £10 plus expenses – overcame his reservations about hanging women, particularly women who, like Mrs Thompson, were innocent of the crime with which they'd been charged. (Hanging an innocent man, or a guilty woman, might for Ellis have been morally less confusing.) In the event, he was able to confirm that he would arrive at Holloway on Monday 8 January. If he had planned to take his whippets out on the Tuesday, Mrs Thompson would have been hanged four days earlier – not that that would have made much difference to her.

For Ellis, however, there were unforeseen consequences of a disagreeable nature. At three minutes to nine on Tuesday 9 January he took up his position and heard a low moan from the condemned cell. The prison chaplain, the Reverend Glanville Murray, was, according to his Christian principles, trying to console Mrs Thompson. Two warders picked her up and carried her towards the scaffold. Her head was sunk on her chest and Ellis suspected that she had been doped with brandy instead of being revived by it at the proper time, as he always requested. The warders were obliged to hold her upright on the trap doors while Ellis placed a bag over her head and adjusted the noose. He pulled the lever and Mrs Thompson's troubles were over.

All those involved in the execution, including Ellis, were quite affected. The Reverend Glanville Murray, who was prone to dizzy spells and had asked for a chair to sit on throughout his ordeal, later declared that he had been 'seized by an impulse to rush in and save her' – an impulse which, luckily, he had been able to resist. Ellis, who described the experience as one of the most nerve-wracking he had ever endured, now suffered a deterioration in his health. The neuritis with which he had long been afflicted was getting worse, and he was beginning to suffer from sleepless nights. In March 1924 he sent a letter of resignation to the prison commissioners.

Retirement was not an easy time for the celebrated executioner of Dr Hawley Harvey CRIPPEN and Sir Roger Casement. He opened a pub which he called The Jolly Butcher, but this was not a success. 'Conversation ceases suddenly when I'm about,' Ellis complained. 'Socially it's a bad business being a hangman.' He then tried his hand at hairdressing, but his shop became a tourist attraction, with people coming from as far away as Bombay seeking advice on how to succeed him as public executioner. In December 1927 he played the part of a hangman in *The Life and Adventures of Charles Peace*, a melodrama produced at the Grand Theatre, Gravesend, but his performance offended more people than it pleased.

On 20 September 1932 Ellis cut his throat with a barber's razor and bled to death. At the time of Edith Thompson's execution, Rebecca West had written:

> Humanity has its need to dream. And if you do not give humanity the good music, the good pictures, the good books that will set it dreaming right, it will dream the bad dreams that lead to lies and death.

Perhaps Ellis had dreamed the wrong dreams.

**Ellis, Rose.** *See* DAVIDSON, THE REVEREND HAROLD FRANCIS.

**Ellis, Ruth** (1927–55), model, nightclub manageress and the last woman to be hanged in England. Ellis's execution was judged by many to have been a disgrace, its only saving aspect being that it hastened the abolition of CAPITAL PUNISHMENT in the United Kingdom. Though not a prostitute or a criminal herself, Ellis moved in the twilight world of Mayfair drinking clubs and Paddington abortionists. In 1944 she had a child by a French Canadian serviceman, and in 1950 she married George Ellis, a dentist. They parted in 1952, and she shortly met David Blakely, a racing-car driver with whom she had a stormy relationship for two years. In 1953 she had an abortion, and Blakely offered to marry her. She tried to leave him, but he became highly emotional. In 1955 they moved together into a flat in

Egerton Gardens, South Kensington, but Ellis continued to see other lovers. Blakely began to drink heavily and there is some evidence that he hit her in the stomach shortly before she had a miscarriage in April 1955. The balance of the relationship had changed, and it was now Ellis who was dependent on Blakely. When he tried to extricate himself from the situation, she became furiously jealous. On Good Friday, while still distraught from the effect of the miscarriage, she went to see him at a house in Tanza Road, Hampstead, where he was staying with friends, and the police were called twice to remove her. On Easter Sunday there was a party at the house. Blakely left with a friend at about 9 p.m. to visit a pub called the Magdala. As he came out of the pub, Ellis shot at him six times. One bullet hit a Mrs Gladys Yule in the hand, one missed, and the other four hit Blakely. He died instantly and Ellis was arrested.

At her trial at the Old Bailey in June 1955, her counsel, Melford STEVENSON, seemed to confuse his duties with those of the prosecution, and his decision not to make a closing speech in his client's defence may not have impressed the jury. Ellis was found guilty after 14 minutes, and in spite of a considerable public outcry, was hanged at Holloway prison on 13 July 1955.

Within two years the law was changed under the Homicide Act 1957. Now under section 3 there was an extended defence of provocation by words and deeds. In 1958 Ernest Fantle, who had shot his wife's lover after verbal provocation, was sentenced to three years imprisonment under this section. It seems likely that a jury would have found the same provocation in Ellis's case, Mr Melford Stevenson's efforts on her behalf notwithstanding.

In December 2001, Ruth Ellis's daughter, Georgie, died in a Yorkshire hospice at the age of 50. A former model, her life had not been happy. She had inherited her mother's looks as well as her preference for unsuitable men. Her lovers included the Great Train Robber, Charlie Wilson. Her third husband, the former Yorkshire cricketer, Mike Blackburn, was at her bedside when she died.

**Ellis, Sid 'Jazzer'** (1881–1943), music hall artiste. Ellis was one of the most popular turns on the British vaudeville stage in the early years of the 20th century. He entertained by lying on his back while his 25-stone wife played a piano balanced on his chest. While Mrs Ellis banged out the accompaniment, Sid sang 'Ireland Must Be Heaven Because Mother Comes From There'.

**Ellul, Philip** (1926– ), gangster and contract killer. Ellul was a minor figure in London's underworld, but he is assured of a place in Soho folklore as the man who killed the greatly feared Tommy 'Scarface' Smithson. In June 1956 Smithson, who managed the deceptively named Publishers

Club in Frith Street but whose real occupation was protection, was shot dead in a lodging house in Maida Vale. There were many theories as to why he had been killed. One was that he'd fallen out with the Maltese vice baron, George Caruana. Fay Sadler, later to be involved in the notorious Pen Club killing (*see* NASH, JIMMY), had recently been arrested over some bounced cheques, and Smithson, who was infatuated with her, was trying to raise money for her defence. Caruana had refused to contribute, a fight had taken place and Caruana had been stabbed. The police had a different theory. They believed that Smithson was becoming a nuisance to two new vice overlords, Frank Mifsud and Bernie Silver, and that they wanted him out of the way, while implicating his boss, Caruana.

The actual reason for the killing was rather more mundane, according to the man who actually carried it out, Philip Ellul. Ellul worked for Caruana as an enforcer, and he and Smithson had confronted one another with knives at the time Caruana was cut. The moment had passed, but Ellul later heard that Smithson was looking for him with a gun. 'So I thought to myself, mmm, and I went and got me a gun,' Ellul later recalled:

> The thing is, if you was having bother with Tommy Smithson you had to kill him. He was someone who'd had so much damage done to him that nothing stopped him anymore.

Ellul lay in wait for Smithson at his usual haunts, but when he failed to show up Ellul set off with an associate, Victor Spaminato, for Maida Vale, looking for Caruana, and not expecting to find Smithson:

> I knocked on the door. I didn't go there to kill Smithson. I didn't know he was there. This bird opens the door. She says, 'Tommy's upstairs.' He's sat on a chair, holding a pair of scissors. I was going to let it go at that because sometimes I'm looking for someone and I'm well mad, and the next moment I'm buying them a cup of coffee. I said, 'Listen, Tommy, you carry a gun, you fucking use it. I'm carrying one and I'm going to use it.' And I just – BANG – shot him in the leg. 'Jesus Christ, Philip!' he says. So I hit him and he went right over the bed.

Ellul left the room and Smithson shouted, 'That man's mad!' and locked the door. Spaminato tried to calm things down, but Ellul kicked the door in:

> One kick, you get the strength, I just walked in, put the gun to Tommy's head and BANG. I said, 'Let's go.' I never had any qualms about what I done in there.

Ellul borrowed £2000 from Caruana and hid out in Manchester, but was persuaded to return to London on the understanding that he'd only face a manslaughter charge. After he'd given himself up, however, he was charged with murder, convicted and sentenced to death. He was reprieved 48 hours before the hangman arrived, eventually serving eleven years.

Nearly 20 years later, the head of Scotland Yard's Serious Crimes Squad, Commander Bert Wickstead ('the Old Grey Fox'), tried to put Silver and Mifsud away on a vice charge. When this failed, he decided to fit them up with Smithson's murder. Spaminato was traced to Malta and gave evidence against Silver and Mifsud at the committal hearing in July 1975. It was rumoured that he was paid £30,000 for his services, but it was never established by whom. Meanwhile, Wickstead had been to the United States in pursuit of Ellul, who was then living in San Francisco. Ellul also received a mysterious sum of money, said, in his case, to be £60,000. In return he agreed to accompany Wickstead back to London to testify against Silver and Mifsud.

In the event, he changed his mind. He was given police protection in a flat in Limehouse and was allowed to visit a nearby betting shop to calm his nerves, but within days he said he needed to return to America to have his ulcers treated. He'd be back for the trial, he said, but he was never seen again. Silver and Mifsud went free. Spaminato returned to Malta, where he devoted himself to the welfare of his elderly mother. Ellul's circumstances, while remaining unknown, must have been more agreeable than hitherto thanks to the large windfall organized by the 'Old Grey Fox'.

**Elton, Gladys** (1881–1970), pensioner. In September 1960 a male inmate died of a cardiac arrest and five more were treated for shock after 81-year-old Gladys Elton performed a striptease dance at the Haslemere Home for the Elderly in Great Yarmouth. The following year there were three more deaths after one of the patients, 87-year-old Harry Meadows, dressed up as the Grim Reaper and peered through the window at the other residents brandishing a scythe. This second incident caused the Haslemere to be closed down.

**Elwes, Dominic** (1941–75), playboy and part-time portrait painter. In September 1975 Elwes, a member of a distinguished Catholic family, committed suicide at the age of 44. His death was a consequence of the key role he had played in what was to become the 'Goldenballs' fiasco. This was the libel action brought against *Private Eye* magazine, by the financier, James Goldsmith – a case which, as the novelist and playwright Michael Frayn pointed out, was followed closely by neutral observers in the hope that both sides might lose.

The son of the portrait painter Simon Elwes, Dominic was a young man of some charm for whom little went right. He was expelled from Downside, the Roman Catholic public school, and dismissed from the army, thereafter trying his hand at many things, seldom with much success. He painted portraits of his friends, worked briefly on *Topic*, a short-lived news magazine, wrote a humorous book *Refer to Drawer* (1968) with Nicholas Luard (co-owner with Peter Cook of the Establishment Club in Soho) and, on one occasion stood as a Liberal candidate for Parliament, losing his deposit. Before 1958 his main claim to fame had been the introduction of an exploding cake at Queen Charlotte's Ball, but in the summer of that year he achieved greater notoriety when he eloped with Tessa Kennedy, the heiress to a shipping fortune. They married in Cuba, but were divorced eleven years later.

In the late 1960s Elwes became court jester to the Clermont set, a collection of rich young men who were happy to lose their inheritances at John ASPINALL's Berkeley Square gambling club. When Aspinall's friend Lord LUCAN murdered his wife's nanny in November 1974, the Clermont crowd closed ranks and preserved a wall of silence. It was Elwes who caused this to be breached, with, for him, unhappy consequences. Some weeks after Lucan's disappearance Elwes was approached by his friend James Fox, a journalist on the *Sunday Times*. Fox told him that he intended to write a sympathetic piece about Lucan's circle and Elwes agreed to effect the necessary introductions. Persuaded by Elwes that Fox was 'on their side', Lucan's cronies spoke very freely – particularly John Aspinall, who, among other things, said that if Lady Lucan had been his wife he'd have 'bashed her to death long before'. He also said that he would have been more than willing to have helped Lucan to escape.

In the event, Fox's article was far from sympathetic, and, worse, it was accompanied by a painting by Elwes that showed Lucan's friends – including James Goldsmith – assembled at a commemorative lunch for the vanished peer. Goldsmith, who had not been at the lunch, was furious, and he demanded that Elwes be ostracized henceforth, and permanently, by the Clermont set. This was more than Elwes could bear, apparently, and he committed suicide in September 1975. *Private Eye* wrote the matter up, and were sued by Goldsmith.

On 25 November 1975 a requiem mass was held for Elwes at the Jesuit Church in Farm Street, Mayfair. One of the speakers was John Aspinall, who in his address referred disparagingly to Elwes's genetic inheritance. Tremayne Rodd, a cousin of Elwes's and an Oxford rugger blue, approached Aspinall after the service and boxed him to the ground.

**Elwes, John** (1714–89), politician, landowner and gambler. Elwes's father, a brewer in Suffolk, was renowned as a miser throughout the county. He died in 1718 when his son was 4 years old. John's mother, who had been left £100,000, was so reluctant to dissipate this fortune that she starved herself to death. After Westminster School, where he was a good classical scholar, Elwes completed his education in Geneva. Here he was introduced to Voltaire, to whom he bore a remarkable resemblance. As a young man he displayed none of the miserly qualities that distinguished his family. Indeed, for many years he indulged his huge appetite for gambling. His disposition changed, however, when, after he returned from Europe, he was introduced to his uncle, Sir Harvey Elwes, another celebrated miser.

Although he was worth in excess of £250,000, Sir Harvey had an annual expenditure of less than £100. He ate only fish that could be caught on his own property. His clothes came out of an ancient chest containing costumes belonging to his great-great-grandmother, which he altered as necessary. Since John Elwes hoped to become Sir Harvey's heir, he set out to please him. On visits to Sir Harvey's Suffolk estate, Stoke College, he would stop first at an inn and change from his smart clothes into the workman's rags that his uncle favoured. He would also snatch a meal before sitting down to enjoy the tiny portions provided by Sir Harvey, with one small glass of wine between the two of them. This policy worked so well that he was made Sir Harvey's sole heir and on 22 October 1763 he inherited an estate worth £250,000, including houses in Suffolk and in Marcham, Berkshire.

Thereafter, John Elwes combined miserly behaviour with high standards of honesty and generosity. He often helped friends and neighbours who were in financial difficulties, but went to extraordinary lengths to deliver it in the cheapest way. On one occasion, Elwes, unsolicited, lent Lord Abingdon £7000 to enable him to place a bet at Newmarket. On the day of the race, and in order to furnish Abingdon with the stake money, he journeyed on horseback from Berkshire to Newmarket with nothing to eat for 14 hours except a pancake that he had put into his pocket two months earlier, and which he assured a companion was 'as good as new'.

Elwes's accomplishments were considerable. He built Portman Place, Portman Square and a large part of Marylebone. During his twelve years as MP for Berkshire he gained a reputation for unshakeable integrity. However, as the years passed, his behaviour became even odder. His idea of a journey was to set off on his horse with one hard-boiled egg in his pocket, choose a route with the fewest toll gates, ride only on the grass verge in order to save wear and tear on horseshoes, and refresh himself and the horse by a wayside stream to avoid the expense of an inn. On one occasion he rode to and from London on an errand to help two old ladies in distress. They wanted to reimburse his expenses, but a friend advised them that this would not be necessary. 'Give him sixpence and he makes a profit of twopence by the journey.'

Throughout his life Elwes had been remarkable as much for his generosity of spirit as for the money he gave away to others. On one occasion he was peppered in the course of a partridge shoot by an inexperienced gun. Elwes immediately sought to reassure him. 'I give you joy of your improvement!' he cried. 'I knew you would hit something by and by.'

**embezzlers.** *See* BOTTOMLEY, HORATIO; MCSKIMMEY, BUNTY; MILLER, SIR ERIC.

*See also* FRAUD AND FRAUDSTERS.

**Emmett, Horace** (1810–89), physician. In 1889 Dr Emmett announced in a lecture to the Biology Society of Magdalene College, Cambridge, that he had discovered the elixir of eternal youth. He described how he had ground up the testicles of red squirrels, thereafter injecting himself with the compound. He said that he was now physically 30 years younger and able to 'visit' his wife every day without fail. The lecture caused a stir in the medical establishment, albeit briefly. Two months later Dr Emmett's wife left him for a younger man, and shortly after that he died of a cerebral haemorrhage.

**English, stupidity of the.** *See* WINTLE, LIEUTENANT A.D., and *passim.*

**English governesses stranded in Russia.** *See* GLENCONNER, PAMELA LADY.

**entrenched snobbery.** *See* ELIZABETH II; SOMERSET, CHARLES SEYMOUR, 6TH DUKE OF.

**Eonism.** *See* CROSS-DRESSERS; DE BEAUMONT, CHEVALIER D'EON.

**epistolatory japes, laborious.** *See* BERKELEY, HUMPHREY JOHN; HOOK, THEODORE.

**Epstein, Brian.** *See* DEMPSEY, ANDREW.

**equilibrists.** *See* CHAMPION, SIR CLAUDE; DERING, GEORGE EDWARD; NEWBOROUGH, DENISA LADY.

**Erotology, Forberg's *Manual of Classical*.** *See* CARRINGTON, CHARLES.

**Erotomaniac, The.** *See* ASHBEE, HENRY SPENCER.

**Erskine, General Sir William** (1748–1813), soldier. Before his appointment as one of the duke of Wellington's senior commanders in the Peninsular War, Erskine had twice been confined in an insane asylum. The duke expressed his concern to the military secretary in London, but was reassured by the reply:

No doubt he is a little mad at times, but he is lucid at intervals. I trust he will have no fit during the campaign, though I must say he looked a little mad as he embarked.

A further concern was Erskine's eyesight, which was particularly poor. Before the enemy could be engaged he had to ask a subordinate to point him in the right direction. At the battle of Sabugal in 1811, Erskine, in the absence of other generals, commanded both the cavalry and the light infantry. Each was marched off in the direction the other should have taken and the French were saved from an even heavier defeat.

At the siege of Almeida, Erskine's actions confounded Wellington's battle tactics, causing the duke to protest that 'this was the most disgraceful military event that has yet occurred to us.' The besieged French garrison was allowed to escape because Erskine failed to guard the bridge of Barba de Puerca. Erskine was dining with a colleague when Wellington's order to guard the bridge arrived. Told to send some cavalry and a force of infantry, Erskine despatched a corporal and four privates. A fellow diner, Colonel Packenham, foresaw a difficulty. 'Sir William,' he said, 'you might as well attempt to block up the bridge with a pinch of snuff as to place such a party for such an object.' Seeing the sense of this, Erskine decided to send a whole regiment. He wrote out the order for its colonel and then put the order in his pocket and forgot all about it. On retiring to bed that night, Erskine found the order in his trousers and passed it on to Colonel Bevan. Bevan arrived at the bridge too late to halt the retreating French, and shouldered the blame for this fiasco. Erskine committed suicide in 1813 by jumping out of a window in Lisbon. His last words to bystanders were, 'Why did I do that?'

**escapers, great.** *See* BIGGS, RONALD; EDGAR, HENRY; HILL, BILLY (for Handy Harry); HINDS, ALFRED; SHEPPARD, JACK.

**estate agents.** *See* FERGUSON, ARTHUR; MILES, LOUISA.

**Eton College, bare knuckle fist fights at.** In January 1863 two pupils at Eton College, Charles Wood, who was 17, and Ashley Cooper, who was 15, decided to settle a quarrel with a fist fight. They then fought bare-knuckled for 60 rounds. The fight lasted for more than two hours. Cooper, though sustained throughout by a pint of brandy, was carried away senseless and died the next day. Charles Wood was indicted for manslaughter, but no witnesses could be found against him and he was acquitted.
*See also* QUEENSBERRY, JOHN SHOLTO DOUGLAS, 9TH MARQUESS OF.

**Etonians.** *See* AMHERST, JEFFREY JOHN ARCHER, 5TH EARL; BURGESS, GUY FRANCIS DE MONCY; CLARK, ALAN; COOK, ROBIN; LUCAN, JOHN

BINGHAM, 6TH BARON; THORPE, JEREMY; VIVIAN, ANTHONY CRESPIGNY CLAUDE, 5TH BARON.

**etwee case, Mrs Persuade's.** *See* BRIAN, JOHN HERMAN.

**evangelists, New Age.** *See* CADDY, EILEEN AND WILLIAM.

**Evans, Frank** (1958– ), kitchen fitter and Britain's only qualified bull-fighter. In July 2000 Evans, who at the time ran a kitchen-fitting business in Greater Manchester, was tossed during a *corrida de toros* in Menalmadena, near Malaga. He was dazed but not fatally injured. 'My wife has hit me harder,' said Evans, before being taken to hospital. 'It's like a golf shot. If you don't stand right you can be all over the place.'

Evans is appreciated in Spain more for his cheerful attitude than for his artistry. One critic in Madrid has described him as 'very nice, but without any talent'. In his trademark red, white and blue suit of lights, he looks the part but perhaps lacks the balletic arrogance *en attitude* usually on display in Spanish bullrings.

Evans decided to become a matador after seeing his first fight when on holiday in Spain in the 1960s. After a year at a bullfighting school in Valencia, he served a 25-year apprenticeship, travelling to remote villages all over Spain. During the winter he trains in his local park in Eccles, brandishing a sword and using a shopping trolley as the bull. Plunging the sword into a bale of hay in the trolley counts as a 'kill'.

**Evans, John** (1770–98), scholar and explorer. Evans, a 22-year-old pioneer Methodist from Waenfawr in Caernarfonshire, was caught up in the Madoc fever that gripped Wales in 1792. This had been triggered by William Jones, a country doctor who had gained celebrity by curing himself of scrofula. Jones circulated an address at an eisteddfod in Llanrwst declaring that Welsh-speaking Indians descended from the followers of Prince Madoc (who had discovered America in 1170) had been contacted beyond the Missouri river. They were living there as a free and distinct people who had preserved their language and ancient liberties and, according to Jones, 'some trace of their religion to this very day'. Jones, who modelled himself on Voltaire, disliked Englishmen, Methodists and his neighbour, Sir Watkin Williams Wynn.

News that the Madocians had been discovered caused an upsurge of national feeling that spread across barriers of class and creed. When the liberal Baptist, Morgan John Rhys, who had distributed bibles in revolutionary Paris, launched a new magazine, *Cylchgrawn Cymraeg*, he declared that all the proceeds would be devoted towards an expedition to the distant Missouri. One critic pointed out that a magazine devoted to all the advanced ideas in Wales – more and better eisteddfodau, greater power for druids – would be unlikely to make enough profit to launch a day trip to Swansea. Nevertheless, many were determined to join the expedition, including the bard of Glamorgan, Iolo Morganwg. And he it was who contacted John Evans, arranging with him that each would make his own way to Baltimore where they would meet up and enjoy the hospitality of Welsh Americans before setting off together on the epic search for the Welsh Indians.

Iolo was 46. He suffered from asthma and was in the habit of taking generous amounts of laudanum. Evans, who was himself in poor health, and whose brother had recently died at the age of 25 of tuberculosis, agreed immediately to Iolo's plan. As a Methodist exhorter it was painful to him to think of his long-lost brethren across the water, bereft of William Morgan's Bible and the hymns of Williams Pantycelyn. He approached the Reverend Thomas Charles of Bala, who had taken over leadership of the Welsh Methodists after the death of Williams Williams, and was given encouragement and financial support. Evans moved with speed, and by late October 1792 he was already in Baltimore.

Iolo never joined him. He had gone into training for the arduous journey and had taken to sleeping under hedges in his native Glamorganshire. This had brought on lumbago to add to all his other ailments. Evans, propelled by a sense of destiny, marched westwards on his own into a series of adventures, the worst of which landed him in a Spanish prison in St Louis. Having secured his release through the generous intervention of the king of Spain, he made a hazardous journey of 1000 miles, through territory dominated by hostile tribes, to reach the Mandan villages in the headwaters of the Missouri river.

The Mandans were believed to be the most likely candidates for Welsh descent. They lived in earth lodges, practised agriculture and were reputed to have fair skin and blue eyes. The young missionary from Waenfawr was transformed by his experiences into a professional explorer. He was received by the Mandans as the accredited representative of the king of Spain, spending a winter in the Mandan villages and surviving an assassination attempt by French Canadian fur traders. His only disappointment was the discovery that the Mandans had no Welsh connections. Evans gave his verdict in a letter to a friend in Philadelphia, Dr Samuel Jones:

> Having explored and charted the Missouri for 1000 miles and by my communication with the Indians this side of the Pacific Ocean from 35 to 49 degrees of latitude, I am able to inform you that there are no such people as the Welsh Indians.

Evans never returned to Wales. He died of drink in New Orleans at the age of 28.

*See also* WELSH, THE.

**Evatt, Clive** (1919–93), barrister. Evatt was a respected QC on the northern circuit until an altercation in court in Bradford brought his career to an end in 1979. Charged with a £1.5-million social-security fraud, 153 Greek Cypriot immigrants, together with their wives, children and lawyers, assembled at Bradford Crown Court in June of that year only to be informed that the team of prosecution lawyers had asked for a further year's adjournment because the police had been unable to sort out which of the accused was which.

Before the adjournment was granted, Mr Clive Evatt QC admitted to the court that he couldn't pronounce his client's name. Several women tried to help by shouting it out, one of them adding, 'He committed suicide six months ago.' An argument broke out, during which Evatt and Miss Erika Clooney, also a barrister, discovered that they had both been briefed on behalf of another of the defendants, and they began to fight each other over the papers.

Jumping into the well of the court, another man, who identified himself as 'Achilles X', floored Evatt and held Miss Clooney's hand aloft, crying, 'This is the one for me!'

Miss Clooney claimed that she had never seen the man before, but this caused another argument to break out among the defendants, during which it was established that 'she had known him extremely well for a year'.

'I would have done my best to get the trial under way,' said Judge Frederick Griffin QC. 'However, among the accused we found a Miss Chong Wah Wong-Diamantopoulos who admitted that her husband was among the crowd but that she was unable to identify him at such short notice.'

**executions, mishaps during the course of.** *See* ARMSTRONG, MAJOR HERBERT ROWSE; BIBBY, JOHN; COTTON, MARY ANN; DUELL, WILLIAM; ELLIS, JOHN; FERRERS, ROBERT SHIRLEY, 2ND EARL; FITZGERALD, GEORGE ROBERT; KIDD, WILLIAM; SHEPPARD, JACK.

**exhibitionists.** *See* CHURCH, THE REVEREND JOHN; CREAM, DR THOMAS NEILL; CRIPPLE, MARGARET AND WILLIAM; DRIBERG, TOM; ELTON, GLADYS; FAIRBAIRN, SIR NICHOLAS; GARVIE, SHEILA; HAMILTON, LADY EMMA; REED, OLIVER; RICE-DAVIES, MANDY.

**Eyres, Tony** (1945– ), record producer and drug dealer. While supplying the upper echelons of society with drugs during the 1970s and 1980s, Eyres found time to pursue a secondary career in the music business, recording Tina Charles and Leapy Lee. When he and his partner in the drug-dealing division of the business, Andrew DEMPSEY, also known as Andy from the Sixties, were arrested in 1985, a message from Princess Margaret was discovered on Eyres's answering machine. The investigating officer was advised not to probe too deeply, but he ignored this warning and set off to question Princess Margaret at Kensington Palace. Here he was denied entry by the Royal Protection Squad, and was later transferred to Hong Kong, where he finished his career directing traffic. Eyres agreed not to mention Princess Margaret's name at his trial and received a suspended sentence of 18 months. Dempsey came to no such accommodation with the prosecution and, charged with the same offence, received seven years in prison.

# f

**Fagan, Michael** (1950   ), royal intruder. In 1982, Fagan, from Islington, north London, successfully broke into Buckingham Palace twice within one month. On the second occasion he entered the queen's bedroom and sat chatting with her for ten minutes. No charge could be brought against him for this, since, under English law, it is not a crime to enter the queen's home, or the home of anyone else, unless there is an intention to commit an offence. However, on the earlier occasion he had helped himself to a bottle of Californian white wine, set aside for the prince and princess of Wales. For that he was charged with:

> Burglary contrary to Section 9 (1) of the Theft Act, 1968, the particulars being that between the sixth day and ninth day of June 1982, he entered Buckingham Palace as a trespasser and stole therein a bottle of wine, valued at £3.

On 19 July Fagan appeared at Bow Street magistrates court and was committed to trial at the Old Bailey. As well as the alleged theft of the bottle of wine, he faced two unrelated charges: one of taking a car without the owner's consent on 16 June (to which he pleaded guilty), and another of assaulting his 10-year-old stepson (to which he pleaded not guilty and of which he was subsequently acquitted). It took the jury less than 20 minutes to find him guilty of stealing the wine intended for the prince and princess of Wales, so Judge James Miskin QC ordered him to be detained in an insane asylum, remarking:

> I am confident that the skilled members of the medical profession, in whose charge he will be, are admirably suited to determine the moment when he is safe to be released.

Whether the circumstances of Fagan's two break-ins suggested mental instability seemed, to some jurists, open to doubt. In the course of the first break-in, on 9 June 1982, he scaled the railings round the palace grounds and entered Ambassadors Court, thereafter shinning 50 feet up a drainpipe and peering into Room 151 as he clung to the wall like a human fly above a sheer drop to the yard below. A housemaid, Sarah Jane Carter, who was in bed reading with the curtains open, saw him clearly but she assumed her mind was playing tricks and she returned to her book. Fagan continued with his climb and crawled across a flat roof to break into the royal residence. Once inside he wandered around at his leisure, pausing occasionally to sit on the throne, to admire the portraits in the Picture Gallery and to note the names on the various royal bedrooms before entering Room 108, the Post Room. By this time he felt thirsty, so he helped himself to the prince of Wales's Californian white wine. He then settled down to await what he assumed would be his inevitable arrest. Nothing happened, so he made his way out of the palace and went home.

On the night of 9 July, Fagan entered the palace by the same route, on this occasion making his way to her majesty's bedroom, where she woke to find an intruder sitting on her bed, dripping blood from a hand that he had cut when accidentally dropping an ashtray. She rang her alarm bell but the police guard had gone off duty, her footman was outside in the grounds exercising the corgies and all the housemaids were asleep. With considerable self-control she chatted with Fagan until he asked for a cigarette. This gave her the opportunity to summon help in the form of a young servant, Whybrew, who ushered Fagan into a pantry, where the police finally arrested him. Had he not drunk the prince of Wales's Californian white wine on his previous visit they would have been obliged to let him go.

Throughout his subsequent difficulties Fagan insisted that his motivation had simply been to point up the poor security arrangements at the palace. 'I wanted to prove the queen wasn't safe,' he said. 'I did her a favour.' The chairman of the Mental Health Tribunal that heard Fagan's appeal in October 1982 arrived at much the same conclusion. On 19 January 1983 he was freed from the top-security Park Lane mental hospital in Liverpool. The Tribunal chairman said in a statement that 'while Fagan is not fully recovered, and remains vulnerable to pressure, it is desirable that he should be left alone to re-establish himself in society.'

Outrage was expressed in the usual quarters, but Fagan has since conducted himself in an exemplary fashion.

**Fairbairn, Sir Nicholas** (1933–95), lawyer, politician and libertine. The son of a distinguished Scottish psychiatrist who believed in frequent involuntary releases of tension through sneezing and orgasms, Fairbairn was educated at Loretto and Edinburgh University. He was called to the Scottish Bar in 1957, and entered Parliament in 1974 as Conservative MP for Kinross and Perthshire West. He was appointed solicitor general for Scotland in 1979, but was dismissed in 1982 by the prime minister, Margaret Thatcher, after he had decided not to prosecute in an alleged rape case. Throughout his career he subscribed to the theory that when a woman says 'no' she means 'yes'.

Sir Nicholas, who customarily wore clothes designed by himself, was considered by some to be a wit. Others on coming across his variously anthologized '*mots*', might be embarrassed on his behalf. When the junior health minister Edwina Currie was forced to resign after some incautious remarks about salmonella infection in eggs, Fairbairn suggested that:

> The Hon. lady should remember that she was an egg once; and very many members on all sides of the House may regret that it was ever fertilized.

In the course of a debate at Edinburgh University he told a student that she was 'a silly rude bitch and, since you are a potential breeder, God help the human race'. Ridiculing fellow Tory MP Janet Fooke's kerb-crawling bill, which would make it an offence for a man to solicit for sex from a woman 'in a manner which causes her fear', Fairbairn said:

> I must tell Miss Fookes that I have always been attracted to her. I have never actually dared ask her whether she would go to bed with me, but after the introduction of the Bill I must ask myself how I am to put it to her so that it does not cause her fear.

Reliable parliamentary sketch writers have reported that certain sections of the House were greatly amused by these and other sallies. Sir Nicholas's wit, thanks to the medium of the wireless, could be savoured by the general public too. On *Desert Island Discs* he regretted that women MPs 'lack fragrance on the whole':

> They definitely aren't desert island material. They all look as though they are from the 5th Kiev Stalinist machine-gun parade.

For his luxury item as a castaway, Sir Nicholas chose a photograph of Mrs Khrushchev, wife of the former Soviet leader, 'whose ugliness,' he said, 'would prevent me fantasizing about sex'.

Sex seemed to have been a recurring problem for Sir Nicholas. A Miss Pamela Milne was reported to have tried to hang herself from a lamppost outside his London home after discovering that he was to marry another woman, whose husband had cited Fairbairn as co-respondent. Miss Milne later claimed that he had begged her to become 'the mistress of Forsell' (his castle in Scotland) and had given her an engagement ring. The incident must have taken place between the two marriages on which he did embark: first, in 1962, to Elizabeth Mackay, elder daughter of the 13th Baron Reay, by whom he had four daughters and a son, and, second, in 1983, to Suzanne Mary Wheeler.

**Fairbanks Jnr, Douglas.** *See* ARGYLL, MARGARET DUCHESS OF; KEELER, CHRISTINE.

**fairs, travelling.** Victorian magistrates objected to the presence in their area of travelling fairs because of the amount of violence that accompanied them. The trouble was usually a consequence of rivalry between showmen, as when Hilton's convoy tried to overtake Wombwell's during a race at night to be first at Henley Fair in 1851. According to 'Lord' George Sanger's *Seventy Years a Showman* (1927), the incident occurred on the Oxford Road just outside Reading. One of Hilton's men knocked one of Wombwell's drivers off his seat with a tent pole. A fight broke out when the Fat Man attacked the Living Skeleton with a door hook. The Living Skeleton fought back with a peg mallet and there was a general mêlée. The noise startled the horses that were pulling Wombwell's elephant van, and the elephants escaped. The fight continued until it was time to gather up the injured and take them to hospital in Reading. The elephants were later rounded up and walked into town.

On other occasions the showmen and their families were attacked by local inhabitants. Reports survive of a serious affray in August 1839 after tents, booths and sideshows had been erected on a hill north of Bath. By 10 p.m. the showmen had begun to take down their stalls and sideshows. As they did so they were attacked by a gang of local hooligans led by a red-headed virago known as 'Carrotty Kate'. George Sanger's father, 'Lord' James Sanger, had previously suffered at the hands of Carrotty Kate, whom he described as 'a big brutal animal, caring nothing for magistrates or gaol, and the terror of every respectable person in Bath and the neighbourhood'.

Eventually the mob turned back to the city. The showmen were badly bruised, but about 30 of them, armed with improvised weapons, rode after their attackers and took about a dozen prisoners, including Carrotty Kate. The captive hooligans were then tied together in a 'living chain' and dragged backwards and forwards through a pond. The showmen's intention was to stop short of drowning their former persecutors, but several lost consciousness. Then, two by two, the rioters were tied against wagon wheels and flogged with riding whips.

The leader of the showmen then informed Carrotty Kate that, urgently in need of a tubbing though she was, she would yet be spared immersion in the pond. However, she would be horsewhipped. The face of the 'virago was chalky white against the mass of red hair' as six of the women held her over a trestle while two young women thrashed her until they were exhausted. Later, a party of policemen, who had heard about the riot, set upon suspected town folk with staves. Several were arrested and subsequently transported for their attack on the showmen. One crippled a policeman with an iron bar and was later hanged.

**falling down stairs having been kicked by a junior whip.** *See* BROMLEY-DAVENPORT, LIEUTENANT COLONEL SIR WALTER.

**falling down stairs having been pushed by a fellow diplomat.** *See* BURGESS, GUY FRANCIS DE MONCY.

**falling down stairs having tripped over a dead hippopotamus.** *See* BUCKLAND, FRANCIS TREVELYAN.

**false teeth, incriminating.** *See* HAIGH, JOHN GEORGE.

**fanatical vicars.** *See* WENHAM, JANE (for the Reverend Francis Bragge).

**fancy ladies and their penchants.** *See* NICHOLSON, 'BARON' RENTON.

**Fang, the much-feared.** *See* KINGSLEY, MARY.

**Fanny, Lord.** *See* BRISTOL, FREDERICK WILLIAM JOHN AUGUSTUS HERVEY, 7TH MARQUESS OF, one of whose ancestors was so named.

**farmers, pedagogical.** *See* ALINGTON, JOHN.

**farmers, priapic.** *See* GARVIE, SHEILA.

**Farson, Daniel** (1927–97), journalist, author and broadcaster. The son of the distinguished American journalist, Negley Farson, Dan was a writer of some talent himself, and a prodigious drunk. In what is thought to be his best book, *Soho in the Fifties* (1986), he describes a typical day. This would start with a large drink at the French pub in Soho at 11 a.m., followed by lunch at Wheelers, perhaps, with Francis Bacon as a companion. After lunch he would repair to the Colony Club (*see* BELCHER, MURIEL) where he would drink with friends until the Coach and Horses (*see* BALON, NORMAN) opened again at 5.30 p.m. At closing time he would return to the Colony Club, unintelligible by this time and fighting drunk, thereafter making his way to some such place as the Elephant's Graveyard where he would hope to be beaten up by a queer docker. The next morning he would appear at the French pub covered in cuts – from a fall or a fight or an altercation with a policeman – and the round of alcohol and arguments would start again.

Farson's utter fearlessness was his most obvious quality, perhaps. One afternoon a lorry driver tracked him down to the Coach and Horses and demanded payment for services rendered the night before. Farson stood his ground. 'But you didn't fucking do anything!' he shouted.

In 1962, with money left to him by his father, Farson bought a pub called The Waterman's Arms in London's East End and turned it into a venue for old-fashioned music hall. The venture lasted for little more than a year, but it gave rise to what many people regard as his finest achievement. In 1964 he devised and staged *Nights at the Comedy*, a memorable attempt to combine music hall and pub entertainment in a West End theatre. Although the show contained many excellent turns – including a man who hit himself over the head with a tin tray while singing *Mule Train*, and another, calling himself Demetrious the Gladiator, who blew up hot water bottles while standing on one leg – it was compromised by the fact that Farson broke the first rule of vaudeville, which is never to put the seals on first. Thereafter the stage was as slippery as an ice rink, and the next act, 86-year-old Ida Barr, skated straight across the stage and into the compère, Nicol WILLIAMSON, knocking him into the orchestra pit. Williamson recovered, but the ingénue, on next and singing 'Let me entertain you', skated across the stage and knocked him into the orchestra pit again. Taking himself to be the butt of a joke, Williamson, a fine Shakespearean actor but unused to the hurly-burly of vaudeville, walked out of the show, to be replaced as compère by Mr Jimmy Tarbuck, the Liverpool comedian then at the start of his career. Meanwhile, Mrs Shufflewick, a drag comedian who was popular at the time, took advantage of the fact that Farson had converted the stage into a pub interior dispensing real alcohol and got drunk. Thereafter she remained on stage, offering a derisive running commentary on the quality of the other acts. The least successful in her opinion was Princess Juanita and her snakes. 'Don't put your snakes on the stage, Mrs Worthington,' said Mrs Shufflewick, causing Princess Juanita, like Nicol Williamson before her, to walk out in a huff.

Farson retired to north Devon, where he lived in his parents' house near the sea. His behaviour caused him to be banned from every pub in the Appledore area save one. From time to time he visited London, got drunk earlier and earlier in the day and missed the last train back to Devon. Last-minute accommodation on these occasions always presented a difficulty since he was unwelcome at so many hotels. Shortly before his death he was able to complete his autobiography, *Never a Normal Man* (1997), which was well received.

**Fartleberry, Viscount.** *See* BECKFORD, WILLIAM.

**fate worse than death, avoidance of a.** *See* BAKER, COLONEL VALENTINE.

**father of not being a gentleman, accusing one's.** *See* LUTTRELL, COLONEL JAMES.

**father of pornographic publishing in England, the.** *See* CURLL, EDMOND.

**father's attitude, murderously disliking one's.** *See* BROWN, ERIC.

**Fat Man attacks Living Skeleton.** *See* FAIRS, TRAVELLING.

**Fawkes, Guy** (1570–1606), conspirator. Born of Protestant parents, Fawkes became an ardent Catholic while still at school. There he had learned of Henry VIII's persecution of Catholics 40 years earlier. He was shocked too at the treatment still being meted out to his Catholic friends. In 1592 he fought with the Spanish army in the Netherlands and in 1603 he tried to persuade the king of Spain to invade Protestant England.

Meanwhile, a group of English Catholics, disappointed that James I was no more tolerant of their religion than Elizabeth I had been, decided that violent action was the answer. Their leader was Robert Catesby, a Warwickshire landowner who, as a recusant, had suffered fines and imprisonment under Elizabeth. A charismatic figure, he was able to persuade a number of his impressionable friends to join him in what was later to be known as the Gunpowder Plot. The plan was to blow up the Houses of Parliament on the day it was opened by the king.

Catesby first recruited Thomas Wintour, Jack Wright and Thomas Percy, who hired a cellar under the House of Lords in which he stored 36 barrels of gunpowder. Guy Fawkes joined the conspiracy with the second group, which included Sir Everard Digby and Francis Tresham, the latter being the brother-in-law of Lord Monteagle. In the event, Lord Monteagle received an anonymous letter warning him not to attend Parliament on the 5 November. The letter was shown to the authorities, who invaded the cellar under the House of Lords where they discovered Guy Fawkes alone with the 36 barrels of gunpowder. He was arrested, tortured and executed, though not before he had given up the names of his co-conspirators, all of whom followed him to the block. It is not clear whether those who, to this day, light bonfires on 5 November are celebrating his execution or honouring a man who attempted to blow up the Houses of Parliament.

*Fawlty Towers*, **the inspiration for.** *See* SINCLAIR, DONALD.

**feet cut off to fit into sarcophagus.** *See* HAMILTON, ALEXANDER DOUGLAS, 10TH DUKE OF.

**Ferguson, Arthur** (1883–?), actor and confidence trickster. A mediocre actor by all accounts, Ferguson made an enterprising career change after taking the role of an American in a play in Manchester. This fictional American was easily tricked by an English swindler, and Ferguson began to wonder whether Americans might be just as gullible in the real world.

In about 1920 he moved to London and, being a sober middle-aged man of smart appearance and impeccable address, was able, without the need to act, to persuade American tourists that he was working with the government to pay off war loans to America by selling off valuable parts of London. If his intended victim seemed to be sharper than the average, Ferguson explained that it was only the leasehold that was for sale. Many American tourists viewed Big Ben as a bargain at a shade over £5000; Nelson's Column was marked down to a reasonable £20,000; and Ferguson was able to secure a down payment of £30,000 on Buckingham Palace.

By 1922 Ferguson's activities had come to the attention of the police, so he moved his business to New York. Being unusual among English actors in that he recognized how feeble his performances were, and realizing that tourists from any country other than England would spot him immediately as a bad English actor playing an American, he targeted only English visitors. This policy bore fruit, and it was not long before a hard-headed Yorkshireman on holiday with his wife had handed over a $10,000 downpayment on the Empire State Building, and another had put up an advance rent of $15,000 on the White House.

Other successes followed, and Ferguson became over-confident. Having introduced himself to an Australian visitor as the mayor of New York's district surveyor, he told him of plans to rebuild the city's harbour. The Statue of Liberty would have to be sold off at the knockdown price of $30,000. The Australian was able to recognize an incompetent English actor when he saw one, and he went immediately to the police. Ferguson headed for California, and was not heard of again.

**Ferguson, Major Ronald.** *See* ST CLAIR, LINDI.

**Fernseed, Margaret** (*c*.1560–1608), prostitute, brothel-keeper and murderess. Fernseed was the most resourceful controller of prostitutes in 16th-century London. A pamphlet of 1608, commemorating her execution for the murder of her husband, contains a remarkable account of her methods. Although she claimed to be innocent of the murder, she confessed to having been a whore since puberty and to having run a brothel. Her recruiting methods were precisely planned. She kept close contact with carriers so that she could 'make spoile of yong maidens who were sent out of the countrie by their friends with hope to advance themselves'. These girls were debauched and put on the streets, each being compelled to hand over to Fernseed ten shillings from what they earned. She also recruited married women whom she judged to be unhappy with their lot. She would carefully note 'any breach or discontent' between women and their husbands and would then exacerbate the grievance by persuading the wives that their husbands 'maintained them not sufficiently to expresse their beauty, and according to their owne desserts'. Once these women had been persuaded into prostitution, Fernseed ensured their continued service by threatening to expose them to their husbands if they refused to accommodate her customers.

From *The Arraignment & Burning of Margaret Ferne-seede for the Murther of her Late Husband, Anthony Ferne-seede* (1608), we learn that Mr Fernseed was found dead in Peckham Fields near Lambeth, and that she had 'before attempted to poison him with broth'. We are not told what had caused the rift between them, nor whether he had been party to her brothel-keeping activities. Margaret Fernseed was executed in St George's Field on 28 February 1608.

**Ferrers, Robert Shirley, 2nd Earl** (1729–60), murderer. Ferrers was the first peer to be hanged at Tyburn as a common criminal, rather than to suffer decapitation, which was the usual privilege reserved for aristocrats. The descendant of an ancient and distinguished Leicestershire family, whose seat was Staunton Hall near Ashby-de-la-Zouch, Ferrers drank heavily and had a violent temper. In 1752 he married the younger daughter of Sir William Meredith, but she left him when he kicked her unconscious in front of the servants. The earl had previously kicked a footman so hard in the groin that he was unable to retain water for many weeks thereafter. His offence had been a refusal to confirm that a delivery boy had intentionally supplied Ferrers with bad oysters.

In 1760 Ferrers became convinced that his steward, Johnson, had conspired with his trustees to deprive him of a lucrative coal-mining contract. Johnson was summoned to the house and when he arrived Ferrers shot him. The earl was arrested the following morning and taken to the Tower of London. At his trial by the House of Lords in Westminster Hall, Ferrers conducted his own defence, calling many witnesses to testify that he was insane, which was certainly the case. However, when their lordships dismissed this line of argument, he agreed immediately that it was a poor defence and one to which he had always been averse. He had tried it out, he said, merely at the suggestion of his friends.

Huge crowds gathered to see his execution on 5 May 1760. Ferrers, dressed in his white satin wedding suit, travelled to Tyburn in his landau, attended by his liveried servants and accompanied by an escort of cavalry and infantry. The procession from the Tower to Tyburn took three hours because of the mass of people lining the route.

Popular myth has it that the earl was hanged with a silk rope, but there seems to be no evidence of this. On the scaffold he gave the customary five guineas to the assistant executioner by mistake and the proceedings were held up while the hangman, Thomas Turlis, wrestled his junior to the floor in order to recover the money. When Ferrers was at last hanged, he dangled for a while at the end of the rope because Turlis had measured the drop incorrectly. The assistant hangman took hold of his feet and pulled hard. 'He suffered a little by delay,' wrote Horace Walpole, 'but was dead in four minutes.'

The late earl's descendant, Robert Washington Shirley, 13th Earl Ferrers, PC MA DL (1929– ), a lord-in-waiting from 1962 to 1964, has served as sub-warden of Winchester College since 1983.

For references to other Wykehamists, *see* WYKEHAMISTS.

**ferret called Sir Andrew Large, a defrauding.** *See* CHANEY, SID.

**Field, Brian** (1932–81), solicitor's clerk and train robber. If there was a mastermind behind the Great Train Robbery of 1963 – a theory that has often been advanced – it was the easy-going but sadly disorganized Brian Field. Field was the managing clerk at John Wheater & Co., a firm of London solicitors that represented the train robber Gordon GOODY. According to Goody, Field was 'what we call a "silly bollocks"' – that is to say, a pleasant enough amateur who thought it glamorous to mix with criminals. Plans to rob the Glasgow-to-London mail train had been on offer in the underworld for some time, but it was only when a friend of Field's, who happened to work for the Post Office in Glasgow, gave him vital information concerning times, dates and the quantity of money carried that the plan materialized. Field passed the information on to Goody, and the robbery became a reality.

Thereafter, Field's participation was unfortunate – for himself and for the gang assembled by Goody and Bruce REYNOLDS. His first mistake was to use his own firm, John Wheater & Co., to negotiate the purchase of the gang's hideout, Leatherslade Farm; and his second, which was still more remarkable, was to sign the lease himself. He then failed in his most important duty, which was to burn Leatherslade Farm to the ground after the gang had moved out. This oversight presented Detective Chief Superintendent Tommy BUTLER with half the evidence he needed, allowing him to pursue his customary investigative method, which was to provide the other half himself. Finally, Field was careful to put his share of the proceeds (£100,900) in a hold-all marked 'Brian Field'. When the hold-all was discovered buried in a wood near Dorking, Butler was able to show that the person who had signed the lease on Leatherslade Farm had also been involved in the robbery.

Field was arrested and later sentenced to 25 years in prison, reduced to 5 years on appeal. When released he changed his name and remarried. In 1981 he was killed in a road accident. His new family were surprised to discover his real identity.

**Fight that Never Was, the.** *See* SPOT, JACK.

**Filipanas, young.** *See* MOYNIHAN, ANTONY PATRICK ANDREW CAIRNE BERKELEY, 3RD BARON.

**Finney, Emily** (1861–?), actress. The case of *Finney vs Garmoyle* under the

Breach of Promise of Marriage Act (1753), though successful for Finney, illustrates the danger actresses run when appearing before senior members of the judiciary. The daughter of an impoverished City businessman, Finney was a star with the D'Oyly Carte Opera Company. One night in 1882 Viscount Garmoyle, the son of Lord Cairns, a former lord chancellor, was in the audience. He was immediately attracted to Miss Finney, and a few weeks later he proposed. Miss Finney was able to reciprocate his feelings, but she insisted that he secure his parents' consent to the marriage. His mother approved, but Lord Cairns, a missionary churchman, was less agreeable. He relented in time, but only on condition that his future daughter-in-law give up the stage. This she did. It was then decided that Viscount Garmoyle should join the army as a career, and once again Miss Finney acceded. The blow came when he wrote to her one day breaking off the engagement. She wrote back, asking the reason, and when he failed to reply she departed on a tour abroad, having first instructed her solicitor to sue.

The breach of promise was admitted, but there was an argument over the damages. Miss Finney was asking for £30,000. Lord Cairns, on behalf of his son, offered £2000. Miss Finney said she would leave it to the jury to decide. The hearing took place on 21 November 1884. A consent judgement of £10,000 was entered for Miss Finney, together with a statement in open court that the breakdown in the marriage proposal had in no way been her fault. Lord Garmoyle didn't fare so well, least of all at the hands of the judge. However, there was an unpleasant sting in the tail of his lordship's summing-up:

> He [Lord Garmoyle] is clearly a simpleton and a very weak-minded young man. Notwithstanding that he will become one of our hereditary legislators. The moral of this case is simple and salutary. The exemplary damages which, by mutual consent, have been awarded to the plaintiff will operate as a peremptory admonishment to brainless boobies of position ...

At this point, Miss Finney had nothing to fear, it might have been thought, but his lordship continued:

> ... not to philander after their inferiors and especially after actresses.

Matters have not greatly improved in the last 100 years, as is shown by a more recent impertinence to a young actress delivered by the judiciary. In September 1963, at the height of the Christine KEELER affair, the German scandal magazine *Bild* illustrated an article about Miss Keeler with a photograph of Miss Claire Gordon, a young actress of good reputation who at the time was appearing at the Prince of Wales Theatre, London, opposite Mr Michael Crawford in *Come Blow Your Horn,* a light comedy by Neil Simon. The caption to the photograph read, 'The notorious English call girl, Claire Gordon.'

The libel seemed serious and Miss Gordon was reluctant to accept the sum of £50 that the magazine offered by way of settlement. However, her barrister, Mr Michael Sherrard QC, who later came to prominence when defending James Hanratty, pointed out in his written 'opinion' that she was wearing a bathing suit in the photograph and wasn't in any case 'Dame Sybil Thorndike exactly'. He advised Miss Gordon to accept the £50, which she did.

**fire-eater's assistant, married to a Malayan.** *See* MOYNIHAN, ANTONY PATRICK ANDREW CAIRNE BERKELEY, 3RD BARON.

**firing on unoffending blacks as if they were rabbits.** *See* DE ROUGE-MONT, LOUIS.

**'Fish', a bishop known as.** *See* CECIL, LORD WILLIAM.

**fish, hoping that the girls will behave like.** *See* JONES, JANIE (for 'Mr A').

**fish, methods of fooling gullible.** *See* BIRCH, THOMAS.

**fish, smuggling diamonds in frozen.** *See* RICHARDSON, CHARLIE.

**fish, spending every night eating.** *See* PAGET, DOROTHY.

**fish dishes re-heated by sitting on them.** *See* DANCER, DANIEL.

**Fisher, Kitty.** *See* HERVEY, AUGUSTUS.

**fishing, wearing a tree disguise while.** *See* BIRCH, THOMAS.

**fishing, wearing net stocking while.** *See* MATURIN, CHARLES.

**fist-fighters, unlicensed.** *See* BRADSHAW, BRIAN 'THE MAD GYPSY'; BRONSON, CHARLES; MCLEAN, LENNY ('The Guv'nor').

**Fitzclarence, Captain Lord Adolphus.** *See* THISTLEWOOD, ARTHUR.

**Fitzgerald, George Robert** (1748–86), soldier and duellist. Fitzgerald inherited his fighting disposition from his father, a notorious Irish rake, but the panache with which he carried out his various acts of aggression may have owed something to his Hervey ancestry. His mother was Lady Mary Hervey, the sister of Frederick Hervey, the earl-bishop of Derry (*see* BRISTOL, FREDERICK WILLIAM JOHN AUGUSTUS HERVEY, 7TH MARQUESS

OF). Lady Mary left her husband after five years, returning to her home in England with her two small sons, George Robert and Charles Lionel. Before her marriage she had been maid of honour to Princess Amelia, daughter of George II, and her experience at court had given her a taste for cosmopolitan society. In Mayo her husband took a mistress, whom his neighbours called a harlot and who, amid local indignation, sat on the bench beside him as he performed his duties as judge of assize in Castlebar.

George Robert meanwhile enjoyed every advantage associated with the English aristocracy. He was educated at Eton College and, when he was old enough, he joined the army. He already had a reputation as a hothead. He had fought his first duel at the age of 16 against a Mr French. Mr French, who was absent-minded, had forgotten his powder horn and was obliged to borrow Fitzgerald's before firing could begin. On another occasion Fitzgerald was nearly killed in a duel against a second lieutenant in his regiment. A bullet entered his head and a surgeon had to remove part of his skull. While being operated on, Fitzgerald, semiconscious and streaming blood, implored the surgeon to spare his toupee. His father, informed that his son was dying, was so distracted that a man who offered his condolences was run through with a rapier.

Fitzgerald, though scarred for life, survived and became adept at picking quarrels. In Dublin, when in the mood for a fight, he would strike out at people in the street or snatch their rings and watches. Once he shot off a man's wig. In spite of his uncertain temper he had a reputation for charm and was liked by women. He courted, and in 1772 married, the rich and beautiful Jane Conolly. The couple went on an extended honeymoon in France, where, thanks to the Hervey connection, they had an entrée to the court of Louis XV. However, Fitzgerald was not a success as a courtier. He was accused by the comte d'Artois of using loaded dice in a gambling game, offended against the etiquette of the royal hunt by riding ahead of the king, and, most seriously, slapped one of his creditors in full view of the queen, an action that might have landed him in the Bastille. On another occasion he drew his rapier and ran a man through who had stepped on his dog outside a Parisian coffee house.

In 1775 Fitzgerald returned to Ireland. He had fought 30 duels and his debts amounted to £150,000. His wife preferred to live elsewhere. 'Fitzgerald is completely broke and has gone off to Mayo,' reported his uncle, the bishop of Derry. 'His wife remains in Dublin, in a state of decline brought on by the levities, quarrels and wild doings of her husband.' Fitzgerald remained in love with her, however, and when she died he mounted an exhibition of grief that some people found immoderate.

While Fitzgerald worked to improve Rockingham, his estate north of Castlebar, the duels continued. He quarrelled with his neighbours, to whom he considered himself socially superior. Out hunting he regularly lost his temper, and those who he considered were not of a 'caste' to adorn the sport were simply flogged from the field. The Reverend O'Malley was told to 'go home, you unwieldy porpoise!' For want of better entertainment, he rode over to Westport House one day and took a pot shot at Denis Brown, an influential landlord. He then killed Brown's giant wolfhound, named the Prime Sergeant after Lord Altamont's brother, who held the official position.

Fitzgerald's most enduring quarrel, however, was with his father. When he married he had been promised an allowance of £1000 a year from his father's rents, but the money had all been squandered. He appealed to the Court of the Exchequer, contending that his father was 'sotting and dozing away at Turlogh in unmeaning fullness and inactive stupidity, an existence burdensome to himself and useless to his creditors'. The court ruled that the old man should live with his son, who then did everything possible to make his father's life a misery. Once, when the older Fitzgerald refused to change his will, his son knocked out three of his teeth. On another occasion he manacled him all day to a pet bear.

After his day with the bear, Fitzgerald senior was locked up by his son in a cave near Rockingham. This was too much for the old man's other son, Charles Lionel. George Robert was summoned to Castlebar where he was accused of extreme cruelty. He defended himself on the grounds that his father was 'one of the worst men alive', a defence seconded by his counsel, Remesius Lennon, who suggested that it would be unjust to censure any son for chaining such an obvious public nuisance to a bear. The defence was unsuccessful, and Fitzgerald was sentenced to two years imprisonment and fined £500. Any attempt to confine him, however, failed against a militia of 500 men that he had at his disposal, raised at a time when the threat of invasion by the French had made private armies legal. When the militia assembled outside the jail, Fitzgerald was immediately released.

On his return home, Fitzgerald found that his house had been ransacked in his absence. His neighbours avoided him and no respectable servant would stay in his employ. But his militia survived and for companions he had two disreputable assistants, a Welsh attorney named Timothy Brecknock and a coachman known as Scotch Andrew. Before long he was quarrelling again. His new enemy was Patrick McDonnell, who had been elected as colonel of the Mayo Legion of Volunteers, a position that Fitzgerald had coveted himself. He decided that McDonnell would have to be killed. He concocted a plan with the help of Timothy Brecknock, who told him that it would be perfectly in order to arrest McDonnell legally and then to have him shot while trying to escape. The plan worked well. Fitzgerald's militia was sent to arrest McDonnell and two of his friends. McDonnell was duly despatched, but one of his friends, Mr Gallagher, avoided being murdered by feigning death.

Fitzgerald's behaviour was now judged to be unacceptable. His militia grew frightened and scattered. On 21 February 1786, the day after McDonnell had been shot, a detachment of troops was sent to Fitzgerald's home, where they found him hiding in a chest covered by blankets. His trial for murder opened on 11 June in Dublin. The prosecution was led by the attorney general, John Fitzgibbon (later the earl of Clare), with whom Fitzgerald had once fought a duel. Bets were taken on whether the accused would be hanged or saved by his mother's former connections with the court of George II. There was some surprise when a guilty verdict was returned.

On the day of his execution Fitzgerald drank a bottle of port and was completely composed on the scaffold. However, the rope broke and he was hurled to the ground. 'You see I am once more among you unexpectedly,' he told the crowd. There was some delay while they got not only another rope, but another hangman too, a convict who agreed to do the job for a free pardon. At the second attempt, Fitzgerald was successfully executed. His body was taken to the windowless shell of his old home, which had been so thoroughly looted that not a single candlestick could be found. The coffin was set down amid the shambles, lit by candles thrust into bottles. A story has it that, years later, a search was made for his grave in order to recover a ring he was thought to have been wearing. The flesh had gone from his skull to reveal a great cleft in the bone inflicted during one of his first duels. There was speculation that this wound was the cause of his uncertain temper.

Fitzgerald left a young daughter who died suddenly in 1794. It was said that her death was brought on by shock after reading an account of her father's execution in the *Gentleman's Magazine*.

*See also* DUELLING.

**Fitzgibbon, John** (1970– ), drug dealer. In July 2000 Fitzgibbon, an inmate of Parkhurst, became the laughing stock of the prison system, when, in order to evade a £20,000 contract taken out on him by his former bosses who believed he had cheated them on a drug deal, and thinking that the safest place to be would be in solitary confinement in the punishment wing, he picked a fight with a baby-faced prisoner who seemed guaranteed not to fight back. His victim, who received such a severe beating that he had to be taken to the prison hospital, turned out to be Real IRA terrorist, Darren Mulholland. Mulholland had been jailed at the Old Bailey in May 1999 after a jury convicted him of conspiring to cause explosions. The Real IRA vowed revenge on the man who had beaten up their bomber, with the result that there were now two contracts out on Fitzgibbon instead of only one. Bets have been taken in criminal circles on whether the Real IRA or his aggrieved former associates would get him first.

**flash dancing.** *See* PENNY GAFFS.

**Fleckney, Evelyn** (1965– ), drug dealer and police informer. Throughout the 1990s detectives in the Regional Crime Squad, South East Division, were under the operational control not of their superiors at Scotland Yard but of Evelyn ('Blonde Eve') Fleckney, who dealt in drugs from her luxury flat in London's King's Road. This state of affairs only came to light after one of the squad, Detective Constable Neil Putnam, decided to become an informer against his colleagues.

Soon after he joined the squad in 1991 Putnam discovered that it was involved with Fleckney in a profitable operation whose rules seemed to be similar to those governing the children's game, Postman's Knock. A parcel of drugs would circulate at bewildering speed between the police, Fleckney and various lesser dealers without its contents ever touching the 'street' – the penalty being a prison sentence for whoever was holding the parcel when the music stopped, so long as this wasn't Fleckney or the police.

Fleckney, who happened to be the mistress of Detective Sergeant Bob Clarke, the squad's dominating officer, had got her start as a dealer by informing on her previous boyfriend, Joseph French (street name, Frenchie). When French went to prison, Fleckney and Clarke formed a partnership, using French's stock as their initial capital. The method by which she and Clarke thereafter enriched themselves wasn't original, but they executed it with unusual audacity. Fleckney would have in her possession drugs with a street value of, say, £50,000. These she would sell to Dealer 'A'. Before the drugs could be distributed, Dealer 'A' would get a visit from DS Clarke. Usually Clarke and his colleagues would simply relieve Dealer 'A' of the drugs, together with any cash he happened to have lying around. The drugs would be returned to Fleckney and the cash would be divided up between members of the squad. On rare occasions the squad would bring a charge against Dealer 'A' – to keep the scoreboard ticking, as it were – in which case they would return only half of the confiscated stash to Fleckney, since the other half would be needed as evidence. This was not the preferred method.

The system seemed to work for everyone. The police had a result – at least on such occasions as an arrest was made; the squad's reputation grew and its members were enriched; Fleckney received a constant supply of free drugs – albeit drugs that had been hers in the first place; and, if an arrest was made, she was able to claim the reward money too. Nor was Dealer 'A' too aggrieved. Either he escaped arrest, for which he was grateful, or, if arrested, he was charged on a smaller stock than he had in fact been holding and could therefore expect a lighter sentence. The only people with cause for complaint were users in the Royal Borough of Kensington and Chelsea, since Fleckney and her police associates were too busy passing the same drugs backwards and forwards at a profit to attend to their small needs.

The operation began to go wrong after DS Clarke and his men, acting as usual on a tip-off from Fleckney, ambushed a Surrey dealer known as

'Guildford John' when he had £27,000 worth of cannabis in his transit van. The squad took away his cannabis, later returning it to Fleckney, but they didn't arrest him. 'Guildford John's' disappointment at the loss of his stock was greater than his relief at not being arrested, and when he was picked up by the Surrey police a few weeks later, he said, 'I hope you're not going to do what the last lot did.' The arresting officers on this occasion happened not to be corrupt, and once 'Guildford John' had told them of his misfortune at the hands of Clarke, an investigation was carried out into the squad's activities. DC Putnam became a born-again Christian, thereafter deciding that it was morally preferable to inform on his colleagues than go to prison. DS Clarke and three other members of the squad were sentenced to 12 years in prison after Putnam had testified against them. In March 1997 Fleckney was jailed for 15 years for supplying drugs.

**Fleming, Evelyn.** *See* WINCHESTER, BAPSY MARCHIONESS OF.

**flies called Ilemazar, Eyewackett, Peck-in-the-crown and Grizel-Greedigut.** *See* HOPKINS, MATTHEW.

**flogging a dead horse.** *See* BASS, HARRY 'THE DOCTOR'.

**flogging dope peddlers with dog whips in the Great West Road.** *See* MARKS, HOWARD.

**flogging in church.** *See* DASHWOOD, SIR FRANCIS.

***Flogging in Venereal Affairs, A Treatise of the use of.*** *See* CURLL, EDMOND.

**flogging of Carrotty Kate, the.** *See* FAIRS, TRAVELLING.

**Flood, Matthew** (*c.*1692–1723), pickpocket and highwayman. A minor figure in the 18th-century underworld compared to his contemporaries, Jonathan WILD, Joseph BLAKE and Jack SHEPPARD, Flood is nevertheless remembered for having devised, with his associate, Will the Sailor, an innovative method of street robbery.

Described by the compilers of the *Newgate Calendar* as 'of the meanest origin, a miserable, ignorant, yet most dangerous wretch', Flood, together with his first partner, Richard Oakey, specialized in cutting women's pockets. According to the *Newgate Calendar*, either Flood or Oakey:

> ... would trip up the woman's heels while the other cut off the pocket, and they generally were out of reach of detection before the party could recover her legs.

A more ingenious method was employed after Oakey had become romantically involved with Big Sal, a woman of the town. A rich lady walking in the street would suddenly be seized from behind by Big Sal and lifted off her feet with a cry of 'take care, madam, or the coach will hit you!' In the confusion Flood or Oakey would cut off the rich lady's pocket.

When Flood and Oakey dissolved their partnership, Flood teamed up with Will the Sailor, and the two of them devised the practice for which Flood is still remembered. Will the Sailor, wearing a sword, would insult people in the street, provoking them until they stripped off their expensive outer garments to fight with him. At which point, Flood would make off with their clothes.

Flood and Will the Sailor soon quarrelled, however, and Flood resumed his partnership with Richard Oakey. Oakey had parted from Big Sal and was now a member of Jonathan Wild's gang, which also included John Levey and Joseph Blake, known as Blueskin. One day, Oakey, Levey, Flood and Blake stopped a Mr Kneebone and robbed him of his fowling piece. News of this reached Jonathan Wild, who, deciding that he had no further use of them, acted in his thief-taker's capacity and had them arrested. With the exception of Blake, who gave evidence against the other three (later, and by different means, having his revenge on Wild), all were tried, convicted and sentenced to death.

*Newgate* reports that after conviction 'their behaviour was exceedingly proper for persons in this calamitous situation', and it particularly commends Flood, who confessed on the scaffold that what gave him more concern than all his other offences was the burning of a will he had found in a pocket cut from a lady's side, 'a circumstance,' said Flood, 'which must have proved highly detrimental to its owner.' This was thought to be a graceful admission from someone whose deeper regret might well have been his association with Wild and Blake.

**Flower, Joan** (*c*.1565–1619), witch. Flower had two daughters, Margaret and Philippa, who were employed at Belvoir Castle by Francis Manners, 6th earl of Rutland. When Margaret Flower was dismissed for pilfering, her mother Joan threatened revenge on the earl and countess. Among items stolen from the castle were gloves belonging to the earl's two young sons by his second marriage to Cecilia Hungerford. It was later alleged that one of these gloves was dipped in boiling water by Joan Flower and pierced with pins. Within a week Lord Henry Rosse, heir to the earldom, died of a fever. A glove belonging to Lord Francis Rosse, the younger brother, was then buried in a dunghill, and within weeks Lord Francis was also dead. The boys' step-sister, Katherine, the earl's daughter by his first wife, shortly began to suffer fits, but recovered. Finally, a curse was put on the earl and countess, causing them to become sterile – or so it was alleged.

Joan Flower, her two daughters and three local accomplices were arrested. Joan Flower protested her innocence and challenged her inquisitors to give her bread, declaring that if she was guilty of witchcraft it would choke her. Bread was supplied, Joan took a bite, instantly choked and died. This unexpected turn of events so unnerved the other accused women that they hastily incriminated one another. The trial of the remaining 'Witches of Belvoir' took place in 1619. The women described orgies and meetings in their covens on a hill below the castle, and spoke of imps and familiar spirits that sucked at their breasts. Philippa Flower confessed that she had often heard her mother 'curse the Earle and his lady, and thereupon would boil feathers and blood together using many devilish speeches and strange gestures'. Philippa herself was reputed to have been 'lewdly transported with love' for a man called Simpson and to have caused him to suffer from falling fits when he rejected her.

The Flower sisters and three other women were convicted and hanged at Lincoln prison on 11 March 1619. The earl of Rutland died in 1632 without further issue, and the title passed to his brother, George. His tomb in Bottesford Church bears an inscription to his 'two sonnes, both who dyed in their infancy by wicked practice and sorcerye'.

**Fluffa, delayed in Rio with a girl called.** *See* MILLER, SIR ERIC.

**flying saucers.** *See* CADDY, EILEEN AND PETER; CLANCARTY, WILLIAM FRANCIS BRINSLEY LE POER TRENCH, 8TH EARL OF; KIMBERLEY, JOHN WODEHOUSE, 4TH EARL OF; RAMPA, LOBSANG.

**Flynn, Robert** (1931– ), retired civil servant. In 1992 Flynn, a widower of Farnham in Surrey, sued the electricity board for the loss of his parrot, Lady Winchelsea. He had put the parrot in the freezer, but during a power cut she had decomposed. Flynn won the case and was awarded £200.

*See also* PARROTS.

**follies, architectural.** *See* BECKFORD, WILLIAM; BERNERS, GERALD HUGH TYRWHITT-WILSON, 14TH BARON; JAMES, EDWARD.

**foolery, tom.** *See* BROMLEY-DAVENPORT, LIEUTENANT COLONEL SIR WALTER; FAIRBAIRN, SIR NICHOLAS.

**Fordyce, George** (1736–1802), physician. Fordyce was a popular doctor, but his bedside manner was unorthodox. According to James Caulfield's *Portraits of Remarkable Persons* (1794), he was once called to the sick bed of a titled lady when he had had too much to drink. His condition made it impossible for him to take her pulse since his own was so unsteady. Frustrated, he admonished himself, muttering, 'Drunk, by Jove!' and left. The next day he was again summoned to her bedside and, fearing that he would be reprimanded for his condition on the previous occasion, he went in some trepidation. He was greatly relieved when she begged him to forgive her, confessed that his diagnosis had been correct, gave him £100 and promised that she would never touch alcohol again.

Fordyce's study of the eating habits of lions convinced him that one meal a day was enough for anyone. Accordingly, for 20 years he followed a routine that never changed. At 4 o'clock every afternoon he went to Dolly's Chop House in Paternoster Row where he ordered a one-and-a-half-pound rump steak. While this was being prepared he enjoyed an appetizer of half a chicken and a plate of boned fish. With his meal, he drank a tankard of ale, a quarter pint of brandy and a bottle of port. After leaving Dolly's he went to three coffee houses, one after another, drinking a large brandy at each, before setting out on his medical rounds. He died of gout at the age of 66.

**foreigners 'talking all kinds of gibberish'.** *See* SIBTHORP, COLONEL CHARLES DE LAET WALDO.

**Foreman, Freddie** (1932– ), publican, armed robber, gangster and author. When Century, once a serious publishing house now conglomerated, added *Respect* (1995), the memoirs of Freddie Foreman, to their thriving celebrity gangster list, they marked the occasion with a reception at the Café Royal in London. This was attended by all the leading figures in the associated worlds of crime and letters, with the exception of Foreman's fellow author, Frankie FRASER, who was detained in discussions at the Groucho Club concerning the sale of the film rights in his own memoirs, *Mad Frank* (1994). Fraser was represented by his fiancée, Miss Marilyn Wisbey, the cabaret singer, and daughter of Tommy Wisbey, the Great Train Robber. Miss Wisbey is Foreman's goddaughter and, as a child, was taken on caravan holidays by Foreman, who financed these outings by armed robberies on the way.

Century's party was a fitting tribute to a man who has been centrally involved in most of the serious crimes of the last 40 years, and whose sit-down with the ADAMS family in 1998 suggested that he was still a major figure in London's underworld.

Known as 'the Mean Machine', Foreman is rumoured to have been involved in some capacity in the Great Train Robbery of 1963 – rumours that he has been at no great pains to deny. It is generally supposed, and admitted by Foreman, that he avoided arrest in this connection thanks to a long-standing relationship with Detective Superintendent Frank Williams, second-in-command of the Flying Squad under Detective Chief Superintendent Tommy BUTLER. Within days of the robbery a hold-all containing £60,000 in cash from the proceeds was found in a south London telephone kiosk. This had been put there by Foreman, on his own admission, as a 'drink' for Williams. Williams had second thoughts and handed the money in, but Foreman was never arrested. In November 2000 it emerged that it was Foreman who had organized Ronnie BIGGS's escape from Wandsworth prison and thereafter effected his passage to Australia.

In 1968 Foreman was found not guilty of murdering Frank MITCHELL, who had been sprung from Dartmoor by the KRAYS but had thereafter become an embarrassment to them. He has revealed in his memoirs, however, that it was indeed he and Alfie Gerrard who shot Mitchell in the back of a transit van. In a later, but related, trial he received ten years for disposing of the body of Jack 'The Hat' McVitie (*see* KRAY, REGGIE and RONNIE) after the latter had been stabbed to death by Reggie Kray.

In April 1983 Foreman was one of six masked robbers who broke into the Security Express Headquarters in Curtain Road, Shoreditch (known as Fort Knox since it was thought to be impregnable), tied up the guards and departed with £7 million. Underwriters offered £500,000 as a reward for information, and this led to the arrest of one of the gang, Allen Opiola. Opiola turned queen's evidence and in June 1985 John Knight received 22 years for the robbery and his brother James 8 years. Foreman shortly surfaced in a comfortable villa on Spain's Costa del Sol, where he was a near neighbour of a third brother, Ronnie KNIGHT. After five pleasant years relaxing in the sun, Foreman was arrested and brought back to England. In 1990 he received a nine-year sentence for handling money from the Security Express robbery.

The disappearance, and assumed murder, in January 1965 of a small-time East End thief named Ginger Marks was a long-running underworld mystery. It is now known that this too was carried out by Foreman. According to Frankie Fraser, Freddie Foreman's brother Georgie was having an affair with the wife of a thief called Jimmy Evans.

> So Jimmy goes round one day, the door's opened by George's mother. 'Georgie in?' 'I'll get him.' Georgie comes to the door. Jimmy shoots him in the bollocks.

When Freddie Foreman went after Evans, Marks happened to be with him. Evans got away but, according to Frankie Fraser, 'Ginger Marks made good incinerating material.' Many years later, Jimmy Evans named Freddie Foreman as one of three men who had shot at him and Ginger Marks from a car outside the Carpenters Arms in Cheshire Street in 1965, but on 30 October 1975 Foreman, Alfie Gerrard and Jeremiah Callaghan were acquitted of the shooting by Mr Justice Donaldson. Donaldson said:

> The problems with identification are very real. This crime is ten years old. The first time Mr Evans condescended to say it was these three men who were in the car was last year.

Outside the Old Bailey Freddie Foreman said, 'This is the end of a nightmare. Justice has been done at last.'

Foreman is still greatly respected in the underworld. In 1998 an informal coalition of south and east London gangs asked him to lead them in a war against the increasingly volatile Adams family. He is thought to have declined.

**Forman, Simon** (1552–1611), astrologer, necromancer, quack and general practitioner in all forms of hocus-pocus. Born in Quidhampton, Wiltshire, Forman studied at Magdalen College, Oxford. In 1583 he set up a lucrative practice in London, selling love potions to a fashionable clientele. Described by his enemies as a charlatan and obliged to practise outside the jurisdiction of the College of Physicians, Forman was the model on which Ben Jonson based the character of Subtle in *The Alchemist*. To add credence to his astrological predictions, Forman relied on information passed on by Anne TURNER, who conveniently combined the role of dressmaker to the court of James I with that of bawdy-house proprietor. With Mrs Turner he assisted Lady Frances HOWARD in her marital difficulties by using 'sympathetic magic', but was not involved with Turner and Lady Frances in the murder of Sir Thomas Overbury.

*See also* SEX THERAPISTS.

**Forster, James** (1933– ), lecturer in civil engineering with the Open University and instigator of an unusually persistent poison-pen crusade. In August 2001 a jury at Teesside Crown Court took four hours to find Forster guilty on three charges of sending indecent mail, four of threatening to damage property and one of incitement to burglary. He was cleared of allegations of intimidation and vandalism. These involved throwing paint bombs at pensioners and putting glue in their door locks. The verdict marked the end of a twelve-year campaign during which residents of the Yorkshire village of Manfield had been bombarded with obscene letters, leaflets and posters. Forster branded his neighbour's daughter a prostitute, alleged that the bank manager was a rapist and sent a pornographic magazine to a 13-year-old girl.

Forster's first victim was 88-year-old Molly Christian, who received three obscene letters, starting in June 1997, one of which contained a threat to drop a bomb down her chimneypot. A charge that he had thrown stones at her windows and poured glue into her door locks was dismissed. However, the letters persuaded Miss Christian to put her cottage, Meadowcroft, up for sale. The cottage was bought by Roy and Val Kellett, who moved in with their daughter Joanne, then 21. The Kelletts immediately became the target of sexually abusive letters. Miss Kellett, an accountant, was accused of being a prostitute and was sent a Christmas card showing a naked woman with a whip. Forster also sent an anonymous letter to a man in Darlington suggesting that he burgle the Kelletts' home while they were on holiday.

Forster's campaign then widened to include Eric Collin, the coordinator of the village's Neighbourhood Watch scheme, who had helped the Kellets to install a security system. As accusations and rumours mounted, Forster sent villagers anonymous letters claiming that Mr Collin had reported them to the police. The police, who had been aware of the letters since the late 1980s, arrested Forster in May 1999, when he began to harass Rona Wane, the clerk of the parish council. After receiving a letter that warned her that 'we'll be getting you', Mrs Wane discovered that her 13-year-old daughter Catherine had received a pornographic magazine with the message 'A gift from Manfield'. It was written on paper that matched a pad found by detectives at Forster's home. After his conviction Forster told the court that his various night-time forays had been to 'find a vantage point from which to observe the moons of Jupiter'. Judge David Bryant dubbed the case a most unusual one, 'the like of which we may not see again'.

**Foster, Lady Elizabeth.** *See* BRISTOL, FREDERICK WILLIAM JOHN AUGUSTUS HERVEY, 7TH MARQUESS OF.

**Foulke, William 'Fatty'** (1874–1916), soccer player. Foulke, who weighed 25 stone, is thought to have been the heaviest goalkeeper in the history of the game. On one occasion he sat down to lunch early and ate the food intended for the whole team, and for the opposition too. He wore shirts with 24-inch collars, could punch the ball from his own goal to the halfway line, and had an uncertain temper. During his career, which involved spells with Sheffield United, Chelsea and Bradford City, Foulke was involved in various disagreeable incidents. In the 1898–9 season, when playing for Sheffield United, he picked up the Liverpool centre forward, George Allan, turned him upside down and planted him head first in the mud. The resulting penalty goal altered the course of the game, and Foulke was obliged to apologize to his team-mates. In 1905, and now playing for Chelsea, he picked up a Port Vale forward and threw him into the back of the net. The referee, T.J. Homecroft, gave a penalty and said afterwards, 'I kept a reasonable distance from Foulke for the rest of the game.'

Foulke's size presented problems. He once stopped a game by inadvertently colliding with a goalpost and snapping it in two. If he was injured, six men were needed to carry him off the field since no stretcher was able to bear his weight.

**Fowler, Major Nigel** (1925– ), retired Guards officer. In October 1970, on the last night of Kenneth Tynan's erotic revue *Oh Calcutta!* at the Roundhouse Theatre, Chalk Farm, Major Fowler ran on stage during the nude finale and kissed leading actor Anthony Booth. Mr Booth is the father of

Cherie Booth, now married to the prime minister, Tony Blair. At the time of the incident Booth was the live-in lover of 'Elsie Tanner', a character in the long-running television soap opera *Coronation Street*. Major Fowler said that he had been depressed since leaving the army. 'The only job I've been offered was serving in a live-bait shop. It all got on top of me.'

**fowling piece, the case of Mr Persuade's.** *See* BRIAN, JOHN HERMAN.

**Fox, Charles James** (1749–1806), politician, gambler, alcoholic and rake. The third son of the 1st Lord Holland, Fox managed to combine a distinguished political career with a private life that was profligate even by the standards of the 18th century. While holding high office, and offering formidable opposition to his rival, William Pitt the Younger, he dissipated, through drink and gambling, one of the largest fortunes of the age. For Edmund Burke he was 'the greatest debater the world ever saw'. For his biographer, Christopher Hobhouse:

> Fox was never normal. When he did not rise above the accepted standards of conduct, he fell below them. With public gifts as great as his personal failings, he united all that makes a statesman with all that can undo a politician.

Born to position and wealth – his father had amassed a considerable fortune while occupying the office of paymaster general – Fox was educated at Eton and Oxford, where he alternated periods of serious study with longer intervals spent in whorehouses and gambling rooms. At the age of 18 he wrote to a cousin:

> I have had one pox and one clap this summer, I believe I am the most unlucky rascal in the universe.

The following summer he wrote from the south of France, describing Nice as:

> … perhaps the dullest town in the world, and what is a terrible thing, there are no whores – my poxes and claps have weakened me a good deal, but by means of the cold bath I recover apace.

At the age of 19 Fox became MP for Midhurst in Sussex. His election had presented no great difficulties since the constituency was without eligible voters. All the smallholdings were owned by a Lord Montagu, who could therefore nominate whom he wished as the town's two members of Parliament. Fox was duly 'elected' without having been burdened with the need to visit his constituency. At the time of his election he was amusing himself on a Grand Tour of Italy, where he remained for six months after Parliament had reassembled. When he at last took up his seat, he immediately gained a reputation as a brilliant speaker, and by the age of 21 he had become the youngest member of Lord North's government, first as a lord of the Admiralty and later as a commissioner of the treasury. Fox never allowed these occupations to interfere with his private life, which was marked by reckless profligacy. In the course of three years he demolished a vast fortune. In one night at Almanack's Club he lost £70,000 playing faro. He was an excellent whist player, and an expert judge of a racehorse, often returning from a day at Newmarket several thousand pounds in pocket. But ease of winning seemed to bore him. He preferred games of pure chance, like faro, where his enormous losses easily swallowed up profits accrued elsewhere.

While his elder brother remained childless, Fox's creditors were prepared to indulge the heir to Lord Holland's millions. But in 1773 disaster struck. His brother produced a son and heir. Friends, money lenders, tradesmen and servants all faced ruin themselves with the sudden destruction of Fox's credit. Lord Holland, holding himself responsible for his son's feckless spending, stepped in. He gave instructions for the sale of securities and stock 'to pay and discharge the debts of my son, the Honble. Charles James Fox, not exceeding the sum of £100,000'. Even this estimate proved inadequate. Fox's debts, by the age of 24, amounted to £140,000 – equal to £30 million today.

Fox's political career was as erratic as his private life. Impulsive, gregarious, shamelessly inconsistent and ill-groomed (according to Horace Walpole, 'his bristly black person was rarely purified by ablutions'), Fox was the exact opposite of his rival, William Pitt. In 1775 he became the implacable opponent of his mentor, Lord North, whom he had recently, and as eloquently, supported. In 1782, having destroyed North as a serious political figure, he formed an alliance with him against Pitt, even though their beliefs were diametrically opposed. It was when Pitt came to power that Fox was at his best, using his talents to modify and counterbalance his rival's policies. He was a strenuous opponent of war with post-Revolutionary France, and on Pitt's death he set in motion negotiations for a peace. He died in 1806, his corpulent frame horribly distended by a lifetime of heroic self-indulgence.

**Fox, Samantha.** *See* AITKEN, JONATHAN.

**Fox, the Old Grey** (Commander Bert Wickstead). *See* ELLUL, PHILIP; LAMBTON, ANTONY CLAUD FREDERICK.

**Fox, Winnie** (1921– ), widow. In October 1996, 75-year-old Mrs Fox of south London accidentally put her husband Dennis's ashes out for the refuse collectors. Later, she tried to become reunited with him by searching through tons of rubbish on the Putney council tip. 'I'd recognize him straight away,' she said. 'He was in a Tesco's carrier bag. Dennis was a bloke in a million.'

**fox-hunting, use of bulls and pigs in.** *See* HIRST, JEMMY.

**Franny the Spaniel.** *See* HILL, BILLY.

**Fraser, Francis ('Mad Frankie')** (1924– ), gangster, author and cabaret entertainer. Fraser's long career in crime provides a useful illustrative link between the old-style gangster (*see* DIAMOND GEEZERS) and the new (*see* ADAMS, THOMAS; DANIELS, DUANE). He first gained his unequalled reputation as a hard man when working as Billy HILL's chief enforcer in the 1950s, filled the same role a decade later for Charlie RICHARDSON's south London gang, and was shot in the head as a continuing threat by the ADAMS family in 1991.

Fellow hard men speak of him with awe. In 1964 Eric Mason, a KRAY brothers henchman, was pulled out of London's Astor Club by Fraser and had an axe planted in his head. In 1996 Mason, who survived, said, 'When Frank joined the Richardsons it was like China getting the atom bomb.' According to Mason, it was to counterbalance the threat posed by Fraser that the Krays arranged Frank MITCHELL's escape from Dartmoor in 1966. Other authorities have argued that this would have been unnecessary since most of the Richardson gang, including Fraser, had by then been arrested following the celebrated affray at MR SMITH's club in Catford. Be that as it may, Charlie Richardson himself has testified to his former associate's qualities:

> Frank was one of the most polite, mild-mannered men I've ever met, but he had a bit of a temper on him.

Since the age of 13, when he was sent to an approved school for stealing 40 cigarettes, Fraser has spent 32 years in prison or detention centres. Seemingly impervious to pain, he was moved from one prison to another as various governors found him impossible to control. After he instigated the Parkhurst prison riot of 1969 he was regularly beaten up by prison officers. In *My Manor* (1991), Charlie Richardson writes:

> Nothing ever got to Frank. He was a rock. Once when he was in prison he was in solitary for months – not unusual for Frank. Every day a group of screws would deliver his food but just before the plate was handed to him a screw would spit in it. Frank would throw the plate at him. There would be a fight. Frank would get a terrible beating. This went on for months.

Since the publication of his own widely admired memoirs, *Mad Frank* (1994), no publishing launch party has been judged a success unless attended by Fraser and his attractive fiancée, Marilyn, the daughter of Great Train Robber Tommy Wisbey. He is much in demand, too, as a theatrical entertainer, touring theatres and clubs with his one-man show, *An*

*Evening With Mad Frank.* In this he is sometimes accompanied by Miss Wisbey, who sings standards between the anecdotes. 'Stand By Your Man' and 'My Way' are particularly well received.

Success in the 'straight' world has not persuaded Fraser to betray his strict former principles. Just as he had limped into the Old Bailey's Court Number One in February 1969 to provide Ronnie Kray with a character reference – in spite of the fact that his current incapacity was the upshot of a fire fight with Kray's cousin, Richard Hart – so did he refuse to provide the police with the name of his assailant when in August 1991 the Adams family had him shot in the head outside a south London discotheque. He had quite enjoyed the incident, he said, but was surprised by the amateurish way in which it had been carried out. 'The gunman had to have been a proper mug,' Fraser has said. 'Still, it was good fun, good action, it made for a good night out.'

Those born to advantage are seldom allowed the last word. In 1996 Fraser took the wind out of the sails of a patrician fellow guest on Richard Littlejohn's television 'chat show' by observing:

> You had a better start than me. You went to Winchester, which is without argument the best school in the country – better than Eton, Westminster or St Paul's – whereas I went to Radley.

No one cared to ask him why, in that case, he was wearing an Old Wykehamist tie, given to him earlier by one of his middle-class admirers (*see* BOLLOCKS, A SILLY).

**fraud and fraudsters.** *See* ART FORGERS; CONFIDENCE TRICKSTERS; HOOLEY, ERNEST TERAH; IMPOSTORS; INSURANCE SWINDLES; LITERARY FORGERS; MILLER, SIR ERIC; MOYNIHAN, ANTONY PATRICK ANDREW CAIRNE BERKELEY, 3RD BARON; SAVUNDRA, EMILE; STONEHOUSE, JOHN.

**Free, the Reverend Edward Drax** (1755–1843), priest, academic and extortioner. A document held at Lambeth Palace lists the various complaints made against Dr Free during his ministry as rector of Sutton in Bedfordshire. These include fornication, drunkenness, lewdness and assault. He is further accused of rearing pigs in the churchyard. His ministry ended with a fire fight at the rectory, followed by a ten-day siege.

Dr Free arrived in Sutton in 1898, to the relief of the fellows of St John's College, Oxford, where as dean of arts he had made himself unpopular by various acts of rudeness, including 'violence towards the bursar'. He soon turned Sutton's All Saints Church into a place of exceptional squalor. According to one parishioner, William Hale:

> It was common to see cattle running loose and pigs rooting up the graves. Cows mingled with the mourners at my father's funeral. He

kept sheep in the church porch, which was often strewn with straw and dung.

Free believed that the ministry existed to provide him with revenue. He sold lead stripped from the church roof. He cut down trees and sold them as wood. He collected tithes due to him with startling inhumanity. When Mrs Phoebe Smith, a penniless widow, tried to bury her child, Free demanded four shillings before the service could be carried out. Mrs Smith didn't have the money, so Free relented for the time being. After the burial he followed Mrs Smith home and refused to go until he had been paid.

Though unprepossessing in appearance, Free enjoyed some success with women. Of six housekeepers employed, four became his mistress, between them producing five children, most of whom died young. However, it was not his debauchery, his assaults on church wardens with a horsewhip or his unhygienic farming techniques that caused his downfall, but his decision to pursue a vendetta against the parish's most distinguished resident, Sir Montagu Burgoyne.

Why Free picked a quarrel with Sutton's principal landowner remains unclear. In March 1817 he brought a prosecution against Sir Montagu at the Bedfordshire Lent assizes, citing an Elizabethan statute that made non-attendance in church a crime. This law had been introduced to force Catholics to attend Church of England services and seemed by now to be more or less irrelevant. Those found guilty in Elizabeth's day had been fined £20 for each month in which they had been absent from church. Accordingly, Dr Free demanded that Sir Montagu pay him the sum of £380. He produced one witness who testified that she had never seen Sir Montagu in church. This evidence was weakened when it turned out that it had been provided by one of Free's mistresses. Sir Montagu insisted in any case that it had not been possible to attend Dr Free's services since there had not been any services to attend. Alternatively, when there had been a service, Free's sermon had been a tirade of abuse directed against himself.

Sir Montagu was duly found not guilty. He died shortly after the trial, but the struggle was taken up by his uncle, also Sir Montagu. He was a more formidable opponent than his nephew had been – even advertising in London newspapers to track down women whom Free had debauched – but each time he managed to bring the rector to court on charges of immorality and lewdness, Free successfully argued that the court had no jurisdiction in this particular case. A trial finally took place in June 1829 in the Court of Arches, and Free was sentenced to be deprived from the living of Sutton and to pay the costs.

Free decided not to recognize the verdict. He barricaded himself inside the rectory with his housekeeper and a shotgun. When the archdeacon of Bedford volunteered to act as a negotiator, Free took a shot at him. It was then decided that the safest course would be to starve the rector out. After a ten-day siege, Free emerged. He took refuge in a neighbouring village, and then, since no one would take him there, he walked all the way to London.

Thereafter his circumstances became increasingly wretched. He petitioned to be reinstated as a fellow of his old Oxford college, St John's, but was turned down. In January 1839 *The Times* reported him as saying, 'I have no bed to lie on, and have been three days without food.' On 16 February 1843 he was walking in London when a wheel flew off the carriage of Mr Edward Rolls, of Rolls & Co, varnish manufacturers. Mr Rolls survived, but Dr Free was run down by the wheel. He was taken to hospital, and died of his injuries at two o'clock the following morning.

**Freestone, Verity** (1949– ), verger. In 1995 Miss Freestone, described by the *Daily Mail* as 'a large and lumpy woman', claimed that she had had a brief affair – which she had not enjoyed – with the dean of Lincoln, Dr Brandon Jackson. The dean for his part spoke of 'currents of hate and evil that have been swirling around the cathedral for centuries'. In 1989 the prime minister, Margaret Thatcher, had told Dr Jackson to 'go and sort it out and to get rid of those dreadful canons'. Within months of his arrival at Lincoln Cathedral, Jackson was hardly on speaking terms with the canons, or with the bishop, the Right Reverend Robert Hardy. At the height of the row the bishop arranged for Dr Jackson and four canons to attend group therapy sessions, but no lasting cure was effected. In March 1995 the allegation of an affair with Miss Freestone became public, and Dr Jackson went before the cathedral congregation to deny it. Canon Brian Hebblethwaite retaliated with a sermon on 'selfishness, lust and base desires'. The bishop then decided that there was enough evidence of impropriety for the case to go before a consistory court.

The trial was held in a former lunatic asylum. Miss Freestone claimed that the affair had started soon after the stresses of the job had forced her to resign as a verger. Depressed, she had turned to Dr Jackson for help. 'He put his hand under my dress and gave me a full kiss,' she said. Apparently, the dean, who was a keep-fit enthusiast, had turned up at her house in running shorts and with a bottle of wine, explaining that his wife was away. After he had told Miss Freestone that she 'had bedroom eyes', intercourse had taken place, but this had not been a success. Dr Jackson denied this version of events. He may have blown on the back of Miss Freestone's neck, he admitted, but there was nothing sexual in that. 'I did the same with the chief verger, Mr Gridley,' he said.

The defence pointed to a history of counselling and anti-depressants in Miss Freestone's past, and the court accepted Dr Jackson's claim that the allegation was 'pure fantasy'. Jackson was acquitted and Miss Freestone announced that she had lost her faith. In 1997 she was ordered by a county court to pay, at £4 a month, Dr Jackson's legal bill of £5125.71, an order with which it will take her 107 years to comply.

**freeze, ending up in a deep.** *See* OSBOURNE, COLIN 'DUKE'.

**Fuckingstone, the duchess of.** *See* SALA, GEORGE AUGUSTUS.

**funnymen, troubled.** *See* BARRYMORE, MICHAEL; STANSHALL, VIVIEN.

**furniture, inheriting one's father's.** *See* CLARK, ALAN.

# g

**gaiety of the nation.** Judged to be greatly diminished by the death of a political eccentric, lovable rogue or bar-room buffoon. *See* BERNARD, JEFFREY; BOOTHBY, ROBERT; BROMLEY-DAVENPORT, LIEUTENANT COLONEL SIR WALTER; CLARK, ALAN; FAIRBAIRN, SIR NICHOLAS; REED, OLIVER.

**Gamble, the Reverend Peter** (1920–97), priest and schoolmaster. Gamble's brief career as headmaster of the Anglo-American School in Oxfordshire ended when an outbreak of drug taking compelled him to expel more than half the pupils. Happily, he was able to secure a job as an English teacher at Harrow, where he reported that 'there are many good-looking boys'.

Having left school with no qualifications, Gamble worked first in a menial capacity on various small periodicals, but in 1940 he found himself without employment. His prospects were not helped by the fact that he had had some dealings with the British Union of Fascists, a connection which, on the outbreak of World War II, caused him to be investigated by the police. Having been cleared of Nazi sympathies he registered as a conscientious objector and was taken on as a teacher at a private school in Wimbledon. Here he was strongly attracted to a boy called Julian, who came from Belgium. Their relationship ended when Julian was old enough to join the Belgian navy.

Gamble's teaching career was interrupted when he was posted to Plymouth as a civil defence worker. One day he went absent without leave and was sentenced to a month in Exeter prison. After a stint down a coal mine in Derbyshire, he was released in 1945 to teach at Kingsholme School. Here he made a satisfactory start, but soon got into hot water for kissing the boys. This was smoothed over, and Gamble then discovered that his war service entitled him to a government education grant. Having secured admission to St Catherine's Society to read English, he was encouraged to take holy orders, in spite of the fact that he had no interest in theology and believed little of the Christian faith. This turned out to be not unusual in the Church of England, and by no means a disadvantage in its priests. Having been ordained by the bishop of Birmingham, Dr E.W. Barnes, Gamble was appointed to a curacy at Erdington. This occupied him until 1954. After a year in Paris as assistant chaplain at the embassy church, he returned to London to resume his teaching career and to renew his contacts in Soho's homosexual clubs.

After a brief stint at Milton Abbey, which he left after an argument with the headmaster, and eight years as chaplain and tutor at Millfield in Somerset, Gamble founded the Anglo-American School at Barcote Manor on the Berkshire–Oxfordshire border. It was not to be foreseen that the project would coincide with the developing drug problem among young people. By 1970 the police were showing an interest in the students' extracurricular activities, and Gamble, who, like at least two of the school's panel of patrons – Sir John Gielgud and Sir Douglas Fairbanks Jnr (*see* ARGYLL, MARGARET DUCHESS OF) – enthusiastically upheld traditional moral values, retaliated by expelling 16 out of a total of 31 pupils, thus reducing the school roll to a level at which it was no longer on a financially sound footing. The enterprise was wound up by its creditors, and some months passed before the headmaster of Harrow came to Gamble's rescue with an offer to teach A-level English and Latin. The young marquesses BRISTOL and Blandford were just two who benefited from his experience.

**gamekeepers, shooting of.** *See* ABBOTT, GEORGE.

**gamekeepers who simultaneously poach.** *See* WILD, JONATHAN.

**gangsters.** *See* ADAMS, THOMAS; ARIF, DOGAN; ARISTIDES, SUSAN MARY; BOYLE, JIMMY; DIMES, ALBERT; FOREMAN, FREDDIE; FRASER, FRANCIS ('MAD FRANKIE'); HILL, BILLY; KNIGHT, RONNIE; KRAY, REGGIE AND RONNIE; NASH, JIMMY; RICHARDSON, CHARLIE; SABINI, CHARLES; SPOT, JACK.

**Garber, Steve.** *See* EGAN, JOE.

**Garley, Rachel.** *See* STRACHEY, WILLIAM.

**Garner, Roy** (1943– ), drug dealer, armed robber and police informer. Inquiries at the highest level have never satisfactorily decided whether Garner – described by Detective Superintendent Tony Lundy as 'the most valuable informer in the history of Scotland Yard' – was working for Lundy, or Lundy for Garner. Their association lasted for 14 years, during which time Garner received approximately £500,000 for information leading to the recovery of goods or money. His success allowed him to maintain stables for trotting horses in Britain and Florida, as well as a house in Hertfordshire protected by state-of-the-art surveillance equipment. Detective Superintendent Lundy's circumstances, until ill health forced him to retire to Spain, were less ostentatious, but never less than comfortable.

Garner prospered because criminal associates who used his north London club, Elton's, as a convenient place to discuss their plans didn't recognize him as an informer. The police, in fact, were somewhat quicker to become suspicious about the nature of his relationship with Lundy. In 1974 the two men were seen together at a charity function at the Dorchester Hotel in aid of the Grand Order of Lady Ratlings. Lundy became the subject of a disciplinary investigation that divided opinion at Scotland Yard, and which was summed up by the *Sun* headline, 'BRILLIANT OR BENT?' Most damaging for Lundy was a remark by his superior, Deputy Assistant Commissioner Ron Steventon, 'It is my belief that Mr Lundy is a corrupt officer who has long exploited his relationship with Garner.'

In March 1980 silver bullion worth £3.5 million was hijacked on its way from London to Tilbury Docks. A gang of bogus traffic policemen, led by Micky Gervaise flagged down a security van and held up the guards at gunpoint. Gervaise and his accomplices were arrested within two days by Lundy, and all but £180,000 of the bullion was recovered. Garner claimed, and received, the £300,000 reward offered by the insurers. It was widely assumed that this, as well as the missing bullion, was shared between Garner and Lundy.

In 1988 Garner was arrested with Nikolaus Chrastny over the importation of 57 kilos of cocaine found in Chrastny's Harley Street apartment. Lundy was unable to help Garner on this occasion, deciding, perhaps, that their association had given rise to too much speculation. Chrastny was more fortunate. Having succeeded Garner as Lundy's chief informer, he was granted conditional bail – after urgent representations from Lundy – on the usual terms for a valuable supergrass: residence in a police station. Chrastny was taken to north Yorkshire, where his wife was allowed to give him £500 in cash for his daily needs together with the various sharp instruments he needed to practise his hobby of making model aircraft – and, indeed, to escape from police custody. Within two days, Chrastny was free and out of the country.

At Garner's trial Lundy was cross-examined *in camera* by counsel representing Customs and Excise. According to the *Observer*, which later published an account of the *in camera* part of the trial, Mr Derek Spencer QC for HM Customs accused Lundy of corruption, saying that the nature of the relationship with Garner was one of reciprocal advantage. Garner gave Lundy information to further his career and Lundy gave Garner confidential information concerning the progress of police enquiries. Lundy denied the allegation. On his conviction, Garner received a 22-year sentence for conspiracy to import cocaine. Lundy was allowed to retire on the grounds of ill health. Having vigorously defended himself in a memoir published in the *News of the World*, he moved to Spain.

**Garvie, Sheila** (1934– ), secretary, wife and murderer. In August 1968 Mrs Garvie was accused of murdering her husband, Maxwell Garvie, a prosperous farmer of Kincardineshire, Scotland. Her subsequent trial caused a sensation by reason of the many and varied sexual perversions alleged by the defendant against her victim, including trips to Amsterdam and, as a natural consequence of these, the introduction into the ménage of an Aberdeen policeman.

The couple had married in 1955 and had had three children – two daughters and a son – over the next nine years. However, Maxwell Garvie's trips to Amsterdam awakened an interest in nudism, which in turn led to his making abnormal demands on Mrs Garvie. A fellow member of his nudist club, 22-year-old Brian Tevendale, began to spend weekends at the Garvies' farm, in time introducing them to his sister, Trudy Birse, who was married to the Aberdeen policeman. She too became a frequent visitor at the farm and there was some local gossip about unconventional sexual practices. In March 1968 Sheila Garvie ran away with Tevendale to Bradford, but was persuaded by Garvie to return home.

On 14 May 1968 Garvie attended his nudist club, leaving at about 10 o'clock in the evening. It was the last time he was seen alive. On 19 May his sister Hilda Kerr reported him missing. Mrs Garvie expressed her confidence that he would turn up at the nudist club's next meeting, but when he failed to do so she too conceded that something was wrong. A search was made of local woodlands and a *Police Gazette* notice said of Garvie that he:

> … spends freely, is a heavy drinker and consumer of tranquillizers, is fond of female company but has strong homosexual tendencies. He is often in the company of young men, deals in pornographic material, is an active member of a nudist camp and is known to have visited Amsterdam.

Sheila Garvie finally admitted to her mother, Mrs Watson, that her husband was dead and that Brian Tevendale had killed him. Mrs Watson went to the police, and Tivendale was arrested and charged with the murder. Another young man, Alan Peters, a close friend of Tivendale's, was also arrested. Garvie, Tivendale and Peters were charged on 17 August 1968 with striking Max Garvie on the head with a rifle butt and shooting him. The body had been discovered in an underground tunnel at Lauriston Castle, near St Cyrus.

It was alleged at their trial that the Garvies, together with Tivendale and his sister, Mrs Birse, had indulged in a variety of sexual practices, mainly at Max Garvie's insistence. Mrs Garvie testified that she had found these disagreeable, but Mrs Birse said she 'could cope'. Apparently, Garvie liked to have sex with his wife and Mrs Birse together. On some occasions he and Tevendale tossed a coin to see who should make love to Mrs Garvie first. However, while Garvie was excited by the idea of sharing his wife with Tevendale, he objected strongly when they ran away together. On that occasion he paid to have Tevendale beaten up.

Tevendale's version of events was that he had been called to the farm by Sheila Garvie when Garvie was already dead. As usual, Garvie had been making disagreeable sexual demands, at one point telling his wife that he would shoot her unless she consented to anal intercourse. There had been a struggle for the gun, and Garvie had been shot. Tevendale claimed that he had only helped in the disposal of the body. This story contradicted that of Alan Peters, who testified that he and Tevendale had gone to the farm together, and that Tevendale had shot Garvie after Mrs Garvie had gone to bed. This was also the testimony of Mrs Garvie, who denied being 'extremely cheerful' during the three months between her husband's death and the discovery of his body.

The jury found Sheila Garvie and Brian Tevendale guilty of murder and both were sentenced to life imprisonment. Alan Peters was acquitted under the Scottish verdict of 'not proven'.

The sexual aspects of the case caused great offence in Scotland. During the trial, Trudy Birse and her husband, the Aberdeen policeman, were pursued by an angry mob and had to take refuge in the office of the *Daily Record*.

**Gascoigne, Paul** (1966– ), soccer player. Gascoigne's inebriated exploits, and habit of head-butting his first wife Sheryl when an argument was going against him, brought him much unwelcome publicity in the British press. Dubbed 'as daft as a brush' by his English team mates, he is more respected in France, where, accompanied by his ever-present Boswell, M. Cinq Estomacs, he is known as England's most lucid contemporary poet of disillusion, and where, outside Les Deux Magots in Paris, philosophy students can be found deconstructing *Que signifie Gazza? Les pensées d'un idiot savant* (1996). '*Ecoutez-moi*,' says one of the students:

> *Pensée 27: 'Quand Sheryl m'a dit que je serai un papa, j'ai chié mes pantaloons.' Naturellment, il faut dire que ça va mieux en anglais.*

It is a matter of surprise to his admirers in France – where it has been noted that his name spells 'I have suffered' in Icelandic – that *Que signifie Gazza?* has failed to find an English publisher.

**Gatacre, General William.** *See* BULLER, SIR REDVERS.

**Gaul, John** (1910–89), property dealer and murderer. Gaul first gained notoriety in October 1962 when, as chairman of a publicly quoted property company, he was fined £25,000 for living on the immoral earnings of his tenants. Through a firm called Rent and Management he had been letting accommodation to prostitutes at inflated prices, thereafter entering false rents in the company's accounts. As well as less prestigious properties, he also owned Nell Gwynn House, a luxury block of flats in Sloane Avenue, London, in which several dozen high-class call girls maintained apartments (*see* GREEN, HUGHIE).

In March 1977 Gaul's fourth wife, the model Barbara Gaul, was shot in the car park of the Black Lion Hotel in Brighton, where she had been visiting her daughter Samantha. She died eleven weeks later. On the way from the shooting the murder weapon was dropped from a car that was later traced to a breaker's yard in east London. The contract had been arranged in Norfolk with two East End brothers, Roy and Keith Edgeler. At their trial both denied that it was John Gaul who had put out the contract for which they were to be paid, but never received, £10,000.

On 3 April 1978 Gaul was arrested in Malta, where he was living comfortably on a boat, but the attempt to have him extradited failed. By 1981 it was assumed that he was safe in Malta, where he had forged strong political connections and had built and leased a 240-room hotel. A second attempt to have him extradited failed in July 1981 when a magistrate in Malta ruled that the prosecution case was weak. By April 1984 the British police had given up. Gaul was said to be ill, and medical certificates were sent to the director of public prosecutions, who ordered that the warrant be cancelled. Gaul immediately flew to Switzerland, but returned to Malta for his son Simon's wedding in September 1984. He died in Italy in September 1989.

After Gaul's death, Keith Edgeler, who was by then in Ford open prison, finally confirmed that Gaul, fearful that Barbara was about to expose his various illegal deals, had taken out the contract on her life. Although the police had offered him a deal in return for information, Edgeler had refused to talk on the basis, he told the *Sun* newspaper, that his family was in danger from a man who could have his own wife murdered.

**Gent, Bernard.** *See* KEANE, JOHN.

**'genuine fakes' for £150.** *See* DREWE, JOHN.

**George III alleged to be a bigamist.** *See* WILMOT, OLIVE.

**George IV** (1762–1830), king of Great Britain and Ireland. As a young man, George was handsome and charming. Furthermore, and unlike his philistine Hanoverian predecessors, he had a personal style and taste which found expression in the palaces he built, not least the splendid Brighton Pavilion. By his late thirties, however, a taste for gargantuan meals and heavy drinking had transformed him into the repellent creature depicted in Gillray's cartoon, 'A Voluptuary under the horrors of Digestion'. This shows George's enormous belly bursting from his breeches, his face on the verge of apoplexy. He is surrounded by empty wine bottles, unpaid bills for which an overflowing chamber pot acts as paperweight, and various patent medicines including cures for venereal disease. On George's 50th birthday in 1812, he was described by Leigh Hunt as, 'A libertine over head in debt and disgrace, a despiser of domestic ties, the companion of demi-reps, a man who has just closed half a century without a single claim on the gratitude of his country or the respect of posterity.'

In 1784, George went through a form of marriage with a Catholic widow, Maria Fitzherbert. The Reverend Robert Butt, at the time confined to the debtors' prison, agreed to perform the ceremony on condition that he was given a bishopric when George became king. Though canonically valid, the marriage was null and void under the terms of the 1772 Royal Marriages Act, hastily passed to ensure against just such an eventuality. In 1795, and in order to persuade Parliament to pay off his debts, George agreed to marry his cousin, Caroline of Brunswick. Their initial meeting was not a success. George was appalled by his bride-to-be. His first words were, 'I am not very well, pray get me a glass of brandy.' For her part, Caroline found George, 'very stout and by no means as handsome as his portrait.' The wedding itself was a farce. Throughout the ceremony, George, drunk on brandy, smirked lasciviously at his latest mistress, Lady Jersey. At the reception, he collapsed backwards into the fireplace, where he spent the night. Nine months later, however, Caroline gave birth to their only child, Charlotte. Two days after Charlotte was born, George made a will in which he bequeathed one shilling to Caroline and the rest of his estate to Maria Fitzherbert. Caroline was rumoured to be unwashed, and her favourite toy was a Chinese clockwork figure which had a repertoire of unusual sexual positions. George preferred to visit a brothel run by a Mrs Collett in Portland Place, where he liked to be whipped.

**George VI for one's husband's private secretary, mistaking the future.** *See* TYRRELL, LADY MARGARET-ANN.

**Gerrard, Lew.** *See* EGAN, JOE.

**Ghost, the Stockwell.** *See* ROBINSON, ANNE.

**Ghost Squad, Scotland Yard's.** *See* HINDS, ALFRED; SABINI, CHARLES.

**gifts, recipients of.** *See* BELCHER, HARRY; MILLER, SIR ERIC (for Bobby

Moore and Harold Wilson); POULSON, JOHN (for Reginald Maudling and George Pottinger).

**Gillis, Bernard** (1926– ), circuit judge whose lenient sentencing policy earned him the nickname 'Gillis is good for you'.
*See also* O'MAHONEY, MAURICE.

**Glasgow, James Carr-Boyle, 5th earl of** (1792–1869), breeder and owner of racehorses. Glasgow maintained the largest string of racehorses in the country, and one of the least successful. He refused to give his horses names, and was obstinately loyal to certain blood lines that had been proved useless. However, if a horse failed to come up to expectations he would have it shot on the spot. On some mornings, after a trial gallop, six or seven horses would be on their way to the knacker's yard. Since none of them had been named it was never clear whether the right ones had been shot.

Always unpredictable, the earl on one occasion fell out with one of his trainers, James Godding, over what he perceived as a tasteless remark. While escorting Glasgow on a tour of his stables, Godding pointed to one of the horses, 'That's old Volunteer. He's won 17 races and yet his owner's never seen him.' While the earl puzzled over why an owner should be so uninterested in such a successful horse, Godding added, 'He's as blind as a bat.' Glasgow was outraged and immediately removed his own string from Godding's yard.

Such sensitivity was rare. People as a rule were treated as brutally as his horses. Out hunting it sometimes amused Glasgow to select his own huntsmen as the quarry. One evening he dropped in late at the Doncaster Club and demanded a whisky. To his great indignation there was no service because the steward had retired for the night. Glasgow went upstairs and set fire to the steward's bed.

**Glenconner, Pamela Lady** (1903–88), aristocrat and charity worker. The daughter of Sir Richard Paget, the amateur scientist, and Lady Muriel Finch-Hatton, only daughter of the 12th earl of Winchilsea and Nottingham, Lady Pamela was often required to play a part in her father's experiments. On one occasion she had to throw herself off the top of a bus going at 30 mph down Park Lane. Her father's theory was that the force of air behind her would guarantee that she landed on her feet. In this he was proved correct. In another experiment he filled her ears with treacle when testing the efficiency of a sign language he had recently invented.

Sir Richard was often embarrassed by the exploits of his wife Lady Muriel, who devoted herself to rescuing English governesses stranded in Russia. Once he was asked whether they were related. 'Only by marriage,' he replied. Lady Pamela, on the other hand, dutifully carried on her mother's work and in 1961 she was elected to the Russia Company, which provided financial aid to many of those repatriated in the 1930s. She also inherited her mother's interest in the Invalid Kitchens of London, which later became Meals on Wheels, and she was a greatly admired governor of the North London Polytechnic. In the 1960s she often joined student sit-ins, and developed pneumonia as a result.

In 1935 Lady Pamela married the 2nd Baron Glenconner at a lavish ceremony in Wells Cathedral, designed by Lord Glenconner's brother Stephen Tennant, who attended the service with a tortoise in his pocket. They were divorced in 1949, and Lady Glenconner settled in London, first in Hampstead and then in Campden Hill, where she was a popular figure. She wore hats and whistled in the street.

**goalkeepers.** *See* FOULKE, WILLIAM 'FATTY'; KEECH, WILLIAM.

**goalkeepers, Welsh.** *See* MORGAN, PAUL; ROOSE, DR LEIGH RICHMOND.

**goat, the supposed relics of a saint shown to be the bones of a.** *See* BUCKLAND, FRANCIS TREVELYAN.

**goat in a first-class waiting room, milking a.** *See* DEVONSHIRE, ANDREW ROBERT BUXTON CAVENDISH, 11TH DUKE OF.

**goat's rectum, customs officers shining a torch up a.** *See* RADCLIFFE, CHARLES.

**God and his peers, last person to be tried by.** *See* DE CLIFFORD, LORD EDWARD SOUTHWELL RUSSELL.

**God as a prerequisite of club membership, necessity of formally denying the existence of.** *See* BOLD BUCKS.

**God as the spirit in the highest frequency, etc.** *See* ICKE, DAVID.

**God thanked for Queen Mary's death.** *See* NEWTON, ROBERT.

**Goddard, George** (1875–1940), policeman. In 1928 Goddard, a uniformed sergeant stationed at Vine Street police station, was detailed to clean up vice in the West End of London. Within two years, and on pay of just £6 15s a week, he had saved enough to acquire a £4000 house. It was also discovered that he had £12,000 in a bank account in Pall Mall and £500 in a safety deposit box at Selfridges.

The money represented payoffs from Kate MEYRICK, known in the

upper echelons of London society as 'Ma'. Mrs Meyrick was the celebrated proprietor of, among other establishments, the Silver Slipper Club
and the Bunch of Keys, and was later immortalized as Ma Maybrick in
Evelyn Waugh's *Brideshead Revisited* (1945). She had paid Sergeant
Goddard a regular wage in return for tip-offs about police raids – though
he denied this when he and Meyrick were charged at the Old Bailey in
1929. Goddard claimed that the size of his nest egg could be accounted for
by the fact that he was a successful gambler – £7000 had come from winnings on the turf – and an investor in the music-publishing business, which
had brought him another £5000. He had also invested in a scheme to sell
confectionery at the Wembley Exhibition in 1924, he said, and had
dabbled on the foreign-exchange market. The jury chose to doubt his story,
and he was sentenced to 18 months hard labour.

There was a curious postscript to the case. After Goddard's conviction
the commissioner of the Metropolitan Police had confiscated all his money,
claiming that it was the crown's property. In fact Goddard had been convicted of taking only £900 in bribes from Mrs Meyrick. On his release from
prison he returned to court, this time as a plaintiff, and an order was made
that a substantial part of the money be returned to him. Goddard was able
to retire to the country and live comfortably off his investments.

**Goethe, Johann Wolfgang von.** *See* HAMILTON, LADY EMMA.

**'Goldenballs' fiasco.** *See* ELWES, DOMINIC.

**Golden Goose Killing, the.** *See* KNIGHT, RONNIE.

**Golden Hand, the.** *See* MILES, LOUISA (for Sophie Bluffstein).

**Goldfinger.** *See* NOYE, KENNETH.

**goldfish bowl, unable to adjust to life in a.** *See* BEST, GEORGE;
MCAVENNIE, FRANK; YORK, SARAH MARGARET, THE DUCHESS OF.

**Goldstein, Lilian** (1898–1976), couturier and getaway driver. Goldstein, a
middle-class girl from Wembley, known later as the 'Bobbed-Haired
Bandit', was one of the few women to earn the respect of her criminal
associates in pre-war London. According to a report in the *Daily Mirror* in
June 1926:

> She dresses in a red beret and a motoring coat of the same colour, or
> in an all-green motoring outfit, and she is believed to be the brains
> behind recent country house raids which have netted several thou-
> sand pounds.

Goldstein's partner in these exploits was a dashing smash-and-grab thief called 'Ruby' Sparks, whose getaway driver she became in 1923. It was a dangerous occupation and one that obliged her to act in a secondary capacity as a resourceful but unqualified doctor in the field. When working, the multi-scarred Sparks carried a supply of bulldog clips in a clean handkerchief to close the cuts he received until Goldstein, a former seamstress, could stitch them up.

The police were greatly in awe of her driving skills. 'She could whiz that great long tourer about with the skill of an artist,' recalled Detective Inspector 'Nutty' Sharpe. 'Her trouble was, she ought to have been a boy.' Goldstein would have regarded the latter judgement as a compliment. She took great offence when DI Sharpe greeted her in a Soho pub with a cheery, 'Hullo, doll!'

In 1927 Goldstein and Sparks were arrested and charged with robbery. She was acquitted, but he received a three-year sentence. Other arrests followed and in 1939 he was jailed for five years. He escaped from Dartmoor and hid out in Goldstein's flat in Wembley Park. She was sentenced to six months for harbouring him, but served only three weeks after a sympathetic judge decided that she had 'acted from her womanly duties'. 'I can understand the human element in this case,' his lordship said:

> To the rest of the world the man Sparks was an escaped convict, but that was not how she viewed him.

On his release Sparks repaid Goldstein's loyalty by marrying a respectable woman called Anne, with whom he ran an ice-cream business. After World War II he opened the Penguin Club in Regent Street, where the waitresses dressed as musical-comedy sailors. Goldstein retired too. 'I've had enough of this bandit lark,' she said. She never married.

**Good Fairy Fuck, the.** *See* SALA, GEORGE AUGUSTUS.

**Goodman, Arnold.** *See* BOOTHBY, ROBERT; NEWTON, ARTHUR.

**Goodpasture's syndrome.** *See* BARBER, SUSAN.

**Goody, Gordon** (1932– ), hairdresser and thief. With Bruce REYNOLDS, Goody led the gang that pulled off two of the most audacious robberies of the 20th century: the London Airport Bullion Robbery in 1962, and the Great Train Robbery in 1963. Peta Fordham suggests in her book *The Robbers' Tale* that the first job was undertaken to finance the second. Familiar names taking part on both occasions included Charlie Wilson, Roy 'The Weasel' James, Jimmy White and Buster Edwards. Wilson was the victim of a gangland execution in Marbella in April 1990, and Buster Edwards was impersonated by the pop star Phil Collins in the film *Buster* (1992).

The London Airport Bullion Robbery was first suggested by Charlie Wilson. He had become friendly with an employee at Comet House, London Airport, who was able to tell him about the movement of wages for the staff of BOAC. On 27 November 1962 Goody and his team, disguised as City businessmen in bowler hats and false moustaches, walked into Comet House, coshed the guards and walked out with over £250,000. Within hours Wilson, Goody, James and another man were arrested. An identification parade was held, with the suspects wearing bowler hats and false moustaches. James wasn't picked out, but Goody and Wilson were charged with the robbery.

With the Great Train Robbery only months away, considerable sums of money changed hands to ensure that they would be acquitted when they appeared at the Old Bailey. Three jurors were bribed, and a senior detective was persuaded to change his evidence. In August 1963 Goody led the team that stopped the Glasgow-to-London train and stole mailbags worth an estimated £2.5 million. He was one of the first to be arrested and was sentenced to 30 years in prison.

*See also* FIELD, BRIAN.

**goose and turkey races.** *See* HANGER, GEORGE.

**Gordon, Claire.** *See* FINNEY, EMILY.

**Gordon, Lord George** (1742–94), aristocrat, orator and anti-Catholic agitator. Lord George was the son of Cosmo George, 3rd duke of Gordon, and a distant relation of Lord BYRON via his 16th-century ancestor, the 2nd earl of Huntly. His career began at Eton and ended with a spell of genteel imprisonment in Newgate jail. In between, his sectarian rabble-rousing triggered a spasm of violence that gripped London for six days during the summer of 1780 and represented 18th-century England's worst breakdown of law and order.

Early signs of family instability may be evident in the behaviour of Gordon's mother, who twice rode down an Edinburgh street on a pig. On the death of her husband she conceived a passion for King Stanislav of Poland. She invited him to tea, although they had never met, and arranged that Lord George Gordon, aged 8, should be present dressed as Cupid. When the king arrived, Lord George shot him in the eye with a silver arrow.

After Eton, Lord George became a midshipman in the navy, where he antagonized his peers by opposing the conditions under which ratings lived and by arguing for the more meritocratic society he had encountered on a visit to America. As member of Parliament for the pocket borough of Ludgershall from 1774, he was conspicuous for his indiscriminate and hysterical attacks on both Whigs and Tories. But it was religion that, in the words of one commentator, gave him 'a twist in his head, a certain whirligig which ran away with him'.

On returning to Scotland in 1779 Lord George was taken up by various Protestant associations founded to oppose the Catholic Relief Act passed by Parliament in 1778. Here was a cause to which Lord George could enthusiastically commit himself. His language and actions became increasingly immoderate. 'I have 20,000 men at my back,' he declared, 'convinced that the king is a Papist.' In 1780 he gave notice that he would present to Parliament the Petition of the Protestant Association against religious tolerance of Roman Catholics. He then announced that he would not present the petition unless accompanied by a demonstration of 20,000 men. Instead of the anticipated 20,000, no fewer than 60,000 marchers gathered on 2 June in St George's Fields (now the site of Waterloo Station), and by the time they reached Westminster their ranks had been swollen by criminal elements.

Worried by the size of the crowd, Parliament refused to consider Gordon's petition. Gordon gave orders to the marchers to stop all unpopular members of the House of Lords and to demand that they shout 'No Popery!' twice before allowing them to proceed. Lord Bathurst, lord president of the council, was pulled from his carriage and jeered at for being 'the Pope and a silly old woman', while Lord Mansfield, the lord chief justice, had his hat knocked off. But events swiftly turned from pantomime to mayhem. The mob embarked on a comprehensive programme of destruction, attacking and destroying Catholic chapels and private houses and launching repeated assaults on the Bank of England. The intervention of the army on 7 June left 285 rioters dead and 173 wounded. Many more may have died – shot by the troops, crushed by falling debris or burned alive as they lay stupefied with looted liquor. The 'Gordon Riots', as they came to be known, provided a dramatic backdrop for Charles Dickens's novel *Barnaby Rudge* (1841).

Lord George was arrested under the Tumultuous Petitioning Act and locked in the Tower. Charged with high treason, he owed his acquittal to the masterly efforts of his defence counsel, Thomas Erskine. Apparently unchastened, Lord George continued on his release to court legal controversy. In 1782 his refusal to come forward as a witness in an ecclesiastical dispute led to his excommunication for contempt of court by the archbishop of Canterbury. The following year he was convicted of publishing a libel against Marie Antoinette and the French ambassador in London. This included the claim that the pope had sent two French Jesuits to London to poison him. Gordon fled to Holland to escape imprisonment, but on French representations was ordered to return to England. Sentenced to five years in prison, he was able to buy his own room and to employ two maidservants. He received numerous visitors and at dinner seldom entertained fewer than eight guests: dukes, soldiers, Italian cheese vendors, music hall singers and Polish noblemen. In 1793 he became eligible for release but was unable to find anyone willing to give surety for his good behaviour. He remained in Newgate prison until his death from a fever in 1794.

A surprising development in the mid-1780s was Gordon's conversion to Judaism. He took the name Israel Abraham Gorge Gordon and was seen in the Jewish quarter of Birmingham wearing a false beard and broad-brimmed black hat. He had been circumcised and according to the chronicler, Wraxall, 'preserved the sanguinary proofs of his having undergone the amputation'.

**Gordon Cumming, Colonel Sir William** (1854–1921), soldier. Disgraced, in the 'Baccarat Scandal' of 1890, for allegedly cheating in a game of chance, Gordon Cumming later received some sympathy owing to widespread speculation that he had been deliberately 'framed' by his friend, the prince of Wales (later EDWARD VII) in a dispute over a woman.

On 8 September 1890 the prince of Wales was a guest at Tranby Croft, the home of Arthur Wilson, a well-to-do Hull ship owner. By the prince's special request, Gordon Cumming, at the time a lieutenant colonel in the Scots Guards, had also been invited. After dinner the guests settled down to play baccarat – a game in which players stake money on the turn of a card and must sit with their money, or with counters representing money, in front of them. It was the son of the house, Arthur Stanley Wilson, who thought he saw Gordon Cumming surreptitiously adding a few counters to his stake after the cards had been declared in his favour. The other guests were alerted and it was decided that Gordon Cumming should be watched on the following evening to see if he cheated again. On 9 September Wilson's parents and three other guests – Lycett Green and his wife and Berkeley Levett – were all convinced that Gordon Cumming was cheating. This was serious, not because of the money involved (a mere £228) but because Gordon Cumming was there at the invitation of the prince of Wales. The first thought of his hosts was to save the prince from scandal.

Two other guests, Lord Coventry and his assistant, General Owen Williams, confronted Gordon Cumming in the smoking room and told him that he had been accused of cheating. Gordon Cumming was indignant and said, 'Do you believe a parcel of inexperienced boys?' After dinner, Coventry, Williams and the prince of Wales all confronted Gordon Cumming, who continued to insist on his innocence. Later, however, he signed a document by which, in exchange for the silence of the witnesses against him, he would undertake never again to play cards. By the next day the scandal was being openly discussed at the Doncaster races. And three weeks later, on 27 September 1890, Gordon Cumming received a letter from France saying that it was the talk of Paris and Monte Carlo. Belatedly, he decided to sue and his solicitor issued writs for slander against the Wilsons, the Lycett Greens and Berkeley Levett.

The case opened on 1 June 1891. The defence was one of justification. The prince of Wales appeared as a witness, but his evidence was inconclusive. Gordon Cumming claimed that he had signed the paper 'because it was the only way to avoid a scandal'. The judge's summing-up was against Gordon Cumming and was described by one reporter as 'polished, skilful and fiendishly unfair'. The jury took only 13 minutes to find the defendants not guilty and to award them their costs. The crowd hissed and booed the jurors, and tried to attack the defendants as they left the court. This was due less perhaps to the belief that Gordon Cumming was innocent than to dislike of the prince of Wales. The following day Gordon Cumming married his 21-year-old fiancée, an American heiress named Florence Garner, who had stood by him throughout his ordeal, and who continued to believe that her husband had been 'set up' by the prince of Wales. The Gordon Cummings spent the rest of their lives in Scotland, and were reported to have been reasonably happy.

**Gordon-Gordon, Lord** (1815–73), fraud and impostor. The real identity of one of the 19th century's most resourceful international swindlers has never been reliably established. Rumoured to have been the illegitimate son of a North Country clergyman and the family maid, Gordon-Gordon's outstanding achievement was to disprove the rule 'never promote a promoter'. In his most ambitious operation he targeted and ruined Jay Gould, the most notorious of America's 19th-century share swindlers. In the process, he fleeced the Northern Pacific Railroad and instigated a shooting war between the United States and Canada.

In 1868, as 'Lord Glencairn', Gordon-Gordon swindled the London jeweller Marshall & Son of £25,000. He then departed for America, surfacing in Minneapolis and banking Mr Marshall's £25,000 in the name of Lord Gordon-Gordon – a cousin of the Campbells, a descendant of Lochinvar and of the ancient kings of the Highlands. Officials of the North Pacific Railroad were told that he was in America to buy large tracts of land on which to settle tenants from his overpopulated Scottish estates. After three months of being royally treated by Northern Pacific, who were in urgent need of capital, Lord Gordon-Gordon departed for New York, supposedly to arrange the transfer of funds from Scotland with which to finance his intended purchase. With him he carried a letter of introduction to Jay Gould, who at the time was fighting for control of the Erie Railroad. Lord Gordon-Gordon told Gould that he could help him retain his hold on Erie since he held proxies from several Europeans who had stock in the company. With this added to his own considerable stock he could provide Gould with the margin of victory. Gould was impressed, and agreed at once to an important reciprocal stipulation: that he should present Lord Gordon-Gordon with $1 million in negotiable stock in what he called 'a pooling of interests' – in fact, a bribe.

No sooner had Lord Gordon-Gordon received the stock from Gould than he put it on the market. Realizing that he'd been swindled, Gould sued. Brought to trial in March 1873, Gordon-Gordon provided the court with the names of many European personages whom he was representing in the Erie deal. He was granted bail while these references were taken up, and promptly fled to Canada. There he managed to convince the authorities that these crude allegations brought against him by Jay Gould and the Minnesota railroaders were the result of his having refused to invest in their land. He proposed instead to buy large parts of Manitoba, investments that would bring great prosperity to Canada.

Frustrated in their attempts to force the Canadian authorities to return the Scottish swindler, Gould and his associates set off to kidnap him. They managed to seize Lord Gordon-Gordon in a dawn swoop, but were apprehended by the Northwest Mounted Police as they returned across the border into the United States. The kidnappers, who included in their number two future governors of Minnesota and three future congressmen, were thrown into prison and refused bail.

The affair then took on the proportions of an international incident. The governor of Minnesota demanded the return of the kidnappers and put the state militia on full readiness. Minnesotans in their thousands volunteered for a full military invasion of Canada. Finally, after protracted negotiations between the United States and Canada, the kidnappers were freed on bail. Gordon-Gordon was safe for the time being since under existing treaties the crimes of embezzlement and grand larceny were not thought serious enough to warrant extradition. It was his misfortune, however, that news of the incident received wide coverage in the European press. The jewellery firm Marshall & Son sent a representative to Canada where he readily identified Lord Gordon-Gordon as the missing 'Lord Glencairn'. Gordon-Gordon again pleaded a smear campaign by Jay Gould and his disappointed associates, but lost the argument and was sentenced to deportation. He threw a lavish farewell party in his hotel room, sent his guests home with expensive presents, and shot himself dead.

**Gow, John** (c.1695–1729), pirate. Contemporary accounts suggest that Gow was one of the less competent pirates of his day, entirely lacking that degree of ruthlessness necessary for success (as demonstrated, for example, by Anne BONNY). In the end he allowed himself to be taken by Mr Fea, a former school friend, the latter receiving some assistance from a Mrs Honeyman.

Even before this debacle Gow had been in constant dispute with his second-in-command, Williams, about the proper way to dispose of difficult crew members. Williams, who liked to shoot his shipmates and throw them overboard, was confused by Gow's leniency in this regard, and with reason. At their eventual trial, Williams was able to point out that those about to give evidence against them would not be there to do so had they been tied back to back and tossed into the sea.

Born in the Orkney Islands, Gow studied maritime affairs, in a short time becoming so expert that he was appointed mate of a ship sailing to Santa Cruz. Conditions were bad and a mutiny took place, in the course of which the captain ordered Gow to open fire on the crew. Gow, who had already decided to turn pirate, refused. The captain was killed and Gow was appointed in his place. His first mistake was to make Williams his second-in-command; his next was to spare the lives of those who had preferred not to join the insurrection. Nor was their first capture, a Scottish ship bound for Italy, much of a prize, since its cargo was pickled herrings, when water, which was in short supply, was what they needed. The next day, they saw a French ship bearing towards them and Gow ordered his crew to prepare for a fight. Then, seeing that it was armed with 32 guns and seemed to be proportionately crewed, Gow decided not to engage it. One of his arguments was that they already had more prisoners than they could easily accommodate, at which Williams suggested that the captive Scots and their pickled herrings be brought up singly, have their throats cut and their bodies thrown overboard. When Gow said that too much blood had been spilt already, Williams called him a coward and drew his pistol. Before he could fire, two other pirates shot him in the arm and leg, without either bullet killing him. The next day Gow successfully engaged a ship bound for Bristol, laden with everything his crew needed by way of provisions. Its capture also solved the problem of what to do with Williams. Having helped themselves to the necessary stores, Gow and his men put Williams on board the Bristol ship and ordered the captain to hand him over to the authorities on reaching England.

Further successful engagements followed, at which point Gow decided to sail to the Orkney Isles, where they would be able to sell their booty and retire – in execution of which ambition his former school friend, Mr Fea, would be of great assistance. Having arrived at the Orkneys, and while lying at anchor out to sea, one of the pressed men whose lives had been spared by Gow managed to escape ashore, thereafter making his way to Edinburgh, where he alerted the authorities to the pirates' whereabouts. A message was sent to Mr Fea, who, apart from his neighbour, Mrs Honeyman, was the only resident in that part of the Orkney Isles. Once alerted, Mr Fea was able to make his dispositions before the pirates landed. Obliged to come ashore six at a time because they had only one rowing boat, the first party of pirates called by mistake on Mrs Honeyman, who locked them in her front room while she hurried round to Mr Fea's. When the next six pirates rowed ashore, Mr Fea was waiting for them behind a hedge. He tied them up, stuffed silk scarves into their mouths and stored them one on top of another in a ditch. Once Mr Fea had secured all 28 pirates – including his school friend Gow – he sent word to Edinburgh requesting that constables should be dispatched to escort his prisoners to the city.

Gow and his men were taken from Edinburgh to London by means of the frigate *Greyhound*, and then to the Marshalsea prison. Here they met up again with Williams, who:

> ...though certain of coming to an ignominious end, took a malignant pleasure in seeing his companions in like circumstances of calamity.

Tried at the Old Bailey, Gow, Williams and six others were sentenced to death. In a remarkable act of courage, Gow had refused to plead, in consequence of which he was sentenced to death under pressure. His reason for refusing was that he had an estate which he wanted to pass on to a relation – an inheritance which, under the law, would only become due if he was pressed to death rather than hanged.

**Grace, Dr W(illiam) G(ilbert)** (1848–1915), physician and cricketer. With his towering frame and full black beard, Grace was a commanding figure on the cricket field, dominating the opposition as much by his personality as by his batting and bowling skills. He invented 'sledging' – offering the other side's batsmen advice on technique from his intimidating fielding position at silly mid-on, but never resorting to the lewd offensiveness practised later by Australian cricketers and others. When batting he employed an affable form of gamesmanship. If clean-bowled, Grace had various ways of avoiding the walk back to the pavilion. Skittled once by Spofforth, he replaced the bails and remarked that there was an unusually strong wind for the time of year. 'Carry on, Spofforth,' he commanded. When given out lbw he generally refused to leave the field, pointing out that the spectators had come to see him bat, not to see the umpire putting an officious interpretation on his duties.

Leading his team off the field one day, Grace fell into conversation with one of the umpires, who remarked that the opposition batsman had edged the last ball to the wicketkeeper. 'You should have appealed,' he said. Grace said nothing. Once the teams had taken up their positions on the following day, Grace bellowed, 'How's that?' The umpire was obliged to give the batsman out.

When Grace died, his obituarist in *The Times* pointed out that although he had captained the Gentlemen against the Players on many occasions he was not in fact a gentleman himself. The judgement was not based on his behaviour on the field but arose from his membership, as a doctor, of the professional classes.

**Gracie Fields of the psychic world, the.** *See* STOKES, DORIS.

**Graham, James** (1745–94), sex therapist. Graham was one of the most inventive quacks in the history of British medicine. The son of a Scottish saddler, he studied at Edinburgh University but contrary to his own claims never graduated. After a spell in America, where he was subsidized by Shelley's grandfather and became an enthusiast for medical electricity, he settled in Bath. Here he was patronized by Georgiana, duchess of Devonshire, and by the historian and essayist Catherine Macaulay, who married Graham's brother.

In 1779 Graham moved to London, where he opened his 'Temple of Health' at the fashionable Adelphi, off the Strand. Here he unveiled his 'Celestial Bed', hired out at £50 a night as a specific against impotence, and advertised as offering 'a superior ecstasy never before experienced: the barren must certainly become fruitful when powerfully agitated in the delights of love'. He was assisted in his demonstrations by a *tableau plastique* of young women described as 'the rosy, athletic and truly gigantic Goddesses of Health and of Hymen', an erotic ensemble in which for a short time Amy Lyons, later Emma HAMILTON, played a part. Graham also preached the omnicurative properties of mud, burying himself naked and, fakir-like, fasting for days on end.

More people turned up to gawp than to participate. Henry Angelo, the gossip writer and fencing master, remembered:

> … the carriages drawing up outside this modern Paphos with crowds of gaping sparks hoping to discover who were the visitors, but the ladies' faces were covered, all incognito.

Graham's citing of onanism as the cause of most evils may have disappointed many potential clients:

> I assure the young of both sexes that any seminal emission out of nature's road is an earthquake, a blast, a paralytic stroke enfeebling mind and memory. This infernal, all blasting practice of self-pollution is the aggregate of all vices and curses, bound up in one diabolical bundle.

Graham himself became increasingly irrational, turning, as a contemporary put it, into 'a vaudeville Messiah'. His latter-day Christian behaviour – undressing in the street and giving his clothes to the poor – persuaded some people to call him mad. He died suddenly in Edinburgh, at the age of 49.

For references to some of Graham's professional colleagues through the ages, *see* QUACKS and SEX THERAPISTS.

**grandfather clocks, embalmed bodies in.** *See* BESWICK, HANNAH.

**Gray, Arthur** (1692–?), manservant. The alleged ravishing of Griselda

Murray by a footman was one of the great scandals of its time, and a cause of much salacious society gossip. In 1734 Murray, a noted beauty and a former lady-in-waiting to Queen Caroline, was staying at the house of her father, George Baillie, as was her custom when visiting London. In the middle of the night Gray burst into her room brandishing a sword, which he admitted he had brought with him to 'put her in fear and force her to comply'. At Gray's trial Murray testified that Gray cried:

> Madam, I mean to ravish ye, for I have entertained a violent love for you a long time, but as there is so great a difference betwixt your fortune and mine, I despair of enjoying my wishes by any means but force.

She allegedly spent an hour begging him not to hurt her, but he said:

> No, I have ventured my life for your sake already, and therefore am resolutely bent to go through with my design, let the consequence be what it will – all the rest of the family are asleep, and if I lose this opportunity, I can never expect another.

With that he pulled aside the bedclothes, but in the struggle that followed she was able to alert her parents, and was rescued.

Gray was convicted and sentenced to death, but Griselda Murray procured a pardon for him, thus causing much amusement among her friends, including Lady Mary Wortley Montagu and Lord John Hervey of Ickworth, dubbed 'Lord Fanny' by Alexander Pope on account of his effeminate manner (*see* BRISTOL, FREDERICK WILLIAM JOHN AUGUSTUS HERVEY, 7TH MARQUESS OF). Lord Hervey insinuated that Griselda Murray had always belonged to a racy set and had no doubt encouraged Gray in his affections. Others speculated that Gray had fabricated his passion for Griselda in order to disguise his real motive for coming to her room, which was blackmail. He had hoped to catch her in bed with her alleged lover, the progressive Bishop Butler. Lord Hervey took it as an occasion for a spiteful poem:

> He laid his sword close by her side
> Her heart went pit-apat:
> 'You've but one weapon left,' she cried,
> 'Sure I can deal with that.'
>
> She saw her looby* frighted stand,
> Out of the bed jump'd she,
> Catch'd hold of his so furious hand
> A sight it was to see!
>
> His pistol-hand she held fast clos'd,
> As she remembers well;
> But how the other was dispos'd

There's none alive can tell.

The sword full to his heart she laid,
But yet did not him slay;
For when he saw the shining blade,
God wot, he ran away.

When she was sure the knave was gone,
Out of her father's hall
This virtuous lady straight began
Most grievously to bawl.

[* a looby is a fool or a dullard]

**Gray, Douglas** (1934– ) and **Gray, Tony** (1932– ), musicians and theatrical entertainers, trading as the Alberts. Having left the Bonzo Dog Doo-Dah Band after artistic differences, the Gray brothers were discovered by the stage director Joan Littlewood at a time when they were living in a bus parked in Chiswick and, by way of employment, were delivering the *Daily Mirror* to newsagents at night. Littlewood brought them to the attention of Peter Cook, the 1960s satirist, and he persuaded them to mount their entertainment, *An Evening of British Rubbish*, at his Establishment Club in London's Soho. Their sketches were greatly enjoyed by an audience hungry for satire. In a typical skit, Douglas played a fire-eater who drank the wrong combustible concoction, put a match to a mouthful of liquid paraffin and blew his trousers off.

In February 1963 the entertainment transferred to the Comedy Theatre, London, where it was so successful that the two brothers, who had never been inside a theatre until they performed in one, were advised not only to give up working for the *Daily Mirror* but also to form themselves into a limited company. They resisted both suggestions, the latter on the grounds that before going to prison defendants always describe themselves as 'company directors'. They continued to live in a bus and to deliver the *Daily Mirror* throughout the run of their hit show.

Their second, and last, appearance on a West End stage was in their own version of *The Three Musketeers* at the Arts Theatre in 1966. Apart from their skill as musicians (both could play a dozen or so instruments), the Alberts built all their own scenery and props. Explosives were put to many purposes. The part of d'Artagnan was taken by a Russian dancer in exploding boots. The more he danced, the more his boots exploded, and so on. One day, during rehearsals, the Alberts left their explosives unattended on a windowsill in their dressing room. It was a hot day and the sun shortly ignited several sticks of dynamite, causing all the doors to be blown off their hinges in the gentlemen's cloakroom. This was occupied at the time by the actor Stratford Johns, who had gained popularity as Sergeant, later Detective Chief Superintendent, Barlow in the television soap operas, *Z Cars* and *Softly Softly*.

The new owner of the Arts Theatre, a Mr Birtwhistle from the north of England, was lunching in the restaurant with a party of businessmen whom he hoped to tap for expansion funds. Hurrying to investigate, he ran into the auditorium and was caught in a man-sized mousetrap, which had been built to capture Cardinal Richelieu, and which the Alberts had left lying in the aisle. In spite of his business colleagues' efforts to release him, Mr Birtwhistle was held fast until the Alberts returned from lunch. They have not since mounted their act in an English theatre, but remain popular in Belgium.

**Great Beast, the.** *See* CROWLEY, ALEISTER.

**'Great' Train Robberies.** *See* AGAR, EDWARD; BIGGS, RONALD; BUTLER, DETECTIVE CHIEF SUPERINTENDENT THOMAS; FIELD, BRIAN; FOREMAN, FREDDIE; GOODY, GORDON; KEYHOE, MICKEY; REYNOLDS, BRUCE.

**Greatrakes, Valentine** (1629–83), faith healer. The son of an Englishman who had settled in Affane, County Waterford, Greatrakes had a varied early career that included service in Cromwell's army, followed after the Restoration by an early retirement during which he decided to give himself wholly to 'the study of goodness and mortification'. He also practised a little witch-hunting, on one occasion journeying to Youghal to test the imprisoned Florence Newton. Newton had supposedly bewitched a servant girl, Mary Longdon, by kissing her. As a result Mary had 'vomited up needles, pins, horsenails, stubbs, wool and straw'. The mayor of Youghal disapproved of the old-fashioned water ordeal, whereby the accused could only prove her innocence by sinking (in which case she drowned) so Greatrakes devised other methods. Newton's hands were pricked with a lance and she sat on a stool while a shoemaker busied himself – to what purpose is unclear – with his awl. The tests were judged positive, and Newton went to the stake.

In 1663 the idea came to Greatrakes that he could cure the king's evil (scrofula, once thought to be cured by the touch of a king). He kept this to himself for a while because of 'the extraddiness of it', but eventually he told his wife. Mrs Greatrakes dismissed this as 'a strange imagination'. However, convinced that God had given him the power of healing, he set up in general practice. His first patient was the commanding officer of his old regiment, Colonel Phaire. Within minutes Greatrakes had stroked away the colonel's agonizing gout. His fame spread and people came to him with their diseases from all over Ireland.

In 1666 Greatrakes toured England, where he had mixed success. In London he 'failed at Whitehall before the king and his courtiers'. Already there were those in Ireland who played down his successes, claiming that:

... his patients often relapse, he fails frequently, he can do nothing where there is any decay in nature, and many distempers are disobedient to his touch.

A doggerel ballad entitled 'Rub for Rub' accused him of taking advantage of his women patients. However, he had many admirers, among them a Mr Stubbs, whose eulogy of the Stroker, *The Miraculist Conformist*, made a comparison between Greatrakes's cures and 'those of Jesus Christ and his disciples'.

After returning to Ireland Greatrakes gave up healing, discouraged, perhaps, by the failure of his English tour, or tired of the crowds that followed wherever he went. Until his death in Affane in 1683 he lived the life of a country gentleman, though he was occasionally called in to help a neighbour. One of his last cases was a butler who was tormented by spirits. The butler was held in a room where he was kept under observation by a distinguished panel of experts that included two bishops and the earl of Orrery. In the afternoon the butler was seen to rise from the ground. In spite of the efforts of Greatrakes and another man to hold him down, 'he was carried in the air to and fro over their heads, several of the company running under him to prevent him receiving hurt if he should fall'. The butler must be considered another of Greatrakes's failures.

**Green, Hughie** (1920–97), actor, entertainer and quiz-show host. Green is best remembered as the host of *Opportunity Knocks*, a television talent show that launched the careers of many popular stars, including Peters and Lee, Little and Large and Tom O'Connor, who later made an impact as the compère of *Name That Tune*. A chef who cooked a veal dinner in under three minutes and a sailor who kept tropical fish and danced the hornpipe were less successful. In an early appearance Su Pollard, who later caught the public imagination in the situation comedy, *Hi-de-Hi*, came second to a performing dog.

Born in London to a Scottish father, Green, in contrast to an on-screen personality that some found too ingratiating, was in reality a hard-nosed businessman who continuously fought in the courts for what he took to be his interests. When the BBC refused to transfer the radio version of *Opportunity Knocks* to television, Green sued and went bankrupt. The show was taken up by ITV with great success, but Green was in trouble again in the early 1970s. His new series, *The Sky's the Limit*, was cancelled when he fell out with his producer, Jeff Yates. 'He's trying to introduce an element of sex into the show,' complained Green. 'To my shock and horror Yates said the show needed to be jazzed up and he sacked our singer, Audrey. I know she's no good but the people liked her.' Relations between Green and Yates became so strained that the series had to be abandoned. It later emerged that Green was the actual father of Yates's daughter, Paula.

A man with an unusually strong libido, Green was a frequent visitor to Nell Gwynn House in Sloane Avenue, London, where the popular call-girl Tricia Bell maintained an apartment.

By the end of the 1970s Green's performing career had gone into permanent decline. However, he kept a keen eye on broadcasting standards, continuing to lobby against what he described as 'Communist subversion on television' and to monitor the small screen for 'evil people putting over anti-British propaganda'. In 1989 he went to court again, suing the New Zealand Broadcasting Company for 'pirating' *Opportunity Knocks*. By the time he lost the case in 1990 his costs amounted to £250,000.

In November 2001 Sally Barnes, a customer-services assistant at Tesco in Brighouse, West Yorkshire, spent £2000 on cosmetic surgery to make her look less like Su Pollard.

**Green, Mary** (*c.*1650–?), quack. Mrs Green, who operated from premises in Chancery Lane and claimed to possess a licence from the archbishop of Canterbury, was one of the most resourceful alternative practitioners of her day. In the 17th century, quackery was a branch of the entertainment industry, using a broad and accessible vulgarity to describe diseases and disorders. Thus, in a bill headed *The Woman's Prophecy or the Rare and Wonderful Doctrines* (1677), Mrs Green offered to cure not only stoppage of the stomach, windy vapours and the Scotch disease, but also the 'Glimmering of the Gizzard, the Quavering of the Kidneys and the Wombling Trot'. In keeping with the slapstick nature of her claims, she sometimes advertised her services in the form of light verse. In a bill dated 1685 she offered to cure:

> The Cramp, the Stitch
> The Squirt, the Itch
> The Gout, the Stone, the Pox
> The Mulligrub
> The Bonny Scrubs
> And all Pandora's Box.

Street-corner clowning of this sort ensured Mrs Green considerable popularity, and there is little reason to suppose that her activities did any greater harm than those of more elevated performers such as the sex therapist James GRAHAM.

For further references to fellow professionals, *see* QUACKS.

**Green, Stanley** (1915–94), sandwich-board man. Green worked in the civil service before launching his campaign against the dangers of lust and protein in 1968. Armed with leaflets produced on his own press at a council flat in Northolt, he walked up and down Oxford Street for the next

25 years, explaining why the sex drive is perilously heightened by fish, meat, cheeseburgers, beans and – crucially – by sitting down. It was Green's view that if people ate less and took more exercise the world would be a better place. His own diet consisted of porridge, home-baked bread and barley water mixed with powdered milk. He had learnt from personal experience, he said, that passion can be a great torment.

Until he qualified for his bus pass in 1980, Green bicycled each day from Northolt to Oxford Street. His mission was not without its hazards. He was often arrested, and he wore green overalls as a precaution against being spat at. In spite of the dangers that were part and parcel of his mission, he held no grudges. People only attacked him, he said, because they mistook him for a religious man. He particularly liked to lecture cinema queues at the weekend, when he would remind young ladies that 'they would find it impossible to deceive their grooms that they were virgins on their wedding nights'. He also warned them against 'love play' and told passers-by that to prevent drug taking, promiscuity and vandalism they should spend more time talking to their children.

*See also* MORAL CRUSADERS.

**Gregory, Maundy** (1877–1941), actor, theatrical manager and confidence trickster. Celebrated as David LLOYD GEORGE's chief broker in the sale of honours – the method by which the prime minister hoped to furnish his National Liberal Party with much needed funds at the end of World War I – Gregory was suspected also of having committed two murders.

From an early age, Gregory's great love was the theatre – an enthusiasm he shared with his boyhood friend, Harold DAVIDSON, later notorious as the rector of Stiffkey. At Oxford Gregory practised ventriloquism and, like Davidson, recited comic monologues. Having left Oxford without a degree, he became manager in 1903 of Frank Benson's touring Shakespeare company at £5 a week, but was fired after he was discovered to have had his hand in the till. In 1908 he went into partnership with Davidson, who, through his various charitable activities, had acquired many acquaintances among the aristocracy. Realizing how vulnerable 'new money' was to snobbish instincts, Gregory launched a society magazine called *Mayfair*. Rich industrialists paid heavily for the privilege of having their photographs appear in it next to portraits of their social betters. He also set up a detective agency to establish the credit ratings of guests wishing to register at smart hotels. When World War I interrupted these activities, he put his experience as an information gatherer at the service of MI5, the British counter-intelligence and security service. He later boasted that on one occasion at a public banquet he had impersonated Winston Churchill, then first lord of the Admiralty, when Churchill was in danger of assassination.

In December 1918 Lloyd George, then prime minister at the head of a coalition government consisting mainly of Conservatives, realized that the solution to his own party's lack of funds lay in the sale of honours – knighthoods at £10,000 each and baronetcies, since they could be inherited, at £40,000. Gregory was recommended to Lloyd George by Lord Murray of Elibank, then National Liberal chief whip, as a reliable man to act as chief salesman. In order to disguise his activities, Gregory launched another magazine, *The Whitehall Gazette*, whose ostensible purpose was to fight Bolshevism. He then engaged J. Douglas Moffat, a man with previous experience in the 'honours for sale' business, to approach war profiteers who might be anxious to legitimize themselves by means of a baronetcy or peerage. A meeting would be arranged with Gregory, who in due course would receive 10% of the agreed price. Lloyd George was responsible for 91 new peers – twice the number created by his two predecessors – and Gregory was soon a very rich man.

Some writers have connected Gregory with the mysterious disappearance of Victor Grayson, the Labour member of Parliament for Colne Valley. On the evening of 8 September 1920 Grayson walked out of the Georgian restaurant in Chandos Place, London, and was never seen again. Grayson's biographer, Reg Groves, claims that Gregory's activities were about to be exposed by Grayson and that with the connivance of Lloyd George and MI5 he was lured into a trap by Gregory and killed. A more likely explanation is that Grayson contrived his own disappearance under the strain of his growing alcoholism and homosexuality.

The evidence against Gregory in the case of Edith Rosse, who was his closest friend and alibi for his own homosexual tendencies, is rather more plausible. Rosse, who had been on the stage under the name of Vivienne Pierpont, was married to Frederick Rosse, a composer and director who had been associated with Gregory in his early theatrical ventures. The three were almost inseparable, but in 1923 Rosse and his wife decided to split up. Gregory and Mrs Rosse continued to be close. Over the next few years Gregory's fortunes declined. Parliament passed the Honours (Prevention of Abuses) Act in 1925 and there were times when he was in urgent need of cash. When he asked one of his clients for payment in advance on a peerage, the man agreed but postdated the cheque and signed it with the title he had chosen. A worse blow followed when a man who had paid £30,000 in expectation of a title died before he received it and his executors asked for the return of the money. Gregory refused, but when court proceedings were threatened he averted disaster by repaying the cash in three instalments.

On 19 August 1932 Mrs Rosse complained that she felt unwell. At the time, Gregory was lunching with his friend King George of Greece, but when he received news of Mrs Rosse's indisposition he hurried from the restaurant to her bedside. The doctor had already diagnosed Bright's disease, and now, in the presence of her housekeeper and the doctor, Mrs Rosse asked for paper on which she could write her will. Gregory pulled out a menu card, on which Mrs Rosse wrote that her goods were to be left to Gregory. By 1 September Mrs Rosse seemed to have recovered and she and Gregory went for a drive. Two days later she had a relapse and died on 14 September.

Gregory then behaved in a way that was seen, retrospectively, as suspicious. With some difficulty, and at the cost of 100 guineas, he arranged for Mrs Rosse to be buried near the river at Bisham in Surrey. Having instructed the undertaker not to solder the coffin shut, he told the gravediggers to bury it a mere 18 inches below the surface.

With the £18,000 left to him by Mrs Rosse, Gregory was now able to pay off a proportion of his debts. Further cash was needed, however, and he decided that a certain Lieutenant Commander Leake RN might wish to buy an honour. Leake was approached by Gregory's scout, J. Douglas Moffat, and asked whether he would like a knighthood for £12,000. Leake said he wasn't interested, and reported the matter to Scotland Yard. On 16 February 1933 Gregory was sentenced to two months imprisonment by the Bow Street magistrate and fined £50.

When he came out of prison on 11 April he was told that the police, alerted by a niece of Mrs Rosse, had applied for permission to have her body exhumed. On the advice of certain politicians, Gregory took the first boat from Newhaven to Dieppe. Two weeks later Mrs Rosse's body was exhumed. As soon as he saw the waterlogged nature of the coffin, Dr Roche Lynch, the Home Office analyst, said, 'Not a chance.' If Mrs Rosse had been poisoned, as her niece suspected, the Thames had removed all trace of it from her body. The inquest made it clear that she had never suffered from Bright's disease, but no cause of death could be found.

Gregory retired to Paris, where he seemed never to be short of money in spite of the fact that he had been declared bankrupt. After the German invasion of France in 1940 he was taken to a civilian internment camp at Drancy. He died on 28 September 1941, aged 64.

**Grey Fox, the Old** (Commander Bert Wickstead). *See* ELLUL, PHILIP; LAMBTON, ANTONY CLAUD FREDERICK.

**Grey Owl.** *See* BELANEY, ARCHIBALD ('GREY OWL').

**Griffenburg, Madame.** *See* BALTIMORE, FREDERICK CALVERT, 6TH BARON.

**Griffiths, Dot** (1952– ), housewife and witch, who carries out her business in Milton Keynes. In former times Mrs Griffiths would have suffered trial by ordeal (*see* HOPKINS, MATTHEW; PRICKERS, SCOTTISH), being drowned if innocent and burned at the stake if guilty. In the early years of the 3rd millennium, however, she is able to practise her Wicca magic with her husband Reg untroubled by the authorities, and to pass on to her acolytes her knowledge of spells and potions. Dot also works as a part-time cleaner at the Open University.

**Griffiths, George** (1676–1700), thief. Born in Thetford, Norfolk, the son of a respectable apothecary, Griffith was articled as a young man, and at a generous salary, to a London lawyer, Arbuthnot Fraser. Thereafter, his life and misfortunes might be taken as a warning to young men of good education who, by entertaining social ambitions above their station, meet an untimely end. They should act as a warning, also, to young women who bestow their affections without regard to their parents' wishes.

At first Griffiths discharged his clerk's duties satisfactorily, but was soon tempted into the company of dissolute young men whose lifestyles and preferred recreations he couldn't hope to match. Worse, he fell in love with Fraser's daughter, and she with him. Indeed, Miss Fraser regarded him as her future husband, without telling her father of this attachment. While visiting friends in Windsor, she wrote to Griffiths every day. One of these letters was opened by her father, who, greatly shocked, summoned his daughter on her return and pointed out the grave impropriety of her conduct. She explained that Griffiths was in fact a young man of considerable private means – news which for a time mollified the old lawyer.

It soon came to light, however, that such money as Griffiths possessed had been stolen from sums held by Fraser on behalf of clients. Hoping to cover up this shortfall in the clients' account, Griffiths took advantage of his master's absence on business in Tonbridge to break into his bureau and steal all the cash it contained. On his return, Fraser missed the money, but for some reason didn't suspect Griffiths. Indeed, he now deposited some jewellery in the bureau. A few days later Griffiths, intending to spend the evening with his spendthrift young friends, broke into the bureau once again. Though disappointed not to find any money there, he nevertheless took a diamond ring, sold it to a jeweller for £12 and thereafter joined his louche companions at play. It was his misfortune that the jeweller used the same coffee house as Fraser and, on examining the ring more closely, he became suspicious that it had been illegally come by. The ring was soon identified as belonging to Fraser, and Griffiths was committed to Newgate prison. He pleaded guilty at the next sessions at the Old Bailey and was sentenced to death.

Griffiths died a penitent, and an enduring warning to young people prone to inappropriate ambitions.

**Grim Reaper, impersonating the.** *See* ELTON, GLADYS.

**Guards, the Irish.** *See* THISTLEWOOD, ARTHUR.

**guardsman found with bishop.** *See* JOCELYN, THE REVEREND PERCY.

**Guards tie, hanging oneself with one's.** *See* CORRIGAN, MICHAEL.

**Guerin, Eddie** (1860–1931), thief. Born in London, Guerin emigrated to Chicago with his parents at the age of 10. Thereafter, his international approach to crime was somewhat ahead of its time. His celebrity in the London underworld was based on the belief that having robbed American Express in Paris in 1901 he had escaped from Devil's Island in a rowing boat being obliged thereafter to eat his two companions in order to survive.

Back in Britain after his escape, Guerin tried briefly to earn a living as a tailor in Leeds, before returning to London. In April 1906 he was betrayed by Chicago May (*see* SHARPE, MAY CHURCHILL), a prostitute and former girlfriend with whom he had fallen out. He was arrested in a newsagent in Charlotte Street while reading *Le Matin* to discover whether he was still a wanted man. He succeeded in avoiding extradition to France, but was later shot outside Russell Square underground station by Chicago May and her new lover, who called himself, variously, Charlie Smith and Cubine Jackson. Smith, or Jackson, was jailed for life and Chicago May for 15 years.

Guerin's notoriety won him the admiration of Britain's criminal fraternity, many of whom became his friends. He was on good terms with Billy HILL'S sister Maggie, 'The Queen of the Forty Elephants', and was often to be seen drinking with George and Austin BIDWELL, the leading forgers of the day. In 1917 he was jailed for trying to break into the Metropole Hotel in Brighton. He was less hurt by the time in prison, he said, than by the fact that when he dropped in at the Savoy Hotel's American Bar after his release he was asked to leave as an undesirable.

By 1928 he was able, like all criminals of advanced years, to talk nostalgically of 'the good old days' and of his disappointment with 'the young thieves of today who have no skills or code of conduct' (*see* DIAMOND GEEZERS). In an interesting twist to the usual argument, he blamed the spread of education for declining standards:

> 'Honesty is the best policy' is one of the fundamental principles of the compulsory learning with which the younger generation of today are brought up. I'm afraid people like me are a dying breed.

**Gumbel, the Reverend Nicholas** (1958– ), priest. The charismatic founder of Alpha.

*See* AITKEN, JONATHAN.

**Guppy, Darius** (1961– ), socialite, insurance broker and fraudsman. Guppy, a trusted friend of Princess Diana's brother, Earl Spencer, was imprisoned for five years in 1992 for his part in a £1.8-million insurance fraud. Those who have not read his autobiography, *Roll The Dice* (1995), might dismiss him as a hedonist and chancer. In fact, as he makes clear in his memoir, he in no way fits the caricature constructed for him by the media. Despite his reputation, he disapproves of privilege in all its forms and has no time for what he calls the Royal Ascot and Henley Regatta set, whose sense of self-worth depends, he says, on little more than a mention in Nigel Dempster's *Daily Mail* gossip column. By his own account, Guppy prefers to shoot pheasants on his friends' country estates in winter and to spend the summer in agreeable company on the French Riviera.

Guppy's father, a distinguished botanist, inspired in his son a taste for the natural world – an inherited disposition that he initially tried to satisfy in the London money markets. In his memoir he writes of the stark contrast between the self-centred materialism of City entrepreneurs and his own sensitive character, the latter being best illustrated by his dealings with Muslims. Guppy has a genetic affinity with Islam. His mother's side of the family claims descent from the Prophet and his great-grandfather was the first professor of philosophy at Tehran University. *Roll The Dice* movingly reveals how profoundly Guppy was affected by the humble dignity of an Iranian shoe-shine boy who made the rounds of City firms – a lesson later reinforced by the simple probity of the many Muslims, who, like him, landed up in prison.

Disillusioned by the City's empty pursuit of wealth, Guppy left it to set up a diamond importing business. The firm soon ran into difficulties, a misfortune that he attributes not to any fault of his but to trading conditions maliciously enforced by the government, whose fraudulent incentives he admits he was naïve enough to embrace. With a close friend, Ben Marsh, he was able to stem the haemorrhage of funds by smuggling gold bullion into India in false-bottomed crates. When this venture failed, there was only one course open to him: an insurance fraud so meticulously planned and professionally executed that it would take the New York police two days to solve. In conspiring to defraud Lloyd's of London by staging a fake robbery of gems in a New York Hotel room – a pantomime that required Guppy to be trussed up as if by thieves ('a very English concept', in the somewhat patronizing opinion of the NYPD officer who investigated the crime) – Guppy, as he makes clear in *Roll The Dice*, was merely avenging the bankruptcy of his father who had been lured into becoming a Lloyd's 'name' without being acquainted with all the attendant risks.

Guppy's subsequent prison experiences – most notably his friendship with Abu Hamza, a Tae Kwon champion turned mujahid who defrauded the Department of Social Security of £10,000 and under whose influence Guppy would rise each day for morning prayers – culminated in his eventual reversion to the faith of his forefathers. Visitors to one of London's many mosques have reported Guppy's regular attendance – evidence of his new Sayyed status and his contention, persuasively advanced in his autobiography, that society offers few opportunities to those of traditional virtue. Throughout his various misfortunes Guppy has been supported by his loyal wife, Patricia, formerly a trouser presser in a Sunderland clothes factory.

**Gypsies, a 14-year-old girl hanged for being found in the company of.** *See* CAPITAL PUNISHMENT.

# h

**Hackman, the Reverend James** (1751–79), priest, soldier and murderer. On 7 April 1779 the Reverend James Hackman, vicar of Wireton in Norfolk, shot Martha Ray, the mistress of the earl of Sandwich, as she emerged from the theatre into Covent Garden. His subsequent appearance at Tyburn revived memories of another clergyman, Dr William DODD, hanged there just two years earlier. Dr Dodd had married one mistress of the earl of Sandwich; Hackman had murdered another. For journalists the two cases bore convenient similarities. One publisher was able to use the same woodcut, of a clergyman dangling at the end of a rope, to illustrate both executions.

Hackman had met Martha Ray eight years earlier at a party at Sandwich's country house in Huntingdonshire. He was a young soldier, she was a former dressmaker's assistant, already aged 35 and Sandwich's mistress for the past ten years. He fell instantly in love, but there is no evidence that she returned his feelings. Hoping to impress her he resigned from the army to take holy orders. He was appointed to the living in Wireton, and proposed to Ray in April 1779. When she rejected him he wrote a suicide note to his brother-in-law, Frederick Booth:

> When this reaches you I shall be no more. You know where
> my affections were placed; my having by some means or other
> lost hers (an idea which I could not support) has driven me to
> madness.

There is no mention in the letter of any plans to murder Ray – indeed it finishes with a request to Booth that he look after her – but that same evening, and armed with two pistols, he positioned himself outside the theatre where Ray was attending a performance of *Love in the Village*. When she came out he tugged at her cloak and as she turned he shot her in the head. He then shot himself with the other pistol, but the wound was superficial.

He tried to finish the job by striking the pistol butt repeatedly against his temple, shouting, 'Kill me! Kill me!'

Hackman was arrested and tried at the Old Bailey within a week. The public was charged one guinea to attend, and James Boswell reported in the *St James's Chronicle* that the occasion was 'one of the most remarkable that has ever occurred in the history of human nature'. He was less entertained by Hackman's execution, which took place on the following Monday. 'Saw the execution quite well,' he wrote in his journal. 'Little affected in comparison of what might have been expected.' There was little sympathy for the three protagonists elsewhere. The general feeling was that Ray and the grieving earl of Sandwich had got no more than they deserved. The *London Evening Post* wondered why the public had ever given way to a 'strange kind of sympathy, shedding tears of condolence for the vilest of men to alleviate his distress for the loss of his mistress'. *Love and Madness*, a novel by Herbert Croft based on the incident, was published in 1780 and was an immediate success.

Perhaps the most disagreeable experience was that suffered by Henry Angelo, the gossip writer and fencing master. The day after the trial he visited Surgeon's Hall where Hackman's corpse had been taken for dissection. Angelo later wrote that this had put him off pork chops for life.

**Haigh, John George** (1910–49), self-styled engineer who committed the Acid Bath Murders. In 1949 Haigh was living in a small hotel in Kensington. Here he became friendly with another resident, a wealthy 69-year-old widow, named Olive Durand-Dickson, who told him her ideas for the marketing of cosmetics. Haigh invited her to visit his factory, which was a storeroom in Crawley, Sussex. There he shot Mrs Durand-Dickson through the neck and then put her body in a drum of sulphuric acid. Later, he presented himself at Chelsea Police Station, where he reported Mrs Durand-Dickson missing. The police thought there was something odd about Haigh and they decided to visit his Sussex factory. There they found plastic dentures, identified as belonging to Mrs Durand-Dickson, and a recently fired revolver. Haigh made a statement in which he admitted eight other murders, including three members of a family called McSwan, a Dr and Mrs Henderson and three people whose identities he had never established. Tried at Lewes Assizes in July 1949, Haigh pleaded insanity. This defence failed and he was executed at Wandsworth Prison on 10 August 1949.

**hairdressers who have also worked as hangmen.** *See* ELLIS, JOHN.

**hairdressers who have carried out Great Train Robberies.** *See* BINT, PAUL; GOODY, GORDON.

**Hair** in Holland, the disappointing production of. *See* CONYERS, DAVID.

**Hall, Archibald** (1924– ), jewel thief, confidence trickster and murderer. Hall was the son of a Glasgow post-office clerk. Having spent his entire criminal career as a resourceful, but relatively harmless, fraudsman, he suddenly, and with a variety of blunt instruments, killed five people in as many months, including his brother. Signs of mental instability may have been evident in his boyhood liking for dressing up as his sister, Violet. At the age of 16 he lost his virginity to an older woman, who took him to expensive hotels for meals, thereby instilling an enduring taste for unearned luxury. His parents noticed that he seemed suddenly to have a great deal of money after he became devoted to an old lady in a neighbouring flat. When she died, thousands of pounds in cash were found in a trunk. Hall, who had made this discovery already, may have regretted not taking all of it – perhaps determining not to make this mistake again. In 1941 Hall's mother gave birth to another son, Donald, whom Archibald always disliked. Donald also became a criminal, though entirely lacking his brother's audacity and style.

In August 1941, at the age of 17, Archibald Hall was imprisoned for theft. In 1943, he received another sentence for housebreaking. A psychiatrist declared him unstable and he spent two years in a mental institution. In 1947 he moved to London, where he shortly received another two years for forging cheques and housebreaking – a sentence that could have been regarded as lenient since he had asked for 51 other offences to be taken into consideration.

In 1951 Hall obtained his first job as a butler with a well-to-do Stirlingshire couple – employment to which he was well suited since his manners were impeccable and his dress immaculate. He was an incurable fantasist, however, who saw himself as a master criminal. When his employers went on holiday, Hall discovered in their mail an invitation to a royal garden party at Holyrood Palace, Edinburgh. He hired a dress suit and drove to the occasion in his employer's Bentley. There he met a rich antiques dealer, Mrs Esta Henry, whose shop he later robbed. Having given in his notice to his former employers, he embarked on a career as a full-time confidence trickster, as a rule posing as a lord, running up large bills in hotels, cashing a substantial cheque and then vanishing. In Torquay the mayor invited him to a civic reception and allowed him to wear his gold chain of office, which subsequently disappeared.

It was a career that Hall pursued with great daring but little regard for his own safety, and in January 1956 he received sentences totalling 30 years. Allowed out of Parkhurst to attend his father's funeral, he returned to prison on time and, being judged a man of his word, was released on parole after seven years. He obtained a job as butler at a house in Mayfair, where his only criminal activity was exchanging the diamonds in a guest's jewellery for glass cut by a criminal associate. A position with the property tycoon, Sir Charles Clore, lasted for five days before Clore found out about his criminal past.

Between 1964 and 1976 Hall was in and out of prison, but in 1977 he became butler to Lady Hudson, widow of an MP, near Waterbeck in Dumfriesshire. It was a position he liked, and when an ex-convict, David Wright, came to stay the two fell out over whether Lady Hudson should be robbed. When a valuable ring disappeared, Hall accused Wright of the theft. Wright, who was drunk on Lady Hudson's champagne, jabbed Hall in the face with a rifle. Hall managed to get the rifle away from Wright, who burst into tears and went to bed. The next day Hall took Wright rabbit shooting, shot him three times in the head, dumped his body in a stream and covered it with rocks.

In September 1977 the police told Lady Hudson that her butler had a criminal record and she dismissed him. Hall went to London, where he found a job at the home of a wealthy ex-MP, Walter Travers Scott-Elliott, who was 82, and of his wife Dorothy. The house in Sloane Street was full of priceless antiques and Scott-Elliott had bank accounts all over the world. Hall realized that here was his chance to retire. In November 1977 he happened to meet a former girlfriend, Mary Coggle, in a pub in Baker Street. She was in the company of a man called Michael Kitto, who had recently absconded with £1000 from a public house in Kennington where he had worked as a barman. Hall proposed that Kitto should be his accomplice in robbing the Scott-Elliotts. Kitto would break in, so that it would seem to have been an ordinary burglary. Hall, the trusted butler, would be in the clear, biding his time before committing a major fraud.

The job was planned for 8 December 1977. Scott-Elliott took pills and was a heavy sleeper and his wife was away in a nursing-home – or so they supposed. When Hall and Kitto pushed open the door of Mrs Scott-Elliott's room they were astonished to find her in bed. Hall panicked, and when Mrs Scott-Elliott screamed he suffocated her with a pillow. The following day, Scott-Elliott was told by Hall that his wife had gone out shopping, and was then sent off to his club for lunch. Mary Coggle was then persuaded to impersonate Mrs Scott-Elliott, dressing up in her clothes, including a mink coat and a wig. That evening, Mr Scott-Elliott, befuddled with the sleeping pills that Hall had persuaded him to take earlier than usual, was put into the back seat of his car, where he mistook Mrs Coggle for his wife. The body of Mrs Scott-Elliott was in the boot. They drove north, stayed the night in a cottage Hall had rented in Cumberland and finally buried Mrs Scott-Elliott in a forest in Perthshire, covering her with leaves and bracken.

Planning now to kill Scott-Elliott, and thereafter to help themselves to the contents of his house and to his bank balance, Hall, Kitto and Coggle stayed overnight at a hotel in Perthshire and the next morning drove off with the old gentleman, who thanked the hotel staff 'for a very pleasant stay'. When Scott-Elliott, wishing to relieve himself, got out of the car on a lonely road in Glen Affric, Hall hit him over the head with the spade he had used to dig his wife's grave, and buried him too. Back in Edinburgh, an argument broke out over Mrs Scott-Elliott's mink coat. Mrs Coggle wanted to keep it; Hall thought that this might lead to their detection. When he suggested that the coat should be burned, Mrs Coggle became hysterical. Hall picked up a poker and knocked her to the ground. That night her body was dumped in a stream under a bridge on the Glasgow-to-Carlisle road.

Hall and Kitto, having sold off the contents of the Scott-Elliotts' house, then returned to the rented cottage in Cumberland, where they were joined by Hall's brother, Donald, whom Hall had always regarded as a small-time crook with perverted tastes. On top of which, Donald's curiosity about all the money he and Kitto had made him nervous. One evening Donald boasted that he could secure someone with six inches of string and offered to prove the matter. He told them to tie his thumbs behind his back then to place his feet through his hands. As Donald lay on the floor bent backwards, Hall soaked a pad with chloroform and held it over his face. He and Kitto then drowned him in the bath.

The next morning they drove back to Scotland in search of a suitable burial site. It was snowing heavily and the ground was frozen, so they booked into a hotel in North Berwick. Because they had little or no luggage, the hotel manager thought they might be planning to leave without paying, and he became still more suspicious when they asked for their drinks in the bar to be charged to their account. While they were having dinner, the manager phoned the police and asked them to check on Hall's car – a Ford Granada. This was Hall's undoing. He had switched the car's number plates and having checked with the computer the police discovered that the car with these number plates should be a Ford Escort. Hall and Kitto were taken to the local police station, where Hall went to the lavatory and escaped through a window. He was picked up later in a taxi on the way to Dunbar. By then the police had opened the boot of the Granada and found the body of Donald Hall.

Mary Coggle's body had already been found, but not identified. The Metropolitan CID were investigating the disappearance of the Scott-Elliotts. Hall and Kitto made a full confession and in 1978 were sentenced to life imprisonment at the Old Bailey.

**Hall, Newman** (1821–99), clergyman. Hall, an admired Methodist preacher in the Surrey Chapel, was involved in one of the most popular divorce cases of the 1890s. He had been married for 20 years to Charlotte Graham, a woman younger than himself, when he discovered that she had taken up with her riding master, the youthful Frank Richardson. Defiant rather than embarrassed at having been found out, Charlotte installed Richardson as a guest in the house. She sat up all night smoking with him in the kitchen and accompanied him to Brighton at a time when her husband had asked her to go with him to the Holy Land. Instead, Hall went with a Harriet Knipe, whom he had met there on a previous visit.

In 1873 Hall presented a petition alleging adultery and naming Richardson, but he then had second thoughts and the petition was withdrawn. Six years later he presented a second petition, again naming Richardson. Charlotte Hall cross-petitioned, claiming misconduct with a Mary Wyatt in Llandudno. The petition was heard by the president of the Divorce Division, Sir James Hannen, who made it clear that smoking in the kitchen with one's riding master, when combined with trips to Brighton, was clear proof of infidelity. He was offended, too, by the public gallery's obvious enjoyment of the case. 'Instead of reading the evidence in their own homes where their blushes of shame could not be seen,' protested Sir James, 'the public galleries have been thronged with women.' At least one member of the jury was as shocked as Sir James. At one point Hall's counsel, Sir Henry James, said of Mrs Hall that, 'She even refused her husband his conjugal rights.' 'Surely not!' cried the juryman.

Charlotte Hall defended her position with vigour. She admitted kissing Richardson, but denied adultery. The case was settled against her when a housemaid testified that she had seen Mrs Hall leaving Richardson's bedroom wearing only a bodice. Mary Wyatt was dropped from the case without a stain on her character, and Hall was granted his divorce. He didn't escape unscathed, however. *The Standard* suggested that:

> A middle-aged man who allows his young wife to sit up at night and smoke with her riding master may fairly be said not only to deserve but to have brought about his own disgrace and dishonour.

In the event, Hall's congregation remained loyal, presenting him with a set of psalms and a bust modelled by Onslow Ford. Charlotte Hall's behaviour, on the other hand, was compared to that of a prostitute. For Giles Playfair (*Six Studies in Hypocrisy*):

> She was, if anything rather worse, for she had not only sinned against a divine commandment but violated the earth-made contract (fidelity in return for maintenance) upon which the institution of marriage is based.

News of Hall's impending second marriage came the day after the decree absolute was granted. His fiancée was not Mary Wyatt, his companion in Llandudno, as had been expected, but Harriet Knipe, who had gone with him to the Holy Land. The marriage took place on 17 February 1880, with the infelicitous announcement by the new Mrs Hall that 'A new

stop – *Vox Angelica* – has this day been heard on the preacher's organ.'
    *See* BRIGHTON.

## Hamilton, Alexander Douglas, 10th duke of (1767–1862), Scottish

peer. The 10th duke combined in his person three dukes, two marquesses, three earls and eight barons. As such, he devoted much of his later life to planning a suitable tomb at Hamilton Palace in which to be buried. In 1852 he outbid the British Museum for a magnificent sarcophagus that had been made for an Egyptian princess. When the sarcophagus, for which he paid £11,000, arrived at Hamilton Palace, he was disappointed to discover that at 6ft 6in he was substantially taller than the princess. Attempts to lengthen the sarcophagus were unsuccessful because of the unyielding nature of the stone from which it was made. The duke suffered great anxiety over this and frequently lay down in the sarcophagus to convince himself that he would fit. To distract himself from this prevailing concern, he decided to build a mausoleum that would be an appropriate receptacle for his sarcophagus and serve as the final resting place for all the dukes of Hamilton, past and present. The mausoleum was a domed structure 120 feet high; the floor was marble inlaid with rare stones; the doors were replicas of those carved for the Baptistery in Florence; inside there was an octagonal chapel, numerous statues, the tombs of the first nine dukes, the magnificent sarcophagus of the 10th duke and room for future generations. 'What a grand sight it will be,' the 10th duke would say to guests, 'when twelve dukes of Hamilton rise together here at the Resurrection.'

Like the pharaohs of Egypt the 4th duke chose to be embalmed, and his last journey was to purchase embalming spices. On his death bed, fears that the sarcophagus would be too small returned and his last words were, 'Double me up! Double me up!' His fears were justified: his feet had to be removed and placed in the tomb separately.

The 10th duke's burial arrangements presented a difficulty for his great-grandson, the 13th duke. When his father, the 12th duke, died, the Inland Revenue invited him to find the required death duties by selling the sarcophagus that held his distinguished forebear's remains. Judging that this would be in poor taste, he counter-claimed against the Revenue and only prevailed after the case went to the House of Lords. Prior to this, in May 1941, Rudolf Hess, the Nazi deputy leader, flew to Scotland and parachuted in to the 12th duke's estate, in the mistaken belief that he would be sympathetic to a negotiated peace between the Allies and Germany.

## Hamilton, Lady Emma (1765–1815), mistress of Horatio Nelson. Her

original name was Amy Lyon. Emma's father, a blacksmith who worked for a colliery in the Wirral peninsula near Liverpool, died two months before she was born. She owed everything to her mother, who brought her to London and found her employment as a maidservant in various house-holds. Some accounts have her working as a prostitute in a high-class brothel run by Mrs Kelly in Arlington Street. She certainly stayed with Mrs Kelly for a time. In 1781, at the age of 16, Emma became the mistress of Sir Harry Featherstonehaugh, who installed her in a cottage on his estate at Uppark in Sussex. When Sir Harry tired of this arrangement he passed her on to his friend Charles Greville. Greville set her up in a house in the Edge-ware Road and paid her living expenses on condition that she remained faithful to him. For a while the highlights of Emma's life were occasional visits to the studio of George Romney, who was commissioned by Greville to paint her portrait. Romney was so impressed by her ability to take on different roles that she became his inspiration for a series of pictures in which she appeared as Ariadne, Circe, Juno, Medea and many other women from the stories of classical Greece.

Greville was fond of Emma, but he had severe financial difficulties that he could only relieve by marrying an heiress and persuading his uncle, Sir William Hamilton, to take Emma off his hands. After lengthy negotiations between uncle and nephew it was agreed that, while Greville travelled in Scotland, Emma and her mother would travel to Italy with Sir William, who was to take up the post as British minister in Naples. Emma had been at Sir William's villa overlooking the Bay of Naples for several weeks before she realized that Greville had abandoned her. At first she was inconsolable, but within months Sir William's flattering attentions lifted her spirits. She visited the theatre, she went sailing in the bay, she was painted by many of the artists who were living in the city, and she became a favoured guest at the court of the king and queen of Naples. Sir William provided her with a language master and a music teacher and encouraged her to sing in front of invited audiences. Goethe, visiting Naples in March 1787, recorded his impressions of Emma acting out a series of sketches based on the attitudes and gestures of Greek and Roman statues:

> Sir William Hamilton, after many years of devotion to the arts and the study of nature, has now found the acme of these delights in the person of an English girl of twenty with a beautiful face and a perfect figure. He has had a Greek costume made for her which becomes her extremely. Dressed in this, she lets down her hair and, with a few shawls, gives so much variety to her poses, gestures, expressions etc, that the spectator can scarcely believe his eyes. He sees what thousands of artists would have liked to express realized before him in movements and surprising transformations – standing, kneeling, sitting, reclining. Serious, sad, playful, ecstatic, contrite, alluring, threatening, anxious, one pose follows another without a break.

Emma had become Sir William's mistress in 1786, and five years later, during a visit to London, they were married. He was 60, she was 26. She had become an accomplished hostess, and was celebrated for her unusual theatrical performances, which were known as 'Lady Hamilton's attitudes'.

This was hardly the woman, however, whom Admiral Nelson met in Naples after his victory at the battle of the Nile in 1798, and with whom he thereafter conducted a very public affair. Lady Hamilton was by then 33 and had put on weight. A Swedish diplomat thought she was the fattest woman he had ever set eyes on, but admitted that she had a beautiful face. James Harris, a young English aristocrat, who first saw her when her affair with Nelson had become common knowledge, considered her to be 'without exception the most coarse, ill-mannered, disagreeable woman I ever met with'. Nevertheless, Nelson's relationship with Lady Hamilton had by February 1800 developed from one of mutual admiration to physical intimacy, and on 29 January 1801 she gave birth to twin daughters at a house in Piccadilly. Deciding that she could only cope with one child, Emma sent the other to a foundling hospital in Holborn. Nelson was told that only one baby had survived. She was christened Horatia and Nelson wrote, 'A finer child was never produced by any two persons. In truth a love-begotten child!'

Nelson's wife, the devoted Fanny Nisbet, was now frozen out of his life. After his victory over the Danish fleet at the battle of Copenhagen in 1801 she wrote:

> Let me beg you to believe that no wife ever felt greater affection for her husband than I do. What more can I do to convince you that I am truly your affectionate wife?

Nelson never replied to the letter. He and Emma took up residence at Merton Place, a country house in Surrey. Sir William, who had maintained a courteous indifference to his wife's infatuation with the naval hero, at last began to complain about Emma's lifestyle, telling her that:

> I by no means wish to live in solitary retreat, but to have seldom less than 12 to 14 at table is coming back to what was so irksome to me in Italy during the latter years of our residence in that country.

In the spring of 1803 he died in Emma's arms, with Nelson holding his hand.

After Nelson's death at Trafalgar in 1805 Lady Hamilton appeared to go into a state of shock. When a friend called to see her a week later she was still in bed and seemingly unable to cope with the extent of her loss. She had not been granted a pension and was deserted by all but a few friends. Nelson had left her Merton Place and she had an inheritance from Sir William Hamilton. She should have been able to live in reasonable comfort but was unable to alter her extravagant lifestyle. Soon she was so deep in debt that she was forced to sell Merton Place, and by the spring of 1808 she owed more than £8000. In 1813 she was arrested for debt and spent time in the King's Bench Prison in Southwark. She was drinking heavily by now and was subject to severe depression. By the summer of 1814 she decided that the only way to escape her creditors was to go abroad. She and her daughter Horatia, who was now 13, sailed for Calais. They took lodgings in the town, and Emma died there in January 1815. In 1822 Horatia married the vicar of Tenterden, in Kent. They had nine children and Horatia lived to the age of 80.

**Hamilton, Neil.** *See* BROMLEY-DAVENPORT, LIEUTENANT COLONEL SIR WALTER; PROCTOR, HARVEY.

**Hamilton, Robert** (1743–1829), scholar. A paradigm of the absent-minded academic, Hamilton was appointed professor of philosophy at Aberdeen University in 1799. At the same time, a Mr Copland was appointed to the chair of mathematics. Arriving to take up their duties on the same day, each managed, through absent-mindedness, to proceed to the other's lecture room, thereafter switching chairs, classes and students. For the next 18 years Hamilton taught mathematics, in which he had some skill, and Copland philosophy, which, to the misfortune of his pupils, was beyond him.

Hamilton's students tended to take advantage of his distracted manner, firing at him with peashooters as he wrote his equations on the blackboard. One day they went too far and let off a cracker behind his back. Hamilton, thinking he was under fire from an assassin with a gun, bolted into the corridor. When a delegation of students came out to apologise, he said, 'Gentlemen, I have no objection to the peas, but I entreat you to spare my life.' The students explained the mistake, and Hamilton returned to his equations.

**Hammond, Charles** (1854–?), male prostitute and proprietor of a brothel at 19 Cleveland Street, London. On 4 July 1886 a 17-year-old telegraph boy, Charles Swinscow, was discovered to have 18 shillings on him – a considerably larger sum than he was likely to have saved from his modest wages. Questioned by PC Hanks, Swinscow admitted that he had been recruited by Hammond to allow members of the upper class to 'have a go between my legs' in return for four shillings, and sometimes to 'put their persons into me' for a like sum. Chief Inspector Frederick Abberline applied for a warrant, but before it could be executed Hammond, posing as a clergyman, had fled to the Continent with his wife, a French prostitute known as 'Madame Caroline'.

*See also* CLARENCE, PRINCE ALBERT VICTOR, DUKE OF; NEWTON, ARTHUR.

**Hampson, Keith** (1943– ), politician. In October 1984 Dr Hampson, Tory MP for Leeds North-West, was charged at Southwark Crown Court with 'fondling the thigh' of Luscious Leon, an undercover policeman working as a table dancer at The Gay Theatre Club in Soho. The incident had arisen after Hampson, who was parliamentary private secretary to defence secretary Michael Heseltine, had downed five pints of his favourite drink, known as 'brain damage', while composing a speech for Mr Heseltine. Wishing to unwind, Hampson had later visited the club in Frith Street. There, his attention had been caught by an attractive woman standing at the bar. As Hampson moved in her direction, he had accidentally brushed the thigh of Luscious Leon. Hampson had been charged with indecent assault and escorted from the club.

Throughout the subsequent court case, Hampson denied that he was homosexual, though what difference it would have made if he had been remains unclear. This defence was supported by his wife. Confused perhaps by whether policemen have a right, for purposes of entrapment, to appear as pole dancers in homosexual cabarets, the jury failed to reach a verdict.

The attorney general, Sir Michael Havers, then announced that because of the widespread publicity already received there would not be a retrial. A verdict of not guilty was recorded.

*See also* THIN BLUE JEANS, THE.

**Hanger, George** (1751–1824), gambler, army officer and coal merchant. As a young soldier, Hanger fought numerous duels, married a gypsy and was wounded in the American War of Independence. At the age of 22 he retired from the army, thereafter devoting himself to drinking, gambling and whoring – occupations that shortly won him the friendship of the prince of Wales, later George IV. Apart from his retirement on half-pay, which didn't cover his tailor's bill, gambling was his only source of income. He would bet on anything, on one occasion laying a wager on the result of a ten-mile foot race between 20 turkeys and 20 geese. The turkeys dropped out after three miles and Hanger lost £500.

In 1798 Hanger's debts caught up with him and he was made a prisoner of the King's Bench. Refusing help from wealthy friends who were prepared to maintain him in style in a private cell, he suffered the full degradation of life in a debtors' prison. By the time his friends procured his release after 18 months by paying off his debts, he had undergone a remarkable transformation. He became a coal merchant, and far from finding his new circumstances a humiliation he delighted in embarrassing fashionable society by drawing attention to his new and inferior status. When his brother died in 1814, he officially acceded to the estates and title of Baron Coleraine, but he continued to work as a coal merchant and corrected anyone who addressed him as baron. 'Plain George Hanger, if you please,' he said. This attitude cost him the friendship of the Prince Regent, a loss that caused him no concern. By now he was happier in the company of the lower orders, on one occasion being seen by the artist J.T. Smith helping an old lady sell apples in Portland Road.

Hanger later became famous for his controversial advice to women set forth in *The Life, Adventures and Opinions of Col. George Hanger* (1801). He suggests that they should settle affairs of honour by duelling among themselves rather than involving men in their disputes. He recommends, when eloping, that they should depart through a window rather than a door, since 'this will establish you in your lover's opinion as a woman of spirit'. He applauds the fashion for loose gowns, which 'are admirably suited to conceal pregnancies or for a shop-lifter to hide a bale of goods', and he advises clergymen to supplement their income by hiring out blind men to beggar-women, who will find that a genuinely handicapped companion exerts a greater pull on the purse strings than a child or even a dog. Less controversially, he advocates a tax on Scotsmen who spend more than six months of the year south of the border.

For other coal merchants of note, *see* BRITTON, THOMAS.

**hanging, drawing and quartering.** *See* DESPARD, EDWARD MARCUS; JEFFREYS, GEORGE.

**hanging, surviving or attempting to survive a.** *See* DUELL, WILLIAM; SHEPPARD, JACK.

**hangmen.** *See* ARNETT, RICHARD; DENNIS, EDWARD; ELLIS, JOHN.

**Harcourt-Smith, Florence 'Flockie'.** *See* BACON, FRANCIS.

**hard bastards.** Not to be confused with DIAMOND GEEZERS.

**Harding, Arthur** (1886–1962), gangster and writer. In the early 1900s Harding was a major figure in the underworld and an authoritative chronicler of life in the East End of London. In 1904 he took over the Walker gang after the death of its leader, 'One-Eyed' Charlie Walker. His most respected opponents were the Titanic Mob, which Harding's gang confronted in 1908 following an argument over the protection of a coffee stall in Brick Lane. 'What they done was crafty,' Harding recalled in his memoirs:

> They set a trap for us. They were well in with the police and directly the fight started the police were there. They got hold of us – including Cooper who had a loaded gun on him. It wasn't an offence to carry a gun, but we got a week's remand for causing an affray. I

always had it in for them afterwards. I thought, 'You twisters – you always have the bogies on your side.'

The same offence was committed a few years later by a team led by Isaac Bogard, better known as the Coon. Although he was Jewish, Bogard was so dark-skinned that he was often referred to as a black man. His mob was accordingly known as the Coons. On 10 September 1911 Harding's gang, now known as the Vendettas, attacked the Coons in the Blue Coat Boy in Bishopsgate. 'We did a lot of damage,' recalls Harding. 'The Coon had a face like the map of England. I hit him with a broken glass. He was knocked about terrible.' In spite of his condition, Bogard was arrested with another man, and charged with causing an affray. When they appeared on the following Monday at Old Street Magistrates' Court they broke a cardinal rule in this milieu by asking for police protection. The ensuing drama was later described by the magistrate, Sir Charles Biron, in his autobiography *Without Prejudice* (1921):

> One morning two men were charged before me with disorderly conduct. It was a confusing case. One of them applied for police protection on the ground that there was an armed body of men waiting outside the court to murder them. I had a very shrewd suspicion that there might be something in it. I sent for the Inspector of Police and saw him in my room.
>
> 'Is this true?' I asked him.
>
> 'Yes,' he said. 'These two men, known coons, used to belong to the Harding gang. The gang regards them as deserters and attacked them this morning in the street. I arrested them for their own safety.'
>
> 'Do you mean to tell me,' I said, 'that an armed mob is waiting outside my court to murder these two coons?'
>
> 'Yes,' he said. 'That is so.'
>
> I sent for an overwhelming force of armed police, finished my work for the day and sat in my room awaiting a result. At five o'clock, the police force arrived. 'Now,', I said, 'let the two coons out.' In a second, firing began and the police surrounded the gang. There were five, all armed, and they were the most desperate characters in Hoxton led by their chief, Harding. In a few minutes they were all arrested and that day's work was the beginning of the end of what is hardly an exaggeration to call a reign of terror.

Harding sought the advice of his solicitor, Arthur Phale, whom he held in high regard. 'He was a crooked solicitor,' he wrote in his memoir. 'That is, you could trust him. Any villainy, he'd do it for you.' In spite of Arthur Phale's efforts, Harding was sentenced by Mr Justice Avory to three years for causing an affray and possession of a firearm in a court of law. Bogard recovered from his injuries, fought in World War I, won the Military Medal and ended up working for the former head of the Flying Squad, Fred 'Nutty' Sharp, who had become a bookmaker in Wandsworth.

**Harding, Sir Peter.** *See* BUCK, BIENVENIDA.

**hard men who became sculptors.** *See* BOYLE, JIMMY.

**hard men who wear old Wykehamist ties.** *See* FRASER, FRANCIS ('MAD FRANKIE').

**hard men who were hairdressers.** *See* GOODY, GORDON.

**hard rock devil music.** *See* OSBOURNE, JOHN MICHAEL ('OZZY').

**Hare, William** (1790–1860), body snatcher. With his partner William BURKE, Hare committed a series of murders in Edinburgh, selling the bodies to the anatomist Dr Robert KNOX for dissection purposes. He turned king's evidence, and died in London, a blind beggar.

**harmonium, playing 'Nearer my God to thee' on the.** *See* SMITH, GEORGE JOSEPH.

**Harris, Frank** (1856–1931), journalist, biographer and author of an extended pornographic memoir. Born in Galway, Ireland, Harris ran away to New York at the age of 15 and later studied law at the University of Kansas. On his return to England in 1876 he made an immediate impact on Fleet Street as editor of the *Saturday Review*, *Vanity Fair* and the *Evening News*. He wrote books on Shakespeare, Wilde and Shaw, but is best remembered for his lewd and unreliable autobiography, *My Life and Loves*, written in four volumes between 1923 and 1927. The first volume was printed in Germany and the text was enlivened by photographs of naked women. To evade legal difficulties, publication was ostensibly for private circulation only. Harris's friends were expected to dispose of copies for him, just as they were expected when they visited him in his retirement in the south of France to arrive with old Etonian ties and other upper-class accoutrements with which he hoped to improve his standing.

Harris's last years in Cimiez, high above Nice, were increasingly penurious. In the end he was literally on the run, chased by his creditors from lodging house to lodging house, but always correctly dressed in striped trousers, black jacket, winged collar and white spats. When funds permitted, Harris continued to consume vast meals, later evacuated by means of the stomach pump brought with him from England. At night, he pegged up his dyed black moustache and left it pegged in the morning when he sat in bed at work on his autobiography. An abiding concern was not to squander his sexual resources in the manner of General Skobelef, whom he had encountered years earlier at Plevna. Skobelef had told him that at the age of 14 he had chased every pretty girl he'd met, with the result that at 40 he was impotent. 'What a dreadful fate!' Harris had cried, and he'd resolved to husband his own stock more prudently. Now, when he retired for the night – with all his possessions packed in one case against a necessary sudden exit – he was accustomed to bind himself up to prevent nocturnal wastage. At least he could look back on his life with pride. 'Christ went deeper than I,' he admitted, 'but I have had a wider range of experience.'

**Harris, John** (*c.*1710–65), barman and publisher. Harris, who worked at the Shakespeare's Head, a Covent Garden tavern popular with sea captains, anticipated by some 200 years the publisher of *The Ladies Directory* (1960), which listed the names and telephone numbers of prostitutes and the services they provided. Harris recognized the need for just such a publication in his own day – a medium through which girls who worked from home could bring themselves to the attention of discerning naval officers and other gentlemen who might seek their company. Accordingly he listed the names of these professional women, together with their addresses and details of their physical attributes and special skills, in a variety of publications such as *The Covent Garden Magazine or Amorous Repository*, *The Man of Fashion's Companion* and *The Rangers' Magazine*. The first compilation, which was handwritten by Harris and produced in the 1740s, was so popular that in 1758 he went into print with *Harris's List of Covent Garden Ladies*, selling 8000 copies of the first edition.

Harris died in 1765, but his *Lists* continued to be updated and issued annually until the end of the century. In one copy, issued in 1788, a Miss Johnson of 17 Goodge Street is marketed gymnastically. 'She has such elasticity in her loins she can cast her lover to a pleasing height, and receive him again with the utmost dexterity'. Another entry advises readers that a Miss Corbett, also of Goodge Street, 'always measures a gentleman's *maypole* by a standard of *nine inches*, and expects a guinea for every inch it is short of full measure'. Several of the women who advertised in the slim volumes expressed a preference for sailors. Mrs Crosby, for instance, of 24 George Street, 'being particularly attached to the sons of Neptune', had married an elderly sea captain. The small annuity left to her on his death was not enough to live on so she worked as a part-time prostitute. Readers of *Harris's List* discovered that she could be contacted at home during the day and at the theatre in the evening, where she always sat in a box. She was described as having 'dark hair falling in ringlets down her back, languishing grey eyes and a tolerable complexion'. She charged one guinea for her services.

Mrs Grafton, who lived near Union Stairs in Wapping, also advertised a preference for sea officers, 'since they do not stay long at home and always return fraught with love and presents'. She was described as 'a comely woman of forty who could give more pleasure than a dozen raw girls'. She had acquired 20 years experience working as a prostitute in Portsmouth before settling in London. Against Mrs Crosby, Mrs Grafton's price was 5 shillings, which must have been attractive to most naval officers. A day's pay for the most senior captains at this time was only 20 shillings.

In October 1960 Derek Shaw, publisher of *The Ladies Directory,* was sentenced to one year in prison for conspiracy to corrupt public morals (*Shaw* 1960 QBD 421).

**Harris, Leopold** (1893–1974), insurance assessor, arsonist and swindler. Known as Leo to his distinguished City friends and as 'Chief' or 'The Prince' to his criminal associates, Harris was an expert at setting up businesses and then, for insurance purposes, burning them to the ground. A vain and extravagant man, who drove a Rolls Royce with a silver fireman as a mascot and a silver fire-engine bell mounted on the bonnet, Harris was the respected head of the family firm of assessors that he had joined on leaving school. From this position he was able to assemble a team of criminal associates, each with a part to play in a series of insurance frauds. A typical case involved the Franco-Italian Silk Company. Harris set it up pseudonymously, stocked it with goods, arranged the insurance and then set it alight. The value of the damaged stock was approximately £3000. As assessor to the company that had insured it, Harris was able to arrange a successful claim of £15,000.

When finally arrested in 1933 Harris was charged with 9 cases of arson and 13 cases of obtaining money by false pretences. It was calculated that a quarter of a million pounds had been paid out in false claims. The crucial breakthrough had come when one of the gang, an Italian called Capsoni, turned king's evidence and admitted that he had personally started four of the fires and that three others had been started by his wife. Harris and 15 other defendants were found variously guilty on 49 separate counts, and received sentences that amounted to a total of 280 years. When he was released from jail Harris rejoined the family firm and made it one of the biggest of its kind in the country. In 1972 Tom DRIBERG alleged in the House of Commons that Harris was again running a fraudulent company – an accusation that Harris vigorously denied. 'I have nothing to hide,' he told journalists. 'After my unfortunate troubles of 1933, I was welcomed back into the insurance world.'

**Harrovians.** *See* BRISTOL, FREDERICK WILLIAM JOHN AUGUSTUS HERVEY, 7TH MARQUESS OF; BYRON, GEORGE GORDON, 6TH BARON; CRADOCK, FANNY (for Johnny Cradock); HOOKE, THEODORE; KEELER, CHRISTINE (for John

Profumo); LAMBTON, LORD ANTHONY CLAUD FREDERICK; MYTTON, JOHN; RANKIN, SIR HUGH; SYMONDS, JOHN ADDINGTON.

**Hart, Christabel.** *See* AMPTHILL, JOHN RUSSELL, 3RD BARON.

**Hartley, John Thorneycroft** (1846–?), clergyman and tennis player. In 1879 Hartley, a 33-year-old vicar from north Yorkshire, reached the semi-finals of the All England men's singles championships at Wimbledon. This achievement presented him with a difficulty since the crucial match was to take place on the Monday and he was needed in Yorkshire on the Sunday to conduct the appropriate services. Immediately after his quarter-final match on the Saturday evening, Hartley set off on the 250-mile journey to his Yorkshire parish. Having discharged his duties on the Sunday, he got up at the crack of dawn on Monday and drove by horse and carriage to Thirsk to catch the train to London. The train arrived at King's Cross at 2 p.m., which left him with a 30-minute dash across London to arrive in time for his semi-final match with C.F. Parr, whom he had not previously beaten. Nor did he prevail on this occasion. Exhausted and hungry, Hartley lost 0–6 0–6 0–6 and C.F. Parr went on to win the final.

**hat, a great profit made from selling a.** *See* DANCER, DANIEL.

**hat, almost hanged for denting the king's.** *See* COLLINS, DENNIS.

**hat, hanged for stealing a.** *See* CAPITAL PUNISHMENT.

**hat called Patent Teapot, a.** *See* LOLE, WILLIAM.

**Hatfield, John** (1760–1803), impostor and confidence trickster. Hatfield was already an experienced swindler by the time he met, and bigamously married, Mary Robinson, 'the Beauty of Buttermere'. In 1792 Captain Budsworth had written about the 14-year-old daughter of an innkeeper whom he had encountered on a walking tour of the Lake District:

> Her face was a fine oval with full eyes and lips as red as vermilion … she looked an angel.

When Hatfield met Mary Robinson eight years later, she was even more beautiful and, according to William Wordsworth, unspoilt by the attention lavished on her since the publication of Budsworth's *A Fortnight's Ramble in the Lakes*. For the Romantics – including Thomas de Quincey and Samuel Coleridge as well as William and Dorothy Wordsworth – she came to represent Nature, Beauty and Innocence.

A member of a prosperous family of wool merchants, Hatfield became bored with the business and emigrated to America in the 1770s, where he married the niece of the marquess of Granby. He soon deserted her and settled in London. There, he ran up huge debts and forged drafts against friends who he knew would not have him prosecuted. When his financial difficulties became acute, he persuaded the duke of Rutland, who was related to his wife's family, to pay his debts for the sake of family honour. In 1784 he worked a number of swindles by posing as a relative of the viceroy of India, and once again the duke of Rutland got him out of trouble. In 1792 he was arrested for forgery in Scarborough. This time there was no one to rescue him and he was sent to prison for eight years.

While in prison, Hatfield continued his impersonations, in time managing to attract a rich widow, Mrs Nation, by pretending to be an ill-used aristocrat who had written inflammatory verses against the authorities. When he was released in 1800 he persuaded Mrs Nation to pay off his debts and the two of them were married. Within a year a failed swindle forced him to leave London and flee north. It was there that he met Mary Robinson, the Beauty of Buttermere, to whom Hatfield represented himself as Colonel the Honourable Alexander Augustus Hope, the MP for Linlithgow and brother of the earl of Hopetoun. The Robinsons were delighted by such a potentially prosperous match, unaware that Hatfield already had a wife and family living in Devon, not to mention an earlier wife living in America.

The marriage of Hatfield and Mary Robinson in October 1802 aroused the suspicions of Mary's admirers. Samuel Coleridge, in particular, had doubts about the Hon. Alexander's accent and ungrammatical speech. Enquiries alerted a local judge who happened to know the real Colonel Hope, and Hatfield was exposed. Within three days of the wedding he was on the run again. Mary was heartbroken; still more so when she discovered some letters from the long-deserted Mrs Nation. A reward was posted for Hope/Hatfield, and he was caught and brought to trial in Carlisle in December 1802 on three charges of forgery. This, unlike bigamy, was a capital offence, and in due course Hatfield was hanged for what the judge described as 'crimes of such magnitude as have seldom, if ever, received any mitigation of capital punishment'. The sum involved in the forgeries was £50. The Beauty of Buttermere had given birth to a son in June 1803, but anxiety for her husband had prevented her from nursing it and the child had died of pneumonia after just three weeks. According to a contemporary account, Hatfield died with dignity, 'showing no signs of levity or insensibility'. His deception of Mary Robinson led to melodramas on the London stage, and has inspired several books – a novel, *The Maid of Buttermere*, by Melvyn Bragg being one of the most recent to exploit the story in fiction.

**Hatry, Clarence** (1888–1965), insurance broker and forger. The son of a well-to-do silk merchant, Hatry was educated at St Paul's School, where he was reported to have done well in every subject except mathematics – an academic shortcoming that may have accounted for his subsequent difficulties, although he never made this claim himself. In 1929 he brought about the biggest City crash of the last century, and was jailed for 14 years for fraud, forgery and conspiracy. In spite of this setback, his belief in his abilities was unimpaired. During his lifetime he made and lost three fortunes, bouncing back on each occasion with renewed vigour.

On the death of his father, Hatry was obliged to run the family business, which was already in difficulties, and at the age of 21 he went bankrupt for the first time. He managed to repay all the money he owed within four years and thereafter to build up a successful career as an insurance broker. By the time he was 25 he was earning £20,000 a year. In 1914 he brought off the kind of deal that was to become his trademark. He borrowed £60,000 and took over the City Equitable Insurance Company, later selling it for £250,000. From then on, he bought and sold a wide variety of businesses, cutting costs by asset stripping and indulging in practices such as bulk buying. These devices are now common, but Hatry was considered an innovator. In 1921 he took over a small bank to finance his operations, later boasting that he had bought and sold Leyland Motors in the same evening at a profit of £150,000 to a man who saw the purchase contract lying on his desk.

In the 1920s Hatry had a personal fortune of £2.5 million and – gripped by the strange need to buy large properties that besets the newly enriched but bewilders other people – had acquired a house in Park Lane and an estate in Sussex. In 1928 he set up the deal that was to bring about his downfall. Needing £3 million to take over a clutch of private companies which many years later were to become British Steel, he found he couldn't raise the money. He faked some share certificates that gave him collateral for loans of £1.6 million, which was enough to keep his companies going for the time being. But the rumour spread that he was in difficulties, and shares in his enterprises began to plummet. When the time came for him to exchange the forged certificates for stock, the fraud was discovered. His accountant went through the books and found a deficit of £132 million. Hatry gave himself up to the police, and dealing in all his companies' shares was suspended.

Hatry's arrest on 20 September 1929 caused a sensation. Only a year before his companies had had a combined turnover of £12 million a month. The owner of the second largest yacht in the world, a string of racehorses and a London house with a swimming pool and a pub in the basement, Hatry spent Christmas in Brixton prison awaiting trial. On 24 Januray 1930 he was sentenced to 14 years at the Old Bailey.

Hatry's friends remained loyal. On his release in 1938 he went straight to the City and was greeted warmly by his old associates. He had a holiday in the south of France, and then set about the business of rebuilding his fortunes, this time in publishing and bookselling. He prospered for a time, but in 1951 he went bankrupt for £5000 and had a nervous breakdown. He fought back again, and in 1962 set up the Affiliated Cleaning Amalgamation, which was 'beginning to turn the corner' at the time of his death.

**Havers, Sir Michael.** *See* St Clair, Lindi.

**Havers, Nigel.** *See* St Clair, Lindi.

**Haward, 'Flash' Harry.** *See* Mr Smith's.

**Headless Man, the.** *See* Argyll, Margaret Duchess of; Keeler, Christine.

**Heathrow, the Battle of.** *See* Hill, Billy.

**Heavy Mob, the.** *See* Hill, Billy.

**Heber-Percy, Robert** (1911–87), aesthete, huntsman and soldier. It was said of Heber-Percy that his company was so intoxicating that his friends had no need of narcotics. Known as 'the Mad Boy', and employed variously as an undertaker, a cavalry officer, an extra in Hollywood and, until he spilt soup over a customer, a waiter in a Lyons Corner House, Heber-Percy was paid this compliment by Diana Mosley, wife of the fascist leader, Sir Oswald Mosley:

> His high spirits, elegant appearance and uninhibited behaviour so enchanted Gerald Berners that he no longer needed a drug to give him contentment.'

The youngest son of Algernon Heber-Percy, a kinsman of the duke of Northumberland, and brought up at Hodnet Hall, an Elizabethan pile in Shropshire, Robert was educated at Stowe and commissioned into the King's Dragoon Guards. It was soon clear, however, that a military career wouldn't suit him. He did serve as a private soldier in Saudi Arabia in World War II, albeit one who drove a Buick. He counted this period of his life a success. 'The Arabs like good manners,' he explained. 'And I have good manners in abundance.' In 1950, following the death of his friend Lord Berners, Heber-Percy inherited Faringdon, in Oxfordshire, the elegant Georgian house famous for such idiosyncrasies as fantailed pigeons dyed pink, orange, green and blue. Here he spent many happy hours designing exotic new constructions such as a swimming pool overlooked by giant gryphons.

Heber-Percy had a long-running feud with the society photographer Cecil Beaton, which climaxed in 1974 when, on the occasion of a birthday party in Chelsea for the literary historian Peter Quennell, he boxed Beaton on the jaw. Beaton, who was knocked for six into Cheyne Row, noted in his diary that Heber-Percy 'had waited his chance to take the law into his own hands'. There were other indications that the 'contentment' he afforded friends was not a state he could always achieve himself. After a suicide attempt in Florence he was carried by Lord Berners in a fireman's lift through the lobby of the Excelsior Hotel.

Heber-Percy married first in 1942 (dissolved in 1947) Jennifer, daughter of Sir George Fry, 1st Baronet. In 1985 he married Lady Dorothy ('Coote') Lygon, younger daughter of the 7th Earl Beauchamp, who was the model, supposedly, for Lord Marchmain in Evelyn Waugh's *Brideshead Revisited* (1945). They parted a year later.

**hedgehog, friend of the.** *See* WATERTON, CHARLES.

**'hell, a friendship from'.** *See* MOON, KEITH; REED, OLIVER.

**hell, devising one's own shipboard.** *See* TEACH, EDWARD.

**hell, dinner guests from.** *See* WILLIAMSON, NICOL.

**hell and back, a four-day trip to.** *See* COPPE, ABIEZER.

**Hell-Fire Club, The.** *See* DASHWOOD, SIR FRANCIS; WILKES, JOHN.

**Hell-Fire Club, the Irish.** Founded in 1735 by Richard Parsons, the 1st earl of Rosse. Members, known as 'bucks', met either at the Hunting Lodge on Montpelier Hill, or, more usually, in the Eagle Tavern on Cork Hill, in the heart of Dublin. Here they drank 'scultheen', a mixture of whiskey and butter, and gave themselves over to 'eccentricity and violence'. Rosse himself was described by the historian Gilbert as 'a sorcerer, a dabbler in black magic and a man of humour and frolic'. He admired the half mad duchess of Albemarle, but she preferred Lord Montagu, who, by pretending to be the emperor of China, humoured her belief that she was the empress. As he lay on his deathbed in 1741 Rosse received a letter from his neighbour, a censorious cleric named Dean Madden, reminding him that he was, among other discreditable things, a blasphemer, profligate and gambler. Since these sentiments were addressed simply to 'My Lord', Rosse returned the letter to its envelope and sent it on to the earl of Kildare, a man of virtue and religion.

Other members of the club included Richard Chapell Whaley, who was known as 'Burn Chapell' from his Sunday morning habit of riding about the countryside setting fire to thatched Catholic churches. Colonel Jack St Ledger, who was so obsessed with the duchess of Rutland that he would drink the water in which she had washed her hands, was also a member.

The Hunting Lodge was used as a venue for extended drinking sessions and the performance of a black mass, where defrocked priests acted out parodies of the Catholic mass, sacrificing cats and, on one occasion, a dwarf. One story, perhaps apocryphal, has a footman tripping over a drunken body on the floor and spilling a drink on Whaley's coat. Whaley supposedly poured brandy over the footman and set him alight, causing the whole building to be burned to the ground.

Richard Whaley's exploits were in some respects less extreme than those of his son, Buck Whaley, who in 1789 travelled to Jerusalem for a bet of £10,000 and played handball against the Wailing Wall. In 1796 financial embarrassment, and an encounter with the Devil in St Audoen's Church, Dublin, forced him to flee to the Isle of Man, where he built a house known as 'Whaley's Folly'. The foundations were made of Irish earth, which he brought in by the shipload in order to win a bet that he could live on Irish soil without living in Ireland. He died of cirrhosis of the liver at the age of 34. Among Whaley's contemporaries was Buck English, who once shot a waiter in a restaurant and had him put on the bill for £50.

There was a thriving Hell-Fire Club in Limerick, whose members included a woman called Celinda Blennerhasset, about whom nothing else is known. Hitherto, the gentlemen of Limerick had looked to the Badger's Club for entertainment. The Grand Badger was a very old gentleman who wore a high cap made of badger's skin over a full-powdered wig and sat on a special chair of state. The club produced two celebrated bucks, known as the Child and the Grand Bugle, neither of whom had much interest in normal behaviour. The Child was famous for having turned a theatre performance into an orgy, reserving two rows of seats for food and wine with which to entertain his friends. Since the theatre was a place where rowdiness could be expected (*see* HOOLIGANS, THEATRICAL), the tendency of the audience to jump on to the stage and attack the actors was discouraged by a row of spikes running parallel with the footlights. In 1787 the duke of Leinster impaled himself on one of these and was crippled for life. The more agile spectators often managed to pack the stage in such numbers that the play couldn't proceed. The Grand Bugle, dressed always at the height of French fashion, was renowned as a stage invader. Once he cut a large hole in the scenery through which he pulled faces at the audience. Away from the theatre he was well known for his poor table manners. From time to time he would prod a piece of beef on a fork and throw it over his shoulder for good luck. He died, worn out by every form of dissipation, a debtor in Dublin's Marshalsea prison.

*See also* ROCHE, TIGER.

**hell-raisers, English.** *See* BOLD BUCKS; DASHWOOD, SIR FRANCIS; MOHOCKS, THE; MOON, KEITH; MYTTON, JOHN; OSBOURNE, JOHN

MICHAEL ('OZZY'); REED, OLIVER ('the hell-raiser's hell-raiser'); WILLIAMSON, NICOL; WILKES, JOHN.

**hell-raisers, Irish.** *See* BAGENAL, BEAUCHAMP; BEST, GEORGE; FITZGER-ALD, GEORGE ROBERT; MAGUIRE, BRIAN; ROCHE, TIGER.
*See also* DUELLING; HELL-FIRE CLUB, IRISH.

**hemp said to induce sexual desire in white girls.** *See* MARKS, HOWARD.

**Henley, Anthony** (1700–67), politician. Henley stood out even among 18th-century members of Parliament for the contempt in which he held his constituents. In 1730, as the member for Southampton, he received a respectful request that he should vote against some tax changes proposed in the budget. His reply would be considered offensive by present-day standards:

> I have received your letter about the Excise and I am surprised at your insolence in writing to me at all. You know, as I know, that I bought this constituency. About what you said about the excise: may God's curse light upon you and may it make your women as open and as free to the excise officers as your wives and daughters have always been to me while I have represented your scoundrel corporation. I have the honour to be, my dear sirs, ever your obliged humble servant ...

Henley continued to represent the borough for a further eleven years.

**Herbert, David** (1908–95), interior decorator, actor, playboy and expatriate. The second son of Lord Herbert, himself the second son of the 15th earl of Pembroke, Herbert richly fulfilled Edith Oliver's prediction that he would be a failure in life. He took a different view, however. 'I realize that I may not have achieved much, but I have had a great deal of fun,' he liked to claim.

Herbert spent his childhood in Ireland before his father inherited the earldoms and the family seat at Wilton. During World War I it was used as a hospital, and the young Herbert recalled flirting with the wounded officers. After Eton, and having thwarted his parents' attempts to get him into Sandhurst, he found he had a vocation for acting. The romantic novelist, Elinor Glyn, who was a family friend, got him parts in two films, *Knowing Men* and *The Prices of Things*, in which he played the second lead without making any particular impact.

In the 1930s Herbert gravitated to Berlin, where he shared a flat with Christopher Sykes and Cyril Connolly. Connolly wrote plays that the three of them performed in Harold Nicolson's apartment – a pastime that Herbert greatly enjoyed. After trying his hand as a *kabaret* performer, he returned to England, where he met Peter Spencer, an actor and opium addict. He and Spencer decided to visit New York, where Herbert set himself up as an interior decorator for rich New Yorkers such as the actress, Tallulah Bankhead, and more or less disgraced himself in the company of friends from England. Stephen Tennent and Cecil Beaton were among his circle. He had first met Beaton at a ball at Wilton where the photographer had been thrown into the river.

In 1947 he decided to settle in Morocco, in which 'oriental Cheltenham', as Cecil Beaton described it, he struck up friendships with the native dignitaries, and arranged flowers for the many rooftop parties thrown in the kasbah by Barbara Hutton, the Woolworth's heiress. His own guest room was decorated with a portrait by Cecil Beaton of Mick Jagger's bottom, executed in green and blue. In his final years he took to wearing an ill-fitting wig to protect his head against the sun. When Barbara Hutton married the screen actor Cary Grant, it was Herbert who nick-named them 'Cash and Cary'.

**hermits.** *See* BIGG, JOHN.

**Hervey, Augustus** (1724–79), naval captain and philanderer. Hervey's biography, by M.J.R. Holmes, is appropriately entitled *Augustus Hervey, a Naval Casanova* (1996). His father was the 2nd earl of Bristol, his mother Mary Lepell, a famous beauty who had attracted eulogies from Pope, Gray and Voltaire. As the younger son, he followed the tradition of aristocratic families by joining the navy. His expeditions round the coasts of Europe as captain of a British warship provided him with opportunities to seduce an unusually large number of women. Actresses, opera stars, society beauties, country girls and nuns fell for his charm, money and aristocratic connec-tions. In later life he was caught up in a notorious scandal when his wife engaged in a bigamous marriage with the duke of Kingston. Hervey was by then in his fifties, had inherited the earldom and was living a quiet life in London with his mistress. Society gossip now had him as the cuckolded party – an irony which, after a lifetime spent seducing other men's wives, may have caused him some embarrassment.

His first conquest was Ellena Paghetti, the Italian opera singer, the seduction taking place in 1740 when his ship put in at Lisbon. Hervey, a midshipman, was just 16. In 1744 he married Elizabeth CHUDLEIGH in a ceremony that was to be kept secret for the next 20 years – a consequence of Miss Chudleigh's reluctance to lose her position as maid of honour to the princess of Wales. This would have been inevitable had it become known that she was married. After a few days together the couple sepa-rated, with Hervey embarking on a pattern of life that he was to pursue for as long as he was on active service in the navy.

Whenever possible, Hervey put in at a port within easy reach of Flo-rence, where he found the women to be the most agreeable in Italy and their husbands the least jealous. There he enjoyed himself alternately with the marchesa de Pecori and the marchesa Acciaiola. To show her appreciation, the marchesa de Pecori presented him with her picture and a ring set with diamonds.

In 1748 Hervey's squadron returned to Lisbon, which allowed him to renew his acquaintance with Signora Paghetti, who had seduced him as a 16-year-old. He found her to be 'still very handsome', but by way of variety he paid several visits to the convent at Odivellas, where the regime was unusually liberal. The previous king of Portugal had maintained two mistresses there and had had a child by each of them. Of one visit to the convent, Hervey wrote, 'We stayed late, making love in the *frereatica* way (as they call it).' Looking for contrast, he also visited the local prostitutes. Describing an evening with the duke of Bagnos and Charles Gravier, later comte de Vergennes and foreign minister under Louis XVI, he wrote, 'We went in cloaks to upwards of, I verily believe, thirty ladies' houses – ladies of pleasure, I mean' (*Augustus Hervey's Journal: Being the Intimate Account of the Life of a Captain in the Royal Navy Ashore and Afloat, 1746–1759*, ed. David Erskine, 1953).

In 1749 Hervey spent the summer in Paris, where he was presented to the queen of France, visited Mme de Pompadour and hunted with the duc de Penthièvre, the grandson of Louis XIV. Most importantly he met Susanne-Félix Lescarmot, whom he described as the most beautiful woman in France. She had been groomed to be the mistress of the king, but the duc de Richelieu had secured that position for Mme de Pompadour, so she had been married off to a M. Caze, later to be *secretaire du cabinet*. Hervey met her at a masquerade and fell in love. The relationship blossomed to the point where she gave him a ring with the motto *L'Union en le passe*, later announcing that she was no longer mistress of herself but belonged to him. At first, their attempts to consummate their passion were frustrated by the presence of others, often her husband. On one occasion they were about to embrace when M. Caze entered the room. Hervey was able to conceal his aroused condition under a muff which he happened to have slung from his girdle. M. Caze departed, and life was subsequently made easier for the lovers when he was moved to Versailles as *secretaire du cabinet*. At last Hervey and Mme Caze were able to spend whole days and nights together:

> …giving and receiving the last charming proofs of an unbounded love, and I never tasted such most exquisite delight, nor was I ever more fit for the scene.

During the next four years Hervey had affairs with aristocratic ladies whenever his ship, the *Phoenix*, was long enough in port. In 1754 he embarked on a liaison with Signora Pallinetta Brignole, a handsome woman from a distinguished Genoese family. Since she was married, meetings had to be arranged with some ingenuity. On the first occasion, she feigned an inflammation of the eye which provided her with an excuse to go to bed in a darkened room. Hervey eased his way stealthily into the bedroom and lay down next to her under the quilt. When her husband came to say goodnight, Hervey remained motionless under the quilt. After an anxious few minutes Signor Brignole exited:

> … leaving me in the arms of the loveliest woman that ever was. I lay till near daylight and performed wonders.

This life of self-indulgence was curtailed by the declaration of war in 1756. Over the next seven years, Hervey was on active service with Admiral Keppel at Belle Isle, and during the West Indian campaign he played a major part in the capture of Martinique, St Lucia and Havana. He did find time, when on leave, to have affairs – most notably with Kitty Fisher, a society beauty and courtesan who was a favourite model for Sir Joshua Reynolds, and sat for him as Cleopatra. Returning from the West Indies in 1763 Hervey formed an attachment to Kitty Hunter, the daughter of one of the lords of the Admiralty. She bore him a son, the only child Hervey ever acknowledged. The boy joined the navy at 18 and was killed in action during the relief of Gibraltar.

The last great love of Augustus Hervey's life was Mrs Mary Nesbitt, a woman of humble origins whose beauty and wit had gained her entry into society. She married a City banker and, like Kitty Fisher, was painted by Joshua Reynolds. She was consistently unfaithful to her husband and left him for Hervey in 1770.

When Hervey's wife, the former Elizabeth Chudleigh, was tried for bigamy in 1776, Hervey – now the 3rd earl of Bristol – left the country and throughout the proceedings stayed in Nice. He died three years later on 22 December 1779 at the family's London house in St James's Square.

For other Herveys, *see* BRISTOL, FREDERICK AUGUSTUS HERVEY, 7TH MARQUESS OF.

**Hervey, Lord Frederick.** *See* BRISTOL, FREDERICK AUGUSTUS HERVEY, 7TH MARQUESS OF.

**Hervey, Lord John.** *See* BRISTOL, FREDERICK AUGUSTUS HERVEY, 7TH MARQUESS OF.

**Hervey, Lady Victoria** (1979– ), boutique proprietor and 'posh tart'. *See* BRISTOL, FREDERICK AUGUSTUS HERVEY, 7TH MARQUESS OF.

**Heseltine, Michael.** *See* HAMPSON, KEITH; PROCTOR, HARVEY.

**hiccups cured by setting light to nightshirt.** *See* MYTTON, JOHN.

**highwaymen.** *See* CHILD, BENJAMIN; COLLINS, JONATHAN; DUDLEY, CAPTAIN RICHARD; DU VALL, CLAUDE; FLOOD, MATTHEW; HIND, JAMES; MACLEANE, JAMES; TURPIN, DICK.

**Hill, Billy** (1911–84), gangster. In his autobiography, *Boss of the Underworld* (1955), Hill claims to have become the 'bandit king' of London by winning a historic showdown with the previous holder of the title, Harry White. Faced by 150 men assembled by Hill from the Elephant and Castle, Kilburn, Paddington and parts of Essex, White quickly relinquished all claims to the leadership of gangland. There was certainly a confrontation of sorts, but it may not have been of the epic proportions recalled by Hill. Frankie FRASER, Hill's chief enforcer, remembers only some of White's people being roughed up and Harry White hiding under a table in a club called the Nuthouse.

Hill was born into a distinguished family of criminals. His father had served time for assaulting the police and his mother was a receiver of stolen goods. His brother Jimmy was a leading pickpocket and his sister Maggie, known as 'Queen of the Forty Elephants', led a gang of expert shoplifters. Her sobriquet arose from the fact that her lieutenants were beefy women who relied more on fear than sleight of hand. They would walk into a shop and wheel racks of dresses into the street in full view of the intimidated management.

Hill received his first sentence at the age of 14, and spent 17 years in prison in the course of his career. In the 1930s he formed his own gang, which he called 'the Heavy Mob', and whose income came mainly from safe breaking and smash-and-grab raids. He liked to give its members Runyonesque nicknames like 'Bear's Breath', 'Franny the Spaniel' (Franny Daniels), 'Horrible Harry' and 'Teddy Odd Legs' (Teddy Machin). His lieutenants were a mixed bunch. Apart from Frankie Fraser, the most reliable – until undergoing a religious conversion while serving a stretch in Dartmoor in the 1950s – was an ex-boxer called Bobby Ramsey. Ramsey could be seen mumbling prayers as he marched round the prison yard, and on one occasion he beat up a cynical fellow prisoner who thought his conversion was a pose to fool the chaplain. In fact, it was Ramsey who, in the days before wirelesses and Sunday papers were allowed in prison, advised the chaplain to ensure a full house in the chapel by reading out Saturday's football results during the Sunday service.

The Hill gang's most notorious heist was the celebrated battle of Heathrow. In the summer of 1948 the police were tipped off that a raid was being plotted on a bonded warehouse at London Airport. The plan was to drug the tea of BOAC staff in charge of the warehouse and steal a million dollars worth of bullion and about £500,000 worth of other goods. On 24 July seven of Hill's gang, armed with iron bars but dressed in BOAC uniforms, broke in and found undercover police officers who had taken the place of BOAC staff and were pretending to be drugged. The sleeping policemen allowed themselves to be tied up and gagged. One who didn't seem to be drowsy enough was coshed into unconsciousness. When Hill's men were about to open the safe, the drugged policemen, with one exception, came suddenly to life. 'We are the Flying Squad,' they said. 'Stay where you are.' The ensuing scuffle was complicated by the fact that both sides were wearing BOAC uniforms. Eventually, eight men were arrested and bundled into the back of a van, including two Flying Squad officers, later released. One of Hill's men who did escape became known thereafter as 'Handy Harry' because he had hidden under the police van, clinging to its axle all the way from the airport to Harlesden police station where he made his getaway. Hill later claimed that 'Teddy Odd Legs' (Teddy Machin) also escaped and fell into a ditch where pursuing police failed to see him. Hill himself had not been on the raid. It later transpired that the plane due to deliver the haul had been held up by fog and had been unable to land.

Hill's long dispute with Jack SPOT over which of them ruled the underworld was settled when Frankie Fraser ambushed Spot one night when he was returning to his flat with his wife Rita and knocked him unconscious with a shillelagh. Spot was never the same after that, and Hill had the field to himself, with assistance from the highest echelons of Scotland Yard. 'We had an inside tap,' a surviving member of Hill's gang has recalled. 'One of the assistant commissioners was having it off with a bird on the strength and she used to pass on everything he said.'

Hill's wife, who was greatly admired in criminal circles, only left her husband after 20 long-suffering years. Hill allowed her to keep one of his Soho clubs and, as a going-away present, gave her a poodle called Chico. Hill then took up with Gipsy, an exotic dancer on the edges of the underworld, and in 1959 announced his retirement. 'I plan to sun myself on the Riviera,' he said. In the event he and Gipsy got no further than Sunningdale, where they settled in well. Gipsy had had her own brushes with the law. In 1957 she was acquitted of stabbing a man in the eye in the Miramar Club, Paddington.

**Hill, Stuart** (1943– ), internet company director and round-Britain yachtsman. Hill's attempt to circumnavigate the British Isles in June 2001 earned him the nickname 'Captain Calamity'. As a result of his exploits, the Royal National Lifeboat Institution suggested that in future amateur yachtsmen should contact them before setting sail. Hill suffered his first setback when he had an allergic reaction to the resin he was using on the hull of his 14-foot *Maximum Exposure*. After a month's delay to recover, he launched into the river Stour at Manningtree, Essex, and hit another boat. Six days, and 100 miles, into his journey, he fell asleep from exhaustion and had to be towed ashore by the Cromer coastguards. Hill insisted that he knew what he was doing and that there was no reason for him to give up. After a three-week interval in which to recover, he set sail again into high winds and covered less than three miles in four days, getting as far as Sheringham. A lifeboat and a helicopter went out to rescue him but Hill told them that he wanted to keep going. Three days later he discovered that the winds had blown him back to Trimingham, south of Cromer – last seen four weeks earlier. At this point he told the Great Yarmouth coastguard that he was prepared to give up, but he continued to occupy the emergency services. He sailed 22 miles out to sea into a busy shipping lane and the coastguards were unable to find him. Once he made his way back to the coast, he came in too close and the Lowestoft lifeboat had to warn him that he was in danger of running aground.

Chris Barnes, honorary secretary of the Cromer lifeboat, said it would always go to help, but Mr Hill should never have attempted the voyage. 'My coxswain described it as like putting someone blindfold in the middle of the M1 and telling everyone else to miss them.' Mr Hill's wife, Vi, said:

> He has always been a bit of an adventurer. There was no danger of the boat sinking but he obviously had problems getting it to sail properly. He thought he could go all the way, but was proved wrong.

**Hinchcliff, Grant** (1958– ), Lloyd's underwriter. In June 1988 the marquess and marchioness of Tavistock and an audience of theatre-lovers were enjoying an open-air charity performance of *A Midsummer Night's Dream* in the grounds of Woburn Abbey when a man dressed as Adolf Hitler ran on and cried, 'Wass is going on?'

Speaking later from the dock, Mr Hinchcliff said:

> I had been wandering round looking for a fancy dress ball promised by invitation. I thought I had found it at last.

Mr Herbert Dell, presiding, said, 'We don't like this sort of thing in Woburn. The maximum fine is ten pounds. I fine you ten pounds.'

**Hind, James** (*c.*1619–52), highwayman. Captain Hind, whose 'merry life and mad exploits' were commemorated in a number of ballads and chapbooks, was the prototype Cavalier highwayman, or 'gentleman of the road'. His execution in 1652 was for treason to the republican regime, not for highway robbery. Tradition has it that he only robbed Roundheads, and that Cromwell and Bradshaw were among his victims. Certainly, he was a staunch royalist, who accosted regicides wherever he could, always delivering an admonitory lecture before relieving them of their valuables. To one victim he said:

> I neither fear you nor any king-killing villain alive. I now have as much power over you as you had lately over the king, and I should do God and my country good service, if I made the same use of it; but live, villain, to suffer the pangs of thine own conscience, till

justice shall lay her iron hand upon thee, and require an answer for thy crimes; nevertheless, though I spare thy life as a regicide, be assured, that unless thou deliverest up thy money immediately, thou shalt die for thy obstinacy.

Born in Chipping Norton, in Oxfordshire, Hind displayed a roving disposition at an early age – much to the despair of his father, who had intended him to be a scholar. According to an 18th-century chapbook:

He came to London and there grew acquainted with a company of roaring debauched blades, who by their evil example made him as bad as themselves.

Be that as it may, he soon became celebrated as much for his generosity to the poor as for his courtesy to ladies. On his first expedition as a highwayman he took £15 from his victims and then gave them back £1 for their travel expenses – 'with so much grace and pleasantry,' according to one of those robbed, 'that I would not harm a hair of his head, though it were in my power'.

In 1651 Hind made his way to Scotland where he offered his services to Charles II, thereafter fighting in the duke of Buckingham's troop against Cromwell at Worcester. Later he hid out for five weeks in London, but was betrayed by a barber called Brown. Brown divulged his whereabouts to the Right Honourable Mr Speaker, and on 1 March 1652 Hind was arraigned on an indictment of high treason and sentenced to death. He was taken to Worcester and there hanged and quartered on 24 September. Before he died, Hind proclaimed that he regretted nothing but not living to see his royal master restored.

**Hinds, Alfred** (1917–91), used-car salesman, litigant and thief. In the course of a long struggle to establish his innocence of a shop-breaking charge, Hinds proved himself to be the most resourceful prison escaper of all time, and a more accomplished lawyer than many of those practising at the Bar. In September 1953 Hinds was charged with stealing £30,000 in jewellery and £4700 in cash from Maple's, the furniture store in the Tottenham Court Road. His defence was that he was only in the area to buy some carpets. Lord Goddard, presiding, pointed out that 10.30 at night was an unusual time to be buying carpets and then sentenced him to twelve years in prison.

Hinds was born in Newington Butts, south London, to parents who had both been jailed themselves. His father was sentenced to seven years after a bank raid in Portsmouth in 1935; he also received ten strokes of the cat, which Hinds always believed contributed to his early death. As a young man, skilled in metalwork and machine-turning, and an accomplished safe-breaker, he was in and out of borstal and army detention centres, but after World War II he seemed to have settled down and was working in the demolition business for his brother at the time of his arrest for the robbery at Maple's. He bitterly, and continuously, protested his innocence, and in November 1955 escaped from Nottingham prison with the help of a hacksaw blade and a prison workshop key that he had copied from memory. He was on the run for 245 days, during which time he bombarded the newspapers with indignant letters. Scotland Yard announced that, to effect his capture, it was reconstituting its Ghost Squad, which was credited with extraordinary powers. Hinds responded with a letter to the *Sunday Dispatch* in which he argued that public money would be better spent on an enquiry into his case. He was caught in Dublin on 31 July 1956, extradited to England and charged with breaking out of prison. Defending himself he was more than a match for opposing counsel, and indeed for the judge. 'My Lord, I think I can assist you here' was a frequent, helpful interruption, 'My Lord, you are not quite with me' another. Later he felt able to offer praise. 'My Lord, you have summed up well.' He received only eleven days extra on his sentence for escaping from custody, and was returned to prison to complete his original sentence.

In July of the same year Hinds was back in court, arguing a point in an action against the prison commissioners for illegal arrest. During a break in the proceedings he bundled his guards into the lavatory and locked the door. He escaped through the back of the building, but was quickly caught. He was sent to Chelmsford prison, but in June 1958 he escaped over the wall and into a waiting Morris Minor. This time he evaded capture for two years, establishing himself in Ireland as a successful second-hand car dealer under the name of William Herbert Bishop. In June 1960 he was arrested by customs officials for smuggling cars across the border, and was returned to England to continue his sentence for the Maple's robbery. A prolonged series of legal manoeuvres seemed to be getting him nowhere – until 1964, when he hit on the idea of instigating a libel action against the policeman who had originally arrested him, Superintendent Herbert Sparks. Hinds was awarded £1300 damages and this civil victory forced a reconsideration of the criminal sentence. He was released in November 1965, and took to lecturing at polytechnics and at the National Council for Civil Liberties. Later he settled in Jersey, where in 1973 he reached the semi-finals of a competition to discover the most intelligent person on the island. With an IQ of 150, he made an excellent secretary of the Channel Islands Mensa Society. Superintendent Sparks remained unconvinced by this happy outcome. Hinds, he said, 'was the most cunning and dangerous criminal I ever met'.

**hippopotamuses.** *See* BUCKLAND, FRANCIS TREVELYAN.

**Hirst, Jemmy** (1730–1802), farmer, inventor and sporting gentleman. Sent by his father, a Yorkshire farmer, to a boarding school for future clergy-men, Hirst was expelled for teaching his headmaster's pigs to jump hurdles. He was then sent away as an apprentice tanner, but in 1756 he returned to Rawcliffe, where, to the surprise of many, he made his fortune by speculating in farm produce. Animals were his abiding interest. His constant companions were an otter and a fox, and he kept a bear called Nicholas. He turned out regularly with Lord Beaumont's hunt, riding a bull named Jupiter. He tried to train a litter of pigs as foxhounds, but the experiment was unsuccessful.

When not preoccupied by his animals, Hirst practised as an inventor. He designed a windmill for cutting up turnips. He attached a pair of sails to his carriage and travelled in it from Rawcliffe to Pontefract, where he crashed into a draper's shop. He was a familiar figure at Doncaster races, which he attended in a multicoloured wickerwork carriage drawn by four Andalusian mules and fitted with a wine cellar and a double bed.

In 1767 Hirst received an invitation from George III to appear at court. He decided to accept, but resented Lord Beaumont's advice on how he should behave. 'Damn your fuss, Beaumont,' he said. 'I didn't seek the king's acquaintance, he sought mine.' In the event his visit aroused much curiosity. The crowds that followed his carriage to court were as surprised by his clothes – an otter-skin coat, patchwork breeches, red and white striped stockings, yellow boots – as were the assembled peers. When the duke of Devonshire collapsed with laughter, Hirst, taking this to be an hysterical fit, threw a glass of water in his face. When the king entered, Hirst refused to bow but politely held out his hand. George III was highly entertained, chatted to him about his inventions and sent him away with his carriage filled with wine from the royal cellars.

In his will Hirst left instructions that his coffin should be borne to the grave by twelve young maidens to an accompaniment of bagpipes. Since only two maidens could be found in Rawcliffe, widows were employed instead.

**Hitchin, Charles** (*c*.1681–1727), prison official, thief-taker, receiver, sodomite and moral watchdog. In 1719 Hitchin was ousted as under-marshal of Newgate prison and London's thief-taker general by his protégé, Jonathan WILD. In 1719 he attempted to reassert his authority by publishing an anonymous pamphlet in which he condemned Wild and his methods. Wild retaliated with a pamphlet deriding Hitchin's motives and exposing his homosexuality.

Throughout his pamphlet Wild maintains a tone of outraged innocence. When serving as his assistant, he had been greatly shocked, he claims, to discover that it was Hitchin's practice to act as an *agent provocateur* at homosexual brothels, encouraging the clients in their perverted ways and then arresting them:

One night the Marshall [Hitchin] invited me to a house near the end of the Old Bailey, telling me he would introduce me to a company of he-whores. Not apprehending rightly his meaning, I asked if they were hermaphrodites. 'No, ye fool,' said the Marshall, 'they are sodomites, such as deal in their own sex instead of females.' This being a curiosity I had not hitherto met, I willingly accompanied my master to the house, which we had no sooner entered than the Marshall was complimented by the company with the titles 'Madam' and 'Ladyship'. When I asked the Marshall the occasion of these uncommon devoirs he said that it was a language peculiar to the house. I was not long in the house before I was more surprised than at first. The men calling one another 'My dear', hugging and kissing, tickling and feeling each other and assuming effeminate voices, female airs etc, some telling others that they might be whipped for not coming to school more frequently.

The Marshall was very merry in this assembly and dallied with the young sparks with a great deal of pleasure until some persons came into the house that he little expected to meet there; and finding it out of his power to secure the lads to himself he started up of a sudden in a prodigious rage, telling them he would spoil their obnoxious diversions. So saying, he seized these sporting sodomites and conveyed them to the Compter, some having gowns and petticoats, fine lace shows, furbelow scarves, masks and complete dresses for women; some were dressed like shepherdesses, others like milkmaids ...

From the several accounts before mentioned, which are incontestably true in every particular, the principles and character of the Marshall sufficiently appear.

From 'The Humble Petition of Jonathan Wild to Charles Hitchin, upon his publishing a paper entitled *The Thief-Taker's Proclamation*.'

On this occasion the systematically treacherous Wild was speaking the truth. In 1727 Hitchin, 'that cowardly lump of scandal', was arrested for sodomizing a man who later informed on him. He was convicted, fined £20, given six months in prison and sentenced to stand in the pillory. Well aware of the hostility displayed towards homosexuals, Hitchin took the precaution of wearing a suit of armour when placed in the stocks, but it proved insufficient to protect him and he died of his injuries. He had had the satisfaction, at least, of outliving Wild, who had been hanged two years earlier.

See also MORAL WATCHDOGS; THIN BLUE JEANS, THE.

**Hitler, Adolf.** See BIRDWOOD, JANE, THE DOWAGER LADY; CLARK, ALAN; HINCHCLIFFE, GRANT; LUCAN, JOHN BINGHAM, 6TH BARON; NEWBOROUGH, DENISA LADY.

**hoaxers.** *See* DAWSON, CHARLES; DAY, ALEXANDER; DE ROUGEMONT, LOUIS.

*See also* ART FORGERS; CONFIDENCE TRICKSTERS; IMPOSTORS; LITERARY FORGERS; PRANKSTERS, INVETERATE.

**Hobbs, William Cooper** (*c.*1900– ?), solicitor's clerk and confidence trickster. An expert in the 'BADGER GAME', Hobbs was the mastermind behind many swindles pulled off by himself and his associates in the early years of the 20th century. His gang, each of whom had a key role to play, consisted of a Mrs Robinson, a former ingénue in the musical theatre, 'Major' Arthur, also a former actor, specializing in upper-class roles, and Montagu Noel Newton, a dishonest solicitor of Hobbs's acquaintance.

Usually the badger game is played for comparatively small stakes, but Hobbs raised it to a more ambitious level. In 1919 his 'mark' was Sir Hari Singh, the nephew, and heir presumptive, of the fabulously wealthy maharajah of Jannu and Kashmir. While having a drink in the bar of the Ritz Hotel in Paris, Sir Hari was introduced by 'Major' Arthur to his companion, a lady of great allure played by Mrs Robinson. Sir Hari and Mrs Robinson shortly retired upstairs to Sir Hari's suite, and were in bed when Mr Robinson, played sometimes by Hobbs but on this occasion by Montagu Newton, suddenly entered. 'Major' Arthur advised Sir Hari that a scandal must at all costs be avoided, and the young prince was persuaded to hand over two cheques, each in the sum of £150,000, with the payee's name left blank. Hobbs then deposited these in a bank account which he had opened in the name of Robinson. For reasons that are not clear, the real Mr Robinson, a respectable businessman who had never been part of Hobbs's gang, got to hear about this and came to the conclusion that his wife's share of £21,000 had not been enough. When Hobbs refused to increase it, Mr Robinson reconsidered his position and went to the police. Hobbs was arrested and received two years in prison. Among exponents of the badger game he is still spoken of with awe, on both sides of the Atlantic.

**hocus-pocus.** *See* FORMAN, SIMON; GRAHAM, JAMES; GREATRAKES, VALENTINE; GREEN, MARY.

**Hodges, Bert** (1892–1981), pensioner. Appearing in June 1972 in a senior citizens' away-day talent contest in Bognor Regis, Sussex, 80-year-old Bert Hodges stepped forward and recited:

> A robin redbreast on my sill
> Sang for a crust of bread
> I slowly brought the window down
> And smashed its fucking head.

Mrs Ethel Helmes, talent organizer and chairman of the judges, said that she didn't think material like this was suitable for a holiday audience. 'The verse is well known in theatrical circles,' protested Mr Hodges, who had once been on the halls.

**Hogflesh the cricketer.** *See* HOOLIGANS, THEATRICAL.

**Hogg, Captain Peter** (1936–  ), commercial pilot and carpet retailer. Hogg, an employee of British Airways, became something of a national hero in 1974 when he overcame much bureaucratic red tape to rescue more than 100 passengers who had been stranded at Montreal Airport. It came as a surprise when he was arrested 11 years later after the body of his wife Margaret was discovered by a recreational diver at the bottom of Coniston Water in Cumbria. It was due to Mrs Kay Newnham, a reporter on the *Cranleigh Echo*, that the story behind Mrs Hogg's death eventually emerged. In 1999 Mrs Newnham, a former neighbour of Peter and Margaret Hogg in Cranleigh, Surrey, spoke to BBC Television. She explained to viewers:

> What you've got to understand is that the Sixties arrived in Cranleigh a little late. In the Seventies, there was many a wild party here. All manner of things went on behind drawn curtains. You could say that the Sixties came to Cranleigh in the Seventies.

Mrs Newnham was also able to confirm that Mrs Hogg customarily painted her toenails red – a circumstance that didn't escape the judge at Hogg's trial when ruling that there had been provocation. Hogg was sentenced to seven years in 1985. 'I wanted to headline my story, "The Wild Sex Life of The Lady In The Lake",' Mrs Newnham told the BBC, 'but my editor ruled that this would not reflect well on Cranleigh.' Interviewed on the same programme, Detective Inspector Salt of the Cumbria CID said that Hogg had been a most incompetent offender. Apparently it would have been impossible to identify Mrs Hogg's body if Hogg had remembered to remove a ring with her name on it. He had also been unimpressed by Hogg's attitude when told that his wife's remains had been discovered. 'That's unlucky, isn't it?' he'd said.

**Holliday, Bert** (1891–1953), jewel thief in the Raffles mode. Holliday came from a humble background in London's East End, but was known to associates as the 'Gentleman Cracksman' and 'Johnny the Gent'. He lived in a house called 'Jour de Fete' on Friary Island in the Thames, rode to hounds and mixed in the southern counties set. Sometimes working with 'Poofy' Len Oades, he was an expert climber, always carried a gun and was so successful that he was targeted by police forces in five counties before he was caught stealing a cheese from the Dumb Bell Inn in Taplow, Buckinghamshire, in 1949. When arrested he was released on £2000 bail and disappeared. He then shot himself in a hotel in Virginia Water with a gun concealed in a walking stick. In a farewell note, he regretted that he would be unable to go fishing that day.

**Holme, Lord Richard** (1936– ), peer, politician and moral watchdog. As chairman of the Broadcasting Standards Commission, it was Lord Holme's job to ensure that offensive material was kept off British television screens. But for tireless work by Miss Rebekah Wade, editress of the *News of the World* it might never have come to light that Lord Holme, while carrying out his regulating duties, had two mistresses, one of whom was a blonde and the other an Australian actress who had appeared in *Prisoner Cell Block H*.

According to the *News of the World*, the Liberal Democrat peer was in the habit of telling Kay, his attractive wife of 42 years, that he had to go out on business. He would then secretly rendezvous with mini-skirted 28-year-old Tracey Kelly, a single mother from the Midlands, who called him 'Mr Toad'. Their games involved spanking, and the silver-haired father of four liked to read *Skin 2*, a fetish magazine. On Sunday 22 October 2000 Miss Wade was able to tell her readers that Lord Holme started to date Nicola Paul, the Australian actress, when she was living in Chelsea, west London. The couple had been seen laughing together, and once stayed at the Gravetye Manor Hotel in Turner's Hill, West Sussex. After checking in to the £270-a-night hotel, Lord Holme and Miss Paul enjoyed a relaxed game of croquet. Later, hotel staff remember Nicola wearing a black dress and red stilettos. The following morning the couple enjoyed another game of croquet.

The day after Miss Wade's story appeared the disgraced peer resigned as television's moral watchdog. His wife Kay is believed to have stood by him. Miss Wade is the partner of Mr Ross Kemp, an actor formerly employed in the television soap opera, *EastEnders.*

**Holy Ghost Pie.** *See* BOLD BUCKS.

**honours for sale.** *See* GREGORY, MAUNDY.

**Hook, Theodore** (1770–1841), writer, playboy and prankster. Hook was a successful novelist, playwright and composer, who became editor of *John Bull* and was the model for Mr Wagg in Thackeray's *Vanity Fair* (1847). In 1809, and already notorious for his 'many boisterous buffooneries', he pulled off his most elaborate practical joke, thought by some to have been the inspiration for a scene in the Marx Brothers' film, *A Night In Casablanca*. It would be less to his credit if, as has been suggested, it also inspired a whole series of laborious epistolary japes set in motion in the later years of the 20th century by *The Letters of J. Rochester Sneath*, a collection of spoof correspondence organized by the ill-mannered Tory MP, Humphrey Berkeley.

Hook was walking along Berners Street one day with his friend and fellow playwright, Sam Beazeley, when the latter remarked on what an uncommonly quiet part of town it was. Hook bet him that he could make No 54, a nondescript house owned by an elderly widow by the name of Tottingham, the most famous in the city. Beazeley accepted the wager, and Hook proceeded to write hundreds of letters in Mrs Tottingham's name asking for various goods and services to be provided at a certain time on a certain day. At 9 o'clock on the appointed morning, twelve chimney sweeps arrived at Mrs Tottingham's front door, each explaining that he was there 'upon your esteemed request to clean the chimney'. Then a wagonload of coal drew up, followed by a furniture van, a hearse with a coffin and a train of mourning coaches. Next to arrive were a shipment of beer, a cartload of potatoes and a pipe organ, with six men to unload it. Soon they were joined by confectioners, bakers, wig-makers, opticians, machinists, footmen, cooks and housemaids, all applying for advertised positions. They were followed by a parade of more illustrious personages – the archbishop of Canterbury, a cabinet minister, the lord mayor, and finally the duke of York. The lord mayor had come to receive the dying depositions of Mrs Tottingham, who was about to distribute a considerable fortune. The duke of York, who was the commander in chief of the army, had responded to the information that one of his officers lay gravely ill at No 54 and needed urgently to speak to him.

By now, Berners Street was in a state of chaos. The police were unable to maintain order as fights broke out and vehicles were overturned. Some of the dignatories were jostled and insulted. Only when it grew dark did the exhausted participants begin to fade away. For a time, Hook was so unpopular that he was compelled to leave London, his escape giving rise to the expression, 'to hook it'. He'd won his bet, however, and the prince regent was so amused by the joke that he appointed him accountant general of Mauritius. During his time of office, one of his deputies embezzled a sum of money. Hook was held responsible and he served two years in prison.

**Hooley, Ernest Terah** (1869–1947), fraudsman. It was Hooley's claim that, whereas any fool could sell people what they wanted, he could 'sell them things they neither want nor need'. Not all his companies were fraudulent. He founded Schweppes, and in 1890 he bought the Dunlop Tyre Company, selling it on in a matter of months at a paper profit of £2 million. But his handling of them was always dishonest. Peers were paid a standard rate to sit on his various boards. A duke received £10,000 a year, a baron £5000. By use of judicious bribes he became high sheriff of Cambridgeshire and a member of the Carlton Club. If a client became too awkward, he advised him to see Horatio BOTTOMLEY, rather as a general practitioner might refer a difficult case to a specialist. He was made bankrupt four times, went to prison twice and died penniless in 1947.

**hooligans.**   *See* ALEXANDER, JAMES; ASTON, JOHN; BUCKINGHAM, GEORGE VILLIERS, 2ND DUKE OF; DORSET, CHARLES SACKVILLE, 1ST EARL OF ; JONES, VINNIE; LUKER, ELIZABETH; MOON, KEITH; REED, OLIVER.

**hooligans, theatrical.** Spectators who spat at Noël Coward after the first night of *Sirocco* in 1927, and their successors who, enraged by the sudden arrival on stage of a German philosopher, booed Peter Ustinov's *No Sign of the Dove* just 45 seconds after the curtain had gone up, were merely following a time-honoured tradition of audience hooliganism dating back to the Restoration. Theatres at that time had been closed for 18 years, and when they reopened, audiences, suddenly released from puritanical constraints, were naturally a little boisterous, liking to pelt actors who had displeased them with missiles and abuse, and, when bored, mounting alternative entertainments in the stalls.

One contemporary report reads:

> On Thursday night there was a great riot at Covent Garden, occasioned by the gentry in the upper gallery calling for a hornpipe, though nothing of the sort was expressed in the bills. Then a Mr Goodyear and a Mr Fielding – who had bought highly priced seats near the stage – drew their swords and engaged in a duel, while the play was going on. An orange was thrown at Mr Sheridan, who was playing the character of Aesop, and so well directed that it dented the iron of his false nose and drove it into his head.

Throughout the 18th and 19th centuries even the most respected performers were considered worthy targets of abuse. The supporters of one star – Kean, say, or Kemble – would, for an amusing night out, visit a theatre where another star – David Garrick, for instance – was appearing, merely to cause trouble. Like the football hooligans of later years, however, they were sternly conservative. On one occasion Garrick – trying to suggest Macbeth's inner turmoil – left the buttons of his waistcoat undone. The audience, enraged by this departure from tradition, threw eggs and tomatoes at him, forcing him to leave the stage.

To avoid hooliganism of this sort, actors and playwrights packed the theatres with their own supporters, leaving little room, they hoped, for troublemakers. This system was thought to be foolproof until Charles Lamb, having filled Drury Lane with his friends for the first night of his play *Mr H*, surprised everyone by leading the booing himself. Within minutes of the curtain going up, Lamb decided that he couldn't tolerate the work, which had advertised itself as a farce. Its only joke consisted in the leading character being called Hogflesh, after a famous cricketer of the day. Judging this to be particularly feeble in performance, Lamb jumped up and down on his hat and cried, 'An outrage! A nausea! Ring down the curtain!'

In December 1965 Mother Goose was shot in the foot by a pellet from an air gun during a pantomime performance at the King's Theatre, Southsea. Dick Emery, as Simple Simon, told the audience that the show would not go on unless the shooting stopped. 'Thank you for your cooperation,' he said, and was shot in the shoulder. Police were called after two more members of the cast were hit.

*See also* LUKER, ELIZABETH; STAGE, HOOLIGANISM ON.

**Hopkins, Matthew** (?–1647), lawyer, charlatan and witch-finder. Among the witch-hunters who practised in Europe during the 16th and 17th centuries, Hopkins stands out as the busiest – at least in England. His total of persons exposed and put to death – perhaps 230, including a few Anglican clergymen – was exceeded only by Jacob Sprenger in Germany, who had as many as 500 victims, Cumanus in Italy who burned 41 women in one day, Delric and Boguet in France who had incalculable totals, and Remigious who convicted and burned 900 witches in a period of 15 years.

Little is known about Hopkins before 1644, but it is believed that he practised as a lawyer. In March 1644 he discovered six witches who, he said, were trying to kill him. He forced confessions out of them so successfully that he won instant fame among the credulous, and was appointed 'witch-finder general'. Thereafter, he travelled round the country in a luxurious coach, demanding 20 shillings per visit whether he found any witches or not. For witches found, he charged an extra 20 shillings per witch. He had various methods of discovery, his favourite being to bind and wrap the suspect in a sheet and throw her into a pond. If she sank to the bottom she was innocent – albeit drowned. If she floated she was a witch, and doomed. Hopkins became adept at laying the suspect so carefully in the water that she often floated. Another method was to tie suspects to a chair and set them in the middle of a room. It was assumed that during a 24-hour period one or more of the witch's imps would appear to suck her blood. A hole was made in the window to allow the imps, in the shape of insects, to enter. Hopkins ordered spectators to kill all such insects, but if any managed to escape they must be imps, and the guilt of the accused was proved. In one case, an old woman, who was subjected to torture after such a test, admitted that four flies in the room were named Ilemazar, Eyewackett, Peck-in-the-crown and Grizel-Greedigut. She was sent to the stake.

In his first year in office Hopkins discovered 60 witches, and made a handsome living. Host communities were required to lodge him at the best inn in the village, and at their expense. In time he became so rapacious that he made many enemies, even among the credulous. More and more magistrates refused his services, and ordinary people noticed that not even the most virtuous were safe from his accusations. In August 1647 he was charged with being a wizard. The story spread that he had cheated the Devil out of a memorandum book in which Satan had entered the names of all the witches in England. 'Thus, you find out witches not by God's aid, but by the Devil's,' his enemies declared. It was decided that he should be subjected to one of his own tests. Bound and wrapped in a sheet, he was set down in water with the same care as he had always used. He floated. There is no judicial entry of a subsequent trial, and most historians agree that he was probably lynched on the spot.

**Horrible Harry.** *See* HILL, BILLY.

**horse, riding a man of the lower class as if he were a.** *See* DORSET, CHARLES SACKVILLE, 1ST EARL OF.

**horse, running in the Leith races as a.** *See* DUFF, JAMES.

**horse and riding off with young men, turning oneself into a.** *See* DICKENSON, MOTHER.

**horse in the bedroom.** *See* MYTTON, JOHN.

**Hotten, John Camden** (1832–1907), publisher, bookseller and pornographer. Hotten, like fellow bookmen, Charles CARRINGTON and William DUGDALE, was a leading figure in the sophisticated and well-organized production of pornography for affluent Victorians. Despite his fashionable address in Piccadilly, he was regarded as a rogue who lived by pirating the copyright of American authors and by passing off books as erotic that could have been more honestly described as straightforwardly sado-masochistic. Among these were *Lady Bumtickler's Revels* and *Madam Birchini's Dance*, the former a two-act flagellation opera. To escape the attentions of the police and the Vice Society, Hotten issued these collectively as 'The Library Illustrative of Social Progress'. The historian Donald Thomas has pointed out (*The Victorian Underworld*, 1998) that, with the help of the genteel blackmailer of the Pre-Raphaelite movement, Charles Augustus HOWELL, he hoped that dramas of that genre might be forthcoming from Algernon Charles Swinburne. Among Swinburne's subversive fantasies were such pieces as *La Fille du policeman* and *La Soeur de la reine*, in which Queen Victoria has a twin sister who becomes a Haymarket prostitute. The queen's own 'unfortunate lapse from virtue' is brought about by the elderly William Wordsworth, who manages to seduce her by the smouldering sensuality of his reading of *The Excursion*. The best efforts of Lord John Russell and 'Sir Peel' are then needed to assuage Victoria's ignited sexuality. Hotten judged that such pieces were best circulated privately. He was more courageous on another occasion. When Swinburne's *Poems and Ballads* were withdrawn by Macmillan, after a threatened prosecution for obscenity, he immediately reprinted it.

**Howard, Lady Frances** (1593–1632), adulteress and murderer. With the help of Anne TURNER, a brothel-keeper, and the notorious quack Simon FORMAN, Lady Frances rendered her husband impotent by means of hocus-pocus, and, with the sole assistance of Mrs Turner, killed Sir Thomas Overbury, her lover's closest friend. In 1607, and as part of a scheme to advance the interests of the Howard family, the earl of Northampton arranged the marriage of his 13-year-old great-niece, Frances Howard – an exquisite presence at the court of James I – to the 14-year-old earl of Essex, Robert Devereux. On completion of the ceremony – which was conducted by the king – Essex was bundled off to the Continent to continue his education, while his wife grew into a beautiful, but headstrong and vindictive, woman.

At the age of 16 Frances became infatuated with James's new favourite, Robert Carr, but just as her pursuit of the young Scotsman was beginning to succeed, she received the bad news that Essex was returning from France to claim her as his wife. Also on his way home was Sir Thomas Overbury, Robert Carr's closest friend and adviser. At first Overbury supported Carr in his putative affair with the countess of Essex, helping him with the composition of love letters and appropriate sonnets. Later he advised his friend against the arrangement, and was to pay for such opposition with his life.

Three years on the Continent had done nothing to improve Essex in the eyes of his wife, and her most pressing consideration now was to avoid his attentions. When Essex told her that unless she accompany him to Chartley, his country house, he would take her there by force, Lady Frances fled to her great-uncle at Northampton House, where she knew she would be safe. Here she received the news that Essex had been taken seriously ill, and was confined to his bed at Chartley with 'a most violent disease of a poisonous nature, imputed to, but far transcending, the small-pox'. This stroke of good fortune allowed her to spend the winter at court, pursuing Robert Carr and seeking the advice of experienced women – one of whom, Anne Turner, court dressmaker and bawdy-house proprietor, explained that if Essex could be dissuaded from making love to her she could obtain a divorce on the grounds of non-consummation, leaving her free to marry the man of her choice.

In pursuit of this aim Mrs Turner took Frances to see the fashionable quack, Simon Forman, who gave her a lead figurine of a man and a woman in copulation. This, he assured her, would bring Robert Carr to her bed by sympathetic magic. More importantly, Forman supplied her with a variety of noxious potions which, when put in her husband's food, and sprinkled on his bed sheets, would dampen his sexual instincts. He also gave her a wax model of Essex, into whose genitals he had inserted a thorn, which she must remember to twist and turn each evening. Another of Forman's devices – 'too immodest to express' – was to be worn internally by Lady Frances to prevent penetration. This combined assault on Essex's virility was so severe that he did indeed become impotent, though whether the condition arose from Forman's abracadabra or from dislike of his wife it is impossible to guess.

In the winter of 1611 Frances and Robert Carr at last became lovers – the affair being conducted in secret at one of Mrs Turner's brothels, with Carr slipping away from court, often in disguise. However, the furtive nature of their meetings frustrated Frances and she determined to resolve the problem by obtaining a divorce. Under pressure from the earl of Northampton, and in order to please his favourite, Robert Carr, King James agreed that the possibility of an annulment should be investigated by an assembly of bishops and lawyers. They, in turn, agreed that if Frances could substantiate her claim still to be a virgin they would allow a divorce. This requirement could have posed a problem, but when the time came for her to be examined by a group of matrons and midwives, Frances most resourcefully insisted, through modesty, that the examination take place under cover of numerous veils. At the last moment she exchanged places in the bed with a young virgin, the daughter of Sir Thomas Monson. The deception was successful, and Frances was granted her divorce on the grounds of her husband's impotence.

Meanwhile, Sir Thomas Overbury had come to realize that once Robert Carr was tied by marriage to the powerful Howard family there would be no place for him at his friend's side. He also realized that, were he to bring his knowledge of Robert's affair to the king's attention, Frances would be disgraced and the power of the Howard family broken. He was in a powerful position, but a dangerous one too, since the threat he posed was apparent to Frances's great-uncle, the earl of Northampton. The earl managed to convince Carr that Overbury should be imprisoned in the Tower until Frances's divorce was granted, after which he could be released. Unbeknown to Northampton, however, Overbury had publicly called Frances a whore. By way of retaliation she would see to it that he never came out of the Tower alive. With Anne Turner as her companion she visited alchemists with a shopping list of poisons, including arsenic, catharnides and sublimate of mercury. These were put into tarts and jellies, which Anne Turner then took to Overbury in the Tower.

Carr, meanwhile, had decided that he could best secure his friend's release if his health seemed to be in danger. Accordingly, and without Frances knowing, he sent enemas and 'vomits' to Overbury to make him violently ill. Thus, while Frances was trying to kill Overbury with poisoned food, he was being kept alive by her lover, whose 'vomits' were purging his stomach. Once she had discovered this, Frances sent Overbury an enema of her own concoction, one containing enough sublimate of mercury to kill him outright. The plan worked, and Overbury died in agony.

The divorce commissioners, in the meantime, had found in favour of Frances, who was now free to marry Robert Carr. The wedding took place in the Chapel Royal, with Carr elevated to the earldom of Somerset and Frances allowed to wear her hair loose as proof that she was a virgin bride. Ben Jonson wrote the wedding masque and Dr John Donne the epithalamium. For the next twelve months it seemed that the mysterious death of Sir Thomas Overbury had been hushed up. Then came a startling revelation from an apothecary's assistant named William Reeve. Reeve had delivered the fatal enema to Overbury and had thereafter been sent away to France. Taken seriously ill, and in the belief that he was dying, the boy wanted forgiveness for the sin he had committed. His story of a murder plot reached the English ambassador in Paris, who passed it on to the secretary of state, Sir Ralph Winwood. The king had no alternative but to call in his chief justice, Sir Edward Coke. Frances Howard and Robert Carr were indicted and tried before Coke and Sir Francis BACON. Frances pleaded guilty and placed herself at the king's mercy, but Robert defended himself with vigour. Both were found guilty and sentenced to death. It surprised no one when James pardoned them and confined them to the Tower, from which they were shortly released. They moved to Rotherfield Greys in Oxfordshire, where, scarcely on speaking terms by now, they lived out their lives in lonely isolation, each inhabiting a separate wing of the house and never meeting except when separated by the length of a dining-room table. Sir Thomas Monson was a forebear of the Hon. Nicholas Monson (1954– ), who, in the early 1980s, published a give-away 'lifestyle' magazine without any great success.

**Howell, Charles Augustus** (1837–90), blackmailer. Howell, who was Conan Doyle's model for the blackmailer Charles Augustus Milverton, used the most delicate methods when exploiting his victim's supposed weaknesses – among which were Algernon Swinburne's sexual deviations and Dante Gabriel Rossetti's sensitivity over the exhumation of his wife's body. When Elizabeth Rossetti died in 1862, after overdosing on the laudanum she was taking for her neuralgia, her grief-stricken husband, himself a morphine addict, had a pile of his unpublished manuscripts wrapped in her golden tresses and buried with her. Seven years later he had a change of heart and wanted them back. Howell was the 'friend' who retrieved Rossetti's poems from the coffin and then used the incident against him. In like manner Howell ingratiated himself with Swinburne by accompanying him to homosexual brothels.

Howell's favourite blackmailing technique was to start a correspondence with intended victims, pretending to share sexual obsessions or anxieties. Having acquired a series of indiscreet replies, he would paste them in an album. His correspondent would next hear that Howell had been obliged to pawn the album for a large sum of money. This had only been forthcoming because of the fame enjoyed by the author of the compromising letters. If the victim was unable to lend him the money with which to redeem his pledge, the pawnbroker would sell the album of letters at the best price. Usually, the victim or his family were quick to pay up.

Such methods made Howell unpopular among former friends, and, as a precautionary move, he was in the habit of announcing his own death when matters became too difficult. His actual death occurred in 1890, apparently after a bout of pneumonia, but T.J. Wise, bibliographer of Wilde and Swinburne, reported that in fact he was found dead in the gutter outside a Chelsea public house with his throat cut and a half-sovereign between his teeth – traditionally the reward of a blackmailer.

**how to pick a pervert according to the *Sunday Mirror*.** *See* VASSALL, JOHN.

**Hudson, Jeffrey** (1619–*c*.1680), courtier and adventurer, known as Lord Minimus owing to his having been 19 inches tall. Hudson's father (who was keeper of the duke of Buckingham's baiting bulls), his mother and his eleven siblings were all of normal size. On his 7th birthday Hudson was given as a present to the duchess of Buckingham. She was charmed, and thereafter lavished attention on him. Ensconced in the Buckinghams' palatial residence, Jeffrey was soon caught up in the currents of history. His new mentor, George Villiers, 1st duke of Buckingham, once a penniless member of the gentry, had advanced his fortunes through his relationship with King James I and his later friendship with Charles I. When the duke and duchess of Buckingham entertained Charles and Queen Henrietta Maria, a cold pie was carried to the dining table and out stepped Jeffrey, his miniature sword shimmering in the candlelight.

The queen was delighted with this conceit, and the duchess offered him to her as a present. Jeffrey now found himself at court, in the company of the queen's 'Negro attendants', her monkey Pug, and her giant. He might have remained just another court curio but his wit and intelligence secured him a privileged place. In 1630, at the age of 11, he represented the queen on his inaugural mission to the Caribbean – the first of the two occasions on which he was kidnapped by pirates. At 14 he was painted by Van Dyck, appeared with their majesties in masques designed by Inigo Jones and moved with the court as it hunted, travelled and played. When the Civil War broke out in 1642 Jeffrey fought fearlessly in the royalist cause, sharing all the vicissitudes of the royal family: victory, defeat, discomfort, exile and failure. When he was eventually cast adrift from his royal patrons, Jeffrey's life deteriorated sharply. He died, impoverished and abandoned, some time in the reign of Charles II.

**humbug, hypocrisy, moral decadence and materialism afflicting England.** *See* STONEHOUSE, JOHN.

**humbugs, canting.** *See* NICHOLSON, 'BARON' RENTON.
    *See also* MORAL CRUSADERS; WARD, STEPHEN (a victim of hypocrisy).

**humbugs, obvious.** *See* BESSELL, PETER.

**Humphreys, James** (1928– ), pornographer. Humphreys was not the most powerful gangster in Soho in the 1970s, but he played a key role in what became known as the Fall of Scotland Yard. In the 1960s he had paid bribes to Detective Sergeant Harold 'Tanky' CHALLONER, and in the 1970s, when he and his formidable wife Rusty opened three clubs in Soho (one of which employed a dancer called Norma Levy – later to compromise Lord LAMBTON), he soon discovered that his business partners included not only underworld bosses Frank Mifsud and Bernie Silver but also Commander Wally Virgo, Scotland Yard's senior detective, Commander Ken Drury, head of the Flying Squad, and Detective Superintendent Bill MOODY, head of the Obscene Publications Squad.

For a while these various coalitions prospered, but in February 1972 the *People* published a photograph of Humphreys on holiday in Cyprus with Commander Drury. Drury claimed in the *News of the World* that he had in fact been searching for escaped 'Great' Train Robber, Ronnie BIGGS, but it later emerged that Humphreys and Drury had met 58 times, on which occasions Humphreys had so assiduously serviced the account – feeding Drury with his favourite profiteroles from Soho *gateaux* trolleys – that he had been obliged to buy the commander an exercise bicycle. The original tip-off had come from Joey Pyle, a legendary gangland figure who had recently been 'fitted up' by Drury on a firearms charge. This had so upset Pyle that he had told the *People* about Drury's relationship with Humphreys.

Drury might have got away with this, but in October 1972 Peter Garforth, the former lover of Rusty Humphreys, was attacked and severely cut in the Dauphin Club, Marylebone. It was assumed that this was a warning to him to end his relationship with Rusty. Although he later denied any involvement in the assault, Humphreys departed immediately for Amsterdam, where he was arrested in December 1973. Incensed by an eight-year sentence for a crime he hadn't committed, Humphreys handed his diaries over to the recently established Serious Crimes Squad. These showed that Commander Virgo and Detective Superintendent Moody had received regular payments for their help. Virgo's rate was £2000 a month, with a Christmas bonus of another £2000. In a period of 16 months, Virgo and Moody had each received £53,000. In addition, they and their subordinates had been treated to holidays, cars, clothes and tickets to charity boxing matches at the Grosvenor House Hotel in Park Lane. In all, Humphreys implicated 38 detectives. On 28 February 1976, 13 officers were arrested, including Drury, Virgo and Moody. Virgo and Moody were jailed for twelve years, and Drury for eight. Virgo died in 1980, and Drury in 1984. Humphreys and Rusty separated. He moved to Spain, where he was subsequently involved in property deals. Rusty attempted to revive her career in show business, and on one occasion modelled industrial safety boots in a factory training film.

**Humphreys, William** (*c.*1820–*c.*1890), pimp. As a criminal Humphreys is remembered solely for the part he played in the downfall of Edward AGAR, the organizer of the Great Train Robbery of 1855. After the job had been successfully completed, a year passed during which time Scotland Yard's 'detective police' failed to make an arrest. The South-Eastern Railway Company, under Mr Smiles and his directors, blamed the robbery on the negligence of the Chemin de Fer du Nord and refused to pay insurance claims. Agar and his co-conspirators, William Pierce, James Burgess and George TESTER, invested their wealth with great care in leases, deeds and securities of different sorts. Since the war in the Crimea seemed to be going in the Allies' favour, Burgess chose Turkish bonds, and he sensibly increased his holding in Reid's Brewery, which was about to announce increased profits. Pierce also invested in Turkish bonds, but Tester preferred Spanish Active Bonds, which Agar bought for him on the stock market.

The gang might never have been arrested had not Agar taken a liking to one of Humphreys's girls, 19-year-old Emily Campbell. When she appeared to be returning his affections, Humphreys became furiously jealous. Agar saw a chance to overcome this hostility when Humphreys asked him for a short-term loan of £235. He made the loan, and when he received a message to come to a house in Bloomsbury one August morning in 1857, Agar assumed that it was about to be repaid.

As Agar approached the house he was intercepted by one of Humphreys' thugs, Smith, who was carrying a large bag full of coins and seemed to be in an agitated state. 'Bill sent me to tell you not to come in,' said Smith. 'There's a screw loose.' As Agar took the bag of coins he saw two men approaching, and Smith said, 'Run! You'd better run!' As Agar made his escape, Smith shouted, 'Stop thief! Stop thief!' The two men ran after Agar, shortly catching him and introducing themselves as plain-clothes policemen. The bag of coins was opened and was revealed to contain not £235 in sovereigns but forged coins to a lesser amount. Agar was then arrested on a charge of a forgery he had never committed with people he had never heard of. Agar protested his innocence, but against evidence by witnesses paid for by Humphreys he was not believed. The sentence for forgery was life imprisonment and Agar, who was never charged in connection with the Great Train Robbery, was taken to the convict hulks at Portland Harbour to await transportation to Australia.

**Hunter, the Reverend Thomas** (c.1661–1700), tutor, priest and murderer. Few people when informed on, least of all by a child, exact such a savage revenge as that taken by the Reverend Thomas Hunter on his former pupils. As a commentator noted at the time, 'A crime more premeditated, and more fraught with cruelty, never stained the annals of history.' Born in Fife, Scotland, the son of a rich farmer, Hunter studied divinity at St Andrew's University. After graduating he was appointed chaplain to an eminent merchant, Mr Gordon, whose household consisted of himself, his wife, two sons and a daughter, who were to be Hunter's pupils, and a young woman who served Mrs Gordon and her daughter. Within a short time Hunter and the young woman formed a secret attachment to one another and one day, when Mr and Mrs Gordon were away on a visit, they went as usual to the girl's room, where, since they had left the door unlocked, they were discovered by the children. On the return of his parents, the eldest boy, who was 9 years old, told his father what he had seen. Attributing Hunter's behaviour to the thoughtlessness of youth, Mr Gordon kept him on in his employ, but the girl was immediately dismissed. From then on, Hunter entertained a violent hatred of the children.

The next day Hunter took the two boys on their usual walk in the nearby fields. While they were busy catching butterflies and gathering wild flowers, he took out his knife and told them that he was going to kill them for what they had done. He then placed his knee on the body of one while he cut the throat of the other with his knife, afterwards killing the second in the same way.

Since the act was committed in full view of Edinburgh Castle and in broad daylight, it was witnessed by many people. Hunter, who had made no serious effort to escape, was quickly seized, committed to jail and chained to the floor. At his trial three days later he pleaded guilty, declaring that his only regret was that he had not murdered the daughter too. The sheriff then passed the following sentence:

> That he should be executed on a gibbet, erected for that purpose on the spot where he had committed the murders, but that previous to the execution his right hand should be cut off with a hatchet; that then he should be drawn up to the gibbet by a rope and when he was dead, hung in chains between Edinburgh and Leith, the knife with which he committed the murders being stuck in his hand, which

should be advanced over his head and fixed therewith to the top of the gibbet.

Hunter was executed according to these stipulations on 22 August 1700, but Mr Gordon later requested that his body might be displayed at a more distant spot since its hanging by the side of a road he frequently used was upsetting to Mrs Gordon. This request was complied with and the body was removed to the outskirts of Broughton, a small village near Edinburgh. The Reverend Hunter had died declaring, 'There is no God – or if there is, I hold him in defiance.'

**Hunter-Cowan, Major Betty** (1912–91), soldier. The daughter of an Army officer, Elizabeth Hunter-Cowan was born in Tonbridge Wells and educated at St Felix's, Southwold. A gifted musician, according to her obituary in the *Daily Telegraph*, she was training to be an opera singer when World War II broke out. She was first a FANY (a member of the First Aid Nursing Yeomanry), and from 1942 did 'a man's job' in the supply department of the War Office. After the war, and now in the WRAC, Major Betty served in the Egyptian Canal Zone, where she first met Major Phyllis Heyman. In 1947, the two majors settled in Cyprus, where they were known as the 'Cavewomen'. The sobriquet derived from their residence, Cave House, situated at Tjiklos, a plateau on the north coast of the island. They themselves preferred to be known as 'Wracks' and 'Cranks', Major Phyllis having served in Queen Alexandra's Royal Army Nursing Corps. The two majors remained in place throughout the EOKA troubles, refusing to move even when the United Nations urged them to evacuate themselves during the Turkish invasion of July 1974. Because of its position on the edge of the three-mile pass to Nicosia, Cave House was of tactical significance to both sides. To the rear was the Greek–Cypriot National Guard, ahead was the advancing Turkish Army. The two majors were in their element. At one point some Turkish troops tried to take a short cut through the Cave House estate, but were seen off easily. One Turkish soldier, wounded in the leg, managed to crawl within a few feet of the majors' rosemary and lavender hedgerow and then shot himself. 'He did the soldierly thing,' said Major Phyllis.

By the mid-1970s, more than half the 800-strong British community had left, but, in spite of a shortage of gin, the majors enjoyed a full social life. Once a week they travelled to the British Council in the Greek south to watch an afternoon film, organized at their request to enable them to return home before the 5 p.m. Turkish curfew. They also enjoyed birdwatching, and made the acquaintance of Lawrence Durrell, about whom Major Betty remarked, 'Little men are very aggressive, don't you find?' When Major Phyllis died in 1990, Major Betty returned to live in a nursing home in Edinburgh.

**husband, experts in obtaining a rich.** *See* BUCK, BIENVENIDA.

**hypnotists.** *See* ORLANDO, THE GREAT.

**hypochondriacs.** *See* KIRWAN, RICHARD; SPENCER, HERBERT.

**hypocrisy, a victim of.** *See* WARD, STEPHEN.

# i

**I am a plonker. Not smart.** *See* PALMER-TOMKINSON, TARA.

**Icke, David** (1945– ), sports commentator, parliamentary candidate and
Green Party evangelist. Icke played in goal for Hereford United until
rheumatoid arthritis forced him to retire at the age of 21. He then became a
sports reporter, commentating on snooker tournaments for BBC television. In 1987 he and his wife Linda formed the Isle of Wight branch of the
Green Party, and within months he was one of the party's six national
spokesmen. In 1990 a visit to a medium in Brighton called Betty Shine convinced him that he had a higher calling. Mrs Shine made contact with an
800-year-old Chinese priest who said, 'I have Socrates on the other line.'
The Chinese priest gave way to Socrates, who told Mrs Shine that 'Icke is a
healer who is here to heal the earth and will be world-famous.'

Icke felt greatly honoured, while conceding that it was hard to proclaim yourself the son of God without sounding presumptuous. 'Jesus's
was the last mission,' he said, 'mine is the next. I feel immensely privileged
to be part of a team working in many universes.' He then explained that
our universe consists of good and bad energy, creating vibrations ordinary
mortals can't see. Good energy resonated with the colour turquoise, which
led Icke and his followers to wear turquoise tracksuits. 'I am the son of
God,' he said. 'By God, I mean the spirit in the highest frequency which
has the most perfect balance between the polarities.' After a visit abroad,
clearing blocked energy points in the Middle East, Italy and Canada, he
pointed out that he was more powerful than Jesus, who had not had the
advantage of working with worldwide media.

By 1991 Icke was in a position to announce some sweeping prophecies.
Greece, Cuba, Teesside and Kent would shortly be under water after being
hit by earthquakes measuring 8 on the Richter scale. Much of China and
Sicily would fall victim to disruptive thought vibrations, some of them

caused by the Mafia. The first sign of the cataclysm would be the explosion of Mount Rainier in the USA. The Channel Tunnel and Naples Cathedral would be the next to go, and the Arctic Circle would begin to move south.

Those who derided him were easily dismissed ('Jesus was assailed by the Pharisees and Sadducees. It is just history repeating itself'), and the failure of his forecasts was easily explained:

> It was a karmic experience which was being set up for me. I had to experience extreme ridicule so that I could emerge stronger and wiser. My predictions were meant to be wrong on a massive scale because I have always been scared of ridicule. Unless you have experienced hot and cold you cannot know what lukewarm is.

The stronger and wiser Icke then announced that he had been contacted by the philosopher Francis BACON, who had asked him whether he could 'endure being the Son of God'. He had later persuaded Icke that he, Icke, had been Socrates in a previous existence. Other beliefs were modified. 'Turquoise is an important colour,' Icke revealed, 'but you don't have to wear it all the time.'

**if you want to know the time, ask a policeman.** The phrase has a more cynical origin than is generally supposed. Coined in the 1860s as part of the oral history of distrust felt by the public for the constabulary, it reflected a policeman's skill in taking advantage of a street drunk's condition to relieve him of his watch.

*See* APPLES, BAD.

**impostors.** *See* BAKER, MARY; BARRY, DR JAMES MIRANDA; BELANEY, ARCHIBALD ('GREY OWL'); BONNY, ANNE; DE ROUGEMONT, LOUIS; ORTON, ARTHUR; PSALMANAZAR, GEORGE; SNELL, HANNAH; STANLEY, SARAH; WILSON, SARAH.

**Imrie, Derek** (1969– ), dance teacher and aerobics instructor. Concerned that gay men might sometimes be too diffident to approach one another in public, Imrie, of Earl's Court, London, invented a small vibrating box that could be fitted inside the trousers, like a cricketer's protector. When two gay men passed one another in the street, the box gave off a low humming noise. The commercial prospects seemed promising, but manufacture of the device was temporarily suspended after tests in the countryside showed that various wild animals, particularly badgers, were also attracted by its signal. Mr Imrie was greatly encouraged, however, when he received a large order from Australia.

**Ince, George** (1940– ), armed robber. Ince's most obvious defence when charged with the Barn Restaurant Murder in 1972 was that at the time of the crime he had been in bed with the wife of the East End gangster Charlie Kray, elder brother of Ronnie and Reggie KRAY. This was not a defence Ince cared to put forward.

On 5 November 1972 two gunmen broke into the Barn Restaurant in Braintree, Essex. When the owner, Bob Patience, refused to hand over keys to the safe, one of the gunmen shot Patience, his wife Muriel, who later died, and his daughter Beverley. Within 24 hours of Muriel Patience's death the police had been told that Ince, who had previous convictions for armed robbery, was one of the gunmen. Photofit pictures were prepared from descriptions supplied by Bob Patience and his daughter, and Beverley was able to identify Ince from photographs shown to her by the police.

In May 1973 Ince stood trial for the murder at Chelmsford Crown Court before Mr Justice Melford STEVENSON. Throughout the proceedings Ince, who was defended by Victor Durand QC, protested his innocence. When Beverley Patience testified that he was one of the gunmen, he became so noisily indignant that he was returned to the cells. Having sent a telegram to the lord chancellor asking for Melford Stevenson to be removed on the grounds that he was biased and rude, Ince then sacked Durand and his junior, Robert Flach. Thereafter he stood in the dock with his back to the judge, occasionally interrupting prosecution witnesses. At one point he asked whether he could take a truth drug – a request that Stevenson refused. After retiring for six hours the jury returned to say that they had been unable to reach a verdict.

Within a week Ince was on trial again before a more sympathetic judge, Mr Justice Eveleigh. On this occasion the reinstated Victor Durand was able to call a crucial witness. Dolly Kray, the wife of Charlie Kray, had bravely visited her husband in Maidstone prison, where he was serving a ten-year sentence for his involvement in the killing of Jack 'The Hat' McVitie. To his considerable credit, Kray, who had been unaware of his wife's liaison with Ince, persuaded her that she must provide Ince with his alibi.

On 23 May 1973 the jury acquitted Ince after a three-hour retirement. On 15 June, a small-time thief called Nicholas de Clare Johnson admitted taking part in the Barn Restaurant robbery, but he attributed the murder of Mrs Patience to one John Brook. At the third Barn trial, held at Chelmsford in January 1974, Brook was found guilty of murder and attempted murder and sentenced to life imprisonment. Johnson was found guilty of manslaughter and received ten years. Mr Justice Melford Stevenson retired in 1978.

**incompetent thieves.** BASS, HARRY 'THE DOCTOR'; BICKFORD, CHARLES ARTHUR; EDGAR, HENRY.

**indigestion caused by being contradicted.** *See* SITWELL, SIR GEORGE RERESBY.

**informers.** *See* BLAKE, JOSEPH; FLECKNEY, EVELYN; GARNER, ROY; HITCHIN, CHARLES; O'MAHONEY, MAURICE; ST GERMANS, NICHOLAS RICHARD MICHAEL ELIOT, 9TH EARL OF; SMALLS, BERTIE; WILD, JONATHAN.

**Ingrams, Harold** (1911–86), undertaker. In July 1966 Ingrams was surprised when the corpse he was embalming woke from a deep coma and beat him up. 'None of my friends in the funeral business has ever had anything like this happen,' said Ingrams from his hospital bed.

**Innes.** *See* PSALMANAZAR, GEORGE.

**instruments, blunt.** *See* ALLEN, MARGARET (the hammer-wielding bus conductress); ALLEN, PETER ANTHONY (the poker-wielding dairyman); BLOOD, COLONEL THOMAS (the man with the mallet); GARVIE, SHEILA (a rifle butt); HALL, ARCHIBALD; MAYES, JOY (for the Iron-Bootscraper Murder); QUERIPEL, MICHAEL (a number-nine iron); RATTENBURY, ALMA (another mallet); WILLIAMS, JOHN (a maul); YORK, SARAH MARGARET, DUCHESS OF (for Jane Andrews and the Cricket-Bat Murder).

**instruments, sharp.** *See* HELL-FIRE CLUB, THE IRISH (for the Duke of Leinster).

**insurance swindles.** *See* BELL, TERENCE; COOK, ROBIN; COTTON, MARY ANN; GUPPY, DARIUS; HARRIS, LEOPOLD; LANCEY, JOHN; RICHARDSON, CHARLIE; SAVUNDRA, EMILE; SMITH, GEORGE JOSEPH; STONEHOUSE, JOHN.

**intellect, inheriting one's father's furniture but not his.** *See* CLARK, ALAN.

**interior decorators.** *See* HERBERT, DAVID.

**intoxicating company, pre-empting the need for narcotics.** *See* HEBER-PERCY, ROBERT.

**intravenous drug use, early modern.** *See* WREN, SIR CHRISTOPHER.

**inventors.** *See* GLENCONNER, PAMELA LADY (for her father, Sir Richard Paget); HIRST, JEMMY; PEACE, CHARLES; POCKRICH, RICHARD.

**Ireland, William Henry** (1777–1835), literary forger. At the age of 18, Ireland, a failed poet and the unappreciated son of a London bookseller, read *Love And Madness*, a novel by Herbert Croft. It contained a long passage devoted to the tragic life of Thomas CHATTERTON, who had forged the poems of a 15th-century priest, Thomas Rowley. Chatterton's example, and a desire to impress his father, inspired Ireland to embark on a particularly audacious fraud – the forging of documents and plays attributed to Shakespeare.

In 1796 Ireland's father Samuel published *Miscellaneous Papers and Legal Instruments under the Hand and Seal of William Shakespeare* – allegedly discovered by his son among the ancient family holdings of a gentleman who preferred not to divulge his identity. This was followed by a love poem to 'Anna Hatherrawaye' and then by Ireland's most remarkable find, two manuscripts of 'lost' Shakespeare plays: *Vortigern*, a love story set during the Saxon conquest, and *Henry II*, both in Shakespeare's own hand. Since Ireland's Elizabethan method was to dispense with punctuation and to put an 'e' at the end of every word ('O Manne whatte arte thou whye considereste thou thyselfe this greatlye where are thye great thye attributes buryed ...' can stand as a characteristic example) it is not obvious why scholars and eminent personages, among them William Pitt the younger and Edmund Burke, hastened to authenticate these finds. James Boswell fell to his knees before the fakes and cried, 'I now kiss the invaluable relics of our Bard and thank God I have lived to see them.'

Richard Brinsley Sheridan acquired the rights to produce *Vortigern* at Drury Lane – a decision that brought about Ireland's downfall. The actors found the dialogue to be literally unspeakable, and many withdrew during rehearsals. The play opened, and closed, on 2 April 1796. Those actors who had not walked out nonetheless mocked their lines, delivering them in a shrill falsetto or bombastic bass. At first the audience, accustomed to the peculiar diction and odd posturing favoured by English actors, noticed nothing unusual, and the first half was well received. In the second act things began to go wrong, however. A comedian with an unnaturally prominent nose had been cast to play a touching death scene. The audience began to laugh, and from then on, found everything humorous. When the popular actress, Mrs Jordan, announced that the play would be repeated on the following night, there were cries of protest and fights broke out.

Later in the same year Ireland admitted his fraud in a book called *An Authentic Account of the Shakespearean Manuscripts*. This was so badly written that it confirmed many in the view that the forgeries must have been done by William's father, Samuel – a theory that the latter angrily denied. At the age of 19 the most audacious literary forger since Chatterton was obliged to find new ways to support himself. He survived on small loans based on the possibility that *Henry II* might yet be produced, and he married a girl called Alice Crudge, about whom little else is known.

**Ireland supposedly untouched by homosexual practices.** *See* BYRNE, JAMES.

**Irish fashion, violent in an uncoordinated.** *See* LANGAN, PETER.

**itinerant cut-throats.** *See* ADAM THE LEPER; BLAKE, JOSEPH.

# j

**jackdaws, companionable.** *See* MONTROSE, JAMES ANGUS GRAHAM, 7TH DUKE OF.

**Jackson, Dr Brandon.** *See* FREESTONE, VERITY.

**Jackson, Edmund Haughton** (1861–?), seed merchant. Jackson's treatment of his wife gave the Court of Appeal the chance in 1891 to consider how much force a husband might reasonably use in the recovery of his conjugal rights. Earlier cases had established that he could confine his wife if she was about to 'be guilty of misconduct touching upon the husband's estate or honour'. The decision in *The Queen vs Jackson* suggested that prevailing attitudes had changed by the 1890s, and it could not be assumed thereafter that ownership of a woman's body resided with her husband.

Jackson and his wife, Emily Emma Maude, had married on 5 November 1887. He executed a settlement of his wife's property on 9 November and left for New Zealand the next day. The intention was that Mrs Jackson would join him there after about six months, and in the meantime she went to live with her married sister in Northampton. Instead of joining her husband in New Zealand, however, she asked him by letter to return home. When he did, she refused to join him in Blackburn, Lancashire, where he bought a house. He applied for, and was granted, an order for the restitution of conjugal rights.

When Emily Jackson failed to comply, her husband was obliged to take decisive action. As she was leaving church on 8 March 1891, Edmund Jackson, accompanied by two young men, one of whom was a solicitor's clerk, seized her in full view of the congregation and bundled her into a waiting carriage. Emily Jackson was taken to Edmund Jackson's home in Blackburn, where she was kept prisoner in the charge of the solicitor's clerk and Jackson's sister. It was the appearance, and aggressive behaviour, of Emily Jackson's relatives outside the house that, according to Jackson, necessitated the presence in the house of the solicitor's clerk.

Warrants were taken out against Jackson and the clerk on a charge of assault on Mrs Jackson. The police were called, but they withdrew when Jackson undertook to appear before the local court.

The first judge who heard the case declined to make an order for Mrs Jackson's release, but Lord Halsbury in the Court of Appeal took a different view:

> I do not mean to lay it down as the law that there may not be some acts which might give the husband some right of physical interference with the wife's freedom – for instance if the wife were on the staircase about to join some person with whom she intended to elope, I could understand that there might be a right to restrain the wife.
>
> However, the husband's contention in this case is that a husband may of his own motion, if the wife withdraws from the conjugal consortium, seize and imprison her person until she consents to restore conjugal rights. I am of the opinion that no such right exists.
>
> *The Queen vs Jackson,* 1891, 1QB. 679–80

*See also* CONJUGAL RIGHTS; SQUIRES, DOROTHY.

**Jackson, John** (1834–1901), cricketer, known as 'Foghorn' from his habit of blowing his nose whenever he took a wicket. Jackson, who played for Nottinghamshire between 1855 and 1866, is credited by some cricket historians with the invention of BODYLINE BOWLING, later exploited so successfully by Douglas JARDINE. Standing well over six foot and weighing 18 stone, Jackson persuaded more than one first-class batsman that the pavilion was the safest place to be. Struck on the foot by a particularly fast delivery, Ludd, of Yorkshire, was given not out. 'Maybe not, but I'm going anyway,' said Ludd and he left the field. Certainly Jackson seemed to get satisfaction from injuring batsmen. On one occasion he was lamenting the fact that he'd never taken all ten wickets in an innings, when he suddenly brightened. Remembering a match against Surrey in 1860 between the north and south, he said, 'I bowled out nine of them and bounced one off Johnny Wisden's head so he couldn't bat. That counts, doesn't it?'

Jackson always insisted on being paid in cash, which he kept in his trouser pocket while he played. In the middle of one match the pocket gave way under the weight of coins and his wages cascaded all over the pitch. When his team-mates offered to recover them, Jackson misinterpreted their motives and a fight broke out. His career was cut short at the age of 33, ironically through injury.

**Jackson, the Reverend William** (1737–95), journalist and priest. Born in Ireland and educated at Oxford University – later becoming chaplain to the earl of Bristol – Jackson played a central role in the most sensational society scandal of the 18th century, thereafter embarking on a career of espionage and high treason, finally committing suicide in the dock of the High Court in Dublin.

Known as 'Dr Viper', and described in the *Morning Chronicle* as 'the libelling, lying, swearing, drunken King's Bench parson', Jackson owed his reputation to the fact that, like the Reverend Henry BATE, he specialized as a journalist in character assassination. His finest passages of sustained invective came when, as editor of the *Public Ledger*, he defended the duchess of Kingston (formerly Elizabeth CHUDLEIGH) after she married the elderly duke in spite of the fact that she was already married to Lieutenant Augustus HERVEY.

Charged with bigamy in 1775, and having discovered that she was to be lampooned by the playwright Samuel Foote in a new comedy, *A Trip To Calais*, the duchess hired Jackson to mount a counterattack. After several weeks of Jackson's unrelenting abuse in the *Public Ledger*, Foote sought an armistice, for his part assuring Jackson that he would cancel *A Trip To Calais* unless obliged to defend himself against Jackson's libels. Jackson responded by insinuating that Foote was a homosexual. Foote thereupon stepped up his campaign, rewriting *A Trip To Calais* as *The Capuchin*, and including in the cast a character called Dr Viper who 'pushed himself into the pay of Lady Deborah Dripping'.

Jackson now began his persecution of Foote in earnest. He managed to track down a former butler, John Savage, who was prepared to claim that the playwright had indecently assaulted him on many occasions. Since sodomy was still a capital offence, Jackson clearly intended to destroy Foote, to the point of having him dead. At Foote's subsequent trial, the judge, Lord Mansfield, advised that the indictment was a conspiracy, and it took the jury a mere two minutes to acquit. However, the ordeal had broken Foote's health and he died within the year.

Meanwhile, the duchess of Kingston, having been found guilty of bigamy and deprived of her title, had departed for St Petersburg, where she struck up a friendship with Catherine the Great. Jackson joined her in St Petersburg, but shortly returned to England with 'a considerable sum of money as a final reward for his services'. The money soon ran out. In 1788, and having announced in the press that he was dead, Jackson fled to France to escape his debts. Here he became a fervent supporter of both the American and French Revolutions. In 1794 he returned to England as a French agent with instructions to discover whether an invasion of England or Ireland might succeed.

Jackson began to sound out potential allies in Dublin, where he was arrested and charged with treason. At this point he revealed a certain nobility of character, hitherto unsuspected. He resisted all efforts, including bribery, to persuade him to turn informer. In court, he was clearly unwell and began to foam at the mouth. The judge ruled that he was too ill to receive sentence and ordered him to be taken down, but he was already dead. An autopsy showed that his stomach contained a pint of arsenic. He had refused to name his co-conspirators, and by killing himself before sentence he had secured his estate for his wife. Had he died on the scaffold this would have been forfeit.

**Jack the Ripper.** Between August and November 1888, a series of gruesome murders took place in the Whitechapel area of London. The victims, all of whom were prostitutes, were Mary Ann Nichols (aka 'Polly', 42), 'Dark Annie' Chapman (47), Elizabeth Stride (aka 'Long Liz', 45), Catherine Eddowes (aka 'Kate Kelly', 43) and Mary Jane Kelly (25). The identity of the murderer was never established, but there has been no lack of engaging speculation. A popular suspect was Queen Victoria's grandson, Prince Albert Victor, the duke of CLARENCE – alternatively, the duke's physician, Sir William Gull, who was often to be found with blood on his clothing and might have framed the duke to cover his own guilt. Many policemen involved in the case, including Sir Melville Macnaghten, the head of the CID at Scotland Yard, suspected a barrister, Montague John DRUITT. Against this theory is the fact that Druitt drowned himself before the last of the Ripper murders. An even less credible suspect is the known murderer of four prostitutes, Dr Thomas Neill CREAM, whose last words as the trapdoor of the Newgate gallows opened under his feet were 'I am Jack the …' That Dr Cream was in a Chicago prison at the time of the Ripper killings rather counts against this theory. Another suspect was Dr Alexander Pedachenko, known to the Russian secret police as 'the boldest of all Russian criminal lunatics'. In 1888 he happened to be living with his sister in Walworth, and the theory is that he was commissioned by the Russian authorities to carry out the Ripper murders in order to discredit the Metropolitan police.

**Jagger's bottom, a portrait of Mick.** *See* HERBERT, DAVID.

**James, Edward** (1907–84), art dealer and frustrated poet, he was rumoured to be the illegitimate son of EDWARD VII and therefore the natural great-uncle of Queen ELIZABETH II. James acquired a fortune by assembling a remarkable collection of surrealist paintings. In 1946 he bought several thousand acres of jungle in Xilitla, Mexico, and built his dream palace, conceived, it is supposed, under the influence of psychedelic mushrooms. Suspended uneasily against a mountainside, it is composed of Greek columns that support nothing, spiral staircases that lead nowhere and doors that don't open. Once completed, James was satisfied with his work. 'When archaeologists come and see this in two or three thousand years' time, they won't know what to make of it,' he maintained.

James liked to stroll naked through the jungle round Xilitla, where he cultivated orchids and kept boa constrictors. It is said that on one occasion, when staying at the Majestic Hotel in Mexico City, he brought his snakes with him, together with the rats that were to be their dinner. When the rats escaped into the corridor, a woman occupying the room next to James's had hysterics and claimed that the hotel was infested. A maid was able to reassure her. 'They are not the hotel's rats,' she said. 'They are food for the gentleman's snakes in the room next door.'

**James I and VI.** *See* ABBOTT, GEORGE; HOWARD, LADY FRANCES; PRICKERS, SCOTTISH.

**Jardine, Douglas** (1900–58), cricketer. A controversial figure in cricket history, Jardine is remembered as the captain of England in the notorious bodyline series of 1932–3, during which he directed his bowlers to aim short-pitched deliveries at the batsmen, supported by a packed leg-side field. The tactic was developed principally to counteract the threat posed by the Australian batsman, Donald Bradman, who was thought to be uncomfortable against fast, rising balls.

Jardine was born in Bombay, the son of a Scottish lawyer who had gone to India to practise. At the age of 6 he was returned to Scotland, where he was brought up by his Aunt Kitty. After Winchester College and Oxford, where he played for the university, he joined Surrey in 1922. He was made captain of Surrey in 1932, and of England in the same year. He was already widely disliked in Australia, where, during the 1928–9 tour he had enraged his hosts by batting in his Harlequins cap, a powerful symbol of English privilege.

The bodyline tour got off to a poor start. Jardine, an aloof man nicknamed 'the Iron Duke', affected disdain for all things Australian: the accent, the women, the wine and particularly the inability of its inhabitants to express themselves in correct English. He was astonished when on the eve of the first test match journalists gathered at the English nets and requested the names of the English team. 'Let me make it perfectly clear once and for all,' said Jardine, 'that I never speak to Australians.'

In the third test at Adelaide, with outrage at boiling point, the English fast bowler Harold Larwood knocked Bill Woodfall over with a sickening blow just above the heart. Ignoring Australia's stricken captain, and deliberately within earshot of Bradman, Jardine said, 'Well bowled, Larwood.' By the fourth test Bradman had devised a way of playing lightning-quick deliveries aimed at him rather than the wicket. He retired in the direction of square leg and swatted the ball on the rise over cover point, but it was already too late and England won the series with ease.

Pointing out that it was quite an achievement to have come close to fracturing an empire with nothing but a cricket ball, the journalist Benny

Green later wrote, 'Jardine was a fine cricketer, a brave man, and a nincompoop of a specifically English sort.'

**Jeffreys, George** (1648–89), judge. 'Malevolent and despotic', according to Lord Macaulay, Jeffreys is secure in his reputation as the most barbaric judge in English legal history:

> To enter his court was to enter the den of a wild beast. The services which the government had expected of him were performed not merely without flinching, but eagerly and triumphantly.

Born in Acton, Clwyd, Wales, Jeffreys was called to the Bar in 1668. He rose rapidly, was knighted in 1677, and became Recorder of London in 1678. The enthusiasm with which he had hanged and deported his fellow citizens during the Popish Plot prosecutions of the late 1670s was rewarded by James II, who appointed him lord chief justice in 1683, according to Encyclopaedia Britannica. Thereafter he carried out his royal patron's wishes, and was created the 1st Baron of Wem in 1685.

Jeffreys's period in the West Country in the summer of 1685 to try the followers of the duke of Monmouth (Charles II's illegitimate Protestant son who had rebelled against the Catholic King James) became notorious as 'the Bloody Assizes': 74 people were hanged in Dorset, and 253 were hanged, drawn and quartered in Somerset. In his History of England Macaulay wrote:

> At every spot where two roads meet, on every green of every village, which had furnished Monmouth with soldiers, ironed corpses clattering in the wind, or heads and quarters stuck on poles, poisoned the air, and made the traveller sick with horror.

Jeffreys's savagery, grotesque enough when sober, was customarily made worse by drink. His evenings were spent in sordid revelry, surrounded by bar-room buffoons who bantered with one another for his amusement. On these occasions, Jeffreys, feigning familiarity with his low acquaintances, sang vulgar songs, danced jigs and hugged his supposed attendant friends in an excess of drunken camaraderie. The next day he would appear in court bloated and still half asleep from his debauch, his eyes staring like a maniac's. At such times his companions of the preceding night would, if they were wise, keep well clear of him. One of his many unpleasant characteristics was the delight he took in the public humiliation of anyone he had previously encouraged, in a state of maudlin drunkenness, to presume upon his friendship.

The barbarity with which Jeffreys carried out his duties appalled some politicians, but placed him still higher in the esteem of James II, who made him lord chancellor in September 1685. When James fled into exile in 1688, Jeffreys tried to follow him, but was captured and imprisoned in the

Tower of London. There he died, unlamented, in 1689. For his contemporary, Gilbert Burnett, writing in his *History of My Own Times*, 'his impieties would have amazed one if done by a bashaw in Turkey. England had never known anything like it.'

**Jeffries, Mary** (1854–1907), brothel-keeper. In 1884 a bill was debated in Parliament that would raise the age of consent to 16. The member for Whitehaven, Cavendish Bentinck, who was thought to be acting on behalf of Mary Jeffries, talked it out with ease. Jeffries owned three fashionable brothels in Church Street, Kensington, a flagellation house in Hampstead, and a chamber of horrors in Gray's Inn Road. Her clients included the king of the Belgians and, as she described them, 'other patrons of the highest social order'. She was also rumoured to have a 'white slave house' by the river at Kew, from which drugged victims were exported to foreign parts in closed coffins drilled with air holes.

Attempts to prosecute Jeffries had always failed, but in 1885 she was caught up in an attempt to discredit the campaigning journalist, W.T. Stead. In June of that year Stead bought a 14-year-old girl, Eliza Armstrong, from her drunken mother for £5, later taking her to one of Jeffries's brothels, where, on examination by Jeffries, her virginity was confirmed. From there she was taken by Stead to Paris, where she was placed in the care of a Swiss Salvationist, Madame Combe. Stead had successfully demonstrated the dangers faced by young girls, but he had committed a criminal offence.

Charged with having taken Eliza Armstrong out of her parents' possession when she was under the age of 16, and with indecent assault – which related to the examination by Jeffries   Stead was sentenced to three months in prison. On 16 April 1885 Mrs Jeffries was committed to Middlesex Sessions on a charge of keeping a disorderly house. She arrived at court in a brougham presented to her by a member of the House of Lords and pleaded guilty after a hurried consultation between judge and counsel. 'The White Slave Widow', as she was called in the newspapers, was fined £200, and ordered to produce another £200 as surety. She paid the fine at once, and in cash. A titled Guards officer stood surety for her, and she was back in business before the day was over. It was generally supposed that the authorities had conspired in the guilty plea so that the names of her eminent clients would not be revealed in court. By the time her latter-day representative, Janie JONES, was tried nearly 100 years later, the prosecution had discovered a better way of avoiding embarrassment. Miss Jones's girls were obliged to take the stand under their own names, but their titled clients were allowed to appear as letters of the alphabet.

**Jesus, a wider range of experience than.** *See* HARRIS, FRANK.

**Jesus, believing oneself to be having carnal relations with.** *See* EDINBURGH, PRINCE PHILIP, DUKE OF.

**Jesus might be found walking in Piccadilly, possibility that.** *See* DAVIDSON, THE REVEREND HAROLD FRANCIS (the rector of Stiffkey).

**Jesus unlikely to need a shower.** *See* PANACEA SOCIETY, THE.

**Jesus was a walking mushroom, theory that.** *See* ALLEGRO, JOHN.

**Jocelyn, the Reverend Percy** (1764–1843), priest and sodomite. In July 1822 Percy Jocelyn, bishop of Clodagh, was discovered in the back room of a public house in the Haymarket, and in compromising circumstances, with a soldier named John Moverley. The ensuing scandal was so great that for some days, according to the archbishop of Canterbury, it was not safe for a bishop to show his face in public. For George Dawson, private secretary to the home secretary, Robert Peel:

> No event in the last century is more to be lamented both on private and public grounds – it will raise up the lower orders against the higher and it will do more to injure the Established church than all the united efforts of its enemies could have effected in a century.

Jocelyn was ordained after leaving Trinity College, Dublin, and in due course became rector of Tamlaght. He seems not to have held any religious beliefs, but this in no way hindered the smooth progress of his career, which culminated in his appointment as bishop of Clodagh in 1820. His rise had been entirely due to family connections. The grandson of the lord chancellor of Ireland, he was the younger brother of the 2nd earl of Roden, and uncle to the 3rd. Inherited influence was unable to save him, however, after his fateful encounter with the 22-year-old guardsman, John Moverley.

After a day at the House of Lords the bishop met the soldier by previous arrangement and they went immediately into the back room of the White Lion public house. This seemed suspicious to the landlord's son-in-law, James Plant, who positioned himself in the backyard and peered through a window. Seeing Jocelyn and Moverley in what George Dawson later described as 'a state of licentiousness only made human by the descriptions in the most abandoned of the French school', he informed the landlord, Mr Lea, who ordered him to fetch a watchman. Soon Plant, Lea and the watchman were gathered round the window, shortly to be joined by some dozen of Mr Lea's regulars. When told by Mr Lea what he had witnessed, the bishop cried, 'I am undone! Could you let me go?' He then tried to make a run for it, but the landlord held him firm. The diarist Charles Greville believed that 'if his breeches had not been down he would have got away'. Jocelyn and Moverley were taken to the St James's watch house, attended by a jeering mob. As they passed Carlton House, Jocelyn was set upon. 'The reverend was kicked about with contempt,' according to Greville, 'and the soldier also received a drubbing.'

The next morning Jocelyn and Moverley appeared at Marlborough Street Magistrates Court. The bishop was described as being 'stout, with powdered hair, a pointed nose, and a black eye'. The guardsman was of 'effeminate appearance', and dressed in military uniform. Both wept. Jocelyn was bound over to appear at Clerkenwell sessions and immediately fled to the Continent. The government was as keen as the bishop to avoid a public trial. The only solution was to get Moverley out of the country too – a suggestion that originated with the home secretary. The matter was arranged, and Moverley was not heard of again.

The government had a good reason for wanting the scandal contained. The foreign secretary, Viscount Castlereagh, had recently been involved in a similar offence. He had picked up a soldier, later claiming that he thought he was a woman. Driven by a fear that he was about to experience a public humiliation as grievous as the bishop's, Castlereagh cut his throat on 12 August 1822.

A cover-up of Jocelyn's case was impossible, however. It now came to light that while bishop of Ferns and Leighlin, Jocelyn had been accused of the same offence. A coachman named James BYRNE had made the allegation in a letter to the lord mayor of Dublin, and for his pains had been prosecuted for malicious libel. After an infamously unjust trial, he had been sentenced to be whipped three times through the streets of Dublin. Indulging in practices 'only made human in the descriptions of the most abandoned of the French school' could just be tolerated; causing a man to be whipped within an inch of his life without good cause was not something the Establishment could easily condone. 'With mingled feelings of sorrow, humiliation and disgust,' *The Times* wondered whether to be relieved or outraged that Jocelyn had 'quit forever the country which his presence has polluted'.

Jocelyn's disgrace brought about James Byrne's rehabilitation. On the anniversary of his flogging a formal dinner was held in his honour at the Horns' Tavern in Kennington. 'Great good will come to us all from the heroic conduct of this humble man,' declared William Cobbett, who presided at the dinner. A public subscription set up for Byrne's benefit raised £300. Meanwhile, the Metropolitan Court of Armagh posted citations for Jocelyn to appear before it. On the day of the trial he was called for three times, and then, in his absence, sentenced to be deprived of his bishopric and of his episcopal order and authority. Two years later he was officially declared an outlaw. He had quietly moved to Scotland, where he lived with his sister under the name of Thomas Wilson, and masqueraded as a butler. He died there on 20 December 1843.

**John, Augustus** (1878–1961), painter and womanizer. While walking in Chelsea or Fitzrovia, John was said to pat any child encountered on the head in case it might be one of his. Among his known offspring were Admiral Casper John, who was able to beat his father in a fight, but lost both his legs in World War II, and Edwin, who became middleweight boxing champion of Wales. When his first wife, Ada, died, Augustus was too drunk to attend her cremation. His second wife, Dorelia 'Dodo' McNeil, was a gypsy and after the marriage he sometimes signed his name in Romany, 'Gustavus Janik'. Among John's conquests was the model and dancer, Caitlin Macnamara, who later married Dylan THOMAS. Caitlin claimed that John 'leaped on her, ripped her clothes off and penetrated her like some mindless old goat'. For his part, John said that Dylan Thomas became 'repetitive and tiresome when drunk'.

**Johnny the Gent.** *See* HOLLIDAY, BERT.

**Johnson, Samuel.** *See* CHATTERTON, THOMAS; DODD, THE REVEREND WILLIAM; LAUDER, WILLIAM; MACPHERSON, JAMES; PAYNE, CYNTHIA; PSALMANAZAR, GEORGE.

**Jones, Charles Horace** (1906–98), poet. For 45 years Jones distributed his poems in the streets of Merthyr Tydfil, Glamorganshire. His targets, which he denounced with increasing fury, were all things Welsh: BBC Wales, the Church of Wales and Welsh politicians in particular. Taking up his position in the marketplace, with an hour off for lunch, Jones attracted some support at first with his lampoons against lawyers, policemen, magistrates, bailiffs, tax commissioners and members of the Labour-controlled council. But as his onslaughts widened to include customs dear to the hearts of passers-by, support dried up. A poem about Welsh rugby that gave particular offence appeared on the day of an international in 1956, and blasphemously suggested that Wales was a nation that had:

> Lost its nerve and found it all
> In the blown-up bladder
> Of a rubber ball.

A gang of rugby supporters confronted Jones outside a butcher's shop. He escaped through a side door, but after that experience he always carried a knuckle-duster in his trousers. On another occasion he was knocked unconscious by a local businessman, who then tried to set fire to him. Again, Jones managed to escape.

When Jones was 5 his father was killed in a mining accident, and, at his mother's insistence, he left school at the age of 12 to work in the pits. By 1950 he was earning £150 a week running a crafts business, but he gave this up after he experienced a compulsion in the middle of the night to write his first poem on the back of a cigarette packet. Thereafter he was supported by his wife Delia, who took a part-time job in a baker's shop. He first came to public attention in 1955, when the Gorsedd of Bards threw him out of the National Eisteddfod at Cardiff for distributing a collection of satirical verses entitled *A Dose of Salts* and containing such aphorisms as, 'The Eisteddfod is a cultural circus where everything is Welsh except the money.' People had been buying it for a shilling in the belief that it was the official programme. On another occasion Jones appeared before the magistrate after he had refused to complete a census form. He came to court dressed in black and told the bench that he was attending the funeral of a man's freedom. He was fined £2.

In 1966 a collection of Jones's work, *The Challenger*, was published by Merthyr Tydfil council at a cost to themselves of £152 10s. The day after it appeared, Jones took up his position by a lamppost in the market place and abused the council for wasting tax payers' money. Asked why he always stood next to the lamppost, he explained that it meant he could only be assaulted from one side.

**Jones, Elizabeth Maud** (1926– ), cabaret artiste and murderess. Jones achieved the brief moment of celebrity she craved when, in 1944, she was involved in what came to be called the Cleft Chin Murder. In October of that year, and then aged 18, she met Karl Gustav Hulten, a deserter from a US parachute regiment based in Britain. He was posing as Lieutenant Ricky Hulten and she as an actress. In reality she was a striptease dancer, working under the name of Georgina Grayson and living in one room near Hammersmith Broadway. Together they lived out a romantic fantasy derived from the cinema, in which he imagined himself to be a gangster in the manner of James Cagney, she a gangster's moll in the style of Veronica Lake, who popularized the peek-a-boo hairstyle.

Their reign of terror in west London, during which they attempted to rob pedestrians and cyclists, was short-lived. One woman was hit repeatedly with an iron bar, nearly strangled and thrown into the Thames. Then, on 7 October, they hailed a taxi driven by George Edward Heath. In the course of the subsequent journey Hulten shot Heath dead and robbed him of 19 shillings, a silver pencil and a cigarette case.

Hulten and Jones then drove the cab to Staines, where they dumped Heath's body in a ditch. Although it was discovered the next morning, and a description of his taxi circulated, Hulten and Jones continued to drive around for five days until Hulten was arrested in the Fulham Palace Road. A few days later Jones struck up a conversation with a stranger in a Hammersmith café. He remarked on how pale she was looking, to which she replied, 'You'd look pale if you'd seen someone do what I've seen done.' Her companion turned out to be a policeman and Jones was arrested.

Jones and Hulten were both sentenced to death, and Hulten was hanged on 8 March 1945. Jones was reprieved on the grounds of her youth, a decision apparently deplored by Winston Churchill. A film about the case, *Chicago Joe and the Showgirl*, was released in 1992. Written by David Yallop, and starring Kiefer Sutherland and Emily Lloyd (the daughter of Roger Lloyd-Pack, who took the role of Trigger in the enduringly popular television series, *Only Fools and Horses*), it was generally judged to be a flop.

**Jones, Janie** (1941– ), recording artiste and madam. Sending Miss Jones to prison for seven years in 1974 for controlling prostitutes, Judge King-Hamilton QC called her 'the most evil woman I have ever had before me'. Some jurists were as surprised by the severity of this description as by the length of the sentence. In the same year Mrs Jean Horn, a far more influential madam than Jones and the representative of Norma Levy in the scandal involving Lord LAMBTON, was fined £100 for the same offence. One explanation for the conspicuous disparity in sentencing policy was that Mrs Horn had not irritated the police by driving round London in a pink Rolls Royce, nor had she failed to ask them to her celebrated Friday night musical evenings, at which Miss Zelda Plum danced with a chinchilla on her head. Later, Jones's guests would assemble in front of an artfully sited two-way mirror while another of her guests – unaware that he was being watched – performed on its other side with Franie Kum, later to marry the BBC Radio presenter, Johnnie Walker.

Jones was born Marion Mitchell, a miner's daughter, in Seaham, County Durham. At the age of 5 she won a clog-dancing competition. When she was 16 she came to London, where she soon obtained employment as a fan dancer at the Windmill Theatre. While trying to launch a singing career she met the film producer Michael Klinger, who was trying to drum up publicity for *London in the Raw*, which was about to open in Piccadilly. Jones suggested that she attend the first night topless. Later she was fined £25 at Bow Street Magistrates Court for 'committing an act of indecency to the annoyance of the general public'. In 1965 she released a record called 'Witches' Brew'. She sang it on television, wearing a pointed hat, and it reached number 37 in the charts.

The following year Jones was charged with blackmail – the first of various court appearances, amusingly documented by Paul Foot in his book *The Trials of Janie Jones* (1978). On this, as on later occasions, her former customers were allowed to take the stand as letters of the alphabet. Mr A, who had had sex with six of Jones's girls – Nina, Janice, Tessa, Crystal, Maureen and Tania – claimed that she had threatened to tell his wife if he didn't give her £1200. Mr A admitted to being 'nominally a sadist'. He had hoped that some of the girls would get into a pool and behave like fish, though it is unclear what that had to do with the blackmail allegation. It came as no great surprise when the jury acquitted Jones after retiring for half an hour.

A month later Jones was arrested again, charged this time with running a brothel. At her trial the police said that they had kept watch on her flat from a balcony on the house opposite and had seen Jones sitting on a US serviceman's lap. When Mr Victor Durand QC for the defence pointed out that there wasn't a balcony on the house opposite – indeed, that there wasn't even a house – the case collapsed. Why the police were not charged with perjury and attempting to pervert the course of justice was never explained. Perhaps they would have given up at this point, but in June 1971 the *News of the World* printed a story about a payola scandal at the BBC. This claimed that Jones was running a call-girl ring and that her girls, believing that they were auditioning for parts on radio and television, were being tricked by her into having sex with disc jockeys and producers. In December 1973 Jones was charged at the Old Bailey on 21 counts, the most serious of which was that she had blackmailed a peer, known as Lord Y. Nina, Janice, Tessa, Crystal, Maureen and Tania again put in appearances as themselves, on this occasion testifying that Lord Y carried a teddy bear and liked them to dress as schoolgirls. Some were no longer in their first youth, a circumstance made more inconvenient by Lord Y's habit of suddenly asking them the date of their birth. If they got this wrong they were asked to leave. They would then walk around the block and return, to Lord Y's complete satisfaction, as their own younger sister. Again it came as no surprise when Janie was acquitted of the blackmail charge, but she was sentenced anyway by King-Hamilton to seven years for the minor offence of controlling prostitutes.

In October 1974 Janie came second in the Holloway song contest, and in April 1977 she was freed on parole. She returned to her old home in Kensington with Denise, a warder from Holloway. As a precaution against further police interest in her affairs she let the basement of her house to three Carmelite nuns. In 1987 *Private Eye* alleged that Judge King-Hamilton had been a client of Miss Lindi ST CLAIR, the Earls Court dominatrix, celebrated for her arguments with the Inland Revenue.

**Jones, Vinnie** (1953– ), footballer and film actor. A hard man by his own account – a claim believed by few since his scrawny build would stand him in poor stead in a bar-room brawl or rugby scrummage – Jones was a footballer of negligible talent. His conduct as a player was a disgrace, but Jones himself has few regrets. He recalls with pride the incident when he took a grip on Paul GASCOIGNE's groin. 'I wanted to kill him. Literally rip off his arms and legs and head. That was the mood I was in. The rolling eyes and everything.' On the other hand, the photograph that appeared in the *Daily Mirror* the day after he had tried to bite a football journalist's nose off did cause him some embarrassment. Indeed, he even contemplated suicide. 'I lost respect for myself. I took my shotgun into the woods. Then my little dog licked my nose. He broke me out of it.'

The short journey from making a fool of himself on the football field to doing the same in films such as *Lock, Stock and Two Smoking Barrels* (1998) has not proved difficult. Judged to have 'screen presence', Jones now divides his time between London and Los Angeles, appearing on 'Celebrity Ready, Steady, Cook' and considering which film script to accept on his way to fulfilling his ambition, which is to be 'the next Brad Pitt'.

**Jones, William** (*c*.1739–?), doctor, antiquarian and one of the scholars caught up in the Madoc fever that gripped Wales in 1792. In that year, Jones circulated an address declaring that Welsh-speaking Indians – descended from the followers of Prince Madoc – had been contacted in Missouri. This turned out not to be the case (*see* EVANS, JOHN).

**Jordan, John** (1950– ), secretary of the British Boomerang Society, founded in 1979 in anticipation of the demise of the Society for the Promotion and Avoidance of Boomerangs. While the SPAB had been successful in at least one of its aims (offering advice on how to avoid boomerangs) the interests of its members had proved to be too limited. Since its formation the BBS has made its mark on the international world of boomerangs in a variety of ways. To increase its members' enjoyment of throwing, catching and avoiding boomerangs, the society publishes *The British Boomerang Society Journal*, which is packed with competition news, historical articles and up-to-date information on materials needed to make boomerangs (aviation plywood and Paxolin).

'Among our ranks', says Jordan, 'you will find casual throwers, dedicated throwers, and some addicted boomerholics. What marks the genuine enthusiast is his willingness to share his knowledge of boomerangs with others.'

**'judge and jury' shows.** *See* NICHOLSON, 'BARON' RENTON.

**judge confuses witness with Marilyn Monroe.** *See* RICE-DAVIES, MANDY.

**judge laughs.** *See* NICHOLSON, 'BARON' RENTON (for Sir John Jervis).

**judges, odd, vicious or wrong-headed.** *See* ARGYLE, MICHAEL; BIGAMY (for Lord Maul); BILLING, PEMBERTON (for Lord Darling); BLACKBURN, RAYMOND (for Lord Chief Goddard); BOTTOMLEY, HORATIO (for Mr Justice Hawkins); BRAUN, HEIDE (for Mr Justice Butler); CLONMELL, JOHN SCOTT, 1ST EARL OF; HALL, NEWMAN (for Sir James Hannen);

JEFFREYS, GEORGE; JONES, JANIE (for Judge King-Hamilton QC); KEELER, CHRISTINE (for Lord Denning); NORBURY, JOHN TOLER, 1ST BARON; STEVENSON, SIR MELFORD; THOMPSON, EDITH (for Mr Justice Shearman).

**judges, sensible.** *See* BOULTON, ERNEST (for Lord Chief Justice Cockburn); FAGAN, MICHAEL (for Judge James Miskin QC); NASH, JIMMY (for Mr Justice Gorman); WENHAM, JANE (for Mr Justice Powell).

**judges, tooled up.** *See* BIDWELL, GEORGE.

**judges, unamused.** *See* the cases of: BIGGAR, JOSEPH; BINT, PAUL.

**judge's morals compared to those of a bashaw in Turkey, a.** *See* JEFFREYS, GEORGE.

**judges who makes jokes.** *See* STEVENSON, SIR MELFORD.

**Julian of Norwich** (*c.*1342–*c.*1413), mystic. Strangely enough, she was a nun. She was blessed with the gift of seeing the whole world in a hazelnut.

**junk, a description of a Chinese.** *See* TRELAWNY, EDWARD.

**justice, miscarriages of.** *See* BRIAN, JOHN HERMAN; ELLIS RUTH; JONES, JANIE; WARD, STEPHEN.

# k

**Kagan, Lord Joseph** (1915–95), textile manufacturer and fraud. Joseph Kagan arrived in Britain as a refugee in 1946. In time he became a millionaire, a friend of Harold Wilson and a life peer. In 1980 he served a ten-month sentence for fraud in Rudgate open prison – a setback that he survived with great resilience. Some suspected him of being a KGB agent, but this was unlikely to have been the case.

Kagan was born in Lithuania and later sent by his father to Leeds University, where he took a degree in commerce. World War II broke out when he was visiting Lithuania and he was interned for the duration. After the war he persuaded the British mission in Bucharest to allow him to come to England. He claimed later that he had been penniless when he arrived but in fact his father had transferred part of his business to Elland in Yorkshire, where Kagan took a job as a salesman. After various projects, none of which got off the ground, he made his fortune with Gannex cloth, in which air was sealed between nylon and wool linings to create a lightweight fabric that was also warm and waterproof. This received wide publicity when Harold Wilson wore a Gannex raincoat on a visit to Russia in 1966. In the same year Kagan pulled off a remarkable promotional coup when he persuaded the duke of Edinburgh's valet to order a Gannex coat from Harrods, which immediately placed a large order.

To capitalize on Wilson's patronage, Kagan became a major contributor to Labour Party funds, and he helped to finance Wilson's private office. His reward was to be created a life peer in Wilson's resignation honours list of 1976.

Kagan's eventual business difficulties stemmed, perhaps, from a temperamental preference for short cuts over long-term planning. When sales of Gannex fell away, he entered the expanding market for denim. For a time he prospered, but in 1978 he was charged with the theft of indigo dye and with defrauding the public revenue. He abandoned his wife and child and fled the country. He first sought asylum in Israel, claiming that he had been the victim of British anti-Semitism, but he was turned away. He next tried Spain, which at the time had no extradition treaty with Britain, but on a trip to Paris he was informed on by a disaffected mistress. Back in Britain he insisted that customs inspectors interview him in the ante-room of the House of Lords. 'My full title is Baron Kagan of Elland,' he informed them, 'but you may call me Lord Kagan.' He described his subsequent ten-month prison sentence as 'a fascinating experience which I am glad not to have missed'. On his release from jail he returned immediately to the House of Lords. 'I do not feel disgraced in any way,' he declared.

**Kaggs, John** (*c.*1790–*c.*1870), distinguished patriarch of the Kaggs family whose members were among the most creative confidence tricksters in Victorian London. Mr Kaggs had begun his career as a domestic servant. Having risen to the rank of butler, he had run off with, and married, the daughter of his employer. They had several children, of whom Betsy, the eldest, was an accomplished actress. Attended by a servant, Betsy would call at the house of a philanthropic lady, to whom she would introduce herself as the daughter of a gallant but ailing army officer now reduced to poverty. To raise a little money, she was offering her few possessions for sale to ladies known for their charitable works.

In some cases this led to a visit from the benefactress to the Kaggs home. Mr Kaggs was put to bed in the garret, his face made up to suggest that he was mortally ill. The Kaggs family in fact occupied the entire house, but this affecting tableau suggested that they were confined to its sparsely furnished upper reaches. Medicine bottles, a bible and an army newspaper were placed by the bed. Another daughter was dressed as a nurse. The visitor would be told that the stricken Mr Kaggs had been wounded at Barrosa in the Peninsular War and discharged from the army. An unworldly half-lieutenant, he had been persuaded to invest his small savings in railway shares, only to be cheated out of them by an absconding broker. His old wound, received at Barrosa, had broken out again and laid him low. The two youngest Kaggs children sat by the bed, dressed in black.

It was a faultless performance, and the Kaggs family prospered until they became too widely known. Deciding that they should leave for Australia, Mr Kaggs put an advertisement in *The Times* informing readers that 'a poor but respectable family required a small sum to enable them to make up the amount of their passage to Australia, and that they could give the highest references as to character.' The response to this was so generous that Mr Kaggs and his family were able to live for another two years in London, before finally departing for Melbourne.

**kangaroo courts.** *See* EDINBURGH, PRINCE PHILIP, DUKE OF.

**Kate, Carrotty.** *See* FAIRS, TRAVELLING.

**Kay, Fanny.** *See* AGAR, EDWARD.

**Kean, Edmund** (*c.*1789–1833), actor, philanderer and drunk. One of the most popular performers of his day, excelling in villainous rather than heroic roles, Kean in the end lost favour with a public that had grown impatient with his drunken absences and other mishaps. By the 1820s it was necessary to sober him up before a performance by holding his head under a jet of cold water. If this didn't work he sat in a box and heckled his understudy. One night, when Kean was booked to play Hamlet at Drury Lane, the dousing failed to have the necessary effect and the management had to announce that the play would proceed without the prince. Sir Walter Scott, who was in the audience, said later that it had been greatly improved.

Born in London, Kean was thought to be the illegitimate son of Anne Carey, an actress and entertainer, and granddaughter of the musician and playwright Henry Carey. Carey wrote the music hall song 'Sally in our Alley', and invented the phrase 'Namby Pamby' as a nickname for Ambrose Philips. Kean's father was probably Edmund Kean, an actor and drunk who committed suicide when his son was an infant. The young Kean was taken into care by Charlotte Tidswell, an actress of no great accomplishment, who was formerly the mistress of Kean's Uncle Moses, a ventriloquist. As a child he was taught singing, dancing, fencing and elocution, and by the age of 8 he had made several appearances on stage at Drury Lane.

In 1804 Kean became an itinerant player, and in 1808 he married an actress, Mary Chambers, by whom he had two sons. His first major role was Shylock at Drury Lane in 1814. Thereafter his performances as Macbeth, Richard III and Iago won him great popularity, which he regularly lost through drunkenness and debauchery. In the United States, which he first visited in 1820, there was a similar pattern. During a performance of Macbeth in New York he was so drunk he could hardly stagger through the opening scenes. At the interval the stage manager was forced to tell the audience that the play would have to proceed without Mr Kean, who was suffering from malaria. A dissatisfied customer announced from the stalls that he could do with a bottle of that himself.

Kean's last performance was with his son Charles, at Drury Lane on 25 March 1833. He collapsed while playing Othello to his son's Iago, and died a few weeks later. On this occasion at least he had avoided the mistake made by one of his most distinguished successors in the role. During the 1955 season at the Old Vic, Richard Burton and John Neville alternated the parts of Othello and Iago. One day they went out to celebrate between the matinee and the evening performance, returned to the theatre and both played Iago.

*See also* NEWTON, ROBERT.

**Keane, John** (1938– ), policeman. On 26 October 1980 City businessmen, enjoying a quiet drink at the Albion public house in Ludgate Circus, were surprised when a fight broke out between two of their number. In fact, one was Detective Superintendent John Keane and the other Detective Inspector Bernard Gent of the Metropolitan Police. The fight was started when Keane, the older man, tried to snatch a tape recorder from Gent's pocket. He had correctly guessed that Gent was taping the conversation, which had recorded a request by Keane that Gent, in return for a bribe of £10,000, would 'lose' the evidence that might convict a man charged with a substantial robbery. Inspector Gent was eventually able to secure Keane in a headlock from which the superintendent was unable to break free. The tape recording was safe and Keane subsequently went to prison for three years.

**Keating, Tom** (1917–84), art forger. Born in London, Keating had ambitions to be a great artist from the age of 10, when he won a paintbox in a school competition. Invalided out of the navy in 1947, he took a course at Goldsmith's College, London, where he failed his exams. This setback left him with a lifelong grudge against the art establishment, which he saw as a self-perpetuating elite. Unable to sell his own paintings, he found employment on the more suspect fringes of 'restoration' work, and finally took up outright forgery. He was exposed in 1976 when the art critic of *The Times* suggested that a Samuel Palmer sold at auction was not genuine. Keating admitted that a series of nine pictures, bearing Palmer's signature, had in fact been drawn by him. He estimated that there were some 2000 of his fakes in circulation. In 1979 he was put on trial at the Old Bailey, but the charges were eventually dropped because of his failing health. He was able, however, to appear in an award-winning television series, in which he demonstrated the techniques of different painters, from Titian to Degas.

Keating and his forgeries enjoyed a growing popularity, and after his death in 1984 a sale of his work brought in £274,000. He insisted to the end that his activities had been a protest against the exploitation of artists by dealers – a protest to which Palmer himself must have been party since Keating always claimed that his copies were guided by the spirit of the artist:

> I'd sit in my little sketching room waiting for something to happen.
> I have never drawn a sheep from life but then Palmer's sheep would
> begin to appear on the paper. With Sam's permission, I sometimes
> signed them with his name, but they were his, not mine. It was his
> hand that guided the pen.

The art establishment retaliated by pointing out that Keating's forgeries had never been very good.

**Keech, William** (c.1860–?), footballer. In the 1890s 'Lord' George Sanger's celebrated travelling fair had as its main attractions an elephant that took penalty kicks. The elephant was a formidable opponent, both at taking penalties and at saving them. The feeling grew that the elephant was unbeatable.

When the fair reached Leicestershire the elephant was challenged by four professional soccer players from Leicester Fosse FC. The first three failed to beat the elephant, and it was left to Keech to retrieve the club's honour. Faced with a goalkeeper of this size, Keech realized that his only hope was to work a dummy, sending the elephant the wrong way. He therefore performed a little shimmy in his run-up and as the elephant dived to the right in anticipation of the shot, Keech placed the ball in the top left-hand corner. Using these tactics Keech held the elephant to a 2–2 draw, winning the rematch 3–2.

**Keeler, Christine** (1942–  ), nightclub dancer, alleged call girl and central figure in the Profumo scandal that kept the public entertained throughout the summer of 1963. It has been suggested that, with the benefit of hindsight, the antics of the leading participants can be seen as merely comic – as they were seen as comic at the time – but this is to overlook the fact that they destroyed the life of an innocent man, the society osteopath, Stephen WARD.

The events that led to Ward's death began in July 1961, when he introduced Keeler to John Profumo, then secretary of state for war, at Cliveden, the home of Lord Astor. Another guest was Captain Eugene Ivanov, a Soviet naval attaché and a KGB agent. For a short time thereafter Keeler entertained both Profumo and Ivanov at Stephen Ward's flat in Wimpole Mews, London. In spite of what was later alleged, no money changed hands. In fact, prostitution, had she ever tried it, was not a profession at which Miss Keeler would have prospered. Unlike her exhibitionist friend, Mandy RICE-DAVIS, Keeler had an introspective disposition and her sexual appetite was sporadic but – which would have been a considerable disadvantage in a professional – intense. When aroused it took as its object black men only – a circumstance but for which there might not have been a scandal. In December 1962 one of her Jamaican lovers, Johnny Edgecombe, disappointed at having been replaced in her affections by Lucky Gordon, a jazz singer, fired a gun outside her flat. When Keeler failed to appear at Edgecombe's Old Bailey trial the rumour circulated that someone had been paid to take her out of the country (see MANN, PAUL). On 22 March 1963 Profumo made the statement in the Commons that was to put an end to his career. 'There was no impropriety whatsoever,' he said, 'in my acquaintance with Miss Keeler.'

Two months later Profumo admitted that this had been a lie and he resigned, causing widespread speculation about the morals of the government, of whom it was said that at least half practised sexual perversions. The master of the rolls, Lord Denning, was invited to conduct an inquiry, and on 22 July 1963 Stephen Ward appeared at the Old Bailey charged with living off the immoral earnings of Christine Keeler and Mandy Rice-Davies. Believing that the case was going against him, and while the judge was still summing up, Ward took an overdose of drugs. The jury convicted him in his absence and sentence was postponed until he was fit to appear. Ward never recovered consciousness and he died on 3 August. There were six mourners at his funeral, and two wreaths. One was from his family. The other contained 100 white carnations and was from Kenneth Tynan, John Osborne, Annie Ross, Arnold Wesker, Penelope Gilliatt and Joe Orton. The card on it read, 'To Stephen Ward, Victim of Hypocrisy'.

*The Denning Report*, published on 26 October 1963, was an immediate success, with 4000 copies sold in the first hour. It was generally taken to be a whitewash, laying the blame for the scandal squarely at the feet of Stephen Ward. 'He was utterly immoral,' Denning found, 'a man who kept pornographic photographs and attended parties where there were sexual orgies of a revolting nature.' Some critics felt that Denning had been more interested in the sexual aspects of the affair than its security implications – but this was the sensible choice. It is unlikely that Profumo discussed state secrets with Keeler in the course of their few brief meetings, even less likely that she would have remembered them if he had, and unlikeliest of all that, even if she had remembered them and subsequently passed them on to Ivanov, they would have proved of any assistance to the Russians.

Of the many rumours flying round London, there were two that Lord Denning was most concerned to investigate: the first that a cabinet minister was attending orgies naked but for a small apron; the second that the same cabinet minister, or someone equally distinguished, was the reality behind the ghostly 'Headless Man' who had featured so notably in the duchess of ARGYLL's divorce. On the matter of orgies, Denning wrote:

> There is a great deal of evidence which satisfied me that there is a group of people who hold parties in private of a perverted nature. At some of these parties, the man who serves dinner is nearly naked except for a small square lace apron round his waist such as a waitress might wear. He wears a black mask over his head with slits for eye-holes. He cannot therefore be recognized by any of the guests. Some reports stop there and say that nothing evil takes place. This may well be so at some of the parties. But at others I am satisfied that it is followed by perverted sex orgies: that the man in the mask is a 'slave' who is whipped: that guests undress and indulge in sexual

intercourse one with the other: and indulge in other sexual activities of a vile and revolting nature. My only concern in my inquiry was to see whether any minister was present at these parties; for, if he were, he would, I should think, be exposing himself to blackmail.

Denning was later able to say that the name of the 'Man in the Mask' had been disclosed to him, and that, happily, he was not a cabinet minister. In order to nail the rumour identifying the same minister (in fact Duncan Sandys) as the 'Headless Man' featured in the duchess of Argyll's divorce, Denning took the unusual step of having the minister's penis examined in chambers by a Harley Street consultant. It is not known whether Denning discovered – as it has since been discovered – that the 'Headless Man' was in fact the film actor, Douglas Fairbanks Jnr.

Miss Keeler's subsequent life appears not to have been happy. She has a son from each of two failed marriages and survives modestly in south London on the proceeds of her 1989 autobiography, *Scandal*, which was later filmed. The part of Keeler was taken by Joanna Kilmer Whaley, that of Mandy Rice-Davies by the American actress Bridget Fonda. Sir Ian McKellan appeared in a bald wig, and to excellent comic effect, as John Profumo.

**Kelaher, Detective Chief Inspector Victor** (1935– ), policeman. Of the various successful raids carried out by Customs and Excise officers in the late 1960s, the one that gave them most satisfaction occurred when they found the head of Scotland Yard's Drugs Squad, Detective Chief Inspector Kelaher, in the Holland Park flat of a prostitute, Mrs Roberts. Mrs Roberts's former husband, a Ghanaian diplomat, had been arrested by Kelaher for importing drugs in 1967. For some time Customs and Excise had been keeping a closer watch on Kelaher's activities than on those of major dealers, so this was a significant victory. They confiscated some jewellery that Kelaher had given Mrs Roberts, but on this occasion he escaped prosecution.

Shortly after this incident, two Arabs arranged for a shipment of cannabis to be delivered in London to a Bahamian pimp, Basil Sands. Kelaher and Sands had known one another for some years. The consignment arrived in the middle of a postal strike and Sands's call to British European Airways to check on the delay was tapped by Customs and Excise. They discovered that Sands had arranged with Kelaher that the drugs should be delivered to the Melba House Hotel in Earl's Court, which was owned by Ghassan Idriss, a friend of Mr and Mrs Roberts. On 5 March 1971 Customs officers surrounded the hotel and arrested Sands, Idriss, Mr and Mrs Roberts, and, when he arrived at the hotel later in the evening, DCI Kelaher was questioned by Customs for five hours, and then released.

A power struggle then took place between Customs, the Home Office and Scotland Yard. Home Office officials wanted a full investigation into the Drugs Squad, but this was blocked by Deputy Assistant Commissioner Dick Chitty, who argued that a prosecution of Kelaher would do little to improve relations between Customs and the police. The argument was accepted, and Kelaher was transferred to administrative duties at Tintagel House.

At his trial Sands claimed that he was an informant for Kelaher, who, with three other Drug Squad detectives, Pilcher, Prichard and Lilley, gave evidence for the defence. John Marriage, representing Customs, questioned Kelaher's credibility, and in his summing-up Judge Alan Trapnell said:

> A forthright attack had been made on the character of Chief Inspector Kelaher, but the jury must not let their opinion of the inspector sway their verdict even if in private they believe he was in the middle of the smuggling ring. If he is to be judged, let him be judged properly by another tribunal on some other occasion.

Pilcher, Prichard and Lilley were later imprisoned for perjury. Kelaher, who had spent a year attending St Thomas's Hospital for treatment of a nervous complaint, was allowed to resign and given a medical discharge.

*See also* LILLEY, DETECTIVE CONSTABLE NIGEL.

**Kelly, Shanghai** (1835–?), sailor, crimp and kidnapper. In the history of crimping – the supplying of sailors by means of kidnap – Kelly, a stubby, red-bearded Irishman, stands out as the most resourceful operator. Forced to flee England after a man was stabbed to death in a drunken brawl in Portsmouth, he set up as a crimp on San Francisco's Barbary Coast. During the 1870s he was estimated to have provided sailing vessels with as many as 10,000 unwilling seamen. As a rule his stock would have been gathered by means of drink or drugs, but sometimes more ingenious methods were required.

On one occasion Kelly was contracted to supply three ships, all of which were putting to sea on the same day, each requiring 90 sailors. This was an unusually large order, but Kelly was not confounded. Having rented an old paddle steamer, on which he installed several bar tenders and a dozen 'ladies of the docks', he advertised a 'sex excursion', held to celebrate his birthday. Customers were promised three days of unconstrained abandonment with as much drink and feminine company as they might require.

In spite of the large admission fee charged by Kelly, there was a rush for tickets. As soon as he had 90 passengers on board, Kelly raised the gang-plank and the steamer paddled out to sea. Barrels of drugged beer and whisky were opened and in no time the celebrating customers were out cold, later to be transferred, at the going rate of $100 a body, to the three ships in need of crews. Kelly had enriched himself twice over: once by the sex excursion that never was, and once by providing men with a long sea voyage they hadn't expected.

Another technique perfected by Kelly was the inclusion of a corpse or two among the drugged bodies, and if a corpse wasn't immediately available, he improvised by mixing in a dummy: a dirty old suit of clothes was stuffed with straw and the 'head' concealed under a muffler. Legend has it that no dummy designed by Kelly was ever discovered by a captain, such was the care that had gone into its creation. One sophisticated touch was to sew a live rat into each of its coat sleeves. As the dummy lay in a heap among the drugged bodies, the efforts of the rats to escape made the dummy seem to twitch, and their muffled squeaks sounded like the groans of a semiconscious drunk.

Kelly became so notorious that he was forced eventually to take up other criminal pursuits. He remained an inspiration, however, to crimps who came after him. One of them, Nikko the Laplander, sometimes included a cigar-store Indian among his wares instead of a corpse, though it is unclear why.

**Kensington, fashionable brothels in.** *See* JEFFRIES, MARY.

**Kensington, visions in South.** *See* CLANCARTY, WILLIAM FRANCIS BRINSLEY LE POER TRENCH, 8TH EARL OF.

*See also* CHELSEA, AGGRIEVED DRUG USERS OF; CHELSEA, PHILANDERING MPS WHO HAVE REPRESENTED; CHELSEA FOOTBALL CLUB SHIRT, MAKING LOVE IN A; CHELSEA PUBLIC HOUSE WITH ONE'S THROAT CUT, FOUND OUTSIDE A.

**Kensington, West.** *See* MELLOR, DAVID.

**Keppel, Mrs.** *See* EDWARD VII.

**Keyhoe, Mickey** (1935–87), bank robber and alleged informer. Underworld opinion is divided on whether Keyhoe is the most successful informer in criminal history, or greatly maligned. Experts agree that the leading participants in the Great Train Robbery of 1963 were informed on to Detective Chief Superintendent Tommy BUTLER within days of the job, and that his investigative task thereafter was the comparatively simple one of supplying the evidence that would put them away. Commander John Cunningham, the former head of Scotland Yard's C11 Intelligence Unit, and underworld boss Freddie FOREMAN are at one on this point. Thereafter, they disagree.

Cunningham has revealed that Keyhoe worked for him for many years, and that it was he who informed on the train robbers. He has also confirmed that Butler was corrupt. Foreman agrees that there was an informer. 'Tommy Butler had the names the day after the job,' he has said on BBC television, 'but Mickey Keyhoe? Never. I knew Mickey for years. He was a good bank robber. He was never an informer.' On the same programme Gordon GOODY, one of the leading train robbers, confirmed that Keyhoe was a friend of his, and as straight a villain as you could find. On the other hand, John McVicar, the armed robber turned writer, agrees with Commander Cunningham that Keyhoe was Butler's informer. The matter remains a mystery. Goody and Foreman do not strike impartial observers as naïve, but Cunningham was an impressive witness.

'Mad' Frankie FRASER, when asked for his opinion, said that he agreed with Foreman and Goody. He then revealed that Keyhoe was knocked down and killed by a police motorcyclist who was escorting the queen on a visit to the All England Tennis Club Championships at Wimbledon in 1985. This may be one of Fraser's jokes.

**kicked unconscious in front of the servants.** *See* FERRERS, ROBERT SHIRLEY, 2ND EARL.

**Kidd, William** (1645–1701), pirate. Kidd was a respected sea captain in New York when he was hired by William III in 1695 as a government-commissioned privateer, authorized to seize 'pirates, freebooters and sea-rovers of what nature soever' in the name of the British government. Though celebrated in English literature as one of the most colourful outlaws of all time, Kidd's subsequent career illustrates how dangerous it is to tread the dividing line between thief-taker and thief (*see*, for example, HITCHEN, CHARLES; WILD, JONATHAN).

Born in Renfrewshire, Scotland, Kidd went to sea as a youth, and in the 1680s captained a fleet of trading vessels based in New York. During the war of the League of Augsburg against France (1688–97) he fought as a privateer to protect Anglo-American trade routes in the West Indies. In 1695 he was given command of an expedition against pirates in the Indian Ocean. Early in 1697, he reached Madagascar in his ship the *Adventure Galley*, and it was at some point after his arrival there that he decided to turn pirate. In August 1697 he made an unsuccessful attack on two ships sailing with mocha coffee from Yemen, but later took several smaller ships. His refusal two months later to attack a Dutch ship nearly brought his crew to mutiny, and in an angry exchange he shot and killed his gunner, William Moore.

In 1699 Kidd returned to the West Indies to find he had been denounced as a pirate. He sailed to New York, where he protested his innocence to the earl of Bellomont, then colonial governor of New York City. Although he had been a private backer of Kidd's expedition three years earlier, Bellomont sent him to England for trial.

On 9 May 1701 Kidd was found guilty of the murder of Moore and on five indictments of piracy. He claimed throughout that his men had mutinied and forced him to lead them in acts of piracy. His cause divided MPs and public opinion, with many believing that there had been a miscarriage of justice. The Admiralty had suppressed evidence in Kidd's favour and it was clear that the trial was intended to inculpate his important backers as well as him. Nevertheless, he was hanged on 9 May at Execution Dock, Wapping. The rope broke, and Kidd, still conscious, but very drunk, fell to the ground before being strung up a second time.

Kidd's name has become inseparable from the romanticized concept of the swashbuckling pirate of western fiction. Among the many stories concerning caches of treasure he supposedly buried, Edgar Allen Poe's *The Gold Bug* stands out. Fortune hunters still try – without success – to locate the sunken wreck of the *Adventure Galley*. A film, *Abbott and Costello Meet Captain Kidd* (1952), in which Charles Laughton plays the eponymous pirate, shows the slapstick comedians at the top of their form.

**killers, contract.** *See* ELLUL, PHILIP; FOREMAN, FREDDIE; GAUL, JOHN (for Keith and Roy Edgeler); NGARIMU, TE RANGIMARIA.

**Kimberley, John Wodehouse, 4th earl of** (1923–2002), shark fisherman and bobsleigh champion. Kimberley was proud of his title as Britain's most married peer, having notched up one more wife than had been managed by his two closest rivals, Lord Lilford and the late Lord Waterpark. The count began in 1945 with Diana Legh, whose father was master of George VI's household. She was succeeded by the daughters of an Australian boxer, a Suffolk doctor, a Hertfordshire café proprietor and an army colonel. His sixth wife Janie formerly worked in a beauty parlour. One fiancée, Countess 'Tiger' Cowley, broke off the engagement.

Educated at Eton and Cambridge, and a relative of P.G. Wodehouse, Kimberley came from a land-owning family of Elizabethan origin, but alimony difficulties cost him his Norfolk estate. In his younger days he made many appearances in tabloid gossip columns. 'If you were as drunk as I was,' he explained, 'it was hard to avoid.'

In 1971 he gave up visiting nightclubs and signed on with Alcoholics Anonymous. He subsequently became chairman of the National Council on Alcoholism and was reputed to believe in flying saucers.

**Kincaid, John.** *See* PRICKERS, SCOTTISH.

**King-Hamilton, His Honour Myer Alan Barry.** *See* JONES, JANIE; ST CLAIR, LINDI.

**King Loon.** *See* MOON, KEITH.

**Kingsale, John de Courcy, 35th Baron** (1941– ), Kingsale, who once described himself as '*nouveau pauvre*', is Ireland's premier baron (created 1223), able to trace his family back to before the Norman conquest. When inheriting his title he discovered that his estate consisted of a lighthouse near Cork, which produced an income of £80 a year against rates of £92. This circumstance obliged him to work, variously, as a plumber, a carpenter, a bingo-caller and manufacturer of silage pits in the West Country. He has also been employed on the duke of Bedford's Woburn Abbey estates as a safari park keeper, and in 1964 he played an Egyptian peasant in *Cleopatra*, a Hollywood epic starring Elizabeth Taylor and Richard Burton.

Kingsale's later preoccupation – in which he has so far been unsuccessful – has been to find a suitable bride with whom to continue the family line. Should he fail in this ambition, the title will go to an elderly cousin in New Zealand, who works as a municipal drains inspector.

Kingsale believes that a curse was placed on his ancestor, John de Courcy, who mislaid St Patrick's bones when subduing Ulster in the 12th century. The Nine Bards of Ireland decreed that for this act of carelessness the family would live forever and never prosper.

**Kingsborough, Edward King, 4th Viscount** (1795–1837), politician and author, who, undeterred by the commonly held view that the New World had not been discovered until 1492, devoted his adult life to the proposition that the lost tribes of Israel were to be located in Mexico. With some reason, Kingsborough pointed out that:

> It will not avail those who wish to insinuate that Moses was ignorant of the existence of America, and therefore did not mean to prophesy that the Jews would be scattered about the continent, since this would be to argue absurdly that human knowledge prescribes limits to Divine inspiration.

After a boyhood spent in Ireland, Kingsborough went to Exeter College, Oxford, where in 1818 he gained an undistinguished degree in classics. He served as MP for County Cork until 1826. He then gave up politics, and every sort of pleasure and pastime – including the idea of marriage – to devote his life to the study of Mexico. His interest had been aroused in Oxford when he came across a manuscript called the Mendoza Codex. Not long after the conquest of Mexico, this codex had been captured at sea by the French, and instead of going to the Spanish king (and Holy Roman emperor), Charles V, it had found its way to Paris, where it had been bought by the chaplain to the English embassy. Two hundred years later it turned up in the Bodleian Library, where the sight of it fired Kingsborough with enthusiasm for Mexico and its past. Although he

398 **Kingsborough, Edward King, 4th Viscount**

never found time to visit the country, he was inspired to undertake the colossal task that was to last his lifetime. He decided to trace other Mexican documents that had found their way to Europe over the centuries and to assemble them in a series of volumes that he would publish himself.

Thereafter, his researches turned up material in the royal libraries of Paris, Berlin and Dresden, in the imperial library in Vienna, in the Borgia museums and in the Vatican. The only source of Mexican documents that Kingsborough didn't think to investigate was the most important: since he never went to Spain to inspect the libraries there, his compilation was inevitably incomplete. Not that he would have considered it so. He had never intended that his should be a work of scholarship, which was as well, perhaps, since he had no knowledge of the language in which the documents were written or the background they described. He used them merely to demonstrate his passionate belief in the early Hebrew colonization of America, an idea he had derived from the writings of Montecino:

> We have the authority of a Jew for believing that a colony of Jews had been settled in America long before the age of Columbus. It is certainly remarkable that they should for so many generations have retained a lively recollection of their Christian persecutions, and should consequently have adopted precautions to prevent the Spaniards discovering their retreat. Their repeated utterance of the syllable Ba! accompanied by furious gesticulations and stamping with their feet, afforded proof also of the fanaticism which still animated them.

An important task was to find similarities between Mexicans and Jews in their laws, customs and religion. Kingsborough discovered prohibitions against the eating of pork in both cultures, and similar attitudes to the idea of sacrifice:

> In nothing did the Mexicans more resemble the Jews than in the multitude of their sacrifices. The Jews, it is well known, never tasted blood; and though the Mexicans devoured the flesh of human victims, they were never allowed to taste the blood.

A reference he found in the Old Testament explained away the fact that the Mexican complexion was darker than the Semitic, '"Men whose visages were to become blacker than coal," occurs in the fourth chapter of Jeremiah.' In fact it doesn't, but the broad sweep rather than rigorous scholarship was Kingsborough's purpose.

The first of the massive volumes entitled *Antiquities of Mexico*, paid for by Kingsborough himself, appeared in 1830. It was followed by another every year for seven years, and two more were published after Kingsborough's death. The work was well received, except in certain academic quarters. The historian of Mexico W.H. Prescott considered the presence of Jews in pre-Columbian America to be as fanciful as the stories of Queen Scheherazade in *The Arabian Nights*, and much less entertaining:

> His theory will scarcely become popular, since instead of being exhibited in a clear and comprehensive form, readily embraced by the mind, it is spread over an infinite number of notes, thickly sprinkled with quotations from languages ancient and modern, till the weary reader, floundering about in the ocean of fragments with no light to guide him, feels like Milton's devil working his way through chaos.

The enterprise, which cost Kingsborough £32,000, was not a commercial success. He gave away numerous free copies: nine sets of volumes were sent to the crowned heads of Europe, and two, printed on vellum with coloured plates at a cost of £3000 each, were presented to Oxford University. His obsession cost him his fortune, and perhaps his life. After he had spent all his money on the venture, debts accrued. He couldn't pay his stationer or his printer, and his illustrator, Augustus Aglio, claimed copyright on his work and submitted an enormous bill.

In 1837 Kingsborough was arrested for debt. Thrown into the squalid confines of the Sheriff's Prison in Dublin, he died of typhus on 3 March 1837, at the age of 42 – one year before his father, from whom he would have inherited the earldom and an income of £40,000.

**Kingsland, Gerald** (1930–2000), journalist, writer and castaway. Some people have seen it as Kingsland's misfortune that, to those who never met him, he will be known only from an impersonation on film by the actor Oliver REED. He led an eventful life and may have deserved better.

Born a chauffeur's son in Whitchurch, Buckinghamshire, on the edge of a large estate, the young Kingsland took a strong interest in improving his position, and, by his own account, an even stronger one in the underwear worn by the maids up at the Big House. After a spell in the Parachute Regiment, with which he saw service in Korea, the interest in underwear took him, via Fleet Street, into the pornography industry, where he edited the 'top shelf' magazine *Mayfair*, and started *Curious*. In spite of the cash flow thus generated, and the cars and mistresses it allowed him to acquire, happiness eluded him. An early marriage failed, as did four others. He left the magazine business to grow grapes in Italy, but he had a drink problem by now, and instead of nurturing his grapes he spent much time weeping on a hillside, realizing, as he said, that he'd 'ballsed things up'.

It was then that Kingsland decided to become a modern-day Robinson Crusoe. His first island was Cocos, a near neighbour of the Galapagos. This was ideally challenging, but had recently been declared a national park by Costa Rica. When he discovered that he would have to share his home with six resident guards, he followed the footsteps of Alexander Selkirk – the model for Daniel DEFOE's Crusoe – to the Juan Fernandez Archipelago, off the coast of Chile. But again, he found it already inhabited.

In 1980 Lucy Irvine, a dissatisfied Inland Revenue clerk, answered a newspaper advertisement for 'a female companion in an untouched Eden'. Feeling she had nothing to lose by testing herself in a wilderness setting, she agreed to accompany Kingsland to the uninhabited island of Tuin, situated between Papua New Guinea and the northern coast of Australia. The adventure was described in her book *Castaway* and subsequently filmed by Nicholas Roeg. Irvine, who had the good fortune to be portrayed by Amanda Donohoe, has been generous about Oliver Reed's performance as Kingsland. 'Ollie made a good Gerald – vulnerable, impossible and endearing by turn.' Others may conclude that Kingsland must have been less of a nuisance in real life, and almost certainly a better actor. It was not, in any case, one of Roeg's more successful pieces of work.

When Irvine left Kingsland after a year he returned to Chile and married his fourth wife, who was in her early twenties. Contact between the former castaways became rare, but Irvine did hear that Kingsland had 'finally hung up his coconuts' in Western Samoa with his fifth wife, Kalopa. In the same letter he described himself as 'the pest of the Pacific', and he included an epitaph composed by himself, 'Gerald Kingsland. He caused a lot of trouble.'

**Kingsley, Mary** (1862–1900), anthropologist and explorer of whom Kipling wrote, 'Being human she must have been afraid of something, but no one ever found out what it was.' Not the gorilla that charged her in Gabon, certainly, or the crocodile that managed to get its front feet into her canoe before she dislodged it with her paddle.

Mary Kingsley's father was an anthropologist who travelled widely, and her uncle Gerald a sea captain who went down with all hands following an 18-month ordeal in a fever-ridden ship. She was also a niece of Charles Kingsley, author of the children's classic *The Water Babies* (1863). As a child she liked to carry out scientific experiments. Once, when attempting to make gunpowder, she blew up a tub of manure, showering a laundry line of clean clothes. At the age of 30 she decided to go to Africa to complete some researches her father had left unfinished.

Having no particular aim, Mary concentrated on 'fetish and fish'. She discovered numerous species of the latter, which were subsequently named after her. She was the first European to penetrate the part of Gabon then inhabited by the Fang, a tribe of cannibals feared throughout Africa for their ferocity. Mary Kingsley gained their confidence and secured an escort of Fang warriors through their territory. For the Fang, cannibalism was no mere ritual, but a primary food source. In one village she stayed in a chief's hut surrounded by bags filled with drying human ears, toes, hands and 'other parts'. By the end of her travels with the Fang she considered them to be 'an uncommonly fine sort of human being'.

Mary was determined to do everything a man could do, but better. Other explorers had climbed the 13,760 ft peak of Mount Cameroon but they had all taken the easier, western side of the mountain. She chose the more difficult south-east face. She recorded in her journal, 'I am the third English man [sic] to have ascended the Peak and the first to have ascended it from the south-east.' She died of fever while nursing soldiers in the Boer War.

**King Squealer.** *See* O'MAHONEY, MAURICE.

**Kirwan, Richard** (1720–99), chemist, mineralogist and hypochondriac. After his wife died in 1765 Kirwan, who had a private income of £4000, was able to order his life just as it suited him. He dined alone and ate only ham and milk. Except at mealtimes, he enjoyed company and was an excellent conversationalist. He held soirees twice a week, reclining on a couch to receive his guests and wearing a hat and two coats. At 7 o'clock the door knocker was removed to prevent interruptions by late arrivals. His guests were expected to leave at nine precisely, at which time Kirwan took off his shoes and knee buckles as a persuasive hint that the evening was over.

Born in Galway, Kirwan was educated at the University of Poitiers with the idea of becoming a Jesuit. After practising briefly as a lawyer he spent ten years in London and was elected FRS in 1780. On his return to Ireland he helped to found the Royal Irish Academy, presiding over it from 1799 until his death. He did important work on chemical affinity and the composition of salts, and in 1784 he published the first systematic work on mineralogy in English. When his academic duties obliged him to be out of doors, Kirwan, who believed himself to be in poor health, took all necessary precautions. First, he stood in front of a roaring fire with his coat open to catch the heat. Once outside, he proceeded at great speed and refused to talk to anyone for fear of releasing the heat he had so carefully stored. When indoors, even when lecturing, he always kept his hat on. Asked once why someone who had intended to become a Jesuit was never seen in church, he explained that attendance would oblige him to remove his hat.

Kirwan's most valued companion was his manservant, Pope, who later shared his grave. Kirwan was fond of animals and kept six dogs and an eagle trained to sit on his shoulder. He had an aversion to flies, however, so Pope received a bonus for each dead fly he was able to produce. Kirwan rose at 4 a.m. every day during the summer, but in winter he allowed himself an extra half hour in bed. His sleep may have been less disturbed than Pope's, whose duty it was to get up several times during the night and pour tea down his employer's throat. In spite, or because, of these precautions, Kirwan died peacefully in his bed at the age of 79.

**kiss of life, giving one's Great Dane the.** *See* THORPE, JEREMY.

**'kiss of love, champagne'.** *See* BUCK, BIENVENIDA.

**Kneebone, the robbing of Mr.** *See* BLAKE, JOSEPH; SHEPPARD, JACK.

**Knight, Ronnie** (1934– ), gangster, armed robber and nightclub owner. In June 2000 Knight was fined £200 for stealing a bag of prawns from Waitrose in the Brent Cross shopping centre. It was an ignominious setback for the man who had so assiduously presented himself as a parody of the celebrity-loving 1960s villain – coiffed, medallioned, married to the popular actress Barbara Windsor, and with an amusing way of expressing himself – that his 'life', as much as his autobiography, seemed to have been written by a tabloid journalist. In his memoir, *Black Knight* (1998), he recalls a typical evening at Danny La Rue's Club:

> Noël Coward tinkling away on the ivories for all he was worth ...
> that Russian bloke, Nureyev, poncing about ... Roger Moore
> drawing the birds like flies to a cowpat.

A more dangerous villain than the caricature suggests, Knight at the time was something of a celebrity himself, mainly as the proprietor of the Artists and Repertoire Club in the Charing Cross Road. Here Ronnie and Reggie KRAY and their associates rubbed shoulders with pop stars such as the young Mick Jagger and Freddie Mercury. Another business, in partnership with Micky Regan, was supplying pubs with pool tables. The seriousness of this venture can be gauged from the fact that Freddie FOREMAN acted as rent collector. Knight was also making £3000 a week from Soho peepshows – establishments where cubicled single men could, by shovelling coins into a slot machine, catch a brief glimpse of a naked woman. Micky Regan thought this was obscene, and would have no part of it.

Knight's fortunes began to decline when his brother, David, was murdered in 1970. David had been beaten up in a pub in the Angel by a man called Johnny Isaacs. Seeking revenge, Ronnie and David went looking for Isaacs at the Latin Quarter Club in Soho. Isaacs wasn't there, but a fight broke out, during which David was stabbed through the heart with a carving knife by Alfredo 'Italian Tony' Zomparelli. At his subsequent trial Zomparelli pleaded self-defence and was jailed for four years. On 4 September 1974 Zomparelli was shot four times with a .38 while playing a pinball machine in the Golden Goose amusement arcade in Old Compton Street, Soho. Six years later, Ronnie Knight was arrested for the murder. George 'Maxie' Bradshaw, also known as Maxwell Piggott, had told police that Knight had paid him £1000 to carry out the hit. Barbara Windsor made a celebrity appearance at Knight's trial, and he was acquitted.

By 1983 Knight was divorced from Windsor and living in Fuengirola on the Costa del Sol with Sue Haylock. 'It was paradise found,' he said later. 'Restaurants where there's only roast beef and Yorkshire pudding on the menu – and English mustard.' In 1987 he and Sue were married at Fuengirola town hall by a vicar who later appeared as himself in *Eldorado*, an unsuccessful BBC soap opera. The only shadow hanging over the happy couple was the nagging determination of the British police to charge Knight in connection with the Shoreditch Security Express robbery of 1983, for which his brothers Jimmy and Johnny had already been jailed (for further details, *see* FOREMAN, FREDDIE). The matter was so well publicized that eight Welsh rugby players planned to kidnap Knight for a £60,000 reward by abseiling into his villa and smuggling him to Gibraltar. Others tried to spring a more sophisticated trap. A policeman invited him to his wedding in Loughton on the grounds that detectives had been polite enough to attend Knight's to Miss Haylock. The Knights declined, pleading a prior engagement. A deal offered by the police in 1993, by which Knight would be guaranteed bail if he returned to England of his own accord, was more successful. Leaving Sue in Spain, he flew to London, and later received a seven-year sentence for handling money from the Security Express robbery.

Two interviews given to the *Sun* – one in 1984, the second in 1994 – confirmed the characteristically close relations Knight has always enjoyed with his mother, but also suggested that his days under the Spanish sun may have affected his memory. 'My old mother, Nellie,' he said in 1984, 'she's 86 and very ill with Parkinson's disease.' In 1994 he told the *Sun*, 'My old mother, Nellie, she's 87 and she's got Parkinson's disease and her mind's beginning to wander.'

**Knox, Dr Robert** (1791–1862), anatomist. Knox studied medicine at Edinburgh University, in London, and later in Paris. Having set himself up as an independent anatomist at 10 Surgeon's Square in Edinburgh, his need for a constant supply of cadavers was met by the notorious body snatchers, BURKE and HARE, who charged him £7 10s a corpse. When the scandal broke, he excused himself of all culpability on the grounds that what he had done had been in the interests of science. He also claimed not to have known that Burke and Hare obtained their corpses not merely by robbing graves but by murder.

By most accounts, Knox was as unprepossessing as his main suppliers. In *Murder for Profit* (1926), William Benbow has him as 'a gnarled little fellow, with one blind eye like a grape, with a coffin-shaped forehead; in character a squirming package of malice, jealousy and pawkiness who did not disdain to eke out his undoubted attainments with all the tricks of an advanced quackery.'

Held in contempt by the medical establishment in Scotland, Knox moved to Hackney and managed to obtain some work as a pathologist at the London Cancer Hospital. By one account, he ended up in the position of showman to a tribe of Ojibwa Indians in a travelling circus.

**Kray, Dolly.** *See* INCE, GEORGE.

**Kray, Reggie** (1933–2000) and **Kray, Ronnie** (1933–95), identical twins from London's East End who established a grip on the criminal under-world in the 1960s, and thereafter on the popular imagination. Their main sources of income were long-firm frauds and protection. Their reputation for extreme violence was established in 1955 when Ronnie, armed with a cutlass, scattered a Maltese gang who tried to take over a billiard hall that the twins were protecting in the Mile End Road. Later, both brothers were involved in a pub fight with a group of dockers who had upset Ronnie. The dockers took a severe beating.

The Krays became professional boxers at the age of 17, and the following year they were called up to do their national service. They reacted badly to army discipline and were dishonourably discharged in 1954. In 1957 they opened the 'Double R' club in Bow Road, east London, which became popular with celebrities such as Barbara Windsor, Joan Little-wood, Roger Moore and Victor Spinetti. Ronnie, a sadistic homosexual, was the dominant twin, and earned the nickname 'The Colonel'. He indulged in fantasies of violence and power, based on Al Capone and gangsters from the American cinema. What little business flair the 'Firm' possessed was provided by Reggie.

In 1965 Reggie married Frances Shea, whom he seemed to have loved. He was devastated when she committed suicide in 1967. In an atmosphere of increasing hostility between the 'Firm' and Charlie RICHARDSON's south London gang, the twins arranged the escape from Dartmoor of Frank MITCHELL, the 'Mad Axeman', whose murder they subsequently ordered. On 9 March 1966 Ronnie Kray shot dead George Cornell, a Richardson henchman, in the Blind Beggar public house on the Mile End Road. Cornell's offence had been to call Ronnie 'a fat poof', an insult ex-acerbated by the fact that he was now drinking on Kray 'territory'. In October 1967 Reggie Kray, urged on by the increasingly unbalanced Ronnie, fatally stabbed a small-time, pill-popping thief called Jack 'The Hat' McVitie in a borrowed flat in Stoke Newington. McVitie had shown a lack of respect for the twins by wearing Bermuda shorts in one of their clubs.

After a lengthy investigation – which, because of the number of police-men presumed to be working for the Krays, Detective Superintendent Leonard 'Nipper' Read was obliged to conduct in conditions of the utmost secrecy and away from Scotland Yard – the twins were brought to trial at the Old Bailey in January 1969. After a senior member of the 'Firm',

Albert DONAGHUE, had turned queen's evidence, they were acquitted of the Mitchell killing (*see* FOREMAN, FREDDIE), but they were convicted of murdering Cornell and McVitie. In 1989, while a patient in Broadmoor, Ronnie married Kate Howard, a former stripogram girl. Mrs Kray later wrote *Murder, Madness and Marriage* (1993), in which she recorded that 'everyone who meets Ronnie is impressed by his charm and wit'. She was widowed in 1995 when Ronnie suffered a fatal heart attack. After serving 31 years of his 30-year sentence, Reggie was released from prison on compassionate grounds in September 2000 when suffering from terminal cancer. He died in hospital a few days later.

Connoisseurs of English films found much to be amused by in *The Krays* (1990). The performance of Steven Berkoff in the role of George Cornell was judged particularly comic. The twins were played by Gary and Martin Kemp, formerly of the pop group Spandau Ballet.

*See also* BOOTHBY, ROBERT; DRIBERG, TOM.

**Kray twins referred to as Gert and Daisie.** *See* MITCHELL, FRANK.

**Kruptadia.** A code word used by 19th-century book dealers to denote pornographic material. *See* ASHBEE, HENRY SPENCER.

**Kum, Franie.** *See* JONES, JANIE.

**Kytler, Dame Alice** (*c.*1285–?), witch. In 1325 an inquisition was set up under the control of Bishop de Ledrede of Ossory to investigate seven counts of sorcery practised in Kilkenny by a band of witches led by Dame Alice. She had been married four times, and the charges were brought against her by her sons by her first three marriages. They accused her of murdering their respective fathers magically and presenting her inherited wealth to her favourite son, William Outlawe. Her current husband, they claimed, had been reduced to such a condition by her potions and powders that 'he had become emaciated, his nails had dropped off and there was no hair on his body'.

Much incriminating evidence was discovered among Dame Alice's effects, including a sacrificial wafer with the Devil's name on it and a broomstick on which, according to her disaffected sons, she 'ambled and galloped through thicke and thin, when and in what name she listed'. One of her habits was to sweep clean the streets of Kilkenny, shoving the refuse towards the door of her favoured son, William Outlawe, chanting:

> To the house of William my sonne
> Hie all the wealth of Kilkenny towne.

Worse, she had sacrificed nine red cocks and nine peacock's eyes to her incubus, Art. Art was known to have had carnal knowledge of her in the shape of a cat, a black hairy dog or in the likeness of a Negro (Aethiops). With the aid of influential friends, Dame Alice was able to slip away during the inquisition. She went to England and was never heard of again.

I

**Labouchere, Henry** (1842–1913), politician and journalist. Labouchere was responsible for s11 of the Criminal Law Amendment Act 1885, which made acts of gross indecency between men punishable by a prison term not exceeding two years. It has been known ever since as a blackmailer's charter, and earned its author a posthumous rebuke from the gay rights activist Mr Peter Tatchell as recently as July 2000.

In fact, Labouchere was an enlightened and radical member of Parliament for Northampton, and the campaigning editor of *Truth*, a magazine that exposed many scandals. In 1894 Labouchere was acquitted of criminal libel, on a technicality, after he had suggested in its pages that the duc de Vallombrasa had made his fortune by sending back the corpses of French soldiers to the army as edible meat. For some years he lived with a burlesque dancer, Henrietta Hodson, whose father was landlord of the Duke's Arms, a public house in Westminster. At election meetings his audience liked to enquire, 'How's Henrietta?' Tiring of this, Labouchere adopted the practice of opening his address by saying, 'I wish to convey the gratifying information that Henrietta is quite well, thank you.' Nor was he ever less than frank about his gambling, duelling and brothel visiting.

Thought to be the best speaker in the House of Commons, and the finest wit since Sheridan, Labouchere was able to inspire animosity from many quarters. The prince of Wales (the future EDWARD VII) referred to him as 'that viper Labouchere', and to the prince's mother, (Queen Victoria) he was 'that horrible, lying Labouchere'. The latter judgement was to be expected, since Labouchere obtained a place on a parliamentary committee to vet royal expenditure, and proposed that Victoria should provide for her grandchildren by putting one of her estates – Osborne, Balmoral or Sandringham – up for sale. When the government spokesman suggested that the properties were white elephants since no one could afford their upkeep, Labouchere offered to write out a cheque on the spot for Osborne, the queen's preferred residence.

When Gladstone was returned to office in 1892 Labouchere hoped to obtain cabinet rank, but he had made too many enemies. The queen's antipathy kept him out of office, and the earl of ROSEBERY vetoed his appointment as head of the Washington legation, which had been his second choice.

It is alleged that when he was dying at his villa outside Florence, Labouchere awoke to find a fire had broken out in the corner of his room. 'Surely not so soon,' he is supposed to have said.

**Ladies Directory, The.** *See* HARRIS, JOHN.

**Ladies of Llangollen, the.** *See* BUTLER, LADY ELEANOR.

**Lady Bumtickler's Revels.** *See* HOTTEN, JOHN CAMDEN.

**Lady's Tickler, The New.** *See* CARRINGTON, CHARLES; SELLON, CAPTAIN EDWARD.

**Lady Winchelsea.** A parrot. *See* FLYNN, ROBERT.

**Lamb, Charles.** *See* HOOLIGANS, THEATRICAL.

**Lambourne, Lady Margaret** (*c*.1550–?), aristocrat and failed assassin. Lady Lambourne was so shocked by the beheading of Mary Queen of Scots in 1587 that she decided to kill Queen Elizabeth I. She managed to penetrate the court dressed as a man and with two muskets concealed under her topcoat – one with which to shoot the queen, the other to turn on herself. While she was creeping up on the queen, who was walking in her garden, one of the muskets went off by mistake, killing a peacock. Lady Lambourne was seized, but, when confronted by Elizabeth, she remained defiant. She had been moved to her desperate act by love, she said. 'So,' the queen replied, 'you have done your duty. Now, what do you think my duty is?' 'You must pardon me,' said Lady Lambourne. The queen agreed, and that was the end of the matter.

For another unsuccessful queen's assassin, *see* OXFORD, EDWARD.

**Lambton, Antony Claud Frederick** (1922– ), politician, journalist and author. In 1973 the patrician nonchalance with which Lambton organized his private arrangements caused the Tory government of Mr Edward Heath to suppose that it had a scandal on its hands as serious as the Profumo affair (*see* KEELER, CHRISTINE) that had embarrassed Harold Macmillan in 1963. An investigation followed, which was masterminded by Commander Bert 'the Old Grey Fox' Wickstead and carried out in its day-to-day details by Mr Pulley of West End Central. Mr Pulley was so conscientious in his duties that most of London's working girls decided for safety's sake to return to their previous occupations as hairstylists, airline personnel and on the reception desk at London Weekend Television.

When his father, the 5th earl of Durham, died in 1970, Lord Lambton disclaimed the title to remain in the House of Commons as MP for Berwick-upon-Tweed and parliamentary undersecretary of state at the Ministry of Defence. In the summer of 1972 he regularly disclaimed his other title too when making use of a high-class call-girl service, to whose proprietor, Jean Horn, he preferred to represent himself as 'Mr Lucas'. Among Mrs Horn's girls, his favourite was an ex-dancer called Norma Levy, née Russell, whom he visited once a week in her Maida Vale apartment. Mrs Levy was often partnered at these rendezvous by one or more of her girlfriends, and cannabis was sometimes smoked.

Lambton, for whatever reason, grew careless, and on one occasion paid Mrs Levy with a personal cheque. Perhaps he had supposed that, as a Tory supporter, she wouldn't wish to get him into trouble. 'Tories are my best clients,' she had often told him. It was Lambton's misfortune that her husband Colin, a heavy drinker with a criminal record for dishonesty, had no such scruples. Soon he was cashing in on his wife's connections. By hiding cine equipment and a microphone in her bedroom, he was able to catch the minister on film. On 5 May 1973 he offered the results to the *News of the World* in return for £30,000. Having judged that Levy's pictures were not of a publishable standard, the newspaper installed its own equipment in Mrs Levy's bedroom. On 9 May Levy used a tape recorder, hidden in the nose of a teddy bear, to capture a conversation about drugs between his wife and Lambton. The next day, a *News of the World* photographer hid in a wardrobe behind a two-way mirror and took pictures of Lambton with Mrs Levy and a friend of hers called Gina. For reasons that have never become clear, the newspaper decided not to use the story and, more remarkably, handed over the evidence to Levy. Having failed to sell the story to the German magazine, *Stern*, he offered it to the *Sunday People* for £45,000. They suggested a price of £750, which he accepted. The *Sunday People* gave the material straight to the police.

Just when it seemed likely that Lambton was to benefit from the print media's unaccountable lack of interest in the story, Mrs Levy happened to mention the matter to the proprietor of the Eve Club in Regent Street, where she sometimes worked as a hostess. The proprietor's wife, who was well-connected, contacted James Prior, then leader of the House of Commons, who conveyed his discoveries to the prime minister, Edward Heath. Lambton resigned immediately from the government and from Parliament. Before departing for his agreeable villa in Italy, where he has since occupied himself by writing novels and short stories, he remarked to

Robin Day on a *Panorama* programme that he couldn't 'think what all the fuss was about; surely all men visit whores?'

Lord Lambton is married to Belinda, daughter of Major D.H. Blew-Jones of Westward Ho! in north Devon. They have one son and five daughters.

**lamppost, hanging oneself from a.** *See* FAIRBAIRN, SIR NICHOLAS.

**Lancey, John** (1727–?), sea captain, arsonist and insurance swindler. Lancey was a pirate of a rather modern sort, his crime – setting fire to his ship in order to make an insurance claim – being in sharp contrast to the smash-and-grab tactics preferred by extrovert freebooters such as Henry MORGAN and Edward 'Blackbeard' TEACH.

Born in Biddeford, Devon, and descended from a reputable sea-going family, Lancey worked for ten years as master of different vessels owned by a Mr Benson, and was married to one of Mr Benson's relations. According to *Select Trials* (1764):

> He always behaved suitably to his station, with the utmost integrity, and to the satisfaction of all those with whom he was concerned.

In 1753 Lancey was sent for by Benson, who proposed fitting out Lancey's ship *Nightingale*, making a large insurance on her, and having her destroyed. Lancey was shocked, and, according to *Select Trials*, replied:

> Sir, I flatter myself you have never known me guilty of a bad action since I have been in your service, and surely you mention this now with a view to trying my integrity.

Benson let the matter drop, but later he invited Lancey to dinner and repeated the suggestion. Again, Lancey turned him down, telling him plainly that if compliance was a condition of continuing in Benson's service then he would be obliged to seek alternative employment. Escorting Lancey to a pleasure house in the garden, Benson offered him red wine and reminded him of his obligations to his wife and two children:

> Why will you stand so much in your own light? Consider your circumstances, consider your family; you may now have an opportunity of making them and yourself happy.

Benson's argument prevailed, and Lancey embarked on the course of action that was to lead him to the scaffold. On 6 August 1753, with Lloyd, the chief mate, Anthony Metherall, the second mate, and James Bather, the boatswain, Lancey went, by the direction of Mr Benson, before the notary public, Mr Narcissus Hatherly, and swore that the *Nightingale* had been destroyed by a fire that had not been in their power to prevent and that the loss of the ship and cargo had been total and unavoidable. Lancey then wrote a letter to John Williams, a merchant of Exeter, who had procured him an insurance of £1301 on the voyage, claiming reimbursement. On 29 August he was arrested by the sheriff of Exeter, who told him that, further to information received from Bather, the boatswain, he was to be charged with intent to defraud the insurers.

In December Lancey was removed by habeas corpus to London, where he was examined before Sir Thomas Salisbury, knight judge of the Admiralty. In the course of this examination, a proposal was made to Lancey that, in return for giving evidence against another, he could save his life and liberty. Lancey rejected it, and on 7 June 1754 was hanged at Execution Dock.

**landlords, abusive.** *See* BALON, NORMAN.

**landlords, unscrupulous.** *See* RACHMAN, PETER.

**Langan, Peter** (1941–88), restaurateur. The son of Dan Langan, an Irish rugby full-back, Langan was born in County Clare and educated locally. After working for a while in petrol, he became the chef at Odin's restaurant in Devonshire Street, Marylebone, where he first displayed the idiosyncratic manner that became his trademark.

In 1976 he opened Langan's on the site of the old Coq d'Or off Piccadilly, in partnership with the film actor Michael Caine and Richard Shepherd, formerly chef at the Capital Hotel. Notwithstanding ineradicable memories of the 98 mediocre films in which Caine had appeared, the business thrived. Shepherd's cooking was generally admired, but it was Langan's personality which kept the restaurant in the public eye.

Stories about his unorthodox behaviour were in constant circulation. One concerned a cockroach that a customer found in the ladies' room. Langan examined it closely and then absolved himself of responsibility. 'Madam,' he said, 'this cockroach is dead. All ours are alive.' He then swallowed it, washed down with champagne. When a customer's attitude offended him – which happened frequently – he became violent in an uncoordinated Irish fashion, as a rule falling face down in the cutlery before too much damage was done. Another of his amusing habits was to offer attractive young women limitless champagne in return for stripping naked. Generally, diners were only safe from his attentions once he had passed out on the floor of the gentlemen's lavatory.

In his last years Langan's ambition was to franchise his name in America, where the first transatlantic Langan's Brasserie opened in 1986. Langan himself was barred from the premises. Before this plan could be profitably developed, he went to sleep one night while smoking a cigarette and set fire to the bed and himself.

**lap dancers, bigamous.** *See* BIGAMY.

**Large, Sir Andrew.** A fraudulent ferret. *See* CHANEY, SID.

**Laskey, Colin** (1931–96), Welsh rugby referee and sadomasochist. In 1987 Laskey and 16 other men were charged at the Old Bailey with grievous bodily harm after the police had discovered a collection of home-made videos showing a group of gay men participating in sadomasochistic acts. After he was convicted, Laskey's greatest regret was that invitations to referee rugby matches dried up. Mel Davies, the appointments secretary for the Rhonda and East Glamorgan League, explained why:

> It was the sadomasochism which shocked everyone, you see. You've got to realize that down in the Valleys even being gay is unheard of. We're still a bit behind.

The case was controversial and the defendants took it to the Court of Appeal, the House of Lords, the European Court of Human Rights and back to the House of Lords. When Operation Spanner, as the police called it, originally came before Judge Rant at the Old Bailey, he ruled that consent to grievous bodily harm did not constitute a defence in law, and he handed out substantial terms of imprisonment. In this, he was following established precedent, notably the case of Coney (8QBD 534, 1881), who was convicted of aiding and abetting a public fist fight. The fact that the protagonists on that occasion, two heavyweights named Burke and Mitchell, took up a collection and were none the worse for the entertainment Coney had engaged them to provide was considered irrelevant. In law, Burke and Mitchell could not consent to causing each other grievous bodily harm.

When Laskey's case went to the Court of Appeal the longest sentences were reduced, but the court unanimously upheld Judge Rant's reliance on *Coney*. As a warning, the court declared that the only reason the sentences were being cut was that it was possible that the participants hadn't known what they were doing. In future, sadomasochists could not expect such leniency (but there again, they might not want it – a point the court overlooked). Unsatisfied by this outcome the defendants next took their case to the House of Lords, where Templeman LJ, having listed certain sadomasochistic practices that were legal (*see* PRACTICES, SADOMASOCHISTIC), concluded:

> It is not in the public interest that people should try to cause each other actual bodily harm for no good reason. What may be a good reason is not for us to decide. It is sufficient to say that the sadomasochistic libido does not come within the category of good reason.

Three of the convicted men, including Laskey, went to the European Court of Human Rights, where they fared no better.

Before his death Laskey said that he regarded the activities in question as rather the same as potholing:

> Unless you've done it, you can't experience what the thrill of it is. We would go and stay with each other for the weekend, and then after the fun have a cup of tea or coffee together. Where was the hostile intent in that?

**Lauder, William** (1712–71), schoolmaster and literary forger. A Latin scholar of some ability, Lauder acquired such a hatred for the work of John Milton that he concocted a deception that fooled even Dr Johnson. An expert on the poetry of Arthur Johnston, Lauder had been enraged by Alexander Pope's criticism of Johnston's work, which he had compared unfavourably with Milton's. At the time, Lauder was trying to persuade the schools to put his edition of Johnston's poems on the curriculum.

In 1750 Lauder published *An Essay on Milton's Use of an Imitation of the Moderns in his Paradise Lost*, in which he cited a number of works by Latin poets to demonstrate that Milton was a plagiarist. He also interpolated eight lines in a Latin translation of *Paradise Lost* by one Hogg to suggest that Milton had copied this Dutch priest. Dr Johnson, who was himself no admirer of Milton, was so taken by this attack on the great poet's reputation that he wrote the preface to Lauder's essay. Unfortunately for Johnson's reputation, Lauder's squib was entirely bogus. His Latin poets and Hogg, his Dutch divine, were all fictitious. When a Dr John Douglas disproved Lauder's claims, Dr Johnson was so angry that he wrote the confession that Lauder agreed to sign.

This was not Lauder's last confession. As part of his campaign against Milton he tried to absolve Charles I of plagiarism when the Puritan Milton demonstrated in his *Eikonoklastes* that the king had lifted lines from Sir Philip Sidney's *Arcadia* to use in his own *Eikon Basilike*. (By a further twist, this collection of the king's meditations, published shortly after his execution in 1649, are now thought to be by another hand.) Lauder's attempt impressed no one, and he shortly departed for Barbados. There he opened a grammar school, which failed. He then bought an African woman who helped him to operate a novelty shop. He died in some financial distress at the age of 59.

**lavatories blown up with home-made bombs, hotel.** *See* MOON, KEITH.

**lavatories used tactically in the course of robberies, thefts, etc.**
*See* CAHILL, MARTIN; CHAPMAN, EDDIE; EDGAR, HENRY.

**lavatory, prisoner bundles his guards into the court.** *See* HINDS, ALFRED.

**lavatory, tackling the outside.** *See* ADAMS, TOMMY.

**lavatory attendants who subsequently became celebrated publishers.** *See* CARRINGTON, CHARLES.

**lavatory paper from the ladies' room at Harrods, conducting one's correspondence on.** *See* SACKVILLE, VICTORIA-JOSEPHA, BARONESS.

**Law, John** (1671–1729), adventurer and financier. Law, the son of a Scottish moneylender, is remembered in banking circles as the man whose inflationary money-making schemes bankrupted France. Unsuited by temperament to life on the country estates that he inherited from his father in 1685, Law moved to London, where he fought a duel in Bloomsbury Square with a man called Beau Wilson over a Mrs Lawrence. Wilson was killed, but before he could be convicted of murder, Law escaped to Amsterdam, where he studied banking. In 1700 he returned to Scotland and suggested to the government that they should set up a national bank that would issue easily redeemable paper money instead of gold. Once confidence had been created, the government could increase its wealth by printing more money. The suggestion was rejected.

In 1708 Law went to Paris, where his considerable charm, and skill as a gambler, made him a favourite of the duc d'Orléans, who was quickly convinced that Law was a financial genius. When Louis XIV died in 1715, and since Louis XV was only 5 years old, the duc d'Orléans became regent. Law immediately approached him with the scheme that had been rejected by the hard-headed Scots. The regent was impressed, but the Council of Finance rejected the idea of a national bank. However, they did allow Law to set up a private bank. From an address in the Place Vendôme, Paris, he proceeded to sell shares in the bank at an unusually attractive price: a quarter in gold and the balance in government bonds, which were worth just one-fifth of their face value. Law's only problem was that he had issued 60 millions' worth of francs in notes secured by 6 million francs in gold. To increase his capital to a point where it could withstand a sudden 'run' on the bank, Law persuaded the regent to grant him a monopoly on land in Louisiana, thereafter telling colonists that in the Mississippi basin rocks were made of emeralds. He was also granted a monopoly of the Canadian fur trade, which yielded enormous profits, and he began to absorb other French colonial companies in the East Indies, China and Senegal.

With his fortune thus established, Law was ready to launch his biggest gamble. He offered to pay off all the government's debts with a loan of 1500 million livres, charging interest at only 3% against the usual 4%. The offer was accepted, and the government's former creditors were persuaded to reinvest with Law – with the guarantee that they could 'unload' at six months' notice.

Huge crowds besieged Law's office in the rue Quincampoix, fighting their way to the desk where Law sat with a huge pile of shares to be exchanged for gold. The shares increased in value at such a rate that anyone who could buy a few was able to walk outside and sell them immediately for several times the purchase price. Destitute cobblers became millionaires overnight. Law's coachman approached him with two other coachmen, saying, 'You take the one you want and I'll take the other.' The crime rate soared as people scrambled to get hold of the gold that could be doubled in value in a morning. The comte de Horn lured a speculator to his house and beat him to death for the 150,000 francs the man had about his person. Shrewd speculators, aware that the bubble would burst, began to smuggle their profits out of the country. A Dutch financier dressed up as a farm labourer and departed for Amsterdam with a million francs worth of gold in a farm cart covered in hay.

More seriously for Law, small speculators now took their profits while they could, further draining the bank's resources. He was forced to issue a statement saying that he would not change more than a 100-livre note per person. The crowds who now gathered outside his bank wanted their money back. On 17 July 1720, 1500 people waited all night, and in the morning it was discovered that 16 had died of suffocation. A mob marched on the Palais Royal. They were eventually dispersed, but there had nearly been a revolution.

Law, in a state of shock, escaped to Brussels. There he was approached by the tsar of Russia, Peter the Great, who – idiosyncratically in the circumstances – invited him to reorganize the finances of the Russian empire. Law declined, pleading exhaustion. In 1721 he returned to England, where he was received cordially by George I. It was generally felt that someone who had been so intimate with France's regent should be treated with respect. The regent himself remained on good terms with Law, even arranging a pension for him. When Law asked him in a letter how he had dealt with his country's bankruptcy, he replied, 'I disposed of it by making a bonfire of the documents.' Law's hopes that he would be recalled to France to take charge again of the country's finances were dashed when the regent died in 1723. He survived his final years by betting anyone £1000 to a shilling that they could not throw six double sixes in succession. The number who tried ensured only a modest income and at the age of 58 he died in Venice a poor man.

**Lawless, a gangster's wife called Frances.** *See* CAHILL, MARTIN.

**lawyer considered an ass, a.** *See* NORBURY, JOHN TOLER, 1ST BARON.

**lawyers, crooked and therefore trustworthy.** *See* HARDING, ARTHUR; NEWTON, ARTHUR; SAWARD, JAMES TOWNSHEND.

**lawyers and judges best sent to Botany Bay.** *See* MACKRETH, BOB.

**Leavis, Dr F.R., visited by two uniformed constables.** *See* BODKIN, SIR ARCHIBALD.

**Le Mesurier, John.** *See* THORPE, JEREMY.

**'lesbian love romps with drug fiend's girlfriend'.** *See* MELLOR, DAVID (for Miss de Sancha).

**lesbian prostitute in bondage tragedy, 18-stone.** *See* SWINDELL, PETER GEORGE.

**Leverson, Rachel** (1820–91), prostitute and blackmailer. 'Madame Rachel' was the most resourceful of the many Victorian blackmailers who lurked in the shadows of the vice trade. By the time she was prosecuted by the common sergeant, Sir William Ballantine, in 1868, she owned a fine house in Maddox Street, between Regent Street and Oxford Street, and had a box at Covent Garden for which she paid £400 each season. Ballantine described her business as 'extortion and robbery' and Leverson herself as 'one of the most dangerous of moral pests'.

When she became too old for prostitution, Leverson invited gullible female customers into her premises in New Bond Street by painting a sign on the door that said 'Beautiful For Ever'. From there she dispensed cosmetics such as 'Magnetic Rock Dew' for removing wrinkles, 'Favourite of the Harem's Pearl White Powder for the skin', 'Mount Hymettus Soap' and the 'Bridal Toilet Cabinet' priced at between 20 and 25 guineas. Her largest source of income, however, were 'houses of assignation' (so dubbed by the journalist, Henry Mayhew), which opened the way to genteel prostitution and hence to blackmail. Adjoining her New Bond Street shop were Madam Rachel's Arabian Baths, which offered beauty treatments and, more importantly, facilities for discreet liaisons. Even those who visited her premises quite innocently were easily compromised. On one occasion the wife of a stockbroker emerged from the Arabian Baths to find her diamond earrings missing from the adjoining dressing room. Madame Rachel told her that if she caused trouble her husband would be informed that she had been using the baths to meet her lover. The woman decided that her reputation would be ruined by a court case. The Victorian middle class, as Ballantine later wrote:

> ...consisted of men and women who would sooner submit to felony and fraud than that their names should be exposed to the public.
> From *The Extraordinary Life and Trial of Madame Rachel* (1868).

Madame Rachel's downfall followed a visit to her premises in 1868 by Mary Tucker Borradaile, the widow of an Indian Army major. Mrs Borradaile was first persuaded to buy a selection of preparations, at a cost of £1700, to repair damage done to her complexion by exposure to the tropical sun. She was then led into the Arabian Baths, where she was briefly glimpsed by a middle-aged bachelor, Lord Henry Ranelagh. After a while Madame Rachel entered, greatly concerned that she had allowed Lord Ranelagh to spy on Mrs Borradaile as she bathed. However, there might yet be a happy consequence, she said. Lord Ranelagh had been so overcome by the widow's beauty that he'd quite lost his head and was determined now to marry her. There was just one problem. Because Mrs Borradaile was of a lower social order there would be opposition from Lord Ranelagh's family. For the time being, he would have to communicate with her by letter, and through Madame Rachel, who for this purpose would operate under the code name 'Granny'. Not only did Mrs Borradaile fall for this, she also responded to appeals for money made by 'Lord Ranelagh' in his letters. He was due considerable sums from a family trust, he wrote, but was temporarily embarrassed for cash. It took Rachel Leverson a mere three months to relieve Mrs Borradaile of her entire capital, worth approximately £5000.

When Mrs Borradaile discovered the fraud she embarked on a course of action that none of Madam Rachel's previous victims had risked. In spite of the public humiliation she would suffer when she entered the witness box, she sued Rachel Leverson in the Court of the Queen's Bench, a trial that was shortly overtaken by a prosecution for fraud in the Central Criminal Court in September 1868. According to Sergeant William Ballantine, Mrs Borradaile 'tottered into the witness box as a skeleton, and so to her public martyrdom'. Her ordeal procured the conviction of Rachel Leverson, who was sentenced to five years penal servitude. On her release she revived her Arabian Baths, and was prosecuted again. She received a long term in prison, during which she died.

**Levy, Norma** (1948– ), cabaret dancer and call girl. She was the central figure in the Lambton scandal of 1973 (*see* LAMBTON, ANTONY CLAUD FREDERICK).

**libertines.** *See* CHARTERIS, COLONEL FRANCIS; CLARK, ALAN; CLONMELL, JOHN SCOTT, 1ST EARL OF; DASHWOOD, SIR FRANCIS; FAIRBAIRN, SIR NICHOLAS; LUTTRELL, COLONEL JAMES.
*See also* PHILANDERERS.

**librarians, blackmailing.** *See* DENNIS, CEREDIG DAWYL.

**lifting the dabs.** The method by which the police, with the use of sticky tape, remove a known criminal's fingerprints from an innocent location and place them at the scene of a crime. Equipped with nothing but a roll of Sellotape, John Platt-Mills QC demonstrated the simplicity of the operation to the court when defending Ronnie KRAY at the Old Bailey in 1969. Platt-Mills had been born in a wheelbarrow in Wellington, New Zealand, after his mother – only the fifth woman to become a doctor in New Zealand – had blown a whistle to attract attention while climbing a hill in order to induce the birth.

**lighting £20 notes in public.** *See* OSBOURNE, COLIN 'DUKE'.

**Lilley, Detective Constable Nigel** (1943– ), policeman. As a member of Scotland Yard's Drugs Squad in the late 1960s and early 1970s, Lilley was a key member of the notoriously corrupt crew, under the operational control of Detective Chief Inspector Victor KELAHER and headed by Detective Sergeant 'Nobby' Pilcher.

Survivors from that period remember Lilley and his colleagues arriving unexpectedly in their apartments with a search warrant in one hand and an ounce of cannabis in the other, which they would then produce from nowhere, like a cabaret conjuror plucking doves out of thin air. After the dust settled, and the court proceedings had been concluded, Lilley would return to his new acquaintance's address, on this occasion suggesting that for as little as £25 a week he could ensure that occurrences of this sort wouldn't be repeated.

The climate at the time didn't encourage accusations of corruption against the police, but Lilley and his colleagues had their careers cut short when Sir Robert Mark became commissioner of the Metropolitan Police in 1974. Lilley, Pilcher and two other officers were charged with conspiracy to pervert the course of justice and received prison sentences of up to four years. This may have been of some satisfaction to their high-profile victims, such as the pop singer Mick Jagger, whose quiet evening with Miss Marianne Faithfull and a Mars Bar had famously been interrupted by Lilley and Pilcher in 1969. On his release from prison, Lilley prospered in the head-hunting sector, later marrying the agony aunt, Anna Raeburn.

**literary forgers.** *See* CHATTERTON, THOMAS; IRELAND, WILLIAM HENRY; LAUDER, WILLIAM; MACPHERSON, JAMES.

**litigants, vexatious.** *See* SQUIRES, DOROTHY.

**Littler, Emile** (1903–81), theatrical producer and author. The younger brother of Prince Littler, the distinguished showman and founding chairman of ATV (later Central Television), Emile Littler belonged to one of the two families (the other was the Grades) that dominated light entertainment in Britain for 30 years. His productions included *Lilac Time* and *Zip Goes A Million*. He also produced over 200 pantomimes, the most popular of which was *Mother Goose*.

It is for his extraordinary meanness, however, that Littler will be remembered. It was said of him that he never mounted an entertainment whose set and props would not fit appropriately into his drawing room once the show had closed, and he was careful always to cast as leading man an actor whose measurements were the same as his own. In 1963 he produced at Her Majesty's Theatre a dramatized version of the celebrated 19th-century divorce case involving Sir Charles DILKE, under the title *The Right Honourable Gentleman*. This starred Anthony Quayle as Dilke and Coral Browne as his nemesis, Virginia Crawford. On the first night the cast were disappointed to receive a coat hanger each as a celebratory gift. When Coral Browne's husband, the theatrical agent Philip Pearman, died during the run, she asked Littler, somewhat apprehensively, whether she might miss the matinee on the day of his funeral. She had expected Littler to refuse this request, so she was surprised and grateful when he agreed. At the end of the week, her pay packet was docked by one-eighth to compensate Littler for the missing performance.

In 1964 Littler resigned from the board of the Royal Shakespeare Company in protest against Sir Peter Hall's production of Joe Orton's *Entertaining Mr Sloane*, which he judged obscene. In 1974 he was knighted for his services to the theatre.

**Liverpool Street Station Information Booth Swindle, the.** *See* CORRIGAN, MICHAEL.

**Llangollen, the ladies of.** *See* BUTLER, LADY ELEANOR.

**Lloyd, Sophie** (1956– ), conjuror and impostor. Known as 'the disappearing magician', Lloyd was confronted in the late 1980s with what seemed an insoluble problem. She wanted to join the Magic Circle, the professional association for conjurors, membership of which was necessary for those wanting to prosper in this profession. However, the Magic Circle, as a matter of policy, extended membership only to men. With the help of a sympathetic variety agent, Jenny Winstanley, Lloyd transformed herself into a 16-year-old boy, thereafter performing magic tricks on the northern club circuit under the name of Raymond.

By 1989 Lloyd and Winstanley were confident enough to enter 'Raymond' as an applicant for membership of the Magic Circle. The examination was performed in front of an audience of 200 people, after which Raymond was obliged to mingle and chat informally with members of the Circle. This latter performance was the more stressful of the two, since Lloyd's invented 'life' – complete with family, friends, school and new personality (that of a rather sulky and monosyllabic adolescent) – was under the microscope. The imposture was carried out successfully, but the Circle ruled that Raymond's tricks fell short of the required standard, and 'his' application was turned down.

**Lloyd George, David** (1863–1945), politician. According to Stanley Baldwin, 'Lloyd George spent his whole life in plastering together the true and the false and therefrom extracting the plausible.' The great Liberal leader's gift for plausible presentation ensured that his reputation survived scandals which would have destroyed lesser men.

In 1912 he perjured himself in a libel action against the *People*, swearing that he had not committed adultery with Frances Stevenson, his daughter Megan's tutor. In the same year, Hilaire Belloc and Cecil Chesterton (brother of G.K. Chesterton) of the political weekly, *The Eye Witness*, accused Herbert Samuel, Rufus Isaacs and Lloyd George of corruption. It was suggested that they had profited by buying shares based on knowledge of a government contract granted to the Marconi Company to build a chain of wireless stations. In 1913, a parliamentary enquiry was held into *The Eye Witness*'s claims. It discovered that Rufus Isaacs had bought 10,000 £2 shares in Marconi and immediately resold 1000 of these to Lloyd George. Although the enquiry revealed that Lloyd George, Isaacs and Samuel had profited directly from the policies of the government, it was decided that they had not been guilty of corruption.

At the head of a coalition government after World War I, Lloyd George enjoyed the prime minister's considerable gifts of patronage. There was nothing new in the practice of rewarding a party benefactor with an honour which his good works alone might not have merited. But Lloyd George worked the system with an audacity hitherto undreamed of, hawking titles from a permanent office in Parliament Square. Ostensibly in charge of the operation were the Liberal Chief Whip Freddy Guest and Lloyd George's press agent, Sir William Sutherland. But its chief broker, and the man who enlarged the scandal to the point where it self-destructed, was a failed theatre impresario, Maundy GREGORY.

A knighthood cost £10,000; a baronetcy, since it was hereditary, came at £40,000; a peerage would set its recipient back by as much as £50,000. Business was brisk. Between December 1918 and July 1922 over 1500 knighthoods were awarded, while twice as many peerages and baronetcies were created as in the previous 20 years. By 1922, Lloyd George had collected more than £2 million. Unfortunately for him, his broker Gregory was careless in his choice of clients. Richard Williamson, who received a CBE for 'untiring work in connection with various charities', turned out to be a

Glasgow bookmaker with a criminal record. When Rowland Hodge became a baronet in 1921 'for public services in connection with shipbuilding', no mention was made of his conviction in 1918 for hoarding foodstuffs. Music hall comedians referred to the OBE as 'the Order of the Bad Egg' and London became known as the 'City of the Dreadful Knights'.

Matters came to a head with the Honours List published on 3 June 1922. Sir John Drughorn, a shipowner recommended for a baronetcy, had been convicted in 1915 of trading with the enemy. Sir William Vestey, recommended for the same honour, was a wartime tax dodger. The most scandalous nomination, however, was that of Sir Joseph Robinson, an 82-year-old South African businessman who, as recently as the previous November, had been fined £500,000 for defrauding the shareholders in his mining company. The subsequent outcry helped to destroy an already discredited administration. Lloyd George resigned in October 1922, and his successor, Bonar Law, accepted the need for change. The 1925 Honours (Prevention of Abuses) Act made it a criminal offence to traffic in titles.

In *My Life With Nye* (1980), Jennie Lee writes, 'The only thing Lloyd George was not prepared to do for the poor was to become one of them himself.'

**Loch Ness monster best observed from a balloon.** *See* VENTRY, ARTHUR FREDERICK DAUBENEY EVELEIGH DE MOLEYNS, 7TH BARON.

**loft, occupying the wrong.** *See* THISTLEWOOD, ARTHUR.

**Lole, William** (1800–74), freedom preacher. Although he called himself 'the Hermit of Newton-Burgoland, near Ashby-de-la-Zouche', Lole's personality was hardly reclusive. Holding that 'true hermits throughout the ages have been abettors of freedom', he went to great lengths to advertise his own ideas on religion and politics. All his clothes carried a symbolic message. Each of his hats had a name and proclaimed a motto. Number 17, for example, was called 'Wash Basin of Reform' and had the legend 'white-washed face and blackened heart'. Number 15, named 'Patent Teapot', carried the message, 'To draw out the flavour of the tea best – Union and Goodwill'.

Lole possessed twelve suits, which he also named and decorated with symbols. His favourite was 'Odd Fellows', a loose-fitting ensemble made from white linen, held at the waist by a white belt and adorned with a heart-shaped badge that he called the 'Order of the Star'. On special occasions he wore a military uniform, which he enlivened with a cocked hat. The hat had a horse's ears on either side.

Lole's obsession with symbolism extended to the garden of his home in Leicestershire. On gaining entry via the 'Three Seats of Self-Inquiry', visitors were asked 'Am I Vile?', 'Am I a Hypocrite?', 'Am I a Christian?'

Later, they were confronted by arrangements of different coloured flowers that spelt out such patriotic sentiments as 'God save our Noble Queen' and 'Britons never shall be Slaves'. Flower-covered mounds carried the title 'Graves of the Reformers'. Other arrangements formed tableaux named 'Inquisition' and 'Purgatory'. Lole himself would climb into a tub and preach against popery and oppression.

Lole's neighbours formed the opinion that he did no great harm, and it was through their generous provision of food and money that Lole, who never had a profitable occupation, managed to survive.

**Long, John** (1798–1834), quack. By sticking to a policy of never seeing a patient who was ill, Long, who was without formal qualifications, became the most successful medical practitioner of his day, with consulting rooms in Harley Street and an income in excess of £13,000 a year. His speciality was the treatment of consumption – a fashionable affliction among hypochondriacs at the time – and his liniment of cabbage leaves effected a complete cure except on the two occasions when his patients were actually suffering from the disease, or at least from a disease of some kind.

His first setback was in the case of Katherine Cashin, who turned out to be allergic to his liniment. She died the day after her consultation and Long was accused of manslaughter. In spite of the evidence of his many fashionable patients, who assured the court that his treatment had no effect at all, he was found guilty and fined £250.

His second misfortune occurred when a man approached Long and asked him to treat his wife. Long, who wasn't to know that the woman was indeed unwell, agreed. She too was allergic to his cabbage leaves, and while they in no way contributed to her death – which occurred within a week of Long's visit – he was once again charged with manslaughter. This time he was acquitted, but his practice suffered. In spite of testimonials in the newspapers from nine members of the aristocracy, six generals, five admirals, an ADC to the king and the mayor of Hertford, his career seemed to be over. As a final irony, he contracted tuberculosis himself – presumably from one or other of his two 'real' patients – and died at the age of 36.

**Lonsdale, James Lowther, 1st earl of** (1736–1802), politician known as 'the Bad Earl' and described by Carlyle as 'more detested than any man alive as a shameless political sharper and an intolerable tyrant over his tenants and dependants'. Sir James Lowther's sponsorship of Pitt the Younger earned him a peerage in 1784, but the details of its bestowal were not to Lowther's liking.

Elevated with him were two barons who would by tradition take precedence over a baronet. When the list was published Lowther was enraged to see his name last. He attempted to forswear his title and when he tried to resume his seat in the House of Commons a wrestling match broke out between him and the serjeant-at-arms. The latter prevailed and Lowther was marched out in a headlock. Having become Lord Lonsdale, he was persuaded to forgive Pitt, who demonstrated his gratitude by showering his demanding mentor with further honours.

Lonsdale's overriding preoccupation was the preservation of his fortune. After he died, 16,000 guineas were discovered in his house, neatly sorted into bags of 500, each labelled according to the quality of the coins it contained – 'indifferent', 'perfect' or 'super excellent'. None had been spent on keeping up the appearances appropriate to his rank. Believing that he was above such petty displays, Lonsdale liked to demonstrate his contempt for public opinion by driving around in a rusty carriage drawn by ungroomed horses. He lived in the burnt-out shell of Lowther Hall, a magnificent Queen Anne house that had almost been destroyed by fire in 1720 and which he never bothered to restore.

Lonsdale's many creditors were obliged to follow his example of austerity since he never settled any of his debts. He owed a great deal of money to William Wordsworth's father, whose five children inherited nothing but IOUs due on Lonsdale, none of which had been honoured in his lifetime. The thinking behind this miserliness was at least logical. If those to whom Lonsdale owed money were friends, then he 'knew them to be knaves'. If they were strangers, 'how could he know what they were?'

Only once in his life did he display a capacity for human emotion – when he fell deeply in love with the daughter of one of his tenant farmers. He persuaded her to run away from home, and he remained devoted to her until her death at an early age. Unaccustomed to having his wishes thwarted, even by death, Lonsdale decided to keep her with him. He had her embalmed, thereafter using her glass-topped coffin as a sideboard in his dining room.

**looning.** *See* MOON, KEITH.

**looting Harrods.** *See* PITTS, SHIRLEY.

***Lorna Doone*, an authority on.** *See* OAKELEY, SIR ATHOLL.

**lost tribes of Israel to be found in England.** *See* PANACEA SOCIETY, THE.

**lost tribes of Israel to be found in Mexico.** *See* KINGSBOROUGH, EDWARD KING, 4TH VISCOUNT.

**Love, Abode of.** *See* PRINCE, HENRY.

**love, giving and receiving the last charming proofs of an unbounded.** *See* HERVEY, AUGUSTUS.

**love, powerfully agitated in the delights of.** *See* GRAHAM, JAMES.

**love and presents, fraught with.** *See* HARRIS, JOHN.

**Lovebody, Jane, nightclub hostess and mistress.** *See* BLOOM, JOHN.

**love in broad daylight, alleged unlikelihood of any woman making.** *See* COLLUSION, DIVORCE BY.

**love in ditches, making.** *See* CRIPPLE, MARGARET AND WILLIAM; DAVIDSON, THE REVEREND HAROLD FRANCIS (the rector of Stiffkey).

***Lovesport and Audacious Harry, The Adventures of Lady.*** *See* CARRINGTON, CHARLES.

**love to a German princess, impudently desiring to make.** *See* CARLETON, MARY.

**Lowson, Sir Denys** (1901–75), financier and asset-stripper. When in 1974 the Department of Trade published its report on the recent City activities of Sir Denys Lowson – lord mayor of London in the year of the Festival of Britain – it commented that he had netted for himself twice the amount of money stolen in the Great Train Robbery of 1963. When he died the following year, the *Daily Mirror*'s story was headlined, 'DEATH OF A DISGRACED TYCOON', and concluded that 'he was the last of the City Dinosaurs, an arrogant autocrat who behaved as if time had stood still since the Thirties.'

The son of a wealthy Scottish banker, Lowson had enjoyed a privileged education: Winchester, Oxford and the Bar. After working as a barrister, he moved into banking and the management of unit trusts, and by the time he was 30 his empire was worth £200 million. In 1972 the *Investor's Chronicle* ran an in-depth survey of his companies, and the following year they published an exposé of his most audacious move to date – one that had netted him a personal windfall of £5 million. Sir Denys, his family and friends had bought a controlling interest in the National Group of Unit Trusts – which he happened to manage – by acquiring shares at 62p each between July and September 1972. Six months later they sold their shares at £8.67. Sir Denys had benefited from the inside knowledge that National was to be taken over. The *Sunday Times* commented that Sir Denys, as well as making such unseemly profit from privileged information, was also chairman of the American Association, which had been savagely attacked for its destructive strip mining for coal in Tennessee. The company's activities had devastated whole valleys and driven local inhabitants from their homes.

The government immediately appointed two Department of Trade inspectors to look into Lowson's affairs; 24 hours later he announced that he and his family would be returning their £5 million profit. His lawyer said that the government's action had had no bearing on this decision. By the following year Sir Denys had resigned 16 of his directorships, but he had returned none of the money. When the papers in the case were handed over to the director of public prosecutions, Sir Denys sold his Sussex mansion and departed on a round-the-world cruise.

Lowson returned to England in April 1975 a sick man, and died in the London Clinic on 10 September. Summonses for his arrest on charges of conspiracy to defraud had been issued three hours before his death. He left an overdraft of £300,000 and on 11 November it was reported that he had left nothing in his will. It was assumed that his family had been provided for by a fortune lodged somewhere abroad. His own flat and that of his son were paid for by public companies that he controlled. Members of the public had also paid for his charitable donations, and, since Sir Denys owned his own bank, he had been able to borrow money without interest. The *Guardian's* obituary was headed, 'NO TEARS FOR THE DEAD'.

**Lucan, John Bingham, 6th Baron** (1934–?), gambler and murderer. Apart from an unhealthy, and for their nanny fatal, affection for his children, Lucan's only interest in life was gambling. After Eton and the Guards he worked in a merchant bank, but he abandoned this career when, on the death of his father, he inherited a quarter of a million pounds. By 1974 he was virtually bankrupt, having squandered his fortune playing games of chance at John ASPINALL's Clermont Club.

On the night of 7 November 1974 Lord Lucan killed Sandra Rivett, the nanny of his two children, in the mistaken belief that she was his wife Veronica. He and Veronica had been separated for some time and were in dispute over custody of the children. After attacking his wife too, but failing to kill her, he drove to the house of his friend Susan Maxwell-Scott at Uckfield in Sussex. His car was discovered at Newhaven, but he was never seen again. 'His qualities,' said John Aspinall, 'were the old-fashioned ones of loyalty, honesty and reliability.' Another of Lucan's qualities that might have appealed to Aspinall was an admiration for Adolf Hitler. When searching Lucan's flat for clues, police found records of the German dictator's speeches. To Aspinall, and to his former cronies at the Clermont, Lucan's homicidal attack was entirely pardonable. 'If she'd been my wife,' Aspinall told a *Sunday Times* reporter, 'I'd have bashed her to death years before, and so would you.'

Some social commentators have pointed out that to papers such as the

*Daily Mail* common criminals are on the run, while Lord Lucan is merely missing.

**Luker, Elizabeth** (*c.*1760–*c.*1829), theatregoer and hooligan. It was customary at the time of Luker's offence for theatre audiences to behave like modern-day football supporters, with one group loudly comparing the preferred actor of another group unfavourably with the artiste of their choice. The exchange of insults and missiles was considered to be part of the entertainment, and fist fights between rival supporters were not uncommon. However, Luker's behaviour, as was made clear at her trial, was unacceptable.

In 1789 an intoxicated party, of whom Luker was one, visited a light opera at the Sadlers Wells Theatre and so annoyed another section of the audience by its behaviour that a quarrel broke out. Luker stood up and cried out to her debauched male companions, 'Fight! Fight!' Unhappily, this was mistaken for a cry of, 'Fire! Fire!' Panic caused a stampede to the exits, the avenues of the theatre were choked, and 18 people were trampled to death. The victims were mainly women, and, as was noted at the time, 'the men numbered with the dead were small, and of weak body parts'.

Luker was identified as the cause of the catastrophe, and was thereafter seized, tried and convicted of being:

> ...tumultuously assembled for the purpose of disturbing the King's peace and of having resisted the legal authority to suppress her dangerous conduct in a theatre legally authorized, called Sadlers Wells.

Having lamented the fact that 'hardly a week passes but that disturbances do arise in one or other of our theatres', the magistrate, Mr Mainwaring, regretted that by legal anomaly (in law, Luker had caused the stampede unwittingly) he could only pass a light sentence. Luker was jailed for 14 days.

*See also* HOOLIGANS, THEATRICAL.

**lunch, arriving early for.** *See* BIRD, HAROLD ('DICKIE').

**lunch, five bottles of port before.** *See* MYTTON, JOHN.

**lunch, out to.** *See passim.*

**lunch, wearing one's pyjamas until after.** *See* BROWN, CRAIG.

**lunch before breakfast.** *See* STRACHEY, WILLIAM.

**Luncheon Vouchers Case, Sex for.** *See* PAYNE, CYNTHIA.

**Luscious Leon.** (A member of the THIN BLUE JEANS.) *See* HAMPSON, KEITH.

**lust and protein, dangers of.** *See* GREEN, STANLEY.

**Luttrell, Colonel James** (1725–92), politician and libertine. Luttrell is remembered for the small part he played in the ongoing rivalry between John WILKES and George III's chief minister, Lord Bute. When Wilkes, a radical, hell-raising journalist, stood for Parliament for the fourth time in 1774 as MP for Middlesex, it was necessary to find candidates to stand against him. Prominent among them as the main government protagonist was Colonel Luttrell, who was already sitting as MP for Bosinney, a Cornish pocket borough of Lord Bute's with only 25 registered voters.

Luttrell was a curious choice. He had a reputation for extreme personal violence, of cheating on his many mistresses and seducing the young and innocent. On one occasion he had kidnapped an 11-year-old girl, debauched her and avoided prosecution by bribing witnesses to swear that she was already a prostitute. On another occasion, he was accused of bad taste after turning up at a Mrs Cornely's masque dressed as a corpse, complete with a shroud and a coffin that bore a plate recording that its occupant had died of venereal disease contracted from Mrs Cornely. Finally, he was on poor terms with his father, Lord Irnham, whose challenge to a duel he had once refused on the grounds that 'Lord Irnham is not a gentleman.'

In the event, Wilkes was elected with a majority of 1143 to 296, only for the House to expel him for the fourth time and then to take the extreme step of declaring that Luttrell was duly elected. Edmund Burke called it 'the fifth act of a tragic-comedy acted by His Majesty's servants for the benefit of Mr Wilkes and the expense of the constitution.'

**luxury, an enduring taste for unearned.** *See* HALL, ARCHIBALD.

**LWT, working girls at.** *See* LAMBTON, ANTONY CLAUD FREDERICK.

# m

**McAvennie, Frank** (1958– ), soccer player. According to his former girl-friend, Page-3 model Jenny Blythe, she and McAvennie were, in their day, 'a low-rent version of Posh and Becks' – a reference to David Beckham, the Manchester United soccer player, and his wife Victoria Adams, formerly of the Spice Girls pop group. Some soccer enthusiasts thought at the time that Miss Blythe was being ungenerous to McAvennie and herself. To the impartial observer, they argued, their circumstances seemed to be as agree-able as those later enjoyed by the Beckhams. McAvennie and Blythe had a mock Tudor mansion in Hertfordshire guarded by attack dogs and an elec-tronic security system; both couples displayed a comedic dress sense; had they been blessed with a celebrity toddler, McAvennie and Miss Blythe would no doubt have cherished it – as the Beckhams were later to cherish Brooklyn – as a fashion accessory; in his heyday as a player with West Ham United, Tottenham Hotspur and Scotland, McAvennie seemed to be as accomplished in his various responsibilities on 'the park' as Beckham; and like George BEST before him and Beckham after, his exploits were eventu-ally celebrated in newspapers as 'style' and gossip features rather than on the sports pages.

McAvennie's difficulties began, perhaps, when he tried to express in his private life the *joie de vivre* that was such a feature of his game. Under the harsh glare of the media spotlight, he quickly succumbed to the pitfalls of fame. During his second spell as a player at West Ham in 1989 he became a heavy user of cocaine. His retirement from football set in motion a down-ward spiral of drug-fuelled crime, scandal and reckless behaviour. In 1996 Customs officers in Dover decided that £200,000 discovered in his Land Rover was going to be used to finance a drugs deal in Holland. McAvennie said that he had been duped by unscrupulous business associates. He had supposed that the money was for the purchase of a sailing boat in which he was to take part in a charitable treasure hunt, and was acquitted. In

October 2000 McAvennie was charged at Newcastle Crown Court with conspiracy to supply £110,000 worth of ecstasy tablets. Police had arrested him outside Newcastle station with the drugs in a parcel. McAvennie stated that he had just been handed the drugs by a complete stranger and had no idea of its contents. He was acquitted. Later he told reporters that he now hoped to get a coaching job, perhaps outside the United Kingdom.

*See also* BECKHAM, BROOKLYN.

**McCartney, Sir Paul** (1941– ), singer and composer. Bass guitarist with the 1960s pop group, the Beatles, and later with Wings, McCartney announced in October 2001 that he had proposed marriage to ex-model Heather Mills after he received instructions from an owl. Sir Paul understood that the bird was passing on a message from his first wife Linda, who was giving the couple her blessing from 'the other side'. Sir Paul was once a pupil of Maharishi Mahesh Yogi, and has frequently taken mind-expanding drugs. In India three hoots from an owl mean that a woman is to be married into a family. Nearer home, Edd Prynn, arch druid of Cornwall, has said, 'The owl is a strong messenger.' On the other hand, it has been said that if you are ever tempted to keep an owl as a pet, think twice. Sir Paul's most successful composition is 'Yesterday', which according to *The Guinness Book of Records* has been covered by more artists than any other song. He gave up cocaine after his first wife, Linda, said, 'Why don't you try reality?' This seemed to beg the question since there is no record of Sir Paul and Lady McCartney having first discussed in what sense 'reality' after taking cocaine might count as less 'real' than 'reality' without cocaine.

For a discussion concerning the nature of reality between the philosopher Galen Strawson and the former glamour model Rachel Garley, *see* STRACHEY, WILLIAM.

**McCray, Raymond** (1940– ), bank robber. In January 1983 members of the Robbery Squad interrupted a performance of *Snow White and the Seven Dwarfs* at the Shaftesbury Theatre, London, when they ran on stage and arrested Raymond McCray, a professional wrestler, in connection with a £45,000 bank hold-up in Ilford. Mr McCray, a three-and-a-half-foot dwarf, had been able to avoid surveillance cameras because his head had remained below the counter during the raid.

**Macdonnell, George** (1850–?), master forger. A middle-class rebel with a university education, Macdonnell was a key conspirator with Austin and George BIDWELL in the celebrated attempt in 1872 to rob the Bank of England. But for an extraordinary, and uncharacteristic, mistake by Macdonnell the gang might have got away with £30 million in today's terms.

It was Macdonnell's job to forge bills of exchange supposedly issued by Rothschilds Bank in Paris. His first efforts passed the Bank of England's scrutiny without question. However, when the final bundle of forged bills reached the Bank's Western Branch, the manager, Colonel Francis, handed them over to his discount clerk, who pointed out that the issuing bank, in this case B.W. Blydenstein & Co, had omitted to date two bills for £1000 each. Colonel Francis sent a messenger with the bills to Blydenstein's office in Great St Helen's to have the dates filled in. The next day he received a note saying, 'We have no record of these bills and can only assume that they are forgeries.'

But for Macdonnell's failure to date these two bills, the robbery must have succeeded. He departed immediately for America, but was arrested as he stepped off the ship in New York. Within a month he had been returned to England and was lodged with the Bidwell brothers in Newgate Prison. In August 1873 he was convicted at the Old Bailey and sentenced to imprisonment for life. He was released in 1891 after serving 18 years.

**McGregor, Gregor** (1786–1845), military adventurer and perpetrator of one of the 19th century's most audacious land swindles. Born into a distinguished Scottish family, McGregor served in the British army and then fought in Venezuela for the great liberator, Simon Bolivar, against colonial Spain. He married Bolivar's daughter and in 1820 led a mercenary expedition against Portobello, a Spanish settlement on the Isthmus of Panama. The area was nominally a British protectorate, but because of the poor nature of the land it remained uncolonized. McGregor befriended its only inhabitants, the Poyais Indians, and having returned to England as Gregor I – 'the Prince of the Poyais' – he set up a company to promote the area as an unspoilt paradise. The natives were friendly, he was able to report, the forests were lush, the land fertile, and the developing cities wanted for nothing in terms of amenities and culture. Accompanied by an impressive entourage, Gregor I toured the British Isles, touting the investment opportunities offered by the Poyais nation. William Richardson, an accomplice who had fought with McGregor on his many campaigns, dressed up as an Indian and was received at court as the Poyais ambassador. McGregor himself was knighted by George IV, who wanted to be sure that his re-settled subjects would be ruled by a titled Briton. Investors snapped up holdings on the Isthmus of Panama, a part of the world of which nothing was known other than the beguiling information obtainable at McGregor's land offices in London and Edinburgh. The newly elevated Sir Gregor had no difficulty in persuading the prestigious bankers, Sir John Perring & Co, to extend a £200,000 loan, and shares were floated.

The first settlers landed in 1822. By the time news filtered back that, instead of thriving cities and fertile land tracts, they had found mosquitoes, barren soil and impoverished Indians living in dilapidated huts, Sir Gregor had moved to Paris. Here, he swindled a financial consortium into granting him a loan of £300,000, posting as security the non-existent 'gold mines of Paulaze'.

In 1827 McGregor returned to London, where he was immediately arrested. Remarkably, he was able to persuade some of his former victims to put up his bail, assuring them that their original investments were about to bear fruit. He immediately escaped to France, where he was arrested and imprisoned. In 1839 Venezuela granted McGregor citizenship as a valued campaigner of the revolution. He returned to the scene of his less exceptionable activities, and lived out his remaining years on a general's pension.

**Mackreth, Bob** (1738–1802), waiter, billiard marker and politician. Mackreth, of whose early life little is known, became a member of Parliament in unusual circumstances. The right to vote in the constituency of Castle Rising was vested in the holders of a handful of 'burgage tenements', most of which were owned by a peer of erratic temperament, Robert Walpole, the 3rd earl of Orford. In 1774 Orford was asked by the constituency's returning officer whom he wished to nominate as the potential member. Orford, who had just recovered from a bout of insanity, nominated Bob Mackreth – a waiter and billiard marker at his club, Arthur's, in St James's. Since he had not been able to supply his candidate's first name, however, the election was declared void. Orford persisted in the nomination. Mackreth was able to supply his first name, a fresh election was held, Mackreth prevailed and duly took his seat.

Not everyone was amused by Lord Orford's prank. His son, Horace Walpole, wrote in a letter:

> The interlude of Mackreth has caused so much offence that he has been persuaded to be modest and give up his seat.

In fact, Mackreth was enjoying his new circumstances and had no intention of returning to his former employment in the billiard room at Arthur's. By 1781 he had used his position as MP for Castle Rising to build up a considerable fortune as a usurer, lending money to aristocratic spendthrifts. A problem arose in 1786 when James Fox Lane pleaded before the master of the rolls that Mackreth, who 'supplied young persons of rank and fortune, or expectation of fortune, with money when in distress', had defrauded him, while he was still a minor, of his inheritance, worth £1300 a year. Mackreth was ordered to repay £20,000, a judgement that was confirmed on appeal to the House of Lords. The Lords further imposed on Mackreth the highest costs ever awarded in such a case.

The one-time billiard marker took a poor view of this judgement:

> I had rather be in the prison of an Inquisition than have anything to do with the Court of Chancery. As the law is now administered, it is

a pest to society and a ruin of three parts of the Kingdom. If three thirds of the men of the Law were sent to Botany Bay it would be the greatest blessing that providence could bestow on mankind. The Law is become what the Church was four or five centuries ago – a curse to the country.

Six years later, in Lincoln's Inn Fields, Mackreth ran into Sir John Scott (afterwards Lord Chancellor Eldon), who had been Fox Lane's counsel. He called him 'a liar and a scoundrel', and then challenged him to a duel. Scott refused to accommodate him and instead preferred an indictment against Mackreth, who was fined £100 and imprisoned for six weeks.

These occasional misfortunes failed in the long term to impede Mackreth's career in Parliament. Although his patron, Lord Orford, had died in 1781, Mackreth had no difficulty in obtaining another seat. In 1784 he was elected as MP for Ashburton, a constituency that he served with distinction until his death in 1802.

**Maclean, Donald.** *See* BLUNT, SIR ANTHONY; BURGESS, GUY FRANCIS DE MONCY.

**McLean, Lenny** (1948–97), bare-knuckle boxer, bar-room bouncer, actor and author. A legendary hard man for many years in London's East End, McLean gained wider celebrity among the metropolitan literary/cocktail party set (*see* BOLLOCKS, A SILLY) with the publication of his memoirs, *The Guv'nor* (1997), and his cameo appearances in films such as Guy Ritchie's *Lock Stock and Two Smoking Barrels* (1997) and in the television series, *The Knock* (1995).

*The Guv'nor* chronicled McLean's various unlicensed fist fights, most notably his victory over the previous 'world champion', Roy 'Pretty Boy' Shaw ('I broke his jaw in seven places, I bit his nose off, I'm going at him like a lunatic …') and attendant misadventures such as terms in prison for attempted murder, affray and grievous bodily harm. On one occasion, when employed on the door at the Hippodrome nightclub in Leicester Square, McLean removed one of its customers, a Mr Gary Humphreys, so vigorously that he died later of his injuries. Humphreys had stripped naked, urinated and played with himself on stage. McLean was acquitted of his murder but was sentenced to 18 months in prison for assault. During his time on remand McLean was seen by psychiatrists, who described him as tearful.

*See also* BRADSHAW, BRIAN 'THE MAD GYPSY'.

**Macleane, James** (1711–50), shopkeeper, highwayman and fop. Known as the 'Gentleman Highwayman', Macleane lived in style in St James's, moving in London's most fashionable circles and supporting several mistresses. When the source of his affluence was questioned, he explained that he lived off the revenues of family estates in Ireland. He seems to have lacked the hardness of temperament necessary for success in his chosen profession. On one occasion he stopped the writer Horace Walpole and accidentally fired his pistol. Macleane offered his apologies, and then relieved Walpole of his purse.

The son of a well-to-do Scottish parson, Macleane drifted from one job to another for some years, but, on getting married, set himself up as a grocer and chandler in Welbeck Street, London. Three years later his wife, who had managed the business, died, and Macleane became a gentleman fortune-hunter – an occupation for which he had little natural aptitude. Within a few months he had exhausted his late wife's savings, this downturn in his affairs coinciding with a visit by one Plunkett, a countryman of his, and an apothecary. Plunkett was disappointed by the state of his friend, saying:

> I thought you had spirit, and resolution, with some knowledge of the world. A brave man cannot want; he has a right to live, and need not want the conveniences of life, while the dull, plodding, busy knaves carry cash in their pockets. We must draw upon them to supply our wants; there is need only of impudence, and the getting better of a few idle scruples; there is scarce courage necessary; all we have to deal with are such mere poltroons.

Plunkett then suggested that they should set up in partnership as highwaymen.

According to *Select Trials* (1764) Macleane, though at first reluctant, yielded to temptation, and from that time:

> ... entered into a particular intimacy with Plunkett, agreed to run all risks together and to share all profits; of which, till the fatal discovery, they kept a fair and regular account.

From the same source it can be discovered that during their first enterprise (the robbery of a grazier on Hounslow Heath) Macleane was a passive observer, that he stood by without speaking a word or drawing his pistols, 'but inwardly in greater agony, from the pricks of conscience, than the man who was robbed'. In time however, he grew more resolute, and, to recover the good opinion of Plunkett – who had charged him with pusillanimity – he summoned up his courage one evening and went on his own to Hyde Park where he robbed a gentleman of his watch and wallet.

The partnership prospered, and might have continued to do so had the two not been undone at last by Macleane's inveterate dandyism. On 26 June 1750 they robbed the Salisbury stagecoach of two portmanteaus containing clothes belonging to a Lord Eglington. Even though the missing garments had been advertised and described in newspapers, Macleane couldn't resist appearing in public dressed in one of the most splendid of Lord Eglington's outfits, thereafter calling on Mr Higden, the laceman from whom Lord Eglington had bought the very waistcoat that Macleane was now wearing. Mr Higden recognized his own handiwork immediately, and summoned law enforcement officers. Macleane was arrested, and later confined in Newgate prison. He was hanged for highway robbery in November 1750.

For another coxcomb, *see* MASSEREENE, CLOTWORTHY SKEFFINGTON, 2ND EARL OF.

**MacLeod, Alexander.** *See VERONICA* MUTINEERS, THE.

**MacLiammoir, Michael.** *See* STAGE, HOOLIGANISM ON.

**McNaughton, Daniel** (1805–?), would-be assassin. In 1843 McNaughton, a Scotsman who suffered from a delusion that he was being persecuted by the Tories, attempted to assassinate the prime minister, Sir Robert Peel, but inadvertently shot, and killed, his private secretary Edward Drummond. He was subsequently acquitted on the grounds of partial insanity – the case giving rise to the McNaughton Rules. These established that, to succeed with a defence of insanity, it must be proved that the defendant didn't know the nature or quality of the act he was committing; alternatively, that if he did know, he did not understand that what he was doing was wrong. This became the law in Britain until the Homicide Act of 1957 sought to rectify some of the Rules' imperfections by recognizing the plea of diminished responsibility.

**McNeile, Major Cyril ('Sapper').** *See* MARKS, HOWARD (regarding the flogging of dope peddlers with dog whips in the Great West Road).

**Macpherson, James** (1736–96), an obscure Scottish poet who received greater acclaim for his work than any literary forger in history. Macpherson was declared by Goethe to be the equal of Homer – a comparison that for Napoleon did Macpherson an injustice.

In 1760 the 24-year-old Macpherson, whose own book of poems, *The Highlander*, had been published without success, announced that he had translated parts of a grand epic from scattered Gaelic manuscripts, which he then published as *Fragments of ancient poetry collected in the Highlands and translated from the Gaelic or Erse languages by James Macpherson*. These were the works, he said, of Ossian, who in Gaelic legend was the 3rd-century poet son of the warrior Finn MacCumhail. Some poems allegedly by the real, or legendary, Ossian had appeared in *The Book of Lismore*, compiled by James MacGregor in 1512. Macpherson's find created a literary sensation in Scotland, England, France and Germany. For the Scots the Ossian texts revealed a glorious page from their heroic ancient past.

*Fingal, An Ancient Poem in Six Books, composed by Ossian, the son of Fingal* followed in 1762, and in 1763 Macpherson produced another Ossian epic, *Temora*. He had been financed in his research by donations and fundraising conducted by the poet John Home, and by the distinguished rhetorician, and Presbyterian minister of Edinburgh, Hugh Blair, neither of whom could read Gaelic.

Ossian's works were translated into Italian, Spanish, French, Polish and German. Goethe was so entranced by 'the Homer of the North' that he had his hero, Werther, declare:

> Ossian is nearer my heart than Homer. What a sublime and noble world he has revealed to me!

Goethe's treatise *Ossian and the Poetry of Ancient Races* remains the standard work on the subject. The German philosopher Johann Gottfried Herder declared, after reading Ossian, that:

> To judge by their recently discovered poems and songs, there has never been a race possessed of such powerful and at the same time tender emotions, who, individually, were so heroic, and at the same time, so supremely human as the ancient Scots.

Doubts were expressed in some academic circles, not least because there were no extant writings in Scottish Gaelic from earlier than the 10th century. The English poet Thomas Gray admired the work, but with reservations. The Scottish philosopher David Hume was frankly sceptical (as was his wont). The most formidable opposition, however, came from Samuel Johnson, who travelled to the Hebrides in 1773 to investigate the legends and their sources. In *A Journey to the Western Islands of Scotland* (1775) he said of Macpherson's discoveries:

> I believe they never existed in any other form but that which we have seen. The editor, or author, never could show the original, nor can it be shown by any other.

Macpherson was outraged and said that only Johnson's age prevented him from the challenge of a duel or a thrashing. Johnson famously replied that:

> I hope I shall never be deterred from detecting what I think a cheat, by the meanness of a ruffian. I thought your book an imposture; I think it an imposture still. Your rage I defy. Your abilities, since your Homer, are not so formidable, and what I hear of your morals inclines me to regard, not to what you shall say, but to what you shall prove.

Macpherson was never able to produce the originals on which he had based his translations, in spite of frequent promises that he would do so. Others supported Johnson, most notably Horace Walpole, who had previously exposed Thomas CHATTERTON. Some scholars refuse to allow the fact of Macpherson's forgeries to obscure his genuine contributions to Gaelic studies. Will and Ariel Durant, in their authoritative work *The Story of Civilization* write, 'The deception was not so complete or so heinous as Johnson supposed. Let us call it poetic licence on too grand a scale.'

**McSkimmey, Bunty** (1921–  ), embezzler. A former Sunday-school teacher, McSkimmey took up crime at the age of 76, later offering the explanation that 'my cooker was on its last legs'. In 1998 she became secretary of the Glasgow Tree Lovers' Society. With hindsight, the society's chairman Colonel Archie Carstairs was able to say that the appointment had been a mistake, and that Miss McSkimmey's habit of smoking cigars had aroused the suspicions of a senior member, Mrs Pugh. These reservations had not prevented them from furnishing McSkimmey with a book full of signed blank cheques and wide powers over the society's assets. The latter included stocks and shares valued at £80,000, and £27,000 in a current account with the Royal Bank of Scotland. At the annual general meeting in 1999 Miss McSkimmey was able to blame a discovered fall in the value of the society's shares – to approximately zero – on a volatile market. At the AGM in October 2000, however, the society's accountants asked her why the balance of £27,000, previously with the Royal Bank of Scotland, had vanished. Her explanation that she had been investing in various children's charities was not accepted, and the police were called in. Miss McSkimmey was sentenced to 200 hours community service.

*See also* BUS-PASS BANDITS.

**McVitie, Jack 'The Hat'.** *See* KRAY, REGGIE AND RONNIE.

**madams.** *See* CLAP, MARGARET; DALY, JOSEPHINE; FERNSEED, MARGARET; JEFFRIES, MARY; JONES, JANIE; PAGE, DAMARIS; PAYNE, CYNTHIA; POTTER, SARAH; TURNER, ANNE.

**mad axemen.** *See* BROMLEY-DAVENPORT, LIEUTENANT COLONEL SIR WALTER; FRASER, FRANCIS ('MAD FRANKIE'); MITCHELL, FRANK.

**Mad Boy, the.** *See* HEBER-PERCY, ROBERT.

**Maddock, Will** (1921–90), former landlord of the Aubrey Arms in Ystradgynlais, South Wales. In Ystradgynlais, there are those who believe Maddock murdered his wife Barbara, and those who believe that he didn't. There is agreement, however, that his habits were unorthodox. Dewi Evans, for one, has recalled:

> I was once walking behind him on the way to the Aubrey's toilet, when £3000 fell out of his pocket. In those days the pub was full of

solicitors, police, miners – every type of person. Opening hour was noon, but Will opened at 7 a.m.

Tales of Maddock's drinking exploits are still the talk of Ystradgynlais. By the time he died at the age of 69 he was drinking two bottles of whisky a day. On one occasion, a certain Dai 'Burma' (so called because he had been forced to work on the Burma railway in World War II) keeled over and died on New Year's Day during a morning gathering at the Aubrey. Dewi Evans remembers the occasion:

No one was supposed to be there until noon, so we couldn't report his death until then. We laid him out on the bar, and then Dai Llewellyn, I think it was, said, 'You absolutely sure he's dead?' 'Absolutely,' we says. 'Well then,' says Dai, 'he won't mind if I finish his beer.'

On 28 October 1973 Mrs Maddock disappeared without saying goodbye to her son Hywel or her daughter Jean. She was thought by many to have walked out of the family pub after a spell of depression, possibly to return to Brisbane, Australia, where Will Maddock, a former Royal Navy bosun, had met her after World War II. His parents had run the Aubrey Arms, so when they died and left it to Will, he and Barbara returned to a thriving business.

Those who do not believe that Mr Maddock could have killed his wife point to the fact that he paid money to the Salvation Army each year to keep an eye out for her. 'Why would he have blown £3.50 if he knew she was dead?' asked Arwel Morgan.

Hywel Griffiths, 42 – who took his mother's maiden name because his parents didn't marry until he was 3 – is said locally to have been on bad terms with his father and is now a teetotaller, although he still runs the Aubrey Arms.

See also WELSH, THE.

**Madoc fever of 1792, the.** See EVANS, JOHN.

**mafiosi attend philosophy classes.** See MARKS, HOWARD.

**Maggott, an abandoned woman called.** See SHEPPARD, JACK.

**magicians, cross-dressing.** See LLOYD, SOPHIE.

**magicians, hemp-growing sons of TV.** See DANIELS, PAUL.

**magicians, occult.** See CROWLEY, ALEISTER; FORMAN, SIMON.

**magic lantern, killed by an exploding.** *See* DE COURCY, KENNETH (whose father died thus).

**magnetic, believing oneself to be.** *See* EDINBURGH, PRINCE PHILIP, DUKE OF.

**Magnetic Rock Dew for removing wrinkles.** *See* LEVERSON, RACHEL.

**Maguire, Brian** (*c.*1770–1835), trader and duellist. Maguire, born into the ancient house of Fermanagh in Ireland, joined the East India Company in 1799. While serving in Cochin, a seaport on the Malabar Coast, his success with the few eligible women caused resentment among the other officers. Eventually he was challenged to a duel by a Captain Thuring. The match appeared to be unequal, since Maguire was armed with a billiard cue against the Captain's sword. Maguire prevailed, however, and Thuring was fatally wounded. Delighted by his success, Maguire was addicted thereafter to the art of duelling.

Maguire's return to Dublin and marriage in 1808 served only to strengthen him in his new enthusiasm. He persuaded his wife to help him perfect his skill by holding at arm's length the lighted candle that he used for target practice. His only problem was a shortage of opponents, but he solved this by hanging out of a window and throwing dirt at passers-by. When they looked up, he spat on them, as a rule finding that they now wished to retaliate with a show of arms.

A long and ultimately unsuccessful Chancery suit for the recovery of a fortune due to his wife led to Maguire's eventual impoverishment. His last years were sad. When his son George died at the age of 12 in 1830, Maguire had him embalmed, thereafter keeping him in a glass case, always by his side, until his own death five years later.

**Maidenhead, The Fifteen Plagues of.** *See* CURLL, EDMOND.

**maidens, how to make spoile of yong.** *See* FERNSEED, MARGARET.

**maiden speech, too bored to complete one's.** *See* SALISBURY, ROBERT ARTHUR TALBOT GASCOYNE CECIL, 3RD MARQUESS OF.

**Malcolm, Al.** *See* EGAN, JOE.

**malice, a squirming package of.** *See* KNOX, DR ROBERT.

**malignant pleasure in seeing one's companions in like circumstances of calamity.** *See* GOW, JOHN.

**malignant spirit of railing and scandal, a.** *See* OATES, TITUS.

**Man, the Headless.** *See* ARGYLL, MARGARET DUCHESS OF.

**Mancini, Johnny 'No-Legs'.** *See* BASS, HARRY 'THE DOCTOR'.

**Mancini, Tony** (1917–89), convicted thief and central figure in the notorious Brighton Trunk Murders. In the 1920s and 1930s it was unusual in Brighton for a week to pass without the body of a dead woman turning up in a trunk, but it was rare for two to be found on the same day, as happened on 11 June 1933. The first had been deposited at Brighton railway station eleven days earlier. In the course of the police enquiries, hundreds of people were interviewed, including a petty thief called Tony Mancini. Mancini had recently moved to Brighton with his mistress, an ex-dancer called Violette Kaye. After a quarrel at the Skylark Café, where Mancini worked as a waiter, Miss Kaye had disappeared. When the police visited him in connection with the body at the railway station they found Violette Kaye in a trunk under the bed. Mancini was duly tried for her murder at Lewes Assizes, where he pleaded not guilty. His defence, ingeniously presented by Norman Birkett KC, was that he had found Miss Kaye already dead in their lodgings and in his terrified state of mind had decided to hide the body. Asked why he had not called the police, he replied, 'Where the police are concerned a man who's got convictions never gets a square deal.'

The jury acquitted him, but in 1976 Mancini admitted in the *People* that he had indeed killed Miss Kaye after their quarrel at the Skylark Café. The body in the trunk at Brighton station was never identified.

**Man in the Mask, the.** *See* KEELER, CHRISTINE.

**Mann, Paul** (1936– ), racing driver, road manager and property developer. In the summer of 1963 Mann was paid £3000 to ensure that Christine KEELER, the chief prosecution witness at the trial of her one-time lover, Johnny Edgecombe, and a central figure in the Profumo scandal, was not in the country. Mann drove her to Spain, where they stayed until Edgecombe's trial was over. On their return, Mann was summoned to an unidentifiable building in Whitehall where he was told that if he ever 'talked' he might well regret it. Mann took the threat all the more seriously from its having been delivered by someone who would have been well cast as an intelligence officer in a British film of the period – Robert Morley, say – and for a time he occupied himself inconspicuously as road manager to various pop groups, including the Walker Brothers. He then returned to Spain, where he tried to sell ladies' wigs. This venture was unsuccessful, so he moved to Birmingham. There he prospered in the property market.

The Walker Brothers' recording, 'The Sun Ain't Going To Shine

Anymore', was playing on the juke box in the Blind Beggar public house in Bow when, in 1966, Ronnie KRAY walked in and shot George Cornell.

*See* BOMBS, TICKING TIME.

**Margaret, Princess.** *See* BINDON, JOHN; CONYERS, DAVID; EYRES, TONY.

**marines, female.** *See* SNELL, HANNAH.

**Marks, Howard** (1945– ), philosopher and drug dealer. Born in Kenfig Hill, near Port Talbot steelworks in Wales, the son of a merchant seaman and a school teacher, Marks was educated at Garw Grammar School and Balliol College, Oxford. His subsequent career showed that an independent drug dealer can compete successfully in a business generally thought to be controlled by organized gangs.

While doing a postgraduate course in philosophy, Marks began to deal in small amounts of cannabis for his friends. Soon he was moving much larger quantities into Europe and America in the equipment of rock and roll bands. By the late 1970s he had 43 aliases and 89 telephone lines, and owned 25 companies trading throughout the world. The bars, recording studios and off-shore banks were merely money-laundering vehicles for his chief activity – dealing in drugs.

Marks's success is explained by the fact that until the 1960s the British authorities had not seen drugs as posing a particular threat to the nation's youth. In their report on drugs to the League of Nations in 1928, the government noted that there were 620 drug addicts in Britain, of whom 320 were women. The figure was large enough, however, to alarm some people, notably Major Cyril McNeile, who as 'Sapper' had created the popular Bulldog Drummond adventure stories. According to the *News of the World*, McNeile, 'disgusted by the degenerate parasites of the West End against whom the police are powerless', suggested in an army mess that 'any young man of spunk' should follow Bulldog Drummond's example, form a gang and deal with these degenerates. Subsequently, vigilante groups of young army officers were reported to have rounded up 'dope peddlers and other crooks', taken them to a garage off the Great West Road and flogged them with dog whips.

A drugs squad was set up in the 1930s, with one car at its disposal, but it was soon disbanded. By 1950 the police were satisfied that drugs had ceased to exist except among foreign seamen and West Indian immigrants. Superintendent Robert Fabian, in his memoir *London After Dark* (1956), describes these 'coloured fellows' as being:

> ... like schoolboys, simple folk, believe me, but they so often get bad names through the young trollops who become their 'camp followers' ... they have the brains of children, can only dimly know the

cruel harm they do these teenage girls, who dance with them and try thrilled puffs at those harmless looking marijuana cigarettes.

Chapman Pincher, the *Daily Express*'s experienced crime correspondent, was alert to the danger. 'Coloured men who peddle reefers,' he wrote, 'meet susceptible white teenagers at the boogie-woogie clubs.' In 1957 *The Times* agreed that:

> White girls who become friendly with West Indians are from time to time enticed to smoke hemp ... this is an aspect of the hemp problem – the possibility of its spreading among irresponsible white people – that causes greatest concern to the authorities. The potential moral danger is significant, since a principal motive of the coloured man in smoking hemp is to stimulate sexual desire.

With the 1960s there came a sea change in drug use, and in drug trafficking. A generation that hadn't derived its travelling experience from national service in Cyprus or Aden had, for the first time, the money to take advantage of cheap foreign travel in Morocco or India, Peru or Thailand. Many young people tried their first marijuana 'joint' in Tangier, and some found it easy enough to bring small supplies of the drug into Britain, where drug tsars, sniffer dogs and drug-educated Customs officers were not yet in place. From these young people came the first of the new generation of drug dealers. Many had been to university and, importantly, none had any links with the criminal world.

Of these new entrepreneurs, Marks was the best organized, able to maintain his position as an independent operator even after the governments of the world fell into line with the United States in the 1960s and decided – idiosyncratically in the view of some – that supposedly dangerous drugs should henceforth be prescribed and distributed not by qualified physicians but by criminal gangs.

At the height of his career Marks was smuggling consignments of up to 30 tons of cannabis from Pakistan and Thailand to America and Canada. Eventually, the British, American, Canadian and Spanish police – with assistance from Lord MOYNIHAN, the half-brother of the former Conserva tive minister, Colin Moynihan – combined to put him out of business. Marks and Moynihan had discussed the possibility of setting up a cannabis plantation on an island off the Philippines where Moynihan was working as a corporate pimp, running massage parlours staffed by young Filipinas. In July 1988 the American Drug Enforcement Agency persuaded Moynihan to tape-record a series of incriminating conversations with Marks. Faced with a choice between fighting the ensuing charges and running the risk of a 60-year jail sentence, or pleading guilty and being jailed for 25 years, Marks pleaded guilty. He was moved from the Palm Beach Federal Court in Florida to the federal penitentiary in Terre Haute,

Indiana, to serve his sentence. There he ran a successful philosophy class, attended by mafiosi and members of Colombian drug cartels.

Marks was released in April 1995 after serving seven years of his sentence. His autobiography, *Mr Nice* (1997), in which he claims to have 'made and lost a couple of million – no more than the average yuppie', has been a worldwide bestseller. He is also a popular speaker on the international lecture circuit, arguing for the decriminalization of soft drugs.

**married to a Great Train Robber, unwittingly.** *See* FIELD, BRIAN.

**Massereene, Clotworthy Skeffington, 2nd earl of** (1742–1805), peer, soldier and persistent debtor. Massereene's father died when he was 14. Seven years later, when he came of age, he inherited the family estates in County Antrim. By then he had already settled in Paris, leaving the management of his Irish property in the hands of his mother. The 2nd earl was a dandy, dubbed by the *Gentleman's Magazine*, 'the most superlative coxcomb that Ireland ever bred'. Before a ball he would spend hours dressing in his chambers, keeping his guests waiting until, as Horace Walpole noted, 'Adonis himself at last consented to appear.'

Massereene's behaviour in this respect didn't depart to any great degree from the aristocratic conventions of the day. It was normal, too, that he should get into debt. His generous allowance of £200 a month could not cover his tailor's bills, gambling losses and the demands of his many mistresses. Even so, he might have survived had he not become involved in a speculative business venture put to him by a crooked merchant named Vidari, who was from Italy (or possibly Syria). Vidari proposed to import salt to France from the Barbary Coast, and he invited Massereene to subsidize the idea. Massereene passed a number of bills that in due course, when the business collapsed, he was called upon to honour. While his mother, the dowager Lady Massereene, set about the task of raising the money required to get him out of trouble, Massereene himself languished in jail. His creditors, who were aware of his extensive property in Ireland, assumed that he would shortly tire of imprisonment and pay the £30,000 he owed. There was a difficulty, however. He insisted that the debts had been incurred by means of a fraud against himself, and he refused to acknowledge them. Rather than admit his guilt by means of a settlement, he decided to stay in prison for 25 years, after which time, according to French law, the debt would be cancelled.

While incarcerated in the Châtelet prison Massereene married Marie Anne Barcier, the daughter of the prison governor. The new Lady Massereene assisted him in two attempts to escape, neither of which was successful. After 18 years he was freed from La Force prison by a Revolutionary mob that had been bribed by his wife – his release coinciding with the storming of the Bastille. The young dandy, whose obstinacy had caused him to be locked up for 18 years, emerged from prison bent and grey.

In May 1788 Lord Massereene returned to Antrim Castle, his seat in Ireland, where a frigid reunion took place with his mother, the dowager countess. He showed no interest in the way his estates were being run, but left Antrim after a few days and went to London with Lady Massereene. Here, he was lured into another fraudulent business venture, which resulted in debt and imprisonment once again. Blaming his wife's extravagance for his problems, he deserted her at a time when, crippled by angina, she was facing an early death brought on by her former exertions on his behalf. She was given a pension of £300 a year until she died in 1803.

Lord Massereene's lack of feeling for his wife was the result of a developing relationship with Elizabeth Blackburn, a girl of 19, who was a servant in a house immediately opposite his lodgings. Having a habit of shadow-boxing in the nude, Massereene exposed himself at his window and caught her eye. Soon she was living with him on the promise that he would marry her when his present wife died. Meanwhile he was passing bills to the amount of £9000 in favour of a swindler named Whaley. Afterwards he claimed that he had no recollection of having done so. This adventure landed him twice in prison, where Miss Blackburn was allowed to join him. A loan from his brother-in-law, Lord Leitrim, and a humiliating lawsuit in which he successfully pleaded that he had acted with extreme foolishness, eventually freed him.

In 1797 Lord Massereene returned to Ireland, where he established Miss Blackburn as mistress of Antrim Castle. Although he owed his own liberty to the rebellious spirit inspired by the French Revolution, he had a horror of Jacobinism and now took an active part against the anticipated uprising. He formed a company of yeomen and trained it by his own unorthodox methods. His men were drilled without weapons and presented arms in a complicated pantomime involving a series of hand signals. They were persuaded to simulate rifle shots by clapping their hands. Massereene also developed a number of original drills, giving them such names as the Serpentine Walk and Eel-in-the-Mud. These martial evolutions convinced Massereene that he was a born leader of men, an assessment with which the military establishment of the time disagreed.

Away from the parade ground, Massereene continued to indulge his personal whims. Sometimes he would take it into his head to dine on the roof, and on these occasions it was necessary to hoist up chairs, tables and provisions by means of a pulley. His guests climbed to the roof by means of a small ladder inside the house, but once they had assembled, Massereene usually declared himself dissatisfied with the arrangements and ordered everything to be taken down again. When one of his dogs died, all the local dogs were invited to its funeral at Antrim Castle. Some 50 of them, provided with white scarves, acted as a guard of honour.

Meanwhile, Miss Blackburn had made friends with a disreputable father and son by the name of O'Doran. O'Doran senior had been a Catholic priest, but later joined the Church of Ireland and received from Lord Massereene the living of Killead which was worth £500. O'Doran junior became Miss Blackburn's lover. Other members of the family, including Mrs O'Doran and her three daughters, moved into Antrim Castle, where they were subjected to the earl's naked shadow-boxing and repertoire of obscene songs. Miss Blackburn assumed complete control of the estates and of Lord Massereene's progressively enfeebled mind. She and the O'Dorans ensured that he quarrelled with his neighbours and became estranged from his family. He was particularly hostile towards his mother, refusing to pay her annuity and forcing her to sue him for it. According to the Reverend George Macartney, vicar of Antrim, whom Massereene had once challenged to a duel:

> Miss Blackburn made the earl believe that his mother was a witch and a whore; and so atrocious was her conduct that upon one occasion when sailing in a boat with him, she said, 'I wish we had your mother tied by the legs dragging after us.' His answer was so indecent that I will not repeat it.

On the death of his first wife in 1803 Lord Massereene married Miss Blackburn, at last regularizing a relationship that had caused scandal far beyond the bounds of County Antrim. A year before his own death he was persuaded to leave the whole of the Massereene estate to the former Miss Blackburn, except for a guinea each to his brothers and one to Lady Leitrim.

Massereene died in March 1805, and the following year his brothers contested the will in court. Their case rested on the fact that Massereene had been insane, and many witnesses testified to this. After lengthy litigation the brothers gained a verdict, not on the grounds of insanity, but on his wife's undue influence over him. Lady Massereene (and, by extension, various members of the O'Doran family) was paid off very comfortably with a lump sum of £15,000 and £800 a year for life. The verdict may have been a matter of etiquette: it was not customary to declare peers mad unless there was no alternative.

**Mathew, George** (*c.*1670–1738), landowner and host. A man of a most hospitable disposition, Mathew used his entire private fortune to turn his home, Thomastown Castle in County Tipperary, into a pleasure park for his friends. Inside the castle Mathew created 40 private apartments in which his guests could stay for as long as they pleased. Although there were rooms for visitors' servants, Mathew's own large staff included a personal valet for each guest. There was a rule that servants were not to be tipped, since Mathew judged it would be vulgar to put guests even to this small expense. Instead, he added what would have been a generous tip to a servant's weekly wage.

Once installed in his suite, a guest had merely to express a wish to find it fulfilled. Soon after a new arrival had been shown to his room, the cook knocked at his door to receive instructions for dinner. The cook was followed by the butler with a list of wines from which the guest was asked to select as many as he pleased. Guests could choose whether to take their meals in their rooms, either alone or with friends, or in the dining room with the other guests. Mathew himself ate in the dining room, but inconspicuously. He never sat at the head of the table, since he wished to be treated at all times not as a host but as a fellow guest.

For those of a gregarious disposition, Mathew had replicated a Dublin coffee house at Thomastown where food was available at all hours and where visitors might sit and argue, play chess or read the latest newspapers. Other guests might prefer a replicated Irish tavern, where waiters served them drinks while they played cards or billiards. For guests who liked to be out of doors, there was fishing, shooting and hunting on Mathew's several-thousand-acre estate – with guns, fishing tackle, 20 fine hunters and several packs of hounds provided.

In 1719 Dean Swift was persuaded to visit Thomastown. When he realized that there were so many other guests, Swift wanted to leave, but was eventually persuaded to stay. 'Well, there is no remedy,' he grumbled, 'I must submit, but I have lost a fortnight of my life.' When the chef and butler knocked on his door, Swift chose to avoid his fellow guests and to dine in his room. After five days, during which he was astonished that no one tried to draw him out, he was tempted downstairs by the sound of laughter from the dining room. He joined the other guests with the ungracious observation, 'Ladies and Gentlemen, I am come to live among you and it will be no fault of mine if we do not pass our time pleasantly.' The cantankerous old satirist enjoyed himself so much that he stayed for four months.

**Maturin, Charles Robert** (1782–1824), clergyman and writer. Maturin was an absent-minded Irish priest who wrote plays and novels. The most notable was *Melmoth the Wanderer*, a fiction in the Gothic style, which was lucky to achieve publication since he delivered it as a stack of randomly assembled and unnumbered pages. The patronage of Lord BYRON and Sir Walter Scott brought him some literary recognition, but failed to free him from financial difficulties. These had originally been brought on by his standing security for a bankrupt relative.

When in receipt of funds, Maturin spent on a lavish scale. The ceiling of his house in Dublin was painted with clouds, and scenes from his novels were reproduced on the walls. It was his great joy to see his wife, who was a famous beauty, elaborately turned out, and he insisted on her wearing several layers of rouge. His own dress sense was dictated by a desire to show off his legs, which were in no way remarkable. He favoured tight pantaloons and wore net stockings and evening clothes even when fishing.

Maturin's abiding love was music. He possessed a pleasing after-dinner baritone, and lay claims to being 'the best dancer in the Established Church'. In Dublin he held quadrille parties on several mornings a week. He recognized no distinction between night and day, preferring to live by artificial light. While he was working he liked to be surrounded by people, though sometimes he put a cushion on his head to show that he didn't wish to be disturbed.

Maturin's absent-mindedness sometimes displayed itself even in matters about which he cared deeply, such as dress. He often made social calls in his dressing gown and slippers. On one occasion he visited his publisher wearing a boot on one foot and a shoe on the other.

**Maudling, Reginald.** *See* MILLER, SIR ERIC; POULSON, JOHN.

**mausoleums.** *See* HAMILTON, ALEXANDER DOUGLAS, 10TH DUKE OF.

**Mausprick, the marchioness of.** *See* SALA, GEORGE AUGUSTUS.

**Maxwell, Robert** (1923–91), politician, publisher and embezzler. Maxwell had an unlikeable way of expressing himself. Having landed by helicopter on the roof of his Mirror Group headquarters, he would unzip his trousers and relieve himself over the edge, 'That's what I think of my readers,' he would say to his assembled guests. Mirror Group employees, whose pensions he stole in order to shore up his collapsing empire, might reasonably have felt that they were among those thus urinated over. Described by his *Independent* obituarist as, 'a foul-mouthed, arrogant, gluttonous rogue,' Maxwell specialized in humiliating his senior staff. Peter Jay, the former economics editor of the BBC, had the misfortune to work as his lieutenant. Having been Britain's ambassador to the United States, Jay was treated by Maxwell with contempt. The *Mirror*'s proprietor would sweep into press conferences with his camelhair coat over his shoulders and pause momentarily so that the former diplomat could remove it.

Born Jan Ludvik Hoch in Czechoslovakia and self-educated, Maxwell fought in World War II before founding the Pergamon Press, a publishing company specializing in scientific journals. A former Labour MP (1964–70), he was judged by government inspectors in 1971 as 'not a fit person in our opinion to be relied upon to exercise proper stewardship of a publicly quoted company.' 'The Bouncing Czech', as he was amusingly dubbed by *Private Eye* magazine, was resilient enough to recover from this setback, rescuing the British Printing Corporation from financial collapse in 1980 and rapidly transforming it into the successful British Printing and

Communications Corporation. In 1985 this became the Maxwell Communication Corporation. At his peak, Maxwell controlled an empire that embraced the *Mirror*, the *New York Daily News* and the American publishing house, Macmillan. In November 1991, when cruising off the Canary Islands in his yacht, *Lady Ghislaine*, he fell overboard in mysterious circumstances, leaving a £400 million hole in his employees' pension funds. His lust for money and power was matched by a gargantuan appetite for food, particularly at night. Cleaners at the *Mirror*'s offices were greeted by scenes of astounding gluttony when attempting to clear up the chairman's kitchen. As a rule, the bones of half a dozen chickens were strewn around the floor. His personal lavatory was reported to look as if a horse had been the last to use it.

**May, Betty 'Tiger woman'.** *See* BOSE, DOUGLAS.

**May, Michael** (1966– ), farm labourer and assistant referee. When officiating as a linesman in a Cornish Cub Scouts match between St Erth and Hayle, May walked on to the pitch and head-butted the referee, Martin Rolfe. He had become incensed when his son, who was appearing for the under-10s, was brought down by a cynical late challenge. When Mr Rolfe asked him why he'd done that, May butted him again, breaking his nose. In January 1997 Penzance magistrates put May on a year's probation and ordered him to pay Mr Rolfe £150 compensation. After the court hearing, Mr Rolfe said:

> I have not picked up a whistle since the attack. When you are refereeing children they will accept almost any decision you make. The most you will get back is a little moan. But the people on the touchline – the parents – they go berserk.

**Maybrick, Florence Elizabeth** (1865–1941), alleged murderess. Born in Alabama, the daughter of a Baroness von Roques, Florence married Liverpool trader James Maybrick in 1881. Maybrick was 23 years older than his wife, and a hypochondriac. He regularly took arsenic as an aphrodisiac. The couple lived in a large house in Liverpool, had two children, five servants and a nanny, Alice Yapp. They seemed happy enough, but in 1887 Mrs Maybrick discovered that her husband kept a mistress. She then took a lover herself, a friend of Maybrick's called Alfred Brierley. In March 1889 she and Brierley spent a weekend together in London. When Maybrick found out, a quarrel ensued and he gave his wife a beating.

Two weeks later Mrs Maybrick bought a dozen arsenic-based flypapers from a local chemist. On 28 April 1889 Maybrick became ill. Mrs Maybrick told his doctor that he had been taking a 'white powder'. After rallying briefly, Maybrick died on 11 May. The circumstances aroused the suspicions of the family nanny, Alice Yapp, and having found an excuse for reading Mrs Maybrick's mail, she handed over some compromising letters to Maybrick's brother Edwin. Mrs Maybrick was kept a prisoner in the house while her room was searched. A packet was found labelled 'Arsenic: poison for cats'. Traces of arsenic were found in Maybrick's body, and a coroner's jury returned a verdict of murder.

Mrs Maybrick was tried at Liverpool in July 1889. An exceptionally strong defence suggested that Maybrick died a natural death. Traces of strychnine, hyoscine and morphine found in his stomach pointed to hypochondriac poisoning. However, the defence could not counter the prejudice of the court against an unfaithful wife. The judge, who was later committed to an insane asylum, summed up against her and Mrs Maybrick was found guilty. The death sentence was commuted to life imprisonment, of which she served 15 years. She died in Florida in 1941, aged 76.

**Mayes, Joy** (1911–92), waitress, cleaner and perpetrator of the Iron Bootscraper Murder. It was not until February 1995 that the circumstances surrounding the death of Roderick Mayes at the Boulevard, Weston-super-Mare, came to light. Joy Mayes had worked for many years in a menial capacity to educate her two sons, Sean and Roderick. Sean went to Trinity College, Cambridge, and Roderick to college in Weston. Mrs Mayes had always feared that Roderick would get into bad company and kill himself with LSD. On 8 April 1972 she accordingly dissolved a handful of sleeping pills in a mug of hot chocolate and took them to him in bed. Once he was unconscious, she fractured his skull with the iron bootscraper. Some days later she told her other son, Sean, and her father, Commander Thomas Thompson OBE, what she had done. Sean, who was a member of a rock-and-roll band called Fumble, had been on tour in Switzerland when his brother was killed. He now insisted that Roderick should have a proper burial. He and his grandfather, Commander Thompson, took the body, which Mrs Mayes had wrapped in a candlewick bedspread and hidden under the bed, and buried it in the back garden. Friends were told that Roderick had gone to live with hippies.

Commander Thompson died in 1975 aged 83 and Mrs Mayes in 1992. It was not until Sean, himself dying of AIDS, told the police what had happened that his brother's body was discovered. No charges were brought against Sean Mayes. Commander Thompson had left a diary with entries relating to the killing. On 12 April 1972 he had written, 'Terrific operation. Went like clockwork' – a reference to Roderick's burial. The following day's entry said, 'Such a relief with R and his friends no longer popping in and out all the time.'

**Mayfair drinking clubs, the twilight world of.** *See* ELLIS, RUTH.

**Mean Machine, the.** *See* FOREMAN, FREDDIE.

**mediums.** *See* ICKE, DAVID.

**Meinertzhagen, Richard** (1878–1956), soldier and ornithologist. Meinertzhagen was one of ten children born to wealthy parents. The family had homes in Knightsbridge and the country, and each child was provided with his personal groom. An uncle gave Richard an elephant as a christening gift and Florence Nightingale was a frequent guest at dinner. After school, Richard joined the army, serving with the Royal Fusiliers in Kenya and gaining a reputation for extreme ruthlessness when the circumstances seemed to demand it. As Captain Meinertzhagen he was active in intelligence during the German invasion of British East Africa. When it became possible to incriminate the most important German agent by giving up the names of his own agents, Meinertzhagen applied a utilitarian calculus and sacrificed his men without a qualm.

He had spent the years before World War I in various army assignments, some of which were less orthodox than others. Intelligence work took him to Odessa, in Russia, and while there he rescued a Jewish girl from prison. He became a proponent of a Jewish state in Palestine, and vowed in his diary that he would help the Jews whenever and wherever he could.

At the outbreak of World War I Meinertzhagen was serving in the Middle East as head of intelligence at army headquarters in Gaza. When Beersheeba was targeted as a prelude to an attack on Jerusalem, Meinertzhagen was ordered to confuse the Turks over the British army's real intentions. His most successful tactic was to drop cigarettes over the enemy lines laced with opium. He then rode among the becalmed Turks, distributing false documents, which, in their state of advanced narcosis, they were happy to accept as genuine. The high quality of the fraudulent papers, as much as the high quality of the opium, caused the Turks to shift the focus of their defence to Gaza and away from Beersheeba, as had been intended. Beersheeba was captured with remarkably few casualties, and within a month the British controlled Jersusalem.

After Meinertzhagen retired from the army in 1925 he was able to devote his time to his two enthusiasms – ornithology and the promotion of the Jewish state. In 1948 he was returning to England from a field trip in Saudi Arabia when his ship docked in Haifa. The British mandate in Palestine was to expire in three weeks, and Arabs and Jews were already fighting to control the city. When a detachment of Coldstream Guards disembarked to take control of government stores, Meinertzhagen, though now over 70, helped himself to the weapons and uniform of a soldier who was sick and disembarked with them, taking up his place at the rear of their column. Once ashore he parted company with the Guards and teamed up with a group of Jewish fighters who were engaged in a fire fight with a group of Arabs. Meinertzhagen joined in with enthusiasm, until apprehended by an officer in the Coldstream Guards. 'It mattered not,' he later wrote in his diary, 'since by then I had got off all my 200 rounds.'

In his will, Meinertzhagen left his collection of 25,000 stuffed birds – recognized as one of the best in the world – to the Natural History Museum in South Kensington. There had long been a certain amount of speculation about the methods he had used to assemble this collection, but it caused surprise when in December 1999 *International Wildlife* revealed that Meinertzhagen had put it together by the systematic theft of specimens from a variety of museums and private houses.

**Mellor, David** (1949– ), Tory cabinet minister whose political downfall was brought about in 1992 when the *Sun* newspaper published details of a liaison with Antonia de Sancha, a 31-year-old actress. Among the films in which she had appeared, Miss de Sancha was able to list *The Pieman* (1990), in which she played a one-legged prostitute who has sex with a pizza delivery man. The affair with Mellor had been conducted in a furnished flat in West Kensington. In these, and other, circumstances the cabinet minister felt obliged to resign as secretary of state at the Department of National Heritage in John Major's government. He might have expected the matter to end there, but in January 1996 the *Sunday Mirror* led with a front-page story under the headline 'DAVID MELLOR'S FORMER MISTRESS IN LESBIAN LOVE ROMPS WITH DRUG FIEND'S GIRLFRIEND' – the upshot of an idiosyncratic PR initiative by Miss de Sancha in an attempt to revive her acting career, at that time rather in the doldrums. The article was illustrated with a suggestive photograph of a former model, Michelle Davies – once the common-law wife of gangster, Tommy Roche, now the girlfriend of society drug dealer Andrew DEMPSEY (aka Andy from the Sixties) – who had been paid £4000 by the *Sunday Mirror* to say that she had had a lesbian relationship with Miss de Sancha. In fact, they met for the first time at the photo shoot organized by the paper two days before publication of the story. The incident was thought to have shone an interesting light on the techniques a tabloid newspaper is prepared to use in an attempt further to discredit an old target – in this case David Mellor.

**Merrett, Donald** (1910–1954), thief, forger and murderer. At the age of 17, Merrett murdered his mother for the price of a motor bicycle; 25 years later, and now calling himself Ronald Chesney, he killed his wife and his wife's mother, who together ran an old people's home in Ealing.

In 1927 Merrett was a student at Edinburgh University, living in the city with his mother, who had parted from her husband. Mrs Merrett was delighted with his progress. 'Donald is doing well at the University and is quite settled down to the life here,' she wrote to a friend. In fact, Donald was already forging her name on cheques. In June of that year, Mrs Merrett was found shot behind the ear. Although Donald insisted that she had shot herself, the gun belonged to him. During the 15 days that she lingered between life and death, he forged and cashed several cheques, and was able to make a down payment of £70 on the motor bicycle he'd coveted. When his mother died, he was charged with murder and forgery.

Merrett would certainly have been convicted but for the dogmatic position taken by the eminent pathologist Sir Bernard Spilsbury – who was appearing for the first and last time as a defence witness – over the absence of powder blackening round the wound. The prosecution argued that this proved that Mrs Merrett had not committed suicide, because in that case traces of powder must have been left. Spilsbury denied this, arguing that bleeding and washing the wound would have eliminated them. The jury believed the man who had a reputation for infallibility. Donald Merrett was acquitted of murder, but went to prison for twelve months on the forgery charge.

On his release Merrett changed his name to Ronald Chesney and for the next 25 years he lived by theft and blackmail, with spells in prison. During World War II he became commander of a small merchant ship, which he used for smuggling. In 1954, and now living in Germany, he determined to recover the sum of £8000 that had been settled on the wife he had married when first released from prison in 1928. She had left him shortly afterwards, but they still met occasionally. Chesney shaved off the beard he had grown, removed the piratical gold earring he now affected as a sea captain, put on horn-rimmed spectacles and flew from Germany to England on a false passport. He called on his wife at the old people's home she was running with her mother in Ealing, knocked her out with drink and drowned her in the bath. As he was leaving the house he was intercepted by her mother, so he was obliged to kill her too. He then flew back to Germany. However, he had been seen leaving the old people's home in Ealing, and Scotland Yard put out a 'wanted' notice with Interpol. As the net tightened, Chesney shot himself in the head in a wood near Cologne. Before he died, he confessed to his German girlfriend that his real name was Donald Merrett and that when he was a boy of 17 he had murdered his mother.

**Methuen, Lord.** *See* BULLER, SIR REDVERS.

**Mexico, fantastical palaces in.** *See* JAMES, EDWARD; MONEY, WILLIAM.

**Mexico, lost tribes of Israel to be found in.** *See* KINGSBOROUGH, EDWARD KING, 4TH VISCOUNT.

**Meyrick, Kate** (1877–1933), undisputed queen of the nightclubs in the 1920s, known as 'Ma' to her high society clientele. The deserted wife of a Brighton doctor, Mrs Meyrick became involved in clubs largely to pay for the education of her eight children. Her most famous establishment was the '43', occupying the basement of a house in Gerrard Street, Soho, once the home of the poet John Dryden. Here, the rich, the titled and the gifted – the prince of Wales, Evelyn Waugh, Noël Coward, Tallulah Bankhead – paid inflated prices to drink outside licensing hours and to take part in illegal games of chance. According to legend, it was at the '43' that a celebrated exchange took place between Miss Bankhead and 'Bendor' Westminster. Westminster, who hadn't seen Bankhead for 15 years, greeted her warmly as he passed her table. 'I thought I told you to wait in the car,' she said.

Mrs Meyrick herself was so ordinary in appearance that she seemed to have gained admission by mistake, but she was a woman of good humour and indomitable spirit. The '43' was followed by a succession of other clubs: Bretts, the Manhattan, the Silver Slipper, the Folies Bergères, the Broadway, the New Follies and the Bunch of Keys. All were regularly fined for various breaches of the licensing laws (one of her clubs was described by a magistrate as 'a sink of iniquity') and Mrs Meyrick spent many nights in prison.

In order to avoid constant harassment she formed a business relationship with Detective Sergeant George GODDARD, who was in charge at the time of nightclub prosecutions. Over a period of eight years Mrs Meyrick paid Goddard more than £15,000 to ensure the smooth running of her operation. After an anonymous tip-off to Scotland Yard, Goddard was investigated and a large wad of £10 notes in a safe deposit box at Selfridges was traced back to Mrs Meyrick. At a famous trial in 1929 Goddard was sentenced to 18 months hard labour, and Mrs Meyrick to 15 months. The spell in Holloway broke her health and she announced her retirement from the nightclub business.

When 'Ma' Meyrick died in 1933 at the age of 56, dance bands throughout the West End observed a two-minute silence in her memory. She was rumoured to have earned £500,000 in the previous ten years. She left just £78. Her sons had been educated at Harrow, and her daughters, two of whom married into the aristocracy, at Roedean.

*See also* COLLUSION, DIVORCE BY; DE CLIFFORD, LORD EDWARD SOUTHWELL RUSSELL.

**Miles, Louisa** (1870–1941), confidence trickster. The 'rented-flat swindle', in which Miles specialized, was not her invention, but she was its most celebrated practitioner in the early years of the 20th century. She had learned its basics when apprenticed to Sophie Bluffstein, nicknamed 'the Golden Hand', a Russian woman who operated in the late 1890s, travelling the capitals of Europe, staying in the best hotels and posing as a noblewoman of great wealth. As such, Bluffstein would order gems to be sent to her suite for evaluation. When jewellers called at the hotel to complete the transaction, they would discover that she and the gems had vanished. Bluffstein was eventually caught in Russia and sent to Siberia.

Miles was even more successful than her mentor. On the estimation of Scotland Yard, she pulled off as many as 100 such swindles between 1900 and 1920, when she retired. In a typical operation, she would call in at a Bond Street jeweller as Miss Constance Browne, secretary to 'Lady Campbell', who had an address appropriate to her social standing. 'Lady Campbell' had a niece who was about to be married and she had decided to give her as a wedding gift some diamonds to be set in a brooch. Miss Browne would be greatly obliged if the diamond merchant could arrange for a trusted employee to bring over a dozen or so of the firm's finest gems so that Lady Campbell could make a selection. At Lady Campbell's elegant home, Miss Browne would take the diamonds from the jeweller's representative and instruct him to wait while her ladyship made her choice. After a lengthy interval, the messenger would become suspicious and try the door through which Miss Browne had departed. This would be bolted, as would all the other doors. The man was trapped. Even the front door would now be locked. By the time he had broken the window and summoned assistance, Miss Browne and the diamonds would be on the other side of London. Only then would it be discovered that Miles had rented the house for a week.

Exponents of the rented-flat swindle prospered particularly in the 1980s – a time when Baroness Thatcher of Finchley, as she later became, set the moral tone. Avaricious estate agents encouraged Louisa Miles's successors to sublet luxury apartments for a brief period, this arrangement enabling the latter to make purchases with stolen credit cards – often using the name of the owner of the apartment and their easily obtained credit-card details.

**Miller, Sir Eric** (1921–77), property tycoon and embezzler. At the age of 27, Miller, the son of a Labour councillor, went to work for the Peachey Property Corporation. By the time he was 34 the company, under his chairmanship, had a value of £40 million and Miller himself was a millionaire. In 1976 he was knighted in Harold Wilson's resignation honours list. In the autumn of the following year he shot himself before fraud charges could be brought against him.

Miller's difficulties arose from a tendency to regard Peachey's assets as his own. He could see nothing wrong in using the shareholders' money to buy a racehorse for his wife or a house for the soccer player Bobby Moore. Miller himself had a £700,000 house in the Boltons, a private helicopter, an executive jet, a Rolls Royce and two Ferraris. For his daughter's wedding in 1973 he hired the Grand Hall at the Dorchester Hotel and engaged Ella Fitzgerald and Count Basie to provide the cabaret. For his son's Bar Mitzvah he flew a planeload of guests to Israel at a cost, to Peachey, of a quarter of a million pounds. When the company was hit by the property slump of 1974 the auditors reported unfavourably on his activities, and in March 1977 he resigned as chairman.

Peachey's board, under its new chairman Lord Mais, initiated legal proceedings against Miller for the return of £282,000 that couldn't be accounted for. On 22 May the *News of the World* revealed that Miller had given £130,000 as a commission to Judah Binstock for arranging a deal. This was part of the missing £282,000. The rest consisted of another payment to Binstock in return for shares he had bought on Miller's behalf in a large European company. Binstock – who had links with the American Mafia, and in whose company Miller once met Meyer Lansky, the Mafia's financial adviser and an expert in money laundering – was wanted by the British police in connection with massive currency frauds, and by the French police for tax evasion. Miller, Binstock and Meyer Lansky had visited Brazil together in 1973, the trip being paid for by Peachey's shareholders.

It was only after Miller shot himself on Yom Kippur, 1977, that the full extent of his extravagance at Peachey's expense became clear. A week after his suicide, the *News of the World* revealed that a mansion flat had been put at the disposal of the Tory politician Reginald Maudling at a rent of £2 a week. The former chancellor of the exchequer and home secretary claimed that he had worked as a financial consultant for Peachey in the past and that the flat was remuneration for his services. 'The whole affair is bloody silly,' said Mr Maudling at the time. The following year Peachey issued writs against Miller's widow and the Churchill Hotel, where Miller had arranged for friends and associates to stay at Peachey's expense. His guests had included the Israeli foreign minister, the Israeli defence minister and an English MP. When the Board of Trade released their report on Miller's misuse of Peachey funds, it revealed other examples of his generosity. In 1977 he had organized a surprise retirement party for Harold Wilson at 10 Downing Street at a cost of over £3000. He had given the footballer Bobby Moore £45,000 with which to effect improvements on the house that he had already received as a gift. Maudling had been 'lent' £22,500 for repairs to his home. Beryl Maudling had received a silver chess set for Christmas, and Harold Wilson had been provided with a helicopter for electioneering purposes.

Before his downfall, Miller had sat for some years as a magistrate, once sentencing a pensioner who had been caught shoplifting to 100 hours community service. Under its conditions, the offending senior citizen was obliged to play the piano at a retirement home for fellow pensioners. On one occasion Miller failed to attend court after being delayed in Rio with a girl called Fluffa, with whom he had been celebrating the New Year.

**Minimus, Lord.** *See* HUDSON, JEFFREY.

**misconduct in Llandudno.** *See* HALL, NEWMAN.

**misers.** *See* BARRETT, JOHN; DANCER, DANIEL; ELWES, JOHN; LONSDALE, JAMES LOWTHER, 1ST EARL OF; NEILD, JAMES CAMDEN; SITWELL, SIR GEORGE RERESBY; STRUTT, PATRICIA; WARING, FRANCIS.

**Miss Stevens, the Pig-Faced Lady.** Miss Stevens, in reality a performing bear, was the star attraction at the Hyde Park Fair that celebrated Queen Victoria's coronation in 1838. The bear's face and paws had been shaved to the skin and it wore lace gloves to conceal its claws. Hidden behind the animal was a boy with a stick. When the bear was asked a question, the boy prodded it with the stick, causing it to grunt in reply. The bear was asked if it was 18, whether it was true that it had been born in Preston, Lancashire, whether it was in good health and happy, and whether it was inclined to marry. At each question, a prod from the stick produced a grunt of assent from the bear. As the audience filed out, the showman would shout at the next group of spectators, 'Hear what they say! Hear what they say about Madame Stevens, the wonderful Pig-Faced Lady!'

The authorities intervened after an incident at the Camberwell Fair in 1837 during which Miss Stevens escaped. A contretemps had arisen after Madame Aurelia the Fat Lady attacked the Pipe-smoking Oyster. Miss Stevens made off in the confusion.

*See also* FAIRS, TRAVELLING.

**Mrs Honeyman captures a boatload of pirates.** *See* GOW, JOHN.

**Mr Smith's.** On the night of 7 March 1966 an affray took place at Mr Smith's nightclub in Catford that finally broke the RICHARDSON gang's hold on south London. Eddie Richardson and Frankie FRASER, who were described initially in newspaper reports as 'businessmen having a drink on their way home', were badly injured, and Richard Hart, an associate of Ron and Reggie KRAY, was killed. Ironically, the dispute was over which gang was supposed to be policing the club – the Richardsons or the Hawards.

For some time, the Haward brothers, Billy and 'Flash' Harry, had been minding Mr Smith's in exchange for free drinks. The Hawards owned clubs themselves, and were on reasonable terms with the Richardsons. Recently, however, they had been using Mr Smith's as their headquarters – an arrangement that held little appeal for the club's management. Eddie Richardson had been asked if he could help. In return for getting rid of the Hawards, he and Frankie Fraser had been told they could install their gaming machines in Mr Smith's.

Richardson and Fraser visited Mr Smith's on the afternoon of 7 March, and security was discussed. 'I wanted to take on employees with local knowledge who would keep better order than was being kept,' the club manager explained at the subsequent court proceedings. Eddie Richardson now assumed he had a verbal agreement to police the club. It only remained to explain the new state of affairs to the Haward brothers. After the Hawards arrived later in the evening, the atmosphere for a time remained convivial. By midnight, however, tension was rising and staff noticed that Billy Haward had a .410 shotgun strapped inside his jacket. Dickie Hart was also seen to be carrying a .45 pistol. When James Moody, another of Richardson's henchmen, arrived, the club's manager sent home as many of the staff as possible. The trouble broke out moments later, when Eddie Richardson told the Hawards to finish their drinks. One of Haward's men, Peter Hennessey, called out to Richardson, 'Who do you fucking well think you are?' adding, in case he had not made his meaning clear, 'I'll take you any day, you half-baked fucking ponce.' Richardson smashed his glass on a table and dragged Hennessey on to the dance floor.

Hart fired his gun at Richardson, and missed. Richardson continued to hammer Peter Hennessey, and general fighting broke out between the two factions. According to Billy Gardner, one of Haward's team:

> Harry Rawlins was shot in the arm, and two or three geezers gave Bill a clump with a bayonet across the nut. Bill went to get the gun in his waistband, got it caught in his braces, but let a couple go and all of a sudden it was off. I thought Bill was dead. The blood was pumping out.

Gardner helped Haward to a doctor who, though 'drunk as a sack', stitched his head and gave him some pills. Meanwhile, Hart, who had somehow lost his gun, was chased into Farley Road by Frankie Fraser. Henry Botton, who worked for the Hawards, saw Fraser kicking Hart as he lay on the pavement.

By the time the police arrived, all that was left of the fight was the body of Dickie Hart lying under a lilac tree with his face smashed in. Fraser, who had also been shot in the leg, appeared to have escaped. James Moody had scooped Eddie Richardson up off the dance floor, thereafter driving him away in his Jaguar, together with the seriously wounded Harry Rawlins. Moody and Richardson, whose injuries were superficial by comparison, dumped Rawlins in a child's cot in the casualty department of Dulwich Hospital. George Barker, one of the officers arriving on the scene, recalls finding Fraser:

> I stepped over a wall of a garden and there was a grunting noise. It was Frankie Fraser. I had accidentally trodden on his leg.

Barker stuffed a handkerchief into Fraser's gaping wound, and was then detailed to guard Fraser in hospital. Here Fraser was entertained by the first portable colour television set he had ever seen.

Fraser, Richardson, James Moody, Billy Haward, Harry Rawlins and Henry Botton were arrested. Fraser was charged with Hart's murder, the others with affray. Fraser was acquitted of murder but convicted at the Old Bailey of affray in July 1966, and sentenced to five years in prison. Richardson also received five years, after a retrial, and Billy Haward eight years. Moody was found not guilty.

The Haward gang disbanded after the affray. Peter Hennessey was later murdered while attending a boxing match, and Henry Botton was shot dead at his front door. Some of Billy Haward's friends were disposed to have their revenge on the Richardsons. Ray Rosa got hold of an iron bar and set off for the Reform Club in New Cross where he intended to hit Charlie Richardson on the head. The attack was unsuccessful. 'Ray's eyesight isn't too good,' a bystander explained. 'He laid out Bobby Cannon as he came down the stairs.' Cannon was a friend of Rosa's, and on the firm. Cannon told the police that he had tripped and hit his head against the wall.

**Mitchell, Frank** (1933–67), failed criminal, known as 'the Mad Axeman'. After ordering Mitchell's execution in the back of a transit van, Ronnie KRAY spoke of his old friend in the warmest terms. 'He was as randy as a stoat,' recalled Kray:

> I've never known anything like it. He would give a bird one and then he'd give her another one. Women would queue up just to be given one. The birds couldn't wait for him to give them one. Then another one. And another.

In January 1955 Mitchell was certified insane and sent to Rampton. In January 1957 he escaped, and while on the run he burgled a house, hitting the occupant over the head with an iron bar. He was sent to Broadmoor, escaped and attacked another householder and his wife. On his arrest, he said, 'I want to prove that I'm sane and that I know what I'm doing.' He received ten years imprisonment. For his part in the Hull prison riots in 1962 he was birched and transferred to Dartmoor. His behaviour improved and in July 1963 he was removed from the escape list. In May 1964 he was allowed to work outside the prison walls in the quarry party. In September of that year he was transferred to the honour party, a loosely supervised group, whose shopping expeditions to local villages and visits to public houses were financed by the Krays. On one occasion, Mitchell took a taxi to Tavistock, where he bought a budgerigar. Women were provided by the Krays to help him pass the afternoons. As one prison warder said, 'I turned a blind eye. I couldn't afford to have Mitchell troublesome.'

By the autumn of 1966 the Krays' reputation was in decline. Some members of their gang had taken to referring to them as Gert and Daisy, characters played by Ethel and Doris Waters, a once popular music-hall act. Others thought they were becoming too dangerous for their own good. As James Morton pointed out in *Gangland* (1993), with the RICHARDSON gang in general, and Frankie FRASER in particular, now in prison, the Krays had little use for another 'hard' man on the firm, but Mitchell was needed to demonstrate that the twins were still a force to be reckoned with. Accordingly, on 12 December 1966 two Kray henchmen, 'Big' Albert DON-AGHUE and 'Scotch' Jack Dickson, an ex-marine, picked up Mitchell while he was playing cards in a hut at Bagga Tor, an isolated village on Dartmoor. They then drove him to the Whitechapel flat of a small-time porn merchant, Lennie 'Books' Dunn.

For a few days Mitchell was happy enough. A hostess, 'Blonde' Lisa, was more or less kidnapped from Winston's nightclub and brought to the flat to provide him with sex. He enjoyed impressing her with feats of strength, which included holding members of the 'Firm' above his head two at a time. He soon discovered, however, that he had exchanged one prison cell for another. He wanted to visit his mother at the family home in Bow, and was told that this could be arranged. When nothing came of it he demanded a meeting with the twins, whom he hadn't seen since his escape. On 24 December 1966 Mitchell was told by Donaghue that he was being moved to a new address in Kent. He protested at being separated from 'Blonde' Lisa, but was told that she would be joining him later. He was never seen again. At the Krays' trial for his murder, Donaghue turned queen's evidence and testified that Mitchell had been shot in the back of a van as it left Barking Road by Freddie FOREMAN and Alfie Gerard on orders from the Krays, an account that Foreman corroborated in his memoirs, *Respect* (1995). The Krays were acquitted. Foreman was never charged with this killing, and Gerard departed for Australia at the time of Mitchell's disappearance. He returned to England in the 1970s and died in Brighton in 1983.

**Mitford sisters.** *See* REDESDALE, CLEMENT NAPIER THOMAS FREEMAN MITFORD, 2ND BARON.

**Mohocks, the.** An 18th-century society of gentlemen whose ambition was 'to do the most possible hurt to their fellow creatures'. Like 21st-century vigilantes stirring up hatred against asylum seekers, they jeered at foreigners in the street and pelted them with mud. One Portuguese visitor had his ear nailed to the wall and was later stabbed to death.

*See also* BOLD BUCKS.

**mole-catcher's daughter, murder of a.** *See* CORDER, WILLIAM.

**molly house.** An 18th-century tavern where working-class men could drink, cross-dress and have sex. Also known as a sodomitical house.

See also CLAP, MARGARET; COOKE, JAMES; HAMMOND, CHARLES; HITCHIN, CHARLES.

**Money, Sir Leo Chiozzo** (1870–1941), politician, financial journalist and protagonist in an indecency case that resulted in a textbook police cover-up. According to two plain-clothes officers, 58-year-old Sir Leo, a former Liberal MP and a married man with a daughter, committed an act of indecency in Hyde Park on the evening of 23 April 1928. His willing accomplice in this offence was Irene Savidge, a 22-year-old valve-tester from New Southgate. When arrested, Sir Leo protested, 'I am not the usual riff-raff, I am a man of substance.' At the police station he was allowed to telephone his friend, Sir William Joynson-Hicks, the home secretary.

Sir Leo's defence was to deny that the incident had taken place. After hearing his evidence, Henry Chancellor, the magistrate at Marlborough Street, dismissed the charge against Sir Leo and Miss Savidge, and awarded £10 costs against the police. The divisional superintendent, sensing a conspiracy between social equals, demanded a retrial (thus showing himself to be ignorant of the law of *autrefois acquit*) on the grounds that the magistrate had been biased in favour of Sir Leo. Sir Leo was equally dissatisfied. At his prompting, a Labour MP rose in the Commons to ask the home secretary what he proposed to do about a situation in which a person of position could be charged with such an offence. Sir William decided that the case should be investigated by Chief Inspector Collins, a policeman with an impeccable reputation.

What followed was straightforwardly a cover-up, an exercise in which Collins was greatly assisted by Sir Leo's uncooperative attitude. Sir Leo refused to attend on Collins at Scotland Yard, and when Collins went to him, Sir Leo refused to answer 'roving questions as to the past history of my relationship with Miss Savidge'. Collins reported back to the director of public prosecutions, Sir Archibald Bodkin, who informed Sir Leo that if he didn't cooperate more serious steps would be taken. Sir Leo's response was to ask why Miss Savidge, at her interview, had been alternately cajoled and bullied by Collins for over five hours without a female officer being present.

The matter had now become serious enough for Sir William Joynson-Hicks, the home secretary, to set up a public inquiry, chaired by Sir John Eldon Banks, a former lord justice of appeal. Miss Savidge was represented at the inquiry by Patrick Hastings KC, and the police by Norman Birkett KC. Miss Savidge bore up well during her long cross-examination by Birkett, accusing Collins of distorting her testimony and of putting his arm round her in a reconstruction of what she and Sir Leo had been doing.

She did admit that by going to restaurants and cinemas with Sir Leo she had been deceiving a young man with whom she was walking out, but she insisted that, with regard to a statement that Sir Leo's hand had been on her knee, the chief inspector 'had suggested it' and she let it go as she was 'fed up' by this time and would have 'signed anything to get away'.

Collins's investigative techniques seem to have been a blueprint for subsequent police inquiries, just as the tribunal's complete exoneration of Collins that followed was a model for future cover-ups. Announcing their decision, Sir John Eldon Bankes said:

> We are unable to accept Miss Savidge's statement on the material matters as to which there was a conflict of evidence between her and Chief Inspector Collins and we acquit him of any improper conduct during the taking of Miss Savidge's statement. We are satisfied that the interrogation followed the lines indicated to him by the Director of Public Prosecutions and was not unduly extended.

In September 1933 Sir Leo Money appeared at Epsom Magistrates' Court on two summonses arising out of an incident on a train on the southern region. It was alleged that he had embraced Miss Ivy Ruxton, a 30-year-old shop assistant. Sir Leo was fined 40 shillings.

**Money, William** (1809–83), scientist, traveller and founder of a fundamentalist religion. Born in Edinburgh, Money worked his passage to America as a young man, setting himself up as a naturalist in Mexico. He trekked on his own across the Sonoran desert and into unexplored regions of northern Mexico, drawing hundreds of maps of the area and assembling a large collection of botanical and zoological specimens.

By 1846 Money was living in Los Angeles, then still in Mexico, with his wife, a local girl. When war with the United States seemed imminent, he packed up all his possessions and headed south. One night his camp was ambushed by US troops, and in the ensuing scuffle Money's life's work – all his accumulated specimens and 30,000 pages of notes – was destroyed. The loss unbalanced him. He spent the next 16 years pressing a vexatious claim for a million dollars against the United States government, but only succeeded in losing most of his money, and his family. With what he had left, he built a hacienda near San Gabriel, California, a brick-and-adobe fantasia based on his memories of Holyrood Palace in Edinburgh, complete with turrets, buttresses and bastions. Here he established a new religion, a fundamentalist sect called the Reformed New Testament Church of the Faith of Jesus Christ, with himself as bishop and spiritual leader.

Failing to attract a congregation, Money abandoned metaphysical speculation and resumed his previous devotion to scientific hypotheses. The Mission San Gabriel became the Moneyan Institute. Inscriptions in Greek, Latin and Hebrew on its entrance gate bore witness to the value of learning. His own contribution was a global map that showed a subterranean ocean extending from the North Pole to the South Pole. A hole in the Arctic icecap sucked water from the known seas into the subterranean ocean, where it was heated by volcanic activity. The heated water rushed out at the Antarctic in two-mile-wide streams. He called these the Kuro Siwa, though it is unclear why.

**monkey, kings who have died after being bitten by a.** *See* EDINBURGH, PRINCE PHILIP, DUKE OF.

**monkey called Pug, a queen's.** *See* HUDSON, JEFFREY.

**monkey of a man, almost a.** *See* PEACE, CHARLES.

**Monks of Medmenham, the.** *See* DASHWOOD, SIR FRANCIS.

**Montalk, Count Geoffrey Wladislaw Vaile Potoi** (*c.*1889–?), poet and pornographer. Montalk laid claim to the Polish throne and spent his days drinking in Soho pubs wearing a purple cloak. In 1931 he decided to publish 100 copies of *Here Lies John Penis*, a parody of Verlaine, largely for the amusement of his friends. His printer was offended and showed the manuscript to the police. It was Montalk's misfortune that at his subsequent trial on an obscenity charge he appeared before the recorder of London, Sir Ernest Wild, himself a poet *manqué*. Wild had famously read some of his own verses to counsel representing Colonel Leslie Ivor Gauntlett BARKER before sentencing her to nine months in prison for causing a false entry to be made in a marriage register. Sir Ernest made no mention of his own work on this occasion but was unimpressed when the count swore on Apollo in preference to one of the more conventional authorities, supernatural or otherwise. Nor did he care for the count's work:

> Are you going to allow a man, just because he calls himself a poet, to deflower the English language by popularizing these words? A man may not say he is a poet and be filthy, he has to obey the law just the same as ordinary citizens, and the sooner the highbrows learn that, the better for the morality of our country.

Sir Ernest sentenced Montalk to six months in Wormwood Scrubs, a decision upheld on appeal (Cr App R. 1932. 182) in spite, or perhaps because, of pleas by such highbrows as T.S. Eliot, Aldous Huxley and H.G. Wells.

**Monte Carlo, the man who broke the bank at.** *See* WELLS, CHARLES.

**Montrose, James Angus Graham, 7th duke of** (1907–92), farmer and politician. Montrose brought to Ian Smith's rebel government in Rhodesia appropriately vigorous views on race. 'It is a common observation,' he wrote in an official report:

> ... that the African is a bright and promising little fellow up to the age of puberty. He then becomes hopelessly inadequate and it is well known that this is due to his almost total obsession with matters of sex.

The 7th duke's obituary in the *Daily Telegraph* makes it clear that the Graham family had been marked by a degree of eccentricity for several centuries. The 3rd duke was credited with obtaining permission for Highlanders to wear the kilt again after the Jacobite Rising of 1745. The duchess of the 4th duke publicly booed Queen Victoria for listening to gossip about her husband. The 6th duke invented the aircraft carrier but reduced his estates from 130,000 acres to 10,000 acres in 40 years, and ensured that they produced no income. When he died in 1954 he left an estate of £804. Nevertheless, the 7th duke was sent to Eton, where he boxed for the school and bit Quintin Hogg in the course of the wall game.

After Christ Church, Oxford, Montrose worked for Imperial Chemicals in Newcastle-upon-Tyne. In 1930 he married Isobel, the daughter of Colonel T.B. Sellar, but his financial circumstances soon forced him to move to Salisbury, Rhodesia, where he obtained employment as a seed salesman. He also sparred with the ex-heavyweight boxing champion and future prime minister, Roy Welensky, who rated him as an indifferent opponent. He then set himself up as a successful farmer on 3000 acres of land outside Salisbury. At the outbreak of World War II he enlisted in the Royal Naval Volunteer Reserve, gaining command of *Ludlow*, an American lease-lend warship, and serving on convoy duty in the Atlantic. He insisted that the crew speak Gaelic and kept a jackdaw that sat on his shoulder when summoned.

After the war Montrose returned to Rhodesia, where he was disappointed to discover that the country's politics were changing. At the 1953 general election he stood as a Confederate Party candidate, campaigning for the protection of the white-dominated *status quo*. When he inherited the dukedom in 1954, he preferred to stay in Rhodesia, leaving his Scottish properties to be run by his 18-year-old son, the marquess of Graham. In 1958 he was elected to the parliament of the Federation of Rhodesia and Nyasaland and declared that Southern Rhodesia's premier, Winston Field, should replace Welensky as federal prime minister to ensure that there would be, 'no miserable compromise with London'. When he became agriculture minister in Field's Southern Rhodesian government, it was noted that he was considerably slower on the uptake than many of the Africans about whom he had expressed reservations. Nevertheless, he played an important part in the election of Ian Smith as the Rhodesian Front prime minister, and was rewarded with the post of external affairs minister. As such, he received a stream of visitors, described by Ken Flower, head of Rhodesian Intelligence, as the 'Nuts in May'. Among them were Captain Henry Kerby, a paranoid Tory MP with intelligence contacts, L. Ron Hubbard, leader of the Church of Scientology, and an armorist. The armorist, who styled himself The Gayre of Gayre and Nigg, received some support from Montrose for his belief that the Zimbabwe ruins were too sophisticated to have been produced by Africans.

Difficulties arose when Ian Smith, who was beginning to see UDI as a mistake, found that Montrose was in no mood to compromise. There is little doubt that Montrose played a key role in the rejection of the offers made by the Wilson government on HMS *Tiger* and HMS *Fearless*. A joke circulating in Salisbury had it that it took Smith an hour to explain the British offer to colleagues, who then spent twelve hours trying to explain it to Montrose.

When the Rhodesian rebellion ended in 1980, Montrose moved to Natal. The following year he paid a visit to Scotland, where he attended a retirement party for a gardener, a gamekeeper and a shepherd that had been put off until he could be present. In 1988 he returned home for good. He spent his final years in Kinross, and was hereditary sheriff of Dunbartonshire.

**Moody, Detective Chief Superintendent William** (1931– ), policeman. In 1969 revelations in *The Times* about corruption in the Metropolitan Police led to a full-scale investigation under Sir Frank Williamson, at that time one of her majesty's inspectors of constabulary. Sir Frank soon expressed his concern about the quality of officers seconded to the inquiry, most notably DCS Bill Moody. His reservations about Moody were well founded. While supposedly helping Williamson to identify corrupt officers, Moody, as head of the Obscene Publications Squad, was raking in huge sums of protection money from Soho pornographers.

A typical arrangement was the one he had with James HUMPHREYS. When Humphreys wanted to open a bookshop in Rupert Street he first had to pay Moody a 'licence' fee of £14,000. A further £2000 a month was subsequently paid to prevent raids and closure. Charged at Knightsbridge Crown Court with possessing obscene publications, a Soho shopkeeper called John Mason revealed that Moody had visited his premises once a week to advise on material and stock control. Mason further complained that his monthly 'drink' to the Porn Squad had risen in ten years from £60 to £1000. However, his relationship with Moody had generally been excellent. Moody had even lent him a tie to wear when he visited the basement at Holborn Police Station, where, for a knock-down price, he could buy back material confiscated from rival shopkeepers.

Following a statement from Humphreys, whose diaries showed that he had paid Moody £53,000 in 16 months, Moody was arrested and charged with 27 counts of bribery and corruption totalling £87,485. He was convicted and sentenced to twelve years in prison.

*See also* ROBSON, DETECTIVE INSPECTOR BRIAN.

**Moon, Keith** (1946–78), drummer, also known as 'King Loon'. The nickname derived from *looning*, the practice, at which he excelled, of destroying articles of hardware – sometimes his, more usually other people's. Moon left school at 15 (a tendency to show off had been noted), and at the age of 18 he became drummer for a pop group, The Who. Although described as a talented performer by aficionados of rock and roll, he is best remembered for the number of hotel rooms he 'trashed' in the United Kingdom and abroad. On one occasion he and his young friends carried a two-ton water bed on to the ninth floor of a Copenhagen hotel and from there dropped it into a swimming pool. For some years, anecdotes about such exploits amused audiences on Michael Parkinson's television 'chat show' and enhanced The Who's popularity. He also liked to blow up hotel lavatories with home-made bombs and to leave piranha fish in the bidet.

In 1965 Moon married his 16-year-old Swedish mistress, Kim Kerrigon, and later moved with her into a large house in Surrey, where his next-door neighbour was the film actor Oliver REED. One morning Reed was in the bath when he heard the sound of a helicopter hovering above his lawn. He ran outside with his 12-bore shotgun and fired at the intruder, who was Moon. In no time the two formed what Reed's talented and long-suffering partner, the former Royal Ballet dancer Jacqui Daryl, later described as 'a friendship from hell'.

While appearing together in the film of the rock opera *Tommy*, Moon gave Reed a tortoise. When drinking, they would encourage the tortoise to cover the ground between them with a bottle of whisky on its back – by this method, since the tortoise moved so slowly, managing to reduce their alcohol consumption by several bottles a night. The tortoise, which travelled with them everywhere, was put to other amusing purposes. Sometimes Moon and Reed took their clothes off in the public rooms of hotels and entertained the other guests by wearing the tortoise as a makeshift codpiece. According to Ken Russell, who directed *Tommy,* it looked, when the tortoise stuck its head out, as if the one who was wearing it had an erection. At other times they turned the tortoise upside down and used it as an ashtray.

In 1974 Moon moved to Los Angeles, where he fuelled his antics with alcohol and purple hearts. He died there at the age of 33, having overdosed on the pills he was taking to cure his alcoholism. For some years Reed was unable to speak of him without tears coming to his eyes.

**Moore, Roger.** *See* CONJUGAL RIGHTS; KNIGHT, RONNIE; SQUIRES, DOROTHY.

**moral crusaders.** Social commentators have noted that moral crusaders prefer a proactive role, seeking out spectacles that will give offence, and, by reason of this disposition, are not to be confused with MORAL WATCHDOGS who prefer to remain muzzled and inactive until an unignorable outrage occurs in their constituency.

*See* BLACKBURN, RAYMOND; CHANT, LAURA ORMISTON; GREEN, STANLEY.

**morals of a pair of Choctaw Indians, the.** *See* SCOTT, LADY SELINA.

**moral watchdogs.** *See* ANDERTON, JAMES; BIRDWOOD, JANE, THE DOWAGER LADY; BODKIN, SIR ARCHIBALD; GREEN, HUGHIE; HOLME, LORD RICHARD; JEFFREYS, GEORGE.

**Morgan, Sir Henry** (1635–88), legendary privateer, still honoured in Wales as one of the greatest land captains in the country's history. At sea, Morgan was less successful. He frequently ran aground or hit a reef, and one ship exploded under him when his crew, who were the worse for drink, lit candles near the gunpowder store. Such mishaps notwithstanding, Morgan was held in such high regard by the pirates under his command that they would, on a long march, eat their own boots rather than disappoint him.

Morgan was born in an ancient manor, Llanrumney, in Monmouthshire, into a distinguished military family. One ancestor, the lord of Caerlleon, had lived in the manor in the 12th century. Another, Sir Thomas Morgan of Pencarn, became known as 'the warrior' after commanding English forces overseas in the late 16th century. Sir Thomas's nephew, Sir Matthew Morgan, was wounded at the siege of Rouen in 1591. Sir Matthew's brother, Sir Charles, also served overseas with distinction and became a member of Charles I's privy council.

With this impeccable pedigree, Henry Morgan arrived in the West Indies in 1655, having been ordered to Barbados as a junior officer in an expedition sent out by Oliver Cromwell. This was under the naval command of Vice Admiral Penn, whose eldest son later gave his name to the American state. Thereafter, and as a result of more immediately advantageous family connections, Morgan's circumstances could only improve. One of his uncles, Major General Thomas Morgan, had fought for Cromwell in the Civil War, while another, Colonel Edward Morgan, had supported the crown. After the Restoration Colonel Edward Morgan was appointed lieutenant governor of Jamaica. Under his uncle Edward's patronage, Morgan prospered greatly as a freebooter, plundering Spanish settlements on Cuba and on the South Cays Islands.

In 1663 Morgan embarked on his most ambitious enterprise to date, sailing with 1000 volunteers to attack Campeche on the Mexican coast. The town, defended by two forts and regular Spanish troops, fell in a day, and 14 Spanish ships were seized as prizes. In 1668 Morgan sailed in the *Oxford* – a warship sent out by the British government for the defence of Jamaica – to Cow Island, off the coast of Hispaniola. Here he arrested a French ship, *Cerf Volant*, for piracy. When the *Oxford* was accidentally blown up under him while he dined (with 250 of the crew killed in the explosion) he took over the *Cerf Volant* as his flagship, under the name *Satisfaction*. After cruising along the east coast of Hispaniola and plundering coastal towns on the way, Morgan turned south to sail back across the Caribbean, making for the Gulf of Venezuela. Here he took the towns of Maracaibo and Gibraltar, later adding to his booty by capturing several Spanish warships on the return journey to Jamaica.

In 1670 Morgan decided to strike at Panama City, the golden hub of the Spanish empire. All the riches of the mines of Peru passed through here on the way to Spain, and the city was known to be stocked with treasure. It was a perilous ambition. Without the convenience of the Panama Canal, Morgan's assembled force of 2000 English and French freebooters would have to land at Chagres and cross the isthmus to Panama through thick jungle and over mountains. Sir Francis Drake had failed in a similar undertaking several decades earlier. After a 30-mile trek in conditions that were so bleak that his pirates were reduced to eating their own boots, Morgan reached the great plain in front of Panama City. The Spanish governor, Don Juan, faced him with a force of a comparable size, backed up by a secret weapon – a herd of cows trained to charge enemy marksmen as they prepared to fire their weapons. In the event, the cows lost their sense of direction and, turning through 180 degrees, charged the Spanish. Don Juan's forces were scattered, but not before he had had time to set fire to the city and destroy its treasures. Morgan returned to Jamaica almost empty-handed, but Spain's grip on the New World had been fatally weakened.

The sack of Panama coincided with a political change in England. Fearing an invasion, the government sought to conciliate Spain by arresting Modyford, the governor of Jamaica, and Morgan too. Morgan arrived in London in 1672. There is no record of his having been detained and he seems to have been free to come and go as he pleased. His friendship with the 2nd duke of Albermarle brought him to the notice of King Charles II, and when the English colonies seemed to be under threat again Morgan was knighted and sent back to Jamaica as lieutenant governor.

At the age of 45, Sir Henry, the pirate, was acting governor of Jamaica, vice admiral, commandant of the Port Royal Regiment, judge of the

Admiralty Court and justice of the peace. These grand titles notwithstanding, he preferred the company of old sea dogs and former shipmates in the rum shops of Port Royal. His health deteriorated, his complexion turned yellow and his frame became swollen. He sought the advice of a local black doctor who plastered him in clay. This treatment was unsuccessful, and, having made his will, Morgan died on 25 August 1688.

**Morgan, Paul** (1973– ), convict and goalkeeper. In 1994 Morgan, who was serving two years for wounding, let in 25 goals when keeping goal for Prescoed open prison in South Wales. Spectators suggested that he wasn't trying. 'It was the seventh goal which gave it away,' said one. 'He didn't move, just let the ball trickle past him.' Prison governor Nicolas Evans later explained that Morgan had been harbouring a grudge against the team coach, who had disciplined him for swearing. His slapstick goalkeeping had been his revenge against the system.

Morgan's performance resulted in a 25–3 defeat, and on the way back to prison a fight broke out on the team bus. He was later moved to Cardiff for his own safety. 'The lads here take their football very seriously,' said Governor Evans.

**Morganwg, Iolo.** *See* EVANS, JOHN.

**Morris, William** (1960– ), salesman and cricketer. In August 2000 village cricketer Willie Morris was banned for 25 years for intimidating two Australian players on a rival team. Imported batsmen Geoff Cullen and David Lovell were subjected to abusive remarks such as, 'The Aussie is a homosexual', 'Fuck off down under', and 'We're going to burn your shack down, marmalade-brain'. At a disciplinary hearing Pembrokeshire league officials banned Morris, a wicket-keeper, until the year 2025. Morris called the ban ridiculous. 'I'll be 64 by then so I'm effectively banned for life. All I did was speak my mind.'

*See also* GRACE, DR W(ILLIAM) G(ILBERT); SLEDGING; WELSH, THE.

**Mortimer, John.** *See* ARGYLE, MICHAEL; BIRDWOOD, JANE, THE DOWAGER LADY.

**'Mother' Clap.** *See* CLAP, MARGARET.

**Mother Goose.** *See* HOOLIGANS, THEATRICAL.

**Mother of the Second Messiah.** *See* SOUTHCOTT, JOANNA.

**Mountbatten, Edwina Cynthia Annette, Countess** (1901–60), the wife of Louis, Earl Mountbatten of Burma. The countess preferred black lovers, among whom were the American actor and *basso profundo*, Paul

Robcson (1898–1976), famous for his rendition of 'Ol Man River' from the musical comedy *Showboat* (1927), and the cocktail lounge tenor, Leslie Hutchinson ('Hutch'), who entertained at the London nightclub Quaglinos in the 1940s and 1950s. As Vicereine of India (1947), the countess's work in social welfare brought her the friendship of Mahatma Gandhi and Jawaharial Nehru.

*See also* CHAPMAN, EDDIE.

## Moynihan, Antony Patrick Andrew Cairne Berkeley, 3rd Baron

(1936–91), peer, bongo drummer and pornographer. In his short but eventful life, Lord Moynihan's main accomplishment was to be elsewhere when wanted either by his creditors or the police. He first practised this skill at the age of 20, when he ran away to Australia after his father had taken out a summons against him for assault. The 2nd baron, who had criticized his son over a liaison he had formed with a nightclub hostess, had been punched in the face. At the time, Moynihan was escaping a similar summons by his wife, an actress and nude model.

In Sydney, Moynihan set himself up as a banjo player, shortly meeting a Malayan fire-eater's assistant, who was to become his second wife. He returned to London the following year and, having effected a reconciliation with his first wife, obtained a job as manager of the Condor Club in Soho. The job didn't last, and in 1958 he married the former fire-eater's assistant, now a belly dancer working under Moynihan's management. Soon after the wedding he was obliged to run away again, this time to escape a court appearance over the theft of two bed sheets. With his new bride he moved to Ibiza, where he set up a nightclub. When this failed he returned to England and opened El Toro, a coffee bar with a Spanish bullfighting theme, in Beckenham, Kent. This failed too, so he set off with his wife on a tour of Europe and the Far East. In 1961 they converted to the Persian faith of Baha'ism. 'It propagates the oneness of mankind,' Moynihan explained. This belief notwithstanding, he frequently challenged people to duels. 'Moynihan's behaviour is founded on exhibitionism,' said an Italian, who declined the challenge. 'It has nothing to do with gentlemanly conduct.'

When his father died in 1965, financially embarrassed and facing charges of homosexual importuning, Moynihan took the Liberal whip in the House of Lords, where he strenuously argued that Gibraltar should be returned to Spain. This was a sensible precaution since a need to be on good terms with General Franco's government would shortly arise. By 1970 he faced 57 charges, among them fraudulent trading, false pretences, fraud against a gaming casino and the purchase of a Rolls Royce with a worthless cheque. He escaped once more, this time to Spain's Costa del Sol. When the British authorities sought his extradition, he moved on to the Philippines, where he married his third wife, a Filipino belly dancer.

The new Lady Moynihan's family owned a chain of massage parlours in Manila, where he stayed for much of the rest of his life.

Throughout the 1970s Moynihan lived comfortably as a Filipino pimp under the protection of President Marcos. Marcos was able to get him out of various scrapes, including the murder of a nightclub owner who had married one of Moynihan's ex-wives. After the coup against Marcos in 1986, Moynihan became vulnerable to pressure from the American Drugs Enforcement Agency, who wanted him to help them catch Howard MARKS; at this time Marks, with whom Moynihan was on friendly terms, was estimated to control one-sixth of the global market in marijuana. Moynihan was persuaded to tape-record a conversation with Marks in which they discussed plans to grow marijuana on an island in the Philippines. At Marks's subsequent trial in Florida, Moynihan appeared as the chief prosecution witness. On his return to Manila Lord Moynihan ran a brothel known as the Yellow Brick Road, situated within 100 yards of the British ambassador's residence. In 1988 he claimed that he had been granted immunity from prosecution in England and said that he intended to resume his seat in the House of Lords, this time on the Labour benches.

When Moynihan died suddenly of a heart attack in November 1991, his brother Colin, the one-time Conservative MP for Lewisham East and minister for sport, in John Major's government, said that the two of them had fallen out in 1985 when Moynihan announced that he intended to sell the Victoria Cross won in 1855 by their great-grandfather, Sergeant Andrew Moynihan. Colin Moynihan had been obliged to pay his brother off with a sum of £22,000. The 4th Lord Moynihan is Daniel, the 9-year-old son of the 3rd baron's third wife, the Filipino belly dancer.

**mud, the omni-curative properties of.** *See* GRAHAM, JAMES.

**Murray, Griselda.** *See* GRAY, ARTHUR.

**mushroom, assertion that Jesus was a walking.** *See* ALLEGRO, JOHN.

**mushrooming intelligence services.** *See* BURGESS, GUY FRANCIS DE MONCY.

**mushrooms leading to an outbreak of pathological violence, non-delivery of.** *See* BRONSON, CHARLES.

**mushrooms lead to building of a dream palace, psychedelic.** *See* JAMES, EDWARD.

**Myatt, John.** *See* DREWE, JOHN.

**Mytton, John** (1796–1834), sportsman, politician and profligate. 'Mad Jack' Mytton was high-spirited from an early age. On one occasion his tutor William Owen was obliged to spend the night with a horse that had been coaxed up the stairs by Mytton and into Owen's bedroom. At the age of 10 he persuaded his widowed mother to allow him to have his own pack of hounds. In 1807 he was sent to Westminster School, but was asked to leave after a year for fighting the masters. He was then sent to Harrow, where he lasted for only three days. Destined for Cambridge University, where he had ordered 2000 bottles of port to await his arrival, he thought better of the arrangement at the last minute and set off instead on the Grand Tour.

On his return from the Continent, Mytton joined the 7th Hussars and spent a year gambling, drinking and racing. At the age of 20 he decided to leave the army and to take charge of the family property at Halston, in Shropshire. At a farewell dinner in his honour, he persuaded his horse, Baronet, to vault the fully laden mess table. On achieving his majority he came into a fortune of £60,000 and estates worth £18,000 a year – a sum that was scarcely enough, since in the remaining 17 years of his life he spent more than £500,000.

In 1819 Mytton decided to follow a family tradition and to seek election to Parliament as MP for Shrewsbury. As part of his campaign, he walked among his constituents with ten-pound notes attached to his hat. These were replaced as soon as they were taken, so Mytton spent £10,000 to secure his seat by a majority of 384 votes to 287. The expense was in vain since it was a hot June day when he first attended Parliament, the debate was uninteresting, and he lost patience. He left the House early and never returned.

Mytton had an iron constitution and customarily drank five bottles of port in the morning. He refused to wear warm clothes even in the coldest conditions. On one occasion he was seen running naked over heavy ice in pursuit of a duck. Physically fearless, he drove his carriage with such recklessness that one terrified passenger, his biographer C.J. Apperley, begged him to slow down. 'What?' cried Mytton. 'Never been upset in a gig? What a damned slow fellow you must have been all your life!' He then ran the carriage up a steep incline, causing it to turn over and tip Apperley into a ditch.

Mytton kept 60 cats, which he dressed in the livery suitable to their breed, and 2000 dogs, his favourite being a bull terrier called Tizer. When Tizer was getting the worst of it in a fight with a friend's dog, Mytton seized the other dog's nose in his teeth and held on until it submitted. On another occasion he alarmed his guests by riding into the dining room in full hunting costume on the back of his pet bear, Nell. When he dug in his spurs, Nell bit him in the leg, but he continued to enjoy her company.

Friends and neighbours were obliged to accustom themselves to

Mytton's preferred ways of amusing himself. These included bringing Baronet, his favourite horse, into the house, sitting it by the fire and serving it mulled port; replacing the last few pages of the local vicar's sermon with pages from the *Sporting Magazine*; and getting his horse dealer, Underhill, drunk and putting him into bed with two bull terriers and Nell, the brown bear. On another occasion he gave Underhill a note to a banker in Shrewsbury, ostensibly authorizing him to collect money on Mytton's behalf. Instead, the message to the banker, who was also a governor of the local mental hospital, read:

> Sir, please admit the bearer, George Underhill, to the lunatic asylum.
> Your obedient servant, John Mytton.

At other times, it amused Mytton to dress himself as a highwayman and to rob his own dinner guests on their way home.

Mytton's first wife died in 1820 after two years of marriage. He remarried, but his second wife, Caroline, left him in 1830. At the time of the separation he was in severe financial difficulties, and he decided to escape his creditors by moving to France. One evening, while staying at a hotel in Calais, he suffered an attack of hiccups. Deciding to cure it by giving himself a fright, he picked up a lighted torch and set fire to his nightshirt. 'The hiccup is gone, by God!' he cried and collapsed on the bed, badly burned. Advised by a doctor to stay in bed for a month, he insisted on dining out with his biographer, C.J. Apperley. Apperley disapproved of the idea, but knowing that Mytton couldn't be stopped he arranged for a carriage to fetch him from his hotel. When Mytton, swathed from head to foot in bandages, saw a modest two-horse equipage at the door, he said he would sooner walk than settle for less than four horses. Supported by two men, he covered a mile and a half on foot to keep the rendezvous with his friend.

At the end of 1832 Mytton returned to England to sign some papers and was briefly confined in the King's Bench for debt. On his release he met an attractive young woman on Westminster Bridge. He asked her where she was going, and she said she didn't know. 'Come and live with me, then,' he said, 'and I'll give you £500 a year.' The girl, whose name was Susan, agreed, and together they spent two happy years in Calais. In 1834 Mytton, who was seriously ill by now from years of self-indulgence, was brought back to England by his mother. In February of that year he was again confined in the King's Bench, where he died from alcohol poisoning.

**naked, priests who address their congregations.** *See* COPPE, ABIEZER; PRINCE, HENRY.

**naked Arab under MP's bed.** *See* PROCTOR, HARVEY.

**names, street.**
Harry BASS: The Doctor.
Joseph BLAKE: Blueskin.
Isaac Bogard: Darky the Coon (*see* HARDING, ARTHUR).
Lady Frances Bootle-Wilbraham: Fluffy (*see* CECIL, LORD WILLIAM).
Sophie Bluffstein: The Golden Hand (*see* MILES, LOUISA).
Ernest BOULTON: Lady Arthur Clinton.
Detective Chief Superintendent Thomas BUTLER: One Day Tommy.
Martin CAHILL: The General.
Linda CALVEY: The Black Widow.
Lord William CECIL: Fish.
Detective Sergeant Harold CHALLENOR: Tanky.
John Scott, 1st earl of CLONMELL: Copperfaced Jack.
Charles CURZON: Bang Bang Charlie.
Franny Daniels: Franny the Spaniel (*see* HILL, BILLY).
Andrew DEMPSEY: Andy from the Sixties.
Freddie FOREMAN: The Mean Machine.
Francis FRASER: Mad Frankie.
Lilian GOLDSTEIN: The Bobbed-Haired Bandit.
Robert HEBER-PERCY: The Mad Boy.
Lord John Hervey of Ickworth: Lord Fanny (*see* BRISTOL, FREDERICK WILLIAM JOHN AUGUSTUS HERVEY, 7TH MARQUESS OF).
Maggie Hill: Queen of the Forty Elephants (*see* HILL, BILLY).
Bert HOLLIDAY: Johnny the Gent.

Major Betty HUNTER-COWAN and Major Phyllis Heyman: Wracks and Cranks, or, The Cavewomen.

John JACKSON: Foghorn.

William JACKSON: Dr Viper.

Douglas JARDINE: The Iron Duke.

Mary JEFFRIES: The White Slave Widow.

Reggie and Ronnie KRAY: Gert and Daisie.

Ronnie KRAY: The Colonel.

James, 1st earl of LONSDALE: The Bad Earl.

Teddy Machin: Teddy Odd Legs (see HILL, BILLY).

Johnny Mancini: No Legs (see BASS, HARRY 'THE DOCTOR').

Frank MITCHELL: The Mad Axeman.

Keith MOON: King Loon.

Maurice O'MAHONEY: King Squealer.

Frederick Park: Fanny (see BOULTON, ERNEST).

James Townshend 'Barrister' SAWARD: Jem the Penman.

Tommy Smithson: Scarface (see ELLUL, PHILIP).

Lord Arthur Somerset: Podge (see NEWTON, ARTHUR).

Edward TEACH: Blackbeard.

Alan James Montagu-Wortley-Mackenzie, 4th earl of WHARNCLIFFE: Mad Ike.

Bert Wickstead: The Old Grey Fox (see LAMBTON, ANTONY CLAUD FREDERICK).

Alfredo Zomparelli: Italian Tony (see KNIGHT, RONNIE).

**Nash, Jimmy** (1930– ), gangster, club owner and one of six brothers who, according to the *Sunday Pictorial* (19 February 1961), constituted 'the wickedest family in England'. Commander Bert Wickstead ('the Old Grey Fox') recalls Nash in his memoirs, *Gangbuster* (1985), as eating too many boiled sweets:

> Jimmy Nash had a very quiet voice for such a violent man, but he didn't say anything that seemed worth remembering. He was a man of negative values – he didn't smoke, he didn't drink and he ate a pound of boiled sweets every day. He sat in his cell, chewing boiled sweets.

Holding sway originally in Islington in the late 1950s, the Nash brothers were able to maintain good relations with the KRAYS and the RICHARDSONS, thus establishing a loose cross-London alliance. By the early 1960s they had more than 20 London clubs under their protection, including the Embassy in Regent Street. It was at the Embassy in the 1930s that the prince of Wales, later Edward VIII, had danced to Bert Ambrose and his orchestra. In the 1970s waiters in hot pants served drinks on roller skates to elderly homosexuals and predatory thin women.

The Nash brothers lost their position of strength after a seemingly trivial incident. In February 1960 Selwyn Cooney, the manager of the New Cabinet Club in Gerrard Street, owned by Billy HILL, was involved in an accident with another car, driven by a prostitute known as Blonde Vicky. Blonde Vicky was a friend of Jimmy Nash's younger brother, Ronnie. Cooney sent the bill for £54 9s to Blonde Vicky. She wasn't insured and the bill remained unpaid. Some weeks later, Cooney met Ronnie Nash in a Notting Hill drinking club. Words were exchanged, a scuffle broke out and Nash took a beating. Two days later Cooney went to the Pen Club in Duval Street, which was owned by a former boxer called Billy Ambrose. Jimmy Nash and his girlfriend Doreen Masters arrived at the Pen Club shortly after Cooney. According to witnesses, Jimmy Nash went straight up to Cooney and broke his nose. Cooney fought back, and there was a cry of 'He's got a gun!' According to witnesses, Nash then shot Cooney and Ambrose at point blank range.

Nash and Doreen Masters ran from the club and were quickly driven away. Ambrose, though badly hurt, was able to carry Cooney's body outside and to put it on the pavement at some distance from the club. He then drove himself to hospital, where he said he'd been shot outside a club in Paddington. Asked for its name he said he couldn't remember. Other witnesses were more cooperative. Cooney's girlfriend Joan Bending, a 19-year-old barmaid, and Johnny Simons, a friend of Cooney's, both accused Jimmy Nash of the shooting. Nash's flat in the Charing Cross Road was searched and a mackintosh stained with blood of the same type as Cooney's was found. Two days later Nash surrendered himself at City Road police station, where he and Doreen Masters were charged with the capital murder of Selwyn Cooney.

A remarkable example of witness interference and jury intimidation followed. On 16 March the chief prosecution witness, Johnny Simons, was slashed with a razor in a Paddington café. His face needed 27 stitches. His girlfriend Barbara Ibbotson, a 23-year-old model, was then picked up in Soho, bundled into a car and slashed in the face four times. Three weeks later three men broke into her flat while she was having a bath, held her under water and then slashed her again. She too needed 27 stitches. Simons and Bending were now offered police protection, which they accepted.

Nash's trial, which began on 21 April, was ostentatiously attended by members of the Billy Hill organization, and by the Kray twins. The Nash family turned out in force. The charges against Doreen Masters had been dropped. Of the ten male jurors, one, who was later found to have had several convictions, was seen to nod towards Billy Nash in the public gallery. The police kept a watch on another member of the jury who was rumoured to have been squared by the family. On the first day of the trial he was seen talking to another man, who ran away when the police approached. 'You won't catch me putting a foot wrong now,' the juror said to the police. It was also discovered that one of the two women on the jury had a husband on remand in Brixton. He is alleged to have told Jimmy Nash that his wife had agreed to acquit him. These matters were reported to the judge by the prosecution, and on 25 April Mr Justice Gorman discharged the first jury.

In the second trial Simons and Bending performed courageously for the prosecution, but the defence produced a surprise witness. A club doorman called 'Big' Dave Sammons testified that, at the time Cooney had been shot, Johnny Simons had been drinking at another club; further, that Joan Bending had been so drunk on the evening in question that she had been helped out of the Pen Club before the fight between Cooney and Jimmy Nash had broken out. The all-male jury took just 98 minutes to acquit Nash of Cooney's murder, but at a second trial, which began an hour later, he was found guilty of causing grievous bodily harm and sentenced by Mr Justice Diplock to five years in prison. Cooney's body was taken back to his birthplace, Leeds, to be buried. 'I have heard somewhere that a Mr Billy Hill was going to give Selwyn a funeral,' said Cooney's mother, 'but this is not a circus. He will be buried with dignity.'

Johnny Simons departed for Majorca, where he found work with a Spanish bookmaker. Three months later he was back in England, complaining that he had no money. He went to stay with Cooney's parents in Leeds and was attacked outside the city's bus station. He was cut three times on the face and once on the arm. The publicity that the case had attracted effectively put an end to the Nash's bid for underworld supremacy, and their position was shortly occupied by the Krays.

**Native Americans, fake.** *See* BELANEY, ARCHIBALD ('Grey Owl').

**Native Americans, Welsh-speaking.** *See* EVANS, JOHN.

**Neild, James Camden** (1780–1852), lawyer and miser. At the age of 34, Neild, a barrister by profession, inherited an estate worth £250,000. Unlike his father, who had been a philanthropist, Neild preferred to save his money. His parsimonious habits included sleeping on the floor, saving his clothes by never having them cleaned, walking from his home in Chelsea to inspect his Buckinghamshire estates, and squatting in his tenants' humble cottages to save the expense of a lodging house.

One of Neild's responsibilities was to maintain the local church in North Marston, Berkshire, where he had a property, in good repair. When there was a need to renew the roof of the chancel, he instructed his workmen to re-cover it not in lead but with strips of calico, telling anyone who cared to listen that these would 'last my lifetime'. To ensure that his workmen didn't slink away early, he sat on an adjacent roof watching them until the job was finished.

Thanks to these skills in money management, Neild had doubled his fortune at the time of his death. Making no provision in his will for Mrs Skillett, the housekeeper who had looked after him for 26 years, he left £500,000 to Queen Victoria, 'begging your Majesty's most gracious acceptance of the same for your sole use and benefit'. The bequest was accepted and the queen used it to put a new roof on the church at North Marston, the strips of calico having long since rotted.

**Nell Gwynn House.** *See* GAUL, JOHN; GREEN, HUGHIE.

**neurotic pre-psychotic libidinous condition, diagnosis of a.** *See* EDINBURGH, PRINCE PHILIP, DUKE OF.

**Newborough, Denisa Lady** (1913–87), courtesan. Denisa Lady Newborough's greatest talent was for what she called, 'profitable romance'. In her memoir, *Fire in my Blood* (1958), she wrote, 'I have never believed that jewels, any more than motor cars, can be called vulgar just because they are large.' Her admirers included the kings of Spain and Bulgaria, Adolf Hitler, Benito Mussolini and a sheikh, who gave her 500 sheep. When she lived in Paris she was concurrently the mistress of five men, whom she referred to as her 'shareholders'. Each was unaware of the others' existence, and all were persuaded to give her a flat or a house. In her memoir she wrote, 'I have only refused to be two things in my life. A whore and a spy.' No more than half of that claim seems to be accurate.

Born Denisa Josephine Braun in Subotica, Serbia, the future Lady Newborough ran away in her teens to Budapest, where she pursued a variety of occupations, among them those of fan dancer, wire-walker, nightclub hostess and aeroplane pilot. At the start of World War II she served as a transport officer with the British Red Cross, but was dismissed in 1941 in mysterious circumstances. In 1946, shortly before her divorce from 'Tommy', the 6th Baron Newborough, whom she had married in 1942, she was declared bankrupt with debts of £951. These had been caused by losses at bridge. She eventually restored her financial position by designing hats. In 1958 she published her autobiography. Among the chapter headings were 'Elegant Sin in Bucharest' and 'On the Trail of the White Slavers'.

In 1964 Lady Newborough was convicted of allowing her maisonette in Mayfair to be used for habitual prostitution, but her conviction was quashed on appeal. Her daughter Juno is married to a dentist.

**Newton, Andrew.** *See* JEREMY THORPE.

**Newton, Arthur** (1858–1927), solicitor. Newton came to prominence early in his career when he was instructed by Lord Arthur Somerset in what became known as the Cleveland Street Brothel Scandal. In July 1886 a 15-year-old boy called Arthur Swinscow was arrested and pressed to explain how such a young person, employed in a humble capacity by the Post Office, had 18 shillings on his person. Swinscow admitted that he supplemented his income by working as a prostitute at 19 Cleveland Street, a homosexual brothel run by Charles HAMMOND, and catering for the nobility. He had been taken there, he said, by another telegraph boy, Henry Newlove. At the police station he protested at the injustice of his arrest when men of high position were allowed to walk free. Asked by Inspector ABBERLINE what he meant, he replied, 'Lord Arthur Somersct goes there regularly. So does the earl of Euston and Colonel Jervois.'

Lord 'Podge' Somerset, the son of the duke of Beaufort, was a major in the Royal Horse Guards, and superintendcnt of the prince of Wales's stables. When another teenager, Algernon Allies, also identified him to the police as a frequent visitor to Cleveland Street, Somerset sought the advice of his solicitor, Arthur Newton. Compared by more than one commentator to lawyers such as Sir Arthur Lewis and Arnold Goodman (*see* BOOTHBY, ROBERT), who were able to advance their own careers by becoming the repository of their social superiors' secrets, Newton, in an act of delicate blackmail, suggested to the assistant director of public prosecutions, Hamilton Cuffe, that were Lord Somerset to be prosecuted he would name the duke of CLARENCE, the eldest son of the prince of Wales, as another of the brothel's clients. Cuffe passed the warning on to his superior, Sir Augustus Stephenson, who informed the prime minister, Lord Salisbury. Lord Somerset was never prosecuted, but as a further precaution Newton persuaded him to depart for France.

Newton was less successful in his efforts to conceal the whereabouts of the four boy prostitutes. Arthur Swinscow, Henry Newlove, Algernon Allies and Charles Thickbroom went on trial at the Old Bailey in September 1886. Newlove received nine months hard labour, the others four months. Lord Somerset wasn't mentioned. That, it seemed, was the end of the matter, but the newspapers were disinclined to let it rest. On 16 November 1889 Ernest Parke of the *North London Press* named Lord Somerset and Lord Euston as the aristocrats whose names had been suppressed at the time of the trial.

The earl of Euston, 38-year-old Henry James Fitzroy, immediately instructed his solicitor to sue for libel. Parke's trial opened at the Old Bailey on 15 January 1890. One of the most serious points made against Lord Euston was an allegation in the *North London Press* that at the time of the previous trial he had departed for Peru. Euston had done no such thing. Since his name had not entered the case after Swinscow mentioned it to Inspector Abberline this precaution would not have been necessary.

He did admit that he had been to 19 Cleveland Street, but this, he claimed, had been due to a misunderstanding. He had been in Piccadilly in May or June 1886, when someone had shown him an advertising card. This had promised '*tableaux plastiques*' and gave the address of 19 Cleveland Street. He was admitted by a man who had told him that there were no women there but that he was welcome in any case. 'You infernal scoundrel, if you don't let me out, I'll knock you down,' Euston had said, before departing in a hurry.

Parke called several witnesses who said they had seen Lord Euston at Cleveland Street on many occasions. One, a male prostitute called John Saul, claimed to have been picked up by Lord Euston and taken to Cleveland Street, where his lordship, according to Saul, had turned out to be 'not an actual sodomite, but likes to play with you and spend on your belly'. Saul also worked under the name of 'Evelyn' at the Hundred Guineas, a transvestite club in Portland Place, and in another brothel in Nassau Street, now part of Middlesex Hospital. The judge described Saul as a 'loathsome object' and the jury found Parke guilty of libel without justification. He was sentenced to one year in prison with hard labour.

In December 1889 Arthur Newton was accused on two counts of conspiring to pervert the course of justice. The first charge was that he had tried to obtain an interview with Algernon Allies, the boy who had claimed to be 'Podge' Somerset's frequent lover; the second was that he had sent three of the telegraph boys to a lodging house while he made arrangements for them to leave the country. In his defence, Newton claimed that his clerk, Frederick Taylorson, had met Allies by chance and exchanged a few words with him. As for the second charge, he had indeed installed three of the boys in a lodging house, but that was because Somerset's father, the duke of Beaufort, wanted to interview them to discover whether they had been bullied by the police. The judge took a light view of Newton's offence, sentencing him to six weeks in prison. He soon returned to practice, acting over the years for a number of illustrious, and not so illustrious, clients, including Oscar Wilde and Major Herbert Rowse ARMSTRONG. In 1910 he received much favourable publicity when he defended Dr Hawley Harvey CRIPPEN, but he then conceived the idea of forging a Crippen 'confession' and selling it to a newspaper for £500. Newton was suspended for unprofessional conduct and in 1913 he was charged with being involved in a Canadian lumber fraud. He was sentenced to three years in prison and was struck off the rolls as a solicitor.

Lord Somerset spent the rest of his life abroad under an assumed name, and died in Hyères on the French Riviera in 1926. Lord Euston was appointed an aide-de-camp by King EDWARD VII in 1901. He died of dropsy in 1912.

**Newton, Robert** (1889–1957), actor, drinker and the source of more theatrical anecdotes, perhaps, than any other performer, many of which are thought to be true. Certainly he was a central figure in one of the most frequently anthologized. While on tour in the 1930s in Shakespeare's *Richard II*, he got drunk at lunchtime with another fine actor, and heavy drinker, Wilfred Lawson. Emerging from a public house, they happened to pass a fishmonger's shop. Newton stared for a long time at the rows of dead-eyed cods' heads looking up at them from the slab. 'Dear God, Wilfred!' he said, 'We've got a matinee!' Somehow they got back to the theatre, where Newton staggered on as John of Gaunt. 'If you think I'm pissed,' he told the audience, 'wait till you see the duke of York.'

In 1953 Newton was appearing in a play in Manchester as Queen Mary lay on her death bed. After the matinee the stage manager told the cast that she was unlikely to live through the day, in which case, he said, the evening performance would be cancelled. Newton got very drunk and, on return- ing to the theatre, was disappointed to discover that Queen Mary was still alive. He could hardly remain upright during the first act and the audience was becoming restless when the stage manager ran on stage. 'I have some sad news,' he announced. 'The queen is dead.' 'Thank God!' cried Newton, keeling over with relief.

*See also* KEAN, EDMUND.

**Ngarimu, Te Rangimaria** (1965–   ), contract killer. Miss Ngarimu is believed to have been the first woman to have been employed in this capac- ity in the United Kingdom. In May 1992 Graeme Woodhatch was recovering from an operation to relieve his haemorrhoids at the Royal Free Hospital, Hampstead, when Ngarimu, a 27-year-old barmaid, shot him twice in the head as he was using the telephone. Initially, Woodhatch's business partners, Paul Tubbs and Keith Bridges, were suspected of the murder, but the police lacked the evidence to prosecute. In fact Ngarimu, who was originally from New Zealand, had been approached by Bridges at the public house in Percy Street where she worked and offered the contract for a fee of £7000. She had agreed immediately, since she had ambitions to own a mobile home in Margate.

On her first visit to the Royal Free Hospital, Miss Ngarimu, who had not previously been a contract killer, was unable to find the right ward, so she left. She returned the next day wearing a tracksuit, a baseball cap and gloves, and on this occasion she shot Woodhatch from a distance of three feet while he was on the telephone. She then caught an aeroplane out of the country, having left the clothes and the gun in a hold-all at Bridges's flat in Camden Town. After the killing Bridges asked a friend, 'Ginger' Lynn, to get rid of the hold-all. Lynn looked inside and went straight to the police. Tubbs and Bridges were arrested, later pleading guilty to perverting the course of justice by disposing of the gun and the clothes worn by Miss Ngarimu.

Miss Ngarimu, meanwhile, had been contacted by the police, but had told them, 'I couldn't kill a chicken. I'm a vegetarian'. Over the next two years, however, she had a number of religious experiences, and in 1994 she returned voluntarily to England to clear her conscience. Bridges and Tubbs were re-arrested, this time on a murder charge. They were later convicted, largely on Miss Ngarimu's evidence. Each received life imprisonment. At Miss Ngarimu's trial, her barrister, Oliver Blunt QC, told the judge, Sir Lawrence Verney, that his client now attended bible classes three times a week and that her conversion to Christianity was total. 'She knows that beyond my Lord's sentence, she faces the judgement of her Lord.' Sir Lawrence sentenced her to life imprisonment.

## Nicholson, 'Baron' Renton (1809–61), journalist and impresario.

Nicholson, whose 'judge and jury shows' were among London's bawdier entertainments in the 1850s, overcame destitution as a young man (he had slept on the doorstep of the bishop of London, who had ignored his presence, but survived through the charity of prostitutes) to become the successful editor in the 1830s of *Town*, a scandal sheet specializing in lewd stories. He concurrently edited a High Church newspaper, the *Crown*, deriving much pleasure from dubbing himself a pornographer in *Crown* and denouncing himself as a hypocrite in *Town*.

In 1841 Nicholson produced the first of the 'judge and jury shows' at the Garrick Head in Bow Street. They were to become the sophisticated rivals of PENNY GAFFS and the forerunners of music halls. Nicholson, the 'Lord Chief Baron', dressed in wig and gown and assisted by waitresses in diaphanous underwear, presided over a slapstick re-enactment of the more scandalous of the day's court actions for adultery and CRIMINAL CONVER-SATION. Nicholson's title was borrowed from the Court of Exchequer Chamber, which was presided over by the lord chief baron.

The proceedings began with the entry of a gowned crier holding a staff of office and announcing to the assembled drinkers the arrival of the 'Lord Chief Baron'. Nicholson, in his robes, bowed to the 'bar', took his seat on the 'bench' and called for a cigar and a large brandy. What followed gave serious offence to at least one contemporary observer, J. Ewing Ritchie:

> A jury was selected, the prosecutor opened his case, which, to suit the depraved tastes of the patrons, was invariably one of seduction or crim. con. Witnesses were examined and cross-examined, the females being men dressed in women's clothes, and everything was done that could be to pander to the lowest propensities of depraved humanity. … After the defence came the summing-up, which men about town hold to be a model of wit, but in which the wit bore but small proportion to the obscenity.
>
> From *Rogue's Progress*, Renton Nicholson (1858).

In 1846, after a spell in the Queen's Bench Prison for debt, Nicholson enlivened proceedings with the introduction of teenage girls in flesh-coloured tights. They performed songs behind a curtain and were then revealed in *tableaux plastiques*. This was as far as the performance could go without attracting the attention of the magistrates. The growing popularity of judge and jury shows led to country-wide tours, taking in Birmingham, Manchester, Newcastle and Glasgow. On Derby Day, and at Ascot, 'Lord Nicholson' erected his 'giant pavilion of canvas, containing the good things of this life for the refreshment of the inward man of the sporting community'. At the same time, Nicholson published his *Swell's Night Guide or A Peep Through the Great Metropolis under the Dominion of Nox*. This included information about:

> ... the saloons, the chaffing cribs, the introducing houses, the singing and lushing cribs, the comical clubs and the fancy ladies and their penchants & &. Devised and fully corrected by the Lord Chief Baron, the Arbiter of Fashion and Folly, with numerous Spicy Engravings.

The legitimate courts, in which he frequently appeared, took Nicholson's self-bestowed titles in good part. When cross-examined by Mr Serjeant Byles as a witness in *Bickley vs Tasker* (1860), he was asked if he appeared as 'Baron of the Exchequer' at the Garrick's Head. 'Very barren of exchequer, I am sorry to say,' he replied. There was loud laughter, in which the chief justice, Sir John Jervis, was reported to have joined.

By then Nicholson's career was almost over. He died in 1861 at the age of 52, judged by many to have brought an element of social and political satire to the rougher humour of the penny gaffs, and to have played an important role in the development of music halls.

**Nickerson, Sir Joseph** (1914–90), farmer and plant breeder. In spite of his many achievements in the production of high-yielding cereals, Sir Joseph will be best remembered as a shot, first rising to prominence in 1952 when he set the official British record for the largest number of partridges killed in a single day. Between 9 a.m. and 6 p.m. he and five other guns on his Lincolnshire estate accounted for 1059 brace. Nickerson liked to compare himself with the 2nd marquess of Ripon, who had bagged a total of 187,763 birds in 24 seasons by the time he died in 1923. Sir Joseph's total for a similar period was 188,172 – an average of 7841 birds a year.

In his robust memoir, *A Shooting Man's Creed* (1989), Sir Joseph makes the important point that the true sportsman respects his prey:

> To me shooting has long been something of a religion. As all religions do, it requires discipline, reverence, ritual and, above all, love.

> My reverence is for the splendid quarry, which is something non-shooters find hard to understand.

He later explains that from an early age he taught himself to think like a partridge:

> I imagined myself to be a male hatched on 20 June on the Lincolnshire Wolds with 12 brothers and sisters. My parents were extraordinarily attentive and when weasels were about they ushered us into cover.

He makes no mention in his memoir of the occasion when Viscount Whitelaw, then deputy prime minister, slipped in the butts when a guest of Sir Joseph's, peppering his host and a gamekeeper, Waddle.

Sir Joseph founded the Cotswold Pig Development Company and in 1983 was made an officer of the Order of Leopold II of Belgium.

*See also* ABBOTT, GEORGE.

**Nicolson, Major Herbert.** A silly bollocks. *See* RICHARDSON, CHARLIE.

**nightcap, unorthodox use of.** *See* CHARTERIS, COLONEL FRANCIS.

**Nikko the Laplander.** *See* KELLY, SHANGHAI.

**nincompoops of a specifically English sort.** *See* BODKIN, SIR ARCHIBALD; BULLER, SIR REDVERS; ERSKINE, GENERAL SIR WILLIAM; JARDINE, DOUGLAS.

**Noailles, Helena comtesse de** (1824–1908), health and education expert. In many respects, the comtesse's ideas were ahead of their time. Her opposition to undue academic pressure on children would find support in the present day, as might her dislike of restrictive clothing and her advocacy of fresh air. However, her ideas on how such theories should be put into practice might seem as unorthodox now as they did then. When at teatime one day her son Phil climbed up a tree to eat a bun, she decided that Darwin's theories on man's ancestry had been corroborated, and she ruled that the child must henceforth and always take his tea up a tree.

The daughter of a wealthy English family (her mother was a Baring, half-sister of Lord Revelstoke and of Lord Cromer), Helena married Antonin, the comte de Noailles, in 1849. After three years they decided to live apart, and the comtesse was free to pursue her own experimental interests, chief of which was the belief that the shape of a person's head was the most reliable key to character. Accordingly, she planned to convert one of her houses into a home for the orphaned daughters of Church of England clergymen – with admission to be determined on the basis of an examination by two qualified phrenologists.

Nothing came of this idea, but in 1865 she bought a 9-year-old Spanish girl, Maria Pasqua, for two bags of gold and assumed responsibility for the child's upbringing. Maria was sent to a convent school at St Leonard's, Sussex, but the comtesse insisted that certain conditions be observed. Since the school uniform was restrictive, Maria was to be kitted out in a loose Grecian tunic and open sandals. Instead of following the standard curriculum, Maria was to be taught grammar according to an improved system that the comtesse herself had devised. The school pond, a dangerous breeding ground for insects, must be drained. Maria could only drink milk from a cow that the comtesse had approved.

The comtesse herself followed a rigorous health regimen. A believer in the salutary effects of methane gas, she kept a herd of cows grazing near the house so that she could benefit from their frequent expulsions of wind. At night she slept with two stockings wrapped round her head filled with the corpses of grey squirrels, and with a wildcat skin, imported from Norway, covering her chest. Her cure for bronchitis was a diet of herring roe.

Travelling presented the comtesse with many challenges. She would never set forth in an east wind, and she would stop a train if the weather was not to her liking. To avoid contact with infectious fellow passengers, she always travelled in a private railway car. When travelling on the Continent she used a specially wide carriage, formerly the property of King Louis Philippe, which contained a folding bed and a portable lavatory. Safely arrived at a hotel in France, she insisted that a string of onions be hung outside her room as a specific against infections.

In 1881 the comtesse, by now a widow, married Phillip Shepheard and settled in Norfolk. Before taking up residence she insisted that all the cows be brought into the garden to improve the atmosphere. When Maria, her adopted daughter, married, the comtesse continued to be concerned for her health. Her advice during one pregnancy was to drink only water in which the cones of pine trees had been boiled. And she ensured that her advice be followed even after her death by making Maria's inheritance conditional on never wearing lace shoes. The comtesse lived to the age of 84, sustained in her last years by a diet of champagne and milk.

**Nolan, Finbar** (1945– ), the most successful Irish healer since Valentine GREATRAKES in the 17th century. According to Celtic legend, the seventh son of a seventh son is able to cure conditions such as eczema and asthma, but Nolan, who has the requisite number of uncles and elder brothers, has been treating a much wider range of diseases since the time when, still in his nappies, he put his hands on another child and cured it of ringworm. People flock to Nolan's remote home in County Cavan, where he claims that 75% of his patients notice an improvement in their condition after he has laid hands on them. Since the percentage of people cured by placebos prescribed by their doctors is more or less the same, the claim may well be true.

In the 1980s Nolan visited England, where he appeared on television. His publicity arrangements were organized by Fred Hift, who had previously worked for Raquel Welch. Nolan's television show had mixed success. He announced his belief that rheumatism and arthritis are caused by a worm in the spine. When he was two, he said, his mother had put a worm in his hand and it had immediately died. However, when Nolan handled some worms on television it was noted that they survived. He charges nothing for his services, but grateful patients are not discouraged if they wish to leave a donation in an envelope.

**'No-Legs' Mancini, Johnny.** *See* BASS, HARRY 'THE DOCTOR'.

**Norbury, John Toler, 1st Baron** (1745–1831), jurist, dubbed by some 'Ireland's Judge Jeffreys' (*see* JEFFREYS, GEORGE), and known as 'Puffendorf' from his habit of inflating his cheeks as he spoke. A contemporary described him as 'fat, with small grey cunning eyes, which sparkled with good humour, especially when he was passing sentence of death'. Norbury seemed to confuse his duties with those of a public entertainer, turning his court into a cockpit of slapstick and sadism. 'What have we here?' he said to a manacled defendant. 'A young man in the flower of life. Yet the flower will never come to fruit.' Once, when the distinguished advocate John Philpot Curran rose to speak on behalf of a client, an ass brayed outside the courthouse window. 'One at a time, please, Mr Curran,' Norbury told him.

Norbury, who came from an impoverished family in Tipperary, boasted that he started his legal career with £50 and a pair of hair-trigger duelling pistols. As a prosecuting counsel he knew little about the law, yet he 'breathed such a turbulent spirit of domination' that in 1798 he was appointed attorney general. In 1800, and in spite of the protestations of Lord Clare, who said he was as suited to be an archbishop as a judge, he was made chief justice of the common pleas. Thereafter he presided over what he himself called 'a racket house'. Norbury would waddle into court and place a few of his friends beside him on the bench. Among the most frequently present was a madman named Toby McCormick, who attended Norbury's sessions under the delusion that he and the judge had exchanged identities. McCormick would shout 'Find for the plaintiff!' as soon as the charges were read out. Once the adversorial buffooneries had been completed, and it was time for the sentencing, Norbury would make a long rambling speech to the condemned man, sprinkled with quotations from Shakespeare and Milton. A typical exhortation was described by Sir Jonah Barrington as:

... a wild harangue in which neither the law, method or argument could be discovered. It generally consisted of narratives connected with the history of his early life.

Norbury once appeared in court wearing under his robe a costume he had previously put on to attend a masque given by Lady Castlereagh. It was a hot day so Norbury prematurely discarded his judicial gown and, 'having a great press of death sentences to pass on rebels etc.,' condemned the prisoners before him dressed in 'a green tabinet with mother of pearl buttons, striped yellow and black waistcoat and buff breeches'. His only known act of clemency was towards a murderer whose guilt was obvious. When Norbury recommended the jury to acquit him, the crown prosecutor interrupted to remind the judge that the evidence left no doubt that the man was guilty. 'I realize that,' said Norbury crossly, 'but I hanged six innocent men at the Tipperary assizes so to square matters I'll let this fellow off.'

Away from his court, Norbury was much sought after as a wit and singer, able to render 'Black Eyed Susan' and 'Admiral Benbow' to good effect, as well as parts of many glees and catches. Professionally, a growing tendency to fall asleep in court brought about some loss of reputation. With increasing frequency the gross figure would be heard snoring loudly through the presentation of a capital charge. Various attempts were made to remove him from the bench, including a petition drawn up against him in 1825 by Daniel O'Connell, pointing out that he had slept throughout an important murder trial. None of them was successful. He finally retired at the age of 82, and was rewarded with an earldom.

**Norcott, William** (1770–1820), barrister and Dublin socialite, reduced, by one account, to selling rhubarb in the street. Norcott, was an able lawyer, but he preferred agreeable company to the pursuit of his legal duties. He was an accomplished guest, an amusing mimic, a free thinker and a writer of satirical plays, for the most part unperformed. As a friend of the duke of Richmond, he was in demand at most of the levees and castle entertainments. 'He could,' it was said, 'drink as stoutly as the duke himself, touch the piano as well as a lady or gamble as deeply as any of the gentlemen.'

It was the latter habit that caused his downfall. Norcott had the contempt for money shared by his richer friends, and never allowed prudence to interfere with pleasure. The descent into bankruptcy was swift, but he didn't make too much of his misfortune and, as a consequence, remained popular in his circle. Soon enough, John Wilson Croker, a friend of the duke of Wellington, found Norcott a decent job in Malta, a position which, it was hoped, would provide a short respite before he was able to recover his place in Dublin society. However, within a short time of taking up his appointment, Norcott was in disgrace. The details of his offence are unknown but it is assumed that he accumulated private debts that he was unable to honour. He fled from Malta and went eastwards, disappearing from view.

Conflicting reports of his whereabouts eventually reached Dublin. According to Sir Jonah Barrington, 'the last authentic account described him as selling rhubarb in the streets of Smyrna' (*Historic Memoirs of Ireland*, 1830–2). Then it was learned that he had made his way to Constantinople. One story had it that he was flourishing once again and had become a confidant of the Diwan. The truth was worse than any had dared fear. When discovered, according to R.L. Sheil's *Sketches of the Irish Bar* (1855):

> His dress was at once the emblem of apostasy and of want. It hung in rags about a person which from a robust magnitude of frame had shrunk to a miserable diminution. He carried starvation in his cheeks, ghastliness and misery overspread his features, and despair was glazed in his sunken eye.

Norcott had become not only a beggar but a criminal too. His debts had climbed to the point where the Turkish authorities wouldn't let him leave the country. Then, in 1820, an English visitor to Constantinople gave him the funds with which to make his escape. He didn't get far. The Turkish police were keeping a close eye on this foreign vagabond, and were on to him the moment he left the city. He had only gone a short distance when he was pursued and captured. He was decapitated on the shores of the Bosphorus and his body thrown into the sea. Sir Jonah Barrington provided a disobliging memorial:

> Norcott died a disgraced and blasphemous renegado. This confirms an observation of mine throughout life that a free thinker is ever disposed to be also a free actor. And is restrained from the gratification of all the vices only by those laws which provide a punishment for the commission.

**Norton, George Chapple** (1810–75), lawyer and wife-beater. Norton, who sat as a magistrate at the White Chapel Police Court, had been fortunate, in the opinion of his contemporaries, to have found employment of any kind. He was an idle and disagreeable man who consistently abused his wife Caroline. To help with the family finances, Mrs Norton wrote some 30 novels and a little poetry, the only surviving piece of which is 'An Arab's Farewell to his Horse'. In 1836 Norton brought an action for CRIMINAL CONVERSATION against the prime minister, Lord Melbourne. (Melbourne had been unsuccessfully married to Lady Caroline Lamb, *née* Ponsonby, who had had a famous affair with Lord BYRON in 1812–13. Melbourne and his wife had finally separated in 1825, and she died three years later.) The claim in the present case was that Lord Melbourne had been too close to Mrs Norton, a great beauty who numbered the young Disraeli among her admirers.

Melbourne had already survived a similar charge, brought against him by the gout-ridden divine, Lord Brandon. Brandon suspected that the young and attractive Lady Brandon had left him at Melbourne's instigation and was living in London under an assumed name. That action had failed, but was inevitably remembered to Melbourne's disadvantage when Norton sued in similar circumstances 15 years later. There was no doubt that Melbourne knew Mrs Norton. On one occasion she had written to him seeking help over her husband's appointment to the White Chapel Bench. He called on her frequently, sometimes leaving brief notes, which were held against him now. One was, 'I will call at about half-past four or five – Yours, Melbourne.' According to the etiquette of the time, the note should have begun, 'My Dear Mrs Norton ...' The fact that it didn't suggested adulterous thoughts, if not action. 'Such notes seem to convey much more than the mere words convey,' observed Sir William Follett for George Norton.

The case was heard by Lord Chief Justice Tindal in the Court of Common Pleas at Westminster, with Melbourne represented by the attorney general, Sir John Campbell. Norton's witnesses were an assembly of discharged footmen, pregnant maids and drunken coachmen. One of the latter admitted under cross-examination that, when driving his master and mistress to a ball, he had been so drunk that he had been arrested and kept in custody overnight. Pressed further, he agreed that, to guarantee his appearance here, he had been given £10 by Norton and lodged, pending the case, at the country house of Norton's brother. The jury was unimpressed and, without leaving the box, acquitted Melbourne of all impropriety. *The Times* took a sterner view. 'Lord Melbourne has been acquitted by the verdict of the jury against the laws of God and man.' In the end, his career was unharmed, but Mrs Norton suffered badly:

> A cabal of intrigue and innuendo was levelled at her, and studied and systematic misrepresentation were her lot. Woman-baiting and mud-flinging, it seemed, were popular pastimes among a section of the gutter journalists from whom the general public formed their opinions. Some of the mud stuck.
>
> From *Blotted 'Scutcheons* Horace Wyndham (1936).

With the collapse of his action against Melbourne, Norton was unable to petition for a divorce, but he and Mrs Norton separated. She failed to realize that, by agreeing to a separation, she had forfeited her rights to the children. Norton had sole custody and, characteristically, he denied his wife access except in degrading conditions. He died in 1875, and in March 1877 Caroline married Sir William Sterling-Maxwell, a longtime friend. She died three months later.

*Norton vs Melbourne* was satirized by Dickens as *Bardwell vs Pickwick.*

**Norton, Joshua** (1819–80), merchant and fantasist. For 20 years Norton, at least in his own mind, was emperor of the United States and, less prestigiously, protector of Mexico, a state of affairs to which his subjects in the Bay area of San Francisco, where he had settled, seemed to have no objection.

Born in London, Norton made his fortune in South Africa and then on the west coast of North America, dealing in comestibles and property. In 1853 he gambled a quarter of a million dollars in an attempt to corner the rice market. He bought and stockpiled all the available supplies, thereby inflating the price artificially. His scheme failed when several ships laden with rice sailed into San Francisco Bay, glutting the market. The price of rice plummeted and Norton was ruined. In 1856 he filed for bankruptcy, thereafter appointing himself emperor, first of California, and then of the whole of the United States.

In 1859 Norton inserted a proclamation in the *San Francisco Bulletin*, in which he announced that:

> At the pre-emptory request of a large majority of the citizens of the United States, I, Joshua Norton, do declare myself Emperor of the US and in virtue of the authority thereby in me vested, do hereby order the representatives the different States of the Union to assemble in the Music Hall to make such alteration in the laws of the Union as may ameliorate the evils under which the country is labouring.

Norton discharged the duties of his office with great diligence. He kept in touch with the life of the city, strolling the streets of San Francisco, checking on the amenities and attending a religious service of a different denomination each week in order not to arouse sectarian jealousy.

In response, the citizens tolerated his various decrees and recognized their responsibility to contribute to his upkeep – paying 50 cents a night to maintain him in a lodging house. When he issued a decree about the state of his clothes – 'Know ye that we, Norton the First, have divers complaints from our liege subjects that our Imperial wardrobe is a national disgrace' – the City Council voted funds for a new uniform to be provided by the prestigious tailors, Bullock and Jones. His own currency – 50-cent notes printed by himself – was accepted by restaurants and shopkeepers. He was issued with free passes to theatres, and the audience always stood as he entered. On one occasion a river boat captain ordered Norton ashore for not paying his fare. Norton retaliated by ordering the United States navy to blockade all the company's vessels. Its board of directors hastily offered him an apology and a lifetime of free travel on its ships.

Robert Louis Stevenson admired the people of San Francisco for fostering 'this harmless madman'. Their reasons were obvious. As a judge remarked, when rebuking a policeman who had arrested Norton for lunacy, he had 'shed no blood, robbed no one and despoiled no country, which is more than can be said for most Kings and Emperors'. When Norton died in 1880 the *San Francisco Chronicle* ran the headline, 'LE ROI EST MORT'. The police were summoned to maintain order among the huge crowds that came to pay their respects at the funeral parlour. Flags were flown at half mast throughout the city, and 30,000 mourners attended the graveside service at the Masonic Cemetery.

In fact, Norton had, on at least two occasions, abused his power. When Maximilian assumed the throne of Mexico, which was an imperial protectorate, Norton sentenced him to death as a usurper. More seriously, he once banished a local character called Uncle Freddie for an unspecified misdemeanour. Uncle Freddie took the imperial decree seriously and departed San Francisco, never to be seen again.

**nose, a capital offence to lie in wait with intent to disfigure someone's.** *See* CAPITAL PUNISHMENT.

**nose, cutting off a stranger's.** *See* FITZGERALD, GEORGE ROBERT.

**nose, the denting of a false.** *See* HOOLIGANS, THEATRICAL.

**nose of a fighting dog until it submits, biting the.** *See* MYTTON, JOHN.

**nose off, biting Pretty Boy's.** *See* MCLEAN, LENNY.

**nose off, trying to bite a journalist's.** *See* JONES, VINNIE.

**Noye, Kenneth** (1948– ), gangster, gold smuggler, property developer and murderer. In May 1996, 21-year-old Stephen Cameron was stabbed to death on the M25 near Swanley in Kent in what was described as a road-rage incident, but which was in fact a dispute over a drug deal. His assailant was Kenneth Noye, who for the next two years enjoyed the reputation of being Britain's 'most wanted man'. It was the latest chapter in the long and eventful history of Noye and the police, which had begun with the Brinks-Mat bullion raid of November 1983 (*see* ROBINSON, BRIAN). The robbers on that occasion were soon captured, but the whereabouts of the £26 million of stolen gold remained a mystery.

It was some time after the raid before the police targeted Noye, who was living in a large house in West Kingsdown, Kent, with his wife Brenda and their two children. To outward appearances, he was a clever and ambitious man whose hard work in the haulage business had given him the entrée to the affluent world of charity dinners, Freemasonry and suburban squash clubs. He had convictions for receiving stolen property, however, and once the police had him under surveillance they noted that he was moving large sums of money and buying gold bars in St Helier, Jersey. It was decided that Noye's home should be staked out, and in January 1985 Detective Constables John Fordham and Neil Murphy hid in the grounds in camouflage gear. The operation ended in disaster. Alerted by barking from his two Rottweilers, named Brinks and Mat, Noye stumbled across Fordham in the dark and stabbed him to death. Charged with murder, Noye pleaded self-defence. 'I just froze with horror,' he told the court:

> All I saw when I flashed my torch on this masked man was the two eye-holes. I thought I was going to be a dead man.

He had stabbed the policeman eleven times, but was acquitted of murder.

Five months later Noye was back in court, charged with laundering the Brinks-Mat bullion. His co-defendants were Brian Reader, a longtime associate of Noye's who had been with him on the night Fordham was killed, and Garth Chappell, the managing director of Scadlynn, a bullion company in Bristol. Noye received 14 years, Chappell 10 and Reader 9. A year later the police turned their attention to John Palmer, a property millionaire known as Goldfinger. Part of the haul from the robbery was found to have been melted down in a furnace at his property in Bath. He was eventually charged with conspiracy to handle the bullion, but was acquitted.

Much of the cash from the Brinks-Mat robbery had entered the banking system, but financial experts were able to trace the money and, using the lower standards of proof required by civil courts, together with the threat to seize assets, they were able to persuade 25 people linked to the robbery to pay back £17 million. When he got out of prison, Noye was among those who paid up rather than face a civil case. He agreed to a cash settlement thought to have been in the region of £3 million. Thereafter he prospered, adding to his fortune with shrewd property investments in Spain and Portugal. That he should have thrown everything away in a moment of anger on the M25 might seem inexplicable to those who had never experienced his uncertain temper. The only interesting aspect of a squalid killing is that it suited both prosecution and defence to hide the cause of the dispute. In fact, Noye's victim, Stephen Cameron, was a small-time drug dealer who owed Noye money. When the two men met, quite fortuitously, on the M25, Noye suggested that Cameron repay him. Cameron refused, and Noye, who was getting the worst of the ensuing fight, stabbed him to death. Two years later he was starting a life sentence for murder.

**nudists.** *See* DAVIDSON, THE REVEREND HAROLD FRANCIS; GARVIE, SHEILA; JAMES, EDWARD; MASSEREENE, CLOTWORTHY SKEFFINGTON, 2ND EARL OF; PRINCE, HENRY.

**Nuthouse, gangsters hiding under the table in the.** *See* HILL, BILLY.

**Nuts in May.** *See* MONTROSE, JAMES ANGUS GRAHAM, 7TH DUKE OF.

# O

**Oades, Len 'Poofy'.** *See* HOLLIDAY, BERT.

**Oakeley, Sir Atholl** (1900–87), soldier, impresario and freestyle wrestler. The grandson of Sir Charles Oakeley, 4th Baronet, a Bengal Lancer who was a champion prize-fighter, Sir Atholl was educated at Clifton and Sandhurst, and commissioned in the Oxfordshire and Buckinghamshire Light Infantry. His interest in wrestling was awakened after he got the worst of it at the hands of a saloon-bar ruffian. Although he was only 5ft 9in tall, he managed to build up his body by drinking eleven pints of milk a day for three years. This diet had been recommended to him in an exchange of letters with the famous wrestling champion, George Hackenschmidt. Hackenschmidt later told him that the quantity of milk prescribed had been a misprint. The correct amount was one pint a day.

Sir Atholl preferred to wrestle men who were larger than himself. On one occasion his opponent was a Turkish wrestler of 7ft 6in, whom he bent double with a half-nelson. The hold was only untangled by several other wrestlers sitting on the Turk. A veteran of over 2000 bouts, Sir Atholl was heavyweight champion of Great Britain from 1930 to 1935, of Europe in 1932, and he remained unbeaten on a 17-bout tour of America in 1933. According to his autobiography, *Blue Blood on the Mat* (1971), his distinctive cauliflower ear was the result of a match in Chicago in the course of which 'Bill Bartuch got me in a scissors grip between his knees and wouldn't let go.'

Sir Atholl's active career came to an end in 1935 when he broke his shoulder. He then became a manager. His clients included Jack Sherry, who became world heavyweight champion. Later, he promoted fights at the Harringay Arena. Among the wrestlers he engaged was Gargantua, a 50-stone German with a 90-inch chest, for whom special travelling arrangements had to be made with British Rail.

Sir Atholl was an authority on *Lorna Doone*. In 1969 he published *The Facts on which R.D. Blackmore based Lorna Doone*, and he mounted a successful campaign to change the map of Exmoor, showing that the Doone Valley was sited at Lank Combe rather than Hoccombe.

**Oates, Titus** (1649–1705), priest and conspirator. The notorious inventor of the fictitious 'Popish Plot' against Charles II – supposedly inspired by Jesuits and due to erupt at the end of the 1670s – Oates was named by Lord Macaulay as 'the greatest perjurer in history':

> His voice, uplifted in accusation, instituted a period of terror unparalleled in the history of an ancient people.

Born in Norfolk, Oates was sent to the Merchant Taylors' School in 1665, but was expelled after a year. In 1669 he went up to Gonville and Caius College, Cambridge, where he was declared by his tutor to be a 'great dunce'. After two terms he was invited to leave. 'The plague and he both visited the University in the same year,' wrote a contemporary, Adam Elliot. After being accepted by St John's College, where 'his malignant spirit of railing and scandal was no less obnoxious', he left Cambridge without a degree.

Oates then entered the Church and obtained an appointment as curate at Sandhurst. He was expelled after parishioners complained that he stole their pigs. Seemingly unemployable anywhere else, he retired to All Saints, Hastings, where his father, an Anabaptist preacher, hired him as his curate. Here he demonstrated his remarkable ruthlessness by accusing a schoolmaster, William Parker, of sodomy, and Parker's father of high treason – both offences carrying the death penalty. The charge of high treason was dismissed as absurd, while the younger Parker was able to prove that he was nowhere in the vicinity at the time of the alleged indecency; further, that the young man he was supposed to have committed it with didn't exist. Oates was fined £1000 and jailed for a period in Dover Castle.

After a few months as a chaplain in the navy (from which he was expelled for sodomy), he settled in London. Here, he was introduced to The Pheasant, a louche club in Holborn that was a meeting place for underground Catholics, who, in the paranoid imagination of many, had started the Great Fire of 1666. 'The people thought their enemies were in their bosoms,' wrote the Scottish philosopher, David Hume. 'Each breath and rumour made them start with anxiety. Common sense and common humanity lost all influence over them.'

Oates now worked on the revelations that would become the Popish Plot. To bring some authority to his allegations, he needed to build up his inside knowledge of Catholicism. Once this had been achieved he would concentrate on what was to become his special area of expertise: religious espionage. In 1677 he joined the English College at Valladolid in Spain.

After four months he was expelled – a circumstance that didn't prevent him taking the title of doctor of divinity from the University of Salamanca.

Back in England, and having discovered no evidence of a Catholic plot, Oates was yet able to tap a rich vein of anti-Catholic paranoia. In the Catholic conspiracy that he claimed to have uncovered, Charles II would be assassinated and his Catholic brother James, the duke of York, placed on the throne. English Protestants would be massacred. Enemies of the king were lurking in St James's with pistols and bludgeons. Wishing to implicate the duke of York (later James II), Oates named the duchess of York's private secretary, Edward Coleman, among the plotters. Incriminating letters to a French Catholic priest were found in Coleman's possession. He was arrested and charged with treason. As chief prosecution witness at his trial, Oates invented further incriminating details, among them that he had seen Coleman paying four Irishmen a guinea each to kill the king. It was enough for Lord Chief Justice Scroggs, who sentenced Coleman to:

> ... be drawn to the place of execution, where you shall be hanged by the neck, and be cut down alive, your bowels burnt before your face, and your quarters severed, and your body disposed of as the King thinks fit; and so the Lord have mercy on your soul.

Apropos Scroggs, John Gay, professor of modern history at University College, London, holds that it is a mistake to judge past behaviour by the standards of today, but, as Professor Bernard Williams has pointed out (*Morality*, 1980), not to do so would seem to be a particularly gross example of the relativist fallacy.

To Protestants, Oates was now a hero. Installed in a Whitehall apartment and protected by bodyguards, he was in receipt of a substantial pension from the government. He was viewed by the public as the saviour of the nation. Confident in his new status, he next accused five Catholic peers. All were arrested and sent to the Tower. With hysteria mounting, a London militia was established with powers to stop funeral processions and examine coffins for hidden arms. The Roman Catholic archbishop of Armagh, Oliver Plunket, was among those sentenced to death – in his case on the trumped-up charge of conspiring to bring the French army to Ireland. In November 1680 Viscount Stafford was tried and convicted by his peers, among them seven members of his own family, all of whom voted for his execution. By the summer of 1681, 35 innocent people had been executed.

Gradually a reaction set in. The public noticed that, contrary to Oates's prediction, Charles II was alive, there had been no popish uprising in Scotland, nor had any Protestants had their throats cut. Oates's past began to catch up with him, as news of his perjury indictment in the case of William Parker came to light. On 29 April, the 22nd anniversary of the Restoration, an effigy of Oates was burned in Covent Garden. In 1684 he was charged with slandering the duke of York and tried before Judge JEF-FREYS, who not long before had enthusiastically sent imaginary plotters to the gallows. Oates was fined £100,000, a sum Jeffreys knew he'd be unable to pay. The following year, while Oates languished in prison, Charles II died and was succeeded by James II. With James on the throne and the Popish Plot discounted, Oates was totally discredited.

In May 1685 Oates was tried on two counts of perjury, again before Judge Jeffreys, and found guilty. Since perjury was not a capital offence, he was sentenced to be pilloried and whipped at the cart's tail from Aldgate to Newgate, and, after an interval of two days, whipped again from Newgate to Tyburn. If he was still alive after that, he was to be imprisoned for life and publicly flogged five times a year. On the first day of his sentence Oates survived the pillory, but the next day was flogged so severely that he passed out in a pool of blood. Two days later, and unable to walk – partly through his injuries and partly because he was drunk – he was dragged to Tyburn on a hurdle and the flogging was repeated. A witness recorded that he received 700 strokes.

Remarkably, Oates survived the ordeal. For the next four years he stayed in prison, only leaving when it was time for his next flogging. When the Protestant William of Orange installed himself on the throne in the Glorious Revolution of 1688, Oates was released. He dined with the archbishop of Canterbury, dressed as an Anglican clergyman and called himself Dr Oates of Salamanca University. In 1689, and to the surprise of everyone, he married an heiress. His rehabilitation was short-lived. He was expelled from the Baptist order, which he had recently joined, for defrauding a wealthy widow of her inheritance. He squandered his wife's fortune, and spent a year in a debtors' prison. In July 1702 he was tried at Westminster Hall Quarter sessions for 'scandalizing and assaulting' a woman named Elizabeth James. He died, in some obscurity, in 1705 at the age of 58.

> His short neck, his legs uneven, the vulgar said, as those of a badger, his forehead low as that of a baboon, his purple cheeks, and his monstrous length of chin, had been familiar to all who frequented the courts of law. Wherever he had appeared, men had uncovered their heads to him. The lives and estates of the magnates of the realm had been at his mercy. Times changed, and many who had formerly regarded him as the deliverer of his country, shuddered at the sight of those hideous features on which villainy seemed to be written by the hand of God.
>
> From *The History of England* Lord Macaulay (1849–61).

**obscene, the self-evidently.** *See* BODKIN, SIR ARCHIBALD.

**obscene rituals in Rochdale.** *See* DICKENSON, MOTHER.

**obscene toothpick, publishing an.** *See* BACCHUS, REGINALD.

*Oh Calcutta!* See FOWLER, MAJOR NIGEL.

**Old Grey Fox, The** (Commander Bert Wickstead). *See* ELLUL, PHILIP; LAMBTON, ANTONY CLAUD FREDERICK.

**old ladies onto a fire, throwing.** *See* TURPIN, DICK.

**Old Wykehamists.** In November 2001 the Winchester College magazine, *The Trusty Servant*, reported that:

> Two hots were held during the OWCC tour of Italy. The first, near Lake Como, was declared null and void because Commoners fielded an Old Etonian. The second was in a square in Lugano. OTH drove Commoners back but the arrival of riot police prevented announcement of the winners. The following were imprisoned before being released on bail: The Club President, Patrick Maclure (I, 1952–57), John Thornycroft (H, 1978–83), Bill Holland (F, 1979–83), Caspar Ridley (K, 1980–85), Ben Thornycroft (1981–86), Matt Sabben-Clare (I, 1985–90), Will Poole-Watson (K), Simon Powell-Jackson (B), and Jake Wellesley-Smith (I) all 1986–91, George Close-Brooks (F, 1990–95), Ed Craig (K), Ed Matthews (K) and Tristan Hanson all 1991–96. The Club President, Patrick Maclure, said later that he was unable to recall the incident, or being in Italy at the time.

> *The Trusty Servant* also reported that during a sponsored cycle ride in Russia to raise funds for Downside Up, A.H. Thompson (staff 1964–2000), held a hot in Red Square where he and Thomas Pedrick (Coll, 1983–88) were defeated by Olivier Bazin (A, 1985–90), Charles Garrett (C, 1976–81) and Dominick Summers (I, 1977–82). Henry Thompson played for Coll by virtue of having been awarded Xs stockings and played in College canvas as a jun don. A dinner was later taken with D.S. Pellew (Coll, 1981–86) and C.W.L. Peters (A, 1986–91) at an excellent Georgian restaurant much frequented by the Moscow Mafia. Downside Up now has a website, www.downsideup.org.

> For a list of Wykehamists, *see* WYKEHAMISTS.

**O'Mahoney, Maurice** (1947–   ), gangster and informer. Known as 'King Squealer', O'Mahoney was one of the 'supergrasses' who became prominent in the late 1970s. Born into a large Irish Catholic family, he was active in robbery, extortion and hijacking from an early age. A violent man who had once bitten a victim's finger off to get his diamond ring, he took pleasure on his own admission in beating debtors about the head with a hammer. His reasons for turning supergrass in June 1974 remain unclear. In his autobiography, *King Squealer* (1978), he claims that some of his associates on a recent Securicor robbery had already started to talk; further, that they had threatened not only his girlfriend, Susan Norville, but him too, promising to gouge his eyes out with a toothbrush.

Perhaps the volatile nature of his relationship with Miss Norville was itself a contributory factor. She emerges from *King Squealer* as a difficult woman:

> I used to return in the early hours after a successful evening of villainy, only to find the door locked and bolted like Fort Knox. She had so many security devices on the inside of the front door that there was no way I could get in once she had locked it. I would bang and shout and ring the bell, I often woke the whole street, but she just lay in bed, determined to make me suffer.

It would certainly have been galling for someone who had just breached a bank's security arrangements to be confounded by his partner's precautions in the same regard.

When arrested at gunpoint on 11 June 1974, O'Mahoney, for whatever reason, said, 'I've had enough. Give me a high-ranking officer from Scotland Yard. I want to confess.' Questioned by Assistant Commissioner Ernest Bond and Detective Chief Superintendent Jack Slipper, O'Mahoney admitted 102 offences, including 13 armed robberies and 65 burglaries involving £197,000 in cash. Implicating 27 major criminals, he said, 'I believe that what I am doing now is right. I want to hit right at the heart of the criminal underworld.'

Lodged in what was known as the 'grass house' at Chiswick police station, O'Mahoney received regular visits from Miss Norville, played snooker with his guards and enjoyed fishing trips and rounds of golf. DCS Slipper defended these conditions. 'Supergrasses must have facilities or they would go bonkers,' he explained.

On 19 September 1974 O'Mahoney pleaded guilty at the Old Bailey to 102 offences. Michael Hill QC said that his assistance to the police had been 'incalculable' – and Hill was leading the prosecution. O'Mahoney's own barrister, Kenneth Machin, told the court that 'by his actions he may have already signed his own death warrant.' The judge, Sir Carl Aarvold, sentenced him to five years and O'Mahoney wept with relief. At Oxford prison he was greeted with cries of, 'You're going to be killed, you grass,' and notes threatening his family were put under the door of his cell. On 4 June 1975 he returned to court to give evidence against 13 of his former colleagues who faced charges of armed robbery, conspiracy to rob and conspiracy to pervert the course of justice. The case was heard before Judge Bernard Gillis QC, whose lenient sentencing policy had earned him the nickname 'Gillis is good for you'. O'Mahoney's evidence was convincing, and a further 7 criminals received sentences of 15 years.

O'Mahoney then refused to give the prosecutors any further help. His armed protection was immediately withdrawn, and he called the *Guardian* to complain:

> They've dropped me flat, the canary that fell from its perch. They've told me to go out and get a decent job. The only trade I know is how to break into banks. I'm in a terrible state. I could go round the corner and cry.

In fact, O'Mahoney re-emerged in a variety of occupations: as a security man for pop singers, including Rick Wakeman and David Bowie; as a door-to-door salesman of stolen jewellery; and as a jobbing electrician at the homes of his former Scotland Yard minders. In 1993 he reappeared at the Old Bailey, charged with robbery and possession of firearms after a raid on a post office in Shepherd's Bush. Appearing under his new name of Peter Davies, he claimed that the police had asked him to carry out the robbery so that they could frame another man with the proceeds. He further told the court that the police, still more reprehensibly, had been planning to kill him. They were frightened, he said, that a sequel to *King Squealer* might expose widespread police corruption. He was acquitted, and managed to sell his story to the *Sun*.

**onanism on stage, dangers of indulging in.** *See* MCLEAN, LENNY.

**onanists.** *See* ROBERTS 'BAWDY HOUSE' BOB (for 'Mad Windham'); SALA, GEORGE AUGUSTUS.

**'One Day' Tommy.** *See* BUTLER, DETECTIVE CHIEF SUPERINTENDENT THOMAS.

**'One-Eyed' Charlie Walker.** *See* HARDING, ARTHUR.

**One-Eyed Peg.** *See* BERKLEY, THERESA.

**one-legged man buys trousers.** *See* STANSHALL, VIVIAN.

**one-legged prostitute has sex with pizza delivery man.** *See* MELLOR, DAVID.

**one-piece bathing suits.** *See* BACON, SIR FRANCIS.

**Open University, a witch at the.** *See* GRIFFITHS, DOT.

**orang-utan, the doctored jawbone of an.** *See* DAWSON, CHARLES.

**organ failure attributable to chronic drug abuse, death through multi-.** *See* BRISTOL, FREDERICK WILLIAM JOHN AUGUSTUS HERVEY, 7TH MARQUESS OF.

**organs, angelic.** *See* POCKRICH, RICHARD.

**orgasms and sneezing recommended for the release of tension.** *See* FAIRBAIRN, SIR NICHOLAS.

**orgasms decried as a drain on vital bodily fluids.** *See* SALA, GEORGE AUGUSTUS (for Dr J.L. Milton).

**orgasms during the course of arrest, experiencing.** *See* AMIRI, JULIE.

**orgies, heterosexual.** *See* BIRDWOOD, JANE, THE DOWAGER LADY; FLOWER, JOAN; GARVIE, SHEILA; KEELER, CHRISTINE.

**orgies, homosexual.** *See* BLUNT, SIR ANTHONY; BOOTHBY, ROBERT; BURGESS, GUY FRANCIS DE MONCY; DRIBERG, TOM; VASSALL, JOHN.

**orgies, mixed.** *See* AUDLEY, MERVYN CASTLEFORD, 2ND BARON.

**Orlando, the Great** (1935– ), stage hypnotist. In June 1978, at the Gaumont Theatre, Southampton, the Great Orlando announced that he would put 20 volunteers from the audience into a trance. 'You are going into a deep sleep,' he told the first subject, local electrician Bob Holliday. Mr Holliday remained alert but the Great Orlando appeared to nod off before admitting to being Mr George Rowson, wanted by police in four counties for social-security frauds. Mr Holliday was later reported to have taken up stage hypnotism as a profession.

**Orton, Arthur** (1834–98), impostor. In 1866 Orton, who was then working as a butcher under the name of Castro in Wagga Wagga, Australia, contacted Lady Tichborne claiming to be her son Roger, who had supposedly drowned at sea in 1854. Lady Tichborne, who had always believed that her son was still alive, contacted a former servant, Bogle, who was now living in New South Wales and who had known Roger Tichborne well. Castro managed to convince the elderly Bogle that he was indeed Tichborne, and Lady Tichborne sent Castro money with which to come to Europe with Mrs Castro and their two children. They met in Paris, and Lady Tichborne was immediately convinced that she had recovered her long-lost son. The rest of the family was less convinced, not least, perhaps, because Castro weighed over 21 stone whereas Roger had always been slim; further, he couldn't speak a word of French, a language in which Roger had been fluent. Castro explained this by saying that he had had an illness that had affected part of his memory.

The legal proceedings to establish the inheritance didn't come to trial until 1871, by which time Lady Tichborne had died. More than 100 people who had known Roger testified that Castro was the true claimant. However, Castro himself created a poor impression in the witness box. He didn't know his mother's maiden name; he was unfamiliar with the school that Roger had attended; and, most seriously, he had none of Roger's distinguishing tattoos. His explanation that these had faded over the years was not accepted, and it was then discovered that Castro was in reality Arthur Orton, the son of a butcher in Wapping, and was wanted in Australia under that name for horse theft. The jury rejected the claimant's case and in 1873 Orton/Castro was tried for perjury and sentenced to 14 years in prison. He was released in 1884, still insisting that he was Roger Tichborne. He sold his memoirs to a newspaper, but died penniless in London at the age of 64. His coffin was inscribed, 'Sir Roger Charles Doughty Tichborne'.

In 1998 the story was filmed by Peter Yates under the title *The Tichborne Claimant*. The butler, Bogle, was played by John Kani and the part of Orton was taken by Robert Pugh. Stephen Fry provided solid support in the role of a barrister.

**Osbaldstone, George.** *See* RACEHORSE SWITCHING.

**Osbourne, Colin 'Duke'** (1930–80), accident-prone drug smuggler who ended up in a deep freezer. Osbourne was a minor public schoolboy and gambler who had once been part of Ron and Reggie KRAY's admiring circle of associates (*see* BOLLOCKS, A SILLY). While serving five years in Maidstone prison for a firearms offence he became something of a tobacco baron, thereafter acquiring an ambition to become a major drug smuggler. In 1980 he put together an importation scheme with Lennie 'Silly Eddie' Watkins – the latter's nickname deriving from his habit of lighting his cigars in public with £20 notes. A container lorry, ostensibly carrying sanitary equipment in one direction and sports shoes in the other, set off from Pakistan to London with £2.5 million of high-grade cannabis, known as 'Paki Black', hidden in a false compartment. The operation was monitored from the start by Customs and Excise officers, and as Watkins drove the lorry out of Felixstowe docks he was shadowed by Customs officer Peter Bennett. When the convoy arrived in London's Docklands, Bennett approached the lorry and was shot dead by Watkins.

Customs and police, no less than Watkins's friends, were keen to find

Massage
Parlour
BY APPOINTMENT

FRANKLIN

"WE DON'T SEE THE MAJOR ANY MORE, BUT HIS HORSE IS STILL A REGULAR CUSTOMER!"

ABOVE The destruction of Newgate prison during the Gordon Riots of 1780 – a consequence of the sectarian rabble-rousing of **Lord George Gordon**, a half-mad aristocrat and anti-Catholic agitator.

LEFT A cartoon by Franklin which appeared in the *Sun* after **Major Ronald Ferguson** – Prince Charles's polo manager and the duchess of York's father – had been caught up in the Wigmore Street Massage Parlour Scandal of 1987.

The execution of **Robert Shirley, 2nd Earl Ferrers** at Tyburn in 1760. Ferrers was the first peer to be hanged as a common criminal, rather than suffer decapitation, a privilege reserved for aristocrats.

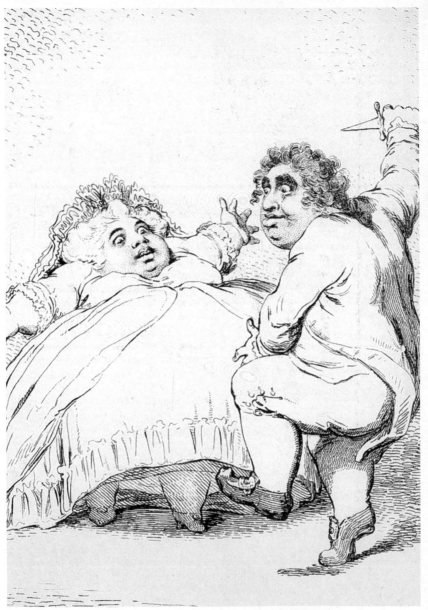

Gillray's cartoon of the politician, gambler and notorious rake **Charles James Fox.** The caption reads, 'Strike home! And I will bless thee for the Blow!'

TOP The legendary gangster **Frankie Fraser** backstage at the Cobden Club, London W10, where he had been giving readings from his most recent book, *Mad Frank's Diary*.

ABOVE **Hughie Green** and fellow light-entertainment artistes (Ted Rogers, Millicent Martin, Tommy Cooper, Barbara Windsor, Frankie Howerd and Eric Sykes) celebrate ITV's 1969 Christmas schedule.

RIGHT Imprisoned for an insurance fraud in 1992, Yuppie socialite **Darius Guppy** is photographed on his release with his loyal wife Patricia.

ABOVE **Dr W.G. Grace**, the most formidable cricketer of his day, ready to face Spofforth, the demon fast bowler from Australia.

RIGHT Admiral Nelson's mistress, **Lady Emma Hamilton**, in a portrait by George Romney.

The savage and malevolent English judge **George Jeffreys** presides at the trial of Richard Baxter, a non-conformist minister accused of libelling James II in a pamphlet.

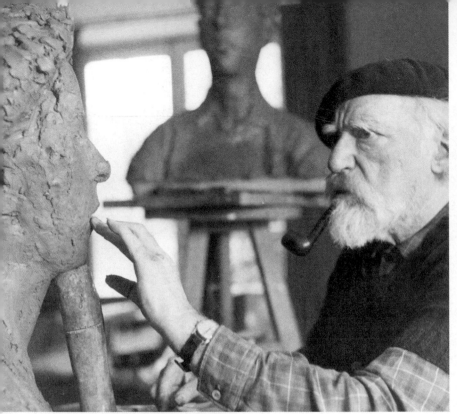

ABOVE In a 1956 photograph taken by the Soho 'character' Daniel Farson, **Augustus John** is seen at work in his studio on a sculpture.

LEFT Formerly a soccer hard man – noted for his violence on and off the pitch – **Vinnie Jones** has recently become a C-list celebrity, style icon and mute participant in gangster films.

RIGHT Before gaining notoriety as a central figure in the Profumo Scandal of 1963, **Christine Keeler** appeared in *tableaux plastiques* at Murray's Cabaret Club in Beak Street, London.

ABOVE East End gangsters, **Ronnie** (right) and **Reggie** (left) **Kray**, photographed in 1965 at the Vallance Road flat of their beloved mother, Violet.

RIGHT **John Bingham, 6th Baron Lucan**, on the occasion of his marriage in 1963 to Veronica Duncan. In 1974, and driven by an unhealthy regard for his children, Lord Lucan tried to kill their mother but instead murdered their nanny. He disappeared and is presumed dead.

Media tycoon and embezzler **Robert Maxwell** attends a ball in Tangiers with his wife Betty (right) and Malcolm Forbes (centre), an American businessman. Only Maxwell appears to have noted that the occasion was fancy dress.

LEFT Having been appointed chairman of the Football Task Force in 1998, the former Tory cabinet minister and West Kensington adulterer **David Mellor** demonstrates his ball skills in a penalty shoot-out in the street.

BELOW The rock and roll drummer **Keith Moon** in party mood with 1960s model Amanda Lear, who was born a man. Miss Lear formerly appeared at Raymond's Revuebar, Soho, as Peki D'Oslo and later became the mistress of Salvador Dali.

ABOVE A force of 2000 English and French freebooters under the leadership of the legendary Welsh pirate **Sir Henry Morgan** sack the city of Panama in 1670. The Spanish governor had hoped to defend his position with a herd of cows trained to charge the enemy but was confounded when the cows changed direction and charged the Spanish.

RIGHT A contemporary print shows **Titus Oates** – notorious inventor of the fictitious 'Popish Plot' against Charles II – standing in the pillory after his conviction for perjury in 1685.

TITUS OATES

RIGHT The celebrated madam **Cynthia Payne** gives the victory salute (albeit back to front) after her release from prison in 1980.

BELOW **Dr William Palmer**, who is thought to have murdered at least 14 people, including his friend Alfred Cook, whom he poisoned at Shrewsbury Races, thereafter picking up his winnings.

LEFT Actor and bar room brawler **Oliver Reed** pulls an amusing face for the camera in 1984.

BELOW Great Train Robbers (from left to right) Buster Edwards, Tommy Wisbey, Jim White, **Bruce Reynolds,** Roger Cordrey, Charlie Wilson and Jim Hussey at their 1979 book launch.

RIGHT The parliamentary eccentric and noted reactionary **Colonel Charles de Laet Waldo Sibthorp** – though only 43 when first elected as MP for Lincoln – dressed in a style which was already 50 years out of date. This contemporary print shows the frock coat and quizzing glass he customarily affected.

BELOW Soho crime boss **Jack Spot** shows off his scars, having got the worst of a street fight with 'Mad Frankie' Fraser.

ABOVE The former leader of the Liberal Party, **Jeremy Thorpe**, arrives at the Old Bailey during his trial in 1979 on a charge of conspiracy and incitement to murder of which he was acquitted. Gay rights activists demonstrate against what they see as anti-homosexual bias in the judicial system.

RIGHT The most celebrated pirate of the 18th century, **Edward Teach** (known as 'Blackbeard'), who stuck lighted matches under his hat and of whom it was said that 'a Fury from Hell could not look more frightful'.

**The duchess of York**, formerly Sarah Ferguson, who, according to royal insider Talbot Church (*101 Things You Didn't Know About The Royal Lovebirds*, 1986), was taught at her Berkshire boarding school 'that P for Personality is more important than looks'.

The famed leader of the Chindits in World War II, **Major-General Orde Charles Wingate**, whose personal arrangements were as unorthodox as his battle plans. On this occasion he is correctly dressed, but he usually held briefing sessions in the nude.

Osbourne, who had disappeared with the drugs. Two days later his body turned up in a freezer in Hackney. An open verdict was recorded at his inquest, and various suggestions were subsequently advanced to explain his death. These include suicide (a theory favoured by Reggie Kray in his book *Villains We Have Known*, 1994), a drug overdose, or a heart attack suffered while being questioned by former colleagues over the whereabouts of the drugs. Lennie 'Silly Eddie' Watkins was sentenced to life imprisonment for the murder of Peter Bennett and committed suicide in Parkhurst.

The case marked a decisive turning point in the distribution of cannabis. With so much money to be made, the business could no longer be left in the hands of minor public schoolboys who liked to read Herman Hesse and listen to the Grateful Dead. As one young graduate, who had made his money in the 1970s, said:

> A Customs guy stopped a lorry, opened the door and got shot. It was a shock. We thought, 'Hullo – We'd better look for another way of earning a living.'

*See also* RADCLIFFE, CHARLIE.

**Osbourne, John Michael ('Ozzy')** (1948– ), musician celebrated for biting the heads off bats. Born into a working-class family in the Midlands, Osbourne was known at school as 'Oz-brain' or 'Ozzie'. After he was expelled he tried to relieve the family's financial difficulties by working first in a slaughterhouse and then in a crematorium. He later claimed that both experiences had influenced his musical style. Neither job brought in enough money, so at the age of 18 he turned to burglary. Since he went to work wearing a pair of gloves with the fingers cut off he was soon arrested, and spent three months in jail. When he came out he stole a 24-inch television set, but while making his escape he fell off a wall and the television set landed on top of him. He was sentenced to six months in Winston Green prison, and while there displayed the recklessness that later distinguished his behaviour on stage and off. He used a sewing needle and a graphite slab to tattoo the letters O–Z–Z–Y on his left knuckles and smiling faces on his knees. He later went to jail again for punching a policeman in the mouth.

Osbourne's most famous band was Black Sabbath, established in 1969 and taking its name from a Boris Karloff film of that name. There are still people who hear the words 'Black Sabbath' and think, 'Hello – hard rock devil music.' This is to be musically ignorant, of course. Black Sabbath was originally a blues band, and there is an unmistakable blues sound on their first album. As their fame spread, a group of Satanists asked Osbourne and the band to play at their 'Night of Satan' at Stonehenge. They refused. Happily, England's head witch, Alec Sanders, was a fan of Black Sabbath and was able to tell the band that the Satanists had placed a hex on them. Osbourne asked his father to make aluminium crosses and then to have them blessed. Thereafter, the cross remained a powerful Black Sabbath symbol.

A feature of the band's act was to be verbally abusive to the audience. This made them very popular, particularly in America. By 1974 Osbourne was enjoying an enviable lifestyle. 'We bought dope and fucked anything that moved,' he recalled later:

> I was something of a madman. I can do nothing in moderation. If it's booze, I drink the place dry. If it's drugs, I take everything and then scrape the carpet for crumbs. I took LSD every day for years. I was spending about $1000 a week on drugs. I overdosed about a dozen times.

The other band members grew tired of Osbourne's unreliability, and in 1978 he was told that he was no longer wanted as their vocalist. He spent the next three months in his hotel room, sending out for pizzas and beer, and having cocaine delivered by his dealer. He was put back onto a more even keel when his girlfriend, Sharon, the daughter of his former manager, Don Arden, suggested that he start a new career as a solo artist. His first solo album, *Blizzard of Ozz*, was an immediate success.

On the American tour to promote his second album, *Diary of a Madman*, Osbourne started to throw raw meat at the audience. As the tour progressed his audiences retaliated with dead frogs, cats and snakes. At a concert in Des Moines, Iowa, someone threw a live bat on stage. Thinking it was a toy bat – or so he claimed later – Osbourne bit its head off. After the show, and for the next seven days, he had to have a rabies shot. The Animal Humane Society boycotted his concerts – an embargo that greatly added to their popularity.

In 1981 Osbourne divorced his first wife, Thelma. They had separated when he came home drunk to find a bailiff at the door and all his belongings in the street. He was told that if he stepped inside the house he would be arrested. Rather than go through complicated divorce proceedings he told Thelma to keep everything. On 4 July 1982 he married Sharon on a Honolulu beach. A few weeks later, while visiting San Antonio, Texas, he drank a bottle of Courvoisier and passed out. Sharon locked his clothes away so that he couldn't go outside and cause trouble. He solved the problem by putting on one of her dresses, later being arrested for relieving himself on the historic Alamo building. He was charged with defiling a national monument and was banned for life from performing in San Antonio.

If the incident with the bat had been an accident, the equally celebrated mishap with a dove could not be so easily explained. Osbourne and Sharon were asked to a meeting with the senior executives of his new record label, CBS, at their offices in Los Angeles. Sharon suggested that Osbourne should make a dramatic entrance, turning up with two doves, which he would release into the air. In the event, Osbourne, who was drunk, didn't like the way the executives were looking at him. Upset that they should regard him as just another product from which they could make money, he threw one dove into the air and bit the head off the other.

Within a week, Sharon had persuaded him to undergo treatment at the Betty Ford addiction centre. She achieved this by telling him that they would 'teach him to drink like a gentleman'. Osbourne took this to mean that the Betty Ford was a place of higher education where he would learn how to drink in a more sophisticated way. Accordingly, he signed in and then asked for directions to the bar.

Osbourne always defended himself against those who accused him of being a menace to society:

> Parents have called me and said, 'When my son died of a drug over-dose, your record was on the turn-table.' I can't help that. These people are freaking out anyway, and they need a vehicle for the freakouts.

'Bark at the Moon' (1983), 'Crazy Babies' (1988), 'Miracle Man' (1988) and 'Symptom of the Universe' (1982) have been among Osbourne's most popular 'tracks'.

**Ossianic epics, forged.** *See* MACPHERSON, JAMES.

**other women.** *See* BRISTOL, FREDERICK WILLIAM JOHN AUGUSTUS HERVEY, 7TH MARQUESS OF (for Lady Elizabeth Foster); BUCK, BIEN-VENIDA; CLARK, ALAN (for 'the Coven'); DE SANCHA, ANTONIA; ELLIOTT, GRACE DALRYMPLE; HAMILTON, LADY EMMA; HAMPSON, DR KEITH (for Lucious Leon); HOLME, LORD (for Tracey Kelly); KEELER, CHRISTINE; LAMBTON, ANTONY CLAUD FREDERICK (for Norma Levy); RAY, MARTHA; RICE-DAVIES, MANDY.

**Overbury, Sir Thomas.** *See* FORMAN, SIMON; HOWARD, LADY FRANCES; TURNER, ANNE.

**Owen Peel, Clarissa** (1879–1961), gambler and protagonist in a case demonstrating the benefits wives once derived from being a chattel in law. A striking and strong-willed woman, Mrs Owen Peel was dominant over her pleasant but ineffectual husband, Major 'Dickie' Owen Peel. When the couple found themselves down on their luck in the early 1920s, Mrs Owen Peel devised a racing swindle that involved backing horses that had already won. The Post Office became suspicious and the Owen Peels were prosecuted. When the case came before Mr Justice Darling, Mrs Owen Peel's lawyer argued that a married woman was irrebuttably presumed to have been coerced into wrongdoing by her husband when they were acting in concert. It was irrelevant that Mrs Owen Peel had devised the fraud and had kept what small profits then accrued. That was the law as set out in a case from 1814 (the last time this defence had been raised) and the prosecution had no answer to it. Mrs Owen Peel had to be acquitted. Captain Owen Peel pleaded guilty and received a nine-month prison sentence. The defence of coercion was no longer available to women after the Criminal Law Act 1925.

**owl sanctions second marriage.** *See* MCCARTNEY, SIR PAUL.

**Oxford, Edward** (1822–?), unsuccessful assassin. There were seven attempts to assassinate Queen Victoria, none of them successful. The first occurred in June 1840, when Oxford, an 18-year-old potboy, fired two pistol shots at the queen and the prince consort on Constitution Hill from a distance of no more than five yards. He missed with both, and the queen moved on to her destination, which was the duchess of Kent's house in Belgrave Square. Lord Palmerston, then foreign secretary, wrote:

> Viscount Palmerston humbly trusts that the failure of this atrocious attempt may be considered as an indication that your Majesty is reserved for a long and prosperous reign.

It is not known what became of Oxford, but it is unlikely that he was forgiven as easily as Lady Margaret LAMBOURNE had been after her attempt on the life of an earlier queen, Elizabeth I.

**Page, Damaris** (*c.*1620–69), the most notorious of the many brothel-keepers who in the 1650s and 1660s ran houses on the Ratcliffe Highway, a street on the river front at Wapping. The neighbourhood had attracted prostitutes of many different nationalities, including Flemish and Venetian courtesans who had a reputation for sexual expertise and were too expensive for ordinary seamen. These foreign virtuosos of the trade were patronized by aristocrats and members of the court. Page's clientele was less exalted. She was described by Samuel Pepys as 'The great bawd of the seamen'.

Born in Stepney, Page became a prostitute in her teens, and in 1640 married a man called William Baker. During the course of the next 15 years she graduated from prostitution to operating brothels. She had one on the Ratcliffe Highway that catered for seamen and dock workers, and later, when this prospered, another in Rosemary Lane for those who could afford her more expensive girls. In 1653 she married for the second time, and a year later faced the Clerkenwell magistrates on two counts. The first, of bigamy, was dismissed on the grounds that her marriage to William Baker had not been sanctified. The second related to the death of a prostitute named Eleanor Pooley while undergoing an abortion with an oyster fork. Page was charged with manslaughter and sentenced to be hanged. However, she was pregnant herself at the time and after being examined by a panel of matrons she escaped the death penalty and spent three years in Newgate prison instead. On her release she took up again as a madam and died a wealthy woman in her house on the Ratcliffe Highway.

For references to other madams, *see* BROTHELS, KEEPERS OF 'CONVENTIONAL'.

**Paget, Dorothy** (1906–60), racehorse owner. In the course of a successful career on the flat and over the jumps, Miss Paget became better known for her appearance and lifestyle than for how her horses performed – although Golden Miller won the Cheltenham Gold Cup five years in succession (1932–6). The daughter of Lord Queensborough, and in possession of a considerable fortune inherited from her maternal grandmother, Miss Paget never changed her outfit in 30 years – dressing always in a blue felt hat and a tent-shaped grey overcoat that reached down to the ground. On two or three occasions she was believed to have bought a new coat, but the replacement was always identical to its predecessor. Not that she was often seen in public. She had her dinner at 7 o'clock in the morning, slept through the day and got up for breakfast at 8.30 p.m. She spent the night telephoning her trainers and eating huge quantities of fish. As a consequence she ballooned to over 20 stone and was obliged to ride side-saddle when hunting or attending a point-to-point.

Miss Paget disliked human company, particularly that of men, which was said to make her vomit. Her last years were sad. She became a recluse, shutting herself away in Chalfont St Giles, Buckinghamshire, and having contact with no one except her small, exclusively female entourage. Such was her horror of outside agencies that when her house caught fire in 1959 while she was in bed she allowed it to be burned to the ground rather than summon help. 'I have no intention of moving until the flames have reached my pyjama legs,' she said. It was only when smoke filled her bedroom that she put on her overcoat and hat and went down to the garden. 'Now you may send for the fire brigade,' she said, observing the ruins of her home from a deckchair on the lawn.

**Paget, Sir Richard** (1876–1949), amateur scientist and inventor of Paget Gorman Signed Speech. *See* GLENCONNER, PAMELA LADY.

**Painter, John the** (1752–77), revolutionary and arsonist. In December 1776 a fire broke out in the rope house at the Royal Navy dockyard in Portsmouth. Six weeks later several warehouses were burned to the ground at Bristol docks. At first, American agents were suspected of starting the fires in order to damage English shipping. The Americans retaliated by blaming Tory *agents provocateurs*. After further investigations, the police arrested an itinerant house painter named James Aitken, later known as 'John the Painter'.

Born in Edinburgh, Aitken had come to London, where, having failed to make a living at his trade, he tried his hand at shoplifting and highway robbery. He had then visited America, and had taken part in the Boston Tea Party. Having returned to England as a supporter of the American Revolution, he had hoped to damage British shipping with the fires at Portsmouth and Bristol. It emerged after his arrest that he was not in the pay of American interests, though he may have been encouraged in his plan by Silas Deane, a member of Congress whom he had met in Paris. Aitken himself admitted:

> I spent two days in the contemplation of this design, and promised myself immortal honour in the accomplishment of it. I was persuaded it would entitle me to the first rank in America, and flattered myself with the ambition of becoming the admiration of the world.

John the Painter fulfilled no such ambition. He was tried at Winchester in March 1777, convicted and sentenced to death. He was hanged at Portsmouth on 10 March and his body was displayed in chains at the harbour mouth.

**Paisley, Ian Richard Kyle** (1926– ), Northern Ireland Protestant cleric and Unionist politician, sometimes referred to as the 'Big Man' due to his impressive physical presence and stentorian voice. In 1951 he founded his own denomination, the Free Presbyterian Church of Ulster. In 1969 he entered the Northern Ireland parliament as Protestant Unionist MP for Bannside, becoming leader of the Opposition in 1972. Staunchly committed to the union with the United Kingdom, his political career has been marked by high drama, protests, resignations and barrel-chested oratory. His behaviour has sometimes been of a kind that might have been better accompanied by a comedian's slapstick. In 1988, he was first pinned to the floor and then frogmarched out of a meeting of the European Parliament, when he interrupted a speech being delivered by Pope John Paul II. As the pope began to speak, Paisley stood up and displayed a red sign on which was painted, 'John Paul II ANTICHRIST'. He accompanied this gesture by shouting, 'I refuse you as an enemy and Antichrist with all your false doctrine.' Enthusiasts of anagrams have noticed that rearranging the letters of 'Ian Paisley' gives, 'Yea pal, I sin!', or, with some licence, 'Vile IRA Pansey' and 'Ideally cranky Irish ape', the latter contributions coming from the Catholic comedian, Dave Allen.

**Palmer, Patsy** (1972– ), troubled actress. She's looking more relaxed now that she's discovered who she really is.
*See* BACK, TO HELL AND.

**Palmer, William** (1824–56), physician and gambler, known as the 'Rugeley Poisoner'. Dr Palmer was a genial man, the owner of several racehorses, a lover of the good life but without the means to support it. His career had been studded with unfortunate fatalities even before the sudden collapse at the races of his friend and fellow owner, Alfred Cook. Among those who had already died were his mother-in-law, from whom he inherited property, a racing friend to whom he owed £800, and his wife, whom he had recently insured for £13,000. All these had gone unremarked, but suspicion was aroused when Alfred Cook was taken ill, and then died in agony, after a visit from Palmer, who gave apoplexy as the cause.

Palmer and Cook had attended Shrewsbury races together. Palmer, who was already in financial difficulties, lost heavily. Cook was on a lucky streak and after his horse won the last race, he and Palmer celebrated at the bar. Cook suddenly keeled over and Palmer, after a show of concern, volunteered to pick up his winnings. With these, he paid off his most pressing debts, and then arranged for Cook to be taken to the Talbot Arms Hotel, which was opposite Palmer's house in Rugeley, Staffordshire. After further treatment by Palmer, Cook died on 21 November 1885. Cook's stepfather was suspicious, and an autopsy conducted by Dr Alfred Taylor – the leading toxicologist of the day and the author of the first standard work on medical jurisprudence – showed traces of antimony in Cook's stomach. Palmer was arrested and tried at the Old Bailey. He was found guilty of Cook's murder and hanged outside Stafford jail on 14 June 1856. It is thought that he may have murdered as many as 14 people.

**Palmer Tomkinson, Tara** (1972– ), self-styled 'It Girl', or 'posh tart'. The former term, current in the later 1920s (after Clara Bow in *It*, 1927), was revived in the 1990s to describe a young woman of noticeable 'sex appeal' who occupied herself by shoe shopping and party-going. The most conspicuous were sometimes rewarded with their own columns in the *Sunday Times*. Literary snobs criticized this practice, but were confounded by the editor, who pointed out that it was unlikely to lower the tone of a paper that already employed Michael Winner (*see* REED, OLIVER). The term 'posh tart' was adopted as an alternative label, to distinguish the type from her equally hedonistic but commoner half-cousin, 'Essex girl'. 'Posh' may nevertheless be an ironic attribution (as in 'Posh' Spice – the cognomen of Victoria Beckham, formerly of the Spice Girls pop group).

An appearance in October 2000 as a guest on a television chat show hosted by the comedian, Frank Skinner, highlighted difficulties Miss Palmer Tomkinson had experienced with drink and drugs. She is reported to be on poor terms with the prince of Wales. Their friendship cooled after she offered Prince William sexual guidance on board a boat. It has been discovered that her name is an anagram of 'I am a plonker. Not smart'.

In the final phase of the assault on the Taliban and al-Qa'ida network in Afghanistan in late 2001, Osama bin Laden's followers mounted a final stand in the Tora Bora cave complex in the southeast of the country. This hideout was referred to by British special forces as 'Tora Bora Tomkinson'. It has been said that Frank Skinner has the appearance of a retired northern jockey.

For another 'posh tart', Lady Victoria Hervey, *see* BRISTOL, FREDERICK WILLIAM JOHN AUGUSTUS HERVEY, 7TH MARQUESS OF.

**Panacea Society, the.** Since the society's foundation in 1929 by Mrs Mabel Barltrop, its members have been doing up a house in Bedford for the use of Christ when he returns for the Second Coming. It has new carpets throughout, and a new kitchen and bathroom, but, as Mrs Ruth Klein, the most elderly of the society's trustees, has pointed out, these renovations may prove unnecessary. 'Christ won't need a shower,' she has explained, 'because he will have a radiant body.'

In 1999 the society found itself under the scrutiny of the Charity Commissioners. They discovered that it had accumulated, at a conservative estimate, £15 million in property and stocks, which generate more than £500,000 a year in income, and was spending none of it. According to the society's treasurer, 85-year-old John Coghill, a hard-headed Scot, the trustees' behaviour in this respect was perfectly proper. All the money was being saved for Christ to spend when he arrived in Bedford. As Mr Coghill has observed, 'The Lord worked as a carpenter the first time. He will still need money this time.'

The Charity Commissioners took a different view of the matter. Accumulating goods and cash for a future event is deemed not to be in accordance with the English law on charitable status. The society was forced to auction large quantities of antiques, jewellery, paintings and other valuables left to it by the 120,000 members it had in its heyday in the 1930s.

However, the society would never agree to sell its most valued possession – a box that once belonged to Joanna SOUTHCOTT, an 18th-century religious figure, described by her followers as a prophet. Southcott, who claimed to receive messages from God, made predictions and sealed them in a box, thereafter ruling that this should only be opened at a time of national emergency and in the presence of 24 bishops of the Church of England. For the past 200 years the holders of the box have been trying to persuade various archbishops of Canterbury to open the box and share Southcott's final visions with the world – a proposal that successive archbishops have rejected. Throughout the 20th century the society placed advertisements in the *Daily Mail* and the *Sunday Telegraph* entreating the public to petition the Anglican Church to change its mind. 'Crime and banditry and the distress of nations and perplexity will continue until the bishops open the box,' has been characteristic copy.

For its part, the church has remained unimpressed by the society's mixture of 19th-century biblical literalism and early 20th-century science, as expounded by senior trustee, Mrs Klein. 'The sin of Adam and Eve was having sex at the wrong time of the month,' Mrs Klein explained on local radio at the time of the auction:

> It's an important eugenic fact. In spite of that, Adam and Eve lived until they were 930. All the patriarchs did. Things went wrong when the people with souls began to intermarry with other races, which

still had animal souls. This brought down their life span, and accounts for the immense cruelty of some races, those with genetic links to races without souls. The Ten Lost Tribes of Israel made their way across Europe – the signs cannot be refuted – and arrived in England as the Angles, Saxons, Danes and Normans. So England is the second Promised Land and Britain has been the great nation which God promised to Abraham.

Mrs Mabel Barltrop, the widow of a vicar, founded the Panacea Society in the 1920s when she began to receive messages from God. With her followers she set up the house in Bedford with 24 bedrooms, furnished and ready for the 24 bishops. Asked why Bedford was chosen, Mrs Klein has explained that it is the site of the Garden of Eden. 'It's a lovely town, very pretty, with the river and everything ...'

It is believed that the society's active membership has dwindled. From 120,000 in the 1930s, it may now be down to 5.

**paper bags, ministers' heads in.** *See* THISTLEWOOD, ARTHUR.

**papering the house.** A term current in theatrical circles to describe the purchase of tickets by an impresario for his own show. The intention is to boost the box-office receipts above the figure at which the theatre's owner can give the visiting producer notice to leave. Since the contract between the theatre owner and the producer always refers to the *bona fide* sale of seats to the public, the practice is a fraud perpetrated by the producer.

One of the least successful attempts to keep a play running by this means involved J.P. Donleavy's *Fairy Tales of New York*, which opened at the Comedy Theatre in March 1961. The reviews were generous and business was encouraging. With the approach of Easter, however, audiences fell away and there seemed a danger that the box-office receipts would drop below the figure at which the theatre's proprietor, Sir Donald Albery, could give the play notice. The producer, David CONYERS, thought that if the play survived this difficult period it might yet run throughout the summer. He therefore decided to inject some £2000 into the box office himself.

Papering the house is not as simple as might be supposed. It would look suspicious if the producer presented himself at the box office with a request for 80 front stalls. The tickets have to be bought in small quantities by apparently genuine theatregoers. Conyers withdrew his last £2000 from the bank and passed it over to his 76-year-old general manager, Bert Leywood. Leywood made his way to Berwick Street fruit market where he distributed the cash among the assembled barrow boys with the instruction that they should go immediately to the Comedy Theatre and buy front stalls for Donleavy's play. An honourable minority did as it had been asked. A sudden queue of greengrocers at the Comedy's box office alerted

Sir Donald Albery, who, to put a stop to any irregularities, posted his son Ian in the foyer. Soon a party of Amish elders from Pennsylvania arrived seeking tickets for that night's performance. Ian Albery, taking them to be actors hired by Conyers, tried to pull their beards off and then drove them from his theatre. Moments later, J.P. Donleavy, who knew nothing of Conyers's plan to keep the play running, arrived at the box office, wishing to buy seats for friends later in the week. Ian Albery stepped forward and accused him of conspiracy in the plot. Donleavy, who had once king-punched Brendan BEHAN unconscious in a Dublin pub, boxed Albery to the floor of his own theatre.

Conyers was later rebuked by Sir Donald Albery, who at the time was papering the house at the Lyric Theatre, Shaftesbury Avenue, in an attempt to extend the run of a musical, *Irma La Douce*, against the wishes of his partner in the enterprise, Hugh 'Binkie' Beaumont. Mr Beaumont wanted the theatre for a production of *How Green Was My Valley* by Emlyn Williams.

**Park, Frederick William.** *See* BOULTON, ERNEST.

**parliamentary candidate of all time, most unsuccessful.** *See* BOAKS, BILL.

**parrots.** *See* BEDFORD, JOHN ROBERT RUSSELL, 12TH DUKE OF; BIGGAR, JOSEPH; FLYNN, ROBERT; RUBELL, IDA.

**parrots that call for a taxi out of the window.** *See* BUCKLAND, FRANCIS TREVELYAN.

**partridge, teaching yourself to think like a.** *See* NICKERSON, SIR JOSEPH.

**partridge shoot, peppered during a.** *See* ELWES, JOHN; NICKERSON, SIR JOSEPH.

**Pavry, Bapsybanoo.** *See* WINCHESTER, BAPSY, MARCHIONESS OF.

**Payne, Cynthia** (1934– ), madam and central figure in the 'Sex for Luncheon Vouchers Case' which caught the public imagination in 1980. 'I have never been interested in sex,' proclaimed Mrs Payne, after her conviction for running a brothel. Evidence at her trial pointed to the same conclusion. Perhaps it was this uncomplicated attitude that brought her the sort of popularity the *Carry On* ... series of films enjoyed, and saved her from the kind of judicial rebuke that, ten years earlier, Miss Janie JONES had received from Judge King-Hamilton QC (*see also* ST CLAIR, LINDI).

On 21 April 1980 Mrs Payne's detached house in Ambleside Avenue, Streatham, was raided by the police. They found 17 men – including a vicar, three accountants, a barrister, a retired wing commander and a member of the House of Lords – queuing in an orderly manner on the stairs. Each was holding a £25 luncheon voucher that they could exchange for sex with three prostitutes supplied by Mrs Payne.

On the first day of Mrs Payne's trial at the Inner London Crown Court before Judge Brian Palmer QC, a police constable described his encounter in the bathroom with a man who was wearing an evening frock, and called himself Amanda. Amanda was sitting on the rim of the bath with a lady at his knee. When the police burst in, she sprang to her feet and Amanda toppled backwards into the bath. The constable acknowledged that it was Amanda's own fault. A sign on the door clearly asked visitors not to fornicate in the bathroom.

On the second day of the trial a man appeared in court dressed as a French maid, and calling himself Isobel. Isobel said he had been groped by a 'very fat guest', who had later turned out to be an undercover policeman (for similar instances, *see* HAMPSON, KEITH; THIN BLUE JEANS, THE). Isobel further alleged that another policeman, PC Taylor, had arrived incognito and in eye makeup and had asked him for a date. PC Taylor described how he had gone upstairs with Isobel, who had explained that his tastes lay in the direction of bondage and humiliation. While PC Taylor and Isobel were queuing for a vacant bedroom, a model named Britt emerged with an elderly man. 'He apologized for taking so long,' said PC Taylor.

On the third day of the trial, items taken from the house were displayed in court, including a kitchen spatula. Judge Palmer remarked that:

> It is notorious that judges lead sheltered lives but I cannot for the moment see the significance of the kitchen spatula – or, for that matter, of the other items.

In a later exchange, Mrs Payne assured the court that she herself never indulged in sex:

> I know it makes some people happy but to me it's like having a cup of tea. One of my slaves said that sex with me would be like growing spuds in a Ming vase.

Police claimed that in the course of twelve days, 249 men and 50 women had visited the Streatham villa for the purposes of sex. Nevertheless, Mrs Payne's neighbours were surprised to discover that she had been anything other than a respectable housewife. It was noted by the press that the house in which Dr Johnson liked Mrs Thrale to 'exercise severity on him' was situated within a stone's throw of Mrs Payne's premises. Amusing comparisons were drawn with the retired wing commander, an ex-bomber pilot, who apparently shared Dr Johnson's tastes. At one point during her testimony, Mrs Payne had described her clients as the sort of men who 'do the housework and in return like to be insulted'.

The judge was unimpressed and Mrs Payne was sentenced to 18 months in prison and a fine of £2000. Some MPs criticized the verdict, pointing out that nuisance should be established in cases of this kind, and arguing that Mrs Payne's operation had been perfectly discreet. On 15 May 1980 her sentence was cut to six months on appeal, but the judge refused to squash it altogether, saying of the ladies involved that, 'some were common prostitutes, while others were married women who were on the premises for the purposes of earning pin money.' Many failed to follow the logic of the argument, and the judge was seen by certain women's groups as somewhat unenlightened. What women, married or otherwise, did to earn pin money seemed not to be the issue at stake.

Mrs Payne emerged from prison in August, declaring that 'I have quit the sex scene.' Some people have argued that the activities at 32 Ambleside Avenue suggested that she had never been part of it. Her many subsequent appearances on early-evening chat shows, together with *Personal Services*, a film of her life starring Julie Walters and directed by Terry Jones, a former member of the 'Monty Python' comedy group, pointed to the same conclusion.

Former distinguished residents of Ambleside Avenue include the comedian Tommy Trinder, and William Meldin, the 14th earl of Streatham who was the inspiration for Tarzan of the Apes. In 1868 Meldin was shipwrecked off the coast of West Africa at the age of 11 and spent 15 years in the jungle before moving to Ambleside Avenue.

**payola scandals.** *See* JONES, JANIE.

**Peace, Charles** (1832–1879), picture framer, thief and murderer. The crime writer and literary critic Julian Symons dubbed Peace 'the greatest and most naturally gifted criminal England has produced.' Born in Manchester, the son of an animal trainer, Peace suffered an accident in childhood that left him crippled. To hide the loss of one finger he wore a false arm made of gutta-percha with a steel plate and a hook on the end of it. Possessing great skill in disguise, he was described in a police notice as 'almost a monkey of a man, with the power of pulling about and altering his features so as to make his face unrecognizable even by his relations and intimates'.

In 1876 Peace shot and killed a policeman who surprised him while he was burgling a house outside Manchester. Two brothers were arrested for the murder, and one of them, William Habron, was sentenced to death. Peace attended the trial, which he later said he had greatly enjoyed. At his home in Sheffield, where he carried on a respectable trade as a picture framer and retailer of musical instruments, he became friendly with a civil engineer named Dyson, and his wife Katherine. Although married himself, Peace pursued Mrs Dyson with some determination. At first she encouraged him, sending him notes when her husband was away. However, when he became too persistent in his advances she began to see him as an embarrassment. To get away from Peace, Mr and Mrs Dyson were obliged to move to another suburb of Sheffield. Peace followed them, accosting Mrs Dyson outside her house with the words, 'I'm here to annoy you, and I'll annoy you wherever you go.' One night she went to the outside lavatory and found Peace standing there with a revolver. Her scream alerted her husband, who chased Peace into the street. Here, Peace fired two shots, one of them entering Dyson's brain.

Peace was now a wanted man. He moved to London, where he rented a villa in Peckham. Notwithstanding the fact that he had established his wife and mistress, Susan Thompson, under one roof, he lived a life of extreme respectability as John Ward, a gentleman of independent means with a taste for dabbling in scientific inventions, such as an improved brush for cleaning railway carriages. By night he practised his profession of thief, driving to do a job in his pony and trap and keeping his tools in a violin case. One night he was caught while carrying out a burglary in Blackheath. He shot at and wounded a policeman before his capture.

The police had no idea who their prisoner was, but Peace was undone by his own ingenuity. He wrote a letter to a fellow inventor, and through it his identity as the respectable Mr Ward became known. His mistress Susan Thompson ('a terrible one for the drink and snuff', according to Peace) then informed the police that Mr Ward was really Charlie Peace. He was sentenced to life imprisonment for wounding the policeman at Blackheath, and then taken to Sheffield to stand trial for killing Arthur Dyson. As the train was nearing Sheffield he escaped through the window of the carriage, which had been opened by his guards so that he could urinate out of it, but he injured himself as he fell and was soon recaptured.

Peace was tried for murder at Leeds assizes, found guilty and sentenced to death. In the condemned cell at Armley Prison he confessed that he had also killed a policeman in Manchester. Fortunately, the death sentence on William Habron had been commuted to life imprisonment, and he was released with a full pardon and awarded £1000 compensation. Before his execution Peace observed to the chaplain who attended him that, 'My great mistake, sir, has been this – in all my career I have used ball cartridge. I ought to have used blank.' On the scaffold he asked the hangman, William Marwood, if he could have a drink. Marwood said no, and pulled the lever. 'I expected difficulties,' Marwood said afterwards, 'because he was such a desperate man, but bless you, my dear sir, he passed away like a summer's eve.'

**peacock shot by would-be assassin.** *See* LAMBOURNE, LADY MARGARET.

**peepshows, Soho.** *See* KNIGHT, RONNIE.

**peer, Britain's most married.** *See* KIMBERLEY, JOHN WODEHOUSE, 4TH EARL OF.

**peer shocked to learn that novel is fiction.** *See* REDESDALE, CLEMENT NAPIER THOMAS FREEMAN MITFORD, 2ND BARON.

**Pen Club Killing, the.** *See* NASH, JIMMY.

**penis, exhibiting one's tattooed.** *See* REED, OLIVER.

***Penis, Here Lies Johnny.*** *See* MONTALK, COUNT GEOFFREY WLADISLAW VAILE POTOI.

**penis, unusual feats achieved with a.** *See* BINDON, JOHN.

**penis examined in chambers by a Harley Street consultant, a government minister's.** *See* KEELER, CHRISTINE.

**penis in the heavens, assertion that the God of the Old Testament was a mighty.** *See* ALLEGRO, JOHN.

**Penman, Jem the.** *See* SAWARD, JAMES TOWNSHEND.

**penny gaffs.** Places of entertainment that disregarded the requirement that, in the interests of 'good manners, decorum and the public peace', stage shows should be subject to censorship by the lord chamberlain. Operating in London in the 19th century as an unlicensed theatrical underworld, they consisted of large shops or warehouses, gutted to their bare walls with a platform at one end to serve as a stage.

A flourishing gaff in Smithfield was visited by the journalist Henry Mayhew in the 1840s. The shopfront had been altered to display crude paintings of comic singers in 'humorous attitudes'. A band was perched on a table playing dance tunes. The audience was young. Mayhew described its members as being between 8 and 20 years old, the girls in polka-dot dresses and with feathers in their bonnets. A boy coming out of an earlier performance was asked whether there had been 'flash dancing' by the girls in the show. He was able to say that there had. 'Lots! Show their legs and all, prime!' The performance consisted of singing and dancing, with the comic songs provided by draymen wearing humorous cravats and the dances by young girls who had more energy than skill.

Mayhew, who was able as a rule to preserve a proper journalistic neutrality when investigating society's disagreeable underside, could not disguise his shock on this occasion. Having deplored a comic song, 'the whole point of which consisted in the mere utterance of some filthy word at the end of each stanza', he went on to describe a ballet 'between a man and a woman dressed as a country clown':

> The most disgusting attitudes were struck, the most immoral attitudes represented, without one dissenting voice ... Here were two ruffians degrading themselves each time they stirred a limb, and forcing into the brains of the childish audience before them thoughts that must embitter a lifetime, and descend from father to child like some bodily infirmity.

Thanks to publishers such as W. West, the songs survived after the penny gaffs themselves were replaced by the great music halls of London. In the 1850s a number of them were collected in *The Rambler's Flash Songster*, *The Flash Chaunter* and *The Cuckold's Nest of Choice Songs*. The *doubles entendres* that had offended Mayhew were staples of such numbers as 'The Slashing Costermonger and his Donkey':

> I'm quite a sporting karacter
> I wisits flashy places,
> Last year, my old voman washed my ass
> An' I went to Ascot races.
>
> I got jist by the royal booth,
> And there – it is no farces, sirs,
> The king, he often bowed at me,
> While the queen looked at my ass, sirs.

*See also* NICHOLSON, 'BARON' RENTON (for 'judge and jury' shows).

**performing plays in Harold Nicolson's apartment.** *See* HERBERT, DAVID.

**'Pervert, How to Pick a'.** (*Sunday Mirror* article.) *See* VASSALL, JOHN.

**philanderers.** *See* BIGGAR, JOSEPH; BLACKBURNE, ARCHBISHOP LANCELOT; BOOTHBY, ROBERT; CHILD, BENJAMIN; CLARK, ALAN; DILKE, SIR CHARLES; GREEN, HUGHIE; HERVEY, AUGUSTUS; ROUSE, ALFRED ARTHUR.
*See also* LIBERTINES.

**philosophers in overalls.** *See* SPENCER, HERBERT.

**physicians, allegedly or actually villainous.** *See* ADAMS, DR JOHN

BODKIN; CREAM, DR THOMAS NEILL; CRIPPEN, DR HAWLEY HARVEY; KNOX, DR ROBERT; PALMER, WILLIAM.
*See also* QUACKS.

**physicians, phoney.** *See* BASS, HARRY 'THE DOCTOR'; BINT, PAUL.
*See also* QUACKS.

**piano, squat-lifting a grand.** *See* DEMPSEY, ANDREW.

**piano at a retirement home, sentenced to play the.** *See* MILLER, SIR ERIC.

**piano balanced on one's chest, singing with a.** *See* ELLIS, SID 'JAZZER'.

**piano down the Cresta Run, riding a grand.** *See* YORK, SARAH MARGARET, DUCHESS OF.

**pickpockets, 'Artful Dodgers' and cut-purses.** *See* BLAKE, JOSEPH; DIVER, JENNY; FLOOD, MATTHEW; PINKINDINDIES.

**pig, riding through Edinburgh on a.** *See* GORDON, LORD GEORGE.

**pig destroys Angelic Organ.** *See* POCKRICH, RICHARD.

**pigeons dyed pink, orange, green and blue.** *See* HEBER-PERCY, ROBERT.

**Pig-Faced Lady, the.** *See* MISS STEVENS, THE PIG-FACED LADY.

**Pigott, Richard** (1851–90), hoax letter writer and instigator of a political smear campaign against Charles Stewart Parnell. In April 1887 *The Times* published a damaging series of articles attacking the Irish leader. These included a letter attributed to Parnell in which he expressed extreme pleasure at the 1882 Phoenix Park Murders, in which Lord Frederick Charles Cavendish – the newly appointed goodwill emissary to Ireland – had been assassinated in Dublin. When *The Times* published further letters confirming Parnell's approval of the killings, outrage was expressed in the House of Commons, and throughout the country. Parnell denounced the letters as forgeries, but was advised by his lawyers not to take legal action. This advice looked sound when a former MP, F.H. O'Donnell, who had also been implicated, sued *The Times* and lost.

In the course of the trial, however, a number of other letters alleged to have been written by Parnell – and which were even more damaging than those already published – surfaced. Parnell now demanded that a select committee be appointed to examine the letters. Parliament eventually agreed to appoint a commission of judges to carry out a full investigation. In court, Parnell's supporters were able to trace the forged letters to their source, one Richard Pigott, who had sold the letters to *The Times* for a considerable sum. During cross-examination by Sir Charles Russell, Pigott was required to write out certain passages from the letters. He repeated the same spelling mistakes as appeared in the texts. The next day he left the country, having left a signed confession with Parnell's supporters. This was introduced in court, and Parnell was exonerated. In composing and selling the letters Pigott's only motive had been money. He committed suicide in a Spanish hotel while waiting to be arrested. *The Times* paid Parnell several thousand pounds in an out-of-court settlement, and £25,000 in costs.

**pigs, priest steals parishioners'.** *See* OATES, TITUS.

**pigs and potatoes, paying the fees at Eton in.** *See* SITWELL, SIR GEORGE RERESBY.

**pigs in fox-hunting, unsuccessful attempt to use.** *See* HIRST, JEMMY.

**pigs rooting up graves.** *See* FREE, THE REVEREND EDWARD DRAX.

**pigs to jump hurdles, teaching the headmaster's.** *See* HIRST, JEMMY.

**Piltdown Man.** *See* DAWSON, CHARLES.

**pinkindindies.** Expert swordsmen, usually the sons of gentlemen, who formed themselves into gangs and ran wild through the streets of 18th-century Dublin. They dressed formally and carried a small sword or, when in undress, a *couteau de chasse*. Violent pickpockets, they robbed their victims by threatening to nick them with the points of their swords. They also engaged in the pastime of abducting prosperous ladies.

　　*See also* ABDUCTION CLUBS; PICKPOCKETS, 'ARTFUL DODGERS' AND CUT-PURSES.

**pinned like a butterfly to a padded ladder.** *See* BERKLEY, THERESA.

**piranhas in the bidet.** *See* MOON, KEITH.

**pirates.** *See* BONNY, ANNE (which article also deals with Mary Read); GOW,

JOHN; KIDD, WILLIAM; LANCEY, JOHN; MORGAN, SIR HENRY; TEACH, EDWARD; TRELAWNY, EDWARD.

**pistol butt, attempting suicide by repeatedly striking one's temple with a.** *See* HACKMAN, THE REVEREND JAMES.

**Pitts, Shirley** (1928–92), thief. Born into a distinguished south London crime family (her brothers were the bank robbers Charlie and Adgie Pitts), Shirley earned the title in the 1950s of 'Queen of the Shoplifters'. She had perfected the art in her teens and by the age of 20 was acknowledged to be the most skilful practitioner in the country. She organized a team that looted Harrods, her favourite target, and other major stores, using two or three accomplices to cause a diversion while she and two others helped themselves to whatever caught their eye at the perfume and jewellery counters. While the European Economic Community was still at the discussion stage, she arranged shoplifting expeditions to Paris, Rome and Berlin.

When she died in 1992 Miss Pitts was buried in a blue Zandra Rhodes creation that she had picked up only the week before. A cortege of 15 Daimlers cruised 20 miles through London to her resting place in a Tooting cemetery where a trumpeter and guitarist played Irving Berlin's 'Heaven, I'm in heaven ...' There was a large floral tribute in the shape of a Harrods shopping bag. Her epitaph was spelled out in flowers on her grave, 'Gone shopping'.

**Plum, Zelda.** *See* JONES, JANIE.

**plumber's body occupied by Tibetan lama.** *See* RAMPA, LOBSANG.

**Pockrich, Richard** (1690–1759), inventor. Pockrich failed at everything he turned his hand to, thereby running through a fortune of £4000 a year left to him by his father. Such was the whimsical nature of his schemes that comparisons were made with Swift's scientists on the island of Laputa. Among them was a project to convert the bishop of Tuam's residence outside Dublin into a tearoom. The bishop refused to move, even after Pockrich had approached him several times with presents of pigeons. Another moneymaking idea was to plant vineyards on undrained stretches of bog land, thus laying the foundations of an Irish wine-making industry. When nothing came of this, Pockrich tried, unsuccessfully, to establish a goose farm in County Wicklow.

More ambitious was Pockrich's proposal for achieving eternal life by means of blood transfusions. Transfusions had been performed on animals, but with mixed results. Pockrich was optimistic, and his instructions precise:

> Take an influx tube in the nature of a siphon, fix it to the extreme ends in the veins of two different people, the one youthful, adult and sanguine, the other aged, decrepit and withered. The redundant fermenting blood of the one will immediately flow like wine decanted into the shrivelled veins of the other. The effects will be no less surprising. The wrinkled skin braces, the flesh plumps up, the eyes sparkle.

Pockrich was aware that the end of death as a human experience might have disadvantages, particularly for doctors and lawyers, so he suggested an act of Parliament laying down that 'anyone attaining the age of 999 years, shall be deemed to all Intents and Purposes dead in law.' This would enable relatives to claim their inheritances, and vicars to go to court to claim burial fees from legally dead 999-year-old parishioners.

In fact, Pockrich did achieve one success – his invention of a musical instrument that he called the Angelic Organ. This consisted of a number of glass tumblers filled with water to different levels and played by running a finger round the rim. Musical glasses were not an original idea. In the *Kama Sutra*, playing on glasses filled with water was one of the 64 practices recommended in the sexual education of a young girl. Pockrich developed his own glasses after disappointing results with an instrument consisting of 20 drums. Varying from the highest treble to the deepest bass, the drums were arranged in a circle to be played by one musician. 'He devoted many months,' a friend wrote, 'wholly to practising upon and the improving of this most extraordinary instrument – to the great mortification of all lovers of martial music.'

Confirmation of the Angelic Organ's power was confirmed for Pockrich when two bailiffs came to arrest him for non-payment of taxes. 'Gentlemen,' Pockrich had said, 'I am your prisoner, but before I do myself the honour to attend you, give me leave as a humble performer in musick to entertain you with a tune.' 'Sir,' one of the bailiffs had answered, 'we came here to execute our warrant, not to hear tunes.' But with the bribe of a bottle of wine they were persuaded to listen to his favourite piece, which he played so affectingly that they were moved to forget their duties, and left without making the arrest.

Shortly after this, Pockrich visited a seaside tavern where he met John Carteret Pilkington, the son of Swift's favourite, Mrs Laetitia Pilkington. By the end of the evening Pilkington, who claimed to be a singer, was offered a job. While Pockrich played the Angelic Organ, Pilkington would sing. For this he would receive £100 a year and board and lodging. In the meantime, however, Pilkington would have to pay for the evening's drinks and also for a coach to return them to Pockrich's lodgings. When they arrived, Pilkington was disappointed to find that Pockrich lived in:

... the most littered and dirty hole I have ever seen; the furniture consisted of an old tawdry bed, one rush-bottomed chair, a frame with a number of large glasses on it, and the case of a violin cello.

Pilkington was not discouraged, however, and during the next few weeks the two of them practised their skills, with Pockrich tapping and rubbing the glasses while Pilkington sang. Once accomplished enough, on their own estimation, to appear in public, they decided to take the instrument to London and hold its debut performance there. Arrangements were made, but disaster overtook the enterprise when, three hours before the first concert, a pig made its way into the auditorium and knocked all the glasses to the floor. The audience had its money refunded, the Angelic Organ was rebuilt and posters were printed advertising a new concert in February 1744. This turned out to be a triumph. After years of failure, Pockrich became famous and moderately well off. The poet Thomas Gray compared the sounds made by the Angelic Organ to the singing of nightingales, and Oliver Goldsmith mentioned them in *The Vicar of Wakefield* (1766). Popular composers of the day wrote music for him. Gluck gave a concert on a refined version of the Organ which used only spring water. And anecdotal evidence suggests that Benjamin Franklin followed suit with a 120-glass Armonica on which he played new compositions provided by Mozart and Beethoven.

A year after the first concert, and temporarily unbalanced, perhaps, by such unaccustomed good fortune, Pockrich, a 50-year-old bachelor, married Mrs Margaret Winter, a widow who had convinced him that she had ample private means, but who brought him nothing but debts. She ran up substantial dressmakers' bills and then ran off with an actor. The couple were drowned in a boat accident off the Scottish coast.

Pockrich thereafter devoted himself to plans for the disposition of his body after death. His executors were directed to preserve his corpse in spirits and place it in a public place for the benefit of future generations. But in 1759, while on a visit to London, he was burned to death in a fire at Hamlin's Coffee House, and nothing remained of him to be displayed.

**poets, anti-Welsh Welsh.** *See* JONES, CHARLES HORACE.

**poets, fraudulent.** *See* CHATTERTON, THOMAS; IRELAND, WILLIAM HENRY; MACPHERSON, JAMES.

**poets, scrounging.** *See* BOYCE, SAMUEL; DERMODY, THOMAS.

**poets whose wives are little better than strumpets.** *See* BOYCE, SAMUEL.

**poisoners, actual or alleged.** *See* ADAMS, DR JOHN BODKIN; ARM-STRONG, MAJOR HERBERT ROWSE; BARBER, SUSAN; BARTLETT, ADELAIDE; COTTON, MARY ANN; CREAM, DR THOMAS NEILL; CRIPPEN, DR HAWLEY HARVEY; EDMUNDS, CHRISTINA; FERNSEED, MARGARET; GREGORY, MAUNDY; HOWARD, LADY FRANCES; MAYBRICK, FLORENCE ELIZABETH; PALMER, WILLIAM; SMITH, MADELEINE; TURNER, ANNE; WAINEWRIGHT, THOMAS GRIFFITHS; YOUNG, GRAHAM.

**poison-pen crusades, perpetrators of.** *See* FORSTER, JAMES.

**Poke, Miss Polly.** *See* SALA, GEORGE AUGUSTUS.

**police, purchasing pornography from the.** *See* MOODY, DETECTIVE CHIEF SUPERINTENDENT WILLIAM.

**Pollard, Su.** *See* GREEN, HUGHIE.

**ponce, inadvisability of calling a gangster a half-baked fucking.** *See* MR SMITH'S.

**ponce turned robber.** *See* SMALLS, BERTIE.

**Ponsonby, Sarah.** *See* BUTLER, LADY ELEANOR.

**'Poofy' Len Oades.** *See* HOLLIDAY, BERT.

**Popay, William Steward** (1801–?), union official and undercover police-man. Disowned by his superiors as 'a bad apple', Popay has been described by at least one authority as 'the true founder of the detective system in Britain' (*British Police and the Democratic Ideal*, C. Reith, 1943). In May 1831 Sergeant Popay, of London's P division, was instructed by his superintendent to attend meetings of the Walworth and Camberwell branch of the National Political Union. Popay took him to mean that he should secretly infiltrate the organization. He therefore became a member of the union, masquerading as a disgruntled coalman who had been put out of work by the Coal Act. Thereafter he seems to have exceeded his brief, though he denied this when his conduct was later investigated. It was said that on one occasion he marched arm in arm with other members to a meeting to celebrate the French Revolution. He urged that the wording of resolutions should be strengthened and encouraged the establishment of an arms depot at which he offered to give members sword practice. His radical speeches and behaviour soon ensured that he became an elected union official – a turn of events that had not been antic-ipated by his superiors.

However, in April 1833 he was comprehensively uncovered when a union member, John Fursey, saw him sitting at his desk in full uniform at Park House police station. A petition was presented to a House of Commons Select Committee by Fursey and others in which they said that Popay had:

> ... urged the members of the Union to use stronger language than they did in their resolutions and other papers; that in his conversation with one of your petitioners particularly, he railed against the Government, damned the Ministers for villains, and said he would expel them from the earth; that he told one of your Petitioners that he would like to establish a shooting-gallery, and wanted some of them to learn the use of the broad-sword, and did give one lesson of the broad-sword to one of your Petitioners.

Popay's conduct was described as 'highly reprehensible' and he was dismissed from the police with ignominy. His superiors argued that they had employed him merely to watch Union meetings, but were criticized for not keeping him under closer control. While the Select Committee accepted the need for a plainclothes force, it deplored 'any approach to the Employment of Spies, in the ordinary acceptance of the terms, as a practice most abhorrent to the feelings of the People and most alien to the spirit of the Constitution'.

Abhorrent or not, the employment of plainclothes detectives became an established practice – though early police forces had an imperfect grasp of how undercover work should best be carried out. In 1840 PC Barnett of the Birmingham police infiltrated the city's Chartists. When not impersonating a Chartist, he was required by his superiors to wear his uniform – a standing order that soon ensured that he was seen at a theatre and exposed as a policeman. Barnett's explanation that he was working in a private capacity as a bouncer for the theatre manager was not accepted.

*See* AGENTS PROVOCATEURS (for further references) and BOW STREET RUNNERS.

**Popish Plot, the.** *See* OATES, TITUS.

**Porlock, a person with business in.** *See* THORPE, JEREMY.

**pornographers.** *See* COOK, ROBIN; CURLL, EDMOND; HARRIS, FRANK; HUMPHREYS, JAMES; MONTALK, COUNT GEOFFREY WLADISLAW VAILE POTOI.

**pornographers, Victorian.** *See* ASHBEE, HENRY SPENCER; BACCHUS, REGINALD; CARRINGTON, CHARLES; DUGDALE, WILLIAM; HOTTEN, JOHN

CAMDEN; SALA, GEORGE AUGUSTUS; SELLON, CAPTAIN EDWARD; STOCK, LIEUTENANT ST GEORGE H.

**porpoise, a priest addressed as a.** *See* FITZGERALD, GEORGE ROBERT.

**porpoise in a railway waiting room, bottle-feeding a.** *See* BUCK-LAND, FRANCIS TREVELYAN.

**port before lunch, five bottles of.** *See* MYTTON, JOHN.

**Porteous, Captain John** (1693–1736), master tailor and constable. Few criminal cases in the 18th century excited greater attention than that of John Porteous, who, having been convicted of murder and sentenced to death, was dragged out of prison and killed by a mob. The magistrates of Edinburgh, where the riot took place, were fined for neglect and dismissed from their posts, and a royal proclamation was issued in which a reward was offered for the discovery of the murderers. It was impossible, however, to identify individuals from such a large crowd.

Born in Edinburgh to humble parents, Porteous was apprenticed to a tailor, shortly reaching the rank of journeyman, and then master. His reputation in the community was such that when a vacancy occurred for a peace officer – or captain, as he was called – it was filled by Porteous by order of the lord provost. Conscientious in his duties, and apparently without fear, he was frequently called upon by the magistrates to suppress any riots that happened in the city. On these occasions he was generally over-robust in his methods, often knocking the delinquents about with his musket and sometimes breaking their arms and legs. As his power grew, his behaviour became worse. If sent to quell a disturbance in a brothel, and notwithstanding the fact that he was a regular visitor to these establishments himself, he took delight in exposing its clients to their families. He seemed to derive pleasure, too, from imprisoning the young ladies whose favours he had recently enjoyed.

His unpopularity was greatly increased when a vacancy occurred at a local church. As the two candidates for this position received the same number of votes, the matter was referred to the presbytery. The decision went in favour of a Mr Dawson. The other candidate, Mr Witherspoon, appealed to the synod, who reversed the order. When Mr Dawson's angry supporters gathered at the church on the day that Mr Witherspoon was to preach his first sermon, Porteous was present to keep the peace. Finding that Mr Dawson had taken possession of the pulpit, Porteous climbed the steps, seized him by the collar and threw him out of the pulpit with such violence that he subsequently died. When Mr Witherspoon arrived, Mr Dawson's enraged supporters beat him in such a manner that he also died, moments after Mr Dawson. Many women and children had been injured in the affray, but Captain Porteous escaped unpunished.

In spite of such incidents the magistrates continued to give Porteous opportunities to exercise his vigorous methods. It was the custom in Scotland at the time to escort condemned criminals to church on Sundays, under the care of the city guards. On the Sunday before their execution, two smugglers, Wilson and Robertson, were on their way to church when Wilson, though handcuffed, assisted Robertson to escape by taking hold of one of the guards with his teeth, at the same time crying out for Robertson to run.

Robertson took off and managed to escape through the city gates just as they were being shut. Porteous was dispatched in search of him, but on the same evening Robertson boarded a ship at Dunbar which took him safely to Holland. (He was still alive in 1756, and kept a public house in Rotterdam.)

In June 1736 a temporary gallows was erected in the Grassmarket for the execution of Wilson, who was ordered to be conducted there by 50 men under the command of Captain Porteous. Afraid that there might be an attempt to rescue Wilson, since he and Robertson enjoyed great popularity in the community, Porteous put in a request that the escort should be augmented by five companies of the Welsh Fusiliers, and this was granted. There was no disturbance, but after Wilson had been hanged, a stone was thrown from the crowd and struck the hangman on the head. Other stones followed, and Porteous panicked. 'Fire and be damned!' he cried, discharging his own gun and shooting a confectioner dead. The Welsh Fusiliers remained calm, firing over the heads of the mob, and inadvertently picking off several spectators leaning out of the windows of a nearby building. As Porteous tried to draw off his men, the mob pressed closer, at which Porteous turned about and fired, killing three more, leaving nine in all dead on the spot, and many wounded.

Assisted by the Welsh Fusiliers, Porteous was able at last to withdraw his men to the guard house, where he was interviewed by the provost. After a long examination, he was committed to prison, charged with murder. On 6 July 1736 the trial opened before the lords of the judiciary. Porteous pleaded self-defence. After lengthy legal arguments about reasonable force when suppressing riots, Porteous was found guilty and sentenced to death. In certain quarters there was a desire to save him, and since George II was in Hanover at the time, the queen, on the advice of her council, and to the fury of the mob, ordered a stay of execution until the king's return. On 7 September, between nine and ten in the evening, a large body of men entered the city of Edinburgh and seized the arms belonging to the guard. They then marched on the Tolbooth prison, hauled Porteous from his cell and dragged him to the Grassmarket where the riot had taken place. Having broken open a shop to find a suitable rope, they hoisted Porteous on a dyer's pole; when he tried to save himself by putting a hand between the halter and his neck, they finished him off with several blows from an axe.

The Porteous Riots are vividly recreated in Sir Walter Scott's *Heart of Midlothian*.

**porthole, pushing a cabaret dancer through a.** *See* CAMB, JAMES.

**Portland, John Cavendish Bentinck-Scott, 5th duke of** (1800–79), peer, architect, builder and recluse. In his younger days as member of Parliament for King's Lynn, Portland had enjoyed something of a public life, but having been spurned in love by the singer Adelaide Kemble he withdrew from society. The staff at Welbeck Abbey, his estate in Nottinghamshire, were instructed to pass him by 'as they would a tree'. He preferred to stay in his bedroom, communicating through a letterbox in the door. Each day he would be posted a roast fowl, lunching off one half of the bird and dining off the other. When obliged to be out of doors, he hid himself under an umbrella. His trousers were secured above the ankle by a piece of string and he balanced a two-foot hat on top of his brown wig.

After his accession to the dukedom in 1854, Portland devoted himself to planning and supervising building schemes at Welbeck Abbey, most of which were carried out underground. At the time of his death there were 15,000 men working on 36 different projects, including a subterranean ballroom 174 feet long and in which 2000 people could have been entertained, had they been invited. Thousands of gas jets supplemented the natural illumination provided by rows of mushroom-shaped skylights. The ballroom was centrally heated, as were other underground chambers such as a series of libraries, one of which had space for twelve billiard tables. All the apartments were painted pink.

There was an underground railway connecting Welbeck to the nearest village, Worksop, and miles of ancillary underground passages linking various buildings on the estate. Above ground was the largest riding school in Europe – its walls covered in mirrors, its ceilings hung with crystal chandeliers. None of these facilities was put to any use apart from a large skating rink. We learn from the 6th duke's half-sister, Ottoline Morrell, that 'the Duke wished his housekeepers to skate, and if he found one of them sweeping the corridor or stairs, the frightened girl was sent out to skate whether she wanted to or not.'

Portland twice refused an offer of the Garter because acceptance would have required him to appear at court. His self-imposed isolation meant that if medical attention was necessary, the doctor had to stand outside his bedroom, questioning, diagnosing and even taking his patient's temperature through the medium of his valet. The few people who did have contact with Portland spoke of him as a kind and intelligent man. Many believed that his passion for building stemmed from a desire to give employment to workers during difficult times, and that he built underground rather than appear ostentatious. The latter fear applied also to the display of his remarkable art collection. When the 6th duke inherited Welbeck, he found unframed masters stacked two or three deep around the huge riding school, and a rare Gobelin tapestry rolled up and packed with peppercorns in an old tin box.

Portland's granddaughter was Lady Victoria Wemyss, who lived to the age of 104 and was an extra woman of the bedchamber to Elizabeth, the Queen Mother.

**posh tarts.** *See* BRISTOL, FREDERICK WILLIAM JOHN AUGUSTUS HERVEY, 7TH MARQUESS OF (for Lady Victoria Hervey); PALMER TOMKINSON, TARA.

**Postman's Knock.** *See* FLECKNEY, EVELYN.

**potholing.** *See* LASKEY, COLIN.

**Potter, Sarah** (1814–73), keeper of a flagellation house where young women were whipped by male clients, sometimes in front of an audience. Potter was prosecuted in 1863 on charges of assault. The case was brought by the Society for the Protection of Females and Young Women, and the complainant was Agnes Thompson, described as 'about fifteen', and therefore three years above the age of consent. A year before she had gone with a man to a house where he had 'effected her ruin'. Since then she had been employed by Mrs Potter at 3 Albion Terrace, King's Road, Chelsea, to solicit in the nearby Cremorne Gardens. Thompson's complaint was that 'I was flogged by gentlemen with birch-rods. I was beaten on my naked flesh.' In addition, and for the gratification of a man known as 'the Count', she had been fastened to a stepladder and flogged. The stepladder was produced in court.

Two other girls, Catherine Kennedy, who was 17, and Alice Smith, who was described in press reports as 'a young woman of considerable personal attractions', underwent similar 'punishments'. Alice's ordeal, for which she wasn't paid, took place in what was called 'the Schoolroom'. Mrs Potter was convicted and sent to prison. According to Henry Spencer ASHBEE's *Index Librorum Prohibitorum* (1877), 'Agnes Thompson returned to Mrs Potter after her release and lived with her for a considerable time in Howland Street.' Mrs Potter is commemorated by an imposing tombstone in Kensal Green Cemetery.

**Potter's Bar Golf Course Murder, the.** *See* QUERIPEL, MICHAEL.

**Pottesman, Soloman** (1904–78), bookseller. Apart from a brief period working in a factory during World War II, Pottesman lived by buying and selling antiquarian books – an occupation that provided few luxuries. He lived alone and never invited colleagues to his flat, which consisted of one room, furnished only with a bed. One acquaintance who managed to gain access was embarrassed to discover that he had been given the only cup while Pottesman drank his tea from a milk bottle.

Potty, as he was known, sold only enough to stay alive. Most of his discoveries, wrapped in brown paper, were stored in bank vaults and safe deposit boxes around London, and he had a private strongroom at Harrods. During rainy seasons he lived in fear that his books would be destroyed by rising tides. As a precaution against this he disconnected his lavatory cistern so that it couldn't burst and flood the room. At such times necessary flushing was carried out with a bucket of water.

Potty's behaviour at auctions was a source of irritation to other bidders, whom he distracted by talking about his latest purchase. Often he became overexcited and bid against himself. When it was time to collect his books, he took at least a quarter of an hour to write out a cheque. Even then he was reluctant to part with it. He kept taking it back for re-examination, explaining that, 'I once made a mistake when writing a cheque.' Finally he would unfold the greasy brown paper he always carried and laboriously wrap his purchases, while a queue formed behind him. When the British Museum introduced security checks, those behind Potty at the guard's desk were obliged to wait for what seemed an eternity while he slowly untied and then re-wrapped his packages for inspection.

Potty was a fan of Nelson Eddy, the Hollywood baritone celebrated for his partnership with Jeanette MacDonald. An acquaintance once saw him coming out of a cinema at which the musical *Rose Marie* was playing. Six days later, passing the cinema again, he saw Potty emerging once more. 'So,' he said, 'you've seen the film twice.' 'No,' Potty replied. 'Seven times. I've been every night this week.'

For other admirers of Nelson Eddy and Jeanette MacDonald, *see* CHENEY, SID.

**Pottinger, 'Gorgeous' George.** *See* POULSON, JOHN.

**Poulson, John** (1910–92), architect and leading figure in one of Britain's most notorious postwar corruption cases. Born in Ferrybridge, Yorkshire, Poulson left school without any qualifications. He joined a firm of architects, but failed his exams and was sacked in 1932. In the same year he set up his own firm in Pontefract with capital of £50. By the 1960s he was running the largest architectural practice in the world outside America, with offices in London, Edinburgh, Lagos and Beirut. He had a staff of 750 and was handling 450 projects a year. He had expanded too ambitiously, and by the end of the decade he was experiencing severe cash-flow problems. His bankruptcy in 1972 implicated many people in public life, the most notable of whom was Reginald Maudling, the Conservative home secretary. When the Metropolitan Police, for which the home secretary has overall responsibility, began to investigate matters arising out of the bankruptcy, Maudling felt obliged to resign as chairman of one of Poulson's companies, though not from the Home Office. He had not received any payment from Poulson, but many thousands of pounds had been pledged to the Adeline Genée Theatre in East Grinstead, of which Mrs Maudling was a trustee. It also came to light that Maudling and his wife had on at least one occasion, and at Poulson's expense, occupied the presidential suite at the George V Hotel in Paris. Maudling's son Martin was also a director of a Poulson company.

In June 1973 Poulson and George Pottinger, a permanent undersecretary at the Scottish Office, were arrested on conspiracy and corruption charges. Poulson had paid Pottinger £30,000 in return for public contracts – including a ski centre at Aviemore whose construction had cost £3 million. Pottinger, who was known as Gorgeous George in the Scottish Office, also admitted that Poulson had built him a house, thereafter giving him a car 'to compensate for errors in the house's design'. Among others subsequently arrested were Andrew Cunningham and T. Dan Smith – both leading figures in the Labour party in the northeast of England – plus two ex-mayors, an NUM official, a hospital secretary, a Coal Board engineer and a journalist.

When the trial opened at Leeds Crown Court in January 1974, evidence from Poulson's bankruptcy became public for the first time. It emerged that when Poulson called on Maudling in September 1969 to discuss money owed to one of his companies, the MP had 'been drunk in his shirt sleeves at four in the afternoon'. The meeting may have been to do with a hospital that Poulson designed on Gozo, an island belonging to Malta. He had been awarded the contract after Maudling had written to the Maltese government in his dual capacity as MP and chairman of a Poulson company, recommending Poulson for the job. The Maltese government later complained that the hospital was 'the wrong design, the wrong size and in the wrong place'. The British government ended up paying the Maltese government £1,625,000 in compensation. Another enjoyable moment in the trial came when Pottinger said that Poulson was a father figure who had bought him clothes because they 'got on well'. The prosecuting QC won himself a place in humorous anthologies by observing, 'Some have greatcoats thrust upon them.' Later, Poulson was sentenced to seven years in prison, T. Dan Smith to six and Pottinger to five (reduced on appeal to four). In the event, Poulson served just three years. He left prison in poor health in 1977.

He was discharged from bankruptcy in 1980, but could no longer work as an architect.

**Powell, Sir John** (*c*.1660–*c*.1730), judge, described by Jonathan Swift as 'the merriest old gentleman I ever saw'.
See WENHAM, JANE.

**pox, accusing one's hostess of giving one the.** See LUTTRELL, COLONEL JAMES.

**pranksters, inveterate.** See BERKELEY, HUMPHREY JOHN; BERNERS, GERALD HUGH TYRWHITT-WILSON, 14TH BARON; COLE, HORACE DE VERE; DOUGLAS-HOME, WILLIAM; HOOK, THEODORE; SPENCER, HERBERT; STAN-SHALL, VIVIAN.

***Prawn, The Amorous.*** See AMPTHILL, JOHN RUSSELL, 3RD BARON.

**prawns, arrested in connection with a bag of.** See KNIGHT, RONNIE.

**predatory thin women.** See NASH, JIMMY.

**Pre-Raphaelite movement, the genteel blackmailer of the.** See HOWELL, CHARLES AUGUSTUS.

**Pretty Police, the.** See HAMPSON, DR KEITH; THIN BLUE JEANS, THE.

**Price, Dilys** (1932– ), Welsh balloonist and skydiver, with some claims to being the oldest person ever to jump from a balloon into 'dead air' over Arizona. Miss Price was born in Cardiff and worked there as a dance teacher until, by her own account, she 'hit a bad patch' at the age of 65. She decided the best therapy would be to take her art into the air. Accordingly, she joined a skydiving school, later mastering the technique of jumping out of an aeroplane and adopting ballet positions during the downward flight.

In search of a greater challenge, Miss Price decided at the age of 69 to switch from aeroplanes to balloons. The experience is altogether different, since from a balloon a person jumps into dead air from 5000 feet – the sensation being similar to stepping into a lift well (though how anyone could have survived the latter experience in order to confirm this remains unclear). Miss Price went to Arizona, which is the best part of the world for dead-air descents. The thermals are unpredictable, and the air is thinner, so the protagonist drops like a stone, accelerating from 0 to 125 mph in 5.7 seconds. Having taken instruction for some weeks from a balloon master, Miss Price made her first successful descent, albeit landing on a cactus. On her second jump she landed in the exercise yard at Arizona State prison, but that was thought to be the fault of the unpredictable thermals.

**Price, William** (1800–93), doctor, Chartist and pioneer of cremation. Price was a conspicuous figure in the district of Pontypridd, Glamorganshire, where, at the Rocking Stone on the common, he performed druidic rites dressed in a white tunic, scarlet waistcoat, green trousers and a fox-skin hat. He also won a wider reputation as a physician and surgeon of great skill.

Price's notoriety was caused as much by his advocacy of free love, vegetarianism and cremation as by his eloquent denunciation of vaccination, vivisection, orthodox religion and the law. After taking part in the Chartist march on Newport in 1839, he escaped to France disguised as a woman, and, in Paris, became acquainted with the poet Heinrich Heine.

Of the many lawsuits in which he was engaged on his return to Wales the most important was his trial at Cardiff assizes in 1884 when he was accused of burning the corpse of his infant son. Dr Price did not believe in the legal bond of marriage, and after the death of his daughter's mother (to whom he had given the name Countess of Glamorgan), he took on as housekeeper Miss Gwenllian Llewellyn, a girl of about 18. She bore him three children – Iesu Grist (Jesus Christ), who died at the age of five months, Penelopen, and Iesu Grist the second. The means by which he attempted to cremate the first Iesu Grist seemed an atrocity to many. He took the body to the summit of a hill on Caerlan Fields at Llantrisant, where he placed it, wrapped in linen, in a cask containing paraffin oil. When he set fire to the cask, the crowd reacted badly. The police were called, Dr Price was arrested and an inquest was held on the child's body. The police sought the coroner's permission to bury the body in the conventional manner, but the coroner was obliged by law to return the child to Price. Subsequently, Price was tried before Mr Justice Stephen at the Cardiff assizes for endeavouring to cremate the body on 13 January 1884, but he was able to show that he had not transgressed the law. His acquittal established the legality of cremation in Britain and paved the way for the passing of the first comprehensive Cremation Act in 1902. In March 1884, Dr Price carried out his intentions unmolested, and Iesu Grist was cremated in half a ton of coals on Caerlan Fields.

Huge crowds attended Price's own funeral at Caerlan Fields, Llantrisant, when his body was cremated in accordance with his detailed instructions. (More information can be found in *A Welsh Heretic* by Islwyn ap Nicholas, 1973.)

**prickers, Scottish.** In the 17th century, 'prickers' roamed the Scottish countryside as witch-hunters, capitalizing on the belief that witches couldn't feel the prick of a pin when it was jabbed into a mark the Devil had left on their bodies. They worked on commission, being paid for each witch they exposed. A 'common pricker', John Kincaid of Dalkeith, was one of the most diligent of his trade, certainly in the collection of his fees. In 1647 he swore before the magistrates that as he had passed the house of one Janet Peaston he had heard her talking to the Devil. Miss Peaston's defence was that she often talked to herself. This was confirmed by her neighbours, albeit without much conviction, since too much expressed sympathy might have marked them out as witches too. Kincaid's statement that no one ever talked to themselves who was not a witch was accepted by the court, and when Miss Peaston showed no pain when he pricked the Devil's marks on her body she was 'convict and brynt'.

The Scottish Parliament continued to fortify the claims of the prickers long after magistrates and ministers became disinclined to accept their evidence. Much of the blame for this must be carried by James VI of Scotland (later James I of England). In 1597 he published his treatise *Demonologie* in which he urged witch-hunters to engage in 'finding of their mark, and trying the sensibilities thereof'. It was not until 1736 that James's penal statutes were repealed. Henceforth, witches could be subjected to the pillory or imprisonment only for their 'crimes'. By this time, pricking had fallen into disrepute even in Scotland.

*See also* GREATRAKES, VALENTINE; HOPKINS, MATTHEW.

**Pridden, Sarah** (1692–1723), courtesan. Pridden, who called herself Sally Salisbury after the surname of one of her lovers, was born into poverty and spent her childhood working the streets of St Giles, one of the poorest parts of London. From *The Genuine History of Mrs Sarah Pridden and her Gallants* (Anon, 1723), we know that at different times she 'shelled beans and peas, cried nose-gays, peeled walnuts and turned bunter [whore], well knowing that a wagging hand always gets a penny'.

Abandoned at the age of 17 by her first lover, the notorious cheat and voluptuary Colonel Francis CHARTERIS, she became a highly paid courtesan for Mother Wisebourne, who ran the most exclusive bordello in London and was noted for keeping a chaplain on the premises. While working for Mother Wisebourne, Sarah easily outshone the other girls. According to her anonymous biographer:

> Immediately upon Sally's entering in a party-coloured petticoat and lovely shift, the spectators were ravished with the sweet assurance of her air, and the symmetrical proportion of her limbs; her leg and foot having powers to excite, like the face and voice of others. When the rivals disputed who should dance first, she refused not, like the rest; but pertly told them that she'd dance first and last. Whereupon, the *beau monde* gave her a universal clap, and she began the wandering contest, like a midnight unctuous fire, bright, but uncertain, that leads uncautious men into bogs and watry places.

Among those affected by this sweet performance were at least two secretaries of state.

One day, Sarah, in a fit of pique, stabbed an admirer who had paid less attention to her than to another girl. Although he survived, and pleaded vigorously for her release, she was convicted of assault and sentenced to a year's imprisonment. Housed for a time in Bridewell, the prison for vagrant women, she suffered unspeakably at the hands of the notorious Captain Whip'em, the sadistic inspector, who according to de Saussure (*A Foreign View of England*):

> ... held a long cane in his hand, about the thickness of my finger, and whenever she was fatigued and ceased working he would rap her on the arms, and in no gentle fashion, I can assure you.

Transferred to Newgate, Sarah died there of brain fever in 1723. Her life served as a model for Hogarth's *Harlot* and for John Cleland's *Fanny Hill* (1750).

**Prince, Henry** (1809–1899), priest. Having declared himself to be the Messiah on New Year's Day 1846, the Reverend Henry Prince, an ordained Anglican priest, shut himself away in a large house in the Somerset village of Spaxton, surrounded by his devoted followers. Few of them doubted his declarations of immortality even when he died. They buried him standing upright in order to facilitate his resurrection.

As a theological student in Wales in the 1830s, Prince attracted a group of fanatical evangelists, many of whom formed the nucleus of the cult that he later instigated, and which he called the Church of the Agapemone. As a curate in Charlinch, Somerset, he soon came into conflict with the church authorities over his decision to divide the congregation into the saved and the damned. Barred from preaching by the bishop of Bath and Wells and dismissed from Charlinch, Prince toured the towns of southern England preaching that the Day of the Lord was nigh. In January 1846 he announced his own divinity to a group of people taking tea in a Weymouth café. In July of the same year, the Dorset county magistrate, Colonel Howarth, wrote to the home secretary reporting that Prince was impersonating the Almighty. The colonel was upset, too, by Prince's habit of addressing his congregation naked. According to the colonel, Prince had already sent three young women to the County Lunatic Asylum 'driven mad by the doctrines they hold'.

Once installed in his mansion in Spaxton, Prince set about the business of persuading his followers to give him their money. After they had done that, they should withdraw from the world, and into the splendour of his 'Abode of Love' – or, more formally, Agapemone. Rumours soon circulated that sexual abandon had replaced all other forms of worship. One of Prince's diversions, it was said, was to place his female devotees on a revolving stage that the men would then spin. Whichever girl landed opposite Prince when the wheel came to a halt would for that week be 'the Bride', or 'Mrs Prince'. There were rumours, too, of the deflowering of virgins in the chapel, which also served as a billiard room.

Prince's public style might have better suited a lord temporal than Jesus come again. He drove round Spaxton in a carriage attended by outriders and preceded by a man in liveried purple who announced his arrival by calling out, 'Blessed is he who cometh in the name of the Lord!' Local shopkeepers, grateful for an increased tourist trade, were happy to submit their accounts to 'My Lord, the Agapemone'.

The Abode of Love nevertheless experienced certain difficulties. While Prince inspired loyalty in his followers, this seldom extended to their relatives. The Nottidge family, whose wealth was swallowed up by Prince through a series of bogus marriages involving five impressionable sisters – Agnes, Clara, Harriet, Louisa and Cornelia – eventually took him to court. Not only had the sisters taken their turn on the revolving stage, they had also on frequent occasions found notes under their dinner plates, such as, 'The Lord hath need of £50, to be used for a special purpose unto His glory. The spirit would have made this known to you. Amen.' The gradual transfer, by this means, of the sisters' estates to Prince culminated in the court case, *Nottidge vs Prince* in 1858. The Nottidge family contended that Prince had obtained the money by 'falsely and blasphemously exercising a powerful and undue domination over the minds of the sisters and by assuming a false character'. The vice chancellor, hearing the case, agreed, and ordered Prince to hand back £6000 with interest. A month later the Reverend Lewis Price (Harriet Nottidge's husband by one of Prince's marriages), who had become disaffected with the Agapemonites and had defected without her, led a raiding party on Spaxton to recover his wife. Scaling the garden walls, the invaders broke down the doors of the house and discovered the Agapemonites barricaded behind furniture, and armed with sticks and guns. However, there was no sign of Harriet, who was hiding in a water cistern, and the rescue mission failed.

In spite of Prince's edicts against death, his followers began to pass away one by one, and he himself died in January 1899. Happily, an alternative Messiah soon emerged. The Reverend John Smyth-Pigott, formerly a member of the Salvation Army, assumed Prince's mantle and within three years the Agapemonites had a new leader. Smyth-Pigott won new followers, first in Reading and Wales, then in Norway and Sweden and finally in Germany, the United States and India. When Smyth-Pigott died in 1926 the Abode of Love became an old people's home. It was visited in 1955 by a reporter from the *Daily Herald*. He found a dozen old women drinking their bedtime cocoa.

**prize-fighters.** In the early years of the 19th century, prize fights were thought to prove that an Englishman's fists were morally superior to the knives and other weaponry of devious foreigners. A fair fist fight appealed to all classes, not least to patrician romantics like Lord BYRON and the prince regent's court. Various legal judgements between 1825 and 1882 outlawed bare-knuckle fist fights, but the sport's reputation for extreme brutality continued to draw crowds to unlicensed challenges. The contests might last for three hours. If a man was knocked down, he was dragged to his corner and allowed 30 seconds to 'toe the mark' or 'come up to scratch'. If necessary, his second and bottle-holder would prop him up at the centre of the ring, where he would go down again at the first punch and thus earn a further 30-second respite.

The public expected the man they had backed to fight until he won or dropped to the ground senseless. To face death in the ring was the true test of a man's courage. The sport's reputation in no way suffered when 'Lips' McKay was killed in 1830 by Simon Byrne, or when Byrne himself died two years later after a fight with 'Deaf' Burke that lasted for 98 rounds. Byrne was carried from the ring and died three days later. Burke and his four seconds were charged with manslaughter, but at Hertford assizes Mr Justice Park directed the jury to acquit all five defendants (*see also* LASKEY, COLIN; PRACTICES, SADOMASOCHISTIC).

An essay written by William Hazlitt in 1820 described a contest in Hungerford when Tom Hickman, 'the Gasman', went down under an onslaught from Bill Neate. After more than 20 rounds, the Gasman appeared to be beaten but he wouldn't give up:

> Neate just then made a tremendous lunge at him, and hit him full in the face. It was doubtful whether he would move backwards or forwards; he hung suspended for a second or two, and then fell back, throwing his hands in the air, and with his face lifted up to the sky. I never saw anything more terrific than his aspect when he fell. All traces of life, of natural expression, were gone from him. His face was like a human skull, a death's head, spouting blood. The eyes were filled with blood, the nose streamed with blood, the mouth gaped blood. He was not like an actual man, but like a pre-ternatural spectral appearance, or like one of the figures in Dante's *Inferno*.

In spite of his condition, the Gasman got up and fought on for several rounds until he fell unconscious for more than 30 seconds and so lost the contest.

*See also* QUEENSBERRY, JOHN SHOLTO DOUGLAS, 9TH MARQUESS OF.

**Proctor, Harvey** (1934– ), politician. The popular Conservative MP for Basildon had his first brush with scandal in September 1981. This followed a misunderstanding with his partner, Terry Woods, a married man with two children. Woods drank too much, a habit that caused him to say things he later regretted. On this occasion, Proctor was obliged to lock him out of the flat they shared in Fulham. The incident led to a story in *Private Eye* magazine which dubbed Proctor a homosexual with a penchant for spanking. Throughout this unfortunate episode he was supported by his constituency party in Basildon, for whom his robust views on race outweighed any reservations they might have about their MP's sexual orientation.

In 1985 allegations appeared in the *People* that were harder to ignore. A young male prostitute described for the newspaper recreational scenarios in which Proctor pretended to be his headmaster:

> I was a pupil who had done something wrong. I had to call him 'sir' at all times and not answer back. He took me into the bedroom and told me to put on a pair of white shorts. Then he spanked me.

While it is not clear why a man should consider himself damaged by suggestions that he is homosexual, Proctor was advised by his friends to sue for libel. He refused on the grounds that he didn't have the capital. The *People*'s next allegation was altogether more serious – that Proctor had had sex with an underage rent boy. Again, Proctor announced that he would not be suing because of the prohibitive costs involved. At this point the *People* passed their material over to Scotland Yard's Vice Squad. Meanwhile, the *Daily Mirror* reported a trip to Morocco by Proctor under the headline, 'NAKED ARAB UNDER MP'S BED'. In April 1987 the Serious Crime Squad arrested Proctor in a dawn raid and took him to Canon Row police station. That night he courageously attended a wine and cheese party at his Essex constituency – now, because of boundary alterations, Billericay. There, and greatly to their credit, local members continued to support him. 'I was in the navy during the war,' said one, 'and I can spot a homosexual at 50 feet. Harvey Proctor is not one of them.'

On 16 May 1987 Proctor pleaded guilty at Bow Street Magistrate's Court to four charges of indecency with two underage rent boys (one was 17, the other 19) whom he believed to be 21. He was convicted and fined £1450 with £250 costs. There was little sympathy for Proctor in serious newspapers, or criticism of the tabloids' methods – a consequence, perhaps, of his right-wing views. However, several of his parliamentary friends – including Michael Heseltine and Neil Hamilton – invested £80,000 in a business venture with which Proctor hoped to recover his fortunes: 'Proctor's Shirts and Ties', of Brewer's Lane, Richmond. The *Spectator* marked the occasion with a cartoon in which the shop bore the sign, 'Shirtlifters will not be prosecuted'. Whether to protect his investment, or out of chivalry, Neil Hamilton came to Proctor's assistance when he was attacked in his shop by a gang of queer-bashers. Hamilton was getting the worst of it, but was rescued by his wife Christine, who chased his assailants down the street. Proctor remains close to his friend, Terry Woods. 'One must plod on,' he says.

**Profumo, John.** *See* KEELER, CHRISTINE.

**Progl, Zoe** (1929– ), burglar and gangster's 'moll'. Known as 'Blonde Mick' and the 'Queen of the Underworld', Progl was the first woman to escape from Holloway prison. In July 1960, during her fourth term of imprisonment for housebreaking, a rope ladder was thrown over the wall and within minutes she was in a car waiting on the other side. While out, she toured the south coast with her boyfriend Barry Harris, her small daughter Tracey and a friend who had helped in the escape, Adelaide de Boer. She was also pictured in the *Daily Express* drinking gin at the Pier Hotel, Chelsea, and offering to give herself up if the home secretary agreed to knock a year off her sentence. Otherwise, she would have plastic surgery, she said, to remove a telltale scar under her left eye.

In the event, she was recaptured five months later in Notting Hill after a police officer noticed a car with the number plate WOP 598. This aroused his suspicions since offensive registrations were not allowed at that time by the licensing authorities. Progl had 18 months added to her sentence, Barry Harris received nine months and Adelaide de Boer, described as having a soft heart and 83 previous convictions, also received nine months. While in prison Progl sued the commissioner of the Metropolitan Police, Sir Joseph Simpson, over a solitaire diamond ring that had been a gift from her former lover, Tommy 'Scarface' Smithson (*see* ELLUL, PHILIP). The police did not oppose the application.

In 1964 Progl, who at the age of 16 had married US Master Sergeant Joseph Progl, announced her engagement to a 24-year-old salesman, Roy Bowman. 'Roy knows about my days as a burglar, as a rich man's mistress, and as a gangster's moll,' she told the *Sunday Mirror*. 'He has decided to give me a chance to become a respectable woman.' It was later reported that the couple had emigrated to Australia.

**Psalmanazar, George** (*c.*1680–1763), impostor. In 1704 the Reverend William Innes, a military chaplain, introduced Psalmanazar to the bishop of London as a converted heathen from Formosa – a country that no Englishman had ever visited. Psalmanazar's handsome appearance, erudition and wit caused him to be lionized by English society. Within a year he had published *An Historical and Geographical Description of Formosa,* which presented bizarre details about his alleged country's language, customs and religion. According to his own account – backed up by the Reverend Innes – Psalmanazar was a member of a princely Formosan family that had some years earlier made its way to Japan and then to the outer world, living for a time in France, where he had been educated and converted to the Christian faith.

Psalmanazar's conversion hadn't cured him entirely of his Formosan past, however, and he remained addicted to eating raw meat. At social and scientific meetings he held audiences spellbound with his stories of Formosan customs and strict laws. One statute read:

> Whosoever shall strike the King, Intendant, or Governor shall be hanged by his feet till he dies, having four dogs fastened to his body to tear it to pieces.

Since the English were greatly taken by accounts of cannibalism, Psalmanazar made his own devotion to the practice a centrepiece of his lectures. Any potentially awkward questions were answered with speed and aplomb. Asked why, as an Oriental, his skin was so fair, he smiled patiently and explained that he, like most members of the Formosan upper class, had passed his life in 'the cool shades or apartments underground'. Only the lower classes toiled in the hot sun and, as a consequence, had their skins tanned yellow.

Soon after the publication of Psalmanazar's first book, the bishop of London sent him to Oxford where he was to lecture on Formosan history. The Anglican Church also commissioned him to translate the Old and New Testaments into Formosan. At Oxford he lectured with a snake wrapped round his neck, an old Formosan custom, he explained for keeping cool. In time, scientific objections were raised to his many stories – not least by Sir Isaac Newton, who accused Psalmanazar of having lifted parts of his book from obscure foreign texts on Formosa, some of which were 40 years old. The Reverend Innes, who had instigated the hoax and had made a fortune from it, realized that it was time to end the masquerade. The mischievous old divine somehow obtained an appointment as chaplain general of the British troops in Portugal, leaving the bogus young Formosan to face his critics on his own.

Psalmanazar was finally exposed as a fraud when the astronomer, Dr Edmund Halley, asked him how long the sun shone down the chimney on a Formosan underground home on an average day in different seasons. Psalmanazar's answers were, from a mathematical point of view, wildly inaccurate. He admitted the hoax and faded away into the English countryside. Not without writing talent, he eventually returned to London, where he produced an annotated edition of the *Book of Psalms*. Among his friends was Dr Samuel Johnson, with whom he had lengthy, ale-house discussions on literature and religion. Johnson always defended the former hoaxer, saying, 'his piety, penitence and virtue exceeded almost what we read as wonderful in the lives of the saints.'

**pygmy cannibals who were no match for English travelling women.** *See* CARSTAIRS, MARION BARBARA; KINGSLEY, MARY.

**pyjamas, buying the chauffeur silk.** *See* RATTENBURY, ALMA.

**pyjamas, photographing actresses in their.** *See* DAVIDSON, THE REVEREND HAROLD FRANCIS (the rector of Stiffkey).

**pyjamas, walking from Land's End to John O'Groats in one's.** *See* SLATER, JOHN.

**Pyle, Joe.** *See* HUMPHREYS, JAMES; ROBSON, DETECTIVE INSPECTOR BRIAN.

**quacks.** *See* FORMAN, SIMON; GRAHAM, JAMES; GREATRAKES, VALENTINE; GREEN, MARY; KNOX, DR ROBERT; NOLAN, FINBAR; SOLOMON SAMUEL.

**quails, curking.** *See* URQUHART, SIR THOMAS.
*See also* NICKERSON, SIR JOSEPH (for someone who taught himself to think like a partridge).

**quavering of the kidneys.** *See* GREEN, MARY.

**Queen, Peter** (1891–1958), a Glasgow bookmaker's assistant, who, unusually, was convicted of murder in spite of expert evidence that his victim had strangled herself. In 1930 Queen was living with a former nursemaid, Chrissie Hall, in the home of a James Burn and his wife. Miss Hall was an alcoholic and often threatened suicide. 'Some day one of you will come home and find me strung up,' was a constant theme. In the summer of 1931 Queen and Miss Hall acquired a home of their own. She continued to drink heavily, and was tormented by the fact that they were 'living in sin'.

On 20 November Queen, in a highly agitated state, ran into a police station and said, 'I think you will find my wife dead.' He was alleged to have added, 'I think I have killed her.' Hall was found in bed, strangled with a clothesline, and Queen was charged with murder. The country's two leading pathologists, Sir Sydney Smith and Sir Bernard Spilsbury, both argued that it was suicide. Their reasons included the fact that there were no signs of a struggle. The jury were unimpressed and returned a verdict of guilty. Death sentence was passed but was later commuted to life imprisonment. After the case, Sir Sydney Smith remarked, 'So, in the only case where Spilsbury and I agreed, the jury believed neither of us.'

**Queen of the Badger Game.** *See* SHARPE, MAY CHURCHILL.

**Queen of the Forty Elephants.** *See* HILL, BILLY.

**Queen of the Shoplifters.** *See* PITTS, SHIRLEY.

**Queen of the Underworld.** *See* PROGL, ZOE.

**Queensberry, John Sholto Douglas, 9th marquess of** (1844–1900), Scottish representative peer, sportsman and bigot. Queensberry supervised the formulation of new conventions to govern professional boxing, since known as the 'Queensberry Rules'. Admired for turning the barbarity of bare-knuckle fist fights into more civilized contests, the marquess was in his own nature quarrelsome and vindictive. In 1895 he appeared before the Marlborough Street magistrates after brawling in Piccadilly with his son and heir, whom he described as 'this squirming skunk Percy'. The following year he was thrown out of the Globe Theatre, London, for his noisy objections to a scene in Tennyson's play *The Promise of May*. When his wife was expecting visitors for the weekend at their country house, Queensberry arrived with a hastily acquired 'mistress' and a gang of sporting toughs, driving Lady Queensberry and her guests from the house. When Lord ROSEBERY, as Gladstone's foreign secretary, arranged a peerage and preferment for his, Queensberry's, second son, Lord Drumlanrig, Queensberry, who suspected Rosebery of homosexuality, followed him to Bad Homburg, where he was taking the waters, and threatened him with a dog whip. The prince of Wales, who was present, failed to calm him down, but the local police commissioner was more successful. With regard to his encounter with the latter, Queensberry later reported, 'In consequence of the entertainment I had with him, found it advisable to part this morning with the 7 o'clock train to Paris.' Rosebery wrote to Queen Victoria, saying that 'I am unhappy at being pursued by a pugilist of unsound mind.' On 18 October 1894 Drumlanrig was found dead from a gunshot wound while attending a shooting party.

Believing that the bad blood in his sons was coming from his wife's side of the family, Queensberry wrote to his brother-in-law, Sir Alfred Montgomery, in ill-considered terms:

> Sir, Now that the first flush of this catastrophe and grief is passed, I write to tell you it is a JUDGEMENT on the WHOLE LOT OF YOU. Montgomerys, The Snob Queers like Roseberry [sic] and certainly Christian hypocrite Gladstone, the whole lot OF YOU. Set my son up against me indeed and make bad blood BETWEEN us, may it devil on your heads that he is gone to his REST, and the quarrel not made up between him and myself. If you and his Mother

did not set up this business with that cur and Jew friend LIAR Rosebery as I always thought – At any rate she [Lady Rosebery] acquiesced in it, which is just as bad ... I smell a Tragedy behind all this and have already GOT WIND of a more STARTLING ONE ... I am in the right track to find out what happened. *CHERCHEZ LA FEME*, when these things happen. I have already heard something that quite accounts FOR IT ALL.

 Queensberry

 Montgomery declined to be drawn. Oscar Wilde was less sensible. On 28 February 1895 Queensberry left a calling card at the Albermarle Club that famously described Wilde as 'posing as a somdomite'. It has never been clear whether the misspelling was another example of the marquess's illiteracy or whether he was shrewdly laying down a technical defence to any action. In any event, he precipitated the greatest scandal of the 1890s. Wilde was provoked into the disastrous action for criminal libel that brought about his ruin. Queensberry himself remains as a paradigm of the sporting gentleman.

**'queen's sister' arrested at gunpoint.** *See* WILSON, SARAH.

**queer dockers.** *See* FARSON, DANIEL.

**Queripel, Michael** (1937– ), trainee civil servant who as the result of a migraine attack murdered a woman on Potter's Bar golf course with a golf club. On the evening of 29 April 1955, a Mr Currell reported that his wife was missing after taking her dog for a walk. The next morning Mrs Currell was found on the 17th tee of Potter's Bar golf course. She had been clubbed to death with a blood-splattered nine iron, which lay next to the body. A palm print discovered on the murder weapon was not in the criminal records. House-to-house checks were made in the area and prints were taken from 9000 local employees. On 19 August a matching print was found, belonging to 17-year-old Michael Queripel, a local-government clerk. At first he told the police that he had merely found the body, but then he said, 'I had a migraine so I hit her.' He pleaded guilty to murder at the Old Bailey and the judge ordered that he be detained during Her Majesty's pleasure.

**Quick-Manning, Reginald.** *See* COTTON, MARY ANNE.

**Quin, James.** *See* STAGE, HOOLIGANISM ON.

**Rabbett, Marmaduke** (*c.*1780–1842), nonconformist minister. In 1823 Rabbett built the Eon Chapel in the Strand as a speculative undertaking business, thereby taking advantage of the fact that the Burial Act of 1850 had not yet ended the practice of cramming the indigent dead into shallow graves. Within 20 years of its construction, 12,000 bodies lay under its wooden floor. In 1838 Rabbett had the even better idea of turning it into a dancing salon, which advertised the novelty of 'Dancing on the Dead – Admission Three Pence. No lady or gentleman admitted unless wearing stockings.' By 1850 the Reverend Rabbett had died and the human remains had, in accordance with the new law, been removed to Norwood Cemetery. The floor had been cemented over and the former chapel now offered clowns and pantomimes 'gaff fashion' (*see* PENNY GAFFS). Within a short while, however, the authorities discovered that the nonconformist entrepreneur and his coffin had been cemented into the floor under the stage on which clowns and dancing girls appeared. The performers were persuaded to take themselves and their properties to an alternative venue – a shed in the Mile End Road.

**rabbit, criminally assaulted by a.** *See* TOFT, MARY.

**racehorse switching.** Systematic fraud by a gang or syndicate entering a horse in a race disguised as another. The practice was particularly common in the early years of the 19th century. When Bloomsbury won the Derby (a race restricted to 3-year-olds) in 1839 at odds of 40–1, the horse was a 4-year-old and in any case not Bloomsbury. There was a similar scandal five years later when the Derby was won easily by a 4-year-old, Maccabeus, entered as the unfancied Running Rein. 'Pulling' a horse to manipulate the odds was less frowned upon; some even considered it not to be cheating. In 1835 George Osbaldston, known as the Squire of All England, decided that the handicapping system had become corrupt. To level the score he bought a horse in Ireland, pulled it in a trial so that its opponent came home at a canter, and then won the actual race with ease. Osbaldston was hissed by the ladies in the stand and challenged to a duel by Lord George Bentinck, who had ridden the loser. Osbaldston had taken odds of 2–1 against himself from Bentinck for the sum of £500. Apart from being an excellent jockey, Osbaldston was a remarkable all-round sportsman. He won boxing matches despite conceding four stones to some opponents; he defeated the French tennis champion using his hand instead of a racquet; and playing cricket for Sussex he once saved a match despite bowling when drunk and suffering from a broken shoulder.

*See also* BARRIE, PADDY; COYLE, FRANCIS; DILL, SIR VICTOR ROBERT COLQHOUN.

**Rachman, Peter** (1919–62), property racketeer with a taste for attack dogs, silk suits and two-way mirrors. By creating one-bedroom slums in Notting Hill and Paddington, Rachman was a major contributor to the race riots of 1958 and 1959. In 1963 Harold Wilson, then leader of the Labour opposition, defined Rachmanism as buying at a low price property that was controlled under the 1957 Rent Act and then bringing about decontrol by evicting tenants by intimidation. The empty property could be sold at a profit to speculators or let at a higher rent either to prostitutes or those suffering from the acute housing shortage. After the Labour victory at the 1964 election, the government introduced the 1965 Rent Act. This gave tenants better protection under the law.

Rachman was born in Poland in 1919, the son of a dentist. During World War II he served with the Polish Free Corps in North Africa, and came to England in 1956. He worked first as a tailor and then in an estate agents' office in Soho, finding accommodation for prostitutes. In 1953 he bought a house full of tenants in Shepherd's Bush that had one empty room. He moved in a black family and persuaded them to make themselves as objectionable as possible to the other tenants. The house was soon vacated and the rooms could now be let at higher rents to people desperate for accommodation.

By 1959 Rachman owned between 80 and 100 houses in the Notting Hill area. He distanced himself from the source of his income, and the manner of its acquisition, by fragmenting his activities into a complex web of interlocking companies. One company would own the house, a second the lease, and three or four other companies would be sub-tenants. He filled up the houses with working girls because they could afford the highest rents. Soon he was running call-girl rackets and supplying protection. From a typical operation – a house in Hereford Road, Paddington – he was receiving rents amounting to £10,000 a year. The house was divided into seven flats, each of which was sub-let to a prostitute at £3 a day, payable every morning at noon. Those behind with their rent were beaten up by Rachman's strong-arm men, who also specialized in removing tenants from properties that Rachman wanted empty. Because no one else would have them, newly arrived immigrants from the West Indies were forced to accept his accommodation, however squalid, at an exorbitant rent.

Because of the libel laws, Rachman's name, and his practices, only became widely known after his death. He was first mentioned in open court in June 1963 at the trial of Stephen WARD, a society osteopath accused of living on the immoral earnings of Christine KEELER and Mandy RICE-DAVIES. Miss Rice-Davies had for two years been Rachman's mistress. Speaking about him on television, she said:

> He was probably a racketeer but not during the two years I knew him. I adored him. I'm a one-guy girl. Only one at a time, that is. I got thousands from him and I've spent it all.

The Labour MP for Paddington, Ben Parkin, had been compiling a dossier on Rachman for years. The Stephen Ward trial gave Parkin the opportunity to raise the issue again. He sought to introduce a private member's bill to prevent abuse of the Rent Act, and Harold Wilson tabled a censure motion on the government. As a result, the Millner-Holland Committee was set up to make a survey of housing in London and to investigate the pressure put on people in rented accommodation.

Rachman preferred to conduct his business from premises in which he felt himself unlikely to be knifed: either a post office or the Daquis Café in South Kensington. When he died he left just £8000, and his name in the dictionary. It has been said of his grave, 'Open it up and you'll find two tenants inside.'

**Rackham, 'Calico' Jack.** *See* BONNY, ANNE.

**Radcliffe, Charles** (1940– ), drug smuggler. The son of an army officer and the product of Wellington College, a military public school, Radcliffe was characteristic of the new generation of student drug dealers that emerged in the 1960s – educated, trusting to the point of naïvety, without criminal associations, and, crucially, users of drugs themselves. It was to satisfy their own small habit, and the habits of their friends, that these unexceptionable young men first became suppliers – travelling the hippie trail through Greece and Turkey to Pakistan and back, or via Spain to Morocco and home again. The level of cooperation between campus dealers of this sort was remarkable. 'There was a phenomenal level of trust between rivals,' Radcliffe has said. 'When Bob Dylan sang "If you live outside the law you've got to be honest," it struck a very resonant chord.'

Since the police had no entrée into this world or understanding of its language, it seemed as if Radcliffe and those like him could operate with impunity. At first, their methods were crude. The simplest hiding place was the space below the side window of a van, since drugs could be packed there without distorting the shape of the vehicle. As Customs officers grew wise to what was going on, smuggling by sea came to seem a more sensible option than running drugs by land through guarded checkpoints. The drugs were taken ashore and driven up to London in hired camper vans. At its height, Radcliffe's operation required a team of about eleven: four on the boat doing the two-week trip from Morocco; two on the landing craft; one in Spain; one in Morocco; two to drive the shipment to London; and one to guard it. On one occasion the boat sank. The crew survived, but the experience shocked Radcliffe profoundly. He decided to pull off 'the big one' and then retire.

The 'big one' ended in disappointment. Radcliffe was woken at 6 a.m. by Customs officers in bullet-proof vests pinning him to the bed and asking for his gun. Then they showed him a photograph of a Customs officer holding one of Radcliffe's goats by the tail and shining a torch up its rectum. The caption read. 'We've searched everywhere.' This appears to have been the case. During what they had called Operation Yashmak, customs officers had collected as evidence £100,000 worth of drugs hidden in Radcliffe's garden in screw-up drainage tubes, £10,000 in small boxes and £40,000 stashed in a safe under the stove along with keys to a safety-deposit box. Having told him that they had already arrested his wife – which they hadn't – the officers proceeded to make the usual threats. 'The council look after children pretty well these days, it's not as bad being in care as it was in Victorian times.' Radcliffe agreed to make a statement if his wife was released, and was shortly sentenced to five years in prison.

While he was on remand, the handless corpse of a dealer who had informed on his colleagues was found in a quarry. Radcliffe was impressed. He thought, 'This isn't like the Round House '66. People are getting hurt.' He decided that it was time to retire.

*See also* MARKS, HOWARD.

**Rae, Edward** (1847–1923). Rae, who introduced the game of cricket to Russian Lapland, died at Birkenhead on 26 June 1923, aged 76.

**raincoats.** *See* KAGAN, LORD JOSEPH.

**Ramensky, Johnny** (1905–71), cracksman. Ramensky was one of the many remarkable criminals recruited during World War II to put their special skills at the disposal of the Allies. Born in Glenboig outside Glasgow, he had followed his father down the Lanarkshire mines, but thieving soon landed him in Polmont Borstal, near Falkirk. From there he graduated to safe-cracking, at which he shortly became expert. Unbalanced, perhaps, by the death of his wife Daisy in 1934, he thereafter pursued his career with a recklessness that his advocate, Sir Nicholas FAIR-BAIRN, once described as 'a lifelong compulsion to break into whatever he was out of and out of whatever he was inside' – a construction that, typically from this source, was inelegant and unhelpful in equal measure.

During World War II Ramensky's skills with gelignite caused him to be dropped behind enemy lines with the commandos, a similar if more active role to that played by Eddie CHAPMAN, his safe-cracking contemporary in England. His job was to break into German safes in captured headquarters, including Goering's, and to release the papers and maps. When the Allies advanced through Italy, he was taken along to blow open the safes in foreign embassies. When the Allies took Rome in 1944, he cracked 14 in one day.

Having won the Military Medal for his services, he returned to Scotland a hero, but was unwilling to forgo his former occupation. For whatever reason, his methods became ever more unpredictable, particularly after he started using Polar Ammon, an explosive whose properties he never properly understood. On one occasion he overdid the gelignite to such an extent that two patrolling policemen, unaware of his activities until that moment, were blown off their feet.

At first judges were lenient to the old war hero because he always pleaded guilty and never attacked the arresting officer except in self-defence. However, the well of sympathy gradually dried up, the sentences grew heavier and Ramensky was never able to reorganize his life in the way that Eddie Chapman had. Released from jail in 1964, he promptly broke into Woolworth's in Paisley. He was caught for the last time in 1971, a frail old man of 66 on the roof of a store in Ayr. He died in prison and was buried with gangland's equivalent of full military honours in St Francis Chapel in the Gorbals.

**Rampa, Lobsang** (1911–75), impostor. In the late 1940s a plumber from Weybridge fell out of a tree and suffered a concussion. When he came round he discovered that his body had been occupied by Dr Lobsang Rampa, a Tibetan lama. In 1956, and as Dr Rampa, the former plumber walked into the London offices of the publishers, Secker and Warburg, and offered his autobiography to the firm's founder, Frederick Warburg. It turned out to be an interesting document, describing how the young Rampa had been singled out by astrologers at the age of 7 to become a monk. At the age of 8 he had had a brain operation that had opened the 'third eye' – the source of man's psychic powers. During this operation a hole had been drilled in Rampa's forehead and a sliver of very hard wood inserted in his brain. This allowed him to see 'spirals of colour and globules of incandescent smoke'. He was told that for the rest of his life he would see people 'as they are and not how they pretend to be'.

Warburg was impressed, but had certain reservations. The prose-style was curiously English, colloquial, even. Various experts, consulted by Warburg, expressed contradictory opinions. When Rampa stood by his story that he was Tibetan, Warburg submitted him to a simple test: a few words of Tibetan. Rampa agreed that he could not understand them, but explained that there was a perfectly good reason. During World War II he had been a prisoner of the Japanese who had tortured him for information about his country. He had used his psychic powers to blot out all his knowledge of Tibet, and its language.

Warburg was satisfied by this explanation and the book was published as *The Third Eye*. It became an immediate bestseller and made Rampa a rich man. However, a group of Tibetan scholars was doubtful about its authenticity and hired a private detective, Clifford Burgess, to investigate Rampa's background. Burgess soon discovered that Rampa was in fact Cyril Hoskins, formerly of Devon, now living in Weybridge. Hoskins had been born in Plymouth and had entered his father's plumbing business. Later, he had become interested in China and claimed to have been taken there as a child. Mr Burgess spoke to a journalist on *Psychic News*, who in turn tracked down a couple, Mr and Mrs Boxall, who had known Hoskins when he was a clerk in Thames Ditton, Surrey. Apparently he had told Mr and Mrs Boxall that he had been a flying instructor in the Chinese air force and had had an accident when his parachute failed to open.

Warburg was unsettled at first by these revelations, but rallied enough to wonder whether 'the whole truth is out? Isn't Rampa perhaps the mouthpiece of a true Lama, as many have alleged?' Journalists went in search of Hoskins and eventually found him in a house outside Dublin, where he was living with a woman whom he had seduced away from her Old Etonian husband. All three declined to be interviewed, but Rampa wrote a second book, *Doctor From Lhasa* (1959), which was published by the Souvenir Press. The publisher's note acknowledged that *The Third Eye* had caused some contention; the explanation was that, since falling out of a tree and suffering a mild concussion, the author had been 'possessed' by the Tibetan lama, Rampa. He had come round to find himself standing beside his physical body, connected to it by a silver cord. Then he had seen a Tibetan walking towards him. 'I have come to you because I want your body,' the Tibetan had said. After thinking it over, Hoskins, for whom things had not been going well, had decided that he might as well hand his body over to someone who would make better use of it. The lama had instructed him to climb the tree and fall on his head again in order to loosen the silver cord. Then another lama had taken Hoskins by the arm and had floated away with him to heaven, leaving Lobsang Rampa to squeeze himself into the vacated body. Rampa had been confronted by such problems as learning to ride a bicycle and claiming unemployment benefit. Life had been difficult and painful until he had met a literary agent and outlined the story of *The Third Eye*.

Hoskins went on to produce several more books, including *Living with the Lama*, *Wisdom of the Ancients* and *My Visit to Venus*, in which he describes how he was taken to Venus in a flying saucer.

**Rankin, Sir Hugh** (1899–1988), variously a riveter's mate in a Belfast shipyard, president of the British Muslim Society and runner-up in the All-Britain Sheep Judging Competition. Sir Hugh was born in the middle of the Tunisian desert, the elder son of Sir Reginald Rankin, a big-game hunter. In India Sir Reginald had shot the largest snow leopard on record, and had survived being frozen asleep in the Andes. Sir Hugh was educated at Harrow, but ran away to work in a Belfast shipyard before joining the 1st Royal Dragon Guards as a trooper. In 1921 he was broad-sword champion of the cavalry. While serving in Ireland during the Troubles – on the wrong side, in his opinion – he was shot by a sniper and invalided out of the army.

Rankin then devoted himself to the study of sheep. When he succeeded to the baronetcy in 1931 he was a sheepshearer in Western Australia, covering the area between Bunbury and Broome. During travels in the Middle East he fell under the influence of the Muslim peer, the 5th Lord Headley, whom he succeeded in 1935 as president of the British Muslim Society. He resigned a few weeks later over a procedural matter, 'They were very rude and knew nothing of law and order. I was disgusted with the whole lot of them.' Since Sir Hugh had always disliked the Christian religion and was now disillusioned with the Muslims, he became a Buddhist. In 1959 he confirmed that Abominable Snowmen existed:

> It is part of our known belief that five Bodhisattvas (Perfected Men) control the destiny of the world. They meet once a year in a cave in the Himalayas to make their decisions. One of them lives in the Scottish Cairngorms.

In 1965 Sir Hugh claimed that he was the only baronet in the United Kingdom who was living on national assistance. Asked what job he might like, he replied, 'Anything except being a butler. I hate snobbishness.' Sir Hugh had no children by either of his marriages, and the baronetcy passed in 1988 to his nephew, Ian Niall Rankin, whose mother, Lady Jean Rankin, was a woman of the bedchamber to the queen mother.

**rape, date.** *See* DIGGLE, ANGUS.

**Rat, the Reverend.** *See* TYLER, THE REVEREND TOM.

**Ratcliffe, Owen** (1923–99), gangster and club proprietor, remembered with respect in gangland circles for having thwarted an attempt by Ron and Reggie KRAY to take over the popular Cromford Club in Manchester. In

1961 Detective Chief Superintendent Frank Williamson, of the Greater Manchester police, received a telephone call from Tabby Booth, a house detective at the Midland Hotel. Two boxers called Gray from the East End of London were making a nuisance of themselves, Booth said, boasting in the hotel bar that they had just thrown the doorman at the Cromford Club down the stairs. The doorman happened to be Jack London, the former heavyweight champion of Britain, and father of Brian London, who once fought Muhammad Ali for the world title without success.

'There was no need for that,' said Williamson later:

> Dear old Jack London, he was no menace by then. I rang the Met and asked about these Grays. They told me they had nothing on them. That was patently false because Grays from the East End who were boxers was an easy link. It was only the next letter in the alphabet. That's the Met for you. Bent as could be.

Williamson and his sergeant, Douglas Nimmo, went round to the Midland Hotel, but the Krays had already left. Owen Ratcliffe had called with a meat cleaver under his Crombie and told them to go away. They never returned. Williamson was later appointed to the position of Her Majesty's Inspector of Constabulary (Crime). In 1969, following allegations in *The Times*, he was called in to investigate widespread corruption in the Metropolitan Police (*see* HUMPHREYS, JAMES; MOODY, DETECTIVE CHIEF SUPERINTENDENT WILLIAM; ROBSON, DETECTIVE INSPECTOR BRIAN).

**Ratcliffe Highway Murder, the.** *See* WILLIAMS, JOHN.

**Rattenbury, Alma** (1897–1935), protagonist in a murder case as sensational in its day, and having many of the same ingredients, as the THOMPSON and Bywaters affair. In 1928 Alma, who had already had two husbands, married a 67-year-old Bournemouth architect, Francis Rattenbury. The differences between the two soon became apparent. Alma was pretty and, by the conventions of Bournemouth, of an outgoing disposition. At the weekly *thé dansant* at the Pavilion she was thought to make herself too conspicuous in the rumba. Rattenbury was dull for his age. In 1934 Alma advertised for a chauffeur, and the job went to George Stoner, an 18-year-old who could neither read nor write. Mrs Rattenbury soon fell for the boy, taking him to stay at a hotel in London, where they became lovers. The next day she bought him some silk pyjamas and a fashionable suit.

On their return to Bournemouth, Stoner was less willing to accept Rattenbury's instructions than he had been, on one occasion refusing to drive the couple to Bridport since the thought of Alma spending the night with her husband was too painful to endure. On the night of 24 March 1935 Alma found Rattenbury with blood streaming from his head. He died later in hospital from a fractured skull. Alma was questioned by the police, but she was incoherent with drink, flirted with the officers and claimed that she 'did it with a mallet'. Meanwhile, Stoner had confessed that it was he who had killed Rattenbury. He and Alma were both arrested, and each remained loyal to the other. She refused to withdraw her confession and Stoner insisted that she had had nothing to do with the murder. At their Old Bailey trial, Stoner was found guilty and sentenced to death. Alma was acquitted. Three days later, and wishing to be with her lover in the hereafter, she committed suicide. A week before he was due to hang, Stoner's sentence was commuted to life imprisonment.

**Rauch, Michael** (1944–83), blackmailer and rent boy involved in the Palace Homosexual Scandal of 1982. In July of that year, when Scotland Yard had only recently recovered from the Intruder in the Palace Fiasco (*see* FAGAN, MICHAEL), the Queen's personal bodyguard, Commander Michael Trestrail, resigned because two of his many homosexual lovers were threatening to reveal the nature of his private life to his employers. One of those who so threatened him was Rauch, who, professionally, called himself Pratt; the other was a Spaniard from the Canary Islands whom Trestrail had met in Hyde Park, and with whom he later went out dancing.

Yorkshire-born Rauch had known the Queen's bodyguard since he was a detective sergeant, and they continued their affair after Trestrail's promotion to the Royal Protection Group. Rauch visited Buckingham Palace on several occasions, and the two men often holidayed abroad together. The commander broke off the relationship when Rauch tried to blackmail him. After reading reports in the press about the Intruder in the Palace Fiasco, Rauch attempted to sell his story to the *News of the World* for £20,000. The paper reported the matter to the Palace and Rauch was interviewed by Scotland Yard detectives on 17 July 1982. The following year, he was found dead in his hotel room in Notting Hill Gate after taking an overdose of drugs. An unnamed friend was quoted as saying:

> No one wanted to know him after he embarrassed the Queen. It's very pro-monarchy, the gay community.

**ravishing of Griselda Murray, the alleged.** *See* GRAY, ARTHUR.

**Ray, Martha** (1734–79), former dressmaker's assistant, debauched when young by the earl of Sandwich, a notorious roué, later living with him as his wife (Sandwich's real wife was mad). Ray was shot dead by the Reverend James HACKMAN, vicar of Wireton, as she emerged from the Covent Garden Theatre, where she had been attending a performance of *Love in the Village*.

**Rayner, Horace** (1880–1953), natural son of William Whiteley, the founder of Britain's first department store. Whiteley's motto was, 'Add conscience to your capital', and he liked to style himself as the 'Universal Provider'. On 24 January 1907 a young man walked into his office and shot him dead. The man, later identified as Horace Rayner, then tried to shoot himself, having first written on a piece of paper, 'To whom it may concern: William Whiteley is my father ...'

Rayner pleaded not guilty to murder at the Old Bailey, maintaining that he had acted while temporarily insane – a condition brought on by the discovery that a woman who he had thought was his Aunt Louisa was in fact his mother. The trial centred less on his sanity than on his illegitimacy. His alleged father, George Rayner, denied that Horace was his son. He admitted that his mistress, Emily Turner, now dead, had been the boy's mother but had improperly registered the birth. He further admitted that he had agreed to act as foster father. Louisa Turner, Emily's sister, then produced a sensation. She said that she had been William Whiteley's mistress for many years. She, Whiteley, George Rayner and her sister Emily had frequently made up a foursome for weekends at BRIGHTON. Both women had illegitimate children. Emily had two by Rayner and she, Louisa, had one by Whiteley. In 1881 Mrs Whiteley had discovered the truth and had sued the Universal Provider for divorce.

Horace Rayner was found guilty and sentenced to death. Within a week 200,000 signatures on a petition for reprieve had persuaded the home secretary to commute the sentence to life imprisonment. Rayner twice tried to commit suicide and was released in 1919.

**Read, Mary.** *See* BONNY, ANNE.

**reality, the nature of.** *See* STRACHEY, WILLIAM.

**reality, the relative merits of.** *See* MCCARTNEY, SIR PAUL.

**recluses.** *See* BECKFORD, WILLIAM; BIGG, JOHN; BRIDGEWATER, FRANCIS HENRY EGERTON, 8TH EARL OF; BRUCE-WALLACE, ANDY; BUTLER, LADY ELEANOR; DERING, GEORGE EDWARD; PAGET, DOROTHY; PORTLAND, JOHN CAVENDISH BENTINCK-SCOTT, 5TH DUKE OF; RUSSELL, JOHN CONRAD, 4TH EARL; SLATER, JOHN.

**rectory, shoot-out at the.** *See* FREE, THE REVEREND EDWARD DRAX.

**Red Barn Murder, the.** *See* CORDER, WILLIAM.

**Redesdale, Clement Napier Thomas Freeman Mitford, 2nd Baron** (1870–1948), aristocrat and animal lover. Redesdale's idiosyncratic perception of his paternal duties was amusingly recreated by Nancy Mitford, one of his seven children, in her novels *The Pursuit of Love* (1945) and *Love in a Cold Climate* (1949). Further evidence was provided by his fifth daughter, Jessica, in her autobiography, *Hons and Rebels* (1960).

Known as Farve to his children, Redesdale was semi-literate and – comparatively – of straightened circumstances, but he made life interesting for the girls, providing them with mongooses as companions, several dogs and a pony. A keen huntsman, he sometimes used the girls as quarry, which they enjoyed. Every few years Redesdale went to Canada to prospect for gold, always unsuccessfully. He had no time for books, or for any form of education that might be acquired from them. His son Tom was sent to school because he was a boy, but the girls weren't educated at all. When Redesdale served at the front during World War I, his eldest daughter Nancy received just one letter which, in its entirety, read:

Dearest Koko, many thanks for your last letter.
Much love
Farv

On one occasion Lady Redesdale read *Tess of the D'Urbervilles* to him. He found it so upsetting that Lady Redesdale felt obliged to tell him that the book was a fiction. Redesdale was astonished. 'What! The damned feller made it up?' He could never be persuaded to look at another book, until Nancy used him as a character in her novels; in these, as 'Uncle Matthew', he would offer such observations as, 'Abroad is unutterably bloody and foreigners are fiends,' and, 'I loathe abroad, nothing would induce me to live there,' and, 'as for foreigners, they are all the same, and they all make me sick.' Later, he was furious to discover that he didn't have a part in her biography of Madame de Pompadour.

Lady Redesdale had some unusual ideas of her own about bringing up children, particularly with regard to health and diet. Although conventionally High Church herself, she insisted that the children observe the ancient Jewish dietary laws. The school food was a welcome relief to Tom, and his first letter home from Eton said, 'We have sossages every day.' At home, the no pig rule was never relaxed. Lady Redesdale called the doctor only in extreme emergencies, but any medicines he prescribed were poured down the drain once he had left.

Their parents' eccentricities notwithstanding, all the girls made their mark in later life. Pam and Deborah married well, the latter becoming the duchess of Devonshire and mistress of Chatsworth (*see* DEVONSHIRE, ANDREW ROBERT BUXTON CAVENDISH, 11TH DUKE OF). The fourth sister, Diana, left her husband for Sir Oswald Mosley, leader of the British Union of Fascists, and spent World War II in prison. Unity, the fifth child, became a personal friend, and possibly a lover, of Adolf Hitler. When Britain declared war against Germany she had a nervous breakdown and shot herself. Jessica, the fifth daughter, eloped with a cousin and ran away to Spain to support the Republican cause in the civil war. In 1939 she moved to California, where she became an American citizen and a member of the Communist Party.

**Reed, Oliver** (1938–99), bibulous show-off, known as 'the hell-raiser's hell-raiser', a title that is thought to have gone to him because no one else wanted it. In a 40-year career, Reed appeared in 108 films, including *The Curse of the Werewolf* (1961), *The Pirates of Blood River* (1962), *Castaway* (1986) and *Fanny Hill* (1984), a soft-core porn movie in which the lead was taken by a Canadian actress, Lisa Raines. *The System* (1963) marked the beginning of a long collaboration with the director Michael Winner. Winner made his reputation with *Some Like It Cool* (1959), which was shot in a nudist camp. With the exception of *Fanny Hill*, Reed's films were judged a disappointment, and he will be remembered best for his off-screen behaviour, which was unusually boorish. When drunk he liked either to be beaten up in pubs by members of the working class or to indulge in acts of unfocused exhibitionism – the latter aspect of his character guaranteeing him many appearances on Michael Parkinson's television 'chat show'. When the occasion was less intellectually demanding, it amused him to take out his penis, which was decorated with a tattoo. In 1973 he stripped naked in a Madrid restaurant and dived into an aquarium. On that occasion he was beaten up by the Spanish police. If there was no one else to fight, he fought himself, once knocking himself out. Reed died in Malta in 1999 while filming a bit part in *Gladiator* for Ridley Scott. He had been relaxing in a pub in Valletta and suffered a fatal heart attack after drinking three bottles of rum and getting the worst of an arm wrestling contest with a local fisherman.

*See also* MOON, KEITH.

**reefers endanger white teenagers at boogie-woogie clubs.** *See* MARKS, HOWARD.

**referee head-butted by linesman, football.** *See* MAY, MICHAEL.

**rent boys.** *See* NEWTON, ARTHUR (for Charles Swinscow); RAUCH, MICHAEL.
   *See also* BROTHELS, KEEPERS OF 'SODOMITICAL'; THIN BLUE JEANS, THE.

**restaurateurs, drunken.** *See* LANGAN, PETER; VIVIAN, ANTHONY CRESPIGNY CLAUDE, 5TH BARON.

**Restoration, aristocratic hooliganism in the.** *See* DORSET, CHARLES SACKVILLE, 1ST EARL OF.

**resurrectionists.** *See* BURKE, WILLIAM; HARE, WILLIAM; BODY SNATCH-
ERS, IRISH.

**revolver, occasional trips to New York equipped with a.** *See*
CARSTAIRS, MARION BARBARA.

**revolver for shooting wasps, a miniature.** *See* SITWELL, SIR GEORGE
RERESBY.

**Reyn-Bardt, Peter** (1919–93), businessman and murderer. In May 1983
two peat cutters working at Lindow Moss, near Wilmslow, Cheshire, dug
up the skull of a middle-aged woman. Police reported the find to Peter
Reyn-Bardt, a former executive with BOAC at Manchester airport,
whose wife Malika had disappeared in 1960. He had married Malika to
hide his homosexuality, and, faced with this discovery, he now confessed
to her murder. He had strangled her, chopped up her body with an axe
and buried the pieces in a Wilmslow peat bog. He was tried at Chester
and sentenced to life imprisonment. After his confession the skull was
sent to Oxford University for radiocarbon dating. The laboratory
reported that the head was that of a woman aged between 30 and 50, and
that she had died in about AD 410, during the last years of the Roman
occupation. In the following year a more complete skeleton was dug up
and this one, to the relief of the police, was more clearly the victim of violence. There was evidence of stab wounds and there was a garotte round
the neck in the form of a knotted thong. Once again experts were consulted at Oxford University. This time they reported that the skeleton was
that of a man who had probably been killed in a ritual sacrifice in approximately 300 BC. Wilmslow's peat bog had yielded Britain's earliest known
murder victim, and Reyn-Bardt had confessed to murder on the discovery
of a prehistoric corpse. The whereabouts of Mrs Reyn-Bardt remain a
mystery.

**Reynolds, Bruce** (1933– ), scholarly and charismatic leader of the notorious South-Western Gang of thieves. In her book *A Robbers' Tale* (1966),
Peta Fordham, wife of the distinguished defence barrister Wilfrid
Fordham QC, names Ernest Watts as the firm's founder and Reynolds's
mentor; others argue that it was Connie Wilkin. 'Watts?' says one:

> A good dresser. A good thief. But as the organizer? No. That was
> Connie Wilkin. He was the business, Connie Wilkin.

Whatever the truth of the matter, once the firm had been taken over by
Reynolds it pulled off two of the most celebrated robberies of the 20th
century: the London Airport bullion robbery in 1962 (*see* GOODY,
GORDON), and, having teamed up with Tommy Wisbey's outfit, the South
Coast Raiders, the Great Train Robbery of 1963.

*See also* BIGGS, RONNIE; BUTLER, DETECTIVE CHIEF SUPERINTENDENT THOMAS; FIELD, BRIAN.

**Rhino-Whip Case, the.** In March 1963 two brothers, Albert and Kenneth Hartley, and a third man, Patrick Bowman, were arrested in the White Horse public house in Malinda Street, Sheffield. Later they were questioned to such good purpose with a rhino whip that all three needed urgent medical attention. The beating followed the establishment under Detective Chief Superintendent George Carnill of a zero-tolerance elite squad set up to deal with Sheffield's rising crime rate. The squad had met with little success at first, and on 14 March its members had been called to a meeting by Carnill at which devotion to duty and the need for hard-nosed methods had been stressed.

Shortly after the meeting, two young constables, Derek Millicheap and Derek Streets, arrested the Hartley brothers and Bowman. According to the *Sheffield Police Appeal Inquiry* (HMSO 1963):

> Apart from a screwdriver and a pair of gloves which we are satisfied were not dropped at the time of the arrest, as claimed by DI Rowley [DCS Carnill's second-in-command], there was no evidence to justify this precipitate action and it is clear that DI Rowley expressed the view that confessions must somehow be obtained or DCS Carnill (using his nickname Chang) would be furious.

The Hartley brothers and Bowman were questioned at CID headquarters in Water Lane, Sheffield. The blinds were drawn and the aim of the interrogation, which included beating with the rhino whip, was to get confessions to break-ins at the Crookes Valley Park Café and the Forum Cinema. The two brothers were charged, but Bowman was released.

When they appeared in court the next morning, Albert Hartley stripped to the waist and showed the marks on his body to the magistrates. All charges against the Hartleys were dropped. After the hearing, the chief constable, Eric Staines, ordered that the matter be dealt with internally. On 27 March Arthur Hewitt, the solicitor for the Hartleys, was granted summonses against Millicheap and Streets under s18 and s20 of the Offences Against the Person Act, 1861.

The first defence concocted was that the bruising on the brothers was the result of self-inflicted sadomasochistic acts. On 2 May Streets and Millicheap pleaded guilty to the lesser charge, s20, and in return the charge under s18 was dropped. Their counsel then put forward a new and improved defence. The Hartleys had been drunk and offensive and had started a fight with others in the public house. As Mr Peter Baker, for the defence, put it:

> They were so truculent, foul-mouthed, obscene and quarrelsome

that they had to be restrained by these two young officers. They did not stop at restraining them, but laid into them and gave them what some might think these men possibly deserved.

No mention was made of the rhino whip, which had long since been 'lost'.

The magistrates believed the defence version of the incident. PC Streets was fined just £75 for his assault on Albert Hartley, on his brother Kenneth and on Patrick Bowman. PC Millicheap pleaded guilty to similar offences against Bowman and Alfred Hartley and was fined £50. Both had been assured by their superiors that the matter would end there. Instead, they were dismissed from the force by Chief Constable Eric Staines. They appealed the decision at a tribunal, chaired by Graham Swanwick, which found that there had been a concerted effort by the Special Crime Squad to explain away the injuries. According to the tribunal report:

> Five days were spent in anxious deliberation by the squad, concocting versions that might meet or mitigate the allegations. The evidence of PC Streets that Detective Inspector Rowley was the main author of the concocted versions is confirmed without a doubt.

Apart from the suggestion – soon dropped – that the injuries had been self-inflicted for sexual gratification, the police put forward three accounts of what had happened: first, that there had been a struggle at the time of the arrest; second, when it was thought that as many as four officers might be charged, that a fight had taken place in the lavatory between Bowman and the Hartley brothers; and third, that this had been broken up by Streets and Millicheap, with DC Rowlands and DI Rowley coming to their assistance. When it was discovered that only Streets and Millicheap were to be charged, they were left to face the music on their own.

The willingness of Streets and Millicheap to accept the blame was based on a fear that if they implicated other officers, the latter would 'gang up against them'. They thought, too, that if they involved senior officers they would not be believed by the magistrates and that any apparent attempt to shift the blame – with the accompanying suggestion of disloyalty – would count against them. Finally, they had been advised to plead guilty by DCS Carnill and DI Rowley, and assured that they would not lose their jobs.

The tribunal accused Chief Constable Eric Staines of living in an ivory tower and concluded that he relied too heavily on DCS Carnill:

> When the appellants were convicted (and indeed before) he shut his eyes to the evidence of the photographs supporting the prosecution version as given in court, and was content to accept the version of the fight in the lavatory without further inquiring into its probable falsity.

DCS Carnill was criticized even more severely, not least in the matter of the 'disappearing rhino whip'.

The appeals of Streets and Millicheap were dismissed, and on 6 November 1963 the Sheffield Watch Committee announced the suspension of Chief Constable Staines and DCS Carnill. Two weeks later DCS Carnill and DI Rowley announced their retirements. Staines resigned on 20 November. He died in Bournemouth in 1979.

**rhubarb in the streets of Smyrna, selling.** *See* NORCOTT, WILLIAM.

**Rice-Davies, Mandy** (1943– ), courtesan, nightclub singer and Christine KEELER's vivacious colleague in the Profumo scandal, the details of which kept the country entertained throughout the summer of 1963. Miss Rice-Davies is remembered for the most quoted riposte in English judicial history. At the trial of Stephen WARD in July 1963 it was put to her that Lord Astor denied that she was a friend of his. 'Well, he would say that, wouldn't he?' she replied. The judge, Sir Archie Pellow Marshall, became so confused that he thereafter referred to her as Marilyn Monroe.

*See also* RACHMAN, PETER.

**Richard III** (1452–85), king of England and chief suspect in what has been called the longest running investigation in criminal history: the mystery of who murdered the Princes in the Tower. As the duke of Gloucester, and brother of King Edward IV, Richard may also have been implicated in the deaths of Prince Edward, the son of Henry VI; in the murder of Henry himself; and in the celebrated drowning in a wine butt of his own brother, the duke of Clarence. His supporters claim that his reputation was blackened in the reign of his successful rival, Henry VII; further, that his character, and even his physical appearance, have such a hold on the public imagination thanks to Shakespeare's demonic creation in *Richard III* that he cannot be judged objectively.

Most historians agree that, while the evidence is inconclusive, it is highly probable that in June 1483, and in order to secure the throne for himself, he did murder his nephew, the 13-year-old Prince Edward, and his younger brother, Prince Richard. To some commentators this was forgivable. In an extraordinary passage in *The Lives of the Kings and Queens of England* (1975), Lady Antonia Fraser writes, 'The murder of two innocent children was a horrible crime even by 15th century standards, but it is difficult to see how Richard could have let them live without risking needless conspiracies in their names. His real failing as a king was his inability to win over the great magnates whose support was crucial to any medieval regime. For all his solid virtues ...' Those who find this point of view congenial could write to Mrs Dorothy Mitchell, 'The Society of Friends of King Richard III', 121 Windsor Drive, Wigginton, York YO32 2RZ. Membership costs £10 (senior citizens, £6, overseas subscribers, £15). The most balanced account of this period is still Anthony Cheetham's *The Life and Times of Richard III* (1972).

**Richardson, Charlie** (1934– ), gangster. With his brother Eddie, Richardson became the dominant figure in the south London underworld in the 1960s. A contemporary of, and in constant dispute with, the East End gang run by Ron and Reggie KRAY, Charlie Richardson was a better businessman than the twins, while sharing their penchant for extreme violence. He was born in Twickenham, the son of a prize-fighter and merchant seaman. Soon after his birth the family moved to Camberwell, and it was from there that Charlie was later to build an empire that was part legal – through his scrap-metal business and foreign investments – and part illegal, through clubs, extortion and long-firm frauds. In 1962 he discovered that still greater profits could be made by setting light to the warehouse buildings used in the frauds and claiming the insurance money – once their contents, which hadn't in any case been paid for, had been sold.

Further income was generated for the family when, on returning from a trip to Manchester, Eddie Richardson and Frankie FRASER – joint proprietors of Atlantic Machines, a juke-box operation – quite fortuitously uncovered a car-parking fiddle at Heathrow airport. Attendants were adjusting the time clocks that marked the visitors' tickets so that cars seemed to have been parked for less time than they actually had. The money that didn't have to be accounted for netted the attendants £1000 a week. This became £500 a week after Fraser and Richardson had introduced themselves and pointed out the merits of their involvement.

While Eddie Richardson was content to work mainly in London, and certainly within England, Charlie Richardson had more ambitious plans. He toyed with the idea of owning a coal tip in Wales, but discarded this on the advice of a Major Herbert Nicolson, an alderman in Bedford and well connected in the Conservative Party (*see* BOLLOCKS, A SILLY). Richardson had heard of the opportunity to obtain the mining rights on 4 million acres in Namaqualand. The group that already had the rights needed finance, and Major Nicolson introduced its principals to Richardson. Once in South Africa, Richardson found a number of opportunities available, including the chance to smuggle diamonds inside frozen fish. However, he was gradually persuaded that there was more money to be made from mining, in particular the possibility of exporting perlite from South Africa. This led to his involvement with BOSS, the South African secret service. In the mid-1960s he met Gordon Winter, a shadowy figure who combined work for South African intelligence with a job on the *Sunday Express*. Winter introduced Richardson to influential figures who were glad to have a man in London prepared to burgle the offices of anti-apartheid groups. In *Rough Justice* (1981), Robert Parker claims that in March 1966 Charlie Richardson organized a break-in at the Anti-Apartheid Movement's headquarters in Charlotte Street and stole files that included the names and addresses of members. The offices of the *Zimbabwe Review* and of Amnesty International were also burgled, both, it is alleged, by Richardson.

From the start of his career Richardson maintained good relations with the police, as he makes clear in his autobiography, *My Manor* (1991):

> The most lucrative, powerful and extensive protection racket ever to exist was administered by the Metropolitan Police. As I got older and became involved in more and more dealings, legal or otherwise, I made regular payments to the police. It was sort of taxation on crime. Sometimes we would pay people to be 'found' committing small crimes so that our friendly local protection racketeer in blue could have somebody to arrest and look like he had been busy.

While there is no reason to doubt the general truth of this, Richardson, like the Krays, eventually discovered that not all the police are corrupt – or, at the very least, that there are some who, from time to time, judge it to be in their interests to make a big arrest rather than a profit. The Richardsons' downfall was the consequence of over-confidence on this score, combined with misdirected violence. For some time Charlie had been in business with a portly conman known as Jack 'the Rat' Duval. Duval's specialities in the late 1950s and early 1960s included the importing of goods in short supply such as silk stockings, a travel company that took advantage of the new appetite for Continental travel, and a small bank in Park Lane, which Richardson had helped him to set up. When Duval withdrew money from this latter enterprise without permission, he was summoned to Richardson's office, where he was beaten up. Duval then passed some dud cheques on Richardson and disappeared. Unable to find Duval, Richardson instead beat up an associate of his, Lucien Harris, an educated man who also compiled crossword puzzles for a living. What happened to Harris formed the cornerstone of the case that eventually brought the Richardsons down. As far as Charlie was concerned, Harris – and others who later gave evidence against the gang – suffered nothing worse than a few slaps, which they more than deserved for taking liberties. According to Harris and the others, they were subjected to systematic and sadistic beatings, involving the use of pliers and a black box that administered electric shocks to their testicles.

Whatever the truth of the allegations, Harris wasn't satisfied with the clean shirt and a handout of £150 that was customarily given to Richardson's victims after a beating. Instead he talked to Gerald McArthur, the chief constable of Hertfordshire, who was beginning to put together a case against the Richardsons. At 5 a.m. on the July morning in 1966 that England were due to play West Germany in the World Cup Final, a team of 60 officers under McArthur arrested 11 members of the Richardson gang, including Charlie.

Eddie Richardson and Frankie Fraser were already in prison, having been convicted in June 1966 on charges of murder and causing an affray at MR SMITH'S club in Catford. On 4 April 1967 Charlie and Eddie Richardson, Frankie Fraser and five others went on trial at the Old Bailey before Mr Justice Lawton. Prosecuting counsel, Sebag Shaw, opened impressively:

> The eight men in the dock are part of a gang of thugs under the leadership of Charles Richardson whose policy and practice over a number of years was to enforce his will and his intentions by violence and intimidation. The case is not about fraud and dishonesty, it is about violence and threats of violence, not, let me say at once, casual acts of violence committed in sudden anger or alarm but vicious and brutal violence systematically inflicted deliberately and cold-bloodedly and with utter and callous ruthlessness.

Charlie Richardson was sent to prison for 25 years, the highest-ever sentence for grievous bodily harm. Fraser and Eddie Richardson both received 10 years. 'Someone swore blind I pulled his teeth out,' said Fraser later. 'In fairness, he gave me a good due as a dentist. Said it was absolutely painless.' Since his release in 1984 Charlie Richardson has occupied himself mainly in the City, whose practices he claims are more dishonest than any he was previously involved in. He has also resumed his interest in Africa, mainly Uganda. In October 1990 at Winchester Crown Court, Eddie Richardson was sentenced to 25 years for conspiracy to smuggle 153 kg of cocaine from Ecuador.

**riding master, committing adultery with the.** *See* HALL, NEWMAN.

**Riots, the Gordon.** *See* DENNIS, EDWARD; GORDON, LORD GEORGE.

**Riots, the Porteous.** *See* PORTEOUS, CAPTAIN JOHN.

**Ripper, Jack the.** *See* JACK THE RIPPER.

**robber barons.** *See* LOWSON, SIR DENYS.

**Robbers, the Great Train.** *See* BIGGS, RONNIE; FIELD, BRIAN; GOODY, GORDON; REYNOLDS, BRUCE.

**robbery, exchange is no.** *See* DUDLEY, CAPTAIN RICHARD.

**Roberts, 'Bawdy House' Bob** (*c*.1825–?), pimp and keeper of a prostitute, Agnes Willoughby, formerly a shop girl in a Regent Street mourning outfitters. In 1861 Roberts sold Agnes in marriage to William Frederick Windham, known as 'Mad' Windham since his days at Eton. In exchange he received the timber on Windham's estate. It was further agreed that Agnes would stay with Roberts until her wedding day. This arrangement gave rise to a lunacy case brought against Windham by his uncles, Lord Bristol, Lord Alfred Hervey and General Windham, known since the Crimean victory at Sebastopol as 'Windham of the Redan'. In their attempt to have 'Mad' Windham committed to an insane asylum, his uncles brought to the Commission in Lunacy reports of the young man's gluttony, incessant masturbation, lack of personal hygiene, a broad Norfolk accent in spite of years at Eton, and his habit of patrolling the West End in a police uniform as a means of 'arresting' such street girls as took his fancy.

The boy's uncles failed to persuade the Commission in Lunacy that young Windham was mad, however odd he might appear. Sir William Hardman, chairman of the Surrey quarter sessions, identified the weakness in the uncles' case as the character of General Windham. The victor of the Redan was known for certain 'foul practices'. He had once been accused of indecent exposure in Hyde Park, and was only got off by a plea of insanity by his counsel. In the event, General Windham was advised to stay silent at the hearing. Despite this precaution, the jurors found his nephew sane.

Four years later 'Mad' Windham died of an obstruction of a pulmonary artery at the age of 26. Agnes, her infant son, who was of disputed paternity, and 'Bawdy House' Roberts remained in possession of Windham's estate at Hanworth, Norfolk, with a sum of £12,000 and rents of more than £5000 a year. These new circumstances allowed 'Bawdy House' Roberts to give up his previous occupation and to pursue the life of a country gentleman.

**Robertson, James** (*c.*1712–90), soldier known as 'the Daft Highland Laird', a sobriquet earned by his serial attempts to be imprisoned. Born in Perthshire, Robertson was a supporter of the Stuart cause and he fought enthusiastically, but with no great distinction, in the Jacobite Rebellion of 1745–6. He was soon captured, but the authorities decided he was harmless and they let him go. He had greatly enjoyed his time in prison, and in his anxiety to be locked up again he did everything he could to bring about his own arrest. He advertised himself in public as a rebel partisan, drank the Pretender's health and tried to whip up treason in the streets, but the authorities continued to ignore him. Crime seemed to be the only recourse left to him, so he had himself imprisoned for refusing to pay his rent. Friends immediately settled the debt, but Robertson refused to leave his cell. In an act of trickery, his desperate captors informed him that he would, after all, be tried for high treason and that a court of judges had been assembled for this purpose. Accordingly, two soldiers came one morning to his cell to escort him to the court. A delighted Robertson walked proudly ahead of them into the street, whereupon the soldiers stepped back into the prison building and locked him out.

The trick seemed to knock the wind out of Robertson's sails, and, for the most part, he occupied himself thereafter in carving likenesses of his enemies in wood. He displayed these in the streets of Edinburgh, at the same time handing out snuff on his daily walk.

**Robinson, Anne** (1750–?), servant girl and perpetrator of the 'Stockwell Ghost' hoax of 1772. In that year Anne and her mistress, an elderly lady called Mrs Golding, became the victims of weird ghostly activities: pots and pans flew up the chimney; hams, cheeses and loaves of bread took up new positions in the kitchen. Mrs Golding became so alarmed that she arranged for several of her neighbours to witness these strange events. As tables and chairs moved of their own accord from one side of the room to the other, the neighbours decided that this was the Devil's work. One by one they departed from Mrs Golding's home, to be followed shortly by Mrs Golding herself, who, for safety's sake and accompanied by her devoted servant girl Anne Robinson, went to live with her widowed sister Marigold on the other side of Stockwell.

The disturbances followed them. Now it was Marigold's crockery, dry goods and provisions that took on a life of their own. Marigold asked her sister and Anne Robinson to return home, which, reluctantly, they did. When the ghostly antics immediately started up again at Mrs Golding's house, she began to suspect some human agency at work. She dismissed Anne Robinson, and the inexplicable happenings stopped. A short time later Anne made a complete confession to a local clergyman, the Reverend Mr Brayfield. Her motive had been to drive Mrs Golding from her home so that she could have it for herself and her lover, a local boy. She had taken as her example the celebrated Cock Lane Ghost hoax of 1762. This had involved the Reverend Mr Moor, a prominent businessman, Mr Slattery, his wife Mary, their 11-year-old daughter Elsie and a servant girl, all of whom had been greatly enriched. Anne Robinson had simply arranged Mrs Golding's crockery so precariously on shelves that it would fall to the floor at the slightest disturbance. To move other objects, she had attached horse hairs to them, which she had been able to tug on from an adjoining room. A contemporary study described her as:

> Exceptionally dextrous at this sort of work. She would have proved a formidable rival to many a juggler by profession.

She was more fortunate, too, than the inventors of the Cock Lane Ghost. At their trial, the Reverend Mr Moor was sentenced to stand three times in the pillory; Mr Slattery received two years in prison, Mrs Slattery one year, and the servant girl six months. There is no record of Anne Robinson having been punished.

**Robinson, Brian** (1944–  ), armed robber. Known as the 'Colonel', Robinson led the gang which on 26 November 1983 broke into the vaults of the Brinks-Mat security company on the Heathrow International Trading Estate, poured petrol over the guards and offered them, as alternatives, incineration or the surrender of the vault's keys. The guards chose the latter. Robinson had expected to find between £1 million and £2 million, which was the usual amount of cash deposited on a Friday night. Instead, the gang discovered £26 million in the form of gold bars waiting to be sent to the Middle and Far East. It was the biggest haul in British criminal history.

The inside man had been Tony Black, a guard at Brinks-Mat who was married to Robinson's sister and whom Robinson had been courting on weekend fishing trips. Black had been given Plasticine and cuttlefish 'bones' so that he could make impressions of the warehouse keys and pass them back to the team assembled by Robinson. He had been promised a substantial reward if the job succeeded but had been told that he would have to work at Brinks-Mat for at least another five years to allay suspicion. That Robinson, an experienced career criminal, had used as an inside man someone so identifiably close to him greatly surprised the police. Black was picked up within 24 hours by the Flying Squad and soon named the robbers. Robinson, Micky McAvoy and an associate called Tony White were arrested. On 17 February 1984 Black pleaded guilty and was sentenced to six years after the court had been told that he would assist in the prosecution of the main conspirators. Robinson, McAvoy and White appeared at the Old Bailey on 25 October. They pleaded not guilty, offered alibis and challenged Black's evidence. White was acquitted, but Robinson and McAvoy were both sentenced to 25 years. The robbery was successfully dramatized on television as *Fools' Gold*, with the popular actor, Sean Bean, appearing in the role of McAvoy.

*See also* NOYE, KENNETH.

**Robson, Detective Inspector Brian** (1930–  ), policeman. Although a very minor criminal compared to others in the Metropolitan Police, Robson contributed significantly to what became known in the 1970s as 'the Fall of Scotland Yard'. On 29 November 1969 *The Times* published an article alleging corruption by Robson, head of a crime-busting operation code-named Coathanger, together with two more junior officers, Detective Sergeants John Symonds and Gordon Harris. According to *The Times*, the three detectives had been practising extortion on Michael Perry, a small-time Peckham thief. On one occasion Robson had threatened to plant gelignite on Perry, the paper claimed, unless he agreed to their demands.

The next day Perry had paid Harris £250 for not telling a court about a previous conviction for receiving, and soon after that, when Robson saw Perry sitting in a car, he had handed him a packet, pretending that it contained a stick of gelignite.

Perry sought the advice of southeast London crime boss Joe Pyle, who had suggested that he give the story to *The Times*. Perry was wired for sound by two senior reporters, Garry Lloyd and Julian Mounter, and his conversations with Robson, Harris and Symonds were subsequently taped. The tapes and statements were handed to the night-duty officer at Scotland Yard at 10 p.m. on 28 November 1969. The investigation that followed was less than exhaustive, a consequence of its being handled by Detective Chief Superintendent Bill MOODY, one of Scotland Yard's most corrupt officers. DCS Moody, who drove a Lancia bought for him by leading Soho pornographer Jimmy HUMPHREYS, and who was later to receive a prison sentence of twelve years, may have enjoyed the irony of investigating colleagues whose dishonesty was amateurish compared with his own. Nor did matters improve when Frank Williamson, an inspector of constabulary and a notably uncorrupt policeman, was appointed as advisor to the inquiry. The problems put in his way were almost insurmountable, as Williamson later made clear:

> By the time I got there, John du Rose [operational head of the Metropolitan CID] had got Moody in to sabotage the whole thing. He was active in the obstruction of *The Times* inquiry right from the start. He had got Moody involved and there was only one reason for that. It wasn't long before du Rose put his ticket in and went to National Car Parks. I can't prove why, but I know why. Because he got the wind up. He realized that the game was partially up. From that moment on, Brodie, who was Assistant Commissioner (Crime) and Waldron, who was the Commissioner, never spoke to me. Brodie said things about me which if I'd been of that frame of mind I'd have taken him to the cleaners.

Although Williamson's investigation was unsuccessful, the reputation of the Metropolitan Police never recovered from the revelations in *The Times*. In 1972 Robson was jailed for seven years and Harris for six. Symonds had fled the country before the Old Bailey trial, but was sentenced to two years when he surrendered in 1979. On his release from prison he sold his story to a Sunday newspaper, claiming that a barrister with close links to the Crown Prosecution Service office was bisexual, and, which seemed less likely, that for the last ten years he, Symonds, had been working for the Soviet KGB in their honey-trap division.

**Roche, Tiger** (1729–?), soldier, duellist and alleged thief, his nickname deriving from the occasion when he attacked a picket guard with his teeth.

Roche was born in Dublin into an ancient and aristocratic Norman family. His brother was Sir Boyle Roche, celebrated for his lateral thinking in a number of anthologized sayings. ('Posterity be damned! What has posterity done for us?') An able and intelligent young man, Roche was offered a commission in the army at the age of 16, but he fell in with a group of bucks such as the earl of Rosse (*see* HELL-FIRE CLUB, THE IRISH) whose riotous pastimes he preferred to soldiering. One night he and his drunken friends killed a night watchman. Roche avoided arrest by boarding a ship to America, where he fought with the French in their wars against the Indians.

When the British and the French declared war on one another, Roche switched to the British army and became an officer. He might have achieved high rank had a fellow officer not accused him of stealing a valuable fowling piece. He was court-martialled and dismissed from service with ignominy. He refused to go quietly, however, challenging the officer who had accused him to a duel, which was refused. He then flew at his guard and tore his throat open with his teeth, thus earning his sobriquet of Tiger.

On his return to Dublin, he married an heiress and became a man about town – his skill as a dancer and the glamour of his nickname adding to his social status. After he had run through her fortune, his wife left him. To escape his Irish debts he returned to London, but his creditors followed him. He was arrested and locked up in the King's Bench prison. Among his fellow prisoners was Buck English, famous for having shot a waiter – thereafter requesting that he be put on the bill for £50.

On his release, Roche enlisted as captain of a company of foot attached to the East India Company, a position that offered some opportunity of recovering his fortune. No sooner had he set sail on the *Vansittart* in May 1773, however, than he had a violent argument with a Captain Ferguson, of the sort that could only be settled by a duel. When the *Vansittart* arrived at Madeira, Captain Ferguson went ashore to discover a firm duelling ground. To his astonishment, Tiger Roche refused to fight. The enclosed circumstances of life on board seemed to have reminded Roche of his former incarceration in the King's Bench prison. He quivered with fright and offered an abject apology. His fellow officers were so disgusted by this performance that for the rest of the voyage they banned him from eating at the captain's table and forced him to mix with the common sailors.

When the *Vansittart* reached Cape Town many of the officers went ashore, including Captain Ferguson. One night Ferguson was found murdered outside his lodgings. Suspicion fell on Tiger Roche, who fled into the bush and sought refuge with the Bushmen. When the *Vansittart* sailed on without him he was put on trial by the Cape authorities, and acquitted. Thereafter Roche, with his fighting instincts recovered, strove to prove his innocence to the world. He had himself shipped back to England, where on 11 December 1775 he stood trial at the Old Bailey for the murder of Captain Ferguson, and was acquitted. The vindication came too late. At the age of 40, impecunious, scarred, half mad and disgraced – the fiasco of the Madeira duel was well known in London – Tiger Roche was no longer wanted in London society. This time he made it all the way to India, where he disappeared, and died.

**Rolls Royces irritating to the police, pink.** *See* JONES, JANIE.

**Rolls Royces waterproofed for underwater driving.** *See* DE COURCY, KENNETH.

**Roose, Dr Leigh Richmond** (1883–1917), footballer. Known as the 'Mad Doctor', Roose played in goal for Everton, Sunderland and Arsenal and was capped on 24 occasions by Wales. Since he was an amateur, he was obliged throughout his career to fill in a weekly expenses sheet. His claims for reimbursement ranged from the extravagant – 'to hire of train from King's Cross to Doncaster, £163 45d ...' (Roose lived in London and preferred not to travel to away matches with the rest of the team) – to the trivial – 'to use of toilet, twice, two pence'. His goalkeeping technique was idiosyncratic. Unless he was kept busy he became distracted, sometimes wandering off and sitting with the crowd. In one international, so little of the play was at his end of the field that he completed the match wearing his overcoat. He much preferred to be fully occupied and on one occasion, when Wales played Ireland at Cardiff in 1909, he fulfilled two roles. The Welsh full-back suffered an injury and, since this was in the days before substitutes were allowed, Wales were reduced to ten men. Normally in such circumstances a forward would have been moved back into defence, but Roose insisted on playing simultaneously in goal and as an overlapping full-back, or wing-back as it would now be called. His many weaving runs into his opponent's half caused Wales to lose their shape and Ireland won the match 8–0.

**Rosebery, Archibald Philip Primrose, 5th earl of** (1847–1929), statesman and racing man. It has been alleged that while serving as foreign secretary in Gladstone's last government (1892–4), Rosebery had a homosexual affair with his 27-year-old private secretary, Viscount Drumlanrig; furthermore, that it was fear that the relationship would become public knowledge that led to Drumlanrig's suicide in 1894.

Rosebery had succeeded his grandfather as 5th earl in 1868 at the age of 21. In 1878 he married Hannah Rothschild, who died twelve years later. In 1881 he entered Gladstone's government as a junior Home Office minister. When the Liberal Party was in dispute with itself over Irish Home Rule, Rosebery remained loyal to Gladstone, and as a reward Gladstone made him foreign secretary in 1892. In the same year Rosebery appointed Viscount Drumlanrig as his private secretary, notwithstanding the fact that the young man lacked all qualifications for the post. He then sought further advancement for his protégé as a lord-in-waiting to the queen. To fill this position, Drumlanrig needed to be made an English peer in his own right, since his father, the bellicose marquess of QUEENSBERRY, had not been re-elected as a representative peer since 1881 and could not sit in the House of Lords. When Queensberry heard that Rosebery planned to elevate his eldest son to the peerage he flew into a rage and informed the queen in a letter that her foreign secretary was a sodomite. Later, he pursued Rosebery to Bad Homburg, where he was taking the baths with the prince of Wales, and threatened him with a dog whip.

Queensberry's behaviour fuelled rumours of Rosebery's homosexuality, which had always been suspected. Nevertheless, when Gladstone resigned in March 1894 Rosebery succeeded him as prime minister. On the weekend of 18 October Drumlanrig, who had become engaged to a young woman called Alix Ellis, stayed at Quantock Lodge near Bridgewater, the home of his new fiancée's uncle, Edward Stanley. While out on a shoot Drumlanrig became separated from the other guns. After a while a shot was heard. His companions ran to investigate and found the young viscount lying dead. The coroner later recorded a verdict of 'accidental death', but it was generally assumed that Drumlanrig had taken his own life under the strain of repressed scandal.

Whatever the truth, the consequences were far reaching. In his rage, and believing that homosexuality was a condition that could be passed on like a virus, Queensberry was prepared to blame Rosebery not only for the death of his favourite son, but also for the relationship of his other son, Lord Alfred Douglas, with Oscar Wilde. He plotted his revenge against the playwright, first trying to interrupt the first night of *The Importance of Being Earnest* in 1895, and, when thwarted in that ambition, leaving his calling card with its celebrated libel at Wilde's London club. At Wilde's first trial for sodomy in April 1895, the jury, amid rumours that they had been influenced in order to protect Rosebery, failed to agree a verdict. Tim Healy, the Irish Nationalists' leader in the Commons, asked the solicitor general, Lockwood, not to try Wilde a second time. Fearing accusations of a cover-up, Lockwood replied, 'I would not but for the abominable rumours against Rosebery.' On 21 May Sir Edward Hamilton, Gladstone's former private secretary, wrote in his diary:

> The Oscar Wilde case has been brought forward again; and unless there is some cantankerous juryman a verdict is expected this time. A verdict of guilty would remove what appears to be a wide-felt impression that the Judge and Jury were on the last occasion got at in order to shield others of a higher status in life.

After Rosebery's government was defeated in the general election of 1895, he remained the leader of the Liberal opposition until his resignation in 1896. His political stance after 1909 was Independent or Conservative. In 1911 he was created earl of Midlothian. His horses won the Derby on three occasions (1894, 1895 and 1905).

**Rosner, Fred** (1922– ), footballer. Playing on the left of midfield for Downham FC in Division Four of the Hackney and Leyton League until 1999, 77-year-old Rosner was thought to be the oldest footballer in England. Sadly, in all his years in the game his only award was a Hackney and Leyton League Cup runners-up medal in 1956–7. His other memories are of three broken noses and a blood clot in his leg. His disciplinary record was good: his name only went into the referee's book once, when he was sent off at the age of 68. The decision still rankled with Rosner nearly ten years later:

> The referee was a woman. No disrespect, but I think it was her first game. When she blew for offside at a corner, I said to her quietly, 'You can't be off-side from a corner'. I was only trying to explain the rules, but she sent me off.

In November 2000 he reported that he had recovered from the blood clot and hoped to play again in the near future. He admitted, however, that although fit, he wasn't match fit.

**Rosse, Richard Parsons, 1st earl of.** See HELL-FIRE CLUB, THE IRISH.

**Rothermere, Lady 'Bubbles'.** See CHATHAM, GEORGE; WOMEN OF HUMBLE ORIGINS WHOSE BEAUTY AND WIT GAINED THEM AN ENTRY INTO SOCIETY.

**Rottweiler inadvertently sits on bomb.** See ARISTIDES, SUSAN MARY.

**Rottweilers, 'playful'.** See DALY, JOSEPHINE.

**Rottweilers named Brinks and Mat, two.** See NOYE, KENNETH.

**Rouse, Alfred Arthur** (1893–1931), commercial traveller, bigamist, womanizer and perpetrator of the Blazing Car Murder. In the early hours of 6 November 1930 William Bailey and Alfred Brown were walking home after a Guy Fawkes party in Hardingstone, Northants, when they came across a Morris Minor that was on fire. As they approached a man scrambled from a ditch and said, 'It looks as if someone has had a bonfire,' before hurrying away. When the blaze was put out, the car was found to contain an incinerated corpse. The body was unidentifiable but the car was traced through its still intact number plate to Alfred Rouse, a commercial traveller living in Finchley, north London. When the police called at that address, Mrs Rouse said that her husband had left early that morning on a business trip.

At first it seemed that Rouse had died in a tragic accident, but the story about the man in the ditch made the police suspicious. A description of Rouse was circulated, and he was shortly identified getting off a bus in Hammersmith. On 7 November he was interviewed by the police. He immediately said, 'In a way, I consider myself responsible. I am glad it's over.' His story was that on a journey to Leicester he had picked up a hitch-hiker on the Great North Road near St Albans. He had stopped the car near Headingstone in order to relieve himself in a field, and he had asked his passenger to fill the tank meanwhile from a spare can of petrol in the boot. Before leaving, he had given the man a cigar and had then set off down the road. He had hardly completed his business when he saw the car go up in flames. He had then panicked. 'I lost my head,' he said.

Rouse was charged with the murder of an unknown man and appeared at Northampton assizes in January 1931. The story that emerged at the trial was of a philanderer and bigamist, who had seduced as many as 80 women in the course of his travels, had countless illegitimate children, and was now struggling under the cost of maintaining several homes. 'My harem takes me to many places,' he had said when first arrested. Rouse was convicted and sentenced to death. After he was hanged at Bedford Prison on 10 March 1931 his confession was published by the *Daily Sketch*. He had planned the whole thing with great care, he said, choosing a victim who would not be missed. He had supposed that the incinerated man, whom he had strangled, would be mistaken for himself, and that he would be free to start a new life. The victim's identity was never established.

**Rowley, Michael** (1934–  ), sales manager and cricket enthusiast. In August 1981 Mildred Rowley was granted a divorce on the grounds that her husband, Michael Rowley, had left the marital home to take up residence in Stourbridge Cricket Club's pavilion. Mrs Rowley, 51-year-old sister in a local nursing home, said:

> I object to cricket being the be-all and end-all. Mike could tell you who scored what years ago and what the weather was like at the time. But he couldn't remember my birthday unless I reminded him.

At the time of the divorce, Rowley, who worked for a steel company in Smethwick, had been the club's scorer for 21 years and had missed only one match – when he went to Headingley to watch England play Australia. He conceded that Stourbridge Cricket Club was the cause of the divorce. 'Cricket is the only life for me,' he said. 'I don't blame Mildred.' Rowley was not in court to hear the termination of his 17-year marriage. He was in

Devon with Stourbridge who, under their touring name of Worcestershire Marauders, were playing Torquay Cricket Club.

**royal family sent sprawling in the sawdust, the Dutch.** *See* CONYERS, DAVID.

**royal garden parties, scoundrels at.** *See* HALL, ARCHIBALD.

**royal intruders.** *See* FAGAN, MICHAEL.

**royals, problematic.** *See* YORK, SARAH MARGARET, DUCHESS OF.

**Rubell, Ida** (1910–91), theatrical landlady. In 1979 Miss Rubell was tried at Leeds crown court for abducting, killing, plucking and cooking a performing parrot called Arthur, before serving it with rice as the dish of the day. 'Arthur was no ordinary performer,' said his owner, George 'Parrots are my Business' Birch, who had been staying at Miss Rubell's guest house. 'He spoke three languages, ate scrambled eggs and had a small but varied repertoire of love songs.'

Miss Rubell admitted that Mr Birch was an excellent guest. 'But I couldn't take the parrot,' she said. 'It waddled round the hall asking for its bill and complaining about the service. It was me or the parrot.' Miss Rubell was bound over to keep the peace.

**rugby players attempt to kidnap gangster, abseiling.** *See* KNIGHT, RONNIE.

**rugby players who tackle parked cars.** *See* ADAMS, TOMMY.

**rumba, making oneself too conspicuous in the.** *See* RATTENBURY, ALMA.

**Russell, John Conrad, 4th Earl** (1921–87), aristocrat, political theorist and writer. Russell, who was the elder son of the logician, Bertrand Russell, was noted for his controversial speeches in the House of Lords. In 1978 he advocated the abolition of law and order, a state of affairs, he argued, which, if achieved, would prevent the police from putting young people into brothels and sending them out to serve other people against their wills. At this point, Russell was interrupted by Lord Wells-Pastell who reminded him of the length of time he had been speaking. Russell immediately left the chamber.

Earlier, and for more than an hour, Russell had spoken of the need for:

... universal leisure for all, and a standing wage sufficient to provide life without working ought to be supplied, so that everyone becomes a leisured aristocrat.

It was from this premise that the earl had inferred the undesirability of a constabulary:

> The police ought to be totally prevented from ever molesting young people at all, from ever putting them into jails and raping them and putting them into brothels.

Changing the direction of his argument, Russell had then said that in a reorganized modern society:

> ...women's lib would be realized by girls being given a house of their own by the age of 12 and three-quarters of the wealth of the State being given to the girls so that marriage would be abolished and the girl could have as many husbands as she liked.

The earl summed up by suggesting that Mr Leonid Brezhnev, the Soviet leader at the time, and Mr Jimmy Carter, the president of the United States, were the same person.

Russell received his early education at his parents' experimental school in Hampshire where there were no compulsory lessons and where the children were encouraged to express themselves by answering their teachers back, to the point of rudeness if candour demanded. After his parents' divorce he lived with his mother, Dora, in America, where he went to Harvard. He worked briefly for the Food and Agriculture Organization of the United Nations in Washington, but after the collapse of his marriage to Susan Lindsay (the daughter of the American poet Vachel Lindsay) he became a recluse, living with his mother in a cottage near Land's End. He occupied himself by writing and – a newly acquired skill – by crocheting. To a visitor in the 1960s he said, 'I like to sit and think and write my thoughts. The few people who have seen my work find it too deep for them.' He then pointed to a pair of trousers hanging on a nail:

> I crocheted those out of string. It took a long time because I didn't have a pattern. I had to keep trying them on.

Lord Russell died while travelling on a train to Penzance.

# S

**Sabini, Charles** (*c.*1880–1950), gang leader and community 'godfather'. By offering bookmakers muscular on-course protection in the 1920s, the Sabini brothers were among the originators in Britain of organized crime and gang warfare in their modern forms. Bookmakers were expected to purchase other services and amenities too, such as stools, race cards, even the chalk with which they posted the odds and the sponges with which they wiped their blackboards clean. Pitched battles between rival gangs were common. A favourite weapon was a razor stitched into the peak of a cap.

By the early 1920s the courses at Newbury, Epsom, Alexandra Palace and Kempton Park were protected by the Sabini family. A Birmingham gang, known as the Brummagem Boys and led by Billy Kimber, dominated most of the Midlands and much of the north. Kimber had ambitions to extend his empire in the south and in 1921 the Brummagem Boys, supported by a gang from Leeds, took on the Sabinis at Epsom on the last day of the Derby meeting. The northern alliance got off to a disappointing start when the Brummagem Boys ambushed their Leeds allies, only realizing their mistake when a Leeds man shouted out, 'You've made a bloomer! We're Leeds men.' The battle, once properly joined, lasted ten minutes, and 23 of the Brummagem Boys were badly injured. They returned to the Midlands and didn't venture south again.

The victorious Sabinis were an Italian immigrant family who had launched the Bookmakers and Backers Racecourse Protection Society to establish their dominance over other London gangs. Rumoured to be connected with the Sicilian Mafia, Charles (usually known as Darby), Joseph, Fred, George and Harry Boy Sabini operated from a base in Clerkenwell, east London, which was the Little Italy of the era. Darby, a former boxer who had worked as a bar-room bouncer in nearby Hoxton, held the position of 'godfather' in the local community. He sorted out disputes and defended the honour of young Italian women against unwelcome attentions from neighbourhood louts.

The family used extreme violence to protect their reputation. According to ex-Detective Chief Superintendent Edward Greeno of the Flying Squad (*War on the Underworld*, 1960), 'Darby Sabini and his thugs used to stand sideways-on to let the bookmakers see the hammers and razors in their pockets.' The most celebrated of their conflicts was the 'battle of Lewes' in June 1936. A gang of 30 Londoners, mainly from Hackney and Hoxton, attacked a Sabini-protected bookie, Alf Solomons, and his clerk, Mark Frater. Frater was fortunate to be wearing his bowler hat, which partly deflected a hatchet blow delivered by Harry 'Moishe' Spinks, the leader of the Hoxton mob. The affray was broken up by the police, and 16 of the participants were later jailed. Mr Justice Hilbery, who was proud of his linguistic skills, addressed the Sabinis in Italian, which none of them could understand. Having informed the jury that the name derived from the Sabines, he then recounted at length the story of the Sabine women (later to become familiar to a wider audience through the high-spirited Hollywood musical *Seven Brides for Seven Brothers*, 1959).

It was the beginning of the end for the Sabinis. After an unflattering profile appeared in the press, Darby sued for libel, lost and was declared bankrupt. When World War II broke out two of the brothers were interned as enemy aliens. When Darby received a short prison sentence for receiving, Harry Boy became head of the family. While Darby was inside, his son, who had joined the Royal Air Force, was killed in action. Darby retired to the south coast and died in Hove in 1950, a broken man. His funeral was a muted affair by gangland standards, but his old adversary, Chief Inspector Jack 'Charlie Artful' Capstick, who had founded the Ghost Squad at Scotland Yard in 1946, was seen to throw a red rose on to the grave. The Sabinis were succeeded by the White family from King's Cross, who in turn gave way to Billy HILL.

**Sackville, Victoria-Josepha, Baroness** (1862–1936), aristocrat and charity fundraiser. The illegitimate child of an Italian ballroom dancer and an English diplomat, Lady Sackville was of a contradictory and unpredictable temperament. Her attitude to money alternated between moods of reckless spending and extreme caution. In possession of a cheque for £20,000 from J.P. Morgan made out to bearer, she left it in a taxi and forgot all about it. On another occasion she was persuaded by a stranger on a train to invest £60,000 in a gold mine. On the other hand, she adopted the habit of piecing together the non-postmarked fragments of used stamps to save the cost of new ones. Another economy was to conduct her correspondence on lavatory paper taken from the ladies' room at Harrods.

An inconvenient idiosyncrasy for her family and guests was Lady Sackville's love of fresh air. She never lit a fire at Knole, her country house in Kent, kept the windows open at all times and insisted that meals should be taken out of doors, whatever the weather. Guests at dinner were obliged to wrap themselves in fur coats and place a hot-water bottle on their laps. Her cure for a sore throat was to tie a pair of the architect Edwin Lutyens' socks round her neck. Unlike her daughter, Vita, who was a distinguished gardener, Lady Sackville preferred artificial flowers, since they were always in bloom and were resistant to slugs. On one occasion when Vita was coming to lunch, and wishing to impress her daughter, she sent out for £30 worth of garishly coloured paper flowers, which she planted in an artistic arrangement in the garden.

Lady Sackville worried constantly that the upkeep of Knole would become too expensive for the family to bear. At the outbreak of World War I, worried that her husband, Lionel, might be called up, she wrote directly to Lord Kitchener pointing out that he must on no account be posted to the front line since Knole would be unable to survive the death duties due if he were killed. Later she wrote again to complain that the call-up policy was decimating her staff:

> I think perhaps you do not realize, my dear Lord K, that we employ five carpenters, four painters, two blacksmiths and two footmen and you are taking them all from us! I do not complain about the footmen, although I must say I had never thought to see parlour-maids at Knole! I am sure you will sympathize with me when I say that parlourmaids are so middle-class. Not at all what you and I are used to. But I do complain about the way you take our workmen from us.

Lady Sackville was not always able to distinguish a charitable enterprise from a profit-making one. Often she solicited funds, without identifying herself as the beneficiary. One of her favourite charities was for 'The Homeless Sleeping on Brighton Beach', which was not registered with the Charity Commissioners and from which only she was enriched. Contributions to the Million Penny Fund, set up to eliminate the National Debt, were solicited in a more open manner. Having checked the newspapers to discover which famous people were celebrating their birthdays, Lady Sackville asked them to send her one penny for each year of their life. The letter she wrote ended with the request:

> Please enclose three stamped envelopes, one for the cost of mine to you, one for having the pleasure of thanking you, and one for a fresh solicitation.

Late in life, she decided to hold a white elephant sale, but, as she said to Vita, 'You know, people have them at bazaars, but I shall have this one for myself.' Then, since elephants came from Siam, she wrote to the king and asked for a white one. He sent her a small but valuable silver elephant.

**sadomasochistic pornography in Europe, the most comprehensive library of.** *See* EDINBURGH, PRINCE PHILIP, DUKE OF.

**sadomasochistic practices.** Following Judge Rant – *Laskey* (1987) QBD – in *re* Operation Spanner, consensual sadomasochistic activities listed by Templeman LJ (*Templeman* HL B278/1988) as being legal included being beaten with leeks, clamped, suspended, stretched, trussed; undergoing colonic irrigation; the use of surgical stirrups, strangulation masks, oranges and paper bags; the participation in violent sports such as boxing, karate and rugby football; and male (but not female) circumcision. *See also* LASKEY, COLIN; SWINDELL, PETER GEORGE.

**safe-crackers, master.** *See* AGAR, EDWARD; CHAPMAN, EDDIE; HINDS, ALFRED; RAMENSKY, JOHNNY.

**Sailor, Will the.** *See* FLOOD, MATTHEW.

**St Albans, Charles Beauclerk, 13th duke of** (1915–88), journalist, film maker and property speculator. The 13th duke's attempt to recover the family's wealth by putting his title to profitable use in commerce ended in disappointment. For many years successive holders of the dukedom of St Albans, created by Charles II for his illegitimate son by his mistress Nell Gwynn, had inherited almost nothing in the way of influence or estates. There was an entitlement to a haunch of venison once a year on the sovereign's birthday, but even that custom was thought to have lapsed. Charles Beauclerk's cousin, and immediate predecessor, 'Obby', the 12th duke, had received a typical setback when claiming his right, as hereditary grand falconer of England, to attend Elizabeth II's coronation in 1953 with a live falcon perched on his arm. When he was told that he could bring only a stuffed bird he returned his invitation. 'Obby' had displayed other eccentricities. It was his custom when invited to stay for the weekend at a country house to arrive with a paper bag containing his pyjamas and a toothbrush. Another oddity was an unwillingness, whether through lassitude or inexperience, to perform tasks requiring any degree of manual or technical dexterity; he used to tell the hall porter at Brooks's Club to 'wind my watch, there's a good fellow'.

At the time he succeeded to the dukedom, Charles Beauclerk, who had previously contributed articles to the *Evening Star* newspaper and had lived in rented accommodation, was employed in the film division of the Central Office of Information. His immediate ambition was to use his title to advance his business prospects, but he showed poor judgement in the company he kept, and after a series of financial scandals he was forced to admit that his involvement in the world of commerce had brought him nothing but problems. In 1973, when chairman of Grendon Trust, a property company, the 13th duke was severely censored in a Department of Trade report. He had sold his holding in the company to a young entrepreneur called Christopher Selmes at a time when the board was trying to secure a higher counter-bid from the Metropolitan Estates and Property Corporation. He was cleared of conspiracy, but the report accused him of having lied to the City Panel on Takeovers and Mergers. St Albans had made £793,000 from the deal.

After the Inland Revenue sued him for £182,000 in 1978, St Albans sold his two houses in Chelsea and went to live in the south of France, where his second wife, Suzanne Fesq, owned property. He returned regularly to London to have his hair cut at the Ritz, and continued to champion the claims of his ancestor, the 17th earl of Oxford, to have written the works of Shakespeare. He was succeeded by Murray de Vere Beauclerk, a chartered accountant.

**St Clair, Lindi** (1951– ), dominatrix. A specialist in what 'rendezvous' magazines advertise as 'correction', and what the French refer to as '*le vice anglais*', Miss St Clair became celebrated in the late 1970s for the vigorous campaigns she waged against the Inland Revenue and Companies House. When Britain joined the European Community it meant that for the first time the Revenue could levy income tax on prostitutes. (British governments had been sensitive until then to accusations of living on immoral earnings.) Miss St Clair immediately understood that her business was no different, from a fiscal point of view, to any other supplying specialized services and that to qualify for legitimate tax relief she must form herself into a limited company. Once incorporated, she would be entitled to recover some of the cost of maintaining her torture chamber in Earl's Court.

Miss St Clair first chose 'Prostitute Ltd' as the title of her business, but was informed by Companies House that this 'would not be appropriate'. Miss St Clair replied that, on the contrary, it would be hard to think of a name that was more appropriate; further, that if her services were respectable enough to be taxed then they were respectable enough to be reflected in the name of her company. Companies House remained opposed to this choice, so she made an application to register a £50,000 limited company in the name of Lindi St Clair (Personal Services) Ltd. The attorney general, Sir Michael Havers, judged that this was a matter in which his department should become involved and in December 1980 he argued in the High Court against the registration of Lindi St Clair (Personal Services) Ltd, on the grounds that it had been formed for 'immoral purposes'. This argument lacked force since Miss St Clair's purposes were immoral or otherwise regardless of their corporate status, but the court ruled in Sir Michael's favour.

Meanwhile, the tax inspectors called in a leading firm of accountants,

Deloitte Touche Ross, to advise them on tax allowances to which prostitutes might be entitled. It was agreed that these could include wear and tear
on the tools of the trade, which, in the opinion of Deloitte Touche Ross,
and following *Templeman* HL B278 1988 (*see* PRACTICES, SADOMASOCHIS-
TIC), included, whips, hawsers, masks, bondage bars, irrigation pumps,
surgical stirrups, rubber suits and suffocation masks. In their turn, Miss St
Clair and her corporate tax lawyers felt they had achieved a result when in
April 1981, and on a turnover of £500,000, she was served with a tax
demand for only £19,781 for the year 1974–5.

While the arguments continued, *Private Eye* magazine revealed that
Miss St Clair had produced a list of her clients for their benefit. One of
them was His Honour Judge Alan King-Hamilton QC, who in 1973 had
sent Janie JONES to prison for seven years, remarking at the time that she
was the most evil woman he had ever sentenced. Sir Michael Havers was
the father of the matinee actor, Nigel Havers, who was caught up some
years later in the Wigmore Street Massage Parlour Scandal. On that occasion, the duchess of York's father, Major Ronald Ferguson, was also
involved.

## St Germans, Nicholas Richard Michael Eliot, 9th earl of

(1914–88), peer, bookmaker, expatriate and police informer. Known as the
'Bookie Peer', the earl's sense of humour was of the kind that runs to contributing amusing entries on oneself to reference books. In *Who's Who* he
described his education as 'at great expense to my parents' and his hobbies
as 'shootin' a line and fishin' for compliments'. Having participated in
horse racing as owner, trainer and bookmaker, St Germans opened a turf
commission agency in 1950 and three years later was called as a witness in
the celebrated Francasal betting coup in which two horses were switched
at Bath (*see* DILL, SIR VICTOR ROBERT COLQHOUN). In his evidence, St
Germans (or Lord Eliot, as he then was) said that one of the conspirators
had come to him with 'quite a childish suggestion'. This turned out to have
been that the wife of the chief constable of Bath should be presented with a
fur coat. The earl went straight to Scotland Yard, where he informed on his
friends.

St Germans succeeded to the title and 6000 acres in 1960 and, having
made the latter over to his son, went as a tax exile to Tangier. Calling
himself the 'Tangerine Earl' and listing his telegraphic address as 'Earls
Court', St Germans was popular among locals but he admitted that there
were things he missed about England. These included treacle tart and a
decent game of backgammon. Perhaps it was depression brought on by a
bout of homesickness that caused him in 1963 to let off an unauthorized
gun in the Safari Bar, after which he spent a night in a police cell.

## Sala, George Augustus (1828–96), journalist, satirist and pornographer.

In what he would have called his 'real life', Sala was a respected foreign correspondent for *Household Words* during the Crimean War and for the *Daily Telegraph* throughout the American Civil War. He was also the chronicler of London life in *Twice Around the Clock* (1858) and of Paris after the Franco-Prussian War in *Paris Herself Again* (1878). He often boasted that the *Telegraph* 'treats me like a king and pays me like an ambassador', so it cannot have been a desire for greater riches that persuaded him to write pornography. A delight in moral subversion was the motivation behind such works as *The Mysteries of Verbena House; or, Miss Bellasis Birched for Thieving* (1882), described by Henry Spencer ASHBEE as 'one of the best and most truthful books of its kind'. The setting is a girls' finishing school in Brighton, where punishable behaviour seems to be the norm among the pupils. Readers with disciplinary tastes are generously provided with scenes of delicate classroom retribution. The school's spiritual adviser, the Reverend Arthur Calvedon, is permitted to watch these acts of chastisement through a spy hole and afterwards to consummate his excitement with Miss Sinclair, the school's proprietor.

Sala's pornography, like that of his friend Algernon Charles Swinburne, was subversive of its natural enemy, the middle class. Condemned in respectable households for the subject matter of his *Poems and Ballads*, Swinburne had retaliated with *La Fille du policeman* and *La Soeur de la reine* in which he gave Queen Victoria a twin sister who was a Haymarket prostitute and created a court for the queen peopled by such characters as the duchess of Fuckingstone, Miss Sarah Butterbottom, the marchioness of Mausprick and Miss Polly Poke. Equally, when Dr J.L. Milton in his *Pathology and Treatment of Spermatorrhoea* (1877) recommended chastity as a discipline to be adopted by the middle classes – arguing that every orgasm drains away vital bodily fluids, condemning abusers to imbecility and an early grave – Sala greeted it with *Harlequin: Prince Cherrytop and the Good Fairy Fuck*, an amusing pantomime containing such deft choruses as:

> Pity us courtiers, who, moanin' and groanin'
> Are forced willy nilly to imitate Onan,
> Daily and monthly it's surely undoing us,
> Seminal weakness will certainly ruin us!

Nor did Sala miss an opportunity to salute the English attachment to corporal punishment as the cornerstone of morality in school and family:

> Lord: Good morning, Lady Clara, you I see,
> Are waiting for the King as well as me.
> Lady: 'As well as I,' is grammar, Sir, I ween,
> Beside, I wait not for the King but Queen.
> Lord: I stand corrected. 'Tis the only way
> That I can stand, excuse the jest, this day.

*See also* BACCHUS, REGINALD; CARRINGTON, CHARLES; HOTTEN, JOHN CAMDEN; SELLON, CAPTAIN EDWARD; STOCK, LIEUTENANT ST GEORGE H.

**Salisbury, Frances Mary, 1st marchioness of** (1750–1835), outspoken aristocrat, whose death was as spectacular as her life. The fire that destroyed the marchioness's home in Hatfield, and in which she perished, was started at the top of her head. Even in old age she wore her hair piled high and decorated with feathers, after the fashion of her youth. Rising from the table one evening, she entangled this inflammable tower with a chandelier and started the blaze that consumed her.

Throughout her life Lady Salisbury had upset the strait-laced with her extravagance, gambling and limited observance of what was thought to be appropriate behaviour on the Sabbath. She did occasionally go to church, but only for social reasons. Arriving late at the Chapel Royal in London once, she found the place full. One of her daughters asked, 'Where shall we go, Mamma?' 'Home again,' the marchioness replied. 'If we can't get in, it is no fault of ours – we have done the civil thing.' Obliged on another occasion to sit through a service by the provision of an empty pew, she was astonished, on hearing the story of Adam and Eve for the first time, to discover that when Adam was rebuked by God for eating from the Tree of Knowledge he had pusillanimously blamed Eve. 'A shabby fellow indeed!' the marchioness exclaimed. In Hatfield she upset conventional opinion by holding card parties on Sunday mornings and concerts in the evening. These conflicted with matins and evensong in the local church. This inconvenience was sometimes overcome by the cancellation of the relevant service – a necessary consequence of the rector of Hatfield's frequent presence at Lady Salisbury's card parties.

The marchioness made no concessions to the passage of time, surrounding herself more and more with young people as the years went by and modelling her dress and behaviour on theirs. At the age of 80 she still hunted, but, like El Cid before his final battle, was bolted upright in the saddle, and, since she was too blind to see where she was going, the horse was attached by a leading rein to a groom. When they came to a hedge the groom would shout out, 'Damn you, my Lady, jump!' and, as often as not, over they went. Happily, she had been hunting on the day her hair caught fire.

**Salisbury, Robert Arthur Talbot Gascoyne Cecil, 3rd marquess of** (1830–1903), Tory party statesman and prime minister (1885–6, 1886–92, 1895–1902). Salisbury was profoundly suspicious of democracy, which he thought a 'dangerous and irrational creed by which two day-labourers shall outvote Baron Rothschild'. Since he represented a small borough dominated by the influence of his cousin, the marquess of Exeter, he was never obliged to participate in a contested election himself, but this didn't prevent him from describing the vote-winning process as:

> ... days and weeks of screwed up smiles and laboured courtesy, the mock geniality, the hearty shake of the filthy hand, the chuckling reply that must be made to the coarse joke, the loathsome, choking compliment that must be paid to the grimy wife and sluttish daughter, the indispensable flattery of the vilest religious prejudices, the wholesale deglutition of hypocritical pledges ...

It can be said in Salisbury's favour that he showed the same unwavering disdain for those in power as for the people they supposedly represented. Two months after he first took his seat as the Tory member for Stamford, he announced that there was 'no escape from taxes, toothache or the statesmanship of Mr Disraeli'. This greatly embarrassed Salisbury's father who was in Disraeli's cabinet. On another occasion he criticized what he saw as a merely pedantic manoeuvre by Gladstone as 'more worthy of an attorney than a statesman'. Gladstone was offended and demanded an apology. For once, Salisbury obliged. His words had been too harsh, he said, and he had done a great injustice to attorneys. Another attractive quality was his indifference to the pursuit of power. In the middle of his maiden speech he paused, yawned and sat down – too bored, it seemed, to continue. On the first two occasions on which he was offered the premiership he turned it down. At the end of his first period as prime minister, his son caught his mood correctly when he telegraphed to his father the message, 'I hear you are turned out. Many congratulations.'

Salisbury's contempt for ambition and display was apparent from the way he dressed. His clothes were so scruffy that he was once arrested in his own grounds on suspicion of being a poacher. In 1886, when he was prime minister, he was refused entry to the casino at Monte Carlo because he was thought to be a tramp. Lady Salisbury wrote that on one occasion his dress 'nearly caused the death from consternation' of the prince of Wales, later EDWARD VII. A combination of absent-mindedness and indifference to his appearance had caused him to call on Edward, who was a stickler for sartorial ethics, in the trousers of one uniform and the tunic of another. When this was pointed out to him, he apologized. 'It was a dark morning and I am afraid, Sir, that my mind must have been occupied by some subject of less importance.'

At the age of 70, Salisbury decided to lose weight by exercising in St James's Park on a tricycle – an enterprise that did more for the fitness levels of his groom, who, since his employer was too infirm to get the machine rolling on his own, was obliged to push start both it and its heavyweight passenger, and, when it lost impetus, to set it off again.

In later life, Salisbury's absent-mindedness and failing eyesight made it difficult for him to recognize even close relations if encountered unexpectedly. Standing next to the queen at a court ceremony, and seeing a young man smiling in his direction, he asked a neighbour, 'Who is that?' He was told that it was Lord Cranborne, his eldest son.

**Salisbury, Sally.** *See* PRIDDEN, SARAH.

**Savundra, Emile** (1923–76), insurance swindler. Savundra was able to induce in himself all the symptoms of a cardiac arrest – a skill that got him out of a tight corner on more than one occasion. When he arrived in London in the late 1950s he had already been imprisoned in Belgium for fraud, but because his obituary had been published in the Belgian press those who might have discouraged his career in Britain thought that he was dead. In 1963 he decided to go into motor insurance, an ambition that was easily realized at the time since under the Road Traffic Act anyone was free to do so who could lay their hands on £50,000. With a front man, Stuart de Quincey Walker, he started Fire, Auto and Marine Insurance. This quickly prospered since its premiums cost half as much as those of its rivals. Within two years, the company had a turnover of £5 million, and Savundra was enjoying an arriviste's customary benefits – a house in Hampstead, a power boat and a fleet of motor cars.

By the end of 1965 it was obvious to everyone except the Board of Trade that claims against Fire, Auto and Marine were exceeding its income, and the British Insurance Association, fearing a crash, asked the Board of Trade to carry out an investigation. The Board of Trade replied that 'there appeared to be no danger of insolvency'. In April 1966 Savundra's co-directors put pressure on him to save the business by selling some of his assets, but he refused. Instead, he resigned from the board and departed for Switzerland, leaving Stuart de Quincey Walker to run the rapidly collapsing enterprise. It was then discovered that the certificates issued by the company were useless. Buried deeply in the small print was a clause that said that no claims would be met if, in the opinion of the company, 'a car in an accident was being driven in an unsafe or unroadworthy condition or manner'. This ruled out every situation except an act of God.

The *Sunday Mirror* pursued Savundra to Switzerland, but when confronted he clutched his chest and lapsed into unconsciousness, thereafter being stretchered to a clinic, from which he shortly disappeared. The Board of Trade now demanded that the company be wound up, which left over a quarter of a million motorists with worthless policies and with over £1.5 million owing in claims. Savundra was found to have paid himself £300,000 during the company's short existence and to have funnelled £900,000 out of its accounts and into a bank in Liechtenstein that he controlled.

For reasons that remain unclear – though vanity may have played a part – Savundra returned to Britain in 1967 to be interviewed on television by

David Frost. In front of a studio audience that was made up of widows who had lost their husbands in car crashes and had not received financial compensation, Frost robustly accused Savundra of having had his hand in the till. Savundra replied that he had delegated foolishly, and was then stretchered from the studio with the symptoms of a heart attack. A week later he was arrested. His lawyers claimed that he had already been tried by David Frost, but he was sentenced to eight years in prison, which he spent in hospital. On his release, Savundra said that he had to take 40 pills a day and that henceforth he would 'live off my wife, like the aristocracy'.

**Saward, James Townshend** (1805–?), lawyer and forger. A defence lawyer with a substantial criminal practice conducted from his Inner Temple chambers, 'Barrister' Saward was the most successful forger of his day, an elusive figure known in the underworld, and to the police, only as 'Jem the Penman'. His anonymity was preserved by the skill with which he had built up a network of accomplices. These had been recruited from the ranks of grateful former clients, who in turn employed other offenders who didn't even know of his existence. In the event of a mishap, there was nothing to connect 'Barrister' Saward to the crime.

Saward's method as a forger was to use professional cracksmen to enter commercial premises and, without leaving evidence of a break-in, to open the safe and steal blank cheques. Once he had the cheques in his possession, Saward went to some lengths to obtain the signature of his victim on a document or letter. With this as a model, he was able to inscribe a near perfect imitation on the stolen cheque.

His chief accomplices were a Shoreditch safe-breaker named Henry Attwell and a confidence trickster, William Salt Hardwicke, who had connections in Australia. Saward eventually overreached himself in September 1856 when he attempted to swindle four firms of Yarmouth solicitors at the same time. The operation was botched by Attwell and Hardwicke, who were arrested by the police at their Yarmouth lodgings and charged with obtaining £1000 by forgery.

The investigation had not yet penetrated Saward's carefully structured anonymity but he judged it time to leave his chambers at 4 Inner Court. It was already too late. When it was put to Hardwicke and Attwell at their trial that they could hardly expect leniency while their co-conspirators remained at large, Attwell immediately informed on Saward. On 26 December 1856, John Moss of the City of London police received a tip-off that Saward was hiding in an Oxford Street coffee shop under the name of 'Hopkins'. A raid was carried out and Saward arrested. On 5 March 1857, he was tried for the various crimes of 'Jem the Penman' at the Central Criminal Court. Henry Attwell and William Hardwicke testified against him, the jury took just five minutes to bring in a guilty verdict and 'Barrister' Saward – destroyed eventually, just as his contemporary and colleague,

Edward AGAR, had been, by that lack of corporate loyalty without which no business enterprise can thrive – received transportation for life.

**Scotch disease, the.** *See* GREEN, MARY.

***Scotch Express, A True Story of a Virtuous Lady Ravished and Chastised on the.*** *See* CARRINGTON, CHARLES.

**Scotland Yard, the Fall of.** *See* HUMPHREYS, JAMES.

**Scotsmen to be taxed for living south of the border.** *See* HANGER, GEORGE.

**Scott, Norman** (1940– ), male model and riding instructor whose alleged homosexual relationship with Jeremy THORPE brought about the latter's downfall.
*See also* BESSELL, PETER.

**Scott, Peter** (1930– ), cat burglar. In the late 1950s Scott inherited George 'Taters' CHATHAM's place at the head of the profession. A loquacious Ulsterman who held his clients in no great respect ('upper-class prats chattering in monosyllables'), Scott always insisted that he was driven by a love of danger rather than by greed. 'Fear is a very private form of excitement,' he explained, 'and it's sexual in context.' His planning was meticulous. Before setting off on a job he always bought a new suit, since he felt uneasy if his clothes were not of a standard one might expect to see in the accommodation he was burgling. Early in his career he had come across a butler laying a table with majestic silverware. 'I felt like a missionary seeing my flock for the first time,' said Scott. 'I realized that this was to be my life's work, persecuting the rich.' He was never modest about his talents:

> As soon as Lester Piggott throws his leg over a horse, you can see the magic. As soon as I threw a leg up a drainpipe, my confederates could see the magic.

On the other hand, and confusingly perhaps, he thought that the term 'cat burglar' had been romanticized:

> You're only a dishonest window cleaner. I often see window cleaners doing much more dangerous things than I've ever done.

Dangerous or not, it was the possibility of capture that excited him. During one break-in, 'a titled lady came to the top of the stairs. "Everything's all right, madam," I shouted up, and she went off to bed thinking I was the butler.' On other occasions when he disturbed a resident he would reassuringly cry, 'It's only me!'

Scott's most celebrated job was the theft of jewellery from Sophia Loren. While making a film in England in the summer of 1960, the Italian actress was staying at the Norwegian Barn, in the Edgewarebury County Club. On 28 May Scott drove into the area in a stolen Jaguar with a press card on its windscreen. A petrol pump attendant, taking him to be a journalist, gave him Miss Loren's exact address. He later saw her putting empty Chianti bottles into a bin and remembers her as 'an attractive peasant girl'. He then broke into her rooms and removed a briefcase containing cash and jewels to a value of approximately £200,000. Miss Loren announced on television that she came from old Gypsy stock and had put a curse on the thief – one that worked, Scott admitted, since he immediately lost everything in a casino.

Scott defended his calling to the end:

> My victims were prestigious people, greedy, predatory people and it's been my privilege to persecute them. I feel I have been an agent of God bringing retribution to the self-satisfied. I have an endemic hatred of them.

In the course of his career, Scott stole, by his own estimation, money and jewellery worth £30 million. In 1985 he retired to a council flat in Islington, north London. His wife Jackie, a model, had already left him.

> You become invisible in poverty. Sometimes a Rolls Royce slows when it sees me. I can feel them thinking, "there's no mileage in talking to Peter now", and it glides away. I gave all my money to headwaiters and tarts.

Scott's career was the subject of a film, *He Who Rides the Tiger* (1970), starring Tom Bell and Judi Dench. He was in Dartmoor when they were shooting the film and he made little money from it.

**Scott, Lady Selina** (1850–1917), blackmailer. When the 2nd Earl Russell, grandson of the prime minister and the elder brother of the philosopher Bertrand Russell, married Mabel Edith, daughter of Selina, Lady Scott, in 1890, he found himself in the clutches of two women whom he later described as 'having the morals of a pair of Choctaw Indians'. Lady Scott, who was already separated from her husband Sir Claude Scott, first tried to divert Russell's attentions away from her daughter and towards herself ('I have had plenty of good offers but must get riches,' she wrote to her friend, the elderly countess of Cardigan), and then attempted to extort money from him by allegations of homosexuality. The details of this scheme were plotted at premises in Cranbourne Street, Leicester Square, where Lady Scott's sister worked as a masseuse and whose proprietor, Arthur Carrez, sold rubber goods and pornography on the ground floor. The manoeuvre was unsuccessful, and in 1896 Lady Scott was imprisoned for criminal libel. In his determination to escape his wife and her mother at any cost, Russell entered into a second marriage in the United States only a month after a Nevada divorce – which wasn't recognized by the English courts. Mabel Edith, urged on by Lady Selina, sued on the grounds of bigamous adultery, and Russell was arrested on 17 June 1901. Having chosen to be tried by his fellow peers in the House of Lords, he pleaded guilty and was sentenced to three months in prison.

The right to trial by peers was abolished by the Criminal Justice Act of 1948 (*see* DE CLIFFORD, LORD EDWARD SOUTHWELL RUSSELL).

**Scottish financial prudence.** *See* LAW, JOHN; PANACEA SOCIETY, THE.

**scrofula.** Also known as the 'king's evil'. *See* GREATRAKES, VALENTINE.

**sculptor's hammer, battered to death with a.** *See* BOSE, DOUGLAS.

**'scultheen', a mixture of whiskey and butter.** *See* HELL-FIRE CLUB, THE IRISH.

**seals on first, putting the.** *See* FARSON, DANIEL.

**Second Coming, expecting oneself to play a maternal role in the.** *See* SOUTHCOTT, JOANNA.

**Second Coming announced in a Weymouth tearoom.** *See* PRINCE, HENRY.

**Second Coming expected in Bedford, the.** *See* PANACEA SOCIETY, THE.

**Second Coming manifests itself in Spaxton, Somerset, the.** *See* PRINCE, HENRY.

**seduction of one female pirate by another, attempted.** *See* BONNY, ANNE.

**Sellon, Captain Edward** (1818–66), officer, gentleman, duellist and pornographer. It was said of Sellon that he might have been a character in an erotic fiction created by himself. His own appetites, which he discharged suddenly and in public – sometimes in railway carriages with young women while their partners dozed – certainly had about them a whiff of make believe. Like many who take their pleasure with strangers in railway carriages, he eventually shot himself in a rented room and received disobliging epitaphs ('by no means devoid of talent, and undoubtedly capable of better things,' in the opinion of his fellow pornographer Henry Spencer ASHBEE).

At the age of 16 Sellon had gone to India as an army cadet, returning to England ten years later as a subaltern but with no other obvious qualifications. While in India he had enjoyed frequent encounters with prostitutes, whose beauty and imaginative skills were unmatched, he thought, by anything available in London. After a brief, uncomfortable marriage, he drifted from one affair to another, supporting himself by driving the mail coach between Cambridge and London. While in this employment he went under an assumed name to protect the reputation of his own. When the growing popularity of rail travel put him out of business he opened a fencing school in London. Sword play had become unfashionable, however, and the venture failed. Already in his forties, and urgently in need of an income, Captain Sellon began to write pornography for the coarse-grained publisher and bookseller William DUGDALE.

As well as novels aimed at a public-school readership – *The New Epicurean* (1865), *The Adventures of a Schoolboy* (1865) and *The New Lady's Tickler* (1866) – he translated Boccaccio and produced at least one scholarly work, *Annotations on the Sacred Writings of the Hindus* (1865). Sellon was a classicist and his was an elegant pornography, described by himself as 'a dream of pleasure without riot, of refined voluptuous enjoyment without alloy'. Henry Spencer Ashbee, who thought Sellon a 'pleasure-seeking scamp', described his work as 'showing an ultra lasciviousness and a cynicism worthy of the Marquis de Sade, barring cruelty, which is never practised' – an omission that must have disappointed Ashbee, whose enthusiasm was flagellation.

Whatever the merits of Sellon's narratives, they were never a source of sufficient funds. In March 1866 he accepted the position of paid companion to a Mr Scarsdale on a tour of Egypt. While waiting alone in Scarsdale's brougham near Wandsworth Road railway station he was unexpectedly joined by a young lady who was being taken on the journey for Scarsdale's amusement. When Sellon teased her as a 'mere baby', she boxed his ears and cried, 'Baby indeed! I'm 15!' Sellon teased her again and their first copulation was successfully completed before Scarsdale, who had stepped out to buy cigars, returned to the carriage.

The first part of the journey was by train and steamer to Dover, Calais and Vienna. At the last stop before Vienna, the other passengers left the compartment and Scarsdale went to sleep. Pulling the girl onto his lap, Sellon made love to her a second time, on this occasion, according to a letter he wrote to Dugdale, 'with her stern towards me', during which exercise, Scarsdale woke up:

> I made a desperate effort to throw her on the opposite seat, but it was no go, he had seen us. A row of course ensued and we pitched into one another with hearty good will. He called me a rascal for tampering

with his fiancée. I called him a scoundrel for seducing so young a girl! And we arrived at Vienna! 'Dammit!' said I as I got out of the train with my lip cut and nose bleeding, 'here's a cursed bit of business.'

Dismissed as companion, and with just £15 to his name, Sellon decided to stay in Vienna while the money lasted. He met the girl once more at the Volksgarten, where 'we had a farewell poke and arranged to rendezvous in England'. The tone of bar-room jocularity failed to disguise his growing despair. He returned to London in April 1866 and booked himself into Webb's Hotel, whose site was later the Criterion in Piccadilly Circus. He wrote a poem of farewell to a woman who had once been kind to him, and then he shot himself.

**Selwyn, George** (1719–91), landed gentleman and melancholic whose only interests were crime, death and executions. His friend Horace Walpole wrote that a lady of Selwyn's acquaintance once rebuked him as a barbarian for going to see a criminal being beheaded. Selwyn replied, 'If that was such a crime, I'm sure I have made amends, for I went to see it sewed on again.' Selwyn's reputation as a wit may bewilder a modern reader. His near contemporary, Lord Holland, appears to have been more gifted in this regard. When Lord Holland lay on his sickbed, and was presumed to be dying, he told his servant, 'The next time Mr Selwyn calls, show him up: if I am alive I shall be delighted to see him, and if I am dead he'll be glad to see me.'

**septuagenarian armed robbers.** *See* CURZON, CHARLES.

**sex excursion that never was, the.** *See* KELLY, SHANGHAI.

**sex therapists.** *See* CLAP, MARGARET; CROWLEY, ALEISTER; DALY, JOSEPHINE; DE SANCHA, ANTONIA; FORMAN, SIMON; GRAHAM, JAMES; GREEN, HUGHIE (for Tricia Bell); GUPPY, DARIUS (for Patricia Guppy); HAMPSON, KEITH (for Luscious Leon); HARRIS, JOHN; JONES, JANIE; LAMBTON, ANTONY CLAUD FREDERICK (for Norma Levy); LEVERSON, RACHEL; NEWBOROUGH, DENISA, LADY; PAGE, DAMARIS; PAYNE, CYNTHIA; POTTER, SARAH; PRIDDEN, SARAH; ST CLAIR, LINDI; SOLOMON, SAMUEL; TURNER, ANNE; WILSON, HARRIET.

**sexual practices in the after life.** *See* STOKES, DORIS.

**sexual resources, not squandering one's.** *See* HARRIS, FRANK.

**shadow boxing in the nude.** *See* MASSEREENE, CLOTWORTHY SKEFFINGTON, 2ND EARL OF.

**shark fishermen, aristocratic.** *See* KIMBERLEY, JOHN WODEHOUSE, 4TH EARL OF.

**Shark of Zanzibar, the dorsal fin of the Sacred.** *See* COLE, HORACE DE VERE.

**Sharpe, May Churchill** (1876–1935), confidence trickster, known as 'Chicago May'. Mrs Sharpe was the most successful exponent of the BADGER GAME in the 1890s. Born into a poor Dublin family, May, whose real name was Beatrice Desmond, shared none of the industrious, law-abiding instincts of her parents. At the age of 13 she stole £60 from her father's strongbox – the family's entire savings – and ran off to America. Here she became the mistress of, and later married, a safe-cracker and cattle rustler named Dalton Churchill Sharpe. Churchill Sharpe took his bride west, where he became a member of the notorious Dalton gang. Within a year he was caught in a train robbery and strung up by vigilantes in Arizona.

A widow at the age of 15, May headed for Chicago, where, under the name of May Churchill Sharpe, she became celebrated as the 'Queen of the Badger Game'. Her technique was to lure her victim to a hotel room, where, with the aid of an associate known as 'a bully', she would rob him and steal his papers. Later she would remind him by letter of 'the good time they had had together' and threaten to take the matter up with his wife unless further payments were forthcoming. The act was then refined by the recruitment of an older woman who posed as her mother. 'Mom', on coming across May and her victim, would start screaming for help, which would shortly appear in the form of a muscular 'relative' or 'neighbour'. By this method, May was reputed to have accumulated £300,000 by the age of 19.

In the 1890s May moved her business to New York, where her favourite field of operations was Conidines, a meeting place for literary, theatrical and sporting luminaries. Here she introduced herself to Mark Twain as Lady May Avery of London and expressed admiration for his work. The couple spent a pleasant evening together, but when she asked him to join her in Connecticut for a week, Twain declined. 'I cannot thank you enough for an amusing time,' he said, 'but I haven't believed a word of your story that you're an English noblewoman.' After this disappointment, May formed an alliance with one of New York's most corrupt police officers, Sergeant Charles Becker, who supplied her with likely targets for 25% of the take. The partnership prospered until the city was taken over by reforming politicians. May got out in time, and headed for London. Becker later went to the electric chair for murder.

In England, May became the lover of Eddie GUERIN, celebrated for his supposed escape from Devil's Island. She had been his accomplice in the

£250,000 robbery of American Express in Paris, but was convicted only of smuggling the proceeds to London. Later they fell out, and in April 1906 she and her new lover, who was known variously as Charlie Smith or Cubine Jackson, shot Guerin outside Russell Street underground station. Smith, or Jackson, was sentenced to life imprisonment, and May received 15 years. On her release she was ordered out of Britain and returned to New York. Now in her forties, she engaged in a number of small confidence tricks, with only limited success. Without police protection, she was arrested many times for theft and petty larceny.

In 1928 May announced that crime didn't pay, and she produced her autobiography. The book sold only moderately, and by the 1930s she could no longer survive by living on her past. Chicago May's last newspaper cutting makes disheartening reading. She was arrested in Detroit for soliciting in the street. Her price was $2.

**sheep, devoted to the study of.** *See* RANKIN, SIR HUGH.

**sheep kept in the church porch.** *See* FREE, THE REVEREND EDWARD DRAX.

**sheep presented by sheikh to courtesan, 500.** *See* NEWBOROUGH, DENISA LADY.

**Sheppard, Jack** (1702–24), thief. No robber in the 18th century achieved greater notoriety than Jack Sheppard. His spectacular escapes from various prisons, including two from Newgate, made him the most glamorous man in London in the weeks before his dramatic execution – an occasion attended by a crowd of weeping women. As the *Newgate Calendar* observed:

> His short career provided employment for the bar, the pulpit and the stage. He was for a considerable time the principal subject of conversation in all ranks of society. A pantomime entertainment was brought forward at the royal theatre of Drury Lane, called *Harlequin Sheppard*, wherein his adventures, prison-breakings and other extraordinary escapes were represented. Another dramatic work was published as a farce of three acts, called *The Prison Breaker; or The Adventures of John Sheppard*; and a part of it, with songs, catches and glees added, was performed at Bartholomew Fair, under the title of *The Quaker's Opera*.

Born in Spitalfields, Sheppard was brought up by his mother. In due course he was apprenticed to a carpenter. At first he worked conscientiously at this profession, but soon fell in with bad company at the notorious Black Lion alehouse in Drury Lane. Here he became acquainted with a group of 'abandoned women', one of them named Maggott, and another Elizabeth Lyon, otherwise known as Edgworth Bess, after the town of Edgworth in Lancashire, where she was born. While he continued to work as a carpenter, Sheppard began to rob the houses in which he was employed, stealing tankards and spoons and later fencing them through Edgworth Bess and Maggott.

Under the influence of his two associates, Sheppard's activities became more ambitious, and he shortly fell in with some of Jonathan WILD's gang, notably Joseph BLAKE, known as Blueskin, with whom he was arrested when robbing a Mr Kneebone of £36. This brought about the first of his two spectacular escapes from Newgate while under sentence of death. At that time there was a small visiting room inside the prison, protected by iron spikes. The room opened on to a dark passage leading to the condemned cell. Sheppard, taking advantage of the fact that prisoners were allowed down to the visiting room to speak with their friends, and having been supplied by an accomplice with the necessary implements, cut one of the spikes so that it could easily be broken off. On the evening of 30 August 1724 Sheppard received a visit from Edgworth Bess and Maggott. He broke off the spike, thrust his head and shoulders through the space provided and was pulled to safety by the two women. He was free for no more than a week. Having robbed a watchmaker in Fleet Street, he hid out in Finchley but was shortly informed on, recaptured and taken back to Newgate.

Sheppard's second escape was even more remarkable, taking place at a time when, in his own words (or in the words of his ghostwriter, Daniel DEFOE, in *A Narrative of all the Robberies, Escapes, &c of John Sheppard*, 1724):

> ... my legs were chain'd together, loaded with heavy irons and stapled down to the floor, and a jolly pair of hand-cuffs were provided. Mr Kneebone was present when they were put on: I with tears begg'd his intercession to the keepers to preserve me from those dreadful manacles, telling him my heart was broken, and that I should be much more miserable than before. Mr Kneebone could not refrain from shedding tears, but all to no purpose, and on they went.

These restraints notwithstanding, Sheppard went to work, Houdini-like, with a concealed nail, and within minutes was free of his handcuffs and had unstapled himself from the prison floor. With his leg-irons still in place, but hidden under his stockings, he escaped up a chimney, through the chapel and over the roof to freedom. Having persuaded a journeyman shoemaker to remove his shackles for a fee of 20 shillings, which remained unpaid, he went to the Haymarket where he mingled with a crowd listening to two ballad singers. Their subject was Jack Sheppard, his adventures and escapes. The next day he broke into the shop of Mr Rawlins, a pawn-broker in Drury Lane, and stole a sword, some snuff boxes, rings, watches and other effects to a considerable value. Growing in confidence, and wishing to cut a dash among his old acquaintances in Drury Lane, Sheppard dressed himself up in a black suit, tie-wig and ruffled shirt. Then, carrying a sword and displaying a gold watch and a diamond ring, he dined with two women at a public house in Newgate Street, thereafter, and in their company, driving under the prison walls in a hackney coach with the windows open. Later, while drinking in Clare Market, he sent for his mother, who fainted at the sight of him. Having brought her round with a quart of brandy, he gave her his word that he would immediately leave the country – a promise he was too drunk to keep, had he meant to in the first place. From then until midnight, he staggered between one gin shop and another, eventually being arrested on information from a potboy who'd recognized him. Stupefied with drink, he offered no resistance, even though he had two pistols about his person.

On the day of Sheppard's execution the route from Newgate to the makeshift stadium at Tyburn was lined with weeping girls dressed in white, throwing flowers at their rebel hero as he passed by on an open cart. When he was hanged, the crowd surged forward to tug at his legs, the means by which they hoped to ensure a quick and painless death, but which foiled the plan Sheppard had hatched with Defoe and Appleby, respectively his future ghostwriter and publisher. Their intention had been to spirit his body away after the allotted 15 minutes had elapsed and there-after to revive him. It was possible to survive a hanging, as the case of William DUELL proves, but the crowd was so determined to prevent their hero from being dissected by the anatomists that a scuffle broke out over the body when Appleby's men tried to carry it away. Later in the day there were riots when attempts were made to remove the corpse for burial, but Sheppard was interred that night in the graveyard of St Martin-in-the-Fields.

Defoe, who thought that sensationalist literature about criminals like Sheppard incited others to crime, agreed to ghostwrite his autobiography on condition that he could attribute to Sheppard feelings of contrition and a sense of right and wrong which, from all accounts, were incompatible with his subject's nature. As well as being the model for William Hogarth's idle apprentice – the gifted wastrel whose choice of crime as a career leads inevitably to the gallows – Sheppard was the inspiration for John Gay's Macheath in *The Beggar's Opera* ('The youth in his cart hath the air of a lord, and we cry, there dies an Adonis') and for Charles Dickens's the Artful Dodger.

**Shine, Betty.** *See* ICKE, DAVID.

**show-offs, bibulous.** *See* REED, OLIVER.

**shrieking sisterhood, a member of the.** *See* CHANT, LAURA ORMISTON.

**Shufflewick, Mrs.** *See* FARSON, DANIEL.

**Sibthorp, Colonel Charles de Laet Waldo** (1783–1855), farmer, politician and enemy of 'progress' in all its forms. Throughout his career,
Sibthorp set a standard of reaction and xenophobia unequalled, perhaps,
in parliamentary history. The *Dictionary of National Biography*, which as a
rule prefers to maintain a respectful tone, has him as 'the embodiment of
old-fashioned prejudice', and continues:

> By an eccentricity that did less than justice to his abilities, he made
> himself for many years rather a notorious than a respected figure in
> political life.

In one of his *Sketches by Boz*, Charles Dickens describes him as 'a militia-
man, with a brain slightly damaged and, quite unintentionally, the most
amusing man in the House'.

Although only 43 when first elected as MP for Lincoln, Sibthorp
dressed in a style that was already out of date, preferring the long coat and
Wellington boots of the Regency, set off by an enormous gold quizzing
glass on a long chain. His opinions were as anachronistic as his dress. He
told the House that 'reform was a thing he detested, as he detested the
Devil', and he denounced innovation as 'at best a dangerous thing – resulting in the Reform Bill, which had done everything to cause a revolution,
railroads and other dangerous novelties'. The most consistent of his many
campaigns was the one he waged against railways. He shared the duke of
Wellington's belief that 'they encourage the working classes to move
about'.

Among the other novelties deplored were the new patent water closets,
which Sibthorp had discovered to be much inferior to the old system. He
also feared that the inquisitorial powers of sanitary inspectors would
authorize them to go into the house of the lord mayor of York and see
what he had had for dinner – further, whether he went sober to bed.
'Which I am sure he always does,' Sibthorp added. On another occasion,
he denounced a bill that would levy rates for the building of free libraries.
He had never cared for reading, he informed the House, and had particularly disliked it when at Oxford.

Sibthorp disapproved of foreigners and deplored:

> ... the sums of money carried out of the country by foreign opera
> dancers and singers. I am sorry to say that the higher classes encour-
> age foreigners, whether of character or not, male or female.

He could see no reason to go abroad other than to wage war. In March 1830 he suggested that absenteeism from the country should be taxed. An account should be made of number of passports issued in the last five years, together with the names of their holders and the countries of destination. If these absentees were taxed, it would 'cause £4,000,000 to be spent at home that was currently spent abroad'. He disapproved of Queen Victoria's marriage to Prince Albert, and proposed that the consort's £50,000 annuity should be reduced to £30,000. To the surprise of the prime minister, Lord Melbourne, who had assured the queen that there would be no difficulties, Sibthorp won the debate by a majority of 104 – the only occasion in his career on which he found himself on the winning side. Queen Victoria never forgave him, and she refused to visit Lincoln while Sibthorp was one of its MPs.

The Great Exhibition of 1851 – 'an absurdity and a wild goose-chase', and the brainchild of Prince Albert – was the occasion for his most celebrated campaign. Sibthorp's first objection was to the cutting down of trees in Hyde Park. 'A gentleman who lives near the Park and pays £110 a year ground rent told me that he was admiring the trees one evening before he went to bed and when he got up in the morning to shave they were gone. The object is to introduce among us foreign stuff of every description.' When the Great Exhibition opened, London would be inundated with foreigners 'talking all kinds of gibberish'. The English people wouldn't understand them and there would be all manner of disturbances:

> Suppose a case: a foreigner called a cabman and told him to drive to a certain place; the cabman could not understand him and before he knew what he was about, he would have something like a stiletto in him.

As well as foreigners, English criminals ('at present scattered over the country') would be attracted to Hyde Park as a favourable field for their operations. That being the case, Sibthorp advised 'persons living near the park to keep a sharp look-out after their silver forks, spoons and servant maids'.

In spite of Sibthorp's warnings, the Crystal Palace was opened by Queen Victoria on 1 May 1851. He himself refused to visit it, and he continued to rail against the Exhibition for the length of its run. On one occasion he brought to the House of Commons examples of 'the foreign trash and trumpery' to be purchased at the Crystal Palace and held up an engraved decanter that cost sixpence:

> How is a man in this country who is accustomed to eat roast beef and drink strong ale, after the manner of a Christian, to compete with those nasty foreigners who live on brown bread and sauerkraut and who manufacture decanters at sixpence a piece?

On 2 May 1855 Sibthorp suffered a stroke in the House while suggesting misappropriation of funds by Lord John Russell on a mission abroad. 'However, I will leave it to the public to draw their own conclusions,' he said. He then keeled over and died.

**Sid Vicious.** *See* BEVERLEY, ANNE.

**Silly Eddie.** *See* OSBOURNE, COLIN 'DUKE'.

**Simon Dee Syndrome.** *See* DEE, SIMON.

**Sinclair, Donald** (1919–78), hotel proprietor. During the 1960s Sinclair was the owner and, with his formidable wife Betty, the manager of the Gleneagles Hotel, Torquay – the model on which John Cleese based his television comedy series *Fawlty Towers.* According to Trixie, a woman from the north of England who worked as a waitress and chambermaid at the Gleneagles Hotel, Cleese 'scraped only the tip of the iceberg'. Donald Sinclair was so rude to the guests and upset his staff to such an extent that Betty Sinclair used to lock him in a broom cupboard. 'If he went into the kitchen in the morning,' Trixie has reported, 'she'd be short of three staff by the evening. She'd lock him in the cupboard and say, "If Donald starts knocking, girls, don't let him out."' An idiosyncratic convention of the establishment was that, while anyone could abuse the guests, only Sinclair could insult the staff. When a couple, who had checked in late one evening, complained that Trixie was giving them dirty looks ('which I was because I had to stay on to give them a late supper'), Sinclair picked them up and, with a cry of, 'How dare you criticize my staff!', carried them into the street.

The actor Michael Palin stayed at the Gleneagles in the 1970s when the *Monty Python* team was filming at nearby Paignton. 'I asked for a wake-up call,' Palin has written:

> Sinclair was astonished. He literally took a step back and his jaw dropped. Not something I'd seen before. 'Why?' he said. At dinner, Terry Gilliam (who is American), left his knife and fork at an angle. Sinclair leant over him, put his knife and fork together and said, 'That is how we do it in England.' I left after one night, but John Cleese and Eric Idle stayed on. That was odd because Sinclair had taken Eric's suitcase and put it in the drive because he thought it had a bomb in it.

The Sinclairs sold the Gleneagles in the mid-1970s, and Donald died soon after. Betty, who has survived into her eighties, gives short shrift to anyone who mentions the *Fawlty Towers* connection. Those who fail in this regard are informed that John Cleese is 'a geek' and that her late husband was a lieutenant commander in the Royal Navy. 'She had no time for him when he was alive,' Trixie has said, 'but she's very loyal to his memory.'

Since 1981 the hotel's proprietor has been Ray Marks, who has associations with another famous comedian; his first cousin was Peter Sellers, to whom he bears a striking resemblance. If asked, Marks will perform the Fawlty goose step, but with reservations – the latter arising from the fact that the Gleneagles now has a thriving relationship with a German tour operator. In other respects, little has changed. Elderly single ladies doze in wicker chairs, children are discouraged and a duo calling themselves Pink Champagne are advertised under 'Forthcoming Entertainment'.

**sitting on a trout while it's cooked.** *See* DANCER, DANIEL.

**Sitwell, Sir George Reresby** (1860–1943), landowner, medievalist and father of Osbert, Sacheverell and Edith Sitwell. Sir George held opinions on many subjects and preferred them not to be challenged. A sign at Renishaw Hall, his house at Eckington in Derbyshire, ran:

> I must ask anyone entering the house never to contradict me in any way, as it interferes with the functioning of the gastric juices and prevents my sleeping at night.

His interests were wide-ranging. Renishaw Hall's seven sitting rooms were piled with specially constructed box files, each containing notes for a future monograph. Among the titles were 'The Black Death at Rotherham', 'The Use of the Bed', 'Osbert's Debts', 'Acorns as an Article of Medieval Diet', 'Sachie's Mistakes', 'My Advice on Poetry' and 'My Inventions'. Among the latter was the Sitwell Egg. With a yolk of smoked meat, a white of compressed rice and a shell of synthetic lime, it aimed to be a nourishing meal for travellers. Having decided to put the marketing of his egg into the experienced hands of Mr Gordon Selfridge, founder of the Oxford Street store, Sir George appeared in Selfridge's office one morning unannounced and said, 'I'm Sir George Sitwell and I have my egg with me.' Selfridge must have been unimpressed since the project was shelved soon after the meeting. Sir George persevered with other inventions, however. There was a musical toothbrush that played 'Annie Laurie' and a miniature revolver for shooting wasps.

A major factor in the development of his three gifted children may have been Sir George's disapproval of everything they did. He strongly advised Osbert against writing a novel. 'You'd better drop that idea at once. My cousin, Stephen Arthington, had a friend who utterly ruined his health writing a novel.' Edith's literary ambitions ran counter to his belief that gymnastics would have been a better occupation. 'There's nothing a man likes so much,' he said, 'as a girl who's good on the parallel bars.' Other sports, too, would have been preferable to poetry. 'Edith's made a great mistake by not going in for lawn tennis,' he said. In general, Sir George's attitude to his children was summed up in a comment to Osbert, 'It is dangerous for you to lose touch with me for a single day. You never know when you may need the benefit of my experience and advice.'

The desire to lose touch with their father for as long as possible so preoccupied Osbert and Sacheverell that they invented a mythical yacht, the *Rover*. They had headed notepaper printed on which they wrote to Sir George regretting that since the yacht's itinerary had not yet been finalized they were unable to give him an address at which they could be contacted. Meanwhile, they remained in London, where there was little chance of their being discovered since Sir George was unable to recognize his children if suddenly encountered outside the home.

Sir George's refusal to acknowledge the conventions of modern life was his prevailing characteristic. He held on to the 14th-century practice of paying in kind, offering pigs and potatoes to Eton College for Sacheverell's school fees. Osbert persuaded his father to pay him his allowance in currency, but the result was disappointing since Sir George arrived at the proper amount by studying the allowance granted to the eldest son of the lord of Eckington Manor at the time of the Black Death. Among his many economies were the banning of electricity from Eckington during his lifetime, limiting guests to two candles apiece, and making the family drink cold boiled water rather than wine when travelling in Italy. On his own in Italy, Sir George preferred to stay at what were little more than doss houses, sharing a dormitory with itinerant tramps. However, on these occasions he was accompanied by his valet, Moat, whose responsibility it was to lay out the formal evening dress in which Sir George liked to appear at dinner.

**skunk, calling one's son and heir a squirming.** *See* QUEENSBERRY, JOHN SHOLTO DOUGLAS, 9TH MARQUESS OF.

**slackness at the ministry.** *See* VASSALL, JOHN.

**Slade, Henry** (1840–1905), spiritualist and con man. Slade was an early practitioner of modern spiritualism – the belief that there is life after death and that 'mediums' have the ability to communicate with those who have 'crossed over'. This pseudo-religion had started, unpromisingly, as a prank, when in 1858 a 15-year-old American girl, Margaret Fox, discovered that she could crack her big toe so that it sounded like someone tapping on wood. Slade was known as the 'slate-writing medium', since his method was to ask questions of his dead wife, Alcinda, and receive mysteriously written answers on a slate.

Slade's career was flourishing until Professor Edwin Lankester, an evolutionary biologist who had been Charles Darwin's student, paid to attend a séance at Slade's London home in the hope of exposing him as a fraud. During the séance Lankester snatched the slate out of Slade's hands and found written on it the answer to a question that hadn't yet been asked. Lankester thereupon hauled Slade through the police courts as a 'common rogue'.

Since Slade's séances had been attended by the cream of society, his trial was among the most popular events of the London season. One of the oddest of the many contradictions that it produced was the appearance on Slade's behalf of Darwin's collaborator, Alfred Russel Wallace. Wallace, a firm believer in spiritualism, found Slade to be 'as sincere as any investigator in a university department of natural science'. Against him, Darwin believed all mediums to be 'mere clever rogues' who exploited the credulous and the bereaved. He and Thomas Henry Huxley had previously tried to expose other fraudulent practitioners, and Darwin told Lankester that he would consider it a public benefit were Slade to be put out of business. To this end he secretly contributed funds to the cost of the prosecution. A stage conjuror, Neville Maskelyne, demonstrated to the court how tricks similar to Slade's might be achieved. Slade was convicted under an old law against palmists and fortune-tellers. He was sentenced to three months imprisonment, but since he was neither a fortune-teller nor a palmist the conviction was overturned on a technicality. Slade left forthwith for the Continent, where he continued his slate-writing séances with mixed success. An attempt to resume his career in England failed when in 1883 a conjuror with the unusual name, for someone who made his career upon the stage, of J.N. Truesdell, used trickery of his own to get hold of Slade's slate during a séance and to write on it confusing messages from Alcinda – such as 'Watch out! The jig's up!' With his reputation in decline, Slade took to drink and moved to America, where he ended up in a run-down New York boarding house. He was finally committed to an asylum in Michigan, where he died in 1905.

**Slater, John** (1947– ), Royal Marine commando, truck driver, driftwood artist and recluse. Slater is believed to be the only person to have walked from Land's End to John O'Groats in his bare feet, wearing only his pyjamas and accompanied by his labrador Guinness. Guinness was kitted out with two pairs of suede boots. When he got home Slater appointed Guinness to a directorship of his tour-guide company.

To raise funds for the conservation of pandas, Slater once volunteered to spend six months in a cage at London Zoo as a human exhibit. The offer, he said, 'was foolishly declined'. At that time, and in order to learn more about himself, he lived in a shop doorway with down-and-outs in London. In 1991 Slater moved to a cave in a remote part of the Western Highlands. He has explained that the silence helps him to think, but the results appear not to have been remarkable:

I gave a friend of mine a brand name for his new wholemeal bakery
– 'Thoroughbred'. And why hasn't anyone marketed a unisex
deodorant called 'Everybody?'

When he got married for the third time in 1994, his new wife, who lived in
a modern stone cottage, gave him an ultimatum, 'It's me or the cave.' Slater
went back to his cave. His motto is, 'Wag your tail at everyone you meet.'

**sledging.** A term used in cricket to describe a fielding side's attempt to
intimidate an opposition batsman with derogatory remarks over a range of
subjects: his looks, his parentage, his sister's morals and so forth. The practice is particularly associated with teams from Australia and New Zealand,
but it was probably invented by the great English cricketer and sportsman,
W.G. GRACE, and perfected by the Welsh – the latter making use of experience gained in the front row of rugby-union scrummages.
*See also* CRICKETERS, INTIMIDATION BY.

**Slipper, Detective Chief Superintendent Jack.** *See* BIGGS, RONALD;
SMALLS, BERTIE.

**Smalls, Bertie** (1935–  ), armed robber and police informer. The title of
Britain's first supergrass – a criminal who gives evidence against his former
colleagues in return for a lenient sentence – is usually bestowed on Bertie
Smalls. Once Smalls had set the fashion in 1973, Sir Robert Mark, the
commissioner of the Metropolitan Police, was able to note that, 'Faced
with trustworthy detectives for the first time in their experience, organized
criminals began to sing.' Further persuasion was provided by a sentencing
policy that more than doubled the standard term for robbery.

Smalls held strong right-wing views, and according to Bobby King –
one of his associates on whom he informed – had a naturally violent disposition. Before turning to robbery, he had been a ponce, an indication, his
betrayed former colleagues suggested, of the decadence of character that
would lead to treachery. In 1973, and faced with a draconian sentence for
his part in a raid on Barclay's Bank, Wembley, in which £138,000 had been
stolen, Smalls chose to cooperate with the police. Detective Chief Superintendent Jack Slipper has said that the decisive moment came when Smalls
lined up at the committal proceedings with fellow members of the gang.
Heavily hung over from the bottle of vodka he had drunk the night before,
he was unamused when Danny Allpress, one of his seven co-defendants,
asked him tauntingly who would be enjoying the company of Mrs Smalls
while he was away.

An agreement was drawn up with the director of public prosecutions,
Sir Norman Skelhorn, granting Smalls immunity in return for his cooperation. Smalls, his wife Diane and their two small children were hidden at a

guarded address. By September 1974 he had helped to jail 21 former associates for a total of 308 years. As he concluded his evidence at the Old Bailey trial, Danny Allpress sang, 'We'll meet again, don't know where, don't know when ...,' a detail used by the screenwriter Peter Prince in *The Hit* (1984), a curiosity directed by Stephen Frears and starring Terence Stamp as a supergrass hiding out in Spain. While serving his sentence of 19 years, Allpress taught his pet budgerigar to say, 'Bertie is a fucking grass.'

*See also* O'MAHONEY, MAURICE.

**Smirke, Charlie** (1906–93), jockey. One of the most talented riders of his era, Smirke, who won eleven British classics (including the Derby four times) flouted most of the sport's rules, including the one that prohibits jockeys from betting. Another flaw in his character was an inability to show deference to his superiors, be they the stewards of the Jockey Club or the champion jockey, Gordon Richards – whom Smirke held in low regard. When a starter at York asked the jockeys whether they were ready, Smirke shouted, 'No, no, Gordon isn't ready!' 'Don't be impertinent, Smirke,' snapped the starter. 'I beg your pardon, sir,' said Smirke. 'Mister Richards isn't ready.'

Smirke's career suffered a setback in July 1928 when he was on the favourite, Welcome Gift, at the old Gatwick course. Welcome Gift was left at the start, and at the subsequent inquiry it was alleged that Smirke had made no attempt to put the horse in the race. He was warned off for five years, returning in 1933 to win the Derby on the Maharajah of Rajpipla's horse Windsor Lad.

A story is told about Smirke and another talented jockey who won and lost several fortunes at casino tables, Michael Beary. Involved one afternoon in a two-horse race at Brighton, Smirke and Beary had each staked a considerable sum of money on the other to win. After two furlongs both were proceeding at a cautious trot. Coming into the straight, Beary slowed his horse to a walking pace. Smirke retaliated by stopping his horse altogether. So Beary fell off. It was the only time that Smirke was thought to have been outwitted.

**Smith, George Joseph** (1872–1915), bigamist and perpetrator of the Brides in the Bath Murders. Smith evidently disliked women, but was unusually attractive to them. He had had little education and always approached women who, as he himself once put it, were a cut above him. He began his criminal career with petty larceny, moved on to bigamy and ended by perfecting a murder method that for a time baffled forensic science.

In 1898 Smith married 19-year-old Beatrice Thornhill. She was to be his only legal wife. In 1910 he met 33-year-old Bessie Mundy, who apparently had £2500 in trust. Later that year he 'married' her at Weymouth, calling himself Henry Williams. The couple set up house in Herne Bay, but when he discovered that Bessie's trust was unbreakable he took her ready cash and moved out, leaving behind a letter in which he accused her of infecting him with a venereal disease. When they met by chance two years later, Bessie took the unusual step of agreeing to live with him again. This time Smith was able to get his hands on her trust fund by persuading her to make a will in his favour. As soon as this had been done, he bought a tin bath of the kind that has to be filled with a bucket. He then took Bessie to a doctor and explained that she suffered from fits. Two days later she was found drowned in the bath, with a cake of soap clutched in her hand. The doctor agreed that she must have had one of her fits. The money from Bessie's trust was paid over, and 'Mr Williams' returned the bath, for which he had no further use. 'Mr Williams' then vanished. Smith sent for his real wife, Beatrice, who believed he was a respectable antique dealer. The two of them departed for a holiday in Margate.

The pattern was twice repeated: with Alice Burnham, whom Smith 'married' in Southsea in November 1913, and with Margaret Lofty, a clergyman's daughter, whom he 'married' in 1914 in Bath, later moving into lodgings in Highgate, London. Neither had much money, and Smith made his profit by insuring their lives. He chose houses with bathrooms (his first question at the Highgate establishment was, 'Have you a bath?') and in both cases he took his wife to a doctor before dispatching her. A newspaper report of Margaret Lofty's death was seen by Alice Burnham's father, who went to the police. They realized that Smith was a murderer, but there was no sign of violence on the bodies. It wasn't until Detective Inspector Neil, on the advice of the pathologist Dr Bernard Spilsbury, had carried out various bathroom experiments with a woman police constable in which he pulled her legs up out of the water and nearly drowned her, that Smith's precise methods were understood. Tried at the Old Bailey in June 1915 for the murder of Bessie Mundy, he was defended by Sir Edward Marshall Hall, who attempted, unsuccessfully, to have evidence of the other two deaths excluded. The landlady at Smith's Highgate lodgings testified that she had heard splashings from the bathroom, and had later heard Smith playing 'Nearer my God to Thee' on the harmonium. Smith was found guilty, sentenced to death and hanged at Maidstone Prison on Friday 13 August 1915.

**Smith, Madeleine** (1835–1928), murderess. When Smith, a respectable 21-year-old Glasgow girl, was tried in June 1857 for allegedly poisoning her foreign lover, the frankness of her love letters scandalized polite Scottish society.

The eldest daughter of James Smith, a successful architect and a pillar of the Glasgow community, Madeleine was an educated and graceful girl whose days were filled with artistic pursuits but little in the way of adventure. In the spring of 1855, while staying at the Smith's country house, she began a secret affair with a 34-year-old packing clerk from Jersey, Pierre Emile l'Angelier. With Madeleine's maid acting as a go-between, the two exchanged letters. Hers were passionate in the extreme, addressed to, 'My own, my beloved husband,' and signed, 'Mimi d'Angelier'. When the Smiths returned to Glasgow, meetings were difficult and the couple adopted the unsatisfactory recourse of conversing through the barred windows of Madeleine's basement bedroom. Had her father known of the arrangement he would have forbidden it, since he was on the lookout for a suitable husband for his daughter. l'Angelier was aware of this, and in a fit of jealousy he returned one of Madeleine's letters. This caused her to break off the relationship, and to ask l'Angelier to return all her letters. His reaction was to threaten to send the letters to her father. Madeleine begged him not to, and in an attempt to appease him she renewed the affair.

In March 1857 l'Angelier became ill. He was confined to his bed at his lodging house and on the evening of 23 March he was suddenly convulsed with pain and died. An autopsy showed that his body contained 82 grains of arsenic. On 31 March, after Madeleine's letters to l'Angelier had been found, she was arrested and charged with murder. She made a statement admitting that she had bought arsenic, but claimed, like Florence MAYBRICK, that she used it as a cosmetic. She was tried at Edinburgh in June 1857. The prosecution case was that she had grown tired of l'Angelier, whom she had come to see as an obstacle to a more suitable marriage, and that she had poisoned him with arsenic administered in a chocolate drink. Her defence counsel did his best to depict l'Angelier as a seducer and a blackmailer, further pointing out that he was known to take arsenic and had a history of stomach complaints. On 9 July the jury brought in the peculiarly Scottish verdict of 'Not Proven', which could have been interpreted as 'almost certainly she did it but he probably deserved it'.

Madeleine was later married twice, first in London to an artist, and second in America, where she died at the age of 93. The gravestone in Mount Hope Cemetery says simply, Lena Sheehy, the name of her second husband.

**Smith, T. Dan.** *See* POULSON, JOHN.

**Smithson, Tommy 'Scarface'.** *See* ELLUL, PHILIP.

**Smyth-Pigott, John Hugh.** *See* PRINCE, HENRY.

**Snell, Hannah** (*c.*1720–89), sailor and impostor. In 1748 a young marine, James Gray, and his shipmates were drinking in a London pub, celebrating their safe return from various engagements at sea. Gray turned to the sailor with whom he had shared sleeping accommodation and said:

> Had you known, Master Moody, who you had between the sheets with you, you would have come to closer quarters. In a word, gentlemen, I am as much a woman as my mother ever was, and my real name is Hannah Snell.

Once the assembled ship's company had got over its surprise, it had nothing but praise and admiration for Master Gray. Master Moody went too far, however. According to R. Walker, *The Female Sailor: or, the Surprising Life and Adventures of Hannah Snell* (1750):

> He carried the testimonies of his respects to a much higher pitch than any of his comrades, for he protested solemnly and seriously that he was become all of a sudden so enamoured of her, on account of her numerous and praiseworthy qualifications, that, if Miss Hannah had as favourable opinion of him as he had of her, he was very ready and willing to commit matrimony with her that very hour as an incontestable demonstration of the sincerity of his love and affection.

Hannah refused the offer. She had been married once already and had determined never to repeat the experience. Indeed, it was because of her husband's behaviour that she herself had masqueraded as a man. At the age of 20 she had married a Dutch sailor, who had abandoned her when she was seven months pregnant. After the baby died, Hannah decided to hunt her husband down. In 1745 she took the name and clothes of her brother-in-law, James Gray, and joined the company of a British warship. For the next five years she served as sailor without her true identity being discovered. Since it was beyond the imagination of the crew that one of their shipmates was a girl, her secret remained safe even when she was stripped to the waist and whipped for a misdemeanour of which she was innocent:

> The boatswain of the ship, taking notice of her breasts, seemed surprised, and said they were the most like a woman's he ever saw; but as no person on board ever had the least suspicion of her sex, the whole dropped without any further notice being taken.

It has been noticed by historians, notably by Sarah Burton (*Imposters: Six Kinds of Liars*, 2000), that when convinced of a person's identity, witnesses to an imposture commonly dismiss the evidence of their own eyes.

After some time at sea, Hannah had learned from a shipmate that her husband had been executed for murder, a discovery that made her 'determined to acquire some honour in the expedition, and so distinguish herself by her intrepid behaviour'. As a child Hannah had shown signs of a fighting spirit. At the age of 9 she had formed her playmates into a company of troops and marched them round Worcester, where she lived. In 1748, at the siege of Pondicherry, India, she experienced the reality on which these childhood games were based. During the engagement she was shot in the leg, and, more dangerously, in the groin. As she lay in hospital, she suffered as much from the mental as the physical ordeal. The pain in her groin would only be relieved by having the shot removed by one of the surgeons, but that she couldn't allow. Rather than have her true sex discovered, she allowed the doctors to treat her leg wounds, but concealed the more serious injury. She eventually extracted the shot herself by digging her finger and thumb into the deep narrow wound and pulling it out.

After she had returned to England in 1750, and had revealed her true identity to her former shipmates, Hannah made her living in the theatre, singing sea shanties and performing military marches dressed in her uniform. Her portrait was painted several times, a biography appeared and she capitalized on her growing fame by opening a public house in Wapping that she called 'The Widow in Masquerade'. Her first biographer, Walker, noted that she did better for herself as a 'man' than she ever could have done under her true identity. During her career on stage:

> She was contracted on a stipend that not one woman in ten thousand of her low extraction and want of literature could by any act of industry (how laborious soever) with any possibility procure.

Her rebuff to Master Moody notwithstanding, Hannah Snell married on two further occasions. She died in 1789 in Bethlehem Hospital ('Bedlam'), to which she had been committed after a sudden bout of insanity.

**Society for the Promotion and Avoidance of Boomerangs, the.** *See* JORDAN, JOHN.

**Sodom and Begorrah.** *See* STAGE, HOOLIGANISM ON.

**sodomized by his Lordship, as was Fitzpatrick, the cook.** *See* AUDLEY, MERVYN CASTLEFORD, 2ND BARON.

**soft heart and 83 previous convictions, a.** *See* PROGL, ZOE.

**Solomon, Samuel** (*c.*1781–*c.*1853), quack. In 1820 Solomon, a boot-polish salesman trading in Liverpool, began to market an elixir known as the Balm of Gilead. Its composition, according to Solomon's sales literature, had been:

> ... sanctioned by the most learned physicians of the age. It has preserved its reputation from the period prior to the birth of Christ, growing in Gilead in Judea in 1730 BC.

Its uses were many: it relieved intestinal problems, improved fertility, and acted as an effective aphrodisiac when applied to the appropriate zones. Frederick the Great (who had died when Solomon was an infant) was advertised nevertheless as having been pleased by its latter properties, and, in a rather different application, it had greatly helped victims of the New York yellow fever epidemic of 1800. It cured, among other ailments, weak or shattered constitutions; horrors of the mind; intemperance; debauchery; and inattention to a properly studious life.

The Balm of Gilead was greatly in demand, and within a short time Solomon had franchised some 400 agencies in Britain and 16 in America. He lived in considerable luxury in a mansion outside Liverpool, but remained available for personal consultations, for which he charged at the rate of just £1 a visit (half price for queries by mail). In time, however, complications developed. Users of the Balm discovered that they were becoming addicted to it. Its composition, which reputedly included a small amount of gold, was discovered on analysis to be 90% pure brandy. One elderly lady, whose husband had become a compulsive alcoholic, waited for Solomon outside his house one night and beat him to the ground. Solomon's recovery after this unpleasant episode was greatly assisted, he claimed, by generous doses of the Balm. This testimony did little, however, to prevent a sharp decline in sales.

**Somerset, Lord Arthur.** *See* NEWTON, ARTHUR.

**Somerset, Charles Seymour, 6th duke of** (1662–1748), aristocrat. Somerset carried dislike of the lower classes to unnecessary lengths. He built houses at intervals along the main roads between London and his various country estates so that he would not be obliged to stay overnight in a public house. Outriders preceded him on his travels to clear commoners from his path. Communication with his servants was necessary but he avoided the intimacy of speech by inventing a sign language.

Somerset's sense of superiority extended even to members of his family. His daughter Charlotte was obliged to watch over her father as he took his afternoon nap on a sofa. One day she wandered off while he slept and he rolled onto the floor. He woke in a fury and ordered the whole household to ostracize her. Thereafter, no one was brave enough to mention Charlotte's name or to ask the duke when they might speak to her again. Later, she was written out of his will for sitting down in his presence.

Somerset's first wife was Elizabeth Percy, heir to the wealth and titles of the earldom of Northumberland. When his second wife, herself the daughter of the earl of Nottingham, tapped him gently with her fan she was instantly rebuked. 'Madame,' he said, 'my first duchess was a Percy and *she* never took such a liberty.'

**sots and the sexually depraved, a society for.** *See* DASHWOOD, SIR FRANCIS.

**Southcott, Joanna** (1750–1814), religious fanatic. In 1792 Joanna Southcott, a farmer's daughter from Devon, announced herself as the Bride of Christ, mentioned in Revelations, Chapter 12. She further declared that in due course she would become the mother of the Second Messiah. She attracted a following of some 100,000 supporters and in 1802 established herself in London. There she supported herself in comfort by selling poorly rhymed prophecies collected in *A Warning* (1803) and *The Book of Wonders* (1813). Her announcement that she would give birth on 19 October 1814 to a second Prince of Peace was received by her followers with devout reverence. As the date approached, Southcott was examined by 21 doctors, 17 of whom confirmed that she was indeed pregnant. The news caused throngs of people to congregate in Manchester Street where she was confined. During the vigil many in the crowd collapsed with exhaustion, and three died.

There was no birth on 19 October. Rather, Joanna Southcott developed a brain tumour, fell into a coma and died in December 1814. She left behind a sealed box of prophecies that would cure all the ills of mankind when opened a century later in the presence of 24 bishops. By 1913, Southcott's followers, now organized as the PANACEA SOCIETY, were demanding that the sealed box be opened in 1914. The archbishop of Canterbury refused to do so. Finally, in 1927, under pressure from the Panacea Society, the bands were broken in the presence of the bishop of Grantham. Among the items removed by the bishop were a lady's nightcap, a horse pistol, a lottery ticket dated 1796 and a novel called *The Surprises of Love*.

The declining membership of the Panacea Society still insists that the wrong box was opened. The right one, they claim, is among their possessions at their headquarters in Bedfordshire, and they continue to demand that it be opened with the required number of bishops in attendance.

**Sowden, Des** (1975– ), professional boxer. In November 2000 Sowden, a welterweight, became a contender for the title of 'worst boxer in the world' after being knocked out in two seconds. Spectators were still taking their seats at the Ebbw Vale Leisure Centre, near Cardiff, when Sowden went down after receiving one punch from his opponent, Russell Rees. Sowden's previous record was eleven fights, with one win and ten losses, and he had already been knocked out in 17, 41 and 86 seconds. His one victory was over an Irishman, Martin 'Wee Barry' Moore, who was disqualified for continuing to punch Des as he lay flat on the canvas.

After the fight in Ebbw Vale, a spokesman for *The Guinness Book of Records* said that the present holder of the title was British fighter, Paul Lloyd, who had been knocked out in 12 seconds by Foudal Moudani, an untutored slugger from Algeria. The spokesman added, 'We're waiting for a video recording of the fight. It certainly sounds like a new world record.'

**Sparks, 'Ruby'** (1894–1972), armed robber. Sparks's father was a bare-knuckle fist fighter and his mother a receiver of stolen goods. Before becoming a cat burglar he served his apprenticeship as a junior mail-train robber, hiding in a hamper with the mailbags and jumping out when the hamper was opened. His nickname derives from a misunderstanding over some stolen rubies. An incompetent receiver had assured him that these were artificial, so he had casually distributed them among strangers whom he was seeking to impress, losing himself thousands of pounds in the process. In 1923 Sparks retired as a cat burglar and famously teamed up as a smash-and-grab robber with the 'Bobbed-Haired Bandit' Lilian GOLD-STEIN. After many vicissitudes, including three long prison sentences, Sparks broke up with Goldstein and married a respectable woman named Anne. With her he ran an ice-cream business and later, after World War II, the Penguin Club in Regent Street, where the waitresses were dressed as musical-comedy soubrettes. His new-found probity would have pleased his mother Winnie, who, despite her occupation as a receiver, had instilled in him the highest standards. Sparks later recalled:

> My uncle Frank was a burglar, and our family never saw any harm in that. But my mother objected to the way he mooched around in baggy trousers. 'I expect him to smarten himself up when he comes visiting here,' my mother used to say, 'as we're very respected in the neighbourhood.'

**Spencer, Herbert** (1820–1903), social philosopher. Spencer's important works on evolution (Charles Darwin called him 'twenty times my superior') took their toll on his always delicate health. When he went for a drive, he would, from time to time, order the coachman to pull up while he took his pulse to determine whether he was still alive. When travelling by train he required at least two attendants to help him with his equipment – a hammock, various rugs and air cushions, as well as his luggage and his current manuscript done up in brown paper and secured to his person by means of a length of string. At the start of the journey the hammock would be slung up in the train compartment, and Spencer would climb in. His preferred wardrobe was a one-piece, over-all costume that he had designed himself. This eliminated the need for separate boots, socks, trousers, shirt and coat, and gave him the appearance of a brown bear.

Spencer could be mischievous, and once played a prolonged practical joke on a fellow scholar, Trimbell. Having acquainted Trimbell with the symptoms of water on the brain, Spencer placed a strip of paper inside his hat, adding another strip every day for a period of weeks so that Trimbell became convinced that his head was growing at a disconcerting rate.

**spendthrifts.** *See* ABERCORN, JOHN JAMES HAMILTON, 1ST MARQUESS OF; BRISTOL, FREDERICK WILLIAM JOHN AUGUSTUS HERVEY, 7TH MARQUESS OF; DERMODY, THOMAS; DODD, THE REVEREND DR WILLIAM; FOX, CHARLES JAMES; LUCAN, JOHN BINGHAM, 6TH BARON; MASSEREENE, CLOTWORTHY SKEFFINGTON, 2ND EARL OF; MYTTON, JOHN; NORCOTT, WILLIAM.

**spies, counter-spies and spymasters.** *See* BLUNT, SIR ANTHONY; BURGESS, GUY FRANCIS DE MONCY (both of which entries also deal with Kim Philby and Donald Maclean); CHAPMAN, EDDIE; DANSEY, COLONEL SIR CLAUDE; DEFOE, DANIEL; DRIBERG, TOM (possibly); JACKSON, JOHN; VASSALL, JOHN.

**spiral of drug-fuelled scandal and reckless behaviour, a downward.** *See* MCAVENNIE, FRANK.

**spiral staircases that lead nowhere.** *See* JAMES, EDWARD.

**spirals of colour and globules of incandescent smoke.** *See* RAMPA, LOBSANG.

**spiritualist 'mediums'.** *See* ICKE, DAVID; SLADE, HENRY; STOKES, DORIS. *See also* HOCUS-POCUS.

**spliff, sharing a.** *See* ATTLEE, MARTIN, 2ND EARL; EYRES, TONY; LAMBTON, ANTONY CLAUD FREDERICK; MARGARET, PRINCESS; MARKS, HOWARD.

**Spong, Mrs Mildred.** *See* CLANCARTY, WILLIAM FRANCIS BRINSLEY LE POER TRENCH, 8TH EARL OF.

**Spot, Jack** (1912– ), gangster. Born into a Polish-Jewish immigrant family in the East End of London, Spot competed with Billy HILL throughout the 1950s for the title 'Boss of the Underworld'. Initially they were allies, and it was the Spot–Hill axis that superseded the White family – who in turn had taken over from the SABINIS – in terms of power and influence.

Spot fought ineffectively in World War II before being discharged on the grounds of mental instability. He spent the rest of the war in Leeds, where he established himself in the criminal community by proving himself to be a capable bouncer at the Regal Gaming Club. In 1945 he returned to London and ran various illegal operations, using the Aldgate Fruit Exchange as a front. By the late 1940s, and now married to Rita, an attractive Irish girl, he was playing the part of gang leader with conspicuous effect. Leonard 'Nipper' Read, the detective who broke up the KRAY empire, described Spot at the height of his power:

> He dressed in beautifully cut suits and always wore a brown fedora and he had a religious way of progressing through the day. He would go to the barbers in Edgware Road station and they would shave him and when he felt immaculate he would walk down the Edgware Road, waving and saying good morning to people. He would go into the Bear Garden in the Cumberland Hotel and would sit there for the rest of the morning. People would come up and ask for advice about various matters and he would give it out in much the same way as Don Corleone in *The Godfather*.

Spot's followers were sometimes in need of more physical instruction. 'I used to knock them out in the lavatory,' he told journalist Robert Murphy. 'That was my surgery. I used to go to the toilet and Bomp! Leave them in the piss.' One of his many offices was the Modernaires Club in Old Compton Street, Soho, which he shared with musicians rehearsing what he called their 'heeby-jeeby music'. When the telephone rang he silenced them with a wave of the hand. He liked reliability. When the trumpeter Denis Rose arrived two hours late, he was taken into the 'surgery' and Bomp! – he was in the piss.

In the early 1950s the uneasy alliance between Spot and Billy Hill began to fall apart, finally collapsing altogether with the celebrated Soho affray involving Spot and a colleague of Hill's, Albert DIMES. Spot had become too powerful, and Hill had been looking for a way to discredit him. He had discovered that in 1937 Spot had given evidence against three men in an assault case. He'd got hold of the depositions of the committal proceedings, which showed Spot up as an informer, and had posted copies in underworld pubs. Believing that a confrontation with Dimes would improve his sinking reputation, Spot went after him with a knife in Frith Street, Soho, on 11 August 1955, stabbing him in the thigh and stomach. Dimes took refuge in a fruit shop on the corner of Old Compton Street, where he hoped to find an industrial can-opener to use as a weapon. Spot pursued Dimes into the shop but the woman who owned it hit him over the head with a set of scales. Taking advantage of this sudden reversal in his opponent's fortunes, Dimes grabbed the knife out of the reeling gangster's hand and stabbed him in the side. Spot collapsed in a nearby barber's shop, and was later taken to the Middlesex Hospital. Dimes was treated in the Charing Cross Hospital. Tried at the Old Bailey for causing an affray, both were acquitted thanks to the intervention of the Reverend Basil ANDREWS, and the incident became known as 'the Fight that Never Was'.

In May 1956 Spot got word that Hill intended, with a single strike, to put him out of business for good. He asked the police for help, but this was not forthcoming. Returning with Rita from a trip to the cinema one night, he was ambushed outside his home by Frankie FRASER, now Hill's chief enforcer. Fraser shouted, 'It's on you, Jack!' and set about Spot with a shillelagh. 'I just whacked him a couple of times,' said Fraser later, 'and that was that.' He had planned to cut a pattern of noughts and crosses on his face 'but unfortunately there wasn't time'.

Fraser was arrested with four other men – Bobby Warren, 'Billy Boy' Blythe, William 'Ginger' Dennis and Bert 'Battles' Rossi. At their trial, Mr Justice Donovan reminded the jury that, 'the civic value of the man Spot is neither here nor there. If this sort of thing is allowed to spread it will not be safe for any of us to walk the streets.' Fraser was sentenced to seven years for the assault, the others to five. As he left the court, Spot, who had not given evidence against his attackers, said, 'I ain't afraid of anyone but I want a quiet life.' Hill had made his point, and the underworld joke of the time – 'Billy's the boss, and Jack was very cut up about it' – marked the end of the Spot era.

**Spudgeon, Nancy (aka Nauseating Nancy).** *See* BEVERLEY, ANNE.

**squints, a cause of moral degeneracy.** *See* CREAM, DR THOMAS NEILL.

**Squires, Dorothy** (1915–98), singer. Her unusually varied career, and volatile temperament, earned Miss Squires as many entries in serious sociological studies, such as James Morton's *Sex, Crimes and Misdemeanours* (1999), as in run-of-the-mill show-business memoirs. She sold many records (one of which, 'Gypsy' was 'covered' by the Ink Spots), married the film star Roger Moore, was bankrupted twice, arrested for assault, declared a vexatious litigant and evicted from her home. In the space of five years she launched 21 High Court actions, none of which she won.

Born in a van parked in a field in Carmarthenshire, Squires became a performer at the age of 16 when she was engaged to sing ballads with the Billy Reid Accordion Band. She and Reid became lovers and they had hit records with two songs composed by Reid, 'Gypsy' and 'I'm Walking Behind You'. The proceeds allowed Reid to buy the Llanelli Theatre and Squires a house. The break-up of their relationship followed a disagreeable altercation in the Llanelli Theatre bar in 1950. Miss Squires's father tried to intervene and was slapped in the face.

In 1952 she met Roger Moore, at that time an out-of-work actor making ends meet by advertising Macleans toothpaste. He was twelve years her junior, and married to Doorn van Steyn, a professional skater. Moore soon left the Streatham council flat he had shared with his wife and moved into Miss Squires's suburban mansion, St Michael's Mount. Moore obtained a divorce, and he and Squires were married in 1953. The newlyweds entertained so frequently that Miss Squires tried to have their home registered as a club. The application was turned down.

In 1956 Moore landed the leading role in the television series *Ivanhoe*. As his career prospered, so his wife's declined – to the detriment of their relationship. In 1961 she had a hit record with 'Say It With Flowers' (accompanied by Russ Conway), but her marriage was in a state of collapse. She began to drink heavily, and Moore frequently preferred to sleep on the lawn in front of the house rather than indoors with his wife. In 1962 he worked in Italy on *The Rape of the Sabine Women* and began an affair with Luisa Mattioli, a starlet. Miss Squires discovered this when she intercepted a letter to Moore with an Italian postmark and had it translated by the head waiter at the Astor Club. Unable to accept that Moore no longer cared for her, she applied for, and was granted, an order 'for the restitution of conjugal rights', but she didn't for the time being present the divorce petition to which the order would have automatically entitled her. Instead, she sued the actor Kenneth More for libel. More, when compèring a charity event, had introduced Moore and Mattioli as 'Mr and Mrs Roger Moore'. Kenneth More insisted that he could hardly have introduced the couple as 'Roger Moore and his mistress of nine years', and Miss Squires lost the case.

Throughout the 1970s Miss Squires appeared more often in court than on the stage. Stopped on one occasion for driving when drunk, she sat on the pavement and wept. Then she attacked the arresting officer, 'punching and kicking him in the face'. In 1971 she assaulted a taxi driver and was fined £50. In 1972 she was in court again, charged with 'kicking a taxi driver in the head'. In 1973 she was in more serious trouble when accused of bribing Jack Dabb, the producer of *Family Favourites*, to play her records on the wireless. She admitted that she had paid Dabb's hotel expenses, but had not expected any favours in return. She was eventually cleared of the charge. In 1977 she wrote her autobiography, *Rain, Rain, Go Away*, and shortly after sued her publisher for money she claimed not to have received for the sale of serial rights. She issued seven writs, and at one point staged a sit-in in his office. 'It's not the principle,' she said. 'It's the money.' It was not until 1979 that it was finally established in court that the publisher owed her nothing.

By now Miss Squires was in severe financial difficulties. A proposed charity concert to which she invited the queen mother and various other members of the royal family didn't work out, and plans to mount a musical, *Old Rowley*, about Charles II, fell through. In 1981 she was declared bankrupt. The following year she was prohibited from starting any further actions without High Court consent. Of the 21 she had launched to date, 9 had been dismissed as 'vexatious'. In 1989 she was made bankrupt again, after walking out on a booking in Swansea. She was evicted from her 17-room house in Bray, Berkshire, and its contents were sold by the trustees in bankruptcy. Her final years were spent in a cottage in Trebanog, South Wales, loaned to her by a fan who owned a fish and chip shop next door.

**squirrel pie and mice cooked in batter, youthful experiments with.** *See* BUCKLAND, FRANCIS TREVELYAN.

**squirrels, ground-up testicles of red.** *See* EMMETT, HORACE.

**squirrels round one's head, wrapping dead.** *See* NOAILLES, HELENA COMTESSE DE.

**squirrels wearing gold chains.** *See* DAY, ALEXANDER.

**squirt, a cure for the.** *See* GREEN, MARY.

**stage, hooliganism on.** In the 18th and 19th centuries bad behaviour in the theatre was not confined to the auditorium (*see* HOOLIGANS, THEATRICAL; LUKER, ELIZABETH). In 1718 James Quin, the leading actor of the day, took the title role in *Cato* at Lincoln's Inn Fields Theatre. A Welshman named Williams was to play the character of Decius, who entered with the line, 'Caesar stands health to Cato.' Instead of the classical pronunciation Quin expected, Williams spoke with a Welsh accent. Quin was astonished. 'Would they had sent me a better messenger!' he cried, and for the rest of the act he made fun of the Welsh. Williams took this badly. In the interval he demanded an apology from Quin for ridiculing him in front of the audience. Quin refused, and kept up the banter for the rest of the evening. After the play, Williams lay in wait for Quin up an alley. As Quin approached, he jumped out with a cry of 'Ho!' and swung his sword. Quin drew his rapier and dropped the Welshman on the spot.

Joseph Jefferson once acted at Drury Lane with the great tragedian, William Charles Macready (1793–1873). Macready was playing Werner, and Jefferson was cast in a minor role. In one scene a number of characters, bearing lighted torches, had to rush off stage in search of a delinquent. All went well until that moment, when Jefferson, to his surprise, found Macready standing exactly in line with his point of exit. There was no time to take evasive action, and as Jefferson ran past Macready, torch in hand, he set fire to his wig. In his memoirs Jefferson wrote:

> The enraged Macready tore the wig from his head and stood staring at it for a moment in helpless wonder. Suddenly he made a rush in my direction. The audience, seeing that he was on the warpath, and that I was his game, cheered at the promise of a chase. I dodged him up and down stage, over rocks and gauze waters. He never would

have caught me but that in my excitement I ran full tilt into the stomach of a fat stage carpenter. Here I was seized, but the enraged Macready was so out of wind that he could only gasp and shake his wig at me.

Macready's last visit to the United States of America was marred by riots (10 May 1849) in which 22 people died. Trouble had broken out when Macready's Macbeth was hissed by supporters of the American actor, Edwin Forrest.

When touring in 1940 in J.B. Priestley's *Cornelius*, Dirk Bogarde was so impressed by a moderately good notice he received in Leeds that on the following night he tried to dominate the stage – posing in doorways, rolling his eyes and employing an elaborately exaggerated diction as if participating in an entertainment directed by George 'Dadie' Rylands for the Marlowe Society, Cambridge. Max Adrian, playing the lead, ran out of patience and brought a heavy ledger down on Bogarde's head with a cry of, '*Never* do that again, I say!' Bogarde cannoned into a wall and slid unconscious to the floor. The audience applauded.

Early in his career Noël Coward was engaged by Mr Cecil Barth to tour in *Charlie's Aunt* with Esme Wynn (known in these circles as Stoj) and Arnold Raynor. Mr Barth refused to let Coward share rooms with Raynor, because, he said, it would give the company a bad name. Coward was paired off with Stoj, while Raynor shared with Norah Howard. In Chester, Coward and Stoj had a row because he used her make-up. In Manchester they had another row because she'd forgotten to book them digs, and in Wolverhampton Stoj finally lost her temper and knocked Coward down just before his entrance in Act III. He had no time to fight back, and went on stage with his collar torn and his tie askew. In the dressing room later he confronted Stoj. 'Now then Stoj,' he said, 'we'd better have this out,' so she knocked him down again. Coward lost his temper and threw his make-up box at her. Then she hit him so hard that he banged his head against the wall and slid to the floor. Arnold Raynor ran in at this point and hit Stoj with a hairbrush. So she knocked him over too. Then they all became friends.

In a BBC memorial programme in 1976 devoted to Coward's life and work, Michael MacLiammoir offered an appropriate tribute. Speaking of the 18-year-old Coward as Slightly in *Peter Pan*, MacLiammoir said, 'He was very bad, even then.' When MacLiammoir and Hylton Edwardes ran the Abbey Theatre, Dublin, they were known as Sodom and Begorrah.

*See also* AMHERST, JEFFREY JOHN ARCHER, 5TH EARL.

**Stanley, Sarah** (*c*.1766–?), soldier, impostor and thief. For reasons which are difficult to uncover, Stanley, like Anne BONNY, Mary Read and Hannah SNELL, found it more comfortable, at one stage of her life, to live as a man. Born Sarah Brindley in the house of a rich Warwickshire landowner by the name of Stratford, to whom her father was steward, she became apprentice to a milliner in Lichfield, and then married a shoe-maker, Stanley. In due course she left her husband and went to London. There she dressed as a man for the first time, and found a job as a clerk in the House of Commons. Whether by accident or design, she met a recruit-ing sergeant in Westminster, and thereafter served in the Ayrshire Fencible Cavalry, a regiment of light horse.

Sarah proved to be an exemplary soldier, rode with great skill and was promoted to the rank of corporal. After two years, and while the regiment was billeted in Carlisle, her imposture was discovered. Eloquent testimony to her ability to interact with men as a man was provided by the fact that recriminations and unpleasantness were avoided. She was honourably dis-charged after 'many marks of friendship [were] shewn to her', as the *Newgate Calendar* later put it, 'not only by Major Horsley, in whose troop she rode, but by the other officers, and many of the inhabitants of Carlisle'.

Sarah returned to London, where, in her new and reduced circum-stances, she stole a cloak, was arrested, tried and convicted. Once again she was treated with considerable sympathy. She was discharged from Newgate, the two under-sheriffs giving her money with which to buy a few necessities, and she left the court 'promising henceforward to seek an honest livelihood, in the proper habit of her sex'. According to the *Newgate Calendar* she was a masculine-looking woman of about 30 years of age.

Sarah had been treated with unusual leniency. In 1722 James Appleby had been hanged at Tyburn for the thefts of three wigs; in 1750 Benjamin Beckonfield had been hanged for stealing a hat; and in 1782 a 14-year-old girl had been hanged for being in the company of Gypsies.

**Stanshall, Vivian** (1943–95), musician and writer. As the Bonzo Dog Doo-Dah Band's lead singer in the 1960s, Stanshall hit the charts with a top-ten single featuring a solo for the hosepipe ('I am the Urban Spaceman', 1968). Other 'tracks' failed to repeat this success. The Doo-Dahs' core group included 'Legs' Larry Smith and Neil Innes, whom Stanshall had met at the Central London School of Art. Originally they had specialized in novelty foxtrots, but as the 1960s wore on the band increasingly produced parodies of mainstream pop. Stanshall was a talented mimic and had in his repertoire accurate impressions of Noël Coward, Jack Buchanan and Elvis Presley. After the Doo-Dahs broke up in 1970 he contributed to Mike Old-field's *Tubular Bells*.

In the 1970s and 1980s, Stanshall went to hell and back. As with many other tormented clowns, his zany antics masked a melancholy disposition. In these unhappy circumstances it was not surprising, perhaps, that he formed a friendship with Keith MOON, a drummer with The Who pop group. The two found solace in a series of practical jokes, among which their favourite was 'the trouser testings'. The prank consisted in Stanshall's entering a gentleman's outfitters and asking to see 'a pair of trousers in the strongest fabric you have'. The request seemed sensible enough, and a range of trousers was soon produced. Stanshall would then enlist the assistance of a bystander (Moon), and together they would test a selected pair so rigorously that it would shortly come apart, leaving each of them holding a leg. At that point, a second accomplice – a one-legged man, hired from a theatrical agency – would appear in the shop, look at the devastation and exclaim, 'Just what I want! Wrap them separately!'

Notwithstanding such alliances, Stanshall was able to recover his fortunes with the cult film *Sir Henry at Rawlinson End* (1980), starring Trevor Howard and based on Stanshall's own radio play. A typical line, written for Sir Henry by Stanshall and having a strong autobiographical undertow, ran, 'If I had all the money I've spent on drink, I'd spend it all on drink.' Barred from the set of his own film, Stanshall went to ground in Chertsey, where he remained for two years, unable to work and so vulnerable to anxiety attacks that he was unable, when in need of provisions, to negotiate one of Chertsey High Street's many shopping precincts. In 1992 he did a total of three hours paid work, but after an appearance on Jools Holland's New Year television show in 1993 he was engaged to write and perform a series of television advertisements for Ruddles Ale, which, unusually, contained scenes of spectacular drunkenness. Stanshall spent his last years in a bedsitting-room in Muswell Hill; alternatively, at his mother's bungalow at Leigh-on-Sea in Essex, which he didn't care for.

**state of licentiousness only made human by the descriptions in the most abandoned writers of the French school.** *See* JOCELYN, THE REVEREND PERCY.

**station, perils of entertaining ambitions above one's.** *See* GRIFFITHS, GEORGE.

**Stevenson, Sir Melford** (1902–87), High Court judge who enjoyed the reputation of being the most robust in his sentencing policy since Lord Chief Justice Goddard. Sir Melford famously named his house in Sussex 'Truncheons', an example, according to fellow members of the Garrick Club – where he was popular – of his sense of humour. More successful jokes, perhaps, arose during the trial of Ronnie and Reggie KRAY, at which he presided. Sir Melford was overheard to say that Ronnie Kray had only spoken the truth twice: once, when he referred to the senior prosecuting counsel as 'a flat slob', and once when he claimed that the judge was biased. A joke that everyone might approve of was made when he stood as the Conservative candidate for Maldon, Essex, at the 1945 General Election. Stevenson opened his campaign by announcing that he wanted a clean fight and would not therefore be alluding to the homosexuality of his opponent, Tom DRIBERG.

Many of Stevenson's court-room observations provoked controversy in politically correct quarters. Of a husband in a divorce case, Sir Melford said, 'He chose to live in Manchester, a wholly incomprehensible choice for any free man to make.' To a man accused of rape he said, 'I see you come from Slough. It is a terrible place. You can go back there.' After a difficult case late in his career he said to the defendant, 'I must confess I cannot tell whether you are innocent or guilty. I am giving you three years. If you are guilty, you have got off lightly, if innocent let this be a lesson to you.' He was married twice, secondly to Rosalind Wagner, sister of Sir Anthony Wagner, the herald and genealogist.

**'stew in the pit of your own juice, may you'.** *See* WINCHESTER, BAPSY, MARCHIONESS OF.

**Stiffkey, the rector of.** *See* DAVIDSON, THE REVEREND HAROLD FRANCIS.

**stoat, randy as a.** *See* MITCHELL, FRANK.

**Stock, Lieutenant St George H.** (*c.*1830–*c.*1895) soldier and pornographer. Stock, an officer in the Queen's Royal Regiment, is among those gentlemen authors who provided middle-class Victorian readers with flagellation literature, and was identified by Henry Spencer ASHBEE in his *Index Librorum Prohibitorum* as the creator of *The Romance of Chastisement: or, Revelations of the School and Bedroom* (1870). The manuscript, which had already appeared in serial form in Dublin, was offered to John Camden HOTTEN – the publisher of such curiosities as George Augustus SALA's *Lady Bumtickler's Revels*, a two-act flagellation opera – but he turned it down. Lieutenant Stock then offered it to Hartcupp & Co., who published English-language pornography in Brussels, until the British ambassador complained to the Belgian authorities. Hartcupp's books were seized and destroyed in 1876. It is not known if Lieutenant Stock wrote other books, or whether his military career prospered.

**'Stockwell Ghost' hoax of 1772.** *See* ROBINSON, ANNE.

**Stokes, Doris** (1920–87), medium, known as 'the Gracie Fields of the psychic world' – a tribute to the unpretentious way she went about her business. (A contemporary incarnation from the world of light entertainment might be Miss Cilla Black.) Appearing on stage in a high-street frock and with her hair styled locally, Mrs Stokes would break the ice, as it were, by making a few jokes about sexual practices in the after life, thereafter passing on reassuring messages from 'Aunt Winnie' and 'Uncle Bert'. She would tell her audiences that she had visited 'the Other Side', whose inhabitants 'were not floating around in white sheets or sitting around on clouds strumming a golden harp'. Mrs Stokes chose not to divulge what they *were* doing, and her audiences seemed to accept this. Occasional slip-ups were immediately repaired. 'He went very quickly,' she assured one member of her audience. 'But he was ill for six months,' came the reply. 'Well he went very quickly at the end, lovey,' said Mrs Stokes. She claimed in her books (*Voices in my Ear, More Voices in my Ear* and so forth) to have helped the police on numerous murder inquiries, though no police force ever confirmed this.

Mrs Stokes lived in a mobile home in Kent. Her followers included Ronnie KRAY, Margaret Thatcher and Derek Jameson, a former editor of the *News of the World* and the *Daily Express*. She had one son, Terry, a bus driver.

**Stoll, Sir Oswald** (1869–35), theatrical manager. On the first night of his newly opened Coliseum Theatre in 1904, and in an effort to outdo the spectacular effects recently organized by his rival impresario George Edwardes (of Gaiety Girl fame), Sir Oswald Stoll planned to re-enact the Derby on a revolving platform, complete with sporting toffs, pickpockets, bookmakers, mounted police and six horses ridden by professional jockeys. Owing to a fault in its braking mechanism, the revolve gradually worked up speed until it was a blur to the eye. Jockeys, horses, bits of scenery, pickpockets, toffs and their ladies hurtled across the footlights, causing the audience to duck for safety under their seats. Miraculously, there was only one fatality. Leading jockey, Fred Dent, in Lord Derby's colours, went like a rocket into the upper circle and died before reaching Charing Cross Hospital. The Derby was run again on the second night with a safety net strung across the footlights. After Sir Oswald's death, Stoll Theatres Ltd amalgamated with Moss Empires under the control of Prince Littler (*see* LITTLER, EMILE).

**stomach pumps.** *See* HARRIS, FRANK.

**Stonehouse, John** (1925–88), politician and fraud. In an attempt to escape financial ruin, Stonehouse in 1974 faked his own death in a drowning accident on a Miami beach. By the time the tragedy was announced on the BBC news, Stonehouse, who had left behind a distraught wife, Barbara, a 25-year-old daughter and a mountain of debts, was celebrating in a topless bar in San Francisco. Meanwhile, Sheila Buckley, his mistress and former House of Commons secretary, was preparing to join him in Australia.

Stonehouse entered Parliament in 1957 as Labour Co-op member for Wednesbury. His managerial abilities impressed Harold Wilson and in 1964 he became parliamentary secretary at the Ministry of Aviation in

Wilson's first administration. After a spell as minister of state at the Ministry of Technology, he was appointed postmaster general in 1968, an office in which he was judged a failure. Dropped from Wilson's front bench after Labour's defeat in 1970, Stonehouse, the member now for Walsall North, turned his energies to making a fortune in the expanding world of fringe banking. Using his undoubted charm, he persuaded such eminent businessmen as Sir Charles Forte to invest in his British Bangladesh Trust. Sir Charles also joined the board of London Capital Group, which fulfilled Stonehouse's ambition to own a secondary bank. None of his co-directors were aware that this apparently sound business structure was what a Board of Trade inquiry later described as 'a debt-ridden pack of cards, saturated with offences, irregularities and improprieties'.

With debts of more than £1 million and reluctant to face a long investigation, Stonehouse, who had salted away £100,000 in Swiss bank accounts, embarked on an elaborate plan to fake his own death. Accordingly, he travelled to Miami in November 1974 as a Mr Joseph Markham, whose passport photograph showed him in an open-necked shirt and glasses, and grinning wildly to distort his features. On 19 November Stonehouse went to Miami's Hotel Fontainbleau, where he struck up a friendship with a 65-year-old beach attendant. She happily agreed to look after the charming Englishman's clothes while he went for a swim in the warm Atlantic Ocean. He never returned, and the following day Stonehouse was reported missing, presumed drowned.

The real 'Joseph Markham' had been one of two Walsall North constituents, men of Stonehouse's own age who had recently died, whose identities Stonehouse had been able to assume. The other had been Donald Mildoon. Before his trip to Miami, Stonehouse had obtained copies of the dead men's birth certificates, using Markham's to acquire a false passport. He had then opened more than 40 bank and credit-card accounts in Markham's name, and some in Mildoon's. Under his own name he had taken out life-insurance policies, with his wife as the beneficiary.

After his supposed death by drowning, Stonehouse in fact went to a disused building where he picked up a hidden suitcase containing money, travellers' cheques, credit cards and clothes. He then flew to San Francisco, where he telephoned his mistress Sheila Buckley with the news that the plan had worked. By the end of the month he was in Melbourne, where he was caught by pure chance. A 22-year-old bank clerk became suspicious of a man who was withdrawing large sums of cash as Markham and depositing them up the road as Mildoon. He informed the police, who were looking out for the vanished Lord LUCAN and were already watching an Englishman who was regularly collecting mail from the post office. Convinced that he was Lord Lucan, the police put Stonehouse under surveillance and then raided his flat. Meanwhile, a detective read about the British politician drowned in Miami and remembered seeing a box of the Hotel Fontainbleau's matches in Stonehouse's apartment. Photographs of Stonehouse and Lord Lucan were wired from London, and on Christmas Eve 1974 Stonehouse was arrested. He later wrote in his autobiography, 'Markham/Muldoon was arrested as an illegal immigrant and the world of Stonehouse was thrust back into the reluctant shell of my body.'

After a six-month battle over extradition, Stonehouse and Sheila Buckley were charged at Bow Street with fraud and conspiracy. Stonehouse adopted the role of martyr, arguing that he was a man of honour who had left his wife of 26 years large insurance payments to collect after his death. Mrs Stonehouse was unimpressed. She said her husband was mad, and started divorce proceedings. He was granted bail, and a few days before his trial at the Old Bailey he made an hour-long speech in the Commons on the 'evils of humbug, hypocrisy, moral decadence and materialism afflicting England'. At the trial, which lasted for 70 days, he conducted his own defence, at great length but to little effect since his legal knowledge was confined to what he had picked up while on remand. Stonehouse was sentenced to seven years imprisonment and Sheila Buckley received a two-year suspended sentence. Mr Justice Eveleigh described her as 'unfortunate' to have met him – an opinion that she seemed not to share. When Stonehouse was released on parole after three years she immediately married him at a secret ceremony at Bishop's Waltham. Later, they had a son.

In spite of the millions of pounds Stonehouse had swindled, none seemed to have been salted away. He and the second Mrs Stonehouse lived modestly on her income as a public-relations consultant, while he turned his hand to fiction writing. His first books were autobiographical – *Death of an Idealist* (1975), *My Trial* (1976) – but he switched to action thrillers with *Ralph* (1982), *The Baring Fault* (1986) and *Oil on the Rift* (1987).

**Strachey, William** (1819–1904), civil servant. The uncle of the writer Lytton Strachey, William Strachey spent some years in Calcutta working for the East India Company. He returned to England in 1843 and for the remaining 61 years of his life he stayed on Calcutta time, which is 5 hours and 54 minutes ahead of Greenwich Mean Time. Strachey was of a gregarious disposition, so this preference caused some inconvenience to his friends, who were invited to take lunch with him before they had got up and to dine at his house in the middle of the afternoon. Seeking to break himself of the habit he bought a mechanical bed that had been advertised at the Paris Exhibition. The bed was connected to an alarm clock and the intention was that at the required time in the morning it would throw Strachey on to the floor. In the event, it ejected him into a carelessly placed cold bath. The experiment was discontinued and Strachey returned to Calcutta time.

One of the more charming passages in Rachel Garley's *Canetti et Moi* (2000) – the former model's collected correspondence with the world's leading philosophers – is thought to have been inspired by her researches into the Strachey clan. In an exchange of letters with Galen Strawson, formerly of Jesus College, Oxford, now professor of philosophy at Reading University, Miss Garley describes the advantages of living on Ibiza time. 'You get up at 6 p.m., loon around, hang out, have breakfast and go to bed at 9 a.m. Since you are no longer available during office hours, all the people who want to get you into trouble – the tax man, your bank manager, the government, your boyfriend's mother – assume that you no longer exist.' This leads to an interesting discussion between Garley and Strawson on the themes of existence and reality, taking in Sartrean reflections on 'Being' and 'Nothingness'. For example, Strawson to Garley, 25 October 1999:

> When you go to your bathroom expecting to see Greg the Tiler there, and he isn't there, he isn't 'not there' in the sense that the Archbishop of Canterbury is 'not there'. Greg the Tiler's 'not being there' is reflected back at you in the bathroom's every particular. His absence is palpable. Nothingness *is*. With regard to your question about 'real people', and, by extension, 'real television', your understanding of the difference between 'real' and 'unreal' is probably as good as it was when you were four years old. When you asked your mother whether Father Christmas was 'real' you may not have known the answer but you knew what the question meant.

Miss Garley has appeared on television in *The Fast Show* and *Harry Enfield and Chums*, and in April 2001 came fourth in the *Sun*'s 'All Time Golden Poll of Page 3 Stunners'. Professor Strawson's books include *Mental Reality* (1994).

**Strawson, Galen.** *See* STRACHEY, WILLIAM.

**striptease artistes, murderous.** *See* JONES, ELIZABETH MAUD.

**striptease artistes, octogenarian.** *See* ELTON, GLADYS.

**Strutt, Patricia** (1911–2000), deerstalker. In a shooting career that spanned seven decades, Mrs Strutt accounted for more than two thousand stags, in this respect outdoing even Alma, marchioness of Breadalbane, who wiped out hundreds of animals towards the end of the Victorian era and in 1907 published *The High Tops of Black Mount*, a volume of reminiscences that became a classic of stalking literature.

Strutt was born Patricia Kebbell, the daughter of a successful sheep farmer in New Zealand, but on her mother's side she was descended from

John Cameron of Corrychoillie, considered by some to be the finest cattle drover Scotland has so far produced. Patricia was sent to school in England, where it was discovered that she excelled at running, skiing and skating. In 1930 she married Arthur Strutt, the son of George Herbert Strutt, a cotton tycoon who had recently bought Kingairloch, one of the wildest and most remote deer forests in Scotland, far to the west of Fort William, across the Corran Ferry and down the Morvern peninsular.

In 1977 Arthur Strutt disappeared. One morning he went out alone with a handsaw to do some pruning and he was never seen again. The police, the army, an RAF helicopter and the mountain rescue team from Glencoe, with dogs trained to detect people trapped in avalanches, were called out, but not a trace of the missing tycoon was found. Five years later, forestry contractors, in the business of making a road, came across Arthur Strutt's skeleton, still clothed, sitting propped against a tree less than half a mile from the house. When his Timex watch was wound up it was discovered to be in good working order. An inquiry was held, but it was not possible for the coroner to establish a cause of death.

Patricia Strutt was quite unaffected by the loss of her husband; her response was to live at Kingairloch all the year round, to become ever more self-sufficient and to improve her shooting skills. According to Iain Thornber, an authority on killing deer and a local historian, she was a matchless shot, fast and consistent. From the same source it is learnt that, like a stag in rut, Mrs Strutt ate practically nothing. If she felt cramp coming on, she would lick her wrists for the salt in her sweat. Although worth millions, she was extremely mean, taking to the hills in an old tweed jacket secured by string. On the rare occasions that she offered a ghillie a dram at the end of a hard day, it was always the cheapest supermarket whisky available. To strangers she seemed to be a daunting, even an unpleasant, woman, an opinion shared by those who knew her well.

**subterranean theories, not widely accepted.** *See* CLANCARTY, WILLIAM FRANCIS BRINSLEY LE POER TRENCH, 8TH EARL OF; MONEY, WILLIAM.

**suicide in the dock by means of a pint of arsenic, committing.** *See* JACKSON, JOHN.

**suicides, ineptly handled.** *See* HACKMAN, THE REVEREND JAMES.

**supergrasses.** *See* INFORMERS.

**Swinburne, Algernon Charles.** *See* HOTTEN, JOHN CAMDEN; HOWELL, CHARLES AUGUSTUS; SALA, GEORGE AUGUSTUS.

**Swindell, Peter George** (1946– ), police constable and bondage enthusiast. The dangers inherent in sexual practices involving restraint were illustrated in 1981, when PC Swindell, who had been part of a detachment guarding Mrs Thatcher at 10 Downing Street, stood trial at the Old Bailey charged with manslaughter. For some years, PC Swindell had persuaded a variety of women, including parking attendants, to allow him to tie them up like Christmas parcels, securing them with elaborately fashioned bows, and then photographing the results. The habit became more dangerous when he progressed to leather, zips and manacles. 'Andy' Krate, an 18-stone lesbian prostitute, choked to death under the burden of her fetters. Swindell was acquitted of manslaughter, but because he had deposited Miss Krate's body in Epping Forest he was charged with hindering the coroner's office and sentenced to five years imprisonment. This was later reduced to three years by the Court of Appeal, who found that:

> First of all, this man presents very little, if any, danger to the public. Secondly, this is an offence which, *ex hypothesi*, is not likely to be repeated by this man. Thirdly, this is not the sort of offence from which it is necessary to deter others, again for obvious reasons.

*See also* LASKEY, COLIN; PRACTICES, SADOMASOCHISTIC.

**swindlers.** *See* MCGREGOR, GREGOR.

*See also* ART FORGERS; CONFIDENCE TRICKSTERS; FRAUD AND FRAUDSTERS; LITERARY FORGERS.

**Symonds, John.** *See* ROBSON, DETECTIVE INSPECTOR BRIAN.

**Symonds, John Addington** (1840–92), writer and Harrovian. Notwithstanding his own adolescent fantasies of wrestling with naked sailors, an affair with a choirboy during the school holidays and a relationship with a 24-year-old gondolier named Angelo, Symonds exposed the Reverend Dr Charles Vaughan as a homosexual, thereby terminating the career of the most distinguished headmaster in the history of Harrow School.

As a pupil there himself for five years from 1854, Symonds had been revolted by the crudity of those around him. In his memoirs, which were unpublished in his lifetime and embargoed for 50 years after his death, he wrote of contemporaries such as Barber ('a good-natured longimanous ape, gibbering on his perch and playing ostentatiously with a prodigiously developed phallus'), Cookson ('a red-faced strumpet, with flabby cheeks and sensual mouth') and the much sought-after Ainslie ('who was dubbed Bum Bathsheba because of his opulent posterior parts').

Symonds, who would have nothing to do with such overt homoeroticism, was greatly shocked when his friend Alfred Pretor showed him a batch of love letters written to him by Dr Vaughan:

> I was disgusted to find such desires lurking in a man holding the highest position of responsibility, consecrated by the Church, entrusted with the welfare of six hundred youths – a man who had recently prepared me for confirmation, from whose hands, kneeling by the side of Alfred Pretor, I received the sacrament, and whom I had been accustomed to regard as the pattern of my conduct.

Just as it comforts sexual herbivores to claim that obsessively active heterosexuals are, as a rule, impotent (or, if they are female, nymphomaniacs), so is it evidence of wishful thinking among homosexuals to claim that those who most vocally condemn the practice are themselves closet homosexuals. Nevertheless, it seems to be the case that Symonds hoped to exorcize what he took to be this weakness in himself by exposing it in his headmaster.

Symonds did nothing immediately, but after he had left Harrow and gone to Oxford the matter continued to obsess him. 'My blood boiled,' he wrote in his memoirs, 'and my nerves stiffened when I thought what mischief life at Harrow was doing daily to young lads under the autocracy of a hypocrite.' Unable to control his indignation, Symonds one day blurted out the story to the professor of Classics at Balliol, John Conington, himself a homosexual. Conington advised Symonds to tell his father. He still had in his possession some of Dr Vaughan's letters to Alfred Pretor, and when he returned to Clifton in the summer of 1859 he showed these to his father. Dr Symonds, an eminent surgeon, wrote to Vaughan saying he had evidence of an improper relationship with a pupil, but would not publicize the matter if Vaughan resigned immediately and accepted no further preferment in the Church. After a visit to Clifton from Vaughan's wife, in the course of which she begged Dr Symonds in vain to suspend execution of his sentence, Vaughan announced his resignation as headmaster of Harrow in a circular to the pupils' parents. The prime minister, Lord Palmerston, immediately offered him the bishopric of Rochester. Vaughan indicated that he would accept it, and a half-holiday was declared at Harrow. When Dr Symonds heard of Vaughan's intentions, however, he sent him a warning telegram. Vaughan withdrew, and the half-holiday was cancelled. At the age of 43, and at the start of a brilliant career in the Church, Vaughan would henceforth refuse every offer of ecclesiastical preferment.

John Addington Symonds, for his part, while aware of some moral ambiguity in his position, was sustained by a clear conscience, and by the Bristol choirboy, perhaps, with whom he had recently started an affair:

I felt that the course I followed was right. But I suffered deeply in both spirit and in health. My brain and moral consciousness never recovered from the weariness of those weeks.

Symonds went on to become a celebrated man of letters, and in Vaughan's obituary in *The Times* was mentioned as an old Harrovian who owed his distinction to Vaughan's abilities as a headmaster.

# t

**tableaux plastiques.** *See* GRAHAM, JAMES; HAMILTON, LADY EMMA; NICHOLSON, 'BARON' RENTON.

**Talbot, Matthew** (1856–1925), ascetic. Described in the prayer for his canonization as a 'model for penance', Talbot spent decades of saintly discomfort, not locked away in a hermitage but on the streets of Dublin. A hodman by occupation, a convivial man who liked a drink – sometimes pawning his boots to pay for a pint of porter – he surprised everyone by suddenly taking the pledge at the age of 28. He read St Augustine and Butler's *Lives of the Saints* – with difficulty, since he was almost illiterate – and greatly admired St Catherine of Siena and St Teresa of Avila, whom he thought 'grand girls'. He particularly studied the latter's injunction on how to pray and as a consequence was never off his knees in the evening, unless he had a visitor. At T. & C. Martin's timber yard, where he took a job creosoting wood, he frequently retired behind the timber stacks to pray. His midday meal, taken at work, was a mixture of tea and cocoa, which he drank cold and without milk or sugar. He slept on a plank, with his head on a wooden block.

For 40 years Talbot fasted and held nightly vigils. Under his clothes he wore chains binding his body and limbs, a habit that was only discovered when in June 1925 he collapsed and died during a heat wave. When attendants in Jervis Street Hospital removed his clothes they found a heavy chain wound round his body, a lighter chain on one arm, another below the knee and a cord knotted around the other arm. They had worn deep grooves in his skin. After death, his body was moved several times but finally came to rest in his old parish church in Gloucester Street, where people still pray at his tomb.

**Tangerine Earl, the.** *See* ST GERMANS, NICHOLAS RICHARD MICHAEL ELIOT, 9TH EARL OF.

**Taste Tickell, Kim de la** (1917–90), innkeeper. Taste Tickell, an old Marlburian, had tried his hand at a number of professions, including amateur theatricals, before becoming the comic landlord of the Tickell Arms at Whittlesford in East Anglia. Wearing jocular knee breeches and buckled shoes, he built up a clientele from among Cambridge University's more idle students and sillier dons. Some people felt that his affected behaviour might have better suited Oxford, but others were well enough amused. He preferred left-wingers, blacks and 'modern' women to steer clear of his premises. In 1962 he claimed that female workers from a local Christmas decorations factory lowered the tone of the village, and he refused to serve them. When he accused them of using bad language, they argued that theirs was nothing to that heard outside the Tickell Arms at closing time. 'You will never hear me using four-letter Lady Chatterley words!' Taste Tickell insisted. One of the factory women reminded him that he had once said, 'Get off my fucking grass!' Then they debagged him, which he seemed not to have minded.

In 1970 Taste Tickell appeared in court after he had armed himself with one of the medieval weapons that decorated his walls, later emerging from the Tickell Arms with the cry, 'I will take on any bugger who disapproves of the way I run my house!' Accused of possessing an offensive weapon with intent to wound, he was acquitted on both charges. A keen supporter of the Arts Theatre, Cambridge, whose first nights he attended in an opera cape and silk scarf, Kim de la Taste Tickell never married.

**Tatchell, Peter.** *See* LABOUCHERE, HENRY.

**tax allowances for wear and tear on whips, bondage bars, and suffocation hoods.** *See* ST CLAIR, LINDI.

**taxi drivers, assaulting.** *See* SQUIRES, DOROTHY.

**tea after the fun, a nice cup of.** *See* LASKEY, COLIN.

**Teach, Edward** (*c.*1680–1718), pirate, known as 'Blackbeard'. Teach was the most celebrated buccaneer of the 18th century. In his *A General History of the Robberies and Murders of the Most Notorious Pyrates* (1724), Captain Johnson wrote that, 'some of his frolicks of wickedness, were so extravagant, it was as if he aimed at making his men believe he was a devil incarnate.' Among these 'frolicks', two stand out. One night when drinking in his cabin with the pilot, Marshall, and Israel Hands, his second-in-command, Blackbeard, without provocation, drew out a pair of pistols and cocked them under the table. When he was ready, he crossed his hands and fired the pistols. The pilot was unharmed, but Israel Hands was shot through the knee and lamed for life. When asked why he had done this, Blackbeard said, 'Damn you all! Unless I now and then kill one of my men, they will forget who I am.' On another occasion, when drunk at sea, he suggested to the crew that 'we make a hell of our own, and try how long we can bear it'; accordingly, he and three others went down into the hold, closed the hatches, filled several pots full of brimstone and other combustible matter, and set it on fire. Blackbeard refused to open the hatches until the men were almost suffocated, 'not a little pleased that he had held out the longest'.

Of Teach's appearance, which from all accounts was horrifying, Captain Johnson wrote:

> The beard was black, which he suffered to grow to an extravagant length; as to breadth, it came up to his eyes. In time of action, he wore a sling over his shoulders, with three brace of pistols hanging in holsters like bandoliers; and stuck lighted matches under his hat, which appearing on each side of his face, his eyes naturally looking fierce and wild, made him altogether such a figure, that imagination cannot form an idea of a Fury from Hell to look more frightful.

Born Edward Drummond in Bristol, he assumed the name Teach, or Tache, when employed as a privateer against the Spanish during the War of the Spanish Succession (1701–13). When the war ended he turned to piracy, first crewing for another pirate in the Bahamas, and then, as captain of his own ship, *Queen Anne's Revenge*, attacking Spanish, French and English vessels throughout the Caribbean. He would blockade harbours for days on end, seizing all the shipping going in and out and terrorizing the planters of the Carolina coast. He formed an alliance with the governor of North Carolina, Charles Eden, and the state collector of taxes, giving them a share of the spoils in return for their protection. Some historians believe that by 1718 Teach had had enough, and that the loss of *Queen Anne's Revenge*, which he ran aground in Beaufort Inlet in June of that year, was intentional. Although retired, he was blamed by Virginia's governor, Alexander Spotswood, for the continuing attacks along the colonial coast. Spotswood put a price on Teach's head and urged the British military and the Virginia Assembly to assist in his capture. On 22 November 1718 Lieutenant Robert Maynard, commanding a British sloop, the *Pearl*, tricked him into battle off Ocracoke. After a savage engagement, in which he sustained 25 wounds, five by shot, Teach eventually fell dead. Lieutenant Maynard cut off Teach's head, as was the custom with a pirate, and hung it on the bowsprit. Of 15 of Teach's men taken prisoner, 13 were later hanged. One of the two who avoided the gallows was Israel Hands. He had not yet recovered from his wounded kneecap, and had taken no part in the engagement.

According to Captain Johnson, Teach had, on the night before the battle, sat up with his men, drinking till morning. One of them asked him whether, in the event of his death in the coming engagement, his wife knew where he had buried his treasure. Teach answered that nobody but himself and the Devil knew where it was, 'and which of us lives longest shall take it all'.

**teachers who have strayed.** *See* CHILD, BENJAMIN; CORDER, WILLIAM; GAMBLE, THE REVEREND PETER; HUNTER, THE REVEREND THOMAS.

**tea makers, suspiciously enthusiastic.** *See* YOUNG, GRAHAM.

**tea shop, announcing your divinity in a Weymouth.** *See* PRINCE, HENRY.

**tea shops, priests banned from.** *See* DAVIDSON, THE REVEREND HAROLD FRANCIS (the rector of Stiffkey).

**'Teasie Weasie' Raymond, Mr.** *See* CHATHAM, GEORGE.

**Teddy Odd Legs.** *See* HILL, BILLY.

**Tennyson, Lionel, 3rd Baron** (1878–1951), cricketer. Lord Tennyson, the grandson of the poet Alfred, Lord Tennyson, was an accomplished enough batsman for the selectors of Hampshire, which he captained, and England to overlook many personal idiosyncrasies. Among these was an insistence that his man servant, Walter Livsey, keep wicket for the county although it was not a skill he ever mastered. Livsey was able to ensure, however, that Lord Lionel's cricket bag had in it sufficient bottles of champagne to celebrate victory or alleviate the disappointment of defeat. He was useful, too, in other respects. On one occasion, when Tennyson's appeal against bad light had been rejected by the umpires, Livsey, the next man in, loyally groped his way to the wicket as if blindfolded, taking guard at square leg with a cry of, 'Where are you, my lord? I can hear you, but I can't see you.' On another occasion the umpires objected to Tennyson coaching Livsey by shouting instructions from the pavilion. Tennyson thereafter made his wishes known by telegram, arranging for a boy in a post office uniform to arrive at the crease with a message in a yellow envelope which read, 'For pity's sake, Livsey, what do you think your bat's for?'

Tennyson may have inherited his autocratic manner and dislike of criticism from his distinguished forebear. When, in 1870, Lord Alfred read his latest unpublished poem to Benjamin Jowett, the Master of Balliol College, Oxford, Jowett said, 'I shouldn't publish that, if I were you, Tennyson.' Tennyson replied, 'If it comes to that, Master, the sherry you gave us at lunch was downright filthy.'

**Tesco's carrier bag, mislaying one's husband's ashes in a.** *See* FOX, WINNIE.

**Tester, William George** (*c*.1821–?), adventurer and dandy. At the time of the Great Train Robbery of 1855 Tester (*see* BOLLOCKS, A SILLY) had found temporary employment in London Bridge's public-traffic department and was thus able to assist the prime conspirator, Edward AGAR.

***thés dansants.*** *See* BOURNEMOUTH.

**thicket, ambushed in a.** *See* DU VALL, CLAUDE.

**Thin Blue Jeans, the.** An elite squad of police officers, so dubbed by the Soviet double agent Oleg Bitov in an article on London in *Literaturnaya Gazeta* (Moscow, 1985). Bitov, it may be remembered, was the centre of a diplomatic storm in September 1984 when, having apparently defected to Britain in 1983 and having subsequently written articles in the *Sunday Telegraph* on the repressive conditions in the Soviet Union, he suddenly disappeared from London and reappeared three weeks later in Moscow, with tales of kidnap, violence and brainwashing at the hands of the British authorities. At Bitov's Moscow press conference it was stated that he would in future write at length for the Soviet public on conditions in Britain.

The relevant passage from *Literaturnaya Gazeta*, in a translation by Dr Donald Hunter of Keele University, runs:

> Now that the Metropolitan Police have given up the unequal struggle against crime, it is estimated that 43 per cent of the single men 'cruising' the Earl's Court area of London are members of Commissioner Newman's Gay Squad, otherwise known as the Thin Blue Jeans or the Pretty Police. In spite of protests from residents, tourists and local businessmen, who have objected to being propositioned in bars and toilets, Sir Kenneth Newman has no intention of discontinuing his anti-vice initiative.

When *Bitov's Britain* – a collection of observations about the United Kingdom, ostensibly written by Bitov – was published by Viking (1985) it was described by espionage experts as 'unreliable'.

*See also* HAMPSON, KEITH.

**thinking man's model.** *See* STRACHEY, WILLIAM (for Rachel Garley).

**Thistlewood, Arthur** (1770–1820), soldier and instigator of the Cato Street Conspiracy of 1820. Born in Tupholme, Lincolnshire, Thistlewood served in the army in the United States, where he was greatly influenced by the revolutionary ideas of Tom Paine. He also spent time in France, and was an admirer of Robespierre. His ambition was to assassinate the widely hated foreign secretary, Lord Castlereagh, and seize power. In November 1816 he instigated a mutiny at Spa Fields at which four radical associates of his – Dr James Watson, his son, also called James, John Hooper and a man named Hunt – all carrying tricoloured cockades in their hats, made inflammatory speeches from a cart. Spasmodic rioting took place, but this was suppressed without difficulty by the army.

By January 1820 the government had learned of a more serious plot, which had as its objective the decapitation of the foreign secretary and the assassination of his cabinet colleagues. For the moment the authorities took no direct action. Following the policy of the time, and in order to secure a conviction, they allowed the conspiracy to mature. Thistlewood had timed his attack to take place on Wednesday 23 February, a day on which Lord Harrowby was entertaining the entire cabinet at his home in Grosvenor Square. A parcel would be delivered at Harrowby's house and when the door was opened, Thistlewood and his men would storm in, bind or kill the servants and proceed to the dining room, where Castlereagh and the other ministers would be massacred. To increase the confusion, hand grenades had been prepared and one of the party had been provided with a paper bag in which he was to bring away the heads of Lords Castlereagh and Sidmouth (the latter being the home secretary, whom Thistlewood had earlier challenged to a duel, and been jailed for his pains in 1818–19).

Through a man named Edwards, who was a police spy, the government discovered that Thistlewood's revolutionary headquarters was a dilapidated tenement in Cato Street, on the Portman Estate in London's West End, the premises consisting of a loft above a stable, protected by a trapdoor and accessible via a rickety ladder. A party of police officers, supported by a detachment of Irish Guards, was ordered to Cato Street under the command of Sir Richard Birnie, the Bow Street magistrate. A Bow Street runner named Ruthven led the way up the ladder, followed by Smithers, shortly bursting through the trapdoor and announcing themselves as peace officers. Thistlewood drew his sword and stabbed Smithers to death, while his accomplices hastily armed themselves with cutlasses, bayonets, pistols and swords. For a time it seemed that the Runners would get the worst of it, their task made no easier by the fact that the detachment of Irish Guards, under the command of Captain Lord Adolphus Fitzclarence, had lost their bearings once they had entered Cato Street and had thereafter occupied the wrong loft. This blunder allowed Thistlewood and some 20 of his men to escape, but they were taken the following day while hiding out in Moorfields.

On 15 April 1820 Thistlewood and ten others – including James Ings, Richard Tidd, John Brunt, John Straw Strange and William Davidson (a man of colour, according to the *Newgate Calendar*) – were charged at the

Old Bailey with high treason and murder. Thistlewood, Ings, Brunt, Davidson and Tidd were found guilty, and on Monday 1 May they were hanged by James Botting, and then decapitated. All had refused religious consolation except Davidson, the man of colour.

**Thomas, Dylan** (1914–53), poet and alcoholic. After four days in a coma, and many years of alcohol abuse, Thomas finally succumbed while on a lecture tour in America. His last words were, 'I've just drunk 18 straight whiskies. I think that's a record.' At Thomas's funeral, the poet Louis Mac-Neice was so drunk that he threw his sandwiches on to the coffin in the belief that they were a bunch of daffodils.

In his lifetime, Thomas had been praised by critics for his striking rhythms, original imagery and technical ingenuity, but he only gained a popular following when his 'play for voices', *Under Milk Wood*, was broadcast on BBC Radio in 1954, the year after his death. The work was filmed in 1971 with a cast which included Richard Burton, Elizabeth Taylor, Peter O'Toole, David Jason, who played Nogood Boyo, and Susan Penhaligon, who appeared as Mae Rose Cottage. After she made her mark as pouting Prue Sorenson in the miniseries *Bouquet of Barbed Wire* (1976), sightings of Miss Penhaligon were rare on television until she was reunited in January 2002 with David Jason in an episode of *A Touch of Frost*.

*See* JOHN, AUGUSTUS.

**Thompson, Edith** (1894–1922), protagonist in a celebrated murder, which later inspired books, plays and endless controversy. Whether Thompson conspired with her lover, Frederick Bywaters, in the death of her husband, Percy Thompson, is far from clear. The marriage had been unsuccessful. Edith, an attractive, outgoing woman, was four years younger than her husband, by whom she felt stifled. Percy Thompson, a shipping clerk, was at best a prig, at worst a wife abuser. In 1921 the 20-year-old Bywaters, a steward on the P&O liner *Morea*, took lodgings with the Thompsons, who were then leading an uneventful life in Ilford, Essex. Edith fell passionately in love with the young steward. Because of his job, Bywaters was abroad for lengthy periods and the letters Edith sent him while he was away became the basis of the prosecution's case at the time of her trial. She destroyed his letters, but Bywaters kept hers – perhaps with the intention of blackmailing her at a later date.

On the evening of 3 October 1922 Edith and Percy Thompson attended a play at the Criterion Theatre in London's West End. As they were returning home, Bywaters attacked and stabbed Percy Thompson. Edith was heard to cry out, 'No! Don't! Don't!' and she tried to help Percy as he lay on the ground. When a doctor at last arrived, she complained furiously that he had not come quickly enough to save her husband. Both she and Bywaters were arrested, and their trial opened at the Old Bailey in

December 1922. She denied that she had known of Bywaters's intentions, but according to one of her letters she herself had tried to kill Percy Thompson on three occasions by putting powdered glass in his food. Sir Bernard Spilsbury, the pathologist, had found no evidence of this, but the judge, Mr Justice Shearman, was clearly against her, reminding the jury that they were 'trying a vulgar, common crime', referring to the letters as 'the outpourings of a silly but at the same time wicked affection' and omitting to mention Spilsbury's very significant testimony.

It has come to be accepted that Edith Thompson was tried and convicted not on the evidence but for adultery. On 9 January 1922 she was hanged by John ELLIS at Holloway prison. Everyone directly involved in her execution was greatly affected by it. The chaplain, who had asked for a chair to be placed at his convenience since he was prone to dizzy spells, suffered some sort of breakdown, and Ellis, the hangman, described the occasion as 'the most nerve-wracking' he had ever endured. He complained later that the neuritis, from which he suffered, had been made worse by the experience. And he was unable for some weeks to pursue his enthusiasm for rugby league, missing several of the Rochdale Hornets' home fixtures.

**Thompson, William 'Bendigo'** (1811–80), boxer and religious convert. The champion bare-knuckle fist-fighter of all England, Thompson became so famous that he had a drink, a racehorse and a town named after him in Australia. He was born in Nottingham, one of 21 children. His mother, who weighed 18 stone and smoked a pipe, nicknamed her triplets Shadrach, Meshach and Abednego. The latter was shortened to 'Bendigo', and it was under this name that Thompson, a bar-room brawler who was in and out of prison, won the British title in 1839. The holder, James 'Deaf' Burke (who had been returned to consciousness in one fight by a second biting off his ear), was disqualified for persistent butting between rounds. Undefeated in his next 38 fights, Thompson was forced to retire when he injured his knee turning somersaults to entertain some children. Thereafter, he continued to spend his time in and out of prison. While serving his 28th sentence for drunken brawling he was greatly moved by the sermons of the prison chaplain and, on his release, joined a religious sect, the Good Templars. Here, he fell under the influence of a hellfire and brimstone preacher, Dick Weaver, known as 'Undaunted Dick'. He claimed that the omnipresent Dick peered at him like a ghostly conscience through the windows of public houses. The converted Thompson spread the word across the land, learning his speeches parrot-fashion since he was illiterate. His career was temporarily interrupted by a nine-month prison sentence following an incident in 1859. At a meeting in Birmingham he was half way through his sermon when he asked for 'five minutes to himself'. He climbed down from the rostrum and, the ghost of

'Undaunted Dick' notwithstanding, knocked out four of his congregation whom he didn't like the look of.

**Thorpe, Jeremy** (1929–  ), former leader of the British Liberal Party and central figure in the greatest political scandal since the Profumo Affair (*see* KEELER, CHRISTINE). The charge against Thorpe was that he had incited three men to murder the former male model, Norman Josiffe – later to be known as Norman Scott – with whom he was alleged to have had a homosexual relationship.

Educated at Eton and Oxford, Thorpe was called to the Bar in 1954. In 1959 he became Liberal MP for North Devon. In the following year he first met Josiffe, then working as a riding instructor. Josiffe was emotionally unstable. He was subject to fits of weeping and tried to arouse pity by inventing poignant stories about his background. In 1961 he was hospitalized after an overdose of Largactil. When he was discharged he visited Thorpe at the House of Commons. Afterwards they went together to Oxted in Surrey, where Thorpe's mother had a house. According to Josiffe, their homosexual affair began that night, at Thorpe's instigation and to Josiffe's distress. 'I just lay there with my dog, crying,' said Josiffe later. As compensation, he was given a job on the staff of Len Smith, a Liberal Party official. He was also set up in a small service flat near the Commons, where it is alleged Thorpe continued the affair. They stayed at Mrs Thorpe's house on several other occasions, and Thorpe entertained Josiffe at the Reform Club and at Chelsea restaurants. At Christmas, Josiffe attended a house party in Thorpe's Devon constituency, and while their hosts were walking in the garden with their other guests, Thorpe allegedly sodomized Josiffe amid the bathroom plumbing. He later wrote him a letter in which he assured him that 'Bunnies *can* (and *will*) go to France'.

In time the relationship cooled, at least on Thorpe's side. He did sort out a problem Josiffe had with a national-insurance card, and he helped him to move into the home of a Dr Keith Lister, but when the doctor wrote to Thorpe with an enquiry about Josiffe's background he was brusquely told that he should consult Josiffe's parents. When Josiffe's dog Tish killed Dr Lister's ducks, Josiffe was asked to leave. This triggered some sort of nervous breakdown. In a fit of self-pity, Josiffe told a friend that he planned to kill Thorpe and commit suicide. As a result, Josiffe was interviewed at Chelsea police station in December 1962, and began a statement, 'I have come to the police to tell you about my homosexual relations with Jeremy Thorpe …' The police took the 'Bunnies will go to France' letter to an assistant commissioner at Scotland Yard, but no attempts were made to follow up Josiffe's allegations of a homosexual affair.

By 1964 Josiffe, who now called himself the Honourable Norman Lianche-Josiffe and claimed that his father was a peer of the realm, was becoming an embarrassment. He bought himself a pair of silk pyjamas on

Thorpe's account at Gieves, the naval outfitter, and wrote to Thorpe's mother, describing the details of his alleged affair with her son and protesting at Thorpe's mistreatment of him. Thorpe's reaction was to confide in his friend and fellow Liberal MP, Peter BESSELL. There followed several anxious years during which the talkative and unreliable Bessell tried, with cash payments and other inducements, to shield Thorpe from Josiffe's more serious accusations – a consideration that became all the more pressing after Thorpe succeeded Jo Grimond as leader of the Liberal Party in January 1967.

In May 1968 Thorpe married 29-year-old Caroline Alpass, but Josiffe, who had become a male model and now called himself Scott, remained an ever-present threat. According to the prosecution case at Thorpe's trial, it was some time in the autumn of 1968 that Thorpe first considered killing Scott/Josiffe. Peter Bessell, who had decided that his own interests were best served by becoming a prosecution witness, testified that a discussion had taken place between him and Thorpe in the House of Commons, in the course of which he had told Thorpe that it was impossible to find Scott a job in America. Thorpe had replied, 'In that case, we have got to get rid of him.' Bessell had then asked, 'Are you suggesting killing him off?' and according to Bessell Thorpe had answered, 'Yes.'

In June 1970 Thorpe suffered a personal tragedy when his wife Caroline was killed in a car crash. A rumour circulated that Scott had previously gone to Thorpe's house, where he had told her the full story of his affair with her husband, and that this had been preying on her mind. Scott denied this, but he continued to pressurize Thorpe. Among other demands, he asked Bessell for further sums of money with which to open a riding school in Wales. Bessell refused to help, and Scott tried to sell his story to the press. 'I was deeply in love with Jeremy,' it began. 'I thought our idyllic friendship would last forever. But he discarded me.' The newspapers declined this opportunity, but Scott was not going to fade away. He no longer had Thorpe's letters, but he had kept all Peter Bessell's, and these constituted strong evidence for his claims. It was decided that Thorpe's friend, David Holmes, should pay Scott £2500 for the 'Bessell file' – a sum that Scott quickly squandered. He was now living in some squalor on the edge of Exmoor, addicted to drink and drugs, and increasingly fearful for his life – a condition aggravated by a series of bizarre incidents. He was beaten up by two unknown men as he emerged from a public house in Barnstaple, and a week later he was approached by a man calling himself Peter Keene, who told him that a contract killer was on his way from Canada to murder him.

On 24 October 1975 'Keene', who was in fact a junior pilot officer with British Airways named Andrew Newton, persuaded Scott to drive with him to Porlock, where he had business. On the edge of the moor Newton stopped the car, saying he was tired. Scott, who was accompanied for safety's sake by his Great Dane, Rinka, offered to drive, got out of the car and walked round to the other side. Newton climbed out and, with the words, 'This is it,' produced a Mauser pistol and shot Rinka dead. He then placed the gun at Scott's head and said, 'It's your turn now.' Scott froze, but the gun failed to go off. Newton said, 'Fuck it,' and as Scott tried to give Rinka the kiss of life, he got back into the car and drove off. Scott was able to flag down another car, whose occupants drove him to a police station.

Newton was arrested and in due course sentenced to two years in prison. In January 1976 Scott was charged with defrauding the Department of Health and Social Security of £58.40. This gave him the opportunity to announce in court that he was being hounded because he had once had a homosexual relationship with Jeremy Thorpe. When Andrew Newton, now out of prison, added to Thorpe's difficulties by selling his story to the *London Evening News* ('I was Hired to Kill Scott'), Thorpe resigned as leader of the Liberal Party. On 2 August 1978 warrants were issued for the arrest of Thorpe, David Holmes and two businessmen from Port Talbot – John Le Mesurier, the proprietor of a discount carpet firm, and George Deakin, who had made money out of one-armed bandits. They subsequently appeared at Minehead magistrates' court, where the chief witness against them was Andrew Newton. The story emerged that in October 1974 David Holmes had mentioned to Le Mesurier that a friend of his was having a problem with a blackmailer. Le Mesurier had introduced him to Deakin, who recommended Newton as someone who could help. Newton had been promised £15,000 to frighten Scott. When he came out of prison in April 1977 he was summoned by Le Mesurier and given just £5000. The magistrate decided that these arrangements amounted to a conspiracy to murder, and Thorpe's trial opened at the Old Bailey on 8 May 1979.

The most telling evidence against Thorpe was provided by his friend Peter Bessell, who described the day in the House of Commons when he said Thorpe had suggested 'getting rid' of Scott. They had also discussed how they should dispose of the body. Thorpe was thought to have suggested that David Holmes, posing as a reporter, should invite Scott to Plymouth, where he would get him drunk in a pub, kill him in a lonely spot and drop his body down a mine shaft in Peter Bessell's Cornish constituency. Bessell had pointed out that shooting Scott would be noisy and messy. 'In that case,' Thorpe is alleged to have said, 'it will have to be poison. You can slip it into his drink in a pub.' Holmes had protested that it might be awkward if Scott dropped dead off his bar stool. When Bessell said, 'You can apologize to the landlord and ask for directions to the nearest mineshaft,' Thorpe is alleged to have snapped, 'This is a serious matter.'

Bessell's testimony was somewhat compromised by the fact that he stood to receive £50,000 from the *Sunday Telegraph* were Thorpe to be convicted, but only £25,000 in the event of an acquittal. In these circumstances George Carman QC, for the defence, had little difficulty in destroying Bessell's credibility. Nor had Bessell impressed the judge, the elderly Mr Justice Cantley, who in his summing-up called him an 'obvious humbug'. He was harsh, too, about Scott, describing him as 'an accomplished liar and crook, with an hysterical and warped personality'. The 'Bunnies can go to France' letter might suggest a homosexual relationship, he conceded, but equally, it might not. 'He is a fraud. He is a sponger. He is a whiner. He is a parasite. But of course, he could still be telling the truth.'

Thorpe was acquitted, the *Daily Mail* described his behaviour as 'statesmanlike' and on the following Sunday a service of thanksgiving was held in his constituency. The church was not as full as had been expected, but the vicar nonetheless thanked God for 'the ministry of his servant, Jeremy, in North Devon. The darkness is now passed and the time of light shines.' Finally, he likened Thorpe's acquittal to the miracle of the Resurrection.

**Threadneedle Street, defrauding the Old Lady of.** *See* BIDWELL, AUSTIN.

**thugs, celebrity.** *See* BINDON, JOHN; JONES, VINNIE.

**Tichborne Inheritance, the.** *See* ORTON, ARTHUR.

**'Tiger' Cowley, Countess.** *See* KIMBERLEY, JOHN WODEHOUSE, 4TH EARL OF.

**Tiger Roche.** *See* ROCHE, TIGER.

**Timbrell, Henry** (*c*.1710–*c*.1780), Methodist preacher and farmer. In 1764 Timbrell was tried in a Wiltshire court for castrating two apprentices, Thomas Hay, aged 16, and Robert Brown, aged 8, in order that he might sell them as opera singers. According to a contemporary report, Timbrell was a man 'who has assumed divers characters to support a life of indolence', and the barbarity of his act had been prompted by financial need. He had made a practice, the report says, of breeding bastard children for a stipulated sum, but had found two of them to be redundant. Having tried to lose them to smallpox, he had had his brain wave vis-à-vis the opera, thereafter taking an opportunity, when the children were in bed, to 'wicker them after the manner in which poor rams are treated. This matter being noised abroad, the hard-hearted rascal was apprehended.'

The court at Salisbury sentenced Timbrell to two years in prison and fined him 13s 4d for each assault. According to the Wiltshire Circuit Records, these were punishments that the crowds outside the court thought too lenient:

This sentence was deemed by the female part of the mob so inadequate to his crime that all the constables of the city, the javelin-men and, in short, the whole civil power, were unable to protect him from their rage.

**Titanic Mob, the.** *See* HARDING, ARTHUR.

**toddlers cherished as fashion accessories as much as for themselves.** *See* BECKHAM, BROOKLYN.

**toenails red was provocation, painting one's.** *See* HOGG, CAPTAIN PETER.

**Toft, Mary** (*c.*1690–?), housewife and mother. In late April 1726 Mary Toft, the wife of a journeyman clothier living in Godalming, Surrey, startled neighbouring women with a strange, scarcely intelligible, story. While weeding a field she had been criminally assaulted, she said, by a rabbit. Normally a woman making such a claim would have been considered insane, but Mrs Toft was respected locally as a sensible person not at all given to flights of fancy. There was the matter, too, of the assault having taken place on St George's Day, a time when occult forces were believed to be at their most powerful.

In the following days Mrs Toft returned to normal. Some five months later, however, she became ill, and her husband Joshua summoned Dr John Howard from nearby Guildford. Dr Howard, a physician of high repute who had been delivering babies for 30 years, examined his patient's abdomen and pronounced that there was life within. Five weeks later he published a report that Mrs Toft had given birth to five rabbits. The news spread and when, a few weeks later, Dr Howard announced that Mrs Toft had produced seven more rabbits, interest in the case gripped the nation.

Sceptical doctors denounced the reports as fraudulent and demanded that Mrs Toft be examined by members of the medical establishment. Nathaniel St André, anatomist to George I and senior surgeon at Westminster Hospital, was nominated by royal order to attend on Mrs Toft. He had already spoken with disdain of the reports and was not readily to be deceived. He arrived at Mrs Toft's bedside just in time to witness the birth of two more rabbits. The next expert to appear was the Honourable Cyriacus Ahlers, surgeon to his majesty's German household. He made the journey to Godalming determined to brand Mrs Toft a fake, but found himself present at the birth of three more rabbits. Before leaving he assured Mrs Toft that she would shortly be in possession of a generous pension from the king.

By now the story had spread through Europe, and the king ordered a final determination to be made by Sir Richard Manningham, fellow of the

Royal College of Surgeons. Sir Richard moved Mrs Toft to a hospital in London, where he sat up with her throughout the night. He noticed that 'there was movement in her belly', but nothing occurred. Having kept her under constant surveillance for several days, so that it was impossible for rabbits to be smuggled into her bed, he was able to issue a report denouncing her as a fraud. Mrs Toft was arrested and later made a full confession. She had hidden the rabbits in the bedding, transferring them to a more appropriate location as needed to confound the doctors. Hogarth engraved a satirical print entitled *The Wise Men of Godalming*, and Mrs Toft's secret pouch method was shortly put to use by conjurors when performing the popular 'rabbit out of a hat trick'.

**toothbrush, a musical.** *See* SITWELL, SIR GEORGE RERESBY.

**toothbrush, threatening to gouge out one's eyes with a.** *See* O'MA-HONEY, MAURICE.

**top hat, death sentence for denting the king's.** *See* COLLINS, DENNIS.

**topknot, hoping to be pulled up to heaven by one's.** *See* BUCHAN, ELSPETH.

**Tories, call girl's best clients.** *See* LAMBTON, ANTONY CLAUD FREDERICK.

**tortoise in one's pocket, attending a wedding with a.** *See* GLENCONNER, PAMELA LADY.

**tortoise serving as a butler, a.** *See* MOON, KEITH.

**tortoise serving as a codpiece, a.** *See* MOON, KEITH.

**towers, useless.** *See* BECKFORD, WILLIAM; BERNERS, GERALD HUGH TYR-WHITT-WILSON, 14TH BARON.

**Tracey, Martha** (*c.*1710–45), serving girl, executed for stealing one guinea in the street. The punishment may seem harsh, but contemporary reports make it clear that Martha was the agent of her own misfortune:

> ... an example of misery caused by that licentiousness, which is of all vices the most destructive of the happiness of females, and so disgraces the British metropolis.
> From the *Newgate Calendar.*

Born in Bristol of poor parents, Martha became the servant of a merchant at the age of 16, later moving to London. Here she obtained work in a lodging house that accommodated single gentlemen, thus placing herself in temptation's path. Soon enough, one of these gentlemen, 'having some designs against her virtue', enticed Martha into his chamber. Martha then compounded this lapse by allowing him to buy her a new dress. When she wore this in church the following Sunday, her mistress asked how she had come by such an expensive garment. Having discovered the truth, she had no alternative but to dismiss Martha from her service on the Monday morning.

Martha wrote to her lover in some distress, begging him to meet her at a public house. This he did, thereafter providing her with lodgings in the Strand, where he would visit her, he said, until their marriage could take place. At first he was as good as his word, visiting her on successive days and buying her new dresses, thus 'lulling asleep the small remains of her virtue'. Soon his visits became less frequent, and when she told him that she was expecting his child, he became angry, declaring that he had never intended to marry her and could no longer maintain her in her present lodgings. Martha packed her bags and moved to another house. When she gave birth, the father took away the child, leaving Martha in a most distressed condition. Having survived for a while by pawning her clothes, she eventually took the advice of a woman of the town, who persuaded her into prostitution – an occupation in which she could only grow more corrupt 'by the conversation of the abandoned wretches who had confined themselves to this horrid course of life'.

In January 1745 Martha was indicted at the Old Bailey for robbing William Humphreys of a guinea on the king's highway. When walking in the Strand she had accosted Mr Humphreys, who, on rejecting her advances, was set upon by two men. In the struggle Mr Humphreys had dropped a guinea, which Martha had concealed in her mouth. Mr Humphreys had been able to seize hold of her, later escorting her to the watch house, where the guinea had been discovered by the constable of the night. Since there was some evidence that she had been an accomplice of the men who had attacked Mr Humphreys, the jury rightly found her guilty. After the conviction she displayed a proper sense of her former guilt and, according to the *Newgate Calendar*, 'died a sincere penitent, lamenting that pride of heart which had first seduced her to destruction'.

**traitors.** *See* BLUNT, SIR ANTHONY; BURGESS, GUY FRANCIS DE MONCY; DESPARD, EDWARD MARCUS; JACKSON, JOHN.

**trash and trumpery, foreign.** *See* SIBTHORP, COLONEL CHARLES DE LAET WALDO.

**tree, son obliged to take his tea up a.** *See* NOAILLES, HELENA
COMTESSE DE.

**Tree Lovers' Society embezzled by pensioner.** *See* MCSKIMMEY,
BUNTY.

**trees by gelignite, demolition of.** *See* CHAPMAN, EDDIE.

**Trelawny, Edward** (1792–1881), pirate and author. In Trelawny's value
system, poaching a neighbour's hares and shooting a Chinese trader, while
activities to be discouraged, were nonetheless morally symmetrical. At the
age of 17 Trelawny left a comfortable home, and an oppressive father, in
search of adventure at sea. After a short spell in the navy he fell in with the
charismatic Dutch-American buccaneer, De Ruyter. For the next five years
they sailed the Asian seas together, targeting for the most part Chinese
junks. In his highly unreliable memoirs, *The Adventures of a Younger Son*
(1831), Trelawny describes one of these as 'a huge tea-chest afloat, flat-
bottomed and flat-sided, and sailed about as well'. The junk's interior
was like a bazaar, in which all manner of trade was going on in beehive-
like cells presided over by 'voluptuous Tartars and tun-bellied Chinese'.
Apparently the 'little, black, greedy twinkling eye of the Chinese, almost
buried in mounds of fat, glistened like a fly flapping in a firkin of butter'.
The Tartar, with a mouth the size of a ship's hatchway, 'seemed to have a
proportionate hold for stowage'.

Rather disgusted by these two, Trelawny went in search of the captain,
whom he eventually discovered stretched out on a bed, smoking opium
through a small reed, watching the compass and chanting, 'Kie! Hooe – Kie!
Chee!' Realizing that 'he might as well address the ship's rudder as the
captain', Trelawny set about looting the junk with a party of his men. First
he conducted a general search, forcing his way into every cabin and causing
scenes of confusion and chattering such as he'd never heard before:

> Added to this was the gibbering of monkeys, apes, parrots,
> mackaws, ducks, pigs and other beasts and birds. The consternation
> and panic among the motley ship's crew and merchant passengers
> are neither to be imagined nor described. They never had dreamed
> that a ship, under the sacred flag of the emperor of the universe, the
> king of kings, the sun of God which enlightens the world, could,
> and in his seas, be thus assailed and overhauled.

A few became bellicose, and tried to defend their property. Some Tartar
soldiers took up their guns and, according to Trelawny, the:

> … big-mouthed Tartar and his comrade, swollen with their feed of
> roast dog and sea-slug, came blowing and spluttering towards me. I

caught the Tartar by his mustachios, and in return he snapped a musket in my face. It missed fire, his jaw expanded and I stopped it forever with my pistol. The bullet entered his mouth and he fell like a fat ox knocked on the head by a sledge-hammer. The Chinese have as much antipathy to saltpetre, except in fireworks, as Hotspur's neat and trimly dressed lord.

(This last is a reference to Shakespeare's *Henry IV, Part One*, in which Hotspur is talking about Richard II, whom he betrayed to Henry.) Trelawny continues:

We then began a regular pillage, and almost turned her inside out. The bulky part of the cargo we left, but silks, copper, selected drugs, a quantity of gold dust, diamonds and a few tiger skins were ours. The philosophic captain, whose business it was to attend to the pilotage of the junk, continued to inhale on his narcotic drug. I cut the bowl from the stem of his pipe, but he continued drawing at the reed, and repeating, 'Kie! Hooe! – Kie! Chee!' On shoving off, as I passed under the stern, I cut the tiller ropes, and the junk broached up in the wind, but I still heard the fellow singing out. 'Kie! Hooe! – Kie! Chee!'

On his travels Trelawny married Zula, a beautiful Arabian girl to whom he was devoted. When she died in 1813 he returned to England. He became a close friend of BYRON, Percy Bysshe Shelley and Mary Shelley, and it was Trelawny who found Shelley's body after his death by drowning in 1822. The following year he and Byron went to Greece together, where they fought for Greek independence. When Trelawny died in 1881, his ashes were buried beside Shelley's in Rome, as he had arranged nearly 60 years earlier.

While claiming in later years that he had never been a pirate in the full sense, he did admit in his memoirs that:

I have poached many hares, and killed a leash or two of Chinese in my time, instigated to commit these crimes by the same excitement – that of their being forbidden and guarded against by vindictive threats of pains and penalties.

**Trestrail, Commander Michael.** *See* RAUCH, MICHAEL.

**tricycle in St James's Park, riding a.** *See* SALISBURY, ROBERT ARTHUR TALBOT GASCOYNE CECIL, 3RD MARQUESS OF.

**troilism, alleged.** *See* DILKE, SIR CHARLES.
*See also* BED, THREE IN A.

**trouser joke, the one-legged.** *See* STANSHALL, VIVIAN.

**trousers, knuckle-duster concealed in poet's.** *See* JONES, CHARLES HORACE.

**trousers, machetes concealed in.** *See* BINDON, JOHN.

**trousers, poetical odes to.** *See* DERMODY, THOMAS.

**trousers, removing a solicitor's.** *See* WINTLE, LIEUTENANT A.D.

**trousers crocheted out of string.** *See* RUSSELL, JOHN CONRAD, 4TH EARL.

**trousers preventing a quick getaway, lowered.** *See* JOCELYN, THE REVEREND PERCY.

**Trumper, Francis** (*c.*1790–*c.*1860), farmer and cricketer. On 21 May 1827 at Harefield Common, near Rickmansworth, Francis Trumper and his sheepdog, Cooper, challenged 'two gentlemen of Middlesex' to a game of cricket, and defeated them. Cooper was a poor batsman, as was to be expected, but the day was won by his agility in the field.

Trumper and Cooper batted first and made 31, with the dog scoring only 3. The two county cricketers expected to improve on this total without difficulty, but were confounded by Cooper's speed in the covers and elsewhere. According to the next day's *Times*:

> The dog always stood near his master when he was going to bowl, and the moment the ball was hit he started off after it; and, on his master running up to the wicket, the dog would carry the ball in his mouth and put it into his master's hand with such wonderful quickness that the gentlemen found it very difficult to get a run even from a very long hit.

**tumultuously assembled, woman convicted of being.** *See* LUKER, ELIZABETH.

**Tumultuous Petitioning Act, the.** *See* GORDON, LORD GEORGE.

**Turner, Anne** (1575–1615), dressmaker to the court of James I, bawdy-house proprietor and conspirator with Lady Frances HOWARD, countess of Essex, in the murder of Sir Thomas Overbury. Turner was the daughter of a Somerset landowner and the widow of George Turner, a distinguished doctor of physic. Obliged by the death of her husband to survive by her wits, she built up a profitable double life. To all appearances she was a leader of court fashion, providing the costumes and backdrops for masques and revels, and famous for having introduced from France a saffron-coloured starch for ruffs and sleeves, which greatly complemented its wearer's alabaster beauty. That, however, was merely Mrs Turner's public reputation. Behind the respectable facade she ran a number of bawdy houses and maintained a network of contacts in London's underworld. Her discreet but well-appointed brothels in Paternoster Row and Hammersmith were a convenient setting for ladies and gentlemen of the court who wished to conduct their various rendezvous and seductions out of the royal spotlight.

Among Turner's underworld contacts there was one who had shown her the uses of magic – both black and white – and had introduced her to Simon FORMAN, the leading magician, astrologer and occultist of the day. Turner and Forman soon became indispensable to one another. Turner would travel up the Thames by boat from Paternoster Row to Lambeth, where Forman, who had been banned from practising medicine in the City of London, had his consulting rooms. Here she would bring him up to date with the latest court gossip, which the old astrologer would later use to impress his fashionable clientele. In return, Forman would stock her up with the various spells, enchantments and love potions that would later augment her visitors' pleasure at Paternoster Row and Hammersmith.

Towards the end of 1610 Lady Frances Howard, who was as desperate to win the love of the king's favourite, Robert Carr, as she was to be rid of her husband Robert Devereux, the earl of Essex, confided in Anne Turner. Turner took her to see Forman, who provided her with a lead figurine of a man and a woman in copulation, which, he assured her, would soon bring Carr to her bed by sympathetic magic. He also gave her a selection of love potions that could be put in Carr's food by servants whom Anne Turner had bribed. The devices worked, and in 1612 Howard and Carr became lovers, often meeting in one of Anne Turner's bawdy houses. Meanwhile, Sir Thomas Overbury, Carr's closest adviser, became increasingly disturbed by the influence Howard was having over his friend. Foolishly – since this involved making an enemy of Frances Howard's great-uncle, the powerful earl of Northampton – Overbury planned her disgrace by publicly calling her a whore. Northampton persuaded the king to imprison Overbury in the Tower, whence, as far as Frances was concerned, he'd depart only in a coffin. With the help of one of Anne Turner's underworld apothecaries, Mr Franklin, she obtained a variety of poisons that would be put into Overbury's food. Each day Anne Turner took a selection of poisoned tarts and jellies to the Tower, where she left them with Sir Gervase d'Elwes.

At the same time as Frances was trying to kill Overbury, her lover Robert Carr had worked out a way to secure his friend's release. Deciding that he would be let out on compassionate grounds were his health to be endangered, he supplied Overbury with daily enemas and 'vomits' that would make him violently sick. Thus, while Overbury was eating poisoned food brought in by Turner – supposedly enough to kill 20 men – evacuation by Carr's enemas was keeping him alive. It was Turner who eventually guessed that Overbury's survival must be the result of stomach cleansing, and it was she who came up with the idea of how to silence him forever. Instead of tarts and jellies, he should be sent an enema of her own concoction, containing enough sublimate of mercury to kill him outright. The plan worked, and Overbury died in agony.

Anne Turner and Frances Howard might have got away with it but for a startling revelation by William Reeve, a boy working for the apothecary, Franklin. Reeve, who had delivered the fatal enema to Overbury, and had thereafter been sent to France, suddenly fell ill, and, believing he was dying, wanted relief from the great sin he had committed. Word of this reached the English ambassador in France, who returned to England to report what he'd heard to the king. James, while reluctant to believe that his favourites, Carr and Frances, could have been involved, was obliged to pass the matter on to his chief justice, Sir Edward Coke. The series of trials that followed rocked the court. First to be examined was Anne Turner, who was found guilty as an accomplice to murder and executed on 12 November 1615. Sir Edward Coke had provided the occasion with mockery as well as horror by stipulating that she be hanged wearing one of her own yellow ruffs and that her executioner wear yellow cuffs and a ruff in addition to his black hood. For their part, Frances Howard and Robert Carr, as befitted their higher stations, received pardons from the king.

**Turpin, Dick** (1706–39), highwayman. Turpin was scarcely the dashing hero he became in legend – his false reputation being due most notably to the 19th-century novelist, William Harrison Ainsworth, who also mythologized Jack SHEPPARD. Ainsworth's melodrama *Rockwood* (1834), which first cast Turpin as a handsome, flamboyant figure, was written at a time when highway robbery could safely be romanticized since it was no longer a crime practised much in Britain.

Born in Essex, Turpin trained as a butcher, thus acquiring an expertise that helped him when he became a sheep and cattle thief: he knew which cuts of meat were valuable, and how to carve up an animal. Having fallen in with an armed robber named Samuel Gregory, he took part in attacks on large, isolated houses. In one farmhouse robbery, an old man had a kettle of boiling water thrown over him and a maidservant was raped. A contemporary woodcut shows Turpin persuading an old lady to yield up her jewels by throwing her onto a fire. He then became a highwayman in partnership with Tom King, a liaison that began after he and King had ambushed one another, neither knowing what the other's business was. Their partnership was discontinued in equally unexpected circumstances: Turpin killed King by mistake when trying to avoid capture.

Turpin's overnight ride from London to York on his horse Black Bess is a key component in his legend, but there is no evidence for it. After the accident with King he did head north, in a more leisurely fashion, surviving for a while by stealing horses and trading them in Lincolnshire and the East Riding of Yorkshire. His downfall was brought about by a minor breach of the peace: through frustration he shot a cockerel, for which offence he was arrested, and later imprisoned in York. His identity was discovered only after he foolishly wrote to his family from York Castle prison. The letter was intercepted by his former schoolmaster, who recognized his handwriting. He was hanged on the Knaves' Mire in York in 1739.

In 1979 the first episode of *Dick Turpin* was broadcast by London Weekend Television in the much coveted 5.35 p.m. slot. The series, starring Richard O'Sullivan in the title role, was written by Richard Carpenter and produced by Paul Knight and Sydney Cole – the team that in 1981 brought Oliver Tobias to the screen in a 13-episode series, *Smuggler*.

**twang.** 18th-century slang for a prostitute's associate whose job it was to pick a client's pocket while he was having intercourse upright in a doorway. *See* WILD, JONATHAN.

## two pounds of Walls pork sausages and a week in Bournemouth.
*See* BELCHER, HARRY.

**two-way mirrors.** *See* JONES, JANIE; LAMBTON, ANTONY CLAUD FREDERICK; RACHMAN, PETER.

**Tyler, the Reverend Tom** (1940– ), country vicar, dubbed 'Reverend Rat' by the *News of the World*. In July 1990, Tyler was confronted in his Henfield vicarage by Mr Edwards, a member of his congregation. 'Have you been fiddling with Mrs Edwards?' said Mr Edwards. Tyler said that he hadn't, but Mr Edwards was unconvinced. 'Did you fiddle with Mrs Edwards's breasts and get your penis out?' Tyler swore on the Bible that he hadn't – an account that no longer stood up after Mrs Edwards compared notes with a Mrs Whittome, also a member of the congregation. Ten years earlier, Tyler, a married man with two grown-up children, had taken Mrs Whittome to one side after a service and had guided her hand under his cassock. Thereafter they had made love in the vicarage, in fields, in service lifts, at Mrs Whittome's home, and in the back of the vicar's Ford Cortina, until Tyler, tiring of Mrs Whittome, lifted up Mrs Edwards's dress one day and kissed her in the vestry. 'We had sex standing up,' said 32-year-old Barbara Edwards. 'It didn't last long.'

Mrs Whittome complained to the bishop of Winchester, and in October 1990 Tyler was charged in a consistory court with 'conduct unbecoming a clerk in holy orders'. The judge excluded the media on the grounds that the case (which was strenuously contested) might cause depravity and corruption if reported, so the public was spared much disagreeable, and contradictory, evidence concerning groins, skin blemishes and body hair. Any inconsistencies in that area failed to derail the prosecution and Tyler was found guilty on all charges. He was deprived of his living, but not unfrocked. Mrs Edwards received £10,000 from the *Daily Mirror* for her story, posing nude under the headline, 'How the Randy Vicar Bedded Me'.

Tyler should have let matters rest, but he continued to insist that both women were lying. He appealed successfully for a new trial and on this occasion – since the public were judged to have been already depraved and corrupted by Mrs Edwards's appearance in the *Daily Mirror* – there were no restrictions on the press. As a consequence, many jocular column inches speculated distastefully on the bagginess or otherwise of the vicar's under-wear, with Mrs Tyler being called as an expert witness in this regard. The trial lasted for a week, and Tyler was found guilty for a second time. He retired to Ipswich with Mrs Tyler and wrote a play about the case, so far unperformed.

**Tyrrell, Lady Margaret-Ann** (1861–1939), diplomat's wife. During Lord Tyrrell's time as British ambassador to France (1928–34), Lady Tyrrell displayed a singular attitude to her duties. She showed no inclination to play the part of hostess at embassy functions, and indeed was seldom in Paris at all. Rather, she spent her time researching a book on the history of the world from 2000 BC. On her rare visits to Paris, she preferred to spend her time up a tree in the embassy garden. She sat in the branches writing and if she wanted something she summoned a footman with an ear-splitting whistle – a skill that had been taught to her by the head doorman at the Ritz Hotel in London. When there was no escape from a reception or formal dinner party, her small absent-minded gaffes were usually forgiven. On one occasion she mistook the future George VI for her husband's private secretary; on another, she talked for several hours with Lord Birkenhead under the impression that he was the Turkish ambassador.

# u

**Ugandan interests.** *See* RICHARDSON, CHARLIE.

**umbrella, feeling uncomfortable without an.** *See* WINTLE, LIEU-
TENANT A.D.

**unclothed white girls, feeling uncomfortable in the presence of.**
*See* DE ROUGEMONT, LOUIS.

**Undaunted Dick.** *See* THOMPSON, WILLIAM 'BENDIGO' (for Dick Weaver).

**underside, society's disagreeable.** *See* PENNY GAFFS; and *passim*.

**undertaker beaten up by corpse.** *See* INGRAMS, HAROLD.

**undress at a ball, a state of.** *See* CHUDLEIGH, ELIZABETH.

**undress in a nightclub, a state of.** *See* BRISTOL, FREDERICK WILLIAM
JOHN AUGUSTUS HERVEY, 7TH MARQUESS OF (for Lady Victoria Hervey).

**universes, privileged to be part of a team working in many.** *See*
ICKE, DAVID.

**Urquhart, Sir Thomas** (1611–60), genealogist, linguist, translator and
writer. Born in Cromarty, Sir Thomas studied at King's College, Aberdeen,
and travelled extensively in France, Spain and Italy. On his return to Scotland he took up arms against the Covenanting party in the north but was
defeated and forced to flee to England. Here he joined the court, and was
knighted by Charles I in 1641. In 1645 he produced his *Trissotetras; or a most
exquisite Table for Resolving Triangles etc*, a study of trigonometry based on

John Napier's invention of logarithms. It was dubbed 'impenetrably obscure' by the *Encyclopaedia Britannica*. In 1649 Urquhart again took up arms in the Royalist cause, and in 1651 was present at the battle of Worcester, where he was captured and imprisoned by Oliver Cromwell. He was soon released, but his property was forfeited – this loss, in the opinion of his biographer Richard Boston (*The Admirable Urquhart,* 1975), acting as the mainspring of his creative genius, since he spent the rest of his life trying to persuade the government to restore his land. He first tried to prove his value with *Pantochrononchanon*, a detailed genealogy of the Urquhart family, which Sir Thomas was able to trace back through 143 generations to 'the red earth from which God framed Adam', with reference on the way to Methuselah, Noah and Pamprosodos Urquhart, whose wife Termuth was the pharaoh's daughter who found Moses in the bullrushes.

This task achieved, Urquhart's next undertaking was the creation of a universal language, which, though never published, Urquhart was able to credit with 64 advantages over anything already in existence. Among these was, 'eighteenthly, every word in this language signifieth as well backward as forward whereby a wonderful facility is obtained in making anagrams'.

Urquhart's other works include his translation of Rabelais's *Gargantua and Pantagruel,* in which he expanded a list of 9 animal sounds to 71, among them the 'curking' of quails and the 'boing' of buffaloes. None of these efforts to restore his name succeeded, and he moved abroad. Family tradition has it that his death in 1660 was caused by an uncontrollable fit of laughter on hearing of the Restoration. (For a contrary reaction, *see* BIGG, JOHN.)

# V

**valetudinarians.** *See* KIRWAN, RICHARD; SPENCER, HERBERT.

**Van Butchell, Martin** (1735–1812), medical practitioner. Van Butchell was the most fashionable dentist of his day, able to charge as much as 80 guineas for a set of false teeth. After a while his interest in the profession palled and he turned his skills to the design of trusses and other necessary supports. He was as successful in this line as he had been in the other, and many fashionable ladies were known to be wearing 'Van Butchell garters'. He became still more celebrated with the death of his first wife in January 1775. Having embalmed her by injecting a carmine dye into her blood vessels, he provided her with glass eyes, dressed her in a lace gown and, advertising her as 'my dear departed', displayed her publicly in his front room in a glass-topped case. Although Van Butchell always claimed that this arrangement represented complete domestic harmony, he eventually married again. The second Mrs Butchell demanded that the remains of the first Mrs Butchell be removed, and they were sent to the Royal College of Surgeons. They were destroyed by enemy action in 1941.

**Vassall, John** (1924– ), Admiralty clerk and spy, known in the office as 'Auntie' – a sobriquet due to his homosexuality, which, paradoxically, nobody had recognized. The *Sunday Mirror* was so struck by this oversight that, after Vassall had been sentenced in October 1962 to 18 years in prison for two offences under the Official Secrets Act, it published 'A Short Course In How To Pick a Pervert'. Vassall could not have been offended by the article since in his autobiography he puts the blame for his difficulties squarely at the door of the security forces who, obviously, he thinks, should have realized he was homosexual.

In the early 1950s, while serving as a junior clerk in the British embassy in Moscow, Vassall was blackmailed into becoming a Soviet spy after he had been drugged and photographed at a homosexual orgy. In 1956 he returned to the Admiralty, and for the next six years was able to supply his London spymaster, Nikolai Korovin, with the navy's secrets, such as they were. His career as an agent came to an end when he aroused the suspicions of an alert Special Branch officer by paying £46 in cash for a Jaeger suit. (Vassall later admitted that he usually wore women's clothes, but not in the West End.) Lord Carrington, first lord of the Admiralty, said that he would take full responsibility if there had been any slackness at the ministry, and Thomas Galbraith, the civil lord of the Admiralty, said that he thought Vassall 'had a screw loose'. Vassall's cleaning lady, Mrs Huggins, told a journalist from the *Daily Express* that she had seen Galbraith come to Vassall's flat and go into the bedroom with him. Later she admitted that she had seen nothing of the kind. Reginald Foster of the *Daily Sketch* and Brendan Mulholland of the *Daily Mail* were sent to prison for refusing to name the source of their information, though it is not clear what their information was. The *Sunday Mirror* published a picture of Vassall with the caption, 'A spy and a homo. A gilt-edged specimen of the type.' It then listed other recognizable types of homos, including 'the fussy dresser', 'the over-clean man', and 'the man who drinks alone'.

Vassall was released from Maidstone prison in 1972, having served ten years of his sentence. He spent a short time in a Catholic monastery, where he wrote his autobiography. A television play was made about his period in Moscow. When he saw a preview Vassall wept.

**Vaughan, Dr Charles.** *See* SYMONDS, JOHN ADDINGTON.

**Vaughan, George** (*c.*1790–?), Bow Street runner. In 1821 a House of Commons Select Committee was set up to consider 'the state of mendacity in the Metropolis'. This was to be the most thorough investigation into the condition of London's police force that Parliament had yet undertaken. It discovered, among much else, that George Vaughan, a member of the foot patrol at Bow Street, had been emulating his notorious predecessor in thief-taking, Jonathan WILD, by carrying out robberies and then arresting his accomplices, two of whom were ex-City of London officers. Vaughan was eventually denounced by a 13-year-old boy whom he'd recruited to burgle a wealthy widow named Mrs Macdonald. He was caught in the act and under questioning named Vaughan. It subsequently emerged that Vaughan had taken part in two previous robberies himself. He was tried, convicted and sentenced to transportation.

**vegetables, talking to.** *See* CADDY, EILEEN AND PETER.

**vegetarian contract killers.** *See* NGARIMU, TE RANGIMARIA.

**Vendettas versus the Coons in the Blue Coat Boy in Bishops-gate.** *See* HARDING, ARTHUR.

**Venereal Affairs, A Treatise of the use of Flogging in.** *See* CURLL, EDMOND.

**venison, annual entitlement to a haunch of.** *See* ST ALBANS, CHARLES BEAUCLERK, 13TH DUKE OF.

**ventriloquism, death by.** *See* BRITTON, THOMAS.

**Ventry, Arthur Frederick Daubeney Eveleigh de Moleyns, 7th Baron** (1898–1987), balloonist. In 1949 Lord Ventry began work on the *Bournemouth*, the first airship to be built in Britain since the ill-fated *R 101* crashed in 1930. By July 1951 the sausage-shaped contraption was ready to make its first flight at Cardington in Bedfordshire. It failed to rise, and the 17-stone Ventry was obliged to disembark in favour of a lighter man. The *Bournemouth* achieved lift-off at its second attempt but then 'pancaked' on the gymnasium roof at RAF Cardington. 'Perfectly ordinary flight,' Ventry was able to report. 'Then one of the handling guy ropes caught on the catwalk of the gymnasium building and there we sat like a broody hen. Chance in a million.'

Ventry had become interested in balloons as a schoolboy at Wellington College. In World War I he transferred from the Irish Guards to No 902 County of London Balloon Squadron in the Auxiliary Air Force. In World War II he served as a flight lieutenant in Balloon Command. After the war he ceaselessly pointed out the many advantages of balloons over aircraft. A balloon, for instance, would be an ideal observation post from which to spot the Loch Ness Monster.

Apart from many articles on ballooning, Ventry also wrote about the Boy Scouts, in which he had served happily under Baden-Powell. 'I spent the happiest days of my life with the Scouts,' he wrote, 'not only in this country, but in Norway, too.' Lord Ventry never married. He was succeeded by his nephew, Andrew Harold Wesley Daubeney de Moleyns.

**Venus, My Visit to.** *See* RAMPA, LOBSANG.

**Venus in the Cloister or the Nun in her Smock.** *See* CURLL, EDMOND.

**Venus of Fifteen, Flossie, A.** *See* CARRINGTON, CHARLES.

**Veronica Mutineers, the.** In October 1902 the *Veronica*, a British sailing barque, was crossing the Gulf of Mexico bound for Montevideo. The captain, Alexander Shaw, was a red-bearded martinet, and the second officer, Alexander MacLeod, a sadist who subjected the crew to physical assaults. Tempers were not improved when rations were cut as a consequence of the slow progress the ship was making. Two of the sailors, Gustav Rau and Otto Monsson, who had managed to smuggle a pair of revolvers aboard, enlisted the help of William Smith and 19-year-old Harry Flohr to take the ship over. On 8 December First Officer MacLeod was thrown overboard, and Captain Shaw, Second Officer Fred Abrahamson and four crewmen were shot and killed. The ship's cook, Moses Thomas, a black man, was allowed to live.

Rau set fire to the *Veronica*, and the four mutineers, together with the cook, made their escape in the ship's boat. When they were picked up by a tramp steamer bound for Liverpool, it was noticed that the cook kept himself somewhat apart from the others. As soon as they docked in Liverpool the cook went to the police with a full account of what had happened. Rau, Monsson, Smith and Flohr were charged with murder, conspiracy, arson, piracy and theft, with the cook as the chief witness against them. The trial was conducted on a charge of murdering Captain Shaw, and an immediate point of interest was the lack of a *corpus delicti*, or body (*see* CAMB, JAMES). Apart from the statement provided by Moses Thomas, the cook, there was no evidence against them. Nevertheless, all four were found guilty, a recommendation of mercy being made in the case of Flohr on account of his youth. Flohr was duly reprieved, and on 2 June 1903 Rau, Smith and Monsson were hanged at Liverpool's Walton prison. Their mistake had been not to shoot the cook.

**vibrating godhead, the.** *See* ICKE, DAVID.

**vibrations in one's trousers.** *See* IMRIE, DEREK.

**vicars, parsons, ministers, etc., errant sons of.** *See* BLUNT, SIR ANTHONY; DAVIDSON, THE REVEREND HAROLD FRANCIS (the rector of Stiffkey); DE COURCY, KENNETH; GORDON-GORDON, LORD (possibly); MACLEANE, JAMES.

**vicars, speedy.** *See* WARING, FRANCIS.

**vicar thrashed in semi-final.** *See* HARTLEY, JOHN THORNEYCROFT.

**vice, immorality and puppet shows, suppression of.** *See* COOK, THOMAS.

**Vice Society, able to hold one's own in a scuffle with the.** *See* DUGDALE, WILLIAM.

**'vice tsar', failed attempt to become Tony Blair's roving.** *See* DALY, JOSEPHINE.

**Vicious, Sid.** *See* BEVERLEY, ANNE.

**vicious disposition that baffled all restraint, a.** *See* DUDLEY, CAPTAIN RICHARD.

**Victoria, Queen.** *See* BAKER, COLONEL VALENTINE; HOTTEN, JOHN CAMDEN; LABOUCHERE, HENRY; MONTROSE, JAMES ANGUS GRAHAM, 7TH DUKE OF; NEILD, JAMES CAMDEN; SALA, GEORGE AUGUSTUS; SIBTHORP, COLONEL CHARLES DE LAET WALDO.

**villain as you could find, as straight a.** *See* KEYHOE, MICKEY.
*See also* LAWYERS, CROOKED AND THEREFORE TRUSTWORTHY.

**Viper, Dr.** *See* JACKSON, JOHN.

**Virgil's *Aeneid* as the speech of Abyssinian princes, passing off.** *See* COLE, HORACE DE VERE.

**virgin, impossibility of deceiving one's bridegroom that one is still a.** *See* GREEN, STANLEY.

**virgin, possibility of deceiving a panel of matrons and midwives that one is still a.** *See* HOWARD, LADY FRANCES.

**virgins in Rawcliff, scarcity of.** *See* HIRST, JEMMY.

**Vivian, Anthony Crespigny Claude, 5th Baron** (1906–91), bandleader, impresario and restaurateur. When charged in 1954 with being 'drunk and indecent' in South Eaton Place, Vivian later gave his occupation as 'peer of the realm'. 'That is a description,' said the magistrate, 'not an occupation.' 'I beg your pardon, sir,' said Vivian. 'I thought it was.'

In fact, Vivian led a busy and eventful life. Six months after this incident he was shot in the stomach by Mavis Wheeler, the wife of the archaeologist Sir Mortimer Wheeler and former mistress of Augustus John. He had been trying to climb through a window at Mrs Wheeler's cottage near Devizes in Wiltshire. Mrs Wheeler was arrested and subsequently charged with attempted murder.

At her trial in Salisbury, she and Lord Vivian gave conflicting accounts of how the shooting had occurred. Mrs Wheeler said that Vivian had pointed the gun at her in fun and that it had gone off when she tried to wrestle it away. Vivian, who gave evidence from his hospital bed, claimed that she had shot him as he re-entered through the window after a visit to the George and Dragon locally. Why he had not come through the front door was unexplained. Thereafter, his memory of what had happened was at best hazy. Between arriving at the cottage in the morning and the shooting in the evening, he had drunk a bottle of wine, three liqueurs, seven or eight glasses of sherry, three or four bottles of stout and 'perhaps two or three other drinks'. He did know he was fed up with Mrs Wheeler being 'pilloried by everyone', however, and it was quite untrue that she had broken up his marriage. Mrs Wheeler was found guilty and sentenced to six months imprisonment.

Lord Vivian, who succeeded to the title in 1940 when his father died in a train on the way to Bodmin, was educated at Eton, thereafter seeking adventure in Canada, where he worked backstage in a Vancouver theatre. On his return to England he became a bandleader, finding employment for 'Tony Vivian and his Band' at the Café Anglais and the Ritz Hotel. After World War II, in which he served as a special constable, he teamed up with the veteran impresario Charles Cochran. Cochran was no longer the force he once had been, and after an initial success – the Vivian Ellis musical, *Bless the Bride* (1947) – the partnership faltered. In the late 1950s Vivian embarked on a career in the scarcely less hazardous restaurant business – first as manager of Charco's in Chelsea, which burned down, and then as a director of La Pavillon, located in the same neck of the woods. After an incident at La Pavillon in which several customers and two waiters were injured, Vivian announced his retirement to Norwood, but in 1963 he became catering adviser on board the *Empress of Canada*, about to embark on a Christmas cruise.

After his death in 1991 Vivian was succeeded by Brigadier Nicholas Crespigny Laurence Vivian, who was born in 1935 – the same year, he likes to say, as Floyd Paterson, the ex-world heavyweight boxing champion, and Elvis Presley. His point is unclear.

**voluptuous Tartars and tun-bellied Chinese.** *See* TRELAWNY, EDWARD.

**Wade, Rebekah.** *See* HOLME, LORD RICHARD. For a list of others who have been vigilant in defence of public morality, *see* MORAL WATCHDOGS.

**Wailing Wall, playing handball against the.** *See* HELL-FIRE CLUB, THE IRISH.

**Wainewright, Thomas Griffiths** (1801–59), soldier, painter, literary dabbler and poisoner. Wainewright was brought up by his grandfather, who had been editor of the *Monthly Review*. At 18 he joined the army, but he tired of this and became a writer and painter, attaching himself to a circle that included De Quincey, Wordsworth, Hazlitt and Lamb. His painting was not without merit. He exhibited at the Royal Academy, where his work was admired by William Blake.

In 1821 Wainewright married Eliza Frances Ward. His extravagant tastes and dissolute lifestyle soon caused him severe financial difficulties. When his trustees refused to sell stock held in his name, he forged all four of their signatures on a document with which he defrauded the Bank of England of more than £2000. In 1829 his grandfather died of a fit, and Wainewright, who was thought to have poisoned him with strychnine, inherited his wealth. This was seized by his creditors, however. In the same year his mother-in-law, Mrs Abercromby, came to live with him and his wife, bringing with her her two other daughters, Madeleine and Helen. Although enjoying some success as a writer now – contributing to the *London Magazine* on art and other matters – poisoning people seemed to have become a habit, and within a year Mrs Abercromby died, no doubt murdered by Wainewright. He then insured his 20-year-old sister-in-law, Helen, for £18,000. When Helen died in 1830 the insurance company was suspicious and Wainewright was obliged to sue for payment. The case went against him and he departed for France, where he poisoned the father of a girl he'd just met, having first insured his life for £3000.

In 1837 Wainewright returned to England, but was soon recognized and arrested. He was put on trial, but only for the forgery of his trustees' signatures in 1821, for which he was sentenced to transportation for life. He died in Tasmania, admitting on his deathbed that he had poisoned his mother-in-law, Mrs Abercromby, because her thick ankles had offended him. His case is sometimes compared to that of Pierre François Lacenaire, a Frenchman who, like Wainewright, had literary pretensions and in the 1830s murdered at least four people for profit. When Lacenaire met his death on the guillotine on 10 January 1836 a malfunction of the apparatus caused the descending blade to stick in its grooves. It was wound back, and his head came off at the second attempt.

**Wainwright, Henry** (1832–75), brush manufacturer and murderer. In 1871 Wainwright, a married man, met Harriet Louisa Lane, a 20-year-old milliner's apprentice, whom he set up as his mistress in a house in Mile End. She bore him two children, and – for reasons that may have been clear to her – styled herself Mrs Percy King. Soon enough, the strain of running his brush business and maintaining two households obliged Wainwright to move Harriet into less expensive accommodation in Sydney Square. One day she was seen leaving Sydney Square carrying only her nightclothes in a parcel. She was not seen alive again. Concerned friends were told that she had gone to Brighton. Later, a letter was produced from an Edward Frieke, who wrote to say that he and Harriet had decided to move to the Continent.

A year after Harriet's disappearance, Wainwright, who had been obliged to sell his shop at 215 Whitechapel Road, engaged a Mr Stokes to help him move a large parcel, wrapped in American cloth, to his new address. After walking a short distance, Stokes complained of the weight, and Wainwright said he would fetch a cab. While he was away in search of one, Stokes undid the parcel and discovered the body of Harriet Lane – or Mrs Percy King, as she preferred to be called. Having parcelled her up again, he said nothing when Wainwright returned with the cab, but decided to follow on foot, tracking the cab to an address near London Bridge, in fact the home of Wainwright's brother Thomas.

A year earlier Henry Wainwright had killed Harriet in his shop and buried her under the floorboards. When the shop was sold, his brother Thomas, who had already played the part of Mr Frieke, allowed him to relocate Harriet under the floorboards at his home. Mr Stokes now judged it time to call the police, and the Wainwrights were arrested. Both were tried at the Old Bailey in November 1875. Thomas received seven years as an accessory to murder, and Henry Wainwright was hanged at Newgate on 21 December. Stokes was awarded £30 for his assistance in Wainwright's arrest.

**waiters in hot pants.** *See* NASH, JIMMY.

**'Walter', suggested identity of.** *See* ASHBEE, HENRY SPENCER.

**Walters, Catherine** (*c*.1850–*c*.1920), courtesan. A striking example of the social mobility prostitutes enjoyed in the 19th century, Catherine 'Skittles' Walters became the wife of the marquess of Hartington, later the 8th duke of Devonshire. She was a friend and former colleague of Kate Cook, who passed as the countess of Euston, and of Margaret Steinheil. Miss Steinheil survived the scandal of being discovered in the bed of Felix Faure, the president of France, who had died from their exertions. She lived until 1954, dying at the coastal resort of Hove in Sussex as the 6th Baroness Abinger.

**Ward, Stephen** (1910–63), osteopath, sketch artist and, allegedly, procurer of women for his famous friends. Ward was the establishment's scapegoat in the 1960s sex scandal known as the Profumo Affair. For some years he had rented a cottage, on peppercorn terms, at Cliveden, the country estate owned by his supposed friend, Lord Astor. Ward's guests were allowed the use of the swimming pool, and it was there that he introduced Christine KEELER to John Profumo, the secretary of state for war in Harold Macmillan's government, and also to an officer in the Soviet KGB, Captain Eugene Ivanov. Later, both Profumo and Ivanov enjoyed rendezvous with Keeler at Ward's flat in Wimpole Mews.

As the scandal unfolded, amid rumours of orgies at which naked cabinet ministers acted as cocktail waitresses, it became clear that the government's embarrassment could only be alleviated by a trumped-up charge against one of the protagonists. On 8 June 1963 Ward was arrested and later accused of 'having knowingly on diverse dates between January 1961 and June 1963 lived wholly or in part on the earnings of prostitution at 17 Wimpole Mews W1'. At his Old Bailey trial in July, the judge, Sir Archie Pellow Marshall QC, summed up against him. When it was only half completed, Ward decided he had heard enough. On the night of 3 July, while staying at the Chelsea flat of a friend, Noel Howard-Jones, he swallowed an overdose of barbiturates. He was taken to St Stephen's Hospital, where he hovered between life and death while the trial continued. He was found guilty on two counts, but died before he could appear before the judge for sentencing.

It later emerged that one of the prosecution witnesses – a prostitute named Ronna Ricardo – had been threatened by the police into giving false evidence. Another witness, Vickie Barrett, broke down after the verdict and admitted to a journalist on the *Daily Express* that she too had been pressured into lying. As the author, Wayland Young, asked:

Why did the police find it necessary to interview 140 people before they moved against Stephen Ward? How many people do they usually think it worth interviewing in order to prepare a charge of poncing?

There were six mourners at Ward's funeral, and two wreaths. One was from his family. The other was made up of 100 white carnations and was from John Osborne, Kenneth Tynan, Annie Ross, Joe Orton and Arnold Wesker. The accompanying card read, 'To Stephen Ward, Victim of Hypocrisy'.

**Waring, Francis** (*c*.1760–1833), parish priest. As vicar of Heybridge in Essex, Waring liked to get through a service as quickly as possible. Having set up a small clock on a ledge, he sped through the lessons, delivered a quick-fire sermon consisting of two aphorisms and a proverb, ran down the aisle, jumped onto his horse and galloped off to repeat the performance at two neighbouring churches. He was noted, too, for an idiosyncratic dress sense, appearing in church in hats of his own devising, and on one occasion being loudly rebuked by his bishop for wearing purple at an important ecclesiastical function. The bishop was handed a card – kept in readiness for just such a purpose – on which was written, 'How very good of you to notice. Do let me recommend my tailor.' Though by no means poor, Waring furnished his vicarage with logs rather than chairs; his children fed from a trough; and he and his wife slept in a wicker cradle suspended from the ceiling.

**watch, inability to wind one's own.** *See* ST ALBANS, CHARLES BEAU-CLERK, 13TH DUKE OF (for the 12th duke).

**Waterton, Charles** (1782–1865), Catholic country squire and friend of the hedgehog. On inheriting the family property at Walton Hall in Yorkshire, Waterton surrounded the 300-acre park with a wall, 16 feet high, to form within it a sanctuary for every form of wildlife, with one exception – brown rats. Catholics believed that brown rats had been introduced into England by the Hanoverians, which had thereafter killed the native black rats, with whom Catholics identified. Waterton tempted the brown rats with a mixture of porridge and treacle laced with arsenic and then watched them die. He also kept a team of ratting cats, led at one time by a large margay wild cat that he had brought home from the forests of Guiana. On one occasion he was seen to catch a brown rat in his hands and, holding it by the tail, to dash its head against a wall, with a cry of 'Death to all Hanoverians!'

Waterton's beloved hedgehogs suffered no such hardships. 'On a summer's evening at about four o'clock,' he wrote:

... you may see my hedgehogs slowly advancing from the woods in quest of food. And if you know how to act, you may approach within two feet of them, and see them thrusting their snouts into the sward, and fetching out fat grubs.

Throughout his life, Waterton was able to survive the most extreme physical conditions. After his wife died he slept in an attic with the window open so that owls and bats could fly in and out as they pleased. It was so cold that the water in the washbasin froze overnight into a block of ice. Having 'long learned that a bed is an absolutely useless luxury', he lay on the bare floor with a wooden pillow. When travelling he left the wooden pillow behind since he had discovered that his portmanteau served just as well. At home, he was always up before dawn and out in the park among his trees and animals. If it had been raining he would come in dripping like a dog, and then sit in front of a fire, lost in the cloud of steam drawn from his clothes by the heat. For breakfast he had a piece of toast and a cup of tea, for lunch a piece of bread with watercress. When he visited the Regent's Park Zoo in London a keeper observed that he 'didn't eat enough to sustain two white mice'. On that occasion, Waterton went into the orang-utan's cage and was 'lost in admiration at the protuberance of his enormous mouth. He most obligingly let me open it, and thus I had the best opportunity of examining his two fine rows of teeth'.

Inmates at the local lunatic asylum were provided by Waterton with telescopes so that they could view his lake and its inhabitants.

**Watkins, Lennie 'Silly Eddie'.** See OSBOURNE, COLIN 'DUKE'.

**Watson, Cynthia.** *See* ACKE, PETER.

**Watson, the Reverend John Selby** (1804–84), cleric and classical scholar for whom the consolations of philosophy failed, even more spectacularly than usual, against personal decrepitude and worldly loss. Watson was ordained in 1839. After a curacy in Somerset he moved to London, where in 1844 he became headmaster of a grammar school. The following year he married Anne Armstrong. His career prospered (he was responsible for a number of highly praised translations) and the marriage was happy enough. But by 1870 the number of the school's pupils had dropped, and the governors gave Watson notice. At the age of 66 he had no prospects, a misfortune that comes to everyone but which he found unacceptable. In October 1871, Ellen Payne, the Watsons' servant, returned from her day off to be told that Mrs Watson had gone on a short visit out of town. Watson then said, 'If you find anything wrong with me in the morning, go for Dr Rugg.' The next day he was discovered unconscious on the floor, and the body of Mrs Watson was found in a locked bedroom. She had severe head wounds. Watson had swallowed some prussic acid, but was revived by Dr Rugg. On his dressing table was a pistol with a bloodstained butt that had been used to kill his wife.

Watson was tried at the Old Bailey in January 1872. The defence was insanity, but this failed against the detailed letters of instruction he left behind concerning his literary remains. He was found guilty with a recommendation of mercy, and reprieved. He served twelve years in Parkhurst prison, where he died at the age of 80.

**wedding suit to one's own execution, wearing one's white satin.**
*See* FERRERS, ROBERT SHIRLEY, 2ND EARL.

**Weldon, Georgina** (1838–1911), singer and fantasist. Mrs Weldon successfully resisted two attempts by her husband to have her kidnapped and consigned to an insane asylum. For this achievement she occupies a small historical niche in the annals of Victorian lunacy reform. On the first occasion she was defended against a posse of male nurses by a large bailiff who, ironically, had been employed by her husband to prevent thefts from the house by the foreign confidence trickster whom Georgina had left in charge. On the second occasion she barricaded herself in the library while the 'mad doctors', sent by her husband, were fought off by her friend, Louisa Lowe, who had herself challenged asylum committal proceedings brought by Mr Lowe.

Born in the year of Victoria's coronation, the daughter of an impoverished (and ultimately insane) gentleman, Georgina spent her girlhood in Florence. There she met, and later married, Harry Weldon, a young army officer who possessed no discernible qualities and thus ended his days as garter king of arms. Georgina's only assets were a strong singing voice and considerable self-belief. When not planning an international solo career on stage, she imagined herself to be a philanthropist, opening her home as a singing academy for orphans. She was also a compulsive flirt. Among the marriage's many bizarre incidents were the months the Weldons spent living *à trois* in Tavistock Square with Charles Gounod, the composer of *Faust*. When this arrangement became too complicated, and after Gounod had returned to his wife, Georgina fell prey to a pair of fraudsters, Angèle and Anarchasis Menier. Under their influence, the Weldon household disintegrated, with Harry Weldon soon preferring his club, his rooms and his mistress. Angèle – a former whore from Clermont-Ferrand – became Georgina's confidante and lover. Together the women took a party of orphans to Normandy, a move that in itself might not have precipitated the lunacy proceedings had it not been for Georgina's mounting debts, for which her husband was responsible.

Having avoided the insane asylum, Georgina devoted her energies to legal battles against anyone who crossed her path, including her husband and her own lawyer. Surprisingly, her constant litigation was not declared vexatious, and she won more cases than she lost. She spent the last twelve years of her life quietly in a French convent, where she wrote a 1500-page memoir. Her biographer, Brian Thompson (*A Monkey Among Crocodiles: the Disastrous Life of Mrs Georgina Weldon*, 2000), has two revelations that suggest more turbulent undercurrents than the farcical surface of her life presents: she told Angèle Menier that she had been molested as a child by the butler, and that one of the orphans had died without a death certificate and was buried in the garden.

**Wellington, believing oneself to be the duke of.** *See* BIBBY, JOHN.

**Wells, Charles** (*c.*1860–*c.*1920), swindler. Wells duped people into investing in far-fetched inventions, among them a musical skipping rope. He was successful enough to buy a yacht equipped with a ballroom and church organ. In 1892, he sailed in it to Monte Carlo, where he had a spectacular win of £16,000 at the casino and was later dubbed 'the man who broke the bank at Monte Carlo'. The attendant notoriety alerted disgruntled former investors to his whereabouts and he was sentenced to eight years hard labour. On his release, he invented a lifebelt, which was demonstrated by a defrocked clergyman.

**Welsh, The.** *See* DAVID, PETER; DENNIS, CEREDIG DAWYL; EVANS, JOHN; JONES, CHARLES HORACE; LASKEY, COLIN; MADDOCK, WILL; MORRIS, WILLIAM; PRICE, WILLIAM; ROOSE, DR LEIGH RICHMOND; STAGE, HOOLIGANISM ON.

**Welsh-speaking Indians beyond the Missouri.** *See* EVANS, JOHN.

**Wenham, Jane** (1642–1730), witch. Wenham, who lived at Walkern in Hertfordshire, was the last person in England to be condemned to death for witchcraft. In 1712 the servant of the village parson, 16-year-old Ann Thorn, said that she had seen Jane Wenham take on the shape of a talking cat, which urged her to kill herself and produced a knife for that purpose. The elderly wise woman was also accused of causing the girl to run half a mile and jump over a five-bar gate even though she had a dislocated knee at the time.

Jane Wenham was arrested and brought to trial before Sir John Powell, whom Jonathan Swift described, unironically, as 'the merriest old gentleman I ever saw'. Among the prosecution witnesses was the Reverend Francis Bragge, the fanatical vicar of Hitchin, who had earlier published a popular pamphlet against witches. Bragge swore that attempts to draw blood from Wenham's arm with a pin had been unsuccessful. He further testified that she could not say the Lord's Prayer, but was able to fly. Mr Justice Powell observed that there was no law against flying, and then summed up in a way that suggested he expected an acquittal. The jury brought in a verdict of guilty, however, and Sir John had no alternative but to pass sentence of death, at the same time making his own feelings clear:

> The same ignorance and superstition which had instigated her accusers to apprehend her, operated in the minds of 12 men, sworn to do justice; and they, to their eternal shame, found her guilty.

Nor did he let the matter rest. He interceded with Queen Anne on Wenham's behalf, and the old lady was granted a reprieve. She lived to the age of 88, though she had to move away from the village of Walkern for her own safety. It was said later that Ann Thorn had made her accusations when down in the dumps. Her bad mood had been occasioned by her boyfriend's attitude, and when this improved she apparently stopped spreading malicious rumours. The furore created by the case certainly contributed to the abolition of the death penalty for witches.

**Westbrook, Daniella** (1973– ), troubled actress. She's looking more relaxed now that she's discovered who she really is.

For others in similar position, *see* BACK, TO HELL AND.

**Wharncliffe, Alan James Montagu-Wortley-Mackenzie, 4th earl of** (1935–87), variously an able seaman in the Royal Navy, a publican, a garage mechanic and a drummer in a rock-and-roll band. Wharncliffe – the only son of the 3rd earl by his wife, the formidable Lady Elfreda Wentworth-Fitzwilliam, who, during World War II had run her own munitions factory and had later become master of the Ecclesfield Beagles – was educated at Eton and thereafter did his national service in the navy. After a spell at the Royal Agricultural College, Cirencester, he became drummer for the Johnny Lenniz rock-and-roll band, among whose members were a fishmonger and a stone merchant. The band 'cut' a disc, *Shake, Rattle and Roll*, in 1957, but this made little impact on the charts – these being dominated at the time by the 'King of Skiffle', Lonnie Donegan.

Wharncliffe had succeeded his father in the earldom in 1953, and in 1960 he appointed himself publican of the Wortley Arms on the family estate in Yorkshire. He was known as 'Mad Ike' by the villagers, whom he had upset by shooting a black and white cat that he discovered in his kitchen. However, Wharncliffe Engineering, a car repair shop that he ran behind the Wortley Arms, was a successful venture. The earl himself was charged with drink-driving on several occasions. In 1976 he vowed never to drink again after he was banned for three years. Fifteen days after this ban ended, his estate car was involved in an accident near Barnsley in which a pub landlady was killed. Wharncliffe, who had himself been seriously injured in the crash, was found guilty of causing death by reckless driving and was jailed for six months. He was reported to have found prison life surprisingly agreeable, and to have persuaded a fellow inmate to act as his valet.

Among Wharncliffe's forebears was the celebrated 18th-century woman of letters, Lady Mary Wortley-Montagu, butt of Alexander Pope and pioneer of inoculation against smallpox. He was succeeded by Alan Ralph Montagu-Stuart-Wortley, who was born in 1927 and was discovered to be living in Connecticut.

**Whateley, Archbishop Richard** (c.1800–90), hyperactive Protestant archbishop of Dublin. Dr Whateley was sometimes to be seen reclining on the chains outside his palace in St Stephen's Green, smoking a long clay pipe. More often he would hasten into the Green and climb a tree in which he hid a handkerchief or some other object for his Newfoundland dog to find. When in need of exercise, the archbishop would swing from the branches. On one occasion two old ladies were watching him as he put the dog through its repertoire of tricks. 'Ah, then Mary,' said one, 'do you know who that is playing with the dog?' 'Truth, I don't, Biddy,' said Mary, 'but he's a fine looking man.' 'That's the archbishop!' said Biddy. 'Do you tell me so?' said Mary. 'God bless the innocent creature! Isn't he easily amused!' 'He's not our archbishop, Mary, he's the Protestant archbishop.' 'Oh!' said Mary. 'The bloody old fool!'

The archbishop was so fidgety that those who allowed him into their homes could expect their furniture to be destroyed. Invited to dinner with Lord Anglesey, the lord lieutenant, Dr Whateley sat down and stretched his legs on the mantelpiece, which was covered with Lady Anglesey's valuable china. In the course of the evening the lord lieutenant lost six of his best chairs to the archbishop's habit of whirling them around on their legs. His attendance at the National Education Board at Antrim House wore a hole in the carpet. Throughout an evening's entertainment his restlessness would be unceasing. After one dinner a fellow guest wrote:

> We were all surprised at the strange way he had of raising his right leg and foot, doubling it back over the thigh of the left one, and grasping his instep with both hands as if he were strangling some unpleasant animal. He did this repeatedly during the evening, especially while telling some good stories to which he did ample justice, and during the process the foot thus raised was on the lap of Provost Lloyd on whose right hand the Archbishop sat.

At a privy council meeting, Chief Justice Doherty put his hand into his pocket for his handkerchief and found the archbishop's foot already in it. Dr Whateley disliked armchairs because they impeded the movement of his arms. He also disliked stiff collars, starch, tight garments and people with flat-topped heads, a condition for which he devised 'a new phrenological test':

Take a handful of peas, drop them on the head of the patient; the extent of the man's dishonesty will depend on the number which remain there. If a large number remain, tell the butler to lock up the plate.

The archbishop was unpopular with many people, less because he was restless than because he was English.

**wheelbarrow, born in a.** *See* LIFTING THE DABS.

**wheelchair, blown up by a land mine in a.** *See* BROWN, ERIC.

**wheelchair, brothel-keepers confined to a.** *See* DALY, JOSEPHINE.

**whip, kicked downstairs by a junior.** *See* BROMLEY-DAVENPORT, LIEUTENANT COLONEL SIR WALTER.

**whip by one's fellow peer, threatened with a dog.** *See* ROSEBERY, ARCHIBALD PHILIP PRIMROSE, 5TH EARL OF.

**Whip'em, Captain.** *See* PRIDDEN, SARAH.

**whipped through the streets.** *See* BYRNE, JAMES; OATES, TITUS.

**whipping the congregation.** *See* DASHWOOD, SIR FRANCIS.

**whipping up treason in the streets.** *See* ROBERTSON, JAMES.

**Whitelaw, William Ian Stephen, 1st Viscount.** *See* NICKERSON, SIR JOSEPH.

**White Slave Widow, the.** *See* JEFFRIES, MARY.

**wickedest family in England, the.** *See* NASH, JIMMY.

**wickedest family in Scotland, the.** *See* BEAN, SAWNEY.

**wickedest man alive (since deceased), the.** *See* CROWLEY, ALEISTER.

**wig, shooting off a man's.** *See* FITZGERALD, GEORGE ROBERT.

**Wigmore Street Massage Parlour Scandal, the.** *See* ST CLAIR, LINDI.

**wigs on fire.** *See* STAGE, HOOLIGANISM ON.

**Wild, Sir Ernest.** *See* BARKER, COLONEL LESLIE IVOR GAUNTLETT.

**Wild, Jonathan** (1683–1725), thief-taker and receiver. Though it is not unusual for a gamekeeper to turn poacher, and vice versa, few people have played both roles simultaneously as successfully as Jonathan Wild. Born in Wolverhampton, where he worked as a buckle maker, Wild deserted his wife and went to London in 1707. In the following year he was imprisoned for debt, his four years inside acting as a useful introduction to the capital's underworld. On his release he opened a brothel with his mistress, Mary Milliner, whom he had met in prison. Initially, he was her 'twang', a prostitute's associate who picks the client's pocket while the latter's attention is otherwise engaged. Wild then served his apprenticeship as a thief-taker under Charles HITCHIN, a City marshal who taught him the trade of receiver. Wild's genius for double-dealing soon enabled him to outstrip Hitchin, and from 1714, when he first set up his own office in Little Old Bailey, until 1724, he controlled London's criminals, playing them off against one another, and against the authorities, in a complicated web of intrigue and influence.

As a law enforcer Wild discovered and pursued thieves with great tenacity, earning large sums of money under the parliamentary reward system. He dressed himself up in a lace coat, carried a silver staff and gave himself the title of 'Thief-Taker General of Great Britain and Ireland'. However, there was even more money to be made by acting as a receiver for London's thieves, while continuing to inform on them to the officers of Newgate. Wild organized them into gangs controlled by himself, planned their crimes and then disposed of the proceeds in a highly original way. Instead of 'fencing' the stolen goods with back-street dealers, he set up a lost-property office and sold the recovered items back to their original owners, who, it seemed, were prepared to pay more for the return of their goods than he would have been able to get from professional receivers. To facilitate this process he instructed his gangs to discover the identities of those they were about to rob so that he could, after a suitable interval, notify the victims that their possessions had been 'recovered'. He paid his thieves poorly, but kept their loyalty by arranging rigged trials when they were caught and by exacting swift revenge if they double-crossed him. He developed, too, an ingenious way of punishing thieves who refused to work for him: when one of his own gang was brought to trial Wild would advise him to turn king's evidence and obtain a pardon by denouncing the maverick crook as an accomplice. In 1720 the government itself was naïve enough to consult him about the rising crime rate. Wild told them they should increase the rewards for capturing criminals – one of his own sources of profit.

Wild's own downfall was heralded in 1724 by that of Jack SHEPPARD, which Wild had engineered because Sheppard had refused to join his gang. Wild, who was approaching middle age, was growing less ambitious, and, most importantly, had made many enemies. Even the government had become aware that the advantages he represented (one's stolen property could usually be recovered; criminals were for the most part kept under control) did not justify his existence. A 'Warrant of Detainder' was prepared, listing his various crimes, but he was finally charged with receiving ten guineas as a reward for helping a Mrs Steham to recover some stolen lace, a theft that he himself had organized. It was an ignominious but fitting end, since the law he had broken was informally known as 'Jonathan Wild's Act'. In his defence he pleaded that he had brought 67 criminals to the gallows.

Wild's own execution was attended by a large crowd, which pelted him with rotten fruit and howled for his blood when the executioner took too long in his preparations – a circumstance brought about, according to the *Newgate Calendar,* by the hangman's decision to allow his client time to recover from a suicide attempt the night before:

> At about two in the morning, Jonathan tried to end his life by drinking laudanum; however, on account of his having fasted a considerable time, no other effect was produced than a kind of stupefaction. The situation of Wild being observed by two of his fellow prisoners, they advised him to rouse his spirits, that he might be able to attend to the devotional exercises; and taking him by the arms they obliged him to walk, which he could not have done alone, being much afflicted with gout. The exercise revived him a little, but he presently grew very faint; a profuse sweating ensued, and soon afterwards his stomach discharged the greatest part of the laudanum. In this state of insensibility, he was put into the cart and conveyed to Tyburn. Upon arrival, the executioner informed him that a reasonable time would be allowed for preparing himself for the important change that he must soon experience. But the populace were so enraged by the indulgence shown him that they threatened the executioner with death if he presumed any longer to delay. He judged it prudent to comply with this demand.

Wild's life was used by political commentators like John Gay in *The Beggar's Opera* (1728) and Henry Fielding in *The Life of Jonathan Wild the Great* (1743).

**Wilkes, John** (1727–97), politician, publisher and rake. Though outrageous in his private behaviour, Wilkes no doubt deserved the epitaph, which he composed himself, 'a friend of liberty'. When a fellow debauchee, Lord Sandwich, told him, 'You will die either on the gallows or of the pox,' Wilkes famously replied, 'That depends upon whether I embrace your lordship's principles or your mistress.' In 1747 Wilkes married Mary Meade, an heiress who owned a large estate at Aylesbury. It was a marriage of convenience and Wilkes preferred to spend his time at the Hell-Fire Club, which indulged in orgies at Medmenham Abbey, the home of Sir Francis DASHWOOD. In 1757 Wilkes and his wife separated permanently and Wilkes, bored with his life of dissolute pleasure, purchased his parliamentary seat in Aylesbury, spending £7000 on an unopposed return.

In 1762 George III arranged for his close friend, the earl of Bute, to replace the elder William Pitt as prime minister. Wilkes considered Bute to be a Scottish nonentity, and wishing to make him a target of constant ridicule he founded a satirical magazine, *The North Briton*, in whose pages he lampooned the Establishment throughout the 1760s. On a visit to Paris Mme de Pompadour asked him, 'How far, then, does the liberty of the press extend in England?' Wilkes replied, 'That, madame, is what I'm trying to find out.'

Wilkes discovered the answer in April 1763 with issue No 45 of *The North Briton*, in which he published a slander on George III, accusing him of lying on behalf of the government in his speech from the throne. Such an attack on the monarch was unprecedented; Wilkes was confined to the Tower and it was ordered that *The North Briton* No 45 should be publicly burnt by the hangman, Thomas Turlis. At noon on the appointed day a bonfire was lit in the presence of the sheriff of London and a large crowd. Turlis was handed the offending magazine, but between sentence and execution the government had fallen, Wilkes had been released from the Tower on the grounds of parliamentary privilege, and the mob was on his side. As Turlis made to drop *The North Briton* into the flames, the crowd surged forward, pelting law officers and the hangman with mud and stones, and destroying the sheriff's coach. Turlis stood his ground long enough to do his duty, but no sooner was the publication in the fire than the mob had rescued it.

Meanwhile, the Lords accused Wilkes additionally of having published a pornographic poem, *The Essay On Woman* (in fact written by Thomas Potter, the son of the archbishop of Canterbury, and privately printed by Wilkes, but never published). This last charge was brought by Lord Sandwich – one of the more depraved of Wilkes's fellow members of the Hell-Fire Club – an action that caused Sir Francis Dashwood, now Lord Despencer, to comment audibly that it was the first time he had heard Satan preaching against sin. A week later, Parliament voted that a member's privilege from arrest did not extend to the writing and publishing of seditious libels. However, before Wilkes could be detained, a group of his friends arranged for him to be taken to Paris.

In 1768 Wilkes suddenly announced his candidature for the City of London in the general election. He came seventh, and bottom, in the poll, but his campaign demonstrated the support he could still expect from the public at large. He immediately announced his candidature for Middlesex, where the election took place five days after that in the City. Wilkes presented himself as a tribune of the people persecuted by an unpopular government. The election was conducted amid scenes of drunken disorder; Wilkes's enemies, Bute and Egremont, had the windows of their houses smashed, and the duke of Northumberland was forced to supply the mob with liquor with which to drink Wilkes's health. On election day Wilkes scored a runaway victory, and his ecstatic supporters ensured that 'Wilkes for Liberty' was chalked on houses and carriages throughout London. The Austrian ambassador, Count de Seilern – reported to be 'the most stately and ceremonious of men' – was dragged from his coach and held upside down while 'Wilkes for liberty' was chalked on the soles of his shoes.

As his first act after his election, Wilkes, who was officially still an outlaw, insisted that he be arrested – a course of action that the government, fearing a civil uprising, was reluctant to pursue. Wilkes was intent on martyrdom, however, and on the first day of the legal term he surrendered himself before Lord Chief Justice Mansfield in the Court of the King's Bench. Mansfield refused to sentence him on the grounds that since Wilkes was an outlaw he could take no notice of his submissions. He must first ask the attorney general to arrest him on a writ of *capias utlagatum ut lagatum* (a warrant to arrest an outlaw at large). Wilkes responded by getting himself arrested by a sheriff's officer and thereafter informing the attorney general that, as he would not do his duty, he had effectively arrested himself. On 10 May 1768 he was taken to the King's Bench prison, where a crowd of around 15,000 assembled in St George's Fields, chanting 'Wilkes and Liberty!', 'No Liberty, No King!' and 'Damn the King, Damn the Government!' Fearing that the crowd would attempt to rescue Wilkes, the government ordered a troop of Scots Guards to open fire. Seven people were killed, including an innocent boy who had been mistaken for a stone thrower. Fury at 'the Massacre of St George's Fields' led to disturbances all over London. One soldier was tried for murder, but a jury at Guildford, packed with government supporters, dismissed the charge. Wilkes retaliated with a pamphlet accusing the government of using Scotch butchers to intimidate freeborn Englishmen.

On 8 June Wilkes was found guilty of libel. He was sentenced to 22 months imprisonment, and fined £1000. He was also expelled from the House of Commons, but in February, March and April 1769 he was re-elected three times for Middlesex – the decision on each occasion being overturned by Parliament. In May the House of Commons voted that Colonel James LUTTRELL, the defeated candidate for Middlesex, should be accepted as the MP. In response, John Horme Tooke and other supporters of Wilkes formed the Bill of Rights Society. At first, the society concentrated its efforts on forcing Parliament to accept the will of the Middlesex electorate. Later, the organization adopted a radical programme of parliamentary reform. Meanwhile, imprisonment was no great hardship for Wilkes. He had excellent rooms and servants, was able to use the shops, coffee house and taverns that were contained within the prison walls, and enjoyed an unlimited supply of visitors from all over the country, and from America.

Wilkes was released from prison in April 1770. Denied a place in the House of Commons, he sought instead a power base in the City of London, becoming an alderman and master of the Joiners' Company. From this vantage point he joined the campaign for the freedom of the press. In February 1771 the House of Commons attempted to prevent several London newspapers from publishing reports of its debates. Wilkes consistently flouted this ruling, forcing the government to retaliate by ordering the arrest of two of his printers. A speaker's warrant was issued and a Commons messenger sent to the City to execute it. There the messenger was himself arrested, charged with assault and brought before the sitting magistrate – who happened to be Alderman Wilkes. Wilkes was summoned to the Bar of the House to answer for his insolence. He refused to attend, unless the summons was made out to him as MP for Middlesex.

Several days of noisy debate ensued, accompanied by riots outside the House. Lord North was dragged from his coach, his hat was sold as a souvenir, and the portly Charles James FOX was rolled in the gutter. Wilkes, meanwhile, decided to strengthen his position in the City by becoming lord mayor. In 1774 this ambition was achieved, and in the same year he was at last re-elected to represent Middlesex in the House of Commons. Paradoxically, success effectively marked the end of his political career. Deprived of the role of martyr and the leadership of the mob, he had little to offer. Respectability was the ruin of him, and he finally lost his power base among the commonality when in 1780, as an alderman, he decided to suppress the anti-Catholic Gordon riots by firing on the mob. In his own words he at once became 'an extinct volcano', and thereafter achieved little of note. Wilkites and Whigs were appalled by his support of William Pitt the Younger's bid to become the king's first minister in 1784, thereby proclaiming himself a tacit supporter of the king. Before long, Wilkes was to be seen at court levees in conversation with George III. He also attended upon the prince of Wales, who detested his father. Called upon to give a toast after a dinner at Carlton House, the prince's home, Wilkes proposed, 'The King – Long life to him'. The prince indignantly asked Wilkes, 'Since when have you been so anxious over my parent's health?' 'Since I had the pleasure of Your Royal Highness's acquaintance,' Wilkes replied. The exchange may have done little to improve the prince's already unsteady disposition. (As George IV he had to take 100 drops of laudanum before finding the strength to face his foreign secretary, Lord Aberdeen.) Though a passionate opponent of the harsh criminal code, Wilkes was not a supporter of universal suffrage, and he grew more conservative – though no less a lover of paradox – as he grew older. On one occasion George III sought his opinion of Serjeant Glynn, who had defended him in many of his legal battles and was later a fellow MP for Middlesex. Wilkes said, 'He was a Wilkite, Sir – which, as Your Majesty knows, I never was.'

**Will the Sailor.** *See* FLOOD, MATTHEW.

**Williams, John** (*c*.1780–1811), labourer and alleged perpetrator of the notorious Ratcliffe Highway Murders. On the night of Saturday 7 December 1811 someone broke into the home of a hosier named Timothy Marr and murdered him, his wife Cecilia, their baby and an apprentice boy of 13, John Gowan. A servant girl, Margaret Jewell, who had been sent out to buy some oysters, discovered the bodies on her return. The family had been killed by blows from a maul – a kind of iron mallet, used by ships' carpenters. The murder weapon, which had the initials 'I.P.' punched into its head, was found by a constable of the river police. He also found two sets of footprints leading away from the house.

Twelve days later there was a second multiple murder in the environs of Ratcliffe Highway, this time at the King's Arms public house in Gravel Lane. The pub was run by a Mr Williamson and his wife, with help from their 14-year-old granddaughter Kitty Sewell and a serving girl, Bridget Harrington. There was also a lodger, 26-year-old John Turner. After the bar had closed at 11 p.m., Williamson served a drink to an old friend, the parish constable, and told him that a man in a brown jacket had been listening at the door, and that if the constable saw him he should take the necessary steps.

Fifteen minutes later John Turner, who had retired to bed, heard Bridget Harrington's voice shouting, 'We are all murdered!' Turner crept downstairs and peered into the living room. He saw a man bending over a body and going through the victim's pockets. Turner went back upstairs, made a rope of sheets and lowered himself out of the window with a cry of 'Murder! murder!' A crowd formed, and the parish constable prised open the metal cover that led to the cellar. At the bottom of the steps lay the body of the landlord, Williamson. His head had been smashed in with a crowbar, which lay beside him. The bodies of Mrs Williamson and Bridget Harrington were discovered in upstairs bedrooms. Their skulls had been beaten in and their throats cut.

Dozens of young men in brown jackets were arrested on suspicion, among them a young sailor named John Williams, who lodged at the Pear Tree public house in nearby Wapping. There was no evidence against him, but when handbills with pictures of the maul were circulated John Williams's landlord, a Mr Vermilloe (who happened to be in Newgate prison for debt), said that he recognized it as belonging to a Swedish sailor named John Peterson. Peterson had a perfect alibi, in that he was away at sea, but he had left his tool chest behind in the care of Mr Vermilloe. Suspicion now fell once more on Williams. He had been seen walking towards the King's Arms on the evening of the murders, and had returned to his lodgings in the early hours of the morning with blood on his shirt – the result, he claimed, of a street fight. Other tenants of Mr Vermilloe said that while Williams had no money on the night of the murders, he had a considerable sum the following day.

Williams was taken to Coldbath Fields House of Correction, but hanged himself on 28 December before charges could be brought. An inquest declared that he alone was responsible for the Ratcliffe Highway murders – a verdict that may be questioned in view of the two pairs of footprints leading away from the Marrs' house. Among many theories current at the time was the suggestion that he had been framed by a sailor named Ablass, a man with a record of violence. Thomas De Quincey dealt with the case in an appendix to his essay *Murder Considered as One of the Fine Arts*.

**Williamson, Nicol** (1940– ), temperamental actor and amateur fist-fighter. Williamson, a talented performer in his younger days, acquired a reputation for missing performances and walking out of an entertainment before its run had ended. In her second volume of memoirs, *Serves Me Right* (1994), the actress Sarah Miles tells of an occasion in 1963 when she and Williamson were appearing at the Royal Court Theatre. Walking to dinner after the show one night, Williamson broke into song in a Knightsbridge square. A man put his head out of an upstairs window and politely asked Williamson to keep his voice down since some people were trying to sleep. 'Come down and say that to my face!' shouted Williamson, who, though physically unimpressive, never avoided a fight. The window closed with a bang and after a few minutes the smallest man Miss Miles had ever seen outside of a circus ring ran into the street. Williamson went into a crouch and the little man knocked him over with one blow. Miss Miles was able to box the little man off, and then to carry Williamson home. On this occasion he missed the next six performances.

In 1975 Williamson was invited to dinner by the theatre critic Kenneth Tynan. He arrived an hour early, catching his hosts before they had bathed or changed. Williamson volunteered to pass the time vacuum-cleaning the floor. Then he asked who else was coming. Tynan told him that one of the guests would be Jonathan Miller. 'Biggest phoney in London,' said Williamson. 'Who else?' Tynan mentioned the name of a young actress who had been having an affair with Roman Polanski, the Polish film director. When the guests arrived Williamson made conversation impossible by producing an LP of the Mamas and Papas and playing it at full volume. In the dining room he munched in silence before addressing the young actress for the first time. 'So you're the girl who was being fucked by Polanski.' 'No,' she said. 'I *am* being fucked by Polanski.' This exchange seemed to annoy Williamson, and a few minutes later he got up and left the room. There was a deafening blast of the Mamas and the Papas, and then the front door slammed. Jonathan Miller made a remark about baboons belonging in zoos, which was feeble by his standards, but the circumstances had been exceptionally trying.

*See also* FARSON, DANIEL.

**Wilmot, Olive** (1772–1834), impostor. Wilmot, whose father was a house painter, had a vivid imagination as a child, displaying in games with other children delusions of grandeur that may have been symptomatic of a psychotic condition. Later, she showed considerable talent as an artist, exhibiting at the Royal Academy and obtaining an appointment as landscape painter to the prince of Wales. Thereafter she invented a chain of improbable events that made her the daughter of Henry Frederick, duke of Cumberland – George III's youngest brother. To support her story she assembled more than 70 documents, including a certificate relating to her mother's marriage to the duke, and a second marriage certificate showing that George III himself had married one Hannah Lightfoot before bigamously marrying Queen Charlotte, thus conveniently destroying the succession.

None of the documents was convincing, and most commentators were scornful of Wilmot's tenacious campaign. The *Leeds Mercury* observed:

> The Lady is famed for dealing in documental evidence, but unfortunately for herself, the writers of all her documents always happen to die before their letters and certificates are produced.

A diarist who attended a City of London dinner in 1820 left a disparaging entry:

> She wore the most brilliant rose-coloured satin gown you ever saw, with fancy shawls flung in different forms over her shoulders, after the manner of the late Lady Hamilton. It turned out that Princess Olivia of Cumberland had made her claim as Princess of the Blood to sit at the right hand of my Lord Mayor. The worthy magistrate, however, with great spirit resisted these pretensions, and after much altercation she was compelled to retreat to another table.

After Wilmot's death, her daughter Lavinia Ryves attempted to sustain the imposture, taking the case to court and claiming the right to the title of the duchess of Lancaster and a legacy of £15,000. Her efforts appear to have been as clumsy as her mother's. *The Times* noted that:

> All the declarations and protestations of the great personages, intro-

duced into the story, are written on mere scraps, and the petitioner attempted to account for their size by alleging that they had been cut so small that they might be easier kept.

The case was thrown out by the lord chief justice.

**Wilson, Harriet** (1789–1846), courtesan. Harriet was the most celebrated of the three sisters, known as the 'Three Graces', who for 20 years enjoyed lives of ease and luxury in Regency London, unconstrained by the conventions that bound the unfortunate wives of the men who kept them. Harriet lived in the grandest houses, threw the best parties, wore the most expensive dresses and jewellery – able to boast, meanwhile, that it was never her irksome duty to preside at her husband's Christmas party for his tenants or distribute alms to the poor. Her lovers included the dukes of Wellington, Leinster and Argyll, and the marquess of Worcester, whose father, the duke of Beaufort, paid her off so she would not marry his heir.

At the end of her career Harriet wrote her memoirs and sent a copy to each of her lovers with a note suggesting that for £200 she would omit their names from the expurgated version. The duke of Wellington famously replied, 'Publish and be damned!' The portrait of him is unflattering, though Harriet admits at the end that 'he had relieved me from the duns [bailiffs], who else had given me vast uneasiness. God bless you Wellington!'

**Wilson, Sarah** (*c.*1750–*c.*1820), serving girl, thief and impostor. When Princess Susanna Carolina Matilda, sister of Queen Charlotte, visited America in the 1770s, ambitious society hostesses competed with one another to entertain her in their homes. It must have been a disappointment to one of them when her royal guest was arrested mid-soiree as an escaped convict and escorted off the premises at gunpoint.

Having left her Staffordshire village in 1771 to come to London, Sarah found employment as a servant to Caroline Vernon, a lady-in-waiting to Queen Charlotte. A compulsive thief, she was soon convicted of stealing certain items from the royal apartments – some jewellery, a fine dress and a portrait of the queen – and was sentenced to death. Vernon intervened on her behalf, however, and the sentence was commuted to transportation to the colonies.

After landing in Baltimore, Sarah was sold into the service of William Devall, a planter of Frederick County. At the first opportunity she ran away, headed south and crossed the border into Virginia. Remarkably, she had managed to retain the items stolen from the royal apartments, which she now used to confirm her identity as Princess Susanna Caroline Matilda, the sister of Queen Charlotte. Virginian society was enchanted. She was here, it was rumoured, as the result of a court scandal. To counter any surprise that the princess, who, like her sister, came originally from Germany, didn't speak in her mother tongue, Princess Susanna explained that she had vowed never to converse in German until she had been restored to her sister's favour. She made it clear, however, that she retained some influence in England and that many prestigious appointments remained in her gift. Those set on improving their positions were more than willing in the circumstances to alleviate any financial difficulties the princess might encounter.

Sarah's imposture lasted for nearly two years, at which point she was undone by its very success. Her notoriety reached the ears of her former master, William Devall, who despatched his agent, Michael Dalton, to recapture her – the latter's arrival, armed and with an appropriate warrant, in the middle of a Virginian soiree causing great dismay. Back in the service of Mr Devall, Sarah endured a menial life for two years, at which point an unusual coincidence sent another English serving girl named Sarah Wilson to the colony. The former princess swapped places with the new arrival and disappeared. She later married a British army officer named William Talbot, whom she set up in business with the money accrued during her imposture. They moved to New York, had a large family and are believed to have lived happily for many years. The historian Sarah Burton has accounted for Wilson's success – against the failure of Olive WILMOT, say – by the fact that she was merely an accomplished actress who never forgot that she was playing a part, whereas Wilmot was obsessive, eventually believing her own fantasy.

## Winchester, Bapsy, marchioness of (1902–95), author and litigant. In 1952 Bapsy, who was born Bapsybanoo Pavry, became the third wife of the 16th marquess of Winchester, then in his 90th year. She spent the next ten years quarrelling in public with his friend, Eve Fleming, the mother of Ian Fleming, author of the James Bond adventure books for children.

The marchioness took particular exception to the marquess's arrangements when, at the age of 90, he visited Mrs Fleming in Nassau in 1953. Lady Winchester followed her husband to Nassau, where she stalked the couple, causing one ill-mannered neighbour to say, 'There was almost always an overweight Indian lady in a sari, pacing the main road, occasionally pausing to raise and shake a fist towards the main house.' Later Lady Winchester wrote angry letters to the marquess, 'May a viper's fangs be forever at your throat, and may you stew in the pit of your own juice.' When she saw Mrs Fleming touch the marquess on the thigh in 1954 she sued her for enticement, and the case eventually came to court before Mr Justice Devlin in 1957. Lady Winchester's counsel told the court that his client was 'a wronged woman distraught, like Dido, with a willow in her hand upon the wild sea banks and wafting her love to come again to Carthage'. Nevertheless, the court found in her favour. Later, however, and to Lady Winchester's considerable indignation, the verdict was overturned on appeal. Lord Winchester and Mrs Fleming went to live in Monte Carlo, where they continued to be harassed by the marchioness.

The marquess died in 1962, at the age of 100. He had not been the most distinguished of his line. The 1st marquess, William Paulet, was lord president of the council under Henry VIII, and served as lord treasurer under Edward VI, Queen Mary and Queen Elizabeth. Montagu Paulet, the younger son of the 14th marquess, who was born in 1801, succeeded as 16th marquess in 1899, when his elder brother was killed in the South African War. His first wife died in 1924, and his second in 1949. He maintained to the end that his father-in-law, far from being high priest of the Parsees in Bombay, as Bapsy, his third wife, claimed, was merely the priest of a fire temple.

After her husband's death, Lady Winchester divided her time between London and Bombay, accompanied by her brother, Dr Jal Pavry. When in London they lodged at the Mayfair Hotel, soliciting invitations to public functions. When Dr Pavry died in 1985, Lady Winchester issued a statement that she had received messages of sympathy from all over the world. Her extensive archives, which she presented to the City of Winchester, did reveal that she had once received a Christmas card from King Olav of Norway and also a photocopied acknowledgement of a letter from her to George Bernard Shaw.

**Windham, 'Mad'.** *See* ROBERTS, 'BAWDY HOUSE' BOB.

**windy vapours.** *See* GREEN, MARY.

**Wingate, Orde Charles** (1903–44), soldier. Wingate was a brilliant tactician who rose from the rank of captain to major general in just six years. In the Burma theatre in World War II he organized and led the Chindits – trained jungle fighters who specialized in counter-penetration. Supplied by air, they thrust far behind the Japanese lines, causing grave disruption to the enemy's logistical arrangements. Throughout his tragically short career, Wingate displayed personal characteristics which were as unorthodox as his battle plans. One of his habits was to hold briefing sessions in the nude. Senior colleagues grew to tolerate this, but foreign dignitaries were often disconcerted. Eliahu Elath, the future ambassador to the Court of St James's, was scarred for life, it was said, by his experience of discussing Zionism for an hour and a half with a completely naked man. Later, Wingate decided that bathing was unhealthy. Instead, he would sit naked on a stool and brush himself clean with a toothbrush – often while receiving callers. Visitors were alerted to the fact that the interview was over by a miniature alarm clock which Wingate wore on his little finger. When this sounded, Wingate would rise and, still unclothed, politely escort his guest to the main gates and, sometimes, beyond. He held other unusual theories about health, one of which was that a man could best survive the tropics on a diet of raw onions. Sometimes he ate nothing but onions for days at a time. He died in an airplane crash in Burma in 1944 at the age of 41. Winston Churchill said that, 'He was a man of genius who might have become a man of destiny.'

**Winner, Michael.** *See* PALMER-TOMKINSON, TARA; REED, OLIVER.

**Winterton, Cecil Tournour, 6th Earl** (1883–1953), politician. Winterton was elected to Parliament in 1904 under his courtesy title, since his father was still alive, of Viscount Tournour. On one occasion he was introduced to a constituent who appeared not to recognize him. 'I'm Winterton,' he said. 'I'm so sorry,' said the constituent, 'I thought you were that ass Tournour.' Winterton had a reputation for being 'difficult', which he enjoyed. During World War II he formed an alliance with Emanuel Shinwell, another irascible personality, albeit on the opposite side of the House. They were known as 'Arsenic and Old Face', a play on the title of a thriller *Arsenic and Old Lace*, running in London's West End and, in 1946, filmed with Cary Grant in the lead.

Whether as Arsenic or Old Face, Winterton would become so worked up about a point of order, or some imagined affront to the dignity of the House, that he would become purple in the face and rub his long, bony hands together so forcefully that on one occasion he dislocated both his thumbs. The Allied cause was not assisted in World War II, he believed, by the 'radio crooner' and 'Forces Sweetheart' Vera Lynn, whose singing he likened to 'the caterwauling of an inebriated cockatoo'. In a letter to *The Times*, he deplored the growing habit among waiters in railway dining cars of saying 'Thank you' and 'Excuse me' when serving a customer:

> The person serving has nothing for which to thank the person whom he is serving, nor is there any reason to excuse himself for carrying out a plain duty. I have been sorely tempted more than once to make an equally irrelevant reply, such as 'Merry Christmas' or 'the same to you, and many of them', but have hitherto refrained from doing so.

**Wintle, Lieutenant-Colonel A.D.** (1892–1958), soldier and parliamentary candidate. As a boy, Wintle was given an umbrella purchased by an aunt at the Army & Navy Stores. Thereafter, he could hardly bear to be parted from it. For some years, he took it to bed with him. An umbrella, for Wintle, symbolized the natural superiority of an Englishman over a foreigner. The difference was that a Frenchman, being intelligent, would consult a barometer in the morning and calculate whether to take an umbrella with him. Since all calculation was vain, he would be soaked in any case. An Englishman, being stupid, couldn't understand barometers and would always have an umbrella with him. However, since a gentleman never unfurled his umbrella, the Englishman would also be soaked. But the thinking was importantly different.

Wintle participated erratically in two world wars. In World War I he trod on an unexploded bomb and lost an eye and several fingers. He discharged himself from hospital and returned to the front line, where he captured 35 German soldiers single-handedly. He was extremely upset when the Armistice was signed and wrote in his diary, '19th November: Great War Peace signed. 20th November: Wintle declares war on Germany.'

Wintle's first action in World War II was to have himself court-martialled. Believing that the war could be prosecuted more vigorously, he decided to fly to France, where he would destroy the French air force rather than let it fall into German hands. Since he didn't have an aeroplane at his disposal, he impersonated the Air Ministry's director of intelligence, Air Commodore Boyle, and commandeered an RAF plane. When stopped by Boyle himself, he waved a pistol in the air commodore's face and said, 'You and your kind should all be shot.' Wintle was arrested and sent to the Tower of London. On the way, the young officer who was escorting him lost the rail warrant for the journey. Infuriated by such incompetence, Wintle told him to keep an eye on the baggage while he went to get another one. Wintle found the Transport Office, asked for a warrant and, since there was no officer present, signed it himself. After a few weeks in the Tower, he was let off with a severe reprimand.

In 1941 Wintle was sent to occupied France as an undercover agent. He was betrayed almost immediately and imprisoned in a Napoleonic fortress near Toulon. There he made such a nuisance of himself that the French commandant, unable to endure Wintle's incessant abuse and challenges, defected from Vichy with 200 men and joined the Resistance.

After the war, Wintle found an outlet for his energies when he suspected that a south-coast solicitor called Nye had bilked his half-sister Marjorie out of an inheritance under her Aunt Kitty's will. Resolved at first to give Nye a public flogging, he was persuaded against this course on the grounds that 'these days there is some outcry from do-gooders and other uninformed liberals against the excellent discipline of corporal punishment.' Instead, he borrowed a friend's flat in Hove and, adopting a fictitious title (the earl of Norbury), he invited Nye to visit him with the promise of a property deal. When he arrived, Wintle removed Nye's trousers and then photographed him in a dunce's hat. He later received six months in prison for assault.

In 1945 Wintle had stood for Parliament as Liberal candidate for Lambeth Norwood on a straightforward platform: that the last person who had entered the House with such good intentions had been Guy Fawkes. Wintle was not elected.

**Wirgham, Thomas.** The publisher of an obscene toothpick. *See* BACCHUS, REGINALD.

**Wisbey, Marilyn.** *See* FOREMAN, FREDDIE; FRASER, FRANCIS 'MAD FRANKIE'.

**Wisbey, Tommy.** *See* REYNOLDS, BRUCE.

**witches.** *See* DICKENSON, MOTHER; FLOWER, JOAN; GRIFFITHS, DOT; KYTLER, DAME ALICE; WENHAM, JANE.

**witch-hunters and -finders.** *See* GREATRAKES, VALENTINE; HOPKINS, MATTHEW; PRICKERS, SCOTTISH.

**witness interference and jury intimidation.** *See* NASH, JIMMY.

**wives regarded as chattels, 'just as a thoroughbred mare or cow'.** *See* BRAUN, HEIDE; OWEN PEEL, CLARISSA.
*See also* CONJUGAL RIGHTS.

**womanly duties, acting from one's.** *See* GOLDSTEIN, LILIAN.

**wombling trot, the.** *See* GREEN, MARY.

**women of humble origin whose beauty and wit gained them an entry into society.** *See* CHATHAM, GEORGE (for 'Bubbles' Rothermere); GUPPY, DARIUS (for Patricia Guppy); HAMILTON, LADY EMMA; JONES, JANIE; HERVEY, AUGUSTUS (for Mary Nesbitt); ST CLAIR, LINDI; WALTERS, CATHERINE; WILSON, HARRIET.

**woodworm with a mallet, concussing.** *See* DEVONSHIRE, ANDREW ROBERT BUXTON CAVENDISH, 11TH DUKE OF.

**WOP 598.** *See* PROGL, ZOE.

**Wracks and Cranks.** *See* HUNTER-COWAN, MAJOR BETTY.

**Wren, Sir Christopher** (1632–1723), architect. Sir Christopher was the first needle-opiate user, albeit not on himself but on his dog, whom he injected with opium, using a hollowed-out quill attached to a bulb.

**wrestlers and naked women at the Vatican, oiled.** *See* BIRDWOOD, JANE, THE DOWAGER LADY.

**wrestling aroused by getting the worst of it at the hands of a saloon-bar ruffian, interest in.** *See* OAKELEY, SIR ATHOLL.

**wrestling with naked sailors, fantasies of.** *See* SYMONDS, JOHN ADDINGTON.

**wrong box, the.** *See* SOUTHCOTT, JOANNA.

**Wykehamists.** *See* BUCKLAND, FRANCIS TREVELYAN; CHENEVIX-TRENCH, DAVID BRIAN ROBERT; DRUITT, MONTAGUE; FERRERS, ROBERT SHIRLEY, 2ND EARL (for the 13th earl); JARDINE, DOUGLAS; LOWSON, SIR DENYS.

# x y z

**xenophobes.** *See* REDESDALE, CLEMENT NAPIER THOMAS FREEMAN MITFORD, 2ND BARON; SIBTHORP, COLONEL CHARLES DE LAET WALDO.

**Yapp, Alice.** *See* MAYBRICK, FLORENCE ELIZABETH.

**'Yeti, the'.** *See* BRUCE-WALLACE, ANDY.

**York, Sarah Margaret, duchess of** (1959– ), problematic royal. Before her marriage to Prince Andrew, the duke of York, in 1986 there had been clear signs that Sarah Ferguson might cause the British royal family some embarrassment in the years ahead – most notably, various incidents and escapades from her past chronicled by Talbot Church ('The man the Royals trust') in his *101 Things You Didn't Know About The Royal Lovebirds* (1986). It is now thought that a close reading of Church's book would have spared the royal family many sleepless nights.

According to Church, 'Flame-haired Fergie's' school reports described her as:

> … an enthusiastic pupil who makes a cheerful contribution to the life of Hurst Lodge. Sarah is lively and full of go, if a little lacking in direction – and she must learn that liveliness should cease with lights.

She failed, apparently, to do herself justice in written work, and when asked in divinity who was born in a stable and had thousands of followers, Sarah replied, 'Red Rum.'

There were early indications too that men would play an important part in Sarah's life. Later in his authoritative book, Church tells us that:

> It was not until she returned from a holiday in America in 1977 that full-of-fun Fergie teamed up with her first serious boyfriend,

26-year-old sports-goods salesman, Kim Smith-Bingham. They met at Klosters, the fashionable Swiss ski resort, where Fergie (always willing to muck in!) was working as a chalet girl. The high-spirited royal-to-be was immediately attracted to Smith-Bingham's extrovert antics on the slopes. 'Kim had a tremendous sense of humour, just like Fergie,' says close friend, Charlotte Twohig, 'and he used to make her burst out laughing with his dare-devil escapades! On one classic occasion, he went down the Cresta Run on a grand piano and he was always doing totally mad things like attaching a cowbell under a girl's bed to make sure there was no chalet-hopping!' Old Harrovian Smith-Bingham is an accomplished, but never unkind, mimic and on more than one occasion he had Fergie in fits of laughter ordering drinks in a comic German accent or lining up all the waiters in a restaurant and teaching them to sing 'Forty Years On' while he conducted them, using a German sausage as a baton!

According to Church, a turning point came for Sarah in the course of a holiday in Ibiza:

'Let's face it,' says Jo Bassett-Turner, a former girlfriend of Jamie, the marquess of Blandford, 'Fergie saw things in Ibiza she didn't like. They're all totally mad out there and on drugs most of the time. Down-to-earth Fergie hated all that. She's absolutely genuine, if you know what I mean; what a racehorse trainer would call "honest". Some of the parties were totally wild. At one of them all the men had to come as Adolf Hitler and all the girls as Eva Braun! The party went on all night and at breakfast time they all staggered into Ibiza Town as high as kites! Suddenly there were 30 Adolf Hitlers having coffee outside the Montesol! The police called the German Consul, who, poor love, had a total nervous breakdown! It was too much for Sarah. She packed her bags and flew back to London. The incident left her with an abiding hatred of drugs. Mind you, she's stood by Jamie Blandford through all his troubles. That's typical of her. She visits him in prison, in the clinic, on parole, on probation, on remand, on the run – wherever he happens to be at the time.'

Evidence of the duchess's continuing lack of judgement was provided by an incident in April 2000 when her former dresser, Jane ANDREWS, was convicted of murdering her lover with a cricket bat.

**Young, Graham** (1948–90), trainee storeman and compulsive poisoner. In 1962 Young, then aged 14, was committed to an institution for the criminally insane after confessing to the poisoning of his stepmother, and the attempted poisoning of his father, his sister and a school friend. Nine years later he was released, having made what was described as 'an extremely full recovery'. Now aged 23, he took a job with John Hadland Ltd, a company making photographic equipment at Bovington in Hertfordshire. In the autumn of 1971 a mystery illness began to affect the workforce. Several of them suffered stomach pains, vomiting and diarrhoea. On 19 November Frederick Biggs, a 60-year-old departmental manager, died in hospital. David Tilson, a clerk, and Jethro Batt, a storeman, were also admitted to hospital. David Tilson's hair began to fall out. No one had forgotten that five months earlier Robert Egle, the firm's chief storeman, had died in St Albans Hospital from what had been certified as broncho-pneumonia.

As alarm spread throughout the company, the management organized a medical investigation. A meeting was arranged in the canteen, at which the doctor in charge confirmed that chemicals used in the company were not to blame. A knowledgeable young trainee storeman – Graham Young – asked the doctor if he thought the symptoms of the mysterious illness were consistent with thallium poisoning. His over-enthusiastic questioning aroused suspicion, and the police were called in. Bob Egle's remains were exhumed for analysis, and both he and Fred Biggs were found to have died from thallium poisoning. Young's background was checked, thallium was found in his possession and he was arrested for the murders of Robert Egle and Frederick Biggs.

Young was tried at St Albans and pleaded not guilty. A diary had been found containing incriminating entries, one of which referred to 'a fatal dose of the special compound to F …' Young claimed that such entries were notes for a novel he was writing. Former colleagues testified that he was an enthusiastic tea maker, but that it often tasted bitter. One storeroom employee, who had not been struck down, always left the tea, which had then been drunk by Bob Egle.

In July 1972 Young was convicted of murder, attempted murder and administering poisons. He was sentenced to life imprisonment and died of a heart attack in Parkhurst in July 1990.

**youth, elixir of eternal.** *See* EMMETT, HORACE.

**zany antics masking a melancholy disposition.** *See* STANSHALL, VIVIAN.

**Zanzibar, the dorsal fin of the Sacred Shark of.** *See* COLE, HORACE DE VERE.

**zebras bagged in Piccadilly, a brace of.** *See* DUNSANY, EDWARD JOHN MORETON DRAX PLUNKETT, 18TH BARON.

**Zomparelli, Alfredo 'Italian Tony'.** *See* KNIGHT, RONNIE.

**zoo, human volunteers to be exhibited in.** *See* SLATER, JOHN.

**zoo keepers.** *See* ASPINALL, JOHN.

**zoophilia, avian.** *See* BROWN, JAMES (a pigeon).

**zoophilia, canine.** *See* CARLTON, SYDNEY (a Staffordshire bull terrier); KYTLER, DAME ALICE (an incubus in the form of a black hairy dog).

# picture credits

**Art Archive** George IV; Lord George Gordon

**Bridgeman Art Library/Sheffield City Art Gallery** Judge George Jeffreys

**Corbis/Francis G. Meyer** Lady Emma Hamilton; **Corbis/Hulton-Deutsch Collection** Ronnie and Reggie Kray

**Hulton Getty Archive** Margaret duchess of Argyll; John Aspinall; Gerald Hugh Tyrwhitt-Wilson, 14th Baron Berners; Horatio Bottomley; Lord Byron; Sir Redvers Buller; Barbara 'Joe' Carstairs; Thomas Chatterton; Prince Albert Victor, duke of Clarence; Aleister Crowley; Louis de Rougement; duke of Edinburgh; Sir Nicholas Fairbairn; Hughie Green; Augustus John; John Bingham, 6th Baron Lucan; Sir Henry Morgan; Cynthia Payne; Dr William Palmer; Oliver Reed; Bruce Reynolds; Jack Spot; Jeremy Thorpe; Edward Teach

**Mary Evans Picture Library** Francis Bacon; Sir Francis Dashwood; Reverend Dr William Dodd; Robert Shirley, 2nd Earl Ferrers; Charles James Fox; Dr. W.G. Grace; Colonel Charles de Laet Waldo Sibthorp

**National Trust Photographic Library/Upton House (Bearstead Collection)/Anglo Hornak** William Beckford

**PA Photos** Jonathan Aitken; Sir Anthony Blunt

**Peter Newark's Historical Pictures** Titus Oates

**Popperfoto** Lord Boothby; Barbara Cartland; Dr Hawley Harvey Crippen; Christine Keeler; Major-General Orde Charles Wingate

**Reuters/Popperfoto** Ronnie Biggs

**Rex Features** Jane Andrews; Jeffrey Archer; Jeffrey Bernard; Peter Bessell; Eddie 'The Eagle' Edwards; Major Ronald Ferguson; Darius Guppy; Robert Maxwell; David Mellor; Keith Moon

**Topham Picturepoint** Alan Clark; Reverend Harold Davidson; Frankie Fraser; Vinnie Jones; duchess of York

**Topham/Press Association** 7th marquess of Bristol

**True Detective Magazine** Burke and Hare